Fahrenheit/Celsius

-40°F	=	-40°C	120°F	=	49°C	320°F	=	160°C
-30°F	=	-34°C	125°F	=	52°C	330°F	=	166°C
-20°F	=	-29°C	130°F	=	54°C	340°F	=	171°C
-10°F	=	-23°C	135°F	=	57°C	350°F	=	177°C
- 5°F	=	-21°C	140°F	=	60°C	360°F	=	182°C
0°F	=	-18°C	145°F	=	63°C	370°F	=	188°C
5°F	=	-15°C	150°F	=	66°C	380°F	=	193°C
10°F	=	-12°C	155°F	=	68°C	390°F	=	199°C
15°F	=	- 9°C	160°F	=	71°C	400°F	=	204°C
20°F	=	- 6°C	165°F	=	74°C	410°F	=	210°C
25°F	=	- 4°C	170°F	=	77°C	420°F	=	216°C
30°F	=	- 1°C	175°F	=	79°C	430°F	=	221°C
32°F	=	0°C	180°F	=	82°C	440°F	=	227°C
35°F	=	2°C	185°F	=	85°C	450°F	=	232°C
40°F	=	4°C	190°F	=	88°C	460°F	=	238°C
45°F	=	7°C	195°F	=	91°C	470°F	=	243°C
50°F	=	10°C	200°F	=	93°C	480°F	=	249°C
55°F	=	13°C	205°F	=	96°C	490°F	=	254°C
60°F	=	16°C	210°F	=	99°C	500°F	=	260°C
65°F	=	18°C	212°F	=	100°C	510°F	=	266°C
70°F	=	21°C	220°F	=	104°C	520°F	=	271°C
75°F	=	24°C	230°F	=	110°C	530°F	=	277°C
80°F	=	27°C	240°F	=	116°C	540°F	=	282°C
85°F	=	29°C	250°F	=	121°C	550°F	=	288°C
90°F	=	32°C	260°F	=	127°C	560°F	=	293°C
95°F	=	35°C	270°F	=	132°C	570°F	=	299°C
100°F	=	38°C	280°F	=	137°C	580°F	=	304°C
105°F	=	41°C	290°F	=	143°C	590°F	=	310°C
110°F	=	43°C	300°F	=	149°C	600°F	=	316°C
115°F	=	46°C	310°F	=	154°C			

POINT LOMA NAZARENE COLLEGE
Ryan Library
3900 Lomaland Drive, San Diego, CA 92106-2899

641.57 K69q2
Knight, John Barton, 1950-
Quantity food production,
planning, and management
217271

Quantity Food Production, Planning, and Management

641.57
K69q²

Quantity Food Production, Planning, and Management

Second Edition

John B. Knight
School of Travel Industry Management
University of Hawaii

Lendal H. Kotschevar
Florida International University

POINT LOMA NAZARENE COLLEGE
WITHDRAWN
217271
RYAN LIBRARY

VAN NOSTRAND REINHOLD
New York

Copyright © 1989 by Van Nostrand Reinhold

Library of Congress Catalog Card Number 88-10085

ISBN 0-442-24016-3

All rights reserved. No part of this work covered by the copyright hereon
may be reproduced or used in any form or by any means — graphic, electronic,
or mechanical, including photocopying, recording, taping, or information
storage and retrieval systems — without written permission of the publisher.

Printed in the United States of America

Van Nostrand Reinhold
115 Fifth Avenue
New York, New York 10003

Chapman & Hall
2-6 Boundary Row
London SE1 8HN, England

Thomas Nelson Australia
102 Dodds Street
South Melbourne, Victoria 3205, Australia

Nelson Canada
1120 Birchmount Road
Scarborough, Ontario M1K 5G4, Canada

16   15   14   13   12   11   10   9   8   7   6   5

Library of Congress Cataloging in Publication Data

Knight, John Barton, 1950-
    Quantity food production, planning, and management / John B. Knight.
Lendal H. Kotschevar. — Rev. ed.
        p.   cm.
    Includes bibliographies and index.
    ISBN 0-442-24016-3 :
    1. Food service.   I. Kotschevar, Lendal Henry, 1908-
II. Title.
TX943.K57 1989
641.5'7'068 — dc19   88-10085

For his love, dedication, and service to God,
country, and mankind, and for his contributions
to the hospitality industry and its students, the
authors dedicate this book to Dr. Lewis J. Minor,
Professor, Michigan State University, and founder
of the L. J. Minor Corporation, Cleveland, Ohio.

And to my loving wife, Whitney, and our three
children, Brad, David, and Jacqueline.

—John B. Knight

CONTENTS

Part III. Quantity Food Management — The Five P's   321

Part IV. Appendices   385

PREFACE

Quantity Food Production, Planning, and Management systematically presents all phases of the foodservice operation. Part I begins with an overview of quantity foodservice, followed by coverage of nutrition, sanitation, and safety—emphasizing the importance of these subjects, which so often are given secondary consideration. Menu planning, as the initial step in designing or operating any foodservice facility, is discussed in the following chapter. The reader then learns about the foodservice equipment needed to prepare the menu successfully. Next, purchasing, receiving, storing, and issuing food are discussed, followed by the subject of serving food. Management principles are presented throughout in a fashion that enables both experienced and inexperienced readers to benefit from the material.

In this revised edition, numerous chapters have been updated to discuss computer applications in the foodservice industry. Part II describes the many preparation techniques and principles relating to foods seen on today's menus—from appetizers to desserts and from salads and salad dressings to beverages. Part III deals with the five P's of management; people, products, plant/property, profits, and promotions. Each chapter covers a different important aspect of the multifaceted job of successfully managing a foodservice.

Vocabulary terms are clearly defined as they appear, and text material is continually highlighted with illustrations. At the end of each chapter, problems and questions are posed to test the reader's ability to apply the information covered and to ensure comprehension of the important subjects discussed.

Special thanks are given to Robert Woods, Tom Petot, and the other graduate students in the School of Hotel Administration, Cornell University, who have greatly assisted in the revision of the manuscript for this second edition of *Quantity Food Production, Planning, and Management*. Their time and consideration are appreciated.

PART I

Quantity Food Planning— A Systems Approach

CHAPTER 1

Overview of Quantity Foodservice

OUTLINE

THE FOODSERVICE INDUSTRY

Foodservice is one of the largest industries, achieving nearly $200 billion in sales in 1987. Foodservices contribute substantially to the mobility of individuals and the flexibility of one's social life.

The foodservice industry employs more people than any other industry. Of every $2.50 spent for food, $1 is spent in foodservices. The industry has enjoyed steady growth since before World War II, with an average increase of about 6 percent per year. Its growth has been the most rapid of all retail industries.

The 500,000 or more foodservices that provide this food are widely dispersed and vary from small snack or take-out shops, drive-ins, and coffee shops to moderate-size restaurants and hotel operations, to huge foodservices such as those serving the

3

military, schools, and large hospital complexes. Airline foodservices alone do millions of dollars in business each year.

Some Characteristics of the Industry

Because the foodservice industry is labor intensive and because it is divided into many small units that must produce in small amounts, it has never been able to obtain the benefits of mass production. The industry is characterized by low productivity, low profit margins, low capital investment, and high labor cost per dollar of sales. The industry also has a high labor turnover rate: workers move from job to job with ease, and each year many move in and many others move out.

The steady flow of workers in and out, plus job-hopping, reduces operating efficiency and is costly. It has been estimated that training a new worker to replace an experienced one can cost the operation as much as 8 percent of the worker's annual salary for the first year. The industry has moved to reduce its labor turnover by trying to provide stable, financially attractive positions for workers. While pay is low in some categories, it is good in others—especially at the supervisory and management levels. Graduates from four-year colleges in the hospitality industry find plenty of jobs available at salaries equal to those offered to beginning engineers.

Many foodservice operations are family-owned or individual-owned enterprises, but this characteristic has been constantly eroding over the last thirty years. Today, massive foodservice chains do most of the dollar business, and the small, single-outlet enterprise's share of the market is shrinking. The large corporate organization is the leader in the industry.

Within the last thirty years, the type of food used in foodservices has gradually changed. More processed foods have found their way into use, some of which are practically ready to serve. Many operations still want to produce their own food, but even they now use more processed foods to do it. Another popular development is the central commissary, where foods are mass-produced and then shipped to satellite units to be served. The problem of maintaining quality while obtaining desirable economies has slowed the growth of central commissary production, however, and some operations that had instituted central commissaries have now discontinued them.

The industry has had to change to meet a changing patron market, too. People eat less, have clearer concerns for their health, are eating out more, and are more discriminating shoppers. The industry has become highly competitive, and its management is now largely composed of people who have had training in business or in specialized schools that teach foodservice management.

TRAINING THE LABOR FORCE

The foodservice industry employs millions of people, and each year several hundred thousand new workers must be found to fill newly created or newly vacated jobs. Until recently, much of this new labor was recruited from "off the streets." These people simply walked in and were assigned jobs whose duties they learned by experience. Their teachers were other workers who may or may not have known how to do the job; as a result, the new worker often learned to do the job incorrectly or inefficiently. Upper-echelon jobs were often filled by promotion from within the operation's existing ranks. Not infrequently, the manager or even the president of a large corporation was once a pot washer or busboy.

Within the last forty years, a sizable educational system for training employees at all levels of the industry has emerged. Unions, too, have concerned themselves with educational courses—in part so that they can certify the job abilities of members better. Unions often work with public schools, but in some cases they have established their own training and certification centers. The government has also been active in promoting short educational programs to train workers for the foodservice industry.

Professional associations have set up programs to give educational opportunities to their members. The Club Managers Association has developed an educational program that must be taken by any member who wishes to use the title CM (Certified

Manager). The American Dietetic Association requires all dietitians to be certified by examination and to continue to accumulate educational and professional points during their professional lives if they intend to use the title RD (Registered Dietitian) after their names. The School Foodservice Association and some of its state organizations now require all workers to gain educational credits in order to be certified. Comparable programs exist in other professional groups in the industry. In addition, the industry sponsors a great many educational scholarships for interested individuals.

Home study courses are popular, too. Many universities and other schools sponsor training programs for workers, supervisors, and managers. At some institutions, 5,000 or more people per year register for correspondence courses. Many high schools offer courses for waiters, waitresses, cooks, and other service positions.

Many community colleges and junior colleges have excellent programs for training workers. The emphasis varies from vocational courses for those wanting to work as chefs or maître d's to economics and management training for people interested in becoming food and beverage managers, sales managers, or catering or banquet managers. Four-year hospitality programs commonly accept credits from these schools.

Universities and colleges often have four-year programs in the area, and some offer master's degrees and a few the doctorate. Over 1,000 graduates from four-year schools are thought to enter the foodservice field each year—and the industry could use twice that number. Each year companies make recruiting visits to educational institutions, offering graduates a three month or longer training program before being moved into supervisory or managerial positions. Because of the rapid growth of many businesses, some graduates hold important positions within four or five years after leaving college. The growth of graduate programs to develop top executives and teachers for the industry has also been significant.

Most four-year programs are offered in the College of Business, but others may be found in the College of Home Economics, or the College of Food Technology, and still others exist as separate schools. The discipline of foodservice management is today well recognized in academic circles. Most academic programs require that students spend many hours working in the industry; internships have been established whereby students gain on-the-job experience and receive academic credit. Such an approach works best because—although many basic facts can be learned in class—the student must be exposed to situations that are related to the real work world in order to develop into a successful manager.

MANAGEMENT AND FOODSERVICES

This text is designed to move the student in a logical, sequential order through the various management steps involved in quantity foodservice (we shall define a *quantity foodservice facility* as one preparing foods in quantity to serve to people within a designated period of time). Management is given first priority in this introductory chapter, although it presents only a brief summary of management's scope and functions. The ensuing chapters consider the basics of planning quantity food production and service, and then take up specifics of food production. Food production issues are viewed from the standpoint of what a manager ought to know to be able to manage these operations well and to ensure that adequate standards in food production and service are satisfied. The management skills needed to operate a foodservice are presented in such a way as to prepare the reader for the responsibilities of an entry-level position in the industry. By integrating planning, preparation, and management in an orderly fashion, this text helps the student, manager, owner/operator, or other interested individual build the skills necessary to operate a successful quantity foodservice facility.

Management Defined

Management is sometimes defined as the element in an enterprise that plans, staffs, organizes, directs, and controls an enterprise so that it reaches its goals. It is management's job to establish goals, plan how to reach them, and then organize, staff, lead, and control so as to reach them. Often these actions are called the *function of management*. Sometimes *management* is defined as reaching goals through people. This is a good definition because it underscores that managers alone cannot make an operation a success; it takes others working with management to accomplish this.

Some workers see management as the boss giving the orders, as the one getting the most pay for doing the least work, or as the sector of the company that knows less about the operation than anyone else. Such opinions are often based on a lack of knowledge about what the manager is or does. Management's failure to inform members of the operation about its essential role can be costly to its image.

Good management often consists of the ability to plan operations intelligently and then to select and direct people so that the plans come to a successful conclusion. The more effectively managers prevail upon others to do a good job, the better management succeeds in its job. Many individuals are involved in achieving an enterprise's goals, and management is responsible for getting the energy of people to go in the right direction.

Levels of Responsibility

The hierarchy in a foodservice has three levels: management; mid-management or supervisory; and workers. To maintain a smooth-functioning facility, employees at each level must adequately perform the essential functions allocated to that level.

Management comprises the chairman and members of the board in a corporation, the president, the manager, and even the assistant managers. Mid-management may reach as high in the organization as the assistant managers and may extend as low as supervisors; sales managers, food and beverage managers, and purchasing department heads are typically considered mid-management, as are chefs, chef stewards, the maître d'hôtel, the catering manager, a food production manager, and a dietitian in charge of a hospital's dietary department. The workers are everybody else. In a traditional continental-cuisine organization, the executive chef is a mid-management person under a food and beverage manager or other manager. The *sous chef* is a supervisor under the executive chef and the *chefs des partis* (heads of production such as the *chef de saucier* in charge of the sauce, gravy, and soup department and the garde manger who heads the cold meat section) are sub-supervisors under the *sous chef*. Under these individuals come workers such as cooks, helpers, and others working in the organization. In most foodservices, the number of people at the worker level far exceeds the number of people at the other two levels.

The management level plans action, the mid-management initiates and supervises action, and the workers carry it out. It is important that all employees in the organization know what type of action they are responsible for. When people at a lower level try to assume the functions of others at a higher level (or vice versa), conflict can occur. The intruding individual is resented as encroaching on someone else's turf. Individuals promoted from one level to a higher one sometimes encounter problems in this regard because they find it difficult to break away from the action patterns learned in the lower level. This is seen when a supervisor promoted from worker ranks fails to supervise without constantly pitching in and doing jobs others should be doing.

ORGANIZATION

Getting people into the right place so they do the right job is called "setting up an organization." A *business organization* may be defined as an arrangement of people in jobs designed to accomplish the goals of the operation. Figures 1-1, 1-2, and 1-3 offer examples of the many ways organization charts can be set up.

Organizational structures vary according to the needs of the enterprise, the jobs done, and the people in the organization.

Organizations should be dynamic, not static. They must be changed as needed, and organizational charts should reflect such changes. Obviously, just setting up an organizational chart does not build an organization. Creating the living organization—by selecting and organizing people on the job—is one of the most important responsibilities of management.

*These jobs may be handled by other workers in small establishments.

Figure 1-1. Organization chart (restaurant).

Types of Organizations

Different organizations are needed to do different things for operations. Basically, there are three kinds of organizations: line, staff, and functional. Most organizations are combinations of these. For example, even though a line organization may be set up, parts of the operation may be strictly based on functional tasks or on staff work that is required to support the line operation.

Line Organization

Military organizations usually are considered the best examples of line organizations. The lines of authority and responsibility flow from the head down through the various mid-management layers to the workers. In a line organization, a manager directs an assistant manager to do something; that person in turn directs a supervisor, who in turn directs a worker or workers. In reverse order, the report of work done or problems encountered flows back up through the same line of authority until it reaches the manager. No bypassing of layers is permitted either on the way down or on the way up. Sometimes this flow of authority and responsibility is called the *chain of command.*

In a line organization, the top position bears full responsibility for everything that happens in the

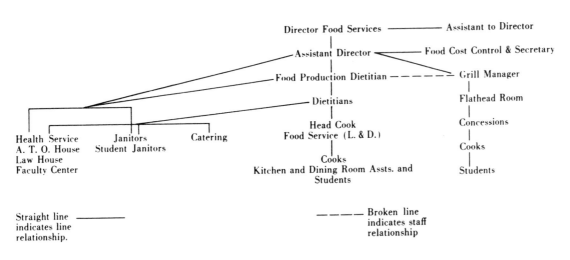

Figure 1-2. Organization chart (foodservice at a university).

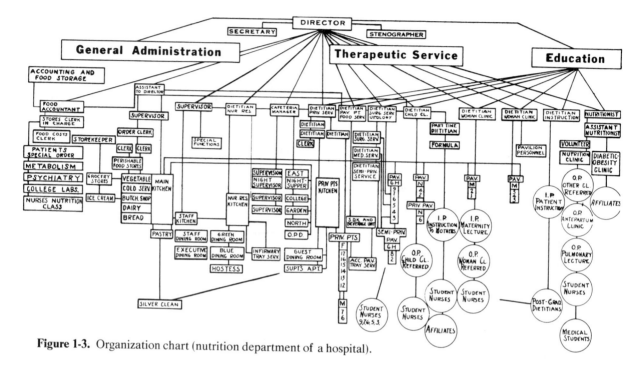

Figure 1-3. Organization chart (nutrition department of a hospital).

organization. Such responsibility cannot be delegated to others. The power to make a decision or do a job can be vested in a subordinate, but the way this duty is discharged by the subordinate remains the responsibility of the chief officer. A good rule is "you can delegate power but you can't delegate responsibility."

Staff Organizations

Staff organizations are usually support organizations established to render a service to the line organization. The staff does not take steps to see that things are done, nor does it have authority to implement any decisions it reaches or to act on any research it gathers. These are tasks for the line organization to perform. Every organization has staff positions—such as a secretary who works for the manager—that carry no line authority. It is improper for such a person to give orders to others in the line. Another staff organization is the accounting department, which renders a service to management by keeping records and furnishing essential financial and accounting data. A consulting

dietitian serves in a staff position in relation to the superintendent of a small hospital or nursing home. Much trouble can occur when staff members step out of their staff roles and assume an unwarranted line role.

Functional Organizations

If a large corporation were to set up its organizational structure on a functional basis, it might set up a division that was in charge of sales, promotion, and advertising; another that was in charge of planning; another that was in charge of procurement; and so on—seeing that all functions needed to bring the operation to its goals were established. The various functional divisions of a corporation coordinate their activities and (usually) report to a high-level line organization. It is possible for line organizations to exist under a functional one. Thus, individual operating foodservices that receive instructions from various functional divisions are set up as line organizations. Functional organizations are best suited to large corporate units.

Management Action

In any foodservice, daily events raise the need for action by management. Management must be prepared to see that the proper decisions are made so that the operation functions efficiently. Poorly devised action or inaction by management can ultimately cause an operation to fail. Proper procedures and records must be maintained. Employees must be selected with care and given adequate training. Personnel records must be established and maintained, complete with job descriptions. Supervisors must be properly instructed as to plans and actions and must be given adequate authority and backing to ensure that the work progresses satisfactorily. Planning, production, and service must flow smoothly so that patrons are satisfied and functions occur when they should. Making the operation run like clockwork requires considerable management skill. Sound decision making is the product of good judgment, practical knowledge, and astute thinking. The foodservice business is a dynamic, fast-changing one, and management must be equal to its demands.

THE COMPUTER AND MANAGEMENT

The job of managing has been considerably assisted by the computer, which has changed many clerical tasks from manual to mechanical processes, giving management more accurate and more reliable information in a shorter time. This permits better decision making and faster action in response to changing conditions or unexpected developments. The overall result of the computer revolution has been better planning, improved organizational control, and more up-to-date and more nearly complete information. Many tasks are simplified, and some are performed almost automatically. Consequently, management has more time to devote to planning and to direct supervision.

While major computer application came relatively late to the foodservice industry, it is now being extended rapidly into many functions. Some of the more common tasks are discussed in the subsections that follow. In some cases, a more complete explanation is given in a later chapter of this text. While various different computer applications are presented, few (if any) operations have yet put together computer programs that include all of the things a computer can do that are discussed here. The use of computers and the coverage they provide in foodservice operations will undoubtedly continue to be extended in the future.

Menu Planning

Early use of the computer in foodservice operations came in the areas of payroll, inventory, accounting, and point-of-sale transactions—largely because systems covering these areas could easily be adapted from other industry computer applications. The first original programs unique to the foodservice industry were programs set up in the 1950s and 1960s for computer planning of menus. These early programs had as their goal the production of menus planned to meet nutritional standards within certain cost constraints; they were largely developed for health-related foodservices.

Today, menu-planning programs are used to produce menus that meet specific patron and operational needs within certain cost limitations. The program can be set to offer a desirable range of individual menu items, such as the following four soups: one a cream soup; another clear; another heavy with vegetables and other items; and the fourth a purée. The menu programming can include instructions to avoid too much repetition of ingredients or flavors, such as having tomatoes appear a limited number of times in dishes on the menu.

Different forms of preparation can also be specified, to ensure that different cooking methods are found in the new items offered, such as a braised meat item, a roast, a broiled meat, and a deep-fried meat item. The computer can also be programmed to present a balance in meat, fish, and poultry offerings. Special combinations can be established, such as having Yorkshire pudding always appear automatically whenever roast ribs of beef are on the menu, having a horseradish sauce always appear with boiled tongue, or having deep-fried onion rings always appear with sautéed calf's liver. The frequency with which menu items reappear from week to week can also be set. If a retirement home wants chicken to appear on the menu for every Sunday dinner, the computer can be instructed to make this happen. The computer can give a print-out of nutritional values for meals so that management can monitor them to ensure that the proper nutrients are being served.

Recipe size can be expanded or reduced automatically. Thus, a recipe can be exploded (increased) from 25 portions to 150, 250, or 1,000 just by giving the computer the right instructions. Other constraints or needs can be input to the computer and it will comply with them in generating its menus. Quite flexible programs are possible, and often management can override the computer by adding, deleting, or otherwise changing what it does. The list of menu items that is entered into the computer to use in menu planning is called the *menu file*. Normally each menu item is identified in the computer by its code number, but some computers can identify items by name as well.

The Standardized Recipe

Many menu items in the menu file require special preparation before service, and so must be backed up by one or more recipes. The recipes listed in this manner are kept on what is called a *recipe file*. Thus, an item titled Baked Cod Mornay may have two recipes: one for baking the cod in a mornay sauce; and one for making the mornay sauce, which is a béchamel sauce to which cheese has been added. (Actually, the mornay sauce might be listed as a variation under the béchamel sauce recipe.) Thus the mornay sauce in the Baked Cod Mornay recipe actually becomes an ingredient in the baked cod recipe. These other recipes for sauces and other items supporting the main recipe are sometimes called *subrecipes*.

Recipes should be standardized to give a known quantity and a known quality at a known cost. Standardization is accomplished by pretesting recipes and precalculating costs.

Recipes should specify the code number or code name, the total amount of food produced and/or the number of portions, the portion size, the ingredients, the amount of each ingredient used, and the method of handling ingredients to produce the recipe. Cooking times, cooking temperatures, panning instructions, and other relevant information should also be given. Variations and substitutions can be listed at the bottom of the recipe. Total cost of the recipe and cost per portion are usually listed, and sometimes menu selling price is, too. In some cases it may be desirable to identify other items that are served with the item produced by that recipe or to include plating or serving instructions. A picture of how the item should appear is sometimes added, and some computers possess the necessary graphics capabilities for this.

Ingredient File

An ingredient file consists of all ingredients listed for recipes. Ingredients are identified in the computer either by their code numbers or their code names. The ingredient code number should either be the same as that used in purchasing or be closely related to it. Thus, a 6/10 case of tomato catsup might have a purchasing and receiving number of P2148, but on the inventory and issue records it is identified as I2148 because the shipping unit (the case) is opened and broken down in the storeroom and issued in individual No. 10 cans. Pricing also differs. The price of P2148 (a case composed of six cans) is $21.60, and the price of I2148 (a single can) is $3.60. The ingredient price and code may require a third set of numbers, since the catsup used in recipes is often measured by volume. Thus, in the recipe, the ingredient code may be R2148 and the cost $0.035 per fluid ounce. If a recipe called for $1\frac{1}{2}$ pints of catsup, the computer would convert $1\frac{1}{2}$ pints into 24 fluid ounces and multiply $24 \times \$0.035$ for a total ingredient cost of $0.84. Some computers cannot easily convert pints into fluid ounces; in such situations the recipe must give the percent of the can to be used. Similarly, in bar work, making conversions from liter bottles into ounce serving portions is difficult for some computers to do, in which case the bar recipes must express quantities of ingredients in milliliter portions.

Changes in recipes or ingredient costs must be input as they occur so that the recipes can be updated and so that the information compiled by the computer reflects what is actually the case. Often a change in the purchase price of one ingredient automatically changes prices in other files.

Recipes often specify the condition in which an ingredient is to be added to others during preparation of the item. For example, a recipe may call for the ingredient to be sifted, beaten, blanched, melted, diced, or strained.

Forecasting

To obtain an estimate of costs and/or profitability of a specific menu mix (group of menu items), management must develop a projection of the number of menu items that will be sold. This projection is called a *forecast.*

Forecasting is still a rather inexact science. The many variables involved in future demand are often difficult to detect and evaluate. Historical data—such as amount sold for the same meal on the same day last week, last month, or last year—can be used. A popularity index can be kept to record how many portions were sold each time the item appeared on the menu. Another technique is to evaluate the other items competing against a particular menu item and estimate how much they add or detract from its sales. An item that might sell well when grouped with some items might not do as well against others.

The effect of weather, events such as conventions, athletic contests, and other independent factors may have to be taken into account. Food-eating trends and other long-term factors deserve consideration, as well. In some foodservices, fairly good estimates of sales can be developed by noting reservations or bookings (such as with hotels or airlines), occupancy projections for dormitories over weekends, normal attendance for sporting events, or other information that indicates what quantity of patrons to expect.

Forecasting, if done with some care, is a better guide to future demand than just plain guessing or playing hunches—although these should not be ruled out entirely. With some practice and experience, prognosticators will find that their forecasts become increasingly precise and increasingly accurate.

Once the forecast is made and input into the computer, the computer can generate cost, profit, and other financial data. The computer will read the menu item, select its proper recipe, calculate from the recipe the ingredient cost and the portion food cost, and multiply the latter cost by the number of portions given in the sales forecast to establish a projected material cost for the menu item. Repeating this process for each item on the menu yields a total food cost figure for the period covered in the projection. If a selling price for each menu item is input into the computer, the forecast number of sales times the selling price gives the expected income from the item; again, when this is done for all menu items, the sum of the income figures will equal the total sales. These computations enable management to estimate how well the menu is going to do. If other cost projections are programmed, the computer can generate a net profit estimate and make other projections that are of great help to management.

Menu Analysis

Menus can be analyzed in various ways, ranging from highly qualitative methods to complex mathematical ones. Subjective menu evaluation, menu counts (popularity indexes), Hurst's menu scoring, menu factor analysis, the matrix analyses of Miller, Smith-Kasavana, Pavesic, and Kotschevar, goal analysis, and break-even analysis are ten common approaches. Some involve radically different aproaches and give different information; and even those that use similar methods vary in the information they give.

A detailed discussion of menu analysis is beyond the scope of this text at this point. However, such a discussion is included in Appendix A for those wishing to delve deeper into this area. Some facets of menu analysis are also discussed later in Chapter

16 under Menu Engineering and in Chapter 18 under Break-even Analysis.

Complementary Computer Applications

The quantity of items to purchase or to issue is determinable when the quantities of ingredients needed to produce the menu are calculated by the computer. These quantities can be further distinguished as quantities needed for immediate use or as quantities to have on inventory. Timely compilation of such information can help operations avoid stock shortfalls and other frustrating food production problems.

When an ordered item is received, the computer can be informed of the date, the item's code number, purveyor, amount, cost, a description of the goods, whether the item went directly to production (directs) or to stores (inventory), and so on. If programmed to do so, the computer adds the new amount to inventory and calculates a new inventory amount. Directs are charged out as, in effect, issues on the receiving date. By having the computer add directs to storeroom issues, management can obtain a food cost for the day; put into ratio with sales, this gives the percentage food cost. Thus, one might see the following:

Storeroom issues	$ 865.74
Directs	46.83
Total food cost	$ 912.57
Sales	$2,944.23
Percentage food cost	31%

Deducting issue values from inventory and adding receipts enables the computer to generate an updated inventory called a *perpetual inventory*. All these programmed tasks are rapidly and accurately performed by the computer, eliminating much slow and tedious manual manipulation and calculation.

Much useful information for making management decisions can be obtained at the cash register, often called POS (point of sale). With this type of POS system, management at any time can ascertain what checks are out, how long checks have been out, what orders remain unfilled, how many items of a particular kind have been sold, what their dollar value is, what volume of sales has been generated by various servers (this is called a *productivity report*), what amounts credit card charges, room charges, and tips come to, and many other things. At the end of a recording period, total sales, total item or food group sales, and other desirable data are at hand. It is now possible for the computer to run an analysis of how well planning projections made prior to production anticipated actual results. This alone is of tremendous value to management as a tool for refining the processes of planning and decision making. In the days when manual compilation of such data was necessary, the results often were unavailable until too long after an actual occurrence for management to take corrective action.

In addition, after all results are in, the computer can transfer essential data to the general ledger file so that important financial reports such as cash flow, balance sheet, and P&L report can be compiled. Thus, almost from cradle to grave, the computer can be effective in food production management. It has changed clerical, decision-making, and other time-consuming tasks into almost automatic operations and has extended management's control and base of information so that better management is achieved.

SUMMARY

The foodservice industry is the fifth largest industry in the United States. It employs more than 8 million people and accounts for 5 to 6 percent of our gross national product. The industry is highly labor intensive and has many problems because of its wide dispersal of operating units, its low productivity, and its need to produce on demand. It is a healthy industry, however, enjoying one of the best and most stable growths of any industry in the nation. It performs important services in our economic, social, and recreational programs. The industry is characterized by family-owned or single-ownership operations, but this is changing rapidly as chains and multiple-type corporations take over.

Training the large number of employees needed to operate the foodservice industry was at one time quite haphazard and unprogrammed. Today, various formal training programs are springing up, bringing a better-trained employee into the industry. Unions as well as professional associations are beginning to develop training programs. Many individuals are also taking foodservice courses in high schools, community or junior colleges, or four-year universities. A number of graduate programs have been started, and correspondence courses are used heavily. Questions still remain as to which way the educational program should go in providing laboratory experiences and actual work experiences.

One of the best definitions of management is *management is the achievement of goals through people.* Three levels of action can be identified in any foodservice organization: management; mid-management or supervision; and workers. It is the job of the first to plan action, of the second to start action, and of the third to act. Proper activity by personnel in each area of action promotes efficiency and smoothness in the foodservice operation.

Management's responsibility is to provide the planning, organizing, staffing, controlling, and leading necessary to bring the enterprise to its goals. Mid-management's responsibility is usually to receive direction from management and see that the required steps are taken to move the enterprise to its goals. Workers' responsibilities are job-related; because they are specific, these duties are best outlined in job classifications.

Foodservices can be organized in three ways: line, staff, and functional. The last two are frequently combined with the first. A line organization is one in which authority and responsibility flow down from the top through various positions. When reversed, the flow proceeds by the same step-by-step process to the top. Staff organizations usually exist to supply information to the line. Functional organizations serve specific functions within the line organization.

Every person holding a position in an organization should have the proper authority and responsibility to discharge the position's requirements. A failure to establish both power and accountability can cause problems in the organization. Delegation is a procedure by which the duty to perform a job is assigned to a subordinate to carry out. In such cases, the proper authority to do the job must be given; but it is not possible for the individual delegating the job to escape responsibility for whether and how well the job is done.

The computer has significantly changed the planning, management, and implementation of quantity food production. Its effectiveness in almost all phases of foodservice operations has helped management refine traditional methods of planning, control, and decision making.

If properly programmed, the computer can plan a menu within specified constraints, print out standardized recipes for any number of portions desired, set up a file of ingredients so that recipes can be priced out, and calculate portion costs. If a forecast of number of portions to be sold is made, the computer can generate a food cost figure; if given the selling price, it can compute the total dollar sales an item will bring in. Other arrangements allow the computer to estimate what total sales will be.

The computer is also useful in performing various menu analyses (which are of special benefit to management for decision making and planning), in calculating quantities to purchase, in totaling inventory, in keeping track of issues and directs, in setting up receiving reports, in maintaining the payroll, and in making many POS calculations.

CHAPTER REVIEW QUESTIONS

1. Mr. R. A. Kroc developed McDonald's from a tiny group of hamburger drive-ins into one of the world's largest foodservice corporations. He had no foodservice experience but was an engineer. One of the reasons for his success was that he approached management

from an engineer's standpoint. Just what is management, how does it work, and why would a person with a strong engineering or scientific background have attributes that might translate into excellent management abilities?

2. A large foodservice operation finds that its menu is in need of improvement: it lacks good profitability, and management feels that it is deficient in patron appeal. You are a shift manager and know that some of the items on the menu do not make a good gross profit because their food cost is too high and some of them are unappealing. You feel you can help the manager by explaining what you feel is wrong with the menu, but you want some proof. What various analytical methods would you use to analyze the menu and to present evidence of your results to the manager?

3. How big is the foodservice industry in dollar sales and as an employer?

4. What are some of the problems in the industry?

5. What educational facilities are available to those who would like to work in the industry? Identify the opportunities for all levels of work and management.

6. What is management?

7. What are the functions of management?

8. Give an example in which a staff organization and a functional organization are both part of a line operation. What would these organizations do for the line operation?

9. What jobs can a computer do for management? How does it perform these jobs?

VOCABULARY

Foodservice industry	Decision making
Processed foods	Menu programming
Functions of management	Standardized recipe
Maître d'hôtel	Ingredient file
Chef des parties	Recipe file
Saucier	Forecast
Garde manger	Menu analysis
Organization	Directs
Line organization	Issues
Staff organization	Perpetual inventory
Functional organization	

ANNOTATED REFERENCES

Koontz, H.; O'Donnell, C.; and Weihrich, H. 1984. *Management.* 8th ed. New York: McGraw-Hill. 1984. (One of the best and most basic books on management.)

Marasciulo, L., and McSweeney, M. 1977. *Nonparametric and Distribution Methods for the Social Sciences.* Monterey, Cal.: Brooks/Cole Publishing. (A book covering various methods of correlation.)

CHAPTER 2

Nutrition

OUTLINE

Food sustains us and enables us to grow. If we select our food well, we take one important step toward having good health. Good nutrition is important to us from the earliest weeks after conception until our death. A good diet is needed not only to promote essential living functions but also to protect against some of our biggest killers—heart attacks, strokes, cancer, diabetes, and others. Seven of the top causes of deaths in this country are diet-related.

In spite of our high standard of living, we are not the healthiest nation in the world: the United States ranks only seventeenth, according to one international standard. Part of the cause could be our diets. Many people in this nation do not eat well, and many eat foods that lead to impaired health.

Studies have shown that poor nutrition is not restricted to the underprivileged (who may not be able to buy the right kind and amount of food); it also afflicts numerous individuals who can afford a good diet but either do not know how to eat properly or do not care. In 1960, a national nutritional survey showed that a large part of our population lacked optimum diets, and the level of nutrition nationwide was found to be poorer than it was in 1950. In more recent years, this trend has been reversed and our diet picture has improved—but not as much as nutritionists would like. Probably this change has come about because of an increasing awareness and concern about how food affects our health.

In 1977, the federal government responded to public concern by publishing some national dietary goals, which included the following points:

1. Eat more complex carbohydrates such as starches and fewer simple carbohydrates such as sugars.
2. Reduce the amount of fat and see that more monounsaturated and polyunsaturated ones are in the diet rather than saturated ones.
3. Increase fiber intake.
4. Reduce salt (sodium) intake.

PUBLIC AWARENESS

Within the last decade or so, people have been hearing more about food and how it affects our health. As a result, many people have become concerned about what they eat, and their dietary patterns have changed. The dietary guidelines of 1977 are being heeded, and many people are following good exercise programs to improve or maintain their health. The convincing evidence that obesity leads to serious health problems has been a stimulus to reduce weight, along with the fact that people feel better and look better when they are thinner. Reducing salt intake is a major step in combating or avoiding hypertension (high blood pressure). The danger of heart problems is lessened by efforts to cut

down on saturated fat and cholesterol intake. We are on a health-diet binge that shows no sign of abating. Most people today want to eat well to be well, and they are aggressively pursuing the dietary way.

One way in which dietary patterns are changing is that people are not consuming as much red meat (beef, lamb, and pork). These meats contain saturated fats that may be harmful in too large amounts. More white meats, such as chicken and fish, are being consumed because their fat is less saturated. Along with eating less red meat, people are reducing their consumption of eggs, butter, and other fatty foods in order to lower their saturated fat, cholesterol, and calorie intake. There is a distinct trend toward eating more fresh fruits and vegetables, although the total quantity of processed and fresh vegetables and fruits consumed has not increased significantly. People are also eating more high-fiber foods such as whole-grain cereals, bran, vegetables, and fruits. Table 2-1 gives the saturated fat, unsaturated fat, cholesterol, and calorie content of some foods.

Public concern has challenged foodservices to become more knowledgeable about nutrition and more careful in planning menus that meet the needs of patrons. Foodservice operations today must have a basic knowledge of how to select and prepare foods in a manner that preserves the nutrients they contain and how to avoid foods that are not desirable for some patrons. It has been found that selling

Table 2-1. Fats, Cholesterol, and Calories in Some Foods

Food	Fat (%)		Cholesterol* (%)	Calories (per 100 g)
	Saturated	Unsaturated		
Milk, whole	2	1	0.01	65
Lamb	12	9	0.07	276
Eggs	4	5	0.50	163
Chicken	2	3	0.06	124
Beef, choice	12	11	0.07	301
Pork, lean	4	4	0.07	185
Salmon	5	5	0.04	222
Veal	5	4	0.09	207
Fish, lean	2	4	0.07	79

*0.07% means that a person receives 70 milligrams of cholesterol in 100 grams (about 3 oz) of product.

nutrition pays, and many foodservices are becoming more expert in nutrition because it improves the bottom line to do so. Educational institutions are also finding it advisable to include instruction on nutrition. Thus, in the future we should see even more attention being paid to nutritional matters. An added impetus is public and governmental pressure. Already the fastfood industry is being pressured by the government to publish the nutritional value of the foods it serves. This requirement could spread throughout the industry.

Unfortunately, there is so much widely circulated misinformation about nutrition and diets in the public mind that foodservices find it difficult to meet all the ideas patrons have about diet and about the foods they should eat. If a foodservice decides to embark on a nutritional program, it should know how to do it, it should set it up carefully, and it should execute a carefully planned strategy to see that it is done right.

How much responsibility do foodservices have in providing nutrition for patrons? Are they responsible for seeing an adequate diet is selected and consumed? There is no easy answer. It depends upon the person selecting and eating the food, the foodservice, and the situation.

The Patron's Responsibility

Patrons eating in foodservices often have primary responsibility for making nutritious choices. Those who freely select where and what they eat should select a foodservice that can provide what they want and need and then should select foods properly. If a patron is not free to select the place and what is consumed, however, the foodservice has some responsibility. Thus, if a person elects to eat at a drive-in every day and always buys a hamburger, a carbonated beverage, and fries, the foodservice should not be blamed for the person's faulty diet; but if the patron is in a hospital or other institution where all food is provided, the foodservice is obliged to see that the diet adequately meets the patron's needs. In short, depending upon circumstances, patrons have a varying responsibility in selecting a diet that is nutritious.

Most commercial operations are subject to free selection of place and of what is consumed. Such operations' responsibility is to ensure that the food offered contains all the nutrients that it should contain—whether or not the food offers a complete and balanced diet. If the operation offers a complete menu where patrons can order a complete meal, it has an obligation to offer items that together constitute a nutritious meal; but if the operation offers only partial meals, no such responsibility attaches. Patrons eating partial meals should ensure on their own that they complete their dietary requirements at some other time during the day. Nonetheless, foodservices must recognize patrons' concerns about nutrition and must try to meet the industry's responsibilities. About 25 percent of our nutrition is provided outside the home, and foodservices thus have a very real responsibility to the nation's welfare and health.

Eating Trends Today

People today eat less because they are less active. Alcohol consumption is dropping. Instead of hard spirits, more wine and lighter alcoholic beverages are selected. A glass of white wine or a glass of orange juice is a common request at a cocktail party. On average, the consumption of rich desserts is down, but many restaurants find that patrons eating out may want to splurge and eat a rich, high-calorie, luscious dessert as a special treat. Many seek foods that for a given number of calories offer a high nutrient yield; often these foods are called *nutrient-dense*, in contrast to *empty-calorie* or *junk* foods that give calories but little or no other nutrients. Calories are not bad in themselves, but eating only calories with little or no accompanying nutrients creates nutritional problems.

The public concern for better nutrition has been felt by foodservices, as is evidenced by changes in patrons' food-selecting habits and by increased demand for specific kinds of foods and preparation. Rich foods are less favored, and a type called *nouvelle cuisine* has become popular. Many hotels and other operations feature low-calorie and low-fat foods. Terms such as "Lean 'n' Light" and "Heart Food" are often at the column head. Some foodservices ask the American Heart Association or American Dietetic Association to approve the recipe for a menu item and then indicate such approval when this food appears on the menu. Some put a small heart after each entrée approved by the American Heart Association. This change in eating patterns has gone beyond being a fad; it is a permanent change.

SOME NUTRITIONAL CONCERNS

People today are interested in weight control, reduced intake of sodium (salt), low-cholesterol or low-fat diets, high-fiber foods, special diets for geriatric eating problems, and alcohol restriction. These and some others are covered in the subsections that follow.

Weight Control

The desire to lose weight is perhaps the most widespread nutritional concern in the United States today. The way for a person to lose weight is to lower caloric intakes below what is needed for the body to function. Exercise increases the body's caloric need. Drugs can help, but this is dangerous and should only be done under medical advice. A person's weight usually increases slowly, and the best way to get rid of excess weight is to embark on a program of losing weight at about the same rate at which it was originally gained. Crash diets are unhealthful and do not usually lead to permanent weight loss. There is also a danger in going below a food intake level of 1,200 calories per day for an adult because below this level it is difficult to get a sufficient supply of all necessary nutrients. Permanent weight control occurs when a person changes from the old diet to a new one and stays on the new one.

Lean meats, fruits, vegetables, low-fat dairy products, and other low-calorie foods should be consumed in place of high-fat foods to reduce

calories. A good daily diet might include the following items:

Two 8-oz glasses of nonfat milk (or equivalent)
Two 2-oz portions of lean meat, fish, or poultry (or other good protein equivalent)
Four 3-oz portions of fruits and vegetables
Four 1-oz portions of grains (or carbohydrate equivalent)—preferably whole grains

This diet is often called the Basic Four Meal Plan or what is sometimes called the 2-2-4-4 plan. To increase calories, select appropriate additional meats, grains, desserts, and other rich foods.

Although some think carbohydrates are fattening, they are not. One gram of carbohydrate contains 4 calories; 1 gram of protein, 4; 1 gram of fat, 9; and 1 gram of alcohol, 7. Thus, fat and alcohol are the big fatteners. Three ounces of lean chicken breast without skin—one of the lowest-calorie meats—has three times more calories than 3 oz of baked potato. Some carbohydrate is essential to dieters when dieting, to burn up fat. If about 500 calories (5 oz) of carbohydrate is not consumed, dangerous byproducts of fat breakdown can induce a ketonic coma and then death.

Some foodservices are misinformed on what foods are low-calorie. They will include a hamburger patty in a low-calorie meal, thinking they have chosen a low-calorie product. But the hamburger contains 325 calories because of its fat. Selecting a lean fish such as cod or sole, a chicken breast, or a lean piece of meat increases the likelihood of keeping a modest meal below 500 calories. A vegetable plate with a poached egg (80 calories) on a thin square of whole-wheat toast, ½ cup each of four vegetables (such as carrots, green peas, baked tomato, and broccoli), ¼ head of lettuce with a low-calorie dressing, and a glass of low-fat milk equals about 350 calories. Topping it off with a low-calorie gelatin dessert with fresh fruit, low-cal canned fruit, or a low-cal sherbet or ice milk keeps the entire meal under 500 calories. Food should not be cooked in fat, and butter or margarine should be used sparingly as a seasoning. Often, if care is taken to hold down fat, the calories in a meal drop considerably.

The Low-salt (Low-sodium) Diet

Too much sodium causes hypertension (high blood pressure) or other health problems in some people. Plant and animal foods contain some natural sodium, but most of our sodium comes from table salt (sodium chloride). About a third of our sodium comes from our own salting of foods, another third comes from processed food we buy, and the final third is present naturally in foods. A normal person can consume 3 to 8.5 grams of salt a day without experiencing any problems. A teaspoon of salt weighs 7 grams. Most normal people have no problem handling a slight sodium excess. Some drinking waters are high in sodium and must be avoided by people observing low-sodium diets. Except in special dietary cases, the salt added to food should contain iodine, an essential nutrient.

Foodservices should undersalt all foods and let patrons add an additional amount to suit their taste. The menu or a table tent may state "We purposely undersalt our foods and provide extra salt at the table for those who wish to add more." Another nice gesture is to put a good salt substitute on the table. Most individuals on a low-sodium diet should be conversant with the sodium content of foods and know which to select. They can also request that there be no salt on foods. Foodservices, too, should be informed as to the sodium content of foods. Many substances contain sodium, including baking powder, baking soda, monosodium glutamate, and sodium sulfite. With normal precautions on both sides, there should not be a problem in satisfying a low-sodium diet in an ordinary foodservice.

Low-fat or Low-cholesterol Diets

It is not difficult to serve a low-fat meal if certain rules are observed. No fried or fatty foods should be served. Butter and margarine should be used sparingly. Foods rich in fat such as pastries and other desserts should be avoided. Foods such as mayonnaise, avocado (about one-quarter fat), and peanut butter contain the same amount of fat per ½ oz as 4 oz of roast beef. It is often desirable to reduce saturated fat and increase unsaturated fat in the diet. A foodservice can meet this need by consulting a good table that indicates the fat content of foods.

It is also wise to refer to a table of food values in planning a low-cholesterol diet. Saturated fats should be restricted, and so (probably) should calories. Unsaturated fats help lower the cholesterol content of the blood. When a person loses weight, a frequent complementary occurrence is the lowering of blood cholesterol levels. The American Heart Association has stated that cholesterol in foods should be limited to less than 300 mg per day. An egg contains 274 mg of cholesterol. Our bodies need about 900 mg of cholesterol per day to make bile, to produce sex and energy hormones, to keep the skin lubricated, to make vitamin D, to use in nerves and brain cells, and to perform other functions. We could not exist without cholesterol. A number of people find that reducing cholesterol in the diet does little good, because the body generates its own to make up for the deficiency. In one test, over 1,800 men who had high blood cholesterol levels were for seven years put on a low-cholesterol diet; the men averaged a 3.5 percent lowering of serum cholesterol. An individual is considered at risk for cardiovascular problems if the serum cholesterol level is higher than 220 milligrams per deciliter of blood. Thus, if a person has a blood cholesterol level of 300 milligrams and reduces it by 3.5 percent, the blood cholesterol level is lowered by 10.5 milligrams but remains at a still-dangerous level of 289.5 milligrams. Exercise, weight reduction, no smoking, spicy foods, garlic, fibers from oatmeal and other grains, fruits and vegetables, hard water, and other food items and dietary changes can help reduce cholesterol. The problem is largely genetic—less than 5 percent of the families in the United States account for around 50 percent of heart-related deaths—and a low-cholesterol diet together with other good living patterns seems to be about the best way to try to lower serum cholesterol. Some people at risk can take drugs, but others cannot because they are vulnerable to bad side effects of the drugs.

Cholesterol is blamed for causing cardiovascular problems because it joins with other substances to form a plaque that accumulates in the artery walls and causes them to harden and become inflexible. Deposits of plaque can develop to such an extent that they severely constrict the interior diameter of an artery or even plug it. All such problems with arteries make the heart work harder. People differ in the kind of cholesterol they carry in the blood. Some carry a lot of high-density lipoproteins (HDL) that are high in protein but low in cholesterol and for this reason are more soluble in the blood and less apt to form plaque deposits. Other people carry a lot of low-density lipoproteins (LDL) that encourage deposits. Eating saturated fats seems to build up low-density lipoproteins, while eating polyunsaturated fats builds up high-density ones. Most vegetable oils contain polyunsaturated fats.

The High-fiber Diet

Fiber is largely composed of a complex carbohydrate called *cellulose.* It occurs in bran, and it forms the skeletal structure of fruits and vegetables, but it is not found in flesh foods. A diet high in fiber can reduce a person's chance of developing intestinal cancer, diverticulosis, constipation, and appendicitis; it can even promote weight loss by displacing other, higher-calorie foods in a normally filling diet. Fiber reduces cholesterol in the digestive tract, thus lowering its chances of being absorbed into the body. There are two ways of identifying fiber amounts. One is in terms of *crude* fiber, which is the fiber that remains in food after treatment with alkalis and acids. The other is in terms of *dietary* fiber, which is the fiber actually present in food in the diet. A person needs about 6 grams of crude fiber (about 15 grams of dietary fiber) per day. A serving (1 oz) of bran flakes contains 6 oz of dietary fiber. A 4-in. piece of corn-on-the-cob contains 6 to 8 oz of dietary fiber. Eating the amount of fruits and vegetables indicated in the 2-2-4-4 diet (discussed

previously) supplies enough fiber, especially if whole-grain cereal products are selected.

It is possible to get too much fiber, since fiber can cause digestive disturbances and can even cause dehydration by pulling too much water out of the body and into the feces. It may also cause foods to pass too quickly through the digestive system, resulting in poor nutrient absorption.

THE NUTRIENTS

Some forty nutrients are needed by the body. These fall into categories such as carbohydrates, proteins, fats, vitamins, and minerals. Water is not a nutrient, but it is essential because it allows the body to carry on its functions. Fiber is not a nutrient, either, but it too is essential. The diet should be designed to allow these items to be consumed in adequate amounts for good health.

The Calorie Nutrients

We get energy from three nutrients—four, if we include alcohol. The three are carbohydrates, proteins, and fats. The body can turn these into calories for energy. Carbohydrates are used almost exclusively for energy, but protein and fat play additional important roles.

Protein

The major material used in making muscle, blood, skin, hair, and the internal organs is protein. Bones and teeth start out as protein substances; then, as minerals replace the protein, they become hard tissues. Proteins are needed to make growth possible, to repair body tissues, and to form hormones, antibodies, vitamins, and other essential substances. Animal products furnish good-quality protein; cereals combined with legumes also furnish fairly good protein; nuts and seeds supply some protein in the diet. Even fruits and vegetables contain some protein, but not in significant amounts.

Protein is made up of units called *amino acids.*

There are twenty-two known amino acids, eight of which the body cannot manufacture and which (as a result) we must get from our diets. We call these eight *essential* amino acids. A *complete* protein is one that contains all eight essential amino acids. An *incomplete* protein is one that lacks one or more essential amino acids or has them in poor balance. When we combine cereals and legumes, we get complete proteins, but each separately has only an incomplete protein makeup. Soybean protein is nearly complete.

We need about 15 percent of our total calories to come from protein; about 25 percent of this should be animal protein. Vegetarians and others are able to live without animal proteins because they combine incomplete plant proteins to produce effectively complete ones.

If the diet lacks calories from fats or carbohydrates, the body breaks down body proteins and uses them for energy. This is an expensive way to get energy; even in weight-loss diets, carbohydrates should be eaten in sufficient amount to spare protein from metabolic attack.

Carbohydrates

Carbohydrates, our main source of energy, come from foods such as cereals, beans, syrups, and sugars. These foods are our cheapest source of energy. Our bodies break down carbohydrates into a simple sugar called *glucose;* this is what we burn for energy and heat. The liver can change glucose into a body starch called *glycogen.* This and the small amount of sugar in our muscles and blood constitute our energy reserve. If we use up the reserve, we have to get the energy we need from fat or protein. About 55 to 65 percent of our total calories should come from carbohydrates. As has been noted, some carbohydrate must be in the diet (about 100 grams per day) to help burn fat in a reducing diet or serious problems can occur.

Carbohydrate is also our most efficient source of energy. An athlete whose diet is high in carbohydrate and not too high in protein has improved stamina and strength. Athletes should not have too much fiber in their diet. For this reason, they do better on carbohydrates from cereals and potatoes than on carbohydrates from fruits and vegetables.

Fats (Lipids)

Fats and fatty substances belong to the family called *lipids.* They are rich sources of energy, but only a few are known to be essential in the diet. In their disfavor, they give a lot of calories and also are associated with cardiovascular disease. The fat-soluble vitamins A, E, D, and K are found in fats. Fatty foods stay in the stomach longest, while carbohydrates stay the shortest time and proteins fall in between (but closer to fats). Thus, we say a meal that is high in fat and protein "sticks to the ribs." Food mixtures of fat, protein, and carbohydrate stay in the stomach just about as long as fatty foods do.

The Body Regulators

Vitamins and minerals are important because they help carry on essential bodily functions. Minerals also have importance because they form a part of hard tissues and constitute important substance-forming materials in many body tissues.

Vitamins

If the body were a machine, the energizing spark provided by vitamins could be compared to the flash of a spark plug that gets the combustion engine of the machine going. If the spark were not there, the machine would not run. Even though vitamins are needed in only minute amounts (like the flash of a spark plug), this amount is vital to good health.

The body cannot make many vitamins; most of them must be gleaned from our food. We know that various vitamins are essential, and we even know how much of some vitamins is needed; on the other hand, we do not know how much of some others is, and as a result, scientists are unsure whether all vitamins have yet been identified.

Because fat-soluble vitamins can be stored in excess in the body, consuming too much of them can cause health problems and even death. Vitamin A is required for tissue health—especially tissues of the nose, ear, throat, and alimentary canal. It is essential to good eyesight, can help fight off infections, helps regulate cell growth, and can delay senility and increase longevity. It is found in yellow and orange fruits and vegetables and in leafy green vegetables as a precursor called *carotene.* Butter and eggs also contain it. It appears in a different form and to a lesser extent in some other foods. Vitamin A is relatively stable in foods and in cooking. We need about 5,000 international units (IU) of this vitamin per day. A green leafy, yellow, or orange vegetable every other day is a good safeguard. Vitamin D is found in milkfat, fish, fish oils, and organ meats. It is often added to margarine and other foods as well. It prevents rickets, helps build bones and teeth, keeps up muscle tone, and reduces the danger of osteomalacia (a rickets-like problem experienced by some adults). Ultraviolet rays from sunlight or lamps striking the skin change egosterol or dehydrocholesterol into vitamin D. Vitamin E, found in many foods but most plentifully in seed and nut oils, functions largely as an antioxidant in the body. Contrary to some people's belief, it does not help prevent infertility in man. It may, however, help prevent damage from smog and other harmful gases in the atmosphere. Vitamin K is required for blood clotting and may have something to do with blood manufacture. It is found in many vegetables, especially the leafy green ones. Of all these fat-soluble vitamins, vitamin D is the most toxic in excess. About 10 micrograms of vitamins D and E per day is sufficient for an adult male. No requirement has been set for vitamin K.

The B-vitamin group is made up of about ten vitamins. They were once identified as a single vitamin, vitamin B, but today we have B vitamins ranging from B_1 to B_{12}. The chemical names are largely used today. Thiamine (B_1) is found in meats, whole-grain or enriched cereals, and legumes. It is needed for muscle action including heart, nerve, and brain functions, good appetite, normal digestion, proper growth, fertility, lactation, the ability to utilize carbohydrates, and avoidance of beriberi (a muscle and nerve disease). Riboflavin (B_2) is found in leafy vegetables, milk products, meats, and cereals. It helps maintain skin, nerves, and eyes; it works

with pyridoxine (vitamin B_6) to change tryptophan (an amino acid) into a vitamin (niacin). It is essential in oxidation reactions in the body. Niacin is found in organ meats, flesh, nuts, and cereals. A diet high in tryptophan provides plenty of niacin. It cures pellagra, works as a coenzyme in removing hydrogen from substances so that the body can use them, and helps maintain skin and the nervous system. Pyridoxine (B_6) is widely distributed in plant and animal foods; flesh, liver, vegetables, and whole-grain cereals are the best sources. It maintains skin, helps prevent anemia, and acts as a coenzyme for many bodily reactions. A lack of pyridoxine causes convulsions. Folacin is widely found in the green part of plants. It works as a coenzyme to further body reactions, helps in the use of amino acids, helps make chole (a vitamin), helps make purines and pyrimidines, and works with vitamin B_{12} and vitamin C to prevent anemia. Vitamin B_{12} (cobalamin) is found only in animal proteins. It is mainly associated with the prevention of pernicious anemia. It is not found in plants and so some vegetarians may lack it. The recommended amount of B vitamins per day in an adult male's diet is as follows: thiamine, 1.4 mg; riboflavin, 1.7 mg; niacin, 18 mg equivalent; pyridoxine, 2.2 mg; folacin, 400 micrograms; and B_{12}, 3 micrograms.

There are no recommended amounts for the other B vitamins. Pantothenic acid is plentiful in most animal and plant foods. It helps to produce energy in the body. Biotin, which is found in organ meats, chicken, eggs, milk, most fresh vegetables, and some fruits, is needed to metabolize carbohydrates, fats, and proteins. Choline is found in brains, organ meats, eggs, yeast, wheat germ, milk products, meats, and vegetables. It functions in protein and fat metabolism. Myoinositol is found in organ meats, brains, whole-grain cereals, and yeast. It probably performs metabolic functions.

Most of the B vitamins are fragile and can be destroyed if cooked too long. Thiamine, pyridoxine, and some others are destroyed if placed in an alkaline medium, such as when soda is added to cooking water. An acidic medium helps preserve them. Riboflavin and some other B vitamins are harmed by the ultraviolet rays of sunlight. Other B vitamins oxidize easily. All are quite soluble in water; for this reason soaking, cooking in water, or otherwise exposing foods to water can lead to a leaching out of the B vitamins. Taking care in the storage, preparation, cooking, and holding of foods rich in B vitamins can do much to preserve the vitamins. Following the 2-2-4-4 diet gives an adequate amount of them all—especially if whole-grain cereals are included in the diet.

Vitamins often join with minerals, enzymes, or other vitamins to do their jobs. When they join an enzyme, the substance is called a *coenzyme*. Many coenzymes perform bodily functions. Some vitamins and minerals work only when other substances are present. Thus, eating just a few of the essential nutrients does not work: a full, balanced group must be consumed to get the job done. The presence of one substance often demands another. Thus, the quantity of thiamine regulates the quantity of energy produced in the body, since thiamine must be present for energy production to occur.

Vitamin C is often called "the sailors' vitamin" because in past centuries sailors who stayed out at sea for long periods of time without vitamin C developed scurvy, "the sailors' disease," evidenced by hemorrhaging under the skin, swollen and bleeding gums, and great weakness. Magellan and a number of his men died of scurvy during the expedition's famous circling of the earth. The disease was caused by the prolonged reliance on a salt meat and biscuit diet with no fresh vegetables. Later, a British physician discovered that the citrus fruit family contained a substance that would cure scurvy, and the British navy ordered all its ships to carry lemons or limes on cruises in order to prevent it. This is why the British sailor is called a *limey*.

Vitamin C is found in good supply in citrus fruits, tomatoes, leafy vegetables of the cabbage family, tropical fruits, and potatoes. It is essential for the production of collagen, the substance that initiates the formation of bones and teeth. It also aids in wound healing and is related to the metabolism of some amino acids and to other bodily functions. It helps the body produce some hormones and helps maintain the bones and teeth.

Vitamin C (also known as ascorbic acid) is very fragile. It can be destroyed by oxidation and cooking (especially in alkaline mediums), and it is so water-soluble that it can easily be leached out of foods. In quantity cooking, much of the ascorbic acid in food tends to be destroyed. Therefore, foodservice operations usually do not plan on having a liberal supply of the vitamin in the foods served; they often advise people to obtain a good source of vitamin C in the morning for breakfast and then not worry about getting it the rest of the day. By eating plenty of fresh fruits and vegetables, however, a person's diet will usually have an adequate amount of vitamin C without such a morning precaution.

Minerals

Minerals participate in many bodily functions. They make body tissues such as bones and teeth. They carry out essential reactions such as the transfer of electrical nerve impulses. Some form parts of vitamins, as cobalt does in vitamin B_{12}; others help make proteins, as sulfur does in the proteins that make up the hair, skin, and nails. Similarly, iron is used in making blood, and iodine is an element in thyroxine, which regulates the body's cell functions. Our muscles contract and relax because of minerals. They are also vital in maintaining a proper acid-alkali balance in the body. Some fifteen minerals are used by the body. We think we know how much iron, zinc, iodine, calcium, and phosphorus are needed, but not how much magnesium, sodium, potassium, copper, cobalt, manganese, sulfur, chlorine, fluorine, molybdenum, chromium, and selenium.

Because of the number of minerals we need, our diet must contain a variety of foods to get all in adequate amounts. Milk and milk products, meat or its equivalent, fruits, vegetables, and cereals together provide the needed variety. Iron is well supplied in dried fruits and meats—especially organ meats. Milk provides calcium and phosphorus; phosphorus can also be supplied by meat, fruits, and vegetables. Iodine is best found in iodized salt, seafoods, and fruits and vegtables grown in soil of good iodine content. If the 2-2-4-4 plan is followed, the diet usually includes enough minerals. The sources of various minerals and the body's use of each mineral are given in table 2-2.

Water

About two-thirds of the body is water. Water is an essential part of cells and forms a major part of body fluids in which many essential processes of the body take place. Water helps regulate temperature through evaporation from the skin. Another important use of water is in digesting foods, after which it must be reabsorbed in the intestines. Water also acts as a lubricant to reduce friction between moving body parts, thus preventing fatigue.

Water is taken into the body in fluids and foods. It is produced when food is converted into energy. The amount of water in the body can vary. Salt and other minerals increase the amount held; lowering their intake causes the body to lose water and thus weight. In some health problems, a swelling of the body called *edema* results when water is retained, making the body appear puffy in parts. A finger pressed against the flesh at such a place leaves a depression that goes away slowly. Prolonged protein deficiency or kidney disease can cause edema.

The body eliminates water through urine, feces, sweat, skin evaporation, and breath. Harm to the kidneys or the buildup of harmful substances in the blood may occur if the body lacks water (a condition called *dehydration*). Excessive perspiration may cause dehydration and, if severe enough, may cause heat exhaustion, heat stroke, or even death. The average individual should have the equivalent of six to eight glasses of water daily in his or her food.

Our Need for Nutrients

From time to time in the above discussion reference has been made to the normal requirement for an individual. These all have been given for an adult male but it can vary because of age, sex, or other factors. Table 2-3 lists the Recommended Daily Dietary Allowances of the Food and Nutrition Board of the National Academy of Sciences. It is evident from this table that people's nutritional needs vary. The data given are for the average person; some individuals with special circumstances

will need more or less than the tabulated amount of some nutrients.

Nutrient Labeling

Many foods today must bear on the package label a listing of nutrients found in one serving of the item. The following information must be given:

Calories	number
Protein	in grams
Carbohydrate	in grams
Fat	in grams
Protein	% of USRDA
Vitamin A	% of USRDA
Vitamin C	% of USRDA
Thiamine	% of USRDA
Riboflavin	% of USRDA
Niacin	% of USRDA
Calcium	% of USRDA
Iron	% of USRDA

Twelve other nutrients may also be shown as a percentage of the USRDA, at the option of the manufacturer. Added substances (additives) must be indicated. Some labels give the quantity of saturated and unsaturated fats, the quantity of sodium, the quantity of cholesterol, or other nutritional information about the product. Some foods may be indicated with two nutrient values—one being a portion of the food in the package, and the other being the nutrient value of the food when it is combined with something else (as occurs when dry cereal is eaten with whole milk). Finally, the label may give the quantity of nutrients for a larger serving than normal. If the quantity of a nutrient is less than 2 percent of a day's requirement, the amount is not stated on the label but is shown as * or 0. The number of portions in the package is also identified.

The U.S. Recommended Daily Allowance (USRDA) list of the Food and Drug Administration (FDA) is used as the basis for judging what a day's proper allowance is (see table 2-4). The values on this list differ from those on the RDA list given in table 2-3.

Table 2-2. Sources and Uses of Minerals

Mineral	Good Source	Use in Body
Iron	Egg yolk, dried legumes, meat, enriched or whole-grain cereals, molasses	Element in blood; found in muscle tissues
Iodine	Seafood, iodized salt, fruits, vegetables	Governs reactions that control the body's speed of metabolism; lack may lead to swelling of the thyroid gland, causing a goiter; lack can cause a pregnant woman to give birth to a mentally deficient child
Calcium	Milk products, shellfish, egg yolk, some fruits and vegetables	Element in bones and teeth; helps muscles function and maintains bones so osteoporosis and osteomalacia do not occur; helps blood coagulate and helps maintain body's acid-base balance; pregnant or lactating women and rapidly growing children need more than do others
Phosphorus	Milk, flesh, egg yolk, cereals, legumes, nuts	Works with calcium to make hard tissues; important in the development of energy; helps maintain body's acid-base balance
Magnesium	Leafy green vegetables, nuts, soybeans, snails	Functions in muscle contraction and nerve reactions
Sodium	Table salt, root vegetables, flesh, processed foods	Maintains fluid and acid-base balances
Potassium	Bran, molasses, potatoes, tea, coffee, legumes, spices, yeast, cocoa	Important in muscle, brain, and nerve cell functioning
Copper	Cocoa, tea, coffee, nuts, beef, liver, pork liver	Helps make blood
Zinc	Eggs, milk products, flesh, peanut butter, whole-grain cereals	Element in insulin and some enzymes; important in the sexual maturation of males and in successful pregnancies
Cobalt	Animal products only	Important part of vitamin B_{12}
Manganese	Nuts, tea, cocoa, coffee, bran, canned pineapple, whole-grain cereals	Helps form blood and some coenzymes
Sulfur	Whole grains, legumes, cheese, lean flesh, nuts	Important part of some essential amino acids
Chlorine	Meats, cheese, table salt	Important part of gastric juices; combines with many of the body's essential substances
Fluorine	Fluoridated water, flesh, plant foods	Helps make and maintain strong teeth and bones
Molybdenum	Organ meats, dark green vegetables, cereals, legumes	Probably involved in the catabolism of some substances in the body
Chromium	Brewer's yeast, flesh, nuts, whole grains, American cheese	Thought to be useful in changing carbohydrate to energy
Selenium	Animal products, whole-grain cereals	Thought to be related to antioxidant reactions

217271

Table 2-3. Recommended Daily Dietary Allowances of the Food and Nutrition Board of the National Academy of Sciences and the National Research Council

	Age (years)	Weight (kg)	Weight (lbs)	Height (cm)	Height (in)	Energy (kcal)[a]	Protein (g)	Vitamin A Activity (RE)[b]	Vitamin A (IU)	Vitamin D (IU)	Vitamin E Activity[d] (IU)	Ascorbic Acid[d] (mg)	Folacin[e] (µg)	Niacin[f] (mg)	Riboflavin (mg)	Thiamin (mg)	Vitamin B₆ (mg)	Vitamin B₁₂ (µg)	Calcium (mg)	Phosphorus (mg)	Iodine (µg)	Iron (mg)	Magnesium (mg)	Zinc (mg)
Infants	0.0–0.5	6	14	60	24	kg × 117	kg × 2.2	420[c]	1,400	400	4	35	50	5	0.4	0.3	0.3	0.3	360	240	35	10	60	3
	0.5–1.0	9	20	71	28	kg × 108	kg × 2.0	400	2,000	400	5	35	50	8	0.6	0.5	0.4	0.3	540	400	45	15	70	5
Children	1–3	13	28	86	34	1,300	23	400	2,000	400	7	40	100	9	0.8	0.7	0.6	1.0	800	800	60	15	150	10
	4–6	20	44	110	44	1,800	30	500	2,500	400	9	40	200	12	1.1	0.9	0.9	1.5	800	800	80	10	200	10
	7–10	30	66	135	54	2,400	36	700	3,500	400	10	40	300	16	1.2	1.2	1.2	2.0	800	800	110	10	250	10
Males	11–14	44	97	158	63	2,800	44	1,000	5,000	400	12	45	400	18	1.5	1.4	1.6	3.0	1,200	1,200	130	18	350	15
	15–18	61	134	172	69	3,000	54	1,000	5,000	400	15	45	400	20	1.8	1.5	2.0	3.0	1,200	1,200	150	18	400	15
	19–22	67	147	172	69	3,000	54	1,000	5,000	400	15	45	400	20	1.8	1.5	2.0	3.0	800	800	140	10	350	15
	23–50	70	154	172	69	2,700	56	1,000	5,000		15	45	400	18	1.6	1.4	2.0	3.0	800	800	130	10	350	15
	51+	70	154	172	69	2,400	56	1,000	5,000		15	45	400	16	1.5	1.2	2.0	3.0	800	800	110	10	350	15
Females	11–14	44	97	155	62	2,400	44	800	4,000	400	12	45	400	16	1.3	1.2	1.6	3.0	1,200	1,200	115	18	300	15
	15–18	54	119	162	65	2,100	48	800	4,000	400	12	45	400	14	1.4	1.1	2.0	3.0	1,200	1,200	115	18	300	15
	19–22	58	128	162	65	2,100	46	800	4,000	400	12	45	400	14	1.4	1.1	2.0	3.0	800	800	100	18	300	15
	23–50	58	128	162	65	2,000	46	800	4,000		12	45	400	13	1.2	1.0	2.0	3.0	800	800	100	18	300	15
	51+	58	128	162	65	1,800	46	800	4,000		12	45	400	12	1.1	1.0	2.0	3.0	800	800	80	10	300	15
Pregnant						+300	+30	1,000	5,000	400	15	60	800	+2	+0.3	+0.3	2.5	4.0	1,200	1,200	125	18+[g]	450	20
Lactating						+500	+20	1,200	6,000	400	15	80	600	+4	+0.5	+0.3	2.5	4.0	1,200	1,200	150	18	450	25

NOTE: The allowances are intended to provide for individual variations among most normal persons as they live in the United States under usual environmental stresses. Diets should be based on a variety of common foods in order to provide other nutrients for which human requirements have been less well defined.

[a] Kilojoules (kJ) = 4.2 × kcal.

[b] Retinol equivalents.

[c] Assumed to be all as retinol in milk during the first six months of life. All subsequent intakes are assumed to be half as retinol and half as β-carotene when calculated from international units. As retinol equivalents, three-fourths are as retinol and one-fourth as β-carotene.

[d] Total vitamin E activity, estimated to be 80 percent as α-tocopherol and 20 percent other tocopherols. See text for variation in allowances.

[e] The folacin allowances refer to dietary sources as determined by *Lactobacillus casei* assay. Pure forms of folacin may be effective in doses less than one fourth of the recommended dietary allowance.

[f] Although allowances are expressed as niacin, it is recognized that on the average 1 mg of niacin is derived from each 60 mg of dietary tryptophan.

[g] This increased requirement cannot be met by ordinary diets; therefore, the use of supplemental iron is recommended.

Table 2-4. Chart of the FDA's U.S. Recommended Daily Allowance (USRDA) for Use in Nutrition Labeling of Foods

	Adults and Children over 4 Yrs.	Children under 4 Yrs.	Infants under 13 Months	Pregnant or Lactating Women
Protein	65 g	28 g	25 g	65 g
Vitamin A	5,000 IU	2,500 IU	2,500 IU	8,000 IU
Vitamin C	60 mg	40 mg	40 mg	60 mg
Thiamine	1.5 mg	0.7 mg	0.7 mg	1.7 mg
Riboflavin	1.7 mg	0.8 mg	0.8 mg	2.0 mg
Niacin	20 mg	9.0 mg	9.0 mg	20 mg
Calcium	1.0 g	0.8 g	0.8 g	1.3 g
Iron	18 mg	10 mg	10 mg	18 mg
Vitamin D	400 IU	400 IU	400 IU	400 IU
Vitamin E	30 IU	10 IU	10 IU	30 IU
Vitamin B_6	2.0 mg	0.7 mg	0.7 mg	2.5 mg
Folacin	0.4 mg	0.2 mg	0.2 mg	0.8 mg
Vitamin B_{12}	6 mcg	3 mcg	3 mcg	8 mcg
Phosphorus	1.0 g	0.8 g	0.8 g	1.3 g
Iodine	150 mcg	70 mcg	70 mcg	150 mcg
Magnesium	400 mg	200 mg	200 mg	450 mg
Zinc	15 mg	8 mg	8 mg	15 mg
Copper	2 mg	1 mg	1 mg	2 mg
Biotin	0.3 mg	0.15 mg	0.15 mg	0.3 mg
Pantothenic acid	10 mg	5 mg	5 mg	10 mg

NOTE: If the protein efficiency ratio of protein is equal to or better than that of casein, USRDA is 45 g for adults and pregnant or lactating women, 20 g for children under 4 years of age, and 18 g for infants.

SUMMARY

Nutrition involves the relationship between the food a person eats and how well this food enables the body to maintain good health. Americans are concerned about the foods they get in foodservices, feeling that the foods offered often fail to provide proper nutrients. The federal government is aware of nutritional problems and has published a list of dietary guidelines that should correct them. Foodservices have responded to public concern (as reflected in a changing pattern of selections by patrons and in the demand for different foods and different methods of food preparation) by offering customers what they want. Red meats are falling out of favor because many people feel they contain undesirable levels of cholesterol and saturated fats. Fewer calories are being consumed. Alcohol con-

sumption is also dropping, in part because it contributes significant calories and in part because problems with alcoholism are being assessed realistically. A *nouvelle cuisine* offering fewer calories and more supposedly healthful foods is now popular.

The foodservice's responsibility for providing nutrition varies, depending on whether or not patrons have free choice to select where they eat and what they eat. It is the responsibility of patrons eating in most commercial operations to know what they should and should not eat and to select meals properly. For their part, such operations should ensure that the nutrients that should be in food at service are there. If an operation does not serve complete meals, it has no obligation to see that the foods served are nutritionally complete; if it does offer a complete menu, the operation should make sure that it is possible to select from the menu a completely nutritious meal. Institutional foodservices have a greater responsibility to ensure that patrons get nutritious food. Health-related operations are obligated to see that patrons get all the nutrients they need in their food.

The major concerns of patrons today are weight control, low-salt or low-sodium diets, low-fat or low-cholesterol diets, and high-fiber diets. It is possible for foodservices to satisfy all of these special concerns.

The nutrients we need are classified as proteins, carbohydrates, fats, vitamins, and minerals. Water and fiber are not nutrients but are essential in a good dietary program. The energy-producing nutrients are carbohydrates, proteins, and fats. Carbohydrates primarily serve to provide energy; proteins and fats do other jobs. Proteins make up muscle and provide the building units for antibodies, hormones, vitamins, and other essential bodily products. For a protein to be completely beneficial, it should contain all of the essential amino acids (the building blocks in proteins that the body cannot manufacture). Proteins in flesh foods and dairy products are largely complete. A complete protein can also be made by combining incomplete proteins —such as those in legumes and cereals—in a single meal. Only one or two fats in their form as lipoproteins are needed by the body. Other fats interchangeably perform the general duties required of fats in the body. For complete metabolization of fats in the body, a person must use some carbohydrate as well.

Vitamins are body regulators that do many things to make bodily functions occur. Minerals also help bodily functions to occur and provide building materials for the body.

Water is needed in the amount of about 1½ qt per day. It is obtained from fluids, foods, and the breakdown of foods in the body. It is eliminated from the body through exhaled air, evaporation from the skin, sweat, urine, and feces. Salts and other regulators determine the quantity of water needed in the body.

The Recommended Daily Dietary Allowances of the National Academy of Sciences is the primary guideline for the desirable nutrient intakes in our diets according to sex, age, and life conditions. The USRDA list offers recommendations about the amounts of nutrients that should be in the American diet. The USRDA quantities are used as a measure of the nutrients provided in many packaged foods.

CHAPTER REVIEW QUESTIONS

1. You are the manager of a restaurant serving yuppies, who want healthful but very good-tasting food. What sort of menu would you offer? How would most of the foods be cooked? Would you use any promotions? Would you try to offer foods for any modified diets?

2. What kind of nutritional information is communicated through newspapers, magazines, TV, and other media? Is it informative? slanted? How well does it agree with known scientific information?

3. What kind of nutritional information can you get from your local American Diabetic Association, American Heart Association, and others? Do they provide information on special diets? What are the basic points in the American Heart Association's publications? How helpful do you think such material is to those who need such information?

4. How well does your own diet agree with the 2-2-4-4 plan? Keep a record for several days to find out.

5. How much responsibility do you think patrons have in deciding their own diets when eating in a commercial operation at which free choice is made as to where and what to eat? Do you agree that fastfood outlets serving only partial meals are not responsible for seeing that patrons eat a complete meal at the operation? How much responsibility does a college dormitory have in this regard when it serves students most of their food? How much responsibility does a retirement home have when it serves all of the food consumed?

6. Do the public health concerns mentioned in this chapter agree with any of yours? Do you agree with the ideas expressed about them?

Vocabulary

Nutrition	Coenzyme
Cholesterol	Carbohydrate
Saturated fat	USRDA
Unsaturated fat	RDA
Fiber	Calcium
Glucose	Iodine
Vitamin	Manganese
Viamins A, K, E, D	Chlorine
Vitamin B_{12}	Vitamin C
Choline	Cobalt
Pantothenic acid	Potassium
Molybdenum	Chromium
Basic Four Plan	Edema
Lipid	Protein
Essential amino acid	Fat-soluble vitamin
Complete protein	Water-soluble vitamin
Thiamine	Phosphorus
Riboflavin	Sulfur
Niacin	Magnesium
Pyridoxine	Sodium
Biotin	Zinc
Myoinositol	Copper
Folacin	Iron
Fluorine	Selenium

Annotated References

American Diabetes Association and American Dietetic Association. 1977. *The Effective Application of Exchange Lists for Meal Planning.* Chicago: ADA and ADA. (How to use the exchange system.)

Alfin-Slater, R., and Aftergood, I. 1973. *Nutrition for Today.* Dubuque, Iowa: Wm C. Brown. (A text dealing with practical nutrition.)

Beloian, A. 1973. "Nutrition Labels: A Great Leap Forward." *FDA Consumer* (July/August 1973). (Describes food labeling regulations, as well as nutrients.)

Deutsch, R. M. 1976. *Realities of Nutrition.* Palo Alto, Cal.: Bull Publishing. (Discusses many nutritional principles from the standpoint of nutritional concerns today.)

Dunn, M. 1983. *Fundamentals of Nutrition.* New York: Van Nostrand Reinhold. (Basic nutrition with pointing toward some of our major nutritional problems.)

Hamilton, E.; Whitney, E.; and Sizer, F. 1985. *Nutrition: Concepts and Controversies.* St. Paul, Minn.: West Publishing. (Discusses nutrition from the standpoint of nutritional concerns today.)

Janssen, W. F., and Waters, E. P. 1973. "What Some Food Labels Don't Tell." *FDA Consumer* (July/August 1973). (Standardized foods and how they came about.)

Lowenberg, M., et al. 1968. *Food and Man.* New York: John Wiley & Sons. (Discussion of world problems in nutrition and steps being taken to solve them.)

Medcom, Inc. 1974. *Atherosclerosis.* Englewood Cliffs, N.J.: Best Foods. (Articles dealing with the problem of cardiovascular diseases.)

Minor, L. 1983. *Nutrition Standards.* Westport, Conn.: Avi Publishing. (Discussion of food product standards, additives, and flavor in food.)

National Academy of Sciences. 1980. *Recommended Dietary Allowances.* 9th ed. Washington, D.C.: NAS. (RDA and the reasoning behind its formulation.)

National Restaurant Association. 1986. *Nutrition and Foodservice: A Current Issues Report.* Washington, D.C.: NRA. (Notes public interest in nutrition in this country and discusses how to meet it.)

Pennington, J., and Church, H. 1966. *Food Values of Portions Commonly Used.* Harper and Row, 1980. (Amounts of nutrients found in commonly used foods.)

Robinson, C. 1970. *Basic Nutrition and Diet.* New York: Macmillan. (Basic nutrition and diet therapy information.)

Stare, F., and McWilliams, M. 1973. *Living Nutrition.* New York: John Wiley. (Another text on basic nutrition.)

U.S. HEW Dept. 1963. *Agricultural Handbook No. 8,* Washington, D.C. (The basic authority on the nutritional value of foods.)

————. 1972. "10-State Nutrition Survey, 1968-1970." Washington, D.C. (A summary of the findings of an important nutrition survey.)

————. 1974. *FDA Consumer,* "The Food Labeling Revolution." Washington, D.C. (Discusses food-labeling regulations.)

————. 1978. "Sodium Content of Your Food." Home and Garden Bulletin No. 233. Washington, D.C. (Identifies the sodium content of various foods.)

Wickham, 1982. *Human Nutrition.* Englewood Cliffs, N.J.: Prentice-Hall. (A self-instructional text that gives basic information on nutrition.)

Wilson, E.; Fisher, K.; and Fuqua, M. 1975. *Principles of Nutrition.* New York: John Wiley. (One of the most widely used books on basic nutrition.)

CHAPTER 3

Sanitation and Safety

OUTLINE

Sanitation and safety in a foodservice operation are the responsibility of every individual working in the establishment. The proper discharge of sanitation and safety duties ensures safe food and freedom from accident or injury.

Sanitation and safety regulations established by local, state, and national bodies must be enforced constantly by management. Sanitary regulations are usually outlined in public health codes, while the Occupational Safety and Health Act (OSHA)

and other state and local regulations specify standards for safety. Proper sanitation and safety, however, do not just happen because a government agency has established appropriate standards; rather, they are made to happen by the concerned and committed personnel of a foodservice.

Proper sanitation results in healthful, clean, and wholesome food, an orderly environment, and pleasant working conditions. Personnel, as part of the working environment, must also be clean and healthy if sanitary conditions are to be maintained. The term *safety* refers to freedom from risk of accident or injury. Clearly, safety and sanitation are related, since unsanitary food can be unsafe and lead to illness. It is best to consider them separately, however, because the basic factors associated with them differ.

SANITATION

There is a difference between the words *clean* and *sanitary,* although both can mean the same thing. *Clean* refers to the lack of soil or dirt on an item. *Sanitary* refers to the lack of organisms that may do harm. Thus, a utensil may look clean and yet not be sanitary, because unseen organisms are present. Conversely, something may be sanitary and yet not look clean. An example would be a utensil coming from a dish machine in which it was sanitized by immersion for 10 seconds in rinse water heated to 180°F (82.2°C): soil may still show on it, but the utensil is sanitary because all harmful microorganisms have been destroyed by the hot rinse. In a good system of sanitation, the aim is to make things clean as well as sanitary.

Microorganisms and Their Classifications

Our world is filled with countless living organisms that are so small we cannot see them without using a microscope. For this reason, they are called *microorganisms.* In order to have sanitary conditions, we must understand how microorganisms live, grow, and reproduce and how they are transported. Employees who know how to keep things sanitary understand the "why" as well as the "how." Some states today require foodservice operations to keep a qualified staff sanitarian on duty at all times. Such a person has satisfactorily completed a sanitation course and is qualified to oversee the maintenance of proper sanitary conditions. Laws and regulations governing sanitation are designed to promote and protect health by requiring adoption of good sanitary practices built on sound microbiological

principles (see fig. 3-1). Some of the common "criminals" in food-borne illnesses are listed in table 3-1.

Microorganisms can be helpful or harmful; as a group, however, microorganisms are dangerous because some can cause serious illness to individuals exposed to them. Microorganisms that cause diphtheria or that develop the powerful poison called *botulinum*—an amount of which small enough to lie on a needle point can kill a person—are examples. Other microorganisms do no harm to humans. Some that live in the soil break down dead organic material, returning the natural substances to the soil so that they are again available to plants. If these microorganisms did not exist, dead trees, leaves, animals, and other matter would accumulate without decomposing. In a remote way, some microorganisms are helpful to human beings; in a sanitary way, they are not.

Many bacteria and other microorganisms are beneficial. Microorganisms in our intestines manufacture vitamin K. Yeasts help leaven bread, ferment wine and beer, and preserve sauerkraut and pickles. Many of our best cheeses are produced (in part) through the action of microorganisms. The holes and flavor in Swiss cheese come from a special bacteria, while Roquefort relies on the working of a particular mold. Some harmless microorganisms may be good indicators that harmful ones are present. Coliform bacteria, for example, are natural and useful inhabitants of the intestinal tract; but when they appear in food, milk, or water or on solid objects, they indicate that harmful (pathogenic) organisms may also be present.

Scientists have classified many thousands of microorganisms, using a classification system that identifies ancestral connections by general category (kingdom and phylum) and then by increasingly specific groups culminating in categories called *genera.* It also is helpful to classify microorganisms on the practical basis of what they do, since this is important in establishing which ones are harmful and which ones are not. A simple classification suited to our purposes categorizes dangerous microorganisms according to whether they are *toxic* or *infectious.*

A *toxic* organism produces harmful toxins in

1. UNSAFE FOOD HOLDING TEMPERATURES	Examples: Holding prepared, potentially hazardous foods at room temperature; unsafe refrigeration temperatures; unsafe hot holding temperatures.
2. POOR PERSONAL HYGIENE	Examples: Failure to wash hands before starting work, after using the toilet, or after touching any soiled object; wearing soiled aprons and outer garments.
3. CROSS CONTAMINATION	Examples: Cutting raw foods and cooked or ready-to-serve foods on same cutting board without sanitizing between changed use; use of slicers, graters, choppers and grinders for more than one food product without cleaning between changed use; same for cook's knives.
4. UNSANITARY DISHWARE, UTENSILS AND EQUIPMENT	Examples: Improperly cleaned and sanitized tableware, utensils, and cutting equipment; failure to protect sanitized ware from contamination.
5. INFECTED FOOD HANDLERS	Examples: Food handlers with infected cuts, burns, or sores; boils or pimples; sore throat; nasal discharge or diarrhea.
6. IMPROPER FOOD HANDLING	Examples: Unnecessary use of hands during preparation and serving; thawing of frozen food at room temperature or in warm water.
7. UNSAFE COLD HOLDING AND REHEATING OF DELAYED-USE FOODS AND LEFTOVERS	Examples: Slow cooling and reheating of foods; large mass food storage in large-quantity containers; failure to reheat food to safe serving temperature; use of holding or warming units to reheat food.
8. IMPROPER FOOD STORAGE	Examples: Uncovered foods on refrigerator shelves; raw foods stored directly on shelves or against refrigerator walls; raw foods stored in direct contact with prepared foods.
9. INSECTS AND RODENTS	Examples: Failure to eliminate pest breeding or entry areas; failure to eliminate grime, spilled food, and trash which become food, breeding, and nesting attractions for pests; failure to report and take control action when pests or evidence of pests is noted.
10. CHEMICALS STORED NEAR FOOD	Examples: Storage of cleaning and sanitizing compounds, solvents, pesticides and other non-food chemicals near food; use of unlabeled containers in kitchen or serving areas.

Figure 3-1. Factors that may lead to an outbreak of food-borne illness.

Table 3-1. Harmful Microorganisms

Criminal	Route to the Customer	Disease
Salmonella group	Food contaminated by unwashed hands, rats	Food infections
Staphylococcus	Food contaminated by sores, boils	
Eberthella typhi	Water, milk, shellfish contaminated at the source; food contaminated by unwashed hands or by flies	Typhoid fever
Endamoeba histolytica	Water contaminated at the source; defective plumbing; food contaminated by unwashed hands or by flies	Amoebic dysentery
Shigella group	Water contaminated at the source; dishes or silverware contaminated by a carrier; food contaminated by unwashed hands or by flies	Bacillary dysentery
Trichinella spiralis	Insufficiently cooked pork	Trichinosis
Clostridium botulinum	Home-canned foods improperly prepared	Botulism
Streptococcus group	Raw milk contaminated at the source	Septic sore throat Scarlet fever
Diphtheria bacillus	Dishes or silverware contaminated by a carrier; sneezing, coughing, and spitting	Diphtheria

food. It is the toxin and not the organism itself that causes the problem. The organism may have been destroyed when the food was cooked, but the toxin still remains when the food is eaten and causes the illness. Illnesses caused by toxins are called *food-borne intoxications.* It is important to understand that, because of toxins, cooking does not always make food safe.

An *infectious* organism must be taken alive into the body in order to grow and cause harm. It may develop a toxin in the body, or it may just multiply in a way that causes illness. Illnesses caused by infectious organisms are called *food-borne infections.* If food is cooked long enough, infectious agents are destroyed, and no harm occurs.

A third classification of microorganisms (similar in many respects to the first) places them into the following five categories: bacteria; virus, parasite; mold; and yeast. These categories are considered in the ensuing subsections.

Bacteria

Bacteria are a common cause of illness in human beings. They are single-celled microorganisms that resemble plant cells but contain no chlorophyll (the green material found in the leaves or blades of plants). Bacteria are so small that, even when hundreds are clustered together, they cannot be seen. Their average size is 1/25,000 inch in diameter.

Bacteria are usually classified by shape. Round individual cells that group into tiny clusters so that under a microscope they look like a bunch of grapes are called *cocci.* Cells having the shape of rods or elongated tubes are called *bacilli;* they may appear as single rods, in pairs, or in chains that resemble sausage links. Some bacilli can change into spores. In the spore stage, bacilli become dormant within a hard shell that protects them from heat and other outside forces that destroy bacteria. When they are in this tiny shell, they do not grow; but when conditions become good for growth outside, they break

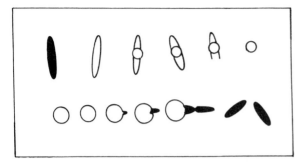

Figure 3-2. Reproduction by a bacillus bacterium through an intermediate spore stage.

out and reproduce living bacteria in the process (see fig. 3-2). Bacteria in spores may successfully withstand normal sanitary treatment, since the spores can withstand temperatures that kill normal bacteria. *Clostridium botulinum*—the bacterium that makes the deadly botulin toxin mentioned previously— forms spores and thus increases in danger. Cells of bacteria that are spiral-shaped are called *spirilla.* These are always single-celled and not grouped. Spirilla are not known to be pathogenic (harmful to human beings).

Bacteria reproduce by dividing from one into two cells. The two single cells then redivide to form four single cells, and so on. Thus, the number of bacteria that can grow from one cell in a very short time is astronomical. The time between divisions can be as little as fifteen to twenty minutes under the right conditions. Poor environmental conditions slow down reproduction. Bacteria in frozen food do not multiply at all, and may gradually die out. However, one should not depend on this happening and think that frozen food has no bacteria. In arctic areas some bacteria have been found that have been frozen for thousands of years.

Bacteria need three things to grow: food, moisture, and temperature. Even if these three are present, other factors may cause bacteria not to grow.

First, bacteria thrive on specific kinds of foods. Most pathogens live on the same types of food that people eat. Some, such as *clostridium perfringens,* are attracted to proteins such as meat, milk, and eggs. Others prefer carbohydrate and protein mixtures such as cream fillings, macaroni and cheese,

and gravies. Some can subsist fairly well on foods they are less attracted to, but they do not prosper as well.

Second, bacteria do not do well in dry food; they need moisture. If salt or sugar is present in sufficient quantity in food, the salt or sugar absorbs so much moisture that bacteria cannot grow in it. Foods containing more than 55 percent sugar or more than 10 percent salt will inhibit the growth of microorganisms.

Third, some bacteria thrive in the cold. They are called *psychrophilic* (cold-loving) bacteria. They rot organic material in the cool soil and do other jobs in a cool atmosphere. Other bacteria prefer high temperatures; they may be found in hot water pools or in the water of geysers, and they are called *thermophilic* (heat-loving) bacteria. Bacteria suited to middle-range temperatures *(mesophiles)* include most types of harmful bacteria. They exist in temperature conditions that are neither too hot nor too cold. Their best growth occurs at temperatures of from 98° to 100°F (36.6° to 37.7°C), but public health authorities have a wider danger zone that extends from 45° to 140°F (7.2° to 60°C).

Food preservation discourages the growth of bacteria and other microorganisms. If food is heated and then sealed airtight while still hot (so that no more microorganisms can get to the food), it will not spoil. Dried food discourages organism growth. An acidity level of around pH 4.5 often is enough to deter bacteria from growing, as is an alcohol content of more than 14 percent. Figure 3-3 illustrates the pH scale and gives pH values for representative foods. Creosote in smoke is a preservative, and spices can also be. Some foods are preserved by a combination of antibacterial agents. Thus, sauerkraut and naturally cured pickles keep because of the combined forces of the salt, the acid, and a cool environment. Smoked meat is first cured with salt, saltpeter, and other substances, and then it is smoked; refrigeration also helps preserve it. An understanding of the effects that various processes or substances can have in protecting foods helps encourage better sanitation.

A bacterium eats by absorbing food through the tiny membrane that surrounds the cell. If the mem-

Figure 3-3. Acidity and alkalinity as measured on the pH scale (7 = neutral).

Strongest Acidity *							Neutral *					Strongest Alkalinity *	
0pH	1pH	2pH	3pH	4pH	5pH	6pH	7pH	8pH	9pH	10pH	11pH	12pH	13pH 14pH

lemon juice 2.0
some vinegars 3.0
tomato juice 4.3
bananas 4.8
fresh bread 5.2

some fruit cakes 6.4
fresh milk 6.8
distilled water 7.0
egg white 7.2
soda cracker 7.8

brane is destroyed, the bacterium dies. Some bacteriacides work by destroying the cell membranes of bacteria.

Viruses

The tiniest known living organism is the virus, some of which cannot be seen even under a regular microscope. Viruses are never toxic; all harmful ones are infectious. They are usually transferred through food or water. Hepatitis, a virus infection of the liver, comes from polluted materials in food and water. Polio, a virus disease, is transferred in milk or other food substances. Ornithosis is a virus in birds that can cause serious illness in people. Birds and animals should not be allowed into foodservices because they may carry dangerous microorganisms.

Viruses thrive in the same living conditions that support bacterial growth, and they are destroyed by the same things. They seem to be cells or some other self-contained life form that reproduces in organic matter, but how they reproduce and how they live are not known. Viruses are highly feared because of their sometimes fatal effect on infected human beings.

Parasites

A third category of harmful microorganisms consists of parasites. Some, such as *Endamoeba histolytica,* are protozoalike organisms that live in water, in the soil, on fruits or vegetables, or in other foods. The intestinal tracts of people and animals can be infested with this parasite and transfer it to water or food. Food handlers can carry it on their hands. Other parasites include trichinae and tapeworms. Trichinae are usually found in pork but also can be in bear, rabbit or other meat. They are small larvae that grow in the body, lay their eggs in the muscles and cause a disease called *trichinosis* that is characterized by nausea, cramps, diarrhea, aching muscles, fever, and chest pain. We cook pork until it is well done to ensure that we destroy any trichinae present. Eggs of the tapeworm in raw meat are usually the source of its infection in the body.

Molds

Molds, which are types of fungus, usually do not cause illness, but they do spoil food. Molds will attack foods that other organisms cannot invade. They can thrive on cured and smoked meats, jellies and jams, and other preserved foods. More difficult to control by low temperatures alone, molds can be found in refrigerated foods.

Molds are threadlike growths that bear spores or seeds at the end of the thread. They appear fuzzy and cottony and are seen in a variety of colors. Mold spores are constantly circulating in the air, and the best form of control is to keep foods fresh. Molds have difficulty growing on highly acidic foods, and most are destroyed by heat above 125°F (51.6°C), although some spores may be resistant to even higher temperatures.

Some molds produce toxic substances, but not all molds are harmful or undesirable. The blue mold found in some cheeses gives the cheese its characteristic flavor and appearance. A similar blue mold is used in the production of the antibiotic penicillin. Mold found on the surface of aged meat can be trimmed off without affecting the wholesomeness of the underlying meat.

Yeasts

As is the case with molds, yeasts (which are also fungi) do not cause illness, but they can cause spoilage of food. Yeasts are single-celled organisms of the fungus kingdom that are present in abundance. In a vineyard, yeasts will quickly group and grow on a ruptured grape.

Yeasts, acting on carbohydrates, cause fermentation. The yeast acts on the sugar present in a carbohydrate to produce alcohol, carbon dioxide, and water. Some yeasts are used in breadmaking, while others are used in the production of alcoholic beverages such as beer. Yeasts can be cultured to perform specific jobs. Breadmakers, for example, use a cultured yeast to obtain predictable results, rather than using wild yeasts present in the air (which might produce an unwanted reaction).

Food-borne Illnesses

People can become ill from poisons in food, from bacteria or viruses, or from parasites. Poisonous substances can be specially manufactured by chemical companies or they can come from substances that normally are not a threat. If a poisonous substance is consumed, illness or death may result.

Chemical Poisons and Poisonous Food

Danger from chemical poisons is ever present. Toxic agents such as cadmium in graniteware or zinc on galvaneal (galvanized iron) can cause illness. Lead, antimony, and even copper can cause metallic poisoning; acids in some fruit drinks or from other food sources can dissolve these metals. Many cleaning or sanitizing solutions are toxic, and some look like food substances. Trisodium phosphate, a cleaning agent, looks like cornmeal. One powerful roach poison looks like powdered milk. Oxalic acid bleaches well but is very poisonous and should not be used around food. Any poisonous agent that must be used around food should be locked up in a separate area and issued only for a fixed period of time to people who know what they are handling. Cleaning agents and other poisons should be stored separately from foods. All poisons should be clearly marked with the word *POISON* and a skull-and-crossbones label.

Chemical poisons can be introduced at other stages of the food production process, as well. Fruits and vegetables may be covered with a film of insecticide spray or other substances that are harmful if ingested. Consequently, careful washing of all foods is a standard procedure in quantity food production. Some food additives, when present in excessive amounts, may cause poisoning. In large quantities, nitrites, niacin, and cobalt can cause illness. Excessive use of monosodium glutamate (MSG) or of the whitener, sodium sulfite,* can trigger allergic reactions in sensitive individuals. Knowledge of the composition of the food being used in an establishment helps prevent an excessive presence of these chemicals.

Some plants are poisonous, such as some mushrooms, some toadstools, water hemlock, jimsonweed, castor bean seeds, and rhubarb leaves. The green substance that appears in potatoes exposed to sunlight is poisonous, but it takes 17 pounds of this green substance (called *solanine*) to kill an adult person. Ergot, a substance in moldy rye, is much more deadly and once killed many people.

Poisons can be found in fish, in shellfish, and even in milk. Some Japanese eat a very poisonous puffer fish that, if prepared correctly, poses no danger. Because mistakes are sometimes made, however, eating it is called playing "Japanese roulette"! A tiny red mite in the ocean can infest shellfish, causing them to become poisonous. If snakeroot forms a significant part of a cow's diet, it makes the milk poisonous.

Purchasing food from sources known to have high standards of purity and sanitation should be a rule in foodservices. Inspection of purveyors' places of business by the buyer is recommended. Public health departments require all commercially offered shellfish to come from beds that it has inspected to ensure sanitation. Vendors can obtain a public health certificate for shellfish taken from such beds. Many original containers are stamped with the

---

*Use of sodium sulfite is no longer permitted in foodservices; its use in processed foods is also restricted and must be shown on the label.

health permit number issued by the public health department.

Ptomaines

Some foods are safe to eat on arrival at the facility, but spoilage afterward makes them unsafe. Ptomaines are products of the putrefaction of proteins. Many people complain that they have suffered ptomaine poisoning, but this is usually not true. Indeed, as far as can be determined, ptomaines are not poisonous. They may cause a person to become ill, however, simply because the thought of eating spoiled food is nauseating. (Foods may be poisonous because they have been intentionally sprayed with insecticides or other potentially harmful substances. "Wash all foods thoroughly before using," is a standard saying in quantity food work.)

Food-borne Infectants

Infectious organisms are often the cause of food-borne illnesses. To cause trouble, these must be alive in the food or drink a person consumes. To prevent infection, the microorganism should be kept out of the item; cooking infected foods at high temperatures for extended periods of time will also render the food safe to eat, but the risk of failing to destroy all of the bacteria usually makes this option unsatisfactory. Meat salads, sandwich salad fillings, and other high-protein foods usually are the source of the poisoning. The basic source of *salmonella* is fecal matter. Food on a block on which chickens have been cut up can pick up the *salmonella* present in the interior cavity of the chicken and become contaminated. Poison symptoms from *salmonella* appear in 12 to 24 hours; fever, abdominal pain, diarrhea, vomiting, and chills are characteristic.

Clostridium perfringens is a species of bacteria found in meats and proteins. Incomplete cooking may leave them in the food. These bacteria form in food and develop a foul odor. Again, the basic source is fecal matter. People become ill in 8 to 22 hours, with acute abdominal pains and diarrhea rather than with nausea, fever, chills, and other usual symptoms of illness. Until recently, these bacteria were unknown.

Shigella, an infection causing diarrhea, is a bacillus that lives in moist foods containing meat, eggs, or other protein. Again, the basic source is fecal matter. Illness is experienced from one to four days after infection.

Different species of *streptococcus* cause strep throat, scarlet fever, and other illnesses. People infected with strep often contaminate food or drink consumed by others, but other causes may bring about infection. Some of these infections are mild; others can be fatal.

Virus infections often come from raw shellfish or other foods that may come into contact with raw sewage. The urine of rats has been known to carry hepatitis and to cause infection. A person may be a carrier—even someone who appears to be healthy but carries germs of the infection that can be spread to others. Most virus infections are dangerous.

Many illnesses are caused by infectants, including the common cold, tuberculosis, scarlet fever, and diphtheria. People who work around food should be in good health. A sneeze or a cough can infect food and spread illness.

This nation is fairly free of food-borne illnesses because of its high sanitation standards. Nevertheless, people still become ill from them because of mistakes and failure to maintain safeguards; and from time to time, outbreaks of poisoning or illness still occur because of bacterial, viral, protozoan, or larval contamination. Clean food, drink, premises, and people are the best safeguards against such contamination.

In areas where municipal drinking water is not used—as in a resort, a rural restaurant or hotel, or a camp—care must be taken to see that the water is potable. Wells and other water sources should be checked by having the public health department examine water samples. If problems exist, chlorination systems should be used. Improper plumbing connections, poor trapping, backwater, blockages, or siphoning can bring sewage water into an area, and contamination can then occur.

Beef, fish, and poultry from uninspected sources may be the source of tapeworms or other larval infections. Raw pork, bear, or rabbit can contain trichinae—a microscopic, wormlike organism that settles in the muscle meat of the host. If diseased meat is improperly processed, consuming it may lead to trichinosis, a serious illness. Federal law requires all sausage or smoked meat that may be eaten uncooked by the consumer to be cooked by the manufacturer during processing to a temperature of 155°F (68.3°C). This is done to ensure that trichinae are destroyed.

Food-borne Intoxicants

Staphylococcus, a genus of cocci, is a common bacterial source of toxic food poisoning. Most people carry staph, but it is also in the air and on most objects. Staph often can be spread by coughing or sneezing, or from infected cuts, boils, pimples, other skin infections, acne, or pus. Foods commonly involved in promoting staph are cooked ham, other cooked meats, cream-filled or custard-filled pastries, potato salad, ham salad, tuna salad, and other carbohydrate-protein foods.

The staph toxin usually causes illness in 1 to 6 hours; symptoms are nausea, vomiting, diarrhea, fever, and abdominal cramps. Individuals in poor physical condition, young children, and old people are relatively susceptible to the poisoning.

It is often found in instances of food-borne illness that some individuals become ill while others eating the same food do not. Those who remain unaffected may have a higher tolerance to infection or be in better physical condition and thus be able to throw off the illness. On the other hand, some people may escape infection because a food bears the harmful microorganisms in only one area, and only some patrons are served the infected portion. This can be true of either infectious agents or toxins in a batch of food. All disease-producing organisms must be controlled by appropriate sanitation procedures.

Clostridium botulinum has been mentioned as a species of bacteria that makes one of the most toxic substances known, botulin. The bacteria grow without oxygen in a neutral, slightly alkaline, or slightly acidic food. Highly acidic foods such as tomatoes, pickles, and fruit juices will not support the bacteria. Pickles of low acidity, however, have been found to contain botulin. Outbreaks of botu-lism have come from canned tunafish and from canned vichyssoise soup. Smoked whitefish placed in plastic wraps that sealed it from the air caused another outbreak. Underprocessed canned food may develop botulin, and home-canned foods have been the cause of deaths from botulism.

A small quantity of botulinum is enough to cause death. Earliest symptoms occur 12 to 36 hours after eating. Dizziness, double vision, muscular weakness, and difficulty in swallowing, speaking, or breathing are characteristic. The toxin attacks the nervous system and—unless an antitoxin is administered in a short time—a painful death occurs.

Preventing Food-borne Illnesses

Food may already be contaminated when purchased or it may be contaminated later by personnel, equipment, utensils, or vermin. A carrier of contamination is called a *vector;* good sanitation procedures call for stopping the vector at its source. The potential for transfer is always present, and safeguards must be established to prevent this from occurring. These safeguards come under four headings: food protection; personal hygiene; facility and equipment sanitation; and rodent and insect control.

Food Protection

Each of the functions performed in the purchasing, storing, preparing, and serving of food should be isolated in establishing a food sanitation program. Each offers a chance for contamination to occur, unless the food is properly handled. Management is responsible for establishing suitable standards and procedures, and the remaining staff is responsible for seeing that these guidelines are carried out. It often is said that food protection is 95 percent people and 5 percent equipment and facilities. **Purchasing Food.** Food should be purchased from purveyors that operate sanitary facilities. Buyers should pay visits to their purveyors to inspect processing conditions. Only food approved for wholesomeness should be purchased. Meat and poultry should carry the round inspected-and-passed stamp. Shellfish should come from beds approved by the public health department, which publishes a semimonthly list of these. Milk should be processed according to prevailing codes. Delivery trucks and delivery procedures should be overseen to ensure that good sanitation is observed. Frozen food should be delivered frozen and refrigerated food should not have an interior temperature that is higher than 40°F (4.5°C). Receiving personnel should be instructed to check the temperatures of incoming perishables, particularly during warm weather.

Operators should ask federal, state, or local agencies about the reliability of food sources. Municipal water is usually considered safe, but private water sources should be checked frequently.

Storing Food. Storage refers to every place where food is kept before preparation, before service, or during service. If contamination occurs at any of these stages, sufficient time may elapse to cause illness in people eating the food. Several rules of thumb can be identified. Rotate stocks, in order to use oldest foods first rather than newer items. Store foods off the floor and away from walls, and maintain correct storage temperatures (see fig. 3-4). Pathogens are most active at about 100°F (38°C) and the danger zone ranges from 45° to 140°F (7° to 60°C). Temperatures below 45°F (7°C) do not kill pathogens, but they do slow down their rate of growth. At temperatures above 45°F (7°C), bacterial growth speeds up, until the optimum of 100°F

Figure 3-4. Proper food storage prevents foodborne illnesses.

(38°C) is reached. Bacteria continue to grow at higher temperatures until the temperature reaches 125° to 140°F (52° to 60°C). At temperatures above 125°F (52°C), most bacteria die. Maintaining correct storage temperatures can do much to reduce food deterioration and contamination.

Fresh fruits and vegetables should be refrigerated. Hot foods from the range or steam table can be cooled quickly if the container is placed in cool water and its contents are stirred. Studies have shown that cooling in this way brings temperatures down as fast as does cooling under refrigeration, until a temperature of around 125°F (52°C) is reached. The item should then be placed under refrigeration to obtain the speediest further cooling.

Factors affecting the rate of cooling include the amount of food in the container, the thickness or density of the food, the velocity with which the cooling medium (movement of air or liquid) strikes the container, the radius of the mass (distance from its outer edge to its center), and whether the food is stirred during cooling. Small amounts of food cool more quickly than large amounts; and the greater the surface area of a given amount of food, the faster the cooling will be. This is why storing food in shallow pans not more than 2 inches deep is recommended for fast cooling and good sanitation. Microorganisms have a good chance of developing in food that stays warm a long time after being cooked. Storing warm containers close together in a refrigerator also favors the growth of microorganisms. Preferably, storage shelves should be slatted, and containers should be placed so as to allow good circulation of air around them. Containers should be covered so that air-borne bacteria and organisms cannot drop into them. Storage areas should be cleaned regularly, and temperatures should be checked frequently. Good air circulation helps to maintain a sanitary storage place.

Certain foods such as meats, eggs, and milk must be given special handling. Store these at 40°F (4.5°C) or below (meat discolors at 31° to 34°F [0° to 1°C]). Hold warm meat, egg, and casserole dishes for service at temperatures above 140°F (60°C)— except perhaps rare meats. Food held within the danger zone longer than several hours can become dangerous. Holding foods in this zone for as short a time as possible is a good idea. Times in the zone are cumulative. A turkey that is left out to cool for 45 minutes, then refrigerated, then brought back out to pick the meat for turkey salad for another 45 minutes, and then made into salad and left standing at room temperature for 1 hour has accumulated 2.5 hours of danger-zone time. For this reason, frozen foods that have thawed should be used as quickly as possible and not be refrozen.

Preparing Food. Following good sanitary practices during food preparation minimizes the likelihood of infecting patrons with a food-borne illness. Many organisms are present on the skin, nose, hair, or body of the preparer and can be transferred to the food. Coughing or sneezing readily transfers germs, and hand contact with food should be avoided. If the hands are used, they should be scrupulously clean. Alternatively, single-service gloves are a good sanitary measure. Foods should be handled with clean utensils, such as tongs, scoops, spoons, or forks, as much as possible. Good hygiene and work habits are absolutely necessary.

All fresh fruits and vegetables should be washed thoroughly and, in some cases, scrubbed to remove any organisms or toxic chemicals on their surface. Soaking, followed by thorough washing in fresh water, is usually sufficient to remove most chemical contaminants.

Proper cooking destroys harmful organisms. Solid or viscous food must be stirred during heating to distribute the heat completely throughout the mass. In quantity food preparation, temperatures never get as high as they do in small-batch cooking, and this may cause problems. A food may appear to be boiling when boiling is actually occurring only near the heat source. Trichinae are destroyed at 138°F (59°C), but pork and other meats that can carry it should be cooked to at least 155°F (68°C) to ensure destruction of the parasites. Figure 3-5 identifies some recommended temperatures for achieving good sanitation.

Serving Food. Opportunities for food contamination to occur are particularly numerous during

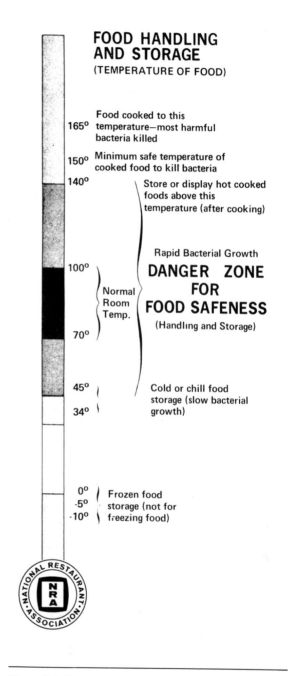

Figure 3-5. Recommended temperatures for food safeness (Fahrenheit scale).

holding for service and during service itself. For this reason, proper holding temperatures must be maintained. The following holding temperatures are recommended:

Soups, thin sauces, coffee, tea	160°F (71°C) and up
Entrées, meats	160°F (71°C)
Rare meats	140°F (60°C)
Chilled foods	35° to 45°F (2° to 7°C)
Frozen foods	8° to 12°F (−13° to −11°C)

Protecting food from contamination during holding is essential. If an item is not being served, it should be covered. If customers are serving themselves, a number of steps must be taken to reduce the risk of contamination. Food on a cafeteria counter should be shielded by a sneeze guard. Silverware and dishes to be used by guests should be placed so that contamination is avoided. Silverware should be placed in containers with the handle up, not the eating end up. Glasses and cups should be upside down in their holders. All necessary precautions should be taken to see that customers do not contaminate food while serving themselves. In all operations, employees should handle dishes, cups, glasses, and eating utensils in such a way that their hands do not touch the eating surfaces. Packaged food—such as packets of sugar, crackers, or salad dressings—should be used if possible, and no opened packages should be reused. Some states or localities do not permit open sugar bowls or other open foods on tables. Local sanitation agents can give information on local recommended practices. Employees should be trained to handle food and equipment properly in front of guests (see figure 3-6).

Personal Hygiene

Good personal hygiene promotes good health and more effective and efficient job performance. It also helps prevent the spread of disease.

Personal hygiene includes getting enough sleep, routinely seeing a doctor or dentist, staying away

Figure 3-6. Good personal hygiene and proper serving techniques are a must for proper sanitation.

from work when sick, and avoiding poor personal habits such as picking the nose or biting the fingernails and then handling food or utensils. Unless the hands are clean, food contamination can occur. A clean handkerchief or tissue should be used to cover the nose and mouth when coughing or sneezing occurs. Employees should wash their hands after sneezing or coughing. Scratching the head, wiping the mouth with the fingers, or wetting the thumb with saliva to pick up a paper napkin or to turn pages of an order are unsanitary habits. Smoking a cigarette, cigar or pipe can transfer organisms from the saliva to the hands or to other items. Smoking should only be permitted in designated areas. Employees should always wash their hands after visiting the rest room, returning from meal breaks, or handling money.

A clean body is the foundation for all the other factors that support a good appearance and proper sanitation. Wearing a cap or hair net is a must to prevent hair from falling into food. Clean hands and nails not only give a good appearance but also protect against contamination. Service personnel make a better impression if they are neat and well-dressed. Makeup may be used sparingly. Nails should be short, well-trimmed, and clean. A well-pressed uniform adds to an employee's appearance of caring about personal hygiene. A healthy, clean person wearing a spotless uniform is more likely to feel like observing good sanitation rules than one who is sloppily dressed, badly groomed, and not particularly clean.

Care is also required in removing soiled dishes and utensils from guests' tables, since these can carry organisms from customers. Table-busing personnel should wash their hands before handling food or clean utensils.

Facility and Equipment Sanitation

Proper cleanliness and sanitation of facilities and equipment is important from both a health standpoint and an aesthetic one. The chances for disease-producing organisms to exist are great in operations where the housekeeping is poor. Customers who are served food on unclean tables or who see a messy, untidy operation will not wish to continue their patronage. A lack of sanitation and cleanliness is repugnant to customers, who are likely to seek a better atmosphere elsewhere. A clean and appealing place is an economic plus to an operation. Foodservices have an ethical responsibility to serve foods that are clean and safe and to maintain an atmosphere that is in keeping with those food standards (see fig. 3-7).

An operation should establish a program for achieving proper standards in the facility and equipment. This should cover at least six areas: the cleanliness of floors, walls, and ceilings; proper ventilation and lighting; garbage and refuse disposal; adequate handwashing and comfort facilities; equipment sanitation; and dishwashing procedures. These rules

Figure 3-7. Well-organized shelves and sanitary working conditions are evident in this kitchen.

and procedures should be established, and then taught to employees.

Cleanliness of Surfaces. The ability to maintain clean floors, walls, and ceilings depends on their construction. Thus the form of sanitation to pursue is established in the original design of the facility. Periodic cleaning should be instituted, preferably in accordance with a written schedule. Walls and ceilings that are smooth and hard are most easily cleaned. Using light-colored surfaces aids in pinpointing soiled surfaces. The surface structure and composition of floors, walls, and ceilings affect how they should be cleaned. Floor surfaces may vary from carpets in the dining room to concrete, terrazzo, ceramic tile, or polyvinyl chloride in other areas. Each requires unique cleaning materials and procedures (see table 3-2).

Employees should be taught to maintain a clean environment as they work. When food is spilled on a surface, it should be cleaned up immediately. Spilled food is a safety hazard, and as it sits and dries out, it becomes progressively more difficult to clean. Keeping a well-organized and clean workplace is often called *mise en place.*

Employees should also maintain equipment well. Any equipment needing repair or attention should be reported at once so that it can be put into proper working order.

Ventilation and Lighting. Proper ventilation and

Table 3-2. Characteristics and Cleaning of Various Floors

Type of Flooring	Hardness	Where Used	Advantages	Disadvantages	Cleaner
Terrazzo	Hard marble chips in cement	Kitchen; dining rooms	Durable	Damaged by alkalies; stained by grease unless well sealed	Use mild cleansers; scrub; rinse; mop dry
Ceramic Tile	Hard	Kitchen; dining rooms	Resists grease stains if glazed; durable	Unglazed tile easily stained by grease; spaces between tile difficult to clean; slippery when wet	Alkaline cleaners are safe; scrub to clean between tiles; rinse; mop dry
Concrete	Hard		Durable	Gives off dust; becomes stained by grease unless well sealed	Alkaline cleaners are safe; scrub, rinse (sealing concrete will make it more cleanable)
Asphalt Tile	Soft	Dining rooms	Durable; nonslippery, even when wet	Poor resistance to grease	Mildly alkaline to neutral cleaners; mop; rinse; mop dry
Rubber Tile	Soft		Durable	Damaged by grease	Mild cleaners; mop; rinse; mop dry; never use strong cleaners
Vinyl	Soft		Nonslippery, even when wet; durable; resistant to grease		Mildly alkaline to neutral cleaner; mop; rinse; mop dry
Vinyl Asbestos	Soft		Durable; resistant to grease		Alkaline cleaners safe; mop, rinse; mop dry
Cork Tile	Soft			Easily damaged by sharp objects; grease will penetrate unless well sealed	Use special cleaners for cork floors (sealing cork tile makes floors more cleanable)

lighting are important aspects of facility and equipment sanitation. Accumulations of grease or dirt on walls and ceilings indicate improperly operated ventilation equipment. A well-designed ventilation and exhaust system removes excessive heat, objectionable odors, and noxious gases. This creates an environment in which patrons can enjoy a meal and workers can function efficiently. Filters and ducts in the ventilation system should be inspected and cleaned frequently. A dirty exhaust system can pose an extreme fire hazard. A fire igniting in greasy ductwork can spread rapidly and be difficult to control.

Good cleaning cannot occur without proper lighting. Something that is visibly dirty is more likely to be cleaned. It is especially important to have good lighting in the kitchen, in storage rooms, and in hand- and dish-washing areas. Where lighting may be low (to create mood and atmosphere), better lighting should be available for after-hours cleaning. Excess lighting is never desirable. Under energy-saving programs, lighting may be reduced—but never so much as to reduce sanitation or safety.

Garbage Disposal. Garbage and refuse disposal are commonly neglected areas of foodservice sanitation. Battered, leaky refuse cans with covers missing are all too frequently seen. Unless a garbage can is actually in use, it should be tightly covered. Garbage cans or containers should be fly-tight and leakproof. Liquid flowing from a garbage can can coat the ground and furnish a breeding place for flies. Plastic liners may help keep cans clean and facilitate disposal. The time saved in cleaning containers may be well worth the extra cost. Garbage grinders, compactors, and incinerators can also simplify refuse and garbage removal and help improve sanitation.

Comfort Facilities. Adequate handwashing facilities and toilets must be provided if the transfer of microorganisms from person to person is to be prevented. Management must supply adequate facilities. Each employee has the responsibility to see that facilities are used properly and are left in a clean condition for the next person. Facilities that are not properly maintained are open to invasion by insects and rodents; these vermin carry disease and filth from toilets to food. Because employees' hands are probably the most common vehicle for transmitting contamination, good handwashing facilities and practices are important. Such facilities should be located near food preparation areas. Employees should not wash their hands in work sinks. Soap, towels, and a waste container should be provided.

Equipment Sanitation. Equipment sanitation comprises the methods, materials, and times required to keep equipment clean. Good maintenance means good operation. Moreover, it helps prevent the transmission of microorganisms. Properly cleaned equipment lasts longer and costs less to operate than badly maintained equipment.

A cleaning schedule and procedure for each major piece of equipment should be developed (see fig. 3-8). In establishing a cleaning schedule to be posted in the foodservice, planners should take the following seven steps:

1. Give the name of the equipment to be cleaned.
2. Have three columns headed *when, how,* and *use.*
3. Include all steps (written as briefly as possible) that are necessary to dismantle, clean, and reassemble the equipment properly.
4. Take into consideration the safety precautions necessary to make the equipment safe and clean.
5. Specify the amount of detergent to use and the temperature of water to use for washing, rinsing, and sanitizing.
6. Stress the need for a clean surface for air drying, and for clean hands for reassembling equipment.
7. Provide a separate procedure if daily cleaning differs from weekly or bimonthly cleaning.

Equipment that disassembles should be taken apart, scraped free of major soil, and washed by machine or by hand. All surfaces that food comes into contact with should be washed with hot detergent water, rinsed in warm water, and sanitized in a final rinse. Equipment can be also sanitized by spraying or wetting its surfaces with a chlorinated solution that is about twice as strong as those used for sanitizing by immersion. Different kinds of soil—grease, carbon, egg, and protein, for example—need different treatment. Proteins and eggs must not be subjected to too high an original temperature or they will be cooked onto the surface. Grease dissolves only at certain washing temperatures.

Water is the primary solvent used in cleaning; a detergent or soap simply makes more things soluble in water. Heat helps to increase solubility, too, and will melt grease. Friction is the main cleaning agent and does about 90 percent of the job; water with detergent does the other 10 percent of the job. After washing, a good rinse in clean water removes detergents and cleaning agents. Sanitizing is the final step. A rinse of 10 seconds in 180°F (82°C) water or of 30 seconds in 170°F (77°C) water is a

Figure 3-8. Sample cleaning schedule for a major piece of foodservice equipment.

PROCEDURE 1.	HOW TO CLEAN FOOD SLICER	
When	How	Use

After each use	1. Turn off machine
	2. Remove electric cord from socket
	3. Set blade control to zero
	4. Remove meat carriage
	  (a) turn knob at bottom of carriage
	5. Remove the back blade guard
	  (a) loosen knob on the guard
	6. Remove the top blade guard
	  (a) loosen knob at center of blade
	7. Take parts to pot-and-pan sink, scrub
	8. Rinse
		Hot machine detergent solution, gong brush, clean hot water, 170°F for 1 minute; use double S hook to remove parts from hot water

	9. Allow parts to air dry on clean surface.
	10. Wash blade and machine shell
	(CAUTION: PROCEED WITH CARE WHILE BLADE IS EXPOSED)
	11. Rinse
	12. Sanitize blade, allow to air dry
	13. Replace front blade guard immediately after cleaning shell
	  (a) tighten knob
	14. Replace back blade guard
	  (a) tighten knob
	15. Replace meat carriage
	  (a) tighten knob
	16. Leave blade control at zero
	17. Replace electric cord in socket
		Use damp bunched cloth* dipped in hot machine detergent solution; clean hot water, clean bunched cloth; clean water, chemical sanitizer, clean bunched cloth

*Fold cloth to several thicknesses.

minimum for sanitizing. Chlorine and other sanitizing agents may be added to the sanitizing rinse to kill any remaining contaminants. Rinse compounds may be used to get better runoff of rinse water, reducing drying time.

Dishwashing Procedures. There are two ways to wash dishes. The first is known as manual or hand dishwashing. The second is mechanical, since a machine is used. Either can give good results, provided that the employee uses proper procedures. The cleaning agents, equipment, work procedures, times, temperatures, and other factors must be correct to get optimum results. Equipment in good operating condition is also required.

Before either manual or mechanical dishwashing can occur, employees must perform the following steps:

1. Separate silverware, glassware, and dishware.
2. Stack trays.
3. Scrape food from utensils.
4. Preflush over a drain. (Using a spray is best; if heated water is used, its temperature should not exceed 120°F [49°C]. If preflushing is done into a disposal, use water no hotter than 110°F [43°C]. Some machines have a preflush built in. If so, this step can be omitted.)
5. Soak silverware in a mild detergent solution.
6. Stack or rack utensils.

Manual dishwashing may require a slightly different procedure than mechanical dishwashing does. The Ohio Department of Health recommends the following manual dishwashing procedures:

PROCEDURE FOR A THREE-COMPARTMENT SINK:
1. Wash, rinse, and give a chemical sanitizing.
2. Wash, rinse, and give a hot-water sanitizing.
3. Prerinse, wash, and use a detergent-sanitizer.
4. Prerinse, wash, and use a hot-water sanitizer.

PROCEDURE FOR A TWO-COMPARTMENT SINK:
1. Wash and use a chemical sanitizer (detergent-sanitizer).
2. Wash and use a hot-water sanitizer.

For mechanical dishwashing, many spray-type machines are available, ranging from the simple single-tank, stationary-rack, -hood, or -door type to the more complex multiple-tank, conveyor type in which dishes move on a conveyor. All are intended to yield a clean and sanitary product, but each must be used correctly to do so.

The temperature of preflush or prerinse water should be below 125°F (52°C) and that of wash water should be between 140° and 160°F (60° and 71°C). Built-in gas, electric, or steam heaters will maintain proper water temperatures. Many machines are built so that the 180°F (82°C) fresh, uncycled final rinse water flows back into the rinse, and water from the rinse area flows back to the wash area, and then back to the prerinse (if the machine has one). This gives a flow of fresh water—from final rinse to rinse, from rinse to wash, and from wash to prerinse—at about the right temperature needed in the machine at each stage.

Detergents are designed for proper cleaning. They are alkaline to help dissolve grease and other products. The alkaline reaction also helps to saponify grease; that is, it helps turn the grease into a soapy substance. Some detergents contain chelating or sequestering agents that hold soil away from utensils once it has been removed. Some detergents contain a sanitizing agent as well, to improve sanitizing. A rinse compound, used to get a better runoff of final rinse water, is usually added separately. The right detergent should be selected for the job, and detergent companies can be helpful in identifying which one is the right one. Sometimes an acid-type detergent may be needed to remove mineral deposits and some stains. Phosphoric acid-containing compounds are used to remove built-up white alkaline salts that form on the surfaces of equipment subjected to hard water. Antispotting compounds or water softeners may be needed in some localities where the water is very hard.

The detergent may be added directly to the wash tank by hand, or it may be dispensed by machine. A light or signal usually indicates when this dispenser is working, and another signal device may warn when the dispenser needs refilling. These dispensers work in different ways but usually do a better job of maintaining a proper detergent-to-water ratio in the wash water than can be achieved by hand addition. Detergents designed for mechanical dispensers may be caustic; they should never be used for manual washing.

Friction in the wash water is produced by a pump forcing water under high pressure through holes in spray arms. The arms may be stationary or moving. Additional friction is generated when spray arms whirl around, throwing the water against the items to be cleaned. The wash water falls, and the soil it carries is collected in strainers or scrap trays. This prevents too much soil from accumulating in the wash water or plugging the machine's spray arms.

After washing is complete, the dishes are given a rinse. The rinse water comes from a tank that is booster-heated to around 190°F (88°C), so it strikes the dishes at about 180°F (82°C). The water should not be heated to 212°F (100°C) because steam produced at that temperature may interfere with the rinsing and cleaning action and because, at such an unnecessarily high temperature, energy is being wasted. In an effort to reduce energy costs and eliminate the need for a booster-heater, some establishments are using low-temperature dish-washers. In these washers, dishes are rinsed in 140°F (60°C) tap water that contains a special chemical sanitizer. The water pressure should be at least 8 psi (pounds per square inch) but not more than 15 psi at the jet, or it should be at least 15 psi but not more than 30 psi in the manifold ahead of the rinse valve. After rinsing is complete, the water flows into the wash section, where it does three things: it helps to keep the wash water hot; it dilutes the wash water, keeping it cleaner; and (as a disadvantage) it dilutes the concentration of the detergent in the wash water.

A drain at the bottom of the wash tank allows for complete draining of the machine. The machine should be cleaned each day. Scrap trays may have to be emptied periodically during the day.

After washing, utensils need to air-dry. This requires space, regardless of whether manual or mechanical washing is done. Sometimes planners set aside one-third of the surface area for soiled dishes and two-thirds of it for clean dishes to dry in. Large operations may need space for five or more drying racks during peak periods. Clean utensils should be removed from racks after drying and stored in dry, clean storage areas above the floor, where they are protected from insects, soil, and other contamination. Employees should take care when handling clean dishes and utensils not to touch eating surfaces.

Rodent and Insect Control

Like people, rodents and insects must have food to live. Because they like much the same foods we do, they seek to feed upon our provisions. In doing so, they contaminate it. The most frequent offenders are rats, mice, flies, and cockroaches. Again, to break the chain of infection or contamination, contact with the vector must be broken. These vermin must be eliminated from the premises.

Even though no single measure completely controls the problems associated with rodents and insects, a good program comprises both basic environmental sanitation and effective chemical or blockage control of the pests. Different methods must be used for each kind.

Rats and Mice. Rats and mice are highly resourceful, highly adaptable contaminating agents. They are extremely intelligent and often can outwit human beings in gaining their ends. It is necessary to be constantly on guard against their invasion and to adopt severe countermeasures when they attempt to invade. The first step is to be able to identify the enemy (see table 3-3). Rats are smarter and more aggressive than mice; but mice, because they are smaller, may gain access where rats cannot.

Rats often enter foodservice areas and reach food by gnawing through wood or other material. They need to gnaw to wear down their long incisors, which grow about 5 inches each year. They have been known to gnaw through concrete and even lead pipe. They are agile and can climb wires, pipes, vertical walls, and even metal barricades. They have excellent balance; if they happen to fall, they can drop 50 feet without injury. They have excellent senses of smell and touch. They create rat runs, blackening surfaces with their oily skins, which helps them rediscover their means of entrance. They locate their nesting places in secure areas such as between walls or in burrows. They can get through a ½-inch opening or burrow to a depth of 4 feet to find food. Rats can be vicious and their bite can cause infection. The life span of a rat is from three to five years.

Control of rats and mice starts with the sanitary disposal of refuse and garbage. Rats and mice will not stay where there is no food. Removing trash and other inviting refuse will eliminate hiding and nesting places. Storage areas should be kept clean so as not to harbor them. Poisoning can be an

Table 3-3. Rodent Pests

Type	Length (head and body)	Weight	Coloring	Appearance	Characteristics
Norway rat	7-10 in.	¾ lb (approx.)	Usually gray, may vary from reddish brown to black	Thick body, blunt head, tail shorter than body	Usually infests old structures, places where food and shelter are near
Roof rat	6-8 in.	½ lb (approx.)	Usually gray or black	Slender head and body, long tail, prominent ears, pointed nose	Good climber; may infest upper floors of buildings
House mouse	4 in. (max.)	less than 1 oz	Gray to brown	Large prominent ears, pointed nose, long very slender tail	Able to enter structures through cracks and holes too small to admit a rat

effective method of control, as well. Mice are much more susceptible to poisoning than rats. Some rats can eat strong poisons and show no ill effects; some even seem to thrive on poisons. Slow-killing poisons, which allow the animal to leave the premises before dying, should be used. Trapping can also be effective.

Rat- or mouse-proofing performed in a competent manner can do much to eliminate them. This is best undertaken when the building is first built. A thoroughgoing effort will include steps in the following areas:

Doors: All doors should be tight-fitting, with no opening greater than ½ inch between the base of the door and the threshold. The base of all rear doors and other doors where rats can gnaw undisturbed should be flashed with metal, or a U-shaped metal channel should be installed around the bottom of the door. Keep rear doors closed or screened when not in use.

Windows: All basement windows and other windows that are opened within 3 feet of the ground should be screened. Hardware cloth screening should be used for all basement windows and for all lower windows of business buildings. Fly screening may be installed in the same frame with the hardware cloth.

Floors: All basement floors and all ground floors of structures with no basements should be made of concrete and should be joined tightly with the walls. Rats find excellent protection and harborage under wooden floors.

Foundations and Walls: Holes in the foundation and the lower walls should be closed with mortar, sheet metal, or other substantial materials. Openings around pipes and wiring should be tightly sealed.

Miscellaneous: Openings on roofs, ventilators, and other building elements should be screened or appropriately closed.

New Buildings: All new buildings should be rat-proofed. Most modern, permanent-type constructions can be made rat-proof at no additional cost.

Curtain Walls: Concrete floors and shallow foundations should be constructed with a curtain wall around the outer edge extending 36 inches into the ground, or in an L shape 24 inches into the ground with a 12-inch lip extending outward at the bottom.

Flies. Houseflies, persistent and ever-present pests, are major spreaders of filth (which they live and breed on) and disease (which they carry on and in their bodies). When a fly walks over filth, some sticks to its hairy body or to a sticky material on the bottom of its feet. (A fly can walk upside down because of this sticky material). Harmful microorganisms also can be ingested into the fly's body when it feeds on filth.

A fly contaminates food by walking on it or by eating it. In order to eat, a fly regurgitates liquid from its stomach onto the food. This dissolves the food and allows the fly to suck it back up. Of course, all that is vomited out is not sucked back in. Since the stomach liquid is likely to contain harmful bacteria, it contaminates the area. Fly specks are fecal matter left by the fly wherever it goes. These too contain harmful bacteria. To combat flies effectively, a person should know something of their life cycle.

Flies come from eggs. An adult female may lay as many as 3,000 in her lifetime. The eggs hatch into larvae called *maggots*—the little white "worms" often seen in decaying matter. In several days, these change into small, hard, brown capsules called pupa from which, after several days, full-grown flies emerge. A single fly could be the progenitor in forty days of more than 7 million offspring weighing en masse around 140 lb (63 kg), if half of each generation's offspring reached adult fly stage.

Management and workers must work together to control flies. Fly control starts with getting rid of breeding places. This means not allowing food to accumulate and decay, and it means removing garbage, manure, and other favorable factors. Flies often travel considerable distances from where they hatch, so controlling the removal of all breeding places may not be possible. Blocking flies from entrance by using screens on doors and windows is a valuable procedure. Screens must be tight-fitting and in good repair. If flies enter when screen doors are opened, sprays, poisons, and other insecticides present acceptable countermeasures only when used correctly. Used improperly, they can be dangerous to workers and can contaminate food. Such chemical methods of control should only be used by qualified individuals and should only be attempted in locations where food and equipment will not be contaminated. An effective alternative is the electric fly catcher, which draws flies to an electric element that electrocutes them. Keeping the premises scrupulously clean also helps to keep flies away.

Cockroaches. Cockroaches are one of the oldest forms of life on earth, and they have adapted well to human habitations. Cockroaches carry many diseases and also bear a characteristic (and offensive) odor. They need moisture and will be found near it—for instance, in a dirty old wet mop or near hidden moisture that accumulates behind a piece of equipment. Roaches contaminate by crawling on dishes, foodstuffs, and other items. Like flies, they contaminate with their bodies, their manner of eating, and their feces. And once again, they can be controlled better if their life cycle and habits are understood.

Cockroach eggs are deposited in a leathery sack that contains from twenty-five to thirty eggs. They may be dropped anywhere, or they may be glued to walls, shelves, or equipment. It takes about one month for the eggs to hatch and about one year for the young to grow to maturity. Their rate of growth is affected by temperature, moisture, and the amount of food available. They prefer warm, dark, damp places, and they hide in cracks, behind equipment, in boxes, and inside walls during the day, emerging to feed at night when it is dark and quiet. If one or more cockroaches are seen in the daytime, it is certain that swarms of them are nearby, waiting to come out at night.

As in combating flies, cleanliness is one of the most important control measures. Besides eliminating their food, frequent cleaning can pick up the egg sacks and thereby reduce the numbers of new cockroaches. Finding their hiding places helps establish where to place the poisons that will control them. Insecticides of the proper type work well, but they should be used by someone who knows how. Usually a pest control company is best equipped to eliminate rats, mice, and cockroaches, and they can also be helpful in getting rid of ants (see fig. 3-9). A program of regular treatments is essential. All deliveries should be examined for cockroaches, since this is one of the most common ways they get into operations. Delivery crates and boxes should be unpacked and disposed of as soon as possible.

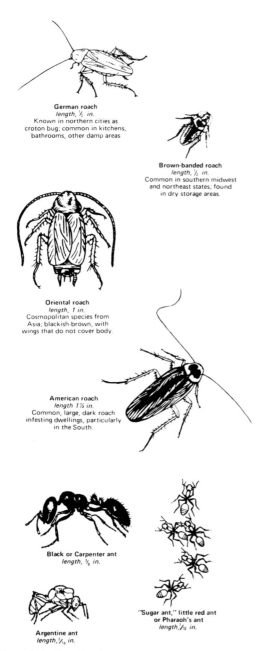

German roach
length, ½ in.
Known in northern cities as
croton bug; common in kitchens,
bathrooms, other damp areas

Brown-banded roach
length, ½ in.
Common in southern midwest
and northeast states; found
in dry storage areas.

Oriental roach
length, 1 in.
Cosmopolitan species from
Asia; blackish-brown, with
wings that do not cover body.

American roach
length 1½ in.
Common, large, dark roach
infesting dwellings, particularly
in the South.

Black or Carpenter ant
length, ⅜ in.

"Sugar ant," little red ant
or Pharaoh's ant
length, 1/10 in.

Argentine ant
length, 1/16 in.

Figure 3-9. Crawling insect pests.

Responsibilities for Sanitation

As with other factors in foodservice operations, different personnel have different responsibilities for maintaining satisfactory sanitary standards. Management's responsibilities in implementing a sanitation program include planning the program and training and supervising the staff; the employees' responsibility is to see that sanitary standards are maintained.

Management must provide the proper facilities, equipment, and resources for maintaining the standards. After establishing appropriate policies and standards, management must train the staff in the proper procedures for implementation. Clearly explained instructions and practical guidance are necessary for success. Supervision of the program calls for monitoring the staff to ensure that standards are met. Equipment maintenance and repair policies and procedures should be part of the sanitation program too. Equipment can easily be monitored and inspected during cleaning.

Employees have a responsibility to develop good working habits, to use care in handling foods, and to know what factors promote or impede the growth of bacteria and other organisms that can contaminate food. Employees must know how to control microorganisms and how to practice good hygiene. They should see that equipment and the facility itself are kept in a sanitary condition.

Foodservices must meet certain standards of sanitation to be legally certified to operate. Federal, state, and local regulations require compliance with such standards. Periodically, inspections are made of operations; those that are found to be substandard are cited for violations and may be fined. Correction of the condition is required within a given time. If conditions remain substandard, the operation may be closed. An operation guilty of repeated violations may also be forced to close. Many states today require that a qualified sanitarian (one who has taken and satisfactorily completed a sanitation course) be on duty at all times. The trend is toward placing more responsibility on the foodservice industry itself for the achievement of satisfactory sanitation standards.

SAFETY

In a modern quantity foodservice, a multiplicity of hazards daily confront both operator and employee. Few occupations, in fact, present so many inherently hazardous features on the job: open flames, hot liquids, high-pressure steam, sharp tools, cutting and grinding machines, and slippery floors are just a few of the unremovable dangers. Accident rates are said to be as high in the foodservice industry as in mining.

Everyone has a responsibility for maintaining good, safe working conditions. Although management is responsible for overall safety guidelines and their enforcement, every person must see that hazards are not created or tolerated out of negligence. Proper observance of safety rules by everyone is essential.

The Employee's Responsibility

One of the most important factors in keeping safe is keeping alert. Inattention, failure to anticipate or plan, ignorance of surprise or danger signals, and just plain loafing are factors that bring about accidents. The Industrial Commission of Ohio's Division of Safety and Hygiene identifies six unsafe acts that frequently result in accidents:

1. Failure to look where one is going: kitchen workers carrying pots, pans, food, or supplies collide with other workers. Result: bumps, bruises, other injuries.
2. Failure to observe surroundings: cooks at the range stand too near the stove, brush against a hot stove, knock over pots and pans. Result: severe burns or other injuries.
3. Failure to handle knives and tools with care: knives are left exposed on open tables instead of being put away in a drawer or other safe place; knives are left protruding from edges of tables and chopping blocks; a knife falls and someone grabs for it. Result: cutting or stabbing.
4. Reaching too high or too low, lifting too heavy a weight, or lifting incorrectly. Result: strained

muscles and sometimes permanent injury. Rule: lift with the leg and thigh muscles, not with the back muscles.
5. Failure to pay attention when using knives, grinders, or other cutting tools: a cook, slicing onions, looks away; a kitchen helper chopping celery in a grinder reaches too far into the grinder. Result: cuts or lost members.
6. Failure to protect hands from hot pans, pots, and plates. Result: burns. Rule: many severe burns result from a failure to use side towels or pot holders.

The Industrial Commission of Ohio's Division of Safety and Hygiene and the Ohio State Restaurant Association cite cuts, slips and falls, burns and scalds, and improper lifting and hauling as the major causes of lost employee time in the foodservice industry. Such lost time would be reduced materially if the suggestions given in the subsections that follow were kept in mind.

Cuts

Cuts mean lost time and lost wages to employees and lost profit to the employer. They are among the most common of accidents in the foodservice industry and, unfortunately, are often caused by carelessness. Important preventive measures include the following:

1. Put knives away when you are finished with them. When cleaning a knife, wipe it with the cutting edge away from you. Slice with the sharp end going away from you, preferably toward a cutting board. Pay attention at all times when using a knife.
2. Always use a food stamper to press food into a grinder. Use all slicers properly, with the guard (not your own hand) holding the food to be sliced. Remember, the slicer is power-driven and will not stop just because your finger gets into it.
3. Keep hands away from all moving cutters on ice-cubing machines.
4. Remove all chipped or broken glass immediately, and keep it in a separate container

provided for this purpose. Many serious cuts are caused by leaving broken glass and broken dishes in the same area with dirty dishes. As figure 3-10 suggests, breakage and resulting accidents can be reduced if employees are made aware of the potential costs and dangers of broken glass.

5. Watch for nails and sharp fasteners when unpacking boxes, crates, cartons, and barrels. Use proper tools, and be careful.

Slips and Falls

Slips and falls are often the result of poor housekeeping. Spilled liquids or foods should be cleaned up immediately. Cluttered aisles and passageways,

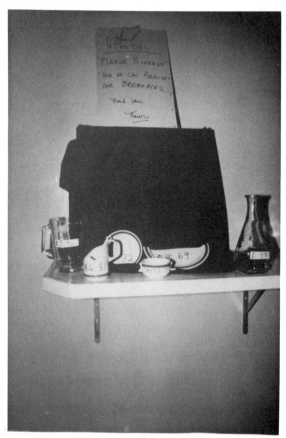

Figure 3-10. The cost and potential dangers of breakage must be understood by all foodservice employees.

torn and loose carpeting, and worn stairways present hazards as well. Caution must be exercised while moving about, climbing stairs, and rounding corners. Overheated work areas can lead to fatigue and increase the likelihood of an accident. Inadequate lighting can exacerbate a hazardous situation. By being alert and aware of potential hazards, employees can increase their chances for maintaining personal safety.

Burns and Scalds

Hot materials or equipment are a part of the foodservice business; the best protection against harm from them is constant awareness and caution. Handling hot food with tongs or long-handled spoons or forks and using hot pads to move hot dishes can help avoid injury. Water temperatures at the spigot should seldom be higher than 160°F (71°C). Because of the need to save energy, high water temperatures are being lowered except where essential for a particular job.

Pots filled with hot food should be lifted carefully. The individual carrying them should look ahead to preview the route of travel and the availability of a proper landing place at journey's end. The handles of hot pots should not project over table or range edges. Knowing how to work around hot ovens, griddles, and steam equipment is a part of job competence. An inexperienced worker can receive a severe burn from lifting the lid of a boiling pot or steam-jacketed kettle without using a long fork or other extension tool. Frequently, burns or scalds occur when workers try to do something with hot equipment or food that cannot be done. For example, a worker may reach into an oven at about shoulder height, pull out a roasting pan full of hot meat and juice, and try to lift this down to a table; the weight of the item at that height is too great to permit good leverage, and the result is often injury. Getting help to lift hot items in such cases is the proper procedure to follow.

Improper Lifting and Hauling

Improper lifting or carrying accounts for 25 percent of lost-time accidents. These accidents occur because workers were not trained to carry or lift properly. More injuries occur while putting objects down than while picking them up. Too many people try to lift objects beyond their strength, often suffering back strains or hernias. A person's ability to lift and carry largely depends on physical condition, build, stature, and experience or training. Heavy lifting can be dangerous to a person handicapped with a weak heart, high blood pressure, or a lung disorder.

Simple rules govern proper lifting. People do not realize that leg muscles, because they are bigger and get more exercise, are stronger than those of the back and abdomen. Instead, people lift with their legs straight and their back bent over, putting most of the strain on the back and thereby causing injury. Some supervisors erroneously believe that everyone knows how to lift or carry, or they simply do not concern themselves with the question. This is a mistake. Supervisors should demonstrate to all new employees the following, correct way to lift:

1. Get a good footing.
2. Make certain no foreign object lies on the floor under your feet.
3. Place your feet about shoulder width apart.
4. Bend at the knees to grasp the weight.
5. Keep your back straight.
6. Get a firm hold.
7. Keep your back as upright as possible.
8. Lift gradually by straightening your legs.
9. When the weight is too heavy or bulky for you to lift comfortably, get help.
10. Place heavy weights on dollies or carts before moving them.

Secondary rules include the following:

1. Inspect the object to be lifted for sharp corners, nails, and other things that might cause injury.
2. Distribute the weight evenly by keeping your hands at opposite corners of the object being lifted.
3. If you must shift the position of the load while carrying it, first rest it on something for support.

Many people readily develop good safety habits, but others do not. Studies have shown that some people are accident-prone whereas others seldom have an accident. Older workers can do much to help build good safety habits in newer workers. They should notice things the new person does that might cause injury and, in a helpful way, show the newcomer the correct procedure. Learning and following safety rules can help prevent injury.

The Manager's Responsibility

Management has primary responsibility for seeing that workers and customers are safe from injury or harm. Customer injuries may translate into claims, lawsuits, or loss of patronage; employee injuries can lead to compensation costs, loss of productivity, and perhaps a lawsuit.

In 1971, the Williams-Steiger Occupational Safety and Health Act became a part of our national labor law. It created the Occupational Safety and Health Administration (OSHA) to administer the act. The purpose of the act was "to assure so far as possible every working man and woman in the nation safe and healthful working conditions and to preserve our human resources." The act performs several functions:

- It encourages employers and employees to reduce hazards in the workplace and to start or improve existing safety and health programs.
- It establishes employer and employee responsibility.
- It authorizes OSHA to set mandatory job safety and health standards.
- It provides an effective enforcement program.
- It encourages the states to assume responsibility for administering and enforcing their own occupational safety and health programs designed to be at least as effective as the federal programs.
- It provides for reporting procedures on job injuries, illnesses, and fatalities.

All employers engaging one or more employees in a business affecting commerce must comply.

Certain federal agencies are exempt. Specific standards have been established; in case they do not apply in a particular situation, a "general duty requirement" covers hazards not otherwise mentioned. It reads, in part, "each employer shall furnish to each of his employees employment and a place of employment which are free from recognized hazards that are causing or likely to cause death or serious physical harm to his employees." Any recognized hazard created in part by a condition not covered in the established specific standards may be cited as a violation under this general duty clause.

The various states have been encouraged to set up laws similar to the federal Occupational Safety and Health Act. If provisions of the state law are more strict than those of the federal government, the former hold precedence; if the federal law is more strict, it takes precedence. Upon inspection, a business can be cited for violations if hazardous conditions are found. In the first five months during which the act was in force, OSHA inspectors of foodservices made 10,668 inspections, found 26,771 violations, and issued 2,141 citations that carried a combined monetary penalty of over $500,000.

The effect of the federal act has been to increase both the responsibility of management for safety and the number of steps management has taken to reduce hazards in foodservices. In some cases the law has brought hardship to a foodservice that was established before the law existed and failed to meet the required standards. Conflict has also developed between foodservices and OSHA inspectors because of interpretations of the law or because of seemingly unreasonable viewpoints of inspectors toward some operational conditions in the industry. So much criticism has been directed against the law and the OSHA administrators by the entire business community of this country that some modification of provisions has occurred. Whatever its shortcomings, the law has brought about a major change in safety in the industries of this nation and has placed upon management a much greater legal responsibility for safety than it ever had before.

It is management's responsibility to see that the plant facilities are safe, to establish rules for safety, and to see that they are enforced. Training programs in safety should be instituted, and meetings should be held to discuss potential hazards and the adequacy of current safety measures. If accidents occur, management should make a careful study of their causes and of possible measures to reduce or eliminate them. A good repair and maintenance schedule should be set up to ensure that equipment and the facility as a whole are kept in top operational shape. All equipment should bear the stamp of approval of the American Gas Association (AGA) or of Underwriters' Laboratories (UL) (see fig. 3-11). Publications of the National Safety Council and others can help management develop and carry out good safety programs.

One of the best ways to encourage safe conditions is to maintain a good safety inspection program. OSHA has safety lists that can be used for this purpose, and the forms inspectors use in making the OSHA inspection can be helpful. To be effective, a safety self-inspection program should include the following four points:

1. Inspection of equipment and physical facilities on a department-by-department or function-by-function basis.
2. Review of the physical fitness of employees to perform assigned duties safely.
3. Review of actual operational procedures and personal practices of employees as they perform their required tasks and of the manner in which employees use hazardous equip-

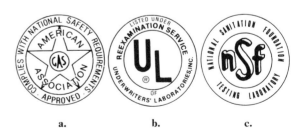

a.   b.   c.

Figure 3-11. Symbols of national testing associations: (a) American Gas Association; (b) Underwriters' Laboratories; (c) National Sanitation Foundation.

ment and work in observance of good safety practices.

4. Check of compliance with safety and health regulations with respect to displaying required permits, posters, and reports and maintaining required reports.

Inspection checks of equipment and facilities should be comprehensive and should include the following fifteen specific areas:

1. Receiving areas for food and supplies.
2. Storage facilities for dry and perishable food and for nonfood supplies.
3. Food preparation areas and equipment.
4. Warewashing and storage facilities.
5. Dining rooms and food serving areas.
6. Exits, stairways, and landings.
7. Customer restrooms.
8. Employee facilities such as toilets, lavatories, locker rooms, and lunch rooms.
9. Storage areas for soaps, detergents, solvents, pesticides, and other hazardous supplies.
10. Garbage and trash storage and disposal areas.
11. Boiler rooms, compressor installations, and other utilities.
12. Exterior surroundings, including parking lots, drive-in service areas, and incinerators.
13. Vehicles for transporting food.
14. Equipment and systems installed or available for fire protection.
15. First-aid supplies.

COMPUTER-ASSISTED SANITATION AND SAFETY PROGRAMS

Computers can be of assistance to management in maintaining a safe, sanitary foodservice environment. With the proper software programs, computers can offer help in two primary areas: training and record keeping.

For any sanitation or safety program to be effective, all personnel must be trained in the proper policies and procedures. The new small-business computers could assist in this training by means of interactive training packages. After reading a booklet or viewing a videotape, the trainee sits at the computer and is quizzed. Right and wrong answers are noted immediately. In the case of a wrong answer, the computer system can backtrack, review material, and lead the student to the correct answer. This type of system can save the manager time by eliminating the need to train each employee personally. In addition, the employee is more receptive to the training because of the immediate feedback on progress and the freedom from any stigma associated with asking "dumb" questions. It allows employees to be trained at their own pace at any time of the day.

As in many other areas of foodservice, sanitation and safety records need to be kept. These necessary records include duct and filter cleaning schedules; pest control schedules related to spraying, fogging, or the placement of traps; employee training records; and accident records. Using a computer to maintain these records renders them readily accessible, easy to update, and space-efficient. The computer can also be programmed to alert the manager to upcoming inspections or periodic cleaning dates.

Clearly, although a computer is not a substitute for a well-planned sanitation and safety program, it can be a useful tool in making an established program more effective.

SUMMARY

Sanitation and safety are the joint responsibility of everyone in a foodservice. Good sanitation ensures that customers are served wholesome food that will neither make them ill nor do other harm. Good safety ensures that the environment confronting both employees and customers is as free as possible from potential sources of harm.

Four kinds of substances cause food poisoning: organisms that infect; organisms that develop toxins that are ingested with food; chemical poisons; and poisonous foods or animals. The first two kinds of substances are living things that belong to a large family called *microorganisms* because they can only be seen with a microscope. Some are harmful, others do no harm, and still others are beneficial. Harmful microorganisms are called *pathogens.* Time, temperature, availability of food and moisture, cleanliness, and the purchase of noncontaminated food are factors that help control them. Bacteria, viruses, parasites, and molds are types of microorganisms that can be pathogenic. Molds and yeasts tend to spoil food, rather than to cause illness in man; however, some few molds can develop toxic substances.

Food-borne intoxication occurs when certain microorganisms contaminate food and produce a toxin in it that causes illness. Thus, the direct cause of illness is the toxin and not the organism itself. Food-borne infection occurs when microorganisms get into the food or drink and are taken live into the body; their growth in the body does the harm. Destroying infectious agents by cooking food thoroughly at a sufficiently high temperature destroys the microorganisms but may not eliminate the danger from toxins.

Chemical poisoning results from errors in handling harmful substances such as cleaning agents, poisons, or other chemical products used in connection with foodservice operations. Such substances should not be used around food and should only be entrusted to employees who know how to use them safely. Chemical poisons should not be stored in the same area where food is stored. Many plants and animals are poisonous, but most of these have been eliminated from our regular food supplies. They do cause problems occasionally, however. For example, eating oysters or clams made poisonous by tiny red mites can cause serious illness. Purchasing food from approved sources can do much to eliminate a person's risk of consuming poisonous food.

Successful prevention of food-borne diseases depends on the factors of food protection, personal hygiene of workers, facility and equipment sanitation, proper ventilation and light, good garbage and refuse disposal, adequate handwashing and toilet facilities, and good pest control.

Purchasing food from approved sources helps ensure that it is safe and wholesome to eat. Following sanitary practices in preparing food is another way to prevent food-borne disease. Storing food under the right conditions is another crucial step, and serving food properly (including holding it for service properly) is the final step in food protection.

Personal hygiene deals with an individual's habits of cleanliness. A failure to follow good hygienic principles endangers food and may cause a loss of patronage; customers do not like to be served by unkempt, unclean personnel.

The foodservice facility and its equipment must be properly maintained to prevent food-borne diseases. Floors, walls, and ceilings should be easy to clean and should be properly maintained. The maintenance requirements depend largely on the original construction of the building. Proper ventilation and lighting are other aspects of physical plant sanitation. Garbage and refuse disposal must be done in a proper manner. Good equipment sanitation ensures that food-borne disease organisms will not be transmitted through improperly cleaned and sanitized equipment.

Adequate control of rodents and insects must occur if good sanitation standards are to be achieved. Elimination of breeding places is an important preventive measure in all cases. Rats and mice are the most resourceful of pests. Keeping them out of the building is one of the best ways to control them. Poisoning and trapping can also be effective. Houseflies carry many diseases. Measures for keeping them out of a facility should include screens and other blockage devices, cleanliness, and elimination if they get inside. Cockroaches, too, can carry disease organisms, and they have a very offensive odor. As with flies, an understanding of their life cycle is an important step in the proper control of these pests.

Both management and employees are responsible for seeing that good sanitation is practiced in an operation. Local, state, and federal sanitary codes must be followed.

Safety is achieved in a foodservice when both employees and management properly perform their duties in this area. Employees should be alert, follow safety rules, work safely, and think safety. Experienced workers can help train newer ones in good safety procedures. Employees should learn to handle tools and materials corectly. In the foodservice industry, the four most common causes of major injuries are cuts, slips and falls, burns and scalds, and improper lifting and hauling. Cuts mean lost time and lost wages to the employee and lost profit to the employer. Slips and falls usually result from poor housekeeping or from inattention. Burns and scalds usually result from carelessness or from a failure to observe good safety rules. Improper lifting and hauling account for the final 25 percent of lost-time accidents. They occur when proper principles of lifting and carrying are not followed.

Management is responsible for seeing that a facility is safe by providing a safe place to work, by keeping equipment in good operating order, by publishing rules for good safety, by making sure that these rules are carried out, and by training employees in good safety principles. The Occupational Safety and Health Act is a law that has established high standards for safety in American industry.

Computer assistance in implementing sanitation and safety programs can be quite helpful. Computers can be used effectively by management for training employees and for maintaining safety and sanitation records.

CHAPTER REVIEW QUESTIONS

1. John Smith is a newly appointed regional manager for Barrt's, a chain of family-style restaurants. In the third week on his new job, John receives a frantic call from Dave Schultz, who is the manager of one of John's units. It seems that Dave's restaurant has just been visited by a county health inspector, and the restaurant failed to pass the inspection. The health inspector has given Dave one week to make corrections, after which the restaurant will be reinspected. After calming Dave down, John asks him about the inspection and learns that there are no major problems—just numerous small ones. John asks Dave about his sanitation and safety programs and is not too surprised when Dave informs him that there is no formal program. John tells Dave to begin addressing the immediate problems and says that he will get back in touch with him in the next few days. John then makes calls to the managers of the other units in his region and discovers that, while some managers have established their own programs, there is no company-directed program. These managers assert, however, that their establishments are clean, safe, and well-maintained. John, knowing how important cleanliness is to Barrt's customers, decides that some action must be taken. What would you suggest he do and how should he do it?

2. List the different kinds of microorganisms that can cause food-borne infections and intoxications. Indicate: (1) how infection and intoxication types differ; (2) the necessary factors that must be present for their growth; and (3) how they can be controlled.

3. Discuss food-borne poisoning from chemicals, plants, and animals. How does such contamination occur? What control measures can be taken to see they do not occur?

4. Food protection, personal hygiene, facility and equipment sanitation, and pest control are important areas in the prevention of food-borne disease. Select one of these and describe how it could be appropriately implemented in an operation of your choice. For example, how would you see that food protection assured good standards if you operated a foodservice? Be specific.

5. Discuss and divide the responsibilities for achieving good sanitation standards between employees, management, and governmental authorities.

6. What are the responsibilities of management

and employees in achieving high safety standards? Can you contribute others you feel are important? Share these in an oral report before the rest of the class.
7. What is OSHA?

VOCABULARY

Clean	Sanitary
Microorganism	Virus
Coliform	Intoxication
Cocci	Botulism
Mesophiles	Amoeba
Hepatitis	Spore
Danger zone	Japanese roulette
Salmonella	UL
OSHA	Bacteria
Infection	Protozoa
Parasite	*Staphylococcus*
Trichinosis	Vector
Pupa	pH
AGA	

ANNOTATED REFERENCES

Coffman, J. P. 1971. *Introduction to Professional Food Service,* pp. 25-58. Boston: CBI Publishing. (Deals with personal safety and sanitation, as well as with food poisoning.)

Guthrie, R. K. 1988. *Food Sanitation.* 3d ed. New York: Van Nostrand Reinhold. (Technical presentation of microbiology and sanitation.)

Longree, K. 1972. *Quantity Food Sanitation.* 2d ed. New York: Wiley-Interscience. (Relatively technical and comprehensive approach to sanitation and safety.)

National Institute for the Foodservice Industry. 1978. *Applied Foodservice Sanitation.* D. C. Heath & Company. (Very practical and informative guide to food-service sanitation.)

Thorner, M. E., and Manning, P. B. 1983. *Quality Control in Foodservice,* pp. 227-263. New York: Van Nostrand Reinhold. (Brief discussion of sanitation, followed by specific recommendations for keeping the workplace clean and sanitary.)

West, B. B. 1977. *Foodservice in Institutions,* pp. 551-629. New York: John Wiley & Sons. (Comprehensive section on sanitation and safety.)

CHAPTER 4

Producing a Menu

OUTLINE

The menu in a modern foodservice operation functions as the operation's primary sales medium. Therefore, it should be written to sell and inform. The content of the menu defines the operation and establishes a direction for management. It determines the items purchased, their cost, the operation's personnel and facility requirements, and the types of service that will be offered. The operation's decor, atmosphere, theme, and service style revolve around the menu as well. At the front of the house and in the heart of the house, the menu establishes the style and content of the operation.

The plan and design of the menu must attract customers to the front of the house and must encourage them to return. Menus that attempt to attract too broad a market are less effective than those that zero in on (or *target*) a specific market. A foodservice cannot be all things to all people: it must be suited to a specific known group or segment of the population. Consequently, the first step in planning a menu is to determine the target market. This clientele's needs and desires must be taken into consideration in constructing the type of menu that will give the operation its best chance for success.

The *front of the house* is the area of the opera-

59

tion in which direct contact with the customer is made; the focal point here is clearly the dining room. Because the front of the house is so vital to an operation's success, management must consider certain front-of-the-house needs in planning a menu. Effective merchandising and selling are the primary objectives of menu planning, and these have an effect on style of service and the variety of menu offerings. Front-of-the-house considerations must be in balance with heart-of-the-house concerns such as food and labor costs, equipment, space and storage, skill of personnel, and availability of foods. Neglecting to establish such a balance can result in a menu failure and an operation that does not achieve desired goals. Therefore, weighing front- and heart-of-the-house considerations is an essential step in the menu-planning process.

ATTRACTING THE CUSTOMER

Every operation should attempt to build an image that it believes will best appeal to the target market. The image is built from a combination of things: food items offered, style of service, pricing, atmosphere, location, type of customer attracted, and personality and philosophy of management. The menu provides a means of conveying these image-building factors to the customer.

The menu must be designed to communicate the operation's ability to satisfy the needs of a specific market. In many cases the wants and needs of a specific market can be identified on the basis of socioeconomic variables such as religious background, age, family size, amount of disposable income, ethnic background, and level of education. These are only a few of the variables that may be considered in defining a target market. The menu planner has a responsibility to study and know the market, so the menu can be designed to meet that market's needs.

In the original planning of a foodservice, the concepts on which a design is based are defined in a *feasibility study*. The feasibility study covers a host of factors, including site selection, type and location of competition, size, cost, financing, budgeting, payback of capital and interest within a

given period, and the number and type of employees, as well as presenting a detailed analysis of the target market and a preliminary menu designed to satisfy the market's needs.

In hospitals and educational institutions, for example, menus are designed to meet a customer's need for three meals per day, seven days a week. A menu in a first-class restaurant may be written for patrons who eat out only on special occasions, such as couples celebrating their anniversaries. One market may be drawn to a menu featuring hamburgers and milkshakes, while another may have special dietary needs. The following questions need to be addressed in targeting a market and designing a menu:

Who are the customers?
Where do they come from?
How much disposable income do they have?
Where do they live?
How do they get here?
How old are they?
What is their ethnic background?
What types of jobs do they have?
How do they spend their leisure time?
How often do they eat out?
In what type of community am I located?
Are there legal or political restraints?
Where else can these customers eat?
Who are the direct competitors?
What does the competition offer?
Should I imitate the competition or be different?
What other types of food or service might be
    successful?

Any menu that does not meet the needs of the market is unlikely to prove successful and should be changed. A precise analysis of the market offers guidelines to management for determining the theme or logo, location, menu structure, equipment needs, and overall image. Recent studies have identified shifts in customer preferences, as well as an increase in the number of meals eaten away from home. The menu planner should be aware of these trends and make adjustments accordingly.

There may be certain limits within which an

operator must work in planning a menu. Some facilities are required to follow specific nutritional guidelines. For example, in a school foodservice covered by federal regulations, a Type A lunch for elementary school students must supply one-third of a child's daily nutritional requirements. Hospitals must provide medically prescribed meals rather than meet personal preferences. This frequently causes problems for a hospital, because people would rather eat what they want instead of what is good for their health.

Restaurants and commercial operations may also face certain constraints. Seasonal availability of some products must be considered—especially in the case of seafood or fresh produce. Many items that were only available on a seasonal basis in the past are now on the market year round. The price of such items (lobster, for example) can still vary considerably, however, and may force certain operations to drop otherwise desirable selections from their menus. Other constraints may be encountered in designing a menu for a preexisting facility. A limited level of skill among workers or a lack of equipment can prevent certain changes from taking place. A new menu must conform to the existing operation; if it does not, confusion and erratic or low-quality performance are likely results.

TYPES OF MENUS

Once a target market has been determined and its needs identified, menu planning begins. There are many different menu types, and each is written for the needs of the particular market it serves. Menus may be à la carte, table d'hôte, *du jour*, limited, cyclical, or other. Some markets may require a combination of menu types.

A La Carte Menu

Food items are priced separately in an à la carte menu, allowing an individual to select precisely the items desired (see fig. 4-1). It is popular in commercial foodservices, since selling separate items brings in more revenue than selling items at a group price.

A semi-à la carte menu may offer an entrée (main dinner offering) with salad, vegetable, and beverage at one price; customers who want an appetizer, a dessert, or other additional food must pay extra.

Another approach is to use à la carte pricing for the entrée as well as semi-à la carte pricing for it in combination with other foods. This is done either by listing entrées separately on an à la carte page or by indicating two prices beside each entrée: one for the entrée alone, and one for the entrée plus the extras. The items included as extras should be clearly indicated, in order not to confuse the customer about what is being offered at à la carte prices. Other menus present two prices: one for an item selected à la carte, and the other for the table d'hôte offering.

Table d'Hôte Menu

A table d'hôte menu is the opposite of an à la carte one (see fig. 4-2). It offers a complete meal at a fixed price, although a choice of some items such as salad, entrée, or dessert may be offered. The table d'hôte offering might include appetizer, salad, soup, entrée, beverage, and perhaps dessert. However, spiraling food and labor costs have caused complete menus of this sort to become quite expensive, and many people want a meal with far fewer calories than they would get with such a repast. Offering a more limited selection on the table d'hôte menu makes it possible to reduce the price and yet give enough food to satisfy the customer's appetite. A table d'hôte menu is desirable in an operation that knows what its customers want and can forecast closely what these needs will be. The ability to predict which items on the menu will be selected is essential. If the number of guests is guaranteed, the prediction may be quite precise. Institutional and industrial operations may find limited menus of this type suitable, whereas elegant restaurants may use a traditional table d'hôte or an à la carte menu.

Du Jour Menu

The term *du jour menu* means the menu of the day. Such a menu must be planned and written

SONNY'S RIBS
115 S. State St.

512-7681

ONION RINGS

Half Loaf	1.95	**Full Loaf**	2.95

APPETIZERS

Fried Cheese — 3.75
Golden browned mozzarella sticks,
seasoned and served with marinara sauce.

Regular Order 2.25 **Large Order** 3.25

Potato Skins
Filled with real bacon and
cheddar cheese.

Regular Order 2.25 **Large Order** 3.75

AND OTHER THINGS

Baked Potato with Butter & Sour Cream	.95
French Fries	.95
Corn on the Cob	.95
Cole Slaw	.95

SALADS

Cobb Salad	4.25
Tossed Salad	1.25
Sliced Tomatoes with Bermuda Onion	1.15

RIBS

All rib entrees are served with cole slaw
and french fries.

Baby Back Ribs — 10.95
House specialty. The choicest lean U.S. ribs
cut from the tenderloin.

St. Louis Style Ribs — 8.95
Select cut U.S. spare ribs. Tender and meaty.

Bountiful Beef Ribs — 8.95
Big, juicy ribs. Hearty and flavorful.

JUMBO PACKS

Each order serves approximately four people.
Does not include cole slaw or french fries.
Barbecue sauce is included.

Baby Back Ribs (40)	38.40
St. Louis Style Ribs (40)	30.40
Bountiful Beef Ribs (16)	27.80
Baby Back Chicken Combo	
(20 ribs, 2 chicken halves)	27.80
St. Louis Chicken Combo	
(20 ribs, 2 chicken halves)	25.90
Chicken (4 halves)	17.80
White Chicken (8 breasts)	19.80
Barbecue Sauce	
Pint	1.95
Quart	3.50
Gallon	15.20

BARBECUE

All entrees are served with cole slaw and
french fries.

Barbecued Shrimp & Baby Back Ribs — 11.95
A skewer of large grilled barbecued shrimp,
served with our Baby Back Ribs.

Barbecued Chicken & Ribs — 9.95
with our Baby Back Ribs (.75 extra).

One Half Barbecued Chicken — 6.45
with White Meat Only (.50 extra).

GRILLED ENTREES

All entrees are served with cole slaw and
french fries.

Marinated Boneless Breasts of Chicken — 7.45
Two boneless breasts of chicken, marinated
then grilled. Served on a bed of rice.

Charbroiled Ribeye Steak — 11.95
U.S.D.A. Choice

Filet Mignon on a Skewer — 7.95
Marinated Kabob with mushrooms, peppers,
onions and tomatoes.

BEVERAGES	DESSERTS
Soft drinks	Chocolate Beast
Iced Tea	Key Lime Pie
Coffee	Cheese Cake
Juices / Milk / Tea	
.85	2.50

$15.00 Minimum Required on all Delivery Orders.

Figure 4-1. Sample à la carte menu.

Figure 4-2. Brennan's table d'hôte menu.

daily, since it will reflect only the foods produced for that day. This offers a convenient way to make use of carry-overs and food bargains; but if it neglects front- and heart-of-the-house considerations, it may not meet the needs of the operation. The *du jour* menu has the advantage of flexibility not only with respect to food items but with respect to the skill of the employee who is to produce them. Usually only a few foods or their combinations are offered. Often an operation offering a *du jour* menu is a specialty one that serves original and special foods to a limited clientele.

Nonetheless, other operations may use such a menu. For example, special foods may be offered on special days to suit market needs. This provides variety along with known foods. On the whole, though, other menus could be more suitable if the only rationale for such a menu hinges on the use of carry-overs and food bargains. The normal rule in a foodservice is that good planning leaves no carryovers.

Limited Menu

The limited menu evolved from more traditional types and may in fact be a hybrid of them. It may or may not offer the same foods every day. The entrée selections are usually limited to between six and twelve items, and some menus may offer only two or three choices. A representative but small selection of appetizers, salads, entrées, and desserts is also offered.

Because of rising costs, limited menus have become increasingly popular as a way to reduce labor costs and food waste so as to improve production control and labor productivity. Planning problems and production complexity are simplified as the menus become more limited. Limited menus must be pointed to relatively specific markets, since

they offer fewer items. They have met with great success in fastfood operations and in specialty restaurants such as steakhouses.

Cyclical Menu

The cyclical menu schedules foods for days within certain time periods, repeating the selections every two to six weeks. It is often wise to change cycles with the seasons and to provide special offerings on certain days. Thus, an operation may have four different cyclical menus to supply meals over the course of four seasons. Sundays and Fridays are days on which people especially remember food, so a slower-running cycle may be used on these days than on other days within the cycle. For example, a menu could be planned with an eighteen-day regular cycle, to which a four-Sunday cycle and a four-Friday cycle are built in (see table 4-1). The eighteen-week or four-season-a-year cyclical menu is the most usual, but cycles within this period may

Table 4-1. Complete Menu Cycle for 13 Weeks or 18 Weeks

Week	Sunday	Monday	Tuesday	Wednesday	Thursday	Friday	Saturday
1st	S-1	D-1	D-2	D-3	D-4	F-1	D-5
2nd	S-2	D-6	D-7	D-8	D-9	F-2	D-10
3rd	S-3	D-11	D-12	D-13	D-14	F-3	D-15
4th	S-4	D-16	D-17	D-18	D-1	F-4	D-2
5th	S-1	D-3	D-4	D-5	D-6	F-1	D-7
6th	S-2	D-8	D-9	D-10	D-11	F-2	D-12
7th	S-3	D-13	D-14	D-15	D-16	F-3	D-17
8th	S-4	D-18	D-1	D-2	D-3	F-4	D-4
9th	S-1	D-5	D-6	D-7	D-8	F-1	D-9
10th	S-2	D-10	D-11	D-12	D-13	F-2	D-14
11th	S-3	D-15	D-16	D-17	D-18	F-3	D-1
12th	S-4	D-2	D-3	D-4	D-5	F-4	D-6
13th	S-1	D-7	D-8	D-9	D-10	F-1	D-11
14th	S-2	D-12	D-13	D-14	D-15	F-2	D-16
15th	S-3	D-17	D-18	D-1	D-2	F-3	D-3
16th	S-4	D-4	D-5	D-6	D-7	F-4	D-8
17th	S-1	D-9	D-10	D-11	D-12	F-1	D-13
18th	S-2	D-14	D-15	D-16	D-17	F-2	D-18

NOTE: This cyclical menu offers no two of the same meals on the same day throughout its 13- or 18-week cycle. Eighteen daily menus (D) have been specified, and four Friday (F) and four Sunday (S) menus have been written to meet the wants and needs of the market that this particular operation serves.

repeat. Flexibility is extremely desirable. A cyclical menu that does not allow for changes or for the use of carry-over foods can become costly and may fail to meet the operation's needs. Cyclical menus do, however, give personnel a greater knowledge of production and quality requirements and more opportunity for better planning. This is because workers are faced with day-to-day changes but at the same time can see a repetition that helps in standardization and reduction of costs. Management forecasts of requirements are often improved as well.

Cyclical menus reduce menu-making time as well as labor time. Most foodservices can adapt cyclical menus, even in a limited fashion. Some hotels operate on a strict seven-day cycle, which makes food production coincide with employees' time on the job. This helps simplify production requirements, since employees prepare the same foods every week and gain proficiency and efficiency with repetition. Management can then more precisely identify costs and quantities needed.

Menu Variety

To capture a market, more than one menu may be required. For instance, there may be a need for separate breakfast, luncheon, and dinner menus or for different menus for different food operations. The menu a coffee shop needs is different from those needed by a bar, a shopping center during tea hours, or a late supper dining room. A child's menu is important for operations wanting to appeal to the family market. Suiting the menu to these needs is an art, and clever merchandising—both with food and with names—can do much to promote customer interest. Suiting the menu to the amount patrons want to spend is very important. Attention to special nutritional needs may attract customers.

DESIGNING THE MENU

One of the first things the customer sees when handed a menu is its design. If the lighting is low, the design of the menu may need to be bolder. In a fastfood operation, the design may be relatively simple and plain. Four factors are especially important in menu construction: menu sequence; the copy, layout, and printing style; the cover; and the flexibility of the menu.

Menu Sequence

The sequence in which foods are placed on the menu usually mirrors the order in which foods are eaten (see table 4-2). Menus are read from the outside pages to the inside, from top to bottom, and from left to right. Many people agree that the best menu position for gaining the reader's attention is on the inside center or inside right-hand page. Entrees should be given the best positions, since they bring in the largest amount of money, but alcoholic beverages should not be neglected in such positioning, because they can earn the largest profit per dollar of sale.

Entrée order is important. The most popular entrées or group of entrées—or the entrées that the operation most wants to sell—should be listed first. The first and last entrée items listed are those most frequently read. Prices should not be arranged in order from least to greatest or from greatest to least. Mixed prices are best (see fig. 4-3). Unless meat, fish, and poultry are offered in separately headed groups, it is not desirable to arrange entrées by animal type or other similar category in an undifferentiated list. Again, mixing is best.

Alcoholic beverages should be listed on the menu in the sequence in which they would be consumed in the course of a meal. Thus, cocktails appear at the beginning, wines in the middle, and after-dinner drinks at the end. Wines identified on a separate wine list card or booklet will not be noticed by customers as often as wines shown on the menu with the food items—unless special attention is brought to it by the server. Some menus list wines on the back of the menu.

The back of the menu is usually used, however, to indicate the operation's address, phone number, days and hours of operation, credit cards honored, and facilities offered. This information informs patrons of important facts relating to the operation.

Table 4-2. Common Menu Sequences for Various Menu Types

Breakfast	Lunch	Dinner		
		Limited Menu *Du Jour Menu*	*À la Carte Menu* *Table d'Hôte Menu*	*French Cuisine Menu*
Juices	Appetizers	Appetizers	Cocktails	Hors d'oeuvres
Fruits	Soups	Soups	Appetizers	Soups
Cereals	Entrées	Entrées	Soups	Eggs
Eggs	Vegetables	Desserts	Entrées	Fish
Omelets	Salads*	Accompaniments[†]	Vegetables	Entrées
Griddle items	Breads		Desserts	Roasted and broiled items
Meats	Desserts		After-dinner drinks	Vegetables and pastas
Vegetables	Beverages		Accompaniments[†]	Cold buffet
Breads				Salads
Beverages				Cheese
				Desserts
				Fruits
				Beverages

* Salads as accompaniments to entrées are usually listed after the entrées on the menu. Salads served alone are usually listed before the entrée selection.
[†] Side orders, salads, sandwiches, beverages, and similar accompaniments should be located on the menu as customer demand dictates.

An interesting bit of history or legend about the foodservice or geographical area can also appear there.

Copy, Layout, and Printing Style

The copy on a menu names and describes each item being offered. The layout of the menu sets individual menu items or groups of items apart from others. The printing style (font) selected can make reading the menu easy or difficult. Appropriate print size and style, effective use of headings, descriptions, and space, and attractive arrangement of the copy can make a menu easy to comprehend. The menu shown in figure 4-3 is relatively difficult to read because of crowding and the kind of print used.

Items or groups of items should bear names people recognize and understand. If a name is unclear or does not give the right connotation, additional descriptive copy is desirable. Such a descriptive explanation can help sell the item; it should be brief and should describe the item realistically. Not everyone is good at writing interesting descriptive

copy. Usually a menu writer/designer familiar with menu terms, culinary words, and ways to enhance a menu's interest should do it. Foreign words should be avoided, unless patrons can be expected to understand them clearly. Simplicity helps improve understanding and broaden communication. Some menus are improved by general descriptive copy built around a special feature, character, or service, or around the history of the establishment or community in which the operation is located. In an operation selling Maryland crab dishes, for example, a story about the Maryland blue crab, how it lives, how it is caught fresh each day by professional crabbers, and how skilled cooks swiftly turn the day's catch into the many delectable dishes on the menu can heighten the customers' interest and build an image of freshness and quality about the product. Using colorful, evocative words is an art; overdoing it can produce garish results.

The advice of a professional menu planner should be used if no one in the operation can put good copy together. Some printing companies make a specialty of planning and setting up menus.

Menu copy should be set in a style of type that is

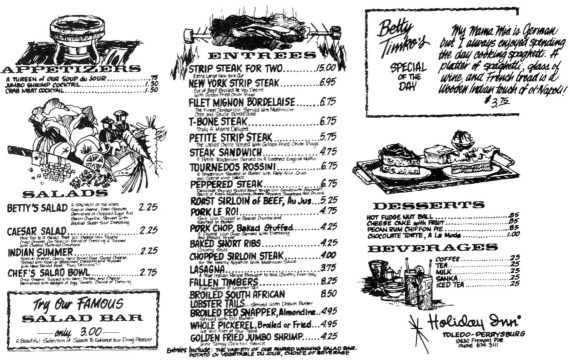

Figure 4-3. Betty Timko's menu, showing good mixing of entrée prices.

easily readable. Plain Bodoni Roman type is one of the best. Type size for regular copy should be 10-point to 14-point, and type size for headings should be as much as 18-point (about ¼ inch high). Adequate spacing between lines should be maintained, since copy can be confusing if lines are too close together. Mixing type among regular, bold, script, and italics may be done to gain emphasis, but too much mixing causes confusion and clutters the menu. Wide margins should be allowed; altogether, they can account for nearly 50 percent of the entire page. In the space used for copy, from one-third to one-half of the area should be left blank. One of the most common faults in menu writing is to try to squeeze too much onto the page. Studies have shown that this defeats the purpose of the menu, which is to quickly convey a message that sells. Too much information on the page confuses patrons, who consequently are not drawn to the menu items the operation particularly wishes to sell.

Emphasis can be added by using borders and boxes. Prices should be clearly presented so that

customers know how much an item or a group of foods will cost.

The color of the menu paper and the color of print can also help to make things stand out. Dark print on light paper is the easiest to read and thus creates the least confusion. Light yellow or light green print on light paper is hard to read. The contrast between paper and ink must be strong to make reading easy and comprehension good. Cafeteria menus and others that are placed on the wall or in places where all customers can see them should be planned so that they quickly give the message the operation wants them to give.

Among the more common mistakes in menu planning are the following:

1. Descriptive copy is left out when it is needed.
2. The wrong emphasis is given. For instance, a cup of tea may receive as much attention as a prime rib entrée.
3. Emphasis is lost because print size and style are not used properly.

4. The menu lacks originality.
5. The menu is designed for the wrong market.
6. Much needed information (such as a listing of certain food or drink items) is omitted.
7. Pricing is not clear.
8. The menu is wrong for the operation.
9. Patrons do not see valuable copy because clip-ons or other added material covers up portions of the menu.

Cover

The cover of the menu should bear a symbol of the operation. A reproduction of a photograph, old print, woodcut, or coat-of-arms can be used for this purpose. This symbol is often called a *logo* and should represent a theme carried through in the decoration of the establishment.

The cover is often planned last because its size depends on the menu's size. Using one color of print on a white background or using two complementary colors is not expensive. Four-color photography produces all colors of the spectrum but is expensive. The cost of using color photography includes obtaining the right color picture to begin with. A professional photographer's fee can add significantly to the expense.

The paper (or *cover stock*) chosen should be heavy, durable, and grease-resistant. Paper that produces too much glare should be avoided, however, since copy is not easily read from it. The cover stock should be stiff enough to remain upright in the hand without bending. The paper used most often for this purpose is called heavy Cover, Bristol, or Tag stock and is at least 0.006 inch thick. Paper used inside the cover for additional copy can be lighter in weight; strong, heavy book paper is usually good enough.

Flexibility

The flexibility of the menu—its ability to withstand changes without having to be discarded—is important in inflationary times (when prices rise rapidly), as well as in an environment where the preferences of patrons change relatively rapidly.

Food fads rise and fall. If an operation tries to keep up fads for merchandising reasons, its menus can become obsolete quickly; and it is expensive to throw away menus.

Some operations resort to the *du jour* menu or even a wall board to obtain needed flexibility. This was a custom in the first restaurants in Paris. A neatly written board told patrons as they entered what was offered that day. Later, wooden boards were hung from the belts of waiters so that they could read to guests what was available at that meal. Printed menus did not come into being until much later.

Today, there is a return to the old plan, but for a different reason—to gain flexibility not only in items but in pricing. Some operations like to change parts of the menu daily or weekly, while leaving other parts the same. A change can be effected by adding a paper insert or attachment to the firmer, harder, printed menu. Appetizers, side dishes, desserts, and beverages do not change frequently, so these can be in print on the harder material; meanwhile, entrées and other offerings that may change more frequently are typed or printed on light paper and can be changed each day. Clip-ons or tip-ins may be used if they are styled to match the menu. Inexpensive inserts can also be used. In many fine dining establishments, it has become customary for waiters to repeat the list of the daily specials to the customer from memory, providing the least costly way of making daily changes.

Presentations other than the traditional printed menu are also becoming more and more prevalent. Alternative approaches include listing menu items on pieces of wood, meat cleavers, or wine bottles. The table tent has been a popular device for merchandising alcoholic beverages and is now being used to promote desserts and other foods. In some establishments that feature buffet menus or salad bars, the operator allows the food to do the selling. Attractive displays and presentations can be a very convincing promotional tool.

Nothing becomes staler faster to the frequent customer than the same menu. Normally menus should be planned to last three months, since after that point customers tire of them. The design should be flexible if new menus are to be created this often.

MAKING A PROFIT

A properly designed and planned menu can increase profits by increasing the size of the average check, minimizing waste, speeding service (to increase dining room turnover), and improving overall operating efficiency. Understanding these factors and their relationship to the menu will help a manager improve the operation's performance and increase profits. In a nonprofit operation, benefits can be measured in terms of reduced costs.

A menu must emphasize popular foods to achieve a high volume of sales. It must also feature high-profit items. The popularity and profitability of each item put on the menu needs to be examined and the item's contribution to total sales must be weighed. Average costs in 1985 in the foodservice industry were approximately 40 percent of gross receipts for food, 28 percent for labor, and 27 percent for other costs. Net profit was 5 percent of gross receipts. Controlling food and labor costs is especially important, since together these consume roughly two-thirds of the operation's income. With the escalation of energy and other costs, however, the need to look at all costs becomes imperative.

The basic cost of food, adjusted to take into account preparation and cooking losses, yields the actual cost of the food. Arriving at a low food cost is not always desirable, since an inexpensive product may require so much additional preparation labor that the final menu item has a higher overall cost and a lower profit. For example, the cabbage used in cole slaw may be cheap, but once the costs of cleaning, shredding, and making the salad are added in, cole slaw may cost more than a salad made from hearts of lettuce, which have a higher food cost but can be prepared more quickly. The selling price of a food is often established on the basis of the food cost. If menu items carry too high a food cost, the result may be a selling price that customers are unwilling to pay. There are many factors to consider in arriving at food costs. Con-

tinued careful analysis must be practiced in selecting items that meet both the foodservice's cost constraints and the price range the customer is willing to pay.

Many operators are turning to convenience foods in an effort to control labor costs. Historically, a change from fresh food to processed (canned, dried, or frozen) food occurred because of the need to improve profits; such a change was not always accompanied by improved or even steadily maintained quality standards. Often, difficult decisions must be made by management when profit margins become too narrow. On the other hand, many of the new convenience foods are of excellent quality.

Since a convenience food incorporates labor, its base price is higher than that of the regular food item the foodservice would use to make it. Consequently, basing the selling price on the cost of the convenience item might make the selling price too high. (If the cost of an item is $1.00 as a raw item but $1.50 as a convenience item, fixing the selling price at 35 percent of food cost would make the same item sell for about $3.00 in the first case and for about $4.50 in the second.) Therefore, some adjustment in setting the selling price must occur when one of these new kinds of foods is used.

Planning for profit requires that a menu be designed to achieve a proper mix of high- and low-profit items. Highly popular, low-profit items on a menu can outperform other items and reduce the operation's profitability. Even though such a popular item may be desirable on the menu, it must be positioned so as not to bury or overwhelm the other offerings. One alternative is to raise the price of the popular item.

PLANNING THE MENU

A menu cannot be planned solely to satisfy front-of-the-house interests. It must also satisfy the needs of the heart-of-the-house. Instead of being concerned with attracting customers, heart-of-the-house considerations are directed toward producing the product and toward accommodating constraints imposed by limits on food availability, equipment, personnel, and cost. Heart-of-the-house activities revolve around purchasing, storing, preparing, holding, and serving food. These constraints and processes must be considered in planning a menu.

Preparation and Service Personnel

The responsibility for planning the menu belongs to management, but the views of other personnel should be sought before final decisions are made. A menu can be set up roughly and then given to the chef or head cook for review and suggestions. Others in the preparation team may also be consulted. An item may not be feasible because of a lack of equipment or because of some other factor that management may not know about. For instance, to make good, hard-crusted bread, there must be steam in the bake oven. Without knowing this (and without having the proper type of oven), management might put this bread on the menu, expecting the bakers to produce it. In this case, the bakers can help by pointing out the hidden factor.

The practicability of producing some item may be open to question for other reasons as well. Sometimes an item cannot be produced properly under the stress of heavy orders during peak periods. The chef or head cook will know this and should advise against its inclusion. Making menu planning a team effort also allows people outside management to feel responsible for the menu and may therefore increase its chances of performing well.

Besides the skill and ability of employees, the efficient distribution of tasks must be considered. A menu can easily overload one employee or one division of the cooking or preparation area, while leaving another section with little or no work to do. The workloads, as dictated by the menu, must be balanced. Employees who are overworked or required to exert a lot of effort to accomplish a particular task tend to do poor work, and the quality of the menu items involved suffers as a result. Management should anticipate changing some production demands seasonally or even by day of the week. Warm weather increases demand for such items as cold plates and complete salad dishes. On a Satur-

day night, the grill may be overwhelmed with fry orders. Shaping the menu to assist in spreading out the work can do much to win the confidence and respect of workers and so to improve work performance and product quality.

Raw Materials

Various food components and raw materials can require different preparation and cooking times. Such variations in time can be critical in deciding whether an item can or cannot be placed on the menu. Customers may not be willing to wait the length of time required for production, or the preparation time may interfere with the production of other items in the kitchen. Quality and cost must also be considered. At certain times of the year, foods are out of season. Although customers may find it pleasing to see them on the menu, either the cost or the quality may make including them impractical.

A menu should present a variety of choices for its customers. People may come to a restaurant for its beef, but if one person in the dining party only eats seafood, the menu should be able to accommodate that person. In establishing a varied menu, availability of the product must be considered. Management must ask, if I cannot get this product, is there a suitable substitute? For instance, a restaurant may offer a halibut mousse with shrimp newburg sauce that is prepared using fresh halibut. If the fresh product were unavailable, a high-quality frozen product could be substituted without a detectable difference in flavor. It should be noted, however, that if the restaurant's menu states that the operation uses fresh halibut, *only* fresh halibut can be used. Truth in menus has become a topic of discussion and legislation in the last few years, as a result of controversy over misleading menu descriptions used by some restaurateurs. If a menu states that a product is fresh, it cannot have been frozen; if an item is described as sautéed in butter, it cannot be sautéed in margarine; if sour cream is specified, an imitation cannot be used. The planner of the menu must have a good knowledge of food products and preparation and must make use of a wide repertoire of dishes to satisfy customer needs and at the same time satisfy the heart of the house.

The form, shape, color, temperature, texture, and overall presentation of a particular dish must be considered when deciding whether to include it in a menu. A dish should be judged both on its own and in relation to other menu offerings. The components that make up a dish should exhibit variety in size, shape, form, and texture, uniting in a harmonious display. Forms and shapes should be definite and varied. An overabundance of cubed items or items cut into hard angles should be avoided. The food on a plate should not be uniformly flat and low; combining various heights produces a more pleasing effect. Proper use of colors can add tremendously to plate appeal. Light-colored items presented together can look bland, but when mixed with brightly colored, complementary vegetables or fruits, they help create an exciting and appetizing display. Contrasts of temperature can bring variety to a dish and enhance flavor as well (hot soups and cold salads, for example). Textures are also significant. A meal consisting of soft foods offers no contrast of textures and, consequently, is unappealing. A meal of soft meat loaf, mashed potatoes, and boiled carrots, for example, does not hold much textural appeal. But replacing the carrots with a crisp salad quickly achieves a nice mix. Adding diced celery to tuna fish salad is another example of mixing textures to enhance interest. Ultimately, all of these elements combine to create a single, overall impression. Judicious use of garnishes can enliven a dull-looking menu item and bring it to life, adding texture, flavor, and color (see table 4-3 and figure 4-4).

Table 4-3. Garnishes and Their Yields

Item	Portion	Yield
Apples, sliced	2 thin wedges	12 wedges per 113-size apple
Apples, ring	1 ring	5 rings per 113-size apple
Apricots	½ or 1 fruit	20 halves or 40 wedges per lb
Avocado	1 slice	30 slices per avocado, 24 per crate size
Banana, split, 1-inch slice	1 or 3 round slices	12 bananas or 2½ c slices per lb AP; 1 banana (3 to lb AP) yields 30 1-inch slices, split
Blackberries	3 berries	1 qt yields 100 berries
Blueberries	3 to 5	1 qt (1½ lb) 360 to 800 berries
Cantaloupe	3 balls or small wedges	30 balls or 45 wedges per 45-size fruit per crate
Capers	1 t	10 to 15 capers per t
Cheese, shredded, moist	1 T (½ oz)	32 portions per lb
Cheese, shredded, dry	1 T (¼ oz)	64 portions per lb
Cheese, cream	2 T (1 oz)	for stuffing celery, 16 portions per lb
Cheese, cottage	1 No. 20 scoop (1½ oz)	10½ scoops per lb
Cherries, maraschino	½ or 1	640 per gal
Cherries, sweet, fresh	1 fruit	40 per lb
Chocolate tidbits	1 T	40 portions per lb
Coconut, long shred	1 T rounded	1 lb equals 6½ c or 60 portions
Currants	3 fruits	1 lb equals 150 currants
Dates	1 fruit	60 dates per lb
Decorettes	1 t	160 portions per lb
Endive, curly	1 leaf	45 per head
Figs	1 fruit	48 per box, 6 lb
Grapes	3 fruits	50 medium-size grapes per lb

Table 4-3. *(cont.)*

Item	Portion	Yield
Grapefruit	1 to 2 sections	12 sections per grapefruit
Kumquats	1 fruit	1 lb equals 24 kumquats
Lemons, wedge	⅙ to ⅛ fruit	1 doz lemons yields 144 rind twists
Limes, wedge	¼ to ⅙ fruit	1 doz limes yields 62 twists or rind
Mint	2 to 3 leaves	300 leaves per bunch
Mushrooms, cap	1 cap	15 to 20 caps per lb AP
Nuts, chopped	1 T	1 lb chopped is 4 c
Nuts, salted for tea	1 T	1 lb nuts is about 4 c; use 3 lb for 100 people
Walnuts, whole	½ nut	8 oz equals 2 c or about 150 halves
Oranges, sections	3	8 to 9 sections per 82-size orange; 1 doz orange rinds yields 164 rind twists
Olives, green	1 or 2 fruits	1 qt (1¼ lb) equals 100 extra-large olives
Olives, stuffed, sliced	1 or 2 fruits	1 medium-size olive yields 6 slices
Olives, ripe	1 or 2 fruits	1 qt small size yields 120 olives
Parsley, curly	1 sprig	80 sprigs per bunch
Peach	1 wedge	8 wedges per medium peach
Pear	1 wedge or slice	12 wedges per 5-oz pear
Pepper, ring	1 ring	10 rings per medium-size pepper
Pickles, sweet, medium (3 in.)*	½ pickle	24 pickles per qt
Pineapple	1 wedge or 2 to 3 diced pieces	60 wedges or 150 diced pieces per 18-size pineapple
Plums, Santa Rosa	1 medium	70 per till (5 × 5 size)
Pomegranate	5 seeds	25 garnishes per pomegranate
Potato chips or shoestring potatoes	¾ oz	1 c; 8 ounces is about 2½ qt
Prunes, dried	1 fruit	30 to 40 per lb AP
Radishes	1 or 2	15 to 20 per bunch; 1 bunch 10 oz; 1½ c topped and tailed equals 8 oz or about 25 radishes
Raspberries	5 berries	1 qt yields 300 berries
Rhubarb	1 or 2 curls	1 lb yields 100 curls
Sardines	1 3 in. long	1 lb yields 48 sardines
Strawberries	1 berry	1 qt yields 60 medium-size berries
Tangerines	3 to 4 sections	10 sections per tangerine
Tomatoes	1 wedge	8 wedges per medium tomato
Watercress	1 sprig	30 sprigs per bunch

* Pickles sized per gallon are frequently used: gherkins, 200; pickle rings or slices, 400; small sweets (3 in.), 80 to 100; large dills (4½ in.), 25.

The flavor of the food item and the resulting blend of flavors in the dish as a whole must be given high priority. An excess of strong flavors will clash and leave an equally strong (and unfavorable) impression. By the same token, a group of bland flavors may not create any impression at all. A combination of complementary flavors—strong and bland—however, can result in a high-quality product. The flavor of roast beef is complemented by a good sharp horseradish sauce. A fruit salad can be improved with the addition of a slightly sweet honey French dressing. A tart, flavorful fruit blend containing strawberries or cherries combines beautifully with cheesecake. Creating interesting flavor

Figure 4-4. Simple garnishes have transformed this open-faced sandwich into an elegant meal.

combinations is part of good menu planning. Many young American chefs are gaining recognition with imaginative new combinations and presentations, resulting in distinctive and outstanding menus.

The key to good menu planning is knowing how to plan a sequence of flavors from the beginning to the end of a meal. Acidic or spicy foods can help whet the taste buds at the start of a meal. A flavorful consommé or bouillon can do the same. Meat flavors stimulate the taste buds in the mouth and start the flow of gastric juices in the stomach, which helps to spur the appetite. Alcohol can also accomplish this, but it destroys the sense of taste, especially if consumed to excess. Sweet or bland foods often are served at the end of the meal to close off the appetite and give a feeling of satisfaction.

Many foods need special flavor combinations. Roast pork is served with applesauce because the tart, sweet sauce helps mask the oiliness of the pork. Cranberries help to modify the sulfury flavor of turkey. Mint sauce masks the pungent flavor of lamb and mutton.

The seasonality of foods needs to be considered in menu planning. Modern methods have gone a long way in extending seasons and in shipping foods from other growing areas during times when they are not available from local supplies. But much variability remains in the market offerings, and some foods are not on the market—either at all or in sufficient supply—at certain times of the year. If foods are purchased out of season, they will cost considerably more and often their quality will be inferior to what it is when the item is at the peak of its season. Many seasonality charts are available that show when foods are apt to be scarce. Seasonality even extends to fish, meat, and poultry. Market reports can also advise menu planners on foods that will be in good supply and foods that will not be. The USDA maintains a market report system that can advise buyers.

Featuring foods when they are in season can do much to brighten up a menu. Thus, a broiled grapefruit in January or February (when this fruit is at its peak) can be a taste treat as well as an unusual dish. A dessert of fresh strawberries with sour cream and light brown sugar in May or June is apt to win customer approval and requires little preparatory labor. Certain fish come onto the market at special times and should be featured during these periods. Eggs are highest in quality and lowest in price in the spring and early summer. A warm-weather omelet festival offering a wide choice of different kinds of omelets can lend a lot of interest to a menu. Promoting certain kinds of foods when people are thinking about them is both smart menu planning and smart merchandising. Pumpkin pie around Halloween takes on a special meaning. A peach shortcake in August with an appropriate descriptive line—"Georgia peaches are here again; try our famous Georgia Gold Shortcake made with mellow, rich, sliced Georgia peaches and our own delicate sponge cake, topped with whipped cream"—may encourage a dessert sale that otherwise would not be made.

As was discussed in chapter 2, nutritional balance is another increasingly important consideration in menu planning. Not only can a menu win friends by offering nutritionally balanced combinations (and even some special diets), it can also draw the attention of customers to principles of good nutrition and thus contribute to increased knowledge on their part.

Facilities and Equipment

A facility should be planned and equipment selected after the menu is written; the menu should not be planned after the facility has been built and the equipment is already in place. If the menu is allowed to determine the design of the production facility and the equipment requirements, lower operating costs and a better product will result. Many foodservices have more space and equipment than they need. As much as 35 percent of some operations' equipment is unnecessary, and many operations allocate space for activities that never take place. Operation and capital costs are far less when a facility is built to meet special menu needs. If proper analysis of the menu occurs, a foodservice in an elementary school may eliminate a broiler and a deep fryer from its plans, since they will rarely be used in producing meals for the children. Some hospital kitchens in Texas were planned with only steamers, steam-jacketed kettles, mixers, ovens, sinks, and tables, since these were the only pieces of equipment needed. A dishwasher was used in the dishroom. Productivity of meals ran well over twenty meals per labor hour, in contrast to the average productivity of four meals per labor hour in many hospitals.

Achieving a proper production flow is necessary if efficient production of food is to occur. Menu items can be selected to ensure a workload that is evenly distributed among different work stations and results in an orderly and timely flow of production. Materials should flow smoothly from storage to preparation and from preparation to service. A well-organized flow between processes will minimize the number of steps that must be walked between work areas. The hazards of poor sanitation may be increased when workflow is poorly organized. A poorly planned menu can result in crowded work stations and a backlog of work. Efficiency is lost; and once this happens, sanitation is usually the first thing overlooked. A broiled steak, for example, is a very perishable item, and it must be moved from the broiler to the consumer as quickly as possible. If the flow of work is so disorganized that the time lag between broiler and service is excessive, the item should not be on the menu. Attempting to send cooked steaks up to a twenty-fifth-floor dining room from a basement kitchen creates an impossible situation—and yet it

is done. Needless to say, customers are rarely happy with the results.

Directing Food Selections

The menu planner can do much to influence customers to select certain foods. Often this can be done by emphasizing the food. Descriptions can help gain attention, as can placing items in boxed areas or giving them special spacing. The items that appear first and last in a group list are the ones most often seen, while those in the center are the ones most often missed. An operation that does not wish to sell steaks, but feels compelled to have a steak listed on the menu, can bury it at the center of the list of entrée items, while placing the higher-gross-profit items at the beginning or end of the column. Special headings or bold type can make something stand out, and clip-ons or tip-ins also have built-in prominence.

Menus should be planned so that foods are balanced between lower-cost and higher-cost items. It is often wise to invite guests to help themselves to liberal portions of salad materials at a salad bar. This helps the "big eater" to fill up, after which a normal or even slightly smaller portion of the more expensive items will suffice to complete the meal later. Serving a good, substantial soup or salad before a meal can accomplish the same result. In planning a buffet, the lower-cost foods should come first, so customers fill their plates with them and have less room for the more expensive ones (such as roast beef) at the end of the buffet.

Lower costs can be realized if sufficient volume is built around items. The cost of materials and labor can be lowered, since it costs just about as much to cook 20 gallons of a product as to cook 40 gallons. Similarly, mixing 30 portions in a mixer takes almost the same amount of energy and time as mixing 300 portions. By planning a menu with these costs in mind and putting items on it that can develop sufficient volume, operational costs can be lowered. Sometimes menu prices may have to be manipulated to achieve better volume. That is, it may be better to sell 500 hamburgers with a gross profit of 12¢ each (giving a $60 margin) than to sell 300 hamburgers with a gross profit of 16¢ each (giving a $48 margin). Management needs good cost information to make informed judgments in these areas. Precosting methods are discussed in detail in chapter 17.

COMPUTERS AND PRODUCING A MENU

Computers can assist the menu planner by maintaining various files on possible menu items and by offering advanced help in all stages of publishing a menu. Files can be created listing menu items, their composition, and any special considerations relating to a specific item. A cross-referenced database can list hundreds or thousands of potential menu items, and the planner has immediate access to this information through a computer terminal. Seasonality of various ingredients can be noted, as well as previous problems encountered in producing an item.

Operations stressing personalized service sometimes maintain files on their customers. Survey responses, birthdays and anniversaries, and names of family members can be kept on file. The survey results can be used to determine shifting preferences, which may lead to menu changes. Customers can be mailed birthday and anniversary greetings, possibly resulting in a return visit to the foodservice for the impending celebration. Greeting the customer and family by name can give the customer a feeling of being appreciated, leading to long-term patronage.

The other front-of-the-house area in which computers are having a major impact is in the publishing of menus. Traditionally, a menu is planned, designed, turned over to a publisher, and finally received for use. This process can take anywhere from several weeks to several months. With the introduction of sophisticated word processing and publishing computer packages, laser printers, and low-priced copiers, however, this process can be completed in a day. As a result, the menu can be changed on a daily basis (or as often as desired), while maintaining high quality in the presentation of the menu.

SUMMARY

The menu is central to the entire foodservice operation. It is the starting point in the planning process and establishes a direction for further planning. The front of the house is designed to meet the needs and wishes of the customer, and the menu must reflect this intention. At the same time, heart-of-the-house needs must also be considered and balanced with those of the front of the house. The goal of a menu is to attract customers. To achieve this, a menu should be designed to appeal to a target market whose demographic characteristics must be identified and whose needs must be determined. This is the first step in the menu planning process, and a good market assessment can contribute a great deal to ultimate success.

The next step in the process is to decide which type of menu to use. A number of different approaches have been used in the past. An à la carte menu prices each food separately. A table d'hôte menu sells foods grouped together for a set price; the group sold as a unit may or may not constitute a complete meal. The *du jour* menu covers only one day's offerings; the next day, a different set of menu items is offered. The limited menu offers between six and twelve entrée or main dinner items, which reduces planning, production, and service problems and strengthens oversight control. Cyclical menus provide daily changes in meals offered over a set period, after which the menu is repeated; the repetition simplifies planning and improves production performance.

Front-of-the-house needs must be addressed in designing the menu. First, the sequence in which menu items are listed on the menu should follow the progression in which foods are presented during a meal. Positioning and location are important in directing patrons' attention to specific items that the operation is most eager to sell. Second, the copy of the menu is important because it can improve communication between patrons and the salespeople as well as enhancing sales. The kind and size of type, its spacing and layout, and other typographic factors can do much to improve menus and help patrons. The cover should be practical and cleanable, and should bear the logo of the operation; it should be completed last, to ensure its compatibility with the menu as planned. Finally, a flexible menu will enable the operator to adjust to changes in customer preferences and eating habits.

Heart-of-the-house considerations involve the purchasing, storage, and preparation of food, as well as the service to the customer. These factors must be considered in the menu planning process.

Making a profit in a profit-oriented operation (or not exceeding budgeted allowances in a nonprofit one) is a primary consideration. Each entrée's popularity must be analyzed against its profitability. The costs of using convenience foods—as opposed to foods requiring full preparation—must be considered.

Planning a menu with due consideration for the needs of the heart of the house requires that a number of factors be taken into account. First, preparation and service personnel should assist in the planning of the menu to ensure that items to be prepared are within the competence of the staff and are not inconsistent with the workload desired. Time factors must also be considered. Issues of high cost, unavailability, or fluctuating supply of raw materials may force menu planners to offer a different set of selections. Facilities and equipment must be rationally related to the number of patrons to be served, the type of service, the availability of equipment, the balancing of menu production requirements and equipment capabilities, and many other factors.

Management must strongly consider the popularity of menu items in deciding which ones to include. Costs can fluctuate with the volume of business and with the volume of materials, machines, and labor used in a foodservice. Management can control these costs by placing specific items on the menu or by keeping them off. The influence of management on profitability by selecting items according to popularity and cost can thus be substantial.

Such factors as reducing waste, increasing productivity, and using food efficiently should be weighed in planning the menu. Standardized recipes that give a known quantity of food of a known quality can be used to maintain standards and control production. Using such recipes also gives an operation greater flexibility. Yield and quantity tests help define the yield that can be expected from quantities purchased and thereby contribute significantly to the process of identifying food costs with precision. Quality of items can also be checked to see if the standards set by the operation are met.

Computers are becoming a useful tool for the menu planner. Information about the type and range of menu item choices can be kept on file. Market information can easily be stored and retrieved, allowing the operation to track customer preferences and to address customers on a personal level. Computers give planners more flexibility, since planning and publishing can be completed in a single day, on the premises—and a new menu can be in the customers' hands that night.

CHAPTER REVIEW QUESTIONS

1. Jennie Hendricks, assistant to the regional manager of OFU Restaurant Group, has just been assigned a project by her boss, Nola Redding. Nola has not been entirely happy with the process by which unit managers have been designing menus for their operations. Some menus have worked better than others, and some operations seem to make the transition to new menus much more easily than others. Nola feels that certain guidelines should be followed in designing a menu, and she is not sure that all of the unit managers are following them. Consequently, she has given Jennie the job of establishing guidelines for designing menus.

   Jennie began work on this project by first analyzing the types of restaurants that the company operates. The OFU Restaurant Group operates a number of different types of properties in different locales, ranging from family-style restaurants located in suburban shopping centers to fine dining establishments in the heart of a city's financial district. Each operation is very different from the next. Taking this into account, Jennie has decided that the guidelines must be very general, so as to be applicable to a wide range of situations. She sees this project developing into a manual that will outline the steps a manager should follow and will identify key points to take into consideration. This is the first project that Jennie has been assigned since she joined the company (after graduating from a restaurant management program) and she hopes to make a strong positive impression on her new boss. Nola has told Jennie that she expects a two-page report on her desk in the next 72 hours detailing the goals, objectives, and major points to be addressed by the finished manual. If you were in Jennie's position, what would be in that report?

2. What are the important questions to answer when doing a feasibility study? Design a questionnaire that could be used by management in determining who its customers are. Assume that the operation is on the main street of a shopping district, and that management will use this questionnaire to request information from patrons finishing their meals.

3. Compare the characteristics of the five menu types listed in this chapter. Give advantages and disadvantages of each. Identify the kind of foodservice in which each would be found. Try to find examples of each type and show them to the class.

4. Analyze the design of a menu by critiquing it with reference to the factors for menu construction: sequence, copy, cover, and flexibility. Is this menu a more effective sales tool because these factors are present or is it lacking because of failures to use them properly? What common menu mistakes does it have? How could its design be improved?

5. Investigate the use of convenience foods as opposed to the use of foods requiring full preparation to see whether the costs and the quality of both are equal. List some of the more popular convenience foods and explain how they can contribute to making a profit in an operation.

6. Discuss planning the menu in light of how it may contribute to making a profit in a specific type of foodservice. Be sure to include such factors as preparation and service personnel, raw materials, and facilities and equipment.

VOCABULARY

Market
Logo
Cycle
Semi-à la carte
Entrée
Copy
Image
Sequence
Heart of the house
Convenience foods
Seasonality

Feasibility study
A la carte
Du jour
Limited menu
Target market
Food cost
Table d'hôte
Front of the house
Selling price
Complementary flavors

ANNOTATED REFERENCES

Eckstein, E. F. 1983. *Menu Planning.* Westport, Conn.: AVI Publishing. (Provides further information on menu planning, use of the computer, and eating habits of American subcultures.)

Kotschevar, L. H. 1986. *Management by Menu,* 2d ed. Chicago: National Institute for the Foodservice Industry. (Covers all details of menu planning and management's job in producing a menu.)

Powers, T. F., and Powers, J. M. 1984. *Foodservice Operations: Planning and Control,* pp. 14-37. New York: John Wiley & Sons. (Good discussion of the various elements involved in menu planning.)

Spears, M. C., and Vaden, A. G. 1985. *Foodservice Organizations: A Managerial and Systems Approach,* pp. 88-119. New York: John Wiley & Sons. (Excellent overview of the major factors involved in planning a menu.)

Restaurant Business, Inc. 1971. *Menu Planning and Food Merchandising.* New York: ITT Educational Services. (Further information on menu planning techniques, as well as on producing and designing menus.)

Visick, H., and Van Kleek, P. 1974. *Menu Planning: A Blueprint for Better Profits.* New York: McGraw-Hill. (Excellent coverage of producing a menu, including many illustrations and examples.)

CHAPTER 5

Foodservice Equipment

OUTLINE

Equipment requirements depend on the basic menu. The menu planner studies recipes and notes the equipment needed to produce the basic menu. Any specialized needs are noted at this point as well, and the equipment involved is added to the list of essential pieces. If a menu item is to be prepared from raw ingredients, equipment needs will differ from those for the same menu item when purchased fully prepared and ready for reheating. Most kitchens contain a variety of different types of equipment aimed at meeting the needs of a specific menu. The needs of a fastfood operator with a standardized menu are quite limited in comparison to the needs of an institutional foodservice whose menu changes daily (see fig. 5-1). The production capacities of the equipment depend on the quantities of food prepared and the preparation times.

Equipment must be selected and arranged in a facility to produce maximum efficiency in the use of labor and high quality in the preparation of food. The ultimate objective is to establish a system that integrates equipment, people, and food to this end.

Operation II

Receiving	Food Cutter	Beverage Dispenser
Scale	Vegetable Slicer	Self-Leveling Dispenser
Storage Freezer	Dicer	Microwave Oven
Storage	Vertical Cutter/Mixer	(Slicer)
Refrigerator-med/low temperature	Slicer	
Refrigerator-Thawing	**Vegetable Cooking**	**Warewashing**
Bake Shop	Low Pressure Steamer	Dishmachine
Refrigerator-Thawing	High Pressure Steam Cooker	Conveyor
Scale		Pulper/Disposer
Convection Oven	Steam-Jacketed Kettle	Booster
Steam Kettle	Oven	(Blower-Dryer)
Hood	Hood	(Condenser)
Mixer/Vertical Cutter/Mixer	(Range)	**Pot Washing**
Meat Preparation	**Salad Preparation**	Pot & Pan Washing Machine
(Meat & Food Chopper)	Pulper/Disposer	Pulper/Disposer
Meat & Fry Cooking	Food Cutter, Vertical Cutter/Mixer	**Sanitation & Waste Removal**
Scale	Mixer	Can Washer/Crusher
Mixer	Vegetable Slicer	Bottle Crusher
Steam Kettle	Dicer	Steam Cleaning Equipment
Braising Pan or Kettle	**Salad Plating**	Pulper/Disposer
Oven	Refrigerator	(Compactor)
Range	**Holding**	**New Equipment**
Griddle	Refrigerator	Microwave Oven
Grill	Roll Warmer	Refrigerator-Thawing
Broiler/Char Broiler	Infra-Red Lamp	Refrigerator-Fast Chilling
Fryer/Pressure Fryer	(Food Warmer)	( ) Optional Equipment
Hood	(Bain Marie)	
Microwave Oven	Serving	
Quartz Oven	Steamtable	
Infra-Red Oven	Sandwich Station	
Vegetable Preparation	Salad Station	
Pulper/Disposer	Dessert Station	
	Coffee Urn	
	Ice Machine	

Operation I

Receiving	Oven	Bain Marie
Scale	Range	Refrigerator
Storage	Griddle	Roll Warmer
Refrigerator-med/low temperature	Grill	Infra-Red Lamp
	Broiler/Char Broiler	**Serving**
Refrigerator-Thawing	Fryer/Pressure Fryer	Steamtable
Bake Shop	Hood	Sandwich Counter
Scale	**Vegetable Preparation**	Slicer
Mixer, Vertical Cutter/Mixer	Peeler	Salad Station
	Pulper/Disposer	Dessert Station
Divider & Rounder	Vertical Cutter/Mixer	Coffee Urn
Dough Roller	Food Cutter	Ice Machine
Proofer	Vegetable Slicer	Beverage Dispenser
Retarder	Dicer	Self-Leveling Dispenser
Doughnut Machine & Fryer	Slicer	**Warewashing**
	Vegetable Cooking	Dishmachine
Oven	Low Pressure Steamer	Conveyor
Steam Kettle	High Pressure Steam Cooker	Pulper/Disposer
Hood		Booster
Refrigerator-Med/Low Temperature	Steam-Jacketed Kettle	Burnisher
	Oven	(Blower-Dryer)
Blast Freezer	Range	(Condenser)
Meat Preparation	Hood	**Pot Washing**
Scale	**Salad Preparation**	Pot Washing Machine
Meat Saw	Food Cutter, Vertical Cutter/Mixer	Pulper/Disposer
Chopper		**Sanitation & Waste Removal**
Grinder	Pulper/Disposer	Can Washer/Crusher
Tenderizer	Mixer	Bottle Crusher
Patty Machine	Dicer	Steam Cleaning Equipment
Slicer	Vegetable Slicer	Pulper/Disposer
Meat & Fry Cooking	**Salad Plating**	Incinerator
Scale	Refrigerator	(Baler)
Mixer	Holding	(Compactor)
Steam Kettle	Food Warmer	( ) Optional Equipment
Braising Pan or Kettle		

Operation III

Receiving	Hood	**Ware & Pot Washing**
Scale	(Slicer)	Conveyor
Storage	**Salad Plating**	Pulper/Disposer
Refrigerator-med/low temperature	Refrigerator	Dishwashing Machine
	Holding	(Blower-Dryer)
Refrigerator-Thawing	Refrigerator	(Condenser)
Fry Cooking	(Food Warmer)	**Sanitation & Waste Removal**
Fryer/Pressure Fryer	(Bain Marie)	Bottle Crusher
Griddle	(Roll Warmer)	Steam Cleaning Equipment
Braising Pan or Kettle	**Serving**	Compactor
Broiler/Char Broiler	Steamtable	Pulper/Disposer
Hood	Sandwich Station	(Can Washer/Crusher)
Heating/Cooking	Salad Station	(Baler)
Convection Oven	Dessert Station	**New Equipment**
Steam Kettle	Coffee Urn	Microwave Oven
High Pressure Steam Cooker	Ice Machine	Refrigerator-Thawing
	Beverage Dispenser	( ) Optional Equipment
Low Pressure Steamer	Microwave Oven	
Microwave Oven	Self-Leveling Dispenser	
Quartz Oven	(Slicer)	
Infra-Red Oven		

Figure 5-1. Recommended necessary equipment for three operations: Operation I, conventional food preparation; Operation II, modified convenience; Operation III, convenience.

Table 5-1. The Systems Approach: Subsystems and Space Allocations under Different Menu Patterns

Subsystem		Conventional		Modified Convenience		Convenience	
Receiving		120 sq. ft	3.00%	120 sq. ft	3.00%	120 sq. ft	3.00%
Storage		1120 sq. ft	28.00%	900 sq. ft	22.50%	700 sq. ft	17.50%
Preparation		1100 sq. ft	27.50%	450 sq. ft	11.25%	300 sq. ft	7.50%
Cooking		470 sq. ft	11.75%	300 sq. ft	7.50%	250 sq. ft	6.25%
Serving		800 sq. ft	20.00%	800 sq. ft	20.00%	800 sq. ft	20.00%
Clean-up		390 sq. ft	9.75%	350 sq. ft	8.75%	350 sq. ft	8.75%
	Subtotal	4000 sq. ft	100.00%	2920 sq. ft	73.00%	2520 sq. ft	63.00%
	Unused Space	—	—	1080 sq. ft	27.00%	1480 sq. ft	37.00%
	(Variable Total)	4000 sq. ft	100.00%	4000 sq. ft	100.00%	4000 sq. ft	100.00%
	Fixed Space*	2000 sq. ft		2000 sq. ft		2000 sq. ft	
	Total	6000 sq. ft		6000 sq. ft		6000 sq. ft	

*Fixed space is required for constant needs and does not vary in any operation. Janitorial storage areas, employee toilets, restrooms, lounge area, and so on would be found in this space.

Every facility exists as a complete system composed of a number of subsystems. Each subsystem uses different equipment, but all equipment in each subsystem must be coordinated with that in the other subsystems if the total system is to work smoothly and give the desired results. A well-planned unit with properly selected equipment functions smoothly; if one subsystem gets out of order or the wrong equipment is put in it, the system as a whole functions badly.

A typical foodservice has six subsystems, each with its own space requirement and each equipped for specific functions: receiving, storage, preparation, cooking, serving, and cleanup (see table 5-1). The equipment required by each can be discussed individually.

RECEIVING EQUIPMENT

Before any food is received, it should be checked for quality, counted, and weighed (if specified in weight). It is then moved to storage or to the using area.

Scales

Scales must give accurate weights down to ounces or even fractions of ounces. A small scale may be used for the latter purpose, and a scale big enough to accommodate the heaviest items is used for pounds and ounces. Large receiving scales usually are able to weigh items in the range from 50 to 1,000 pounds, showing quarter pounds or even ounces. Many scales today also allow the invoice to be stamped showing the time and date of receipt along with the weight of the delivery. Factors to watch for in selecting a scale are durability, compactness, convenient design, accuracy, and a finish that promotes easy cleaning and safe use (see fig. 5-2).

Moving Equipment

Dollies, trucks, and other mobile equipment may be needed to move purchases from the receiving dock to storage. The type to select depends on the kinds and amount of items to be moved. In large operations, an electric or gasoline-driven truck may

Figure 5-2. Receiving-area scales.

be used to move things; it may be equipped with an elevator to load or unload items from stacks. Pallet storage is popular in large operations. The shelving used for storage should be suited to the receiving equipment used.

Miscellaneous Receiving Equipment

Calculators, typewriters, desks, chairs, and file cabinets are also needed for some receiving subsystems. The specific items needed depend on the particular nature of each facility.

STORAGE AREAS

Adequate storage capacity—both dry and cold—is necessary to protect food, ensure proper sanitation, and maintain high food standards. The storage area provided should be designed to receive and hold the specific foods stored in it. Some foods are stored for longer periods of time than others. Fresh foods turn over faster than processed ones. Equipment used to move foods, shelving, and containers must be selected for the specific foods stored. Planning storage facilities prior to planning the menu usually leads to inadequate facilities.

Both dry and cold storage should be located near the receiving dock and the preparation and cooking subsystems. The flow of materials should resemble the pattern shown in figure 5-3.

Refrigeration and Low-temperature Equipment

Refrigeration and low-temperature equipment exist to minimize the deterioration of stored foods and to reduce the likelihood of contamination.

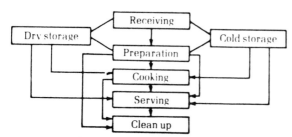

Figure 5-3. Flow chart of movement of materials from the receiving subsystem to the remaining subsystems of the foodservice operation.

This equipment keeps food cool or frozen to preserve flavor, color, texture, and nutritional elements. Chilled foods remain good much longer than foods held at room temperatures, and frozen foods keep much longer still. During the past several decades, foodservices have found it necessary to increase the amount of low-temperature storage provided and to reduce slightly the refrigerated areas. Refrigerators hold foods at temperatures of from about 34° to 40°F (1° to 5°C), whereas low-temperature units hold foods at temperatures of from about 10° to −10°F (−12° to −23°C). Units offering these temperatures come in a variety of types, including reach-in, roll-in, and walk-in models (see fig. 5-4).

Four factors should be considered in comparing different refrigerated storage units: the ability of the unit to hold the relative humidity at 85 percent (to keep foods from drying out); the ability of the unit to control air distribution so that an even temperature is maintained throughout the unit, regardless of loading pattern; precise temperature control within a range necessary to protect the food and hold its quality; and compliance with the design requirements of the National Sanitation Foundation (NSF), including lack of seams, easily cleaned surfaces, and removable parts in interiors to help in cleaning.

Specialized cold-storage equipment may be required, such as quick-chill refrigerators that rapidly reduce the temperature of cooked foods to a safe temperature for storage and blast freezers that freeze foods quickly at −30° to −40°F (−34° to

Figure 5-4. Cold-storage equipment: a roll-in unit.

−40°C). Controlled thawing units offer sanitary and convenient overnight thawing of bulk frozen foods. Many operations today use ice makers. The ice may be block, small or large cube, or crushed. The capacity of these specialized units must be matched to the production needs of the operation.

Shelving and Containers

Shelving and storage containers are important elements in a good storage system. Properly sized adjustable shelving can increase storage space, and easy shelf removal is of primary importance in facilitating good sanitation. Considerations to bear in mind when selecting shelving or mobile storage

a.   b.   c.

Figure 5-5. Food mixers: (a) counter model (5-qt capacity); (b) bench model (20-qt capacity); (c) floor model (140-qt capacity).

equipment (such as carts, dollies, and roll-in racks) include suitability to need, strength, sanitation, safety, size, number needed, and cost. These factors are also applicable to the selection of storage containers; shape and capacity are additional factors to consider in choosing containers.

PREPARATION EQUIPMENT

Tasks such as vegetable and fruit cleaning and cutting, salad preparation, and meat cutting or trimming can be performed speedily and efficiently when the right equipment is properly used in the preparation area. Since the extent to which preparation or fabrication of food takes place on the premises depends on the basic menu pattern, most operations using conventional foods allocate considerably more equipment and space to preparation than do those using convenience foods. If conventional foods are used, efficient and effective food preparation must be achieved through proper equipment selection, location, and use.

Scales

Scales may be a necessary part of the preparation subsystem. Weighing food as it is removed from raw storage (especially in ingredient rooms) is most important. Good accounting records cannot be maintained unless this is done. Portion scales, flat-counter dial scales, and even large scales onto which items are rolled may be used. Accuracy is an important factor in selection as well as ease of use and cleaning. Scales are also important in the cooking area for portioning and for ensuring that the proper amount of each ingredient is added to items being prepared.

Food Mixers

The upright food mixer is available in counter, bench, and floor models of different sizes and capacities (see fig. 5-5). Mixer sizes vary from 5 to 140 quarts. Mashed potatoes, doughs, cake batters, whipped cream, icings, meringues, mayonnaise, and other products are prepared in them. Various a.

b.

c.

d.

e.

Figure 5-6. Commonly used agitators: (a) wire whip; (b) dough arm; (c) pastry knife; (d) flat beater; (e) heavy-duty wire whip.

agitators and attachments are available to speed the preparation of virtually every food item placed in a mixer (see fig. 5-6). Horizontal mixers with interior rotating paddles are used for large-quantity production of such items as breads and cookies. Small units usually do not need them. Many mixers can handle various additional tasks, too. Attach-

ments can be added to perform slicing, grating, grinding, or sausage extrusion.

Food Cutters

One type of food cutter, known as the Buffalo Chopper, consists of a rotating bowl that moves

Figure 5-7. Food cutter.

Figure 5-8. Vertical cutter and mixer.

food into the path of a spinning blade (see fig. 5-7). As the food repeatedly passes through the blades, it is chopped into progressively smaller pieces. The longer the machine is allowed to run, the smaller the particles become. The Buffalo Chopper's basic use is for preparing salad materials, such as chopped onions and cabbage, cheese for toppings, and meat trimmings for croquettes. It is easy to clean and contains no cracks or crevices that could harbor bacteria. Attachments are available for cutting, slicing, grating, shredding, and similar operations.

Another cutter, called the Qualheim cutter, chops, dices, makes strips, and does other work that saves much preparation time. The unit should be used only when there is a large quantity of work to do, since cleanup and reassembly times may be quite lengthy.

The vertical cutter and mixer (known as the VCM) chops, cuts, mixes, blends, emulsifies, purées, and homogenizes foods in a matter of seconds. It works much as a home blender does; the chopping is performed by two knife blades that come up through the bottom of a deep bowl. A baffle extending from the bowl's lid is used for mixing and ensures that items are properly mixed and uniformly cut. The VCM prepares salads and cole slaws, emulsifies salad dressings, mixes batters and doughs, blends meats, chops cheese, and cuts bread crumbs. The operation may be completed in as short a time as it takes to switch the machine on and then off again immediately. It has few movable parts and is

easy to clean. The machine is easily and quickly cleaned by adding water and a cleaning solution to the bowl, flicking the switch on momentarily, draining the wash solution, and rinsing the equipment with a hose as needed. The VCM tilts to facilitate emptying of the bowl. It is available in various sizes. A 25-qt model is sufficient for preparing up to 500 portions, and the 40-qt model is appropriate for preparing more portions than that. Large commissaries use 60-, 80-, or 130-qt sizes (see fig. 5-8).

Similar to the VCM, but considerably smaller and more versatile, is the food processor. It consists of a bowl sitting on top of a small, powerful motor. The motor has the ability to drive any of a number of attachments at very high speed. With the blade attachment, objects can be puréed in a matter of seconds. Grating and slicing attachments are available as well. Batches to be processed can be as small as 1 cup and as large as 1 gallon. The food processor's small size makes it highly portable, and its ability to perform a variety of jobs has contributed to its popularity in many of today's operations.

Food Slicer

The slicer is basically a circular knife on which items such as cheese, boneless meats, luncheon meats, vegetables, and breads can be sliced. A uniform, clean, straight slice of almost any reasonably firm product is possible with this piece of equipment. The machine works on the principle of gravity: the item to be sliced glides back and forth on a carriage feeding into the knife. By adjusting the distance between the plate on which the product rests and the knife itself, the operator can adjust the thickness of the slice as desired. Slicers are available in different sizes, depending on the size of the knife blade. This machine should be obtained in the smallest size that can accommodate the largest item that must be sliced at the foodservice. Safety features should include guards around the blade and few removable parts, all of which can be disassembled easily for thorough cleaning (see fig. 5-9).

Careful prescheduling of the slicer can greatly reduce required cleanup time. For example, prescheduling the slicer would mean cutting such items as celery, cabbage, carrots, and onions first, then progressing to slicing fruits and juicy vegetables, then going on to cheeses and cold meats, and finishing by slicing hot meats and other cooked items. This sort of scheduling allows minimizing cleaning of the machine between each food group; more efficient use of the slicer results. If more than one individual or production area wishes to use the slicer, the machine should be located centrally or placed on a portable cart for easy relocation.

a.

b.

Figure 5-9. Food slicer: (a) in operation; (b) disassembled.

Figure 5-10. Vegetable peeler.

Vegetable Peeler

The vegetable peeler is used when a quantity of vegetables or other hard items must be peeled. Hard root vegetables such as turnips, carrots, and potatoes are rapidly peeled by an abrasive, lightweight disk that spins around, removing the skins. Water flowing into the chamber removes waste as it accumulates. Peelers can handle from 12 to 70 lb in a single batch. A 15-lb machine peels 15 lb of potatoes in 1 to 3 minutes (see fig. 5-10).

Meat-processing Equipment

Meat-processing equipment includes meat saws, choppers, grinders, cubers, and tenderizers (see fig. 5-11). For operations that purchase meats already prepared, such equipment is not required. But some

Figure 5-11. Meat-processing equipment: (a) meat saw; (b) mixer/grinder; (c) chopper; (d) tenderizer.

operations still cut meats from wholesale cuts or larger pieces of meat.

Miscellaneous Preparation Equipment

Other preparation equipment may be needed, as well—blenders, breading machines, can openers, coffee grinders, knife sharpeners, mobile carts, work tables (with locking casters, if mobile), and refrigeration equipment. A proper-size waste disposal or waste collection system must be provided to ensure adequate sanitation and safety.

COOKING EQUIPMENT

The cooking and baking subsystem is the focal point of the food production system. The receiving, storage, preparation, and cleanup subsystems must adequately support the cooking and baking subsystem; therefore, equipment selected for these support subsystems must be designed with the needs of the cooking and baking subsystem in mind.

Ovens

Ovens in foodservices may be as large as several hundred square feet and able to cook food for thousands of portions at one time, or they may be as small as 2 square feet and able to cook only a few portions at a time. There are five different types of ovens: conventional, mechanical, convection, microwave, and reconstituting.

Conventional Ovens

A typical conventional oven is heated by a lower heat source—and perhaps an overhead source as well—in an enclosed chamber. Transfer of heat occurs both by convection (of hot air moving in the chamber) and by conduction (when pans or other equipment in it come into contact with hot surfaces). Variations on the conventional oven include the peel oven (for baking extra-crusty breads), the draw-plate oven, and the deck oven (see fig. 5-12). The deck oven is the most common of these. It consists of a stack of ovens built in decks or tiers, one on top of another. Small ovens situated under range tops may be the only ones used in small operations.

Mechanical Ovens

The mechanical oven evolved from the conventional one. It has a mechanically moving interior that shifts the foods around to different parts of the oven (see fig. 5-13). One variety is the revolving tray or reel oven, which has trays that rotate in a circle around the oven interior. Another variety uses a moving or traveling tray, which passes through a long oven; different temperature ranges are possible within the long area traveled. The shelving on which foods are placed is power-driven and constantly moving. This arrangement offers several advantages: an even distribution of heat; lower costs (because of better heat distribution and more products baked per unit of heat used); and better baking results in terms of volume, color, and texture. Waiting time, temperature recovery time, and goods-shifting time are all said to be lower when these ovens are used—thus reducing costs. Many operations, however, do not have the volume to support these large ovens. The revolving-tray oven holds up to twelve standard-size pans ($18'' \times 26''$) and the traveling tray ovens hold twenty-four such pans or more.

Another type of mechanical oven is the conveyor oven. A moving belt or track carries an uncooked item through a tunnel containing heating elements, and the item emerges from the oven as a finished product. Food can pass through as many as three different temperature zones—for preheating, cooking, and finishing. This oven is geared toward the high-volume operation that has a high peak demand—as exists in many pizza operations.

Convection Ovens

Many conventional ovens have stagnant heat areas where heat does not move. If heat is moved around by forced convection, cooking is more rapid, less heat is needed, and more food can be put into the oven. The convection oven—a conventional oven in which the heat is moved by a fan—allows these results to be achieved. Because of the movement of heat, the convection oven bakes or roasts at 50 Fahrenheit degrees (10 Celsius degrees) lower, with a 25 to 30 percent reduction in cooking time. The amount of food that can be cooked per cubic foot of space is also increased.

Microwave Ovens

Microwaves are a form of electromagnetic energy intermediate in frequency and wave length between radio and infrared waves. When microwaves penetrate food, molecular activity or movement takes place within the food, creating friction that heats the food internally. Metallic materials reflect micro-

a.   b.   c.

d.   e.

Figure 5-12. Conventional ovens: (a) all-purpose oven; (b) reel oven; (c) draw-plate oven; (d) and (e) deck ovens.

Figure 5-13. Mechanical ovens: (a) revolving-tray oven; (b) traveling-tray oven; (c) rotary oven.

waves and should not be used, as they can reflect microwaves back to the microwave tube and destroy it. Microwaves pass through glass and nonmetallic materials, so these materials are used to hold foods being cooked in a microwave oven.

Microwave cooking has not replaced conventional cooking in foodservice operations because they do not allow production of large volumes of food, and because they produce undesirable cooking reactions in some foods. The speed of cooking is often so fast that foods do not respond to heat as they do in other forms of cooking. When it is appropriately used, the unit can bring food from a refrigerated or frozen state to a servable hot state in a few minutes, thus allowing operations to prepare foods on order. The unit also has flexibility.

When properly integrated into the food-production and food-service plan, it can do much to reduce costs and produce foods of high quality.

Reconstituting Ovens

Since many frozen foods are used today in foodservices, there is a major need for a unit that can quickly defrost them without damaging their quality. The reconstituting oven can bring −10°F (−23°C) items to a serving temperature in less than 30 minutes. Some units combine cycles of heat and refrigeration, which reduces drying on the edges while gently thawing the center. Other units use infrared waves and may reach temperatures as high as 850°F (454°C) to bring foods from thawing to serving temperatures. Such energy is called *radiation* because the heat is transferred by infrared waves.

Ranges

The range, a combination of an oven and top-cooking units, was invented by the Chinese more than 5,000 years ago. Modern ranges, heated either by gas or by electricity, are common in today's foodservices. The arrangement of top units may be open, closed, or some combination of the two (see fig. 5-14). The menu of the operation dictates whether a heavyweight, medium-weight, or lightweight model is necessary. The selling price of the range should not be the deciding factor in determining which type of equipment to purchase. Many operations select light equipment because of its lower price, only to find that these units are not suited to the type of production needed. Instead it should be selected on the basis of its capacity, versatility, consistency of temperature, cleanability, serviceability, and dependability.

Griddles

Foodservices use either gas or electric griddles. They can come incorporated as part of a range, or they may stand alone on a platform. Food is cooked on the griddle surface in a small amount of fat,

Figure 5-14. Ranges and range-top combinations: (a) convection oven base with three rectangular hotplates on top; (b) rectangular and high-speed French hotplates on top; (c) griddle on top; (d) electrical coil units on top; (e) backshelf broiler attachable to the back of the range.

much as it would be cooked in a fry or sauté pan. Griddles are used to prepare large quantities of fried products quickly and with a minimum of labor. Splash guards contain grease on the griddle surface; they should be of appropriate height, and the grease troughs must be wide and deep enough to capture excess fat and debris. Griddles can be nicked or scratched, which causes food to stick on the cooking surface. Consequently, care should be taken when using metal utensils, and pots or pans should never be placed on the griddle.

Broilers

Broilers use radiated heat energy to cook. This is the same kind of energy with which the sun heats the earth. Short energy waves, closely associated with light, result from white heat.

Most broilers broil from heat that comes from above, but bottom or side broilers are also found. Heating from the top allows fat to drip down into collectors without flaming. The underheat broiler does not have this advantage, but it often yields a better charred product—one that also shows the markings from the broiler. Side broilers are good

because the product can baste itself while broiling. Whatever broiler is used, the flames from it must not be allowed to burn fat. This could cause the formation of carcinogenic (cancer-producing) substances that could get onto the food. Broilers should be kept very clean since greasy ones can catch fire.

Steam-cooking Equipment

Steam-cooking equipment increases efficiency in many kitchens by reducing cooking times and decreasing the amount of work required to produce certain items (see fig. 5-15). Steam imparts heat rapidly and is economical to use. Because it does not burn food, steam cooking eliminates food scorching and the need for extensive pot-and-pan cleanup. Steam equipment may be self-contained, manufacturing its own steam, or it may receive steam from a central boiler.

Steam Cookers

Some units bring steam into a chamber where it comes directly into contact with the food. The steam vapor circulates in the chamber under pressure, in sufficient volume for good heat distri-

a.   b.   c.   d.

Figure 5-15. Steam cooking equipment: (a) high-compression compartment unit; (b) low-compression compartment unit; (c) convection steamer; (d) tilting steam-jacketed kettle.

bution. Low-compression, compartmented units operating at 5 to 7 psi (pounds per square inch) are used for high-volume production. Some hold up to six $12'' \times 20''$ pans in each compartment. One-, two-, and three-compartment models are available. High-compression, compartmented units operating at 15 to 17 psi use smaller pans but cook much more rapidly. Small quantities can be cooked very quickly, resulting in a high-quality, freshly cooked product. One-compartment models are available as countertop units.

A convection steamer forces steam to circulate in a compartment under normal pressure. The circulating steam disrupts a vapor barrier that is created around cooking food, thereby decreasing cooking time. Since pressure does not build up, the door of the compartment can be opened at any time. Single-compartment capacity for a convection steamer is three $12'' \times 20'' \times 2.5''$ pans.

Steamers work well for many types of foods, with the exception of cakes and pastries. They can be of great use in defrosting frozen goods; covering the food prevents condensing steam from mixing with the product. After defrosting, the food can then undergo normal preparation. If possible, cooking different-flavored foods together should be avoided. Steam transfers flavors between foods, sometimes producing an undesirable combination of tastes. Perforated pans can be used to aid the circulation of steam, again shortening cooking times. The size of steamer to purchase depends on the maximum number of portions to be served and the portion size required per batch.

Steam-jacketed Kettles

The steam-jacketed kettle works much as a double boiler does. Steam is generated and surrounds food contained in a separate compartment. But whereas the steam in the double boiler is not under pressure, the steam in a steam-jacketed kettle is, resulting in higher temperatures. Because the contact surface of the kettle is not at a high heat and because the heat is evenly distributed, food does not scorch easily. Nonetheless, browning meats and performing certain similar processes are possible in these kettles.

Capacities range from 8 quarts to 150 gallons. Steam kettles with capacities of 3,000 or 4,000 gallons are found in central commissaries. Rated capacities must be reduced by 15 to 30 percent to determine actual usable volume. Both stationary kettles, having a standard 1½-inch draw-off valve, and tilting kettles, designed to allow the transfer of foods to smaller vessels, are available. Cold-water cooling systems that inject cold water into the kettle jacket to cool hot items rapidly are optional.

The kettle should be thoroughly cleaned after each use. Bringing water to a boil in a dirty kettle can help loosen stuck-on food for easier cleaning. Stainless steel kettles are more common than aluminum ones; the latter type should not be scoured hard with abrasive materials.

Fryers

Deep-fat fryers are used to cook food in a bath of hot fat, producing a nicely browned, crisp outer coating with a nutty flavor and a completely cooked, moist interior. In the conventional fryer, fat is used to conduct heat from a gas-fired or electrical heat source to the food (see fig. 5-16). The pressure fryer also cooks in deep fat, trapping moisture from food to generate steam, which increases pressure inside the fryer and reduces cooking times. This has proved especially successful for producing tender, moist fried chicken. Both regular and pressure fryers may have automatic, semiautomatic, or hand-operated features. Temperature control is essential, so a precise thermostat should be specified. Temperature recovery must be fast and accurate. Auxiliary safety controls—such as an automatic turn off when the temperature of the fat exceeds 450°F (232°C)—may be needed.

The ratio of food to frying oil varies with the food item. Potatoes can usually be fried with a 1:6 ratio of potatoes to fat, but most other products are fried with a 1:8 ratio. Thus, a 15-lb fryer (holding 15 lb of fat) can fry 2½ lb of potatoes but only about 2 lb of other foods. In selecting the right fryer, the operation's basic menu pattern must be considered, along with the size of the food portion, the number

Figure 5-16. Conventional fryer with thermostatic temperature control.

Figure 5-17. Heavy-duty tilting pan.

of portions required per hour, and the amount of food the fryer can produce in an hour. On average, it is better to have two relatively small fry kettles than one large one, since only one small one need be used during off-peak periods; in this way, savings can be realized on heat and on reduced deterioration of frying oil.

In response to demand from high-volume operators, a conveyor fryer has become available. Food is placed on one end of a conveyor belt, dipped down into hot oil, cooked, brought back out, drained, and dumped into a holding receptacle. This makes possible a continuous flow of hot fried food during periods of peak demand.

Tilting Pans or Skillets

One of the most versatile pieces of equipment in the kitchen is the tilting pan or skillet. It can do the jobs of a range top, griddle, small steam kettle, stock pot, fry pan, and skillet. The tilting pan comes in various sizes. A large, heavy-duty pan has a depth of about 8 or 9 inches (see fig. 5-17). It can tilt up to 90° on a horizontal axis. Stewing, simmering, frying, searing, braising, grilling, sautéing, boiling, defrosting, and roasting can be done in one. A great deal of heavy lifting and transferring of foods from one pan to another can be eliminated by this unit. Temperatures to use for best results are the following:

Simmering:	maximum of 200°F (93°C)
Sautéing:	225° to 275°F (107° to 134°C)
Searing:	300° to 350°F (149° to 177°C)
Frying:	325° to 375°F (163° to 191°C)
Grilling:	350° to 425°F (177° to 218°C)

Models may be mounted on legs, on the wall, on counters, on modular cabinet bases, or on casters. The tilting pan is easily cleaned with a mild detergent. Presoaking is recommended, if possible.

Automated Cooking Equipment

As electronics and computerized technology have become more sophisticated, features not previously available have been added to many types of kitchen equipment. The goal of much of this automation has been to decrease energy costs while increasing worker productivity.

System controls can monitor numerous operations for a piece of equipment. Digital temperature sensors and thermostats are more sensitive than their predecessors and can even anticipate drops in temperature and fire up a piece of equipment before the temperature can drop far enough to affect the quality of the product. When a large batch of food is dropped into a fryer, a radical drop in the oil's temperature can result in a soggy product. A temperature sensor can judge this change immediately and take action to bring the fryer back up to proper cooking temperature rapidly. These systems control oil temperature, gauge the quality of the fat, extend its life, and monitor safety and filtration systems.

It is currently possible to have an oven controlled by a programmable timer. Some foods may require cooking at different temperatures and for different lengths of time. A timer can be set to make these changes automatically. In such an oven coupled with a temperature sensor, a large roast could be placed to cook overnight until done and then be held at the proper temperature for service in the morning.

Small Tools for the Cooking Area

Knives, tools, utensils, pots, pans, and other small equipment are required in the cooking area as well as in other sections. These items must be selected carefully for durability, suitability for the job to be performed, and cost. Good steel is essential in

many cutting tools so that they hold a good edge and wear well (see fig. 5-18). Well-designed handles on utensils and tools help relieve hand fatigue and increase efficiency (see fig. 5-19). Working parts should be firmly fastened to grasps or handles. Weight must be considered in selecting pots and pans (see fig. 5-20).

HOLDING AND SERVING EQUIPMENT

The serving subsystem handles the assembly of food, the holding of food (if necessary) for a short period of time, the arrangement of food on plates and dishes, and the presentation of food to the guest. Thus, the serving subsystem connects the heart of the house with the front of the house. Prior to service, food must be held at the proper temperatures to reduce deterioration and to allow the food to reach guests at its correct serving temperature. Success depends on having the right kind of serving equipment. Tableware, serviceware, napery, decorative items, and uniforms for service personnel are also matters that fall under the purview of this subsystem.

Holding Equipment for Hot Food

Hot foods should be held at temperatures of from 140° to 190°F (60° to 88°C). Each food has its own holding temperature. Entrée and meat dishes usually are held at around 140°F (60°C), sauces and gravies at slightly higher temperatures, and thin soups, beverages, and some other thin liquids at 180° to 190°F (82° to 88°C). Health authorities require hot food to be held at temperatures above 140°F (60°C). Holding equipment for hot foods includes steam tables, pass-through holding units (located between preparation/cooking areas and the service area), undercounter warming drawers, bains-marie, stationary or mobile heated cabinets, and infrared warmers. Some holding cabinets are designed to display the cooked product while in use.

Curved

Spear

Sharp

Clip-point

Wide

Narrow, stiff, and flexible

Wide and stiff

Narrow, flexible, and stiff

Curved

Butcher

Scimitar steak knife

Cleaver

Forged

Regular

Cold meat slicer

Boning knife

Bowl spatula

Offset spatula

Frosting spatula

Figure 5-18. Knives and spatulas.

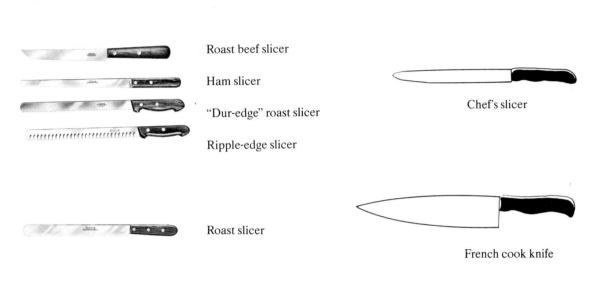

Roast beef slicer

Ham slicer

"Dur-edge" roast slicer

Ripple-edge slicer

Chef's slicer

Roast slicer

French cook knife

Figure 5-18. *(cont.)*

Holding Equipment for Cold Food

To reduce the growth of undesirable microorganisms, cold food should never be held at temperatures above 45°F (7°C). Cold foods should be served at around 40°F (4.5°C), and frozen foods should be served at around 24°F (−4.4°C). Undercounter refrigeration units, pass-through refrigeration systems, mobile refrigerators and freezer cabinets, and refrigerated display cases and storage drawers are among the many pieces that keep foods cold. Again, many units can be used to display and merchandise food, as well as to keep it at the proper temperature (see fig. 5-21).

Serving Equipment

Chafing dishes, mobile carts, and display cases are a few examples of holding equipment that may be used for service. Frequently, holding equipment decorated to please the customer's eye is used to merchandise the product. This is especially true in cafeteria and buffet lines, where guests make their own selections. Hot carts may be used to serve roasted meats and other hot foods. Cold carts may be used to display and sell hors d'oeuvres, salads, or desserts. Other equipment, such as a microwave oven, a reconstituting oven, or a steam cooker, is used for last minute preparation or cooking.

Coffee Machines

Coffee is a popular beverage and should be prepared properly with the right equipment. Many kinds of units are used successfully. Chapter 21 discusses these in detail.

Ice Machines

Ice machines are often installed in the serving subsystem's area to supply ice for such uses as drinking water, bar and beverage service, salads, desserts, and displays of cold foods. The ice pro-

Cook's fork

Broiler fork

Carver fork

Chef's steel

Cookie turner

Dough cutter

Hamburger or cake turner

Pan scraper

Pizza cutter

Pie knife

Sandwich spreader

Figure 5-19. Utensils and tools.

All-purpose disher

Scoop

Collander

Ladle

Wire skimmer

Chinese strainer

Measure

Solid basting spoon
Perforated spoon
Slotted spoon

Piano wire whip

Figure 5-19. *(cont.)*

Double boiler

Steam table insert

Stock pot

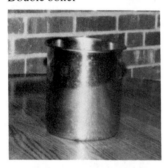

Bain-marie pot

Figure 5-20. Pots and pans.

duced can be in the form of cubes, cubelets, chips, or flakes. Machines are sized and designed as floor-mounted, wall-mounted, compact, or decorator models. The correct model for any particular operation depends on how the ice is used and how much is needed in any one 24-hour period. Among the more popular units are space-saving stacked units, continuous-flow units (machines under which portable bins can be wheeled), and portion-controlled ice maker/water dispenser units.

Beverage Dispensers

Beverage dispensers may dispense milk, punches and fruit-flavored drinks, carbonated beverages, juices, frozen carbonated soft drinks, and soft ice cream shakes. These units, fully automatic or semiautomatic, are easy to operate and require minimal labor input for a fast output of drinks. A wide range of models is available to meet almost any need. Units can be obtained for self-service or behind-the-counter service. All should be appealing and easily cleaned.

CLEANUP

Cleaning up is an ongoing process that begins before each meal and continues throughout preparation, cooking, and service; it is one of the most important subsystems in the total foodservice system, since it can be a determining factor in the success or failure of the operation. High labor costs, excessive breakage and loss of ware, undue maintenance, and poor employee morale can result if the cleanup section is not properly equipped and designed. Customers, too, can be unhappy with poorly maintained equipment.

Waste-removal Equipment

Foodservice operations that prepare and serve large quantities of food generate a considerable amount of waste. Such waste should be easily and quickly removed as it accumulates. Waste and garbage cans often are used for this purpose. If so, they should be thoroughly cleaned each time they

Steam table pan

Loaf pan

Sauce pans

Roast pan

Sauté pan

Fry pan

Straight-sided bake pan

Sheet pan

Pie tin

Layer cake pan

Muffin pan

Figure 5-20. *(cont.)*

Figure 5-21. Food-holding equipment.

are emptied. The use of plastic liners can help make this a simpler process.

Disposers

A disposer can accept food wastes but not cans, bottles, or other hard materials. If only one disposer is used, it should be centrally located near areas where the greatest amount of waste is produced. Smaller units can be put into the individual kitchen sections to save steps, but ready access to disposers can encourage careless employees to waste materials. Disposers should be sized to meet the operation's needs. They should bypass rather than be hooked up to grease traps, since refuse going through the grease trap can clog it. Disposers are frequently used as part of the dishwashing system.

Compactors

A compactor—a box unit into which waste materials are fed—can accept hard materials as well as soft ones. It works by crushing or breaking. A hydraulic ram then compacts the crushed material into a solid mass. Containers holding the compacted materials can then be removed and thrown away. Volume of waste is reduced by up to 98 percent. The compactor usually is located on the loading dock, although portable models are available for movement from one location to another.

Pulpers

A pulper reduces waste by-products into a neat, semidry pulp that is odorless and free of vermin (see fig. 5-22). Garbage volume is reduced by as much as 85 percent as the wastes are pulped underwater, converted into a slurry, and then rendered into a semidry pulp when the water is removed. Waste can be piped in its slurry state to a remote pickup point, eliminating the need for any physical handling. The quantity of waste determines the size of the original pulping unit required. There should be one unit at each of several points of waste generation. Pulpers will not accept metal, glass, crockery, or other hard items. A separate means should be provided for the disposal of such materials.

Dishwashing Equipment

The cleaning of serviceware—china, glass, and silver—is critical to any operation. Customers and health inspectors alike respond poorly to dirty dishes and utensils. To purchase a dishwasher of the proper size requires analysis of the number of pieces of ware to be processed each hour. Manufacturers overstate the capacity of washing machines by 25 to 33 percent. Five different kinds of washing machines are used in foodservices: counter and undercounter models, free-standing models, door models, rack conveyor models, and belt conveyor models (see fig. 5-23).

Dishwashing machines come in one or more

Figure 5-22. Pulper.

sections, usually referred to as *tanks*. A basic one-tank model has two cycles: a wash and a rinse. A two-tank model washes in the first tank and power-rinses in the second. A three-tank model uses one tank for a prewash, another for a wash, and the third for a rinse. Some larger models have a fourth cycle for the final rinse. A blower dryer is an optional unit on some larger models; it serves to speed drying—especially when dishware comes off a short belt at the end and must be removed before much time has been expended on drying.

In many models, the prewash and wash tanks are filled, but water flowing from the rinse section moves down into them, providing fresh water as old water is drained away. Most dishwashers have automatic temperature controls. Prewash units usually operate at around 140° to 150°F (60° to 66°C); wash units, at 160°F (71°C); and the rinse, at 180°F (82°C) for 10 seconds or at 170°F (77°C) for 30 seconds. Too hot a prewash or wash bakes on foods. In some of the newer low temperature dishwashers, rinsing is done with chemical sanitizers at a water temperature of 140°F (60°C). Since this is the nor-

mal temperature of hot tap water, a booster heater (which is required by the 170° to 180°F machines) is unnecessary, allowing energy savings. Many machines have automatic detergent dispensers, which add detergent as needed, and automatic rinse detergent injectors. Rinse detergent is put into the final rinse water to give a better run-off of water for faster drying and reduced water spotting.

Counter and Undercounter Models

The smallest machines used are counter and undercounter dishwashers that are 24 and 30 inches wide. Manufacturers claim that the 24-inch model handles 300 plates or 540 glasses, plus silverware, per hour. The 30-inch model cleans an additional 75 plates or 60 glasses, plus additional silverware, per hour. These models are used in small operations in which only a few dishes must be processed.

Free-standing Models

Roll or hood machines are called *free-standing* models. Manufacturers claim that these models may clean as many as 570 plates or 1,140 glasses per a.

b.

c.

CONDENSER

RACK STORAGE
SHELF   HOOD   PREWASH   POWER   POWER
WASH   RINSE

POWER
RINSE

FINAL RINSE

BLOWER-
DRYER

BOX
SHELF   DRIVE
UNIT

ANGLE
SHELF

WASTE SYSTEM

TROUGH

SLIDING
TRAY LOOP

CONTROL BOX

HANGING
SHELF

d.

Figure 5-23. Dishwashing equipment: (a) undercounter model; (b) roll-type free-standing model; (c) door model; (d) rack conveyor model; (e) belt conveyor model.

e.

Figure 5-23. *(cont.)*

hour, depending on the model. These machines take up relatively little space.

Door Models

Dishwashers called *door* models can handle as many as 1,325 plates or 2,385 glasses per hour. They can be installed for either a straight-through or a corner operation. Corner units load in front and unload at the side (or vice versa). Straight-through units load and unload at opposite sides. This type of model usually satisfies the needs of foodservice operations that have approximately 100 seats.

Rack Conveyor Models

Dishwashers of the rack conveyor model have a belt or drive unit that moves racks filled with ware through the machine. One-, two-, and three-tank models supposedly can do up to 9,000 plates or 16,000 glasses per hour. Machine lengths vary from 40 to 166 inches. Blower dryers, vapor condensers, and vent connections are a few of the optional units that can be used with these larger machines.

Belt Conveyor Models

Flight-type or belt conveyor models have the greatest capacity of all. They are used in big installations where many pieces of ware must be processed each hour. A continuous peg-type belt on the machine eliminates the need for racks, allowing dishes, pots and pans, and other large units to be placed directly onto the belt. Silverware, cups, glasses, and other items are sent through in racks. Silverware is usually placed into canisters, eating end up. When the canister comes from the machine after cleaning, it is inverted into containers so that the handles are up.

According to manufacturers, typical capacities range from 5,000 to 12,500 plates per hour in one-, two-, or three-tank machines. Models may be up to 60 feet long.

NEW EQUIPMENT FEATURES

In some cases, new equipment differs somewhat from the more traditional kinds of equipment described here, and accordingly the mode of food production and equipment handling may have to be changed somewhat. One of the most novel added features in some equipment is its control by computer. Ovens, deep-fat fryers, and other equipment now can have temperature, time, temperature changes, and other functions under computer control. Some deep-fat fryers, for instance, lower on signal and fry at a given temperature, raising the basket at the end of a set time period. Eclair pastes can be put into an oven with a preset temperature of 450°F for 8 minutes and the temperature will then automatically be reset to 350°F for 30 minutes. The use of computer-controlled equipment has made little change in basic techniques or even in modes of cooking. What it has done is give better control and remove the possibility that a worker might forget to set proper temperatures or observe proper times. Better product quality results from such control.

Another feature that has improved equipment performance is the new contact thermostat. It is possible now to have equipment hold temperatures within a very narrow range. Formerly, contact thermostats might allow as much as a 10 to 15 Fahrenheit degree temperature variation above or below the desired one. The new contact thermostat allows more precise control and leads to better results. In some cases, thermocouple control is used, in which thermocouples are inserted into items to register the desired end-temperature of the product—for example, 140°F interior temperature for a rare meat.

Oven insulations have been improved so that heat loss is reduced and heat control is improved. Other types of equipment have also had their insulating qualities improved. Ovens now have heat directors that tend to direct heat from one spot into others. This removes low and high heat spotting in the oven. Some have fans to do this, but reflective materials are also used. Other ovens and equipment have heat recapture systems that capture heat before it is lost and redirect it where it is needed. For example, heat recapture devices can be installed to capture heat and use it for heating water and other needs. This has helped to reduce heat consumption.

There have been many other less notable but still useful changes in equipment to make it more efficient. Teflon-type coatings are now found on some ware, griddles, and tools. Tools have better grips. More use has been made recently of automatic tipping or lifting equipment, thereby reducing the amount of heavy work required of employees. Again, while these are significant changes, their effect on the basic planning or implementation of quantity food production is small.

SUMMARY

The foods served, their quantity, and the type of service given determine equipment needs. If convenience foods are used, the equipment needed is different from that required for preparing foods from scratch. Equipment must be arranged and used properly and must be integrated with other equipment so that the various subsystems of the operation work efficiently. The average foodservice has six subsystems: receiving, storage, preparation, cooking, serving, and cleanup.

Raw materials, supplies, and equipment enter the operation through the receiving subsystem. Ordered food is checked here for quality, count, and weight. Adequate scales should be provided so that the weights of received items can be checked.

In addition, transport equipment is needed to move foods to storage or using areas, and some office equipment is needed to perform various record-keeping tasks.

Storage areas should be planned to give adequate cold and dry storage. Cold storage should be placed near the receiving area and also near the areas that draw materials from it, thus achieving good workflow. Refrigerators, freezers, and other cold-storage equipment preserve food so that it does not deteriorate and lose its nutritional qualities. In the dry-storage area, appropriate shelving and containers are important in order to use storage space efficiently and safeguard the foods stored there. Shelving flexibility and container shape and size are important considerations in designing this area.

The preparation subsystem helps supply foods to the cooking, bakery, and salad units. Preliminary work is done here. Scales, mixers, cutters, slicers, and much other equipment should be selected to do the required jobs and to reduce labor. The vertical cutter/mixer (VCM) is helpful if volume is sufficient to justify its use. Vegetable peelers are used to peel hard root vegetables. Meat-processing equipment—saws, choppers, grinders, and tenderizers—may be needed if the facility does much of its own meat cutting.

The cooking subsystem covers food-cooking areas, the bakeshop, the pantry, and other areas where foods are prepared for service. The receiving, storage, and preparation subsystems, along with the service and cleanup subsystems, should be integrated with this subsystem. Cooking is the core of the entire system. Its equipment includes conventional, convection, mechanical, microwave, and reconstituting ovens; ranges; griddles; broilers; steam-cooking equipment (including steam cookers and steam-jacketed kettles); fryers; tilting skillets; and knives, tools, utensils, pots, and pans.

The serving subsystem is the place where food is assembled, held for service, dished, and served to the customer. This subsystem joins the heart of the house to the front of the house and forms a vital link between what is done for the customer and what the customer experiences. Both hot-food-holding and cold-food-holding equipment are needed. Sometimes such equipment must also be used to display and to help merchandise foods; in this case, attention must be paid to the décor of the equipment. Other major pieces of serving equipment include coffee machines, ice machines, and beverage dispensers.

Cleanup consists of the washing of serviceware and pots and pans, the cleaning of the facility, and the removal of wastes. This is an important area from the standpoint of cost, maintenance of standards, and employee and guest satisfaction. Waste-removal equipment—garbage or waste containers, disposers, compactors, or pulpers—is used for waste removal. The dishwasher used may be a counter or undercounter model, a free-standing model, a door-type model, a rack conveyor model, or a belt conveyor model. The type of dishwasher selected should be based on the quantity of water that must be processed through the washer.

CHAPTER REVIEW QUESTIONS

1. Jim Paige has been working for a major fastfood chain for the last ten years, while nurturing dreams of owning and operating a place of his own. Jim has decided that his nest egg is large enough to begin a serious investigation of his restaurant concept. He wants to open a full-service restaurant that caters to a market segment he is familiar with: the family. He wants to present a medium-priced menu featuring a fairly wide range of selections, while stressing "home-style" cooking. This includes a good seafood selection, steaks, sandwiches, chicken, and a salad bar. This menu will not present exotic dishes but will stick with traditional American preparations. The restaurant will be open for lunch and dinner. Jim knows that one of the first things he must do is get an idea of the cost of his project and its space requirements. Because most of Jim's experience has come in operations and not in restaurant development, his knowledge of equipment is limited to what he has dealt with in his

fastfood operation. Jim has contacted a friend of his who teaches foodservice courses at the local college and has asked if the teacher happens to have a student who would be interested in helping him with his estimates. You are that student (there will be some pay involved!). What Jim is looking for is a rough idea of the equipment he will need for his operation and how it will be arranged in his kitchen (giving him an idea of the space he will need for the kitchen). He would like you to provide a list of necessary equipment, an explanation of your choices, and a rough layout of his kitchen-to-be, showing the placement of storage, work stations, and major pieces of equipment. What would your list, explanations, and sketch look like?

2. Select five pieces of equipment and describe how they work and what factors are important in their selection. Give advantages or disadvantages of various types of this kind of equipment.

3. Compare the equipment found in an operation utilizing conventional foods as opposed to one using convenience foods. Describe the various subsystems in each one.

4. Plan a section (a subsystem) of a kitchen and place the proper equipment in it. Describe what items might be prepared or what might typically occur in this subsystem.

5. Take one piece of equipment and indicate important factors to know in its operation, maintenance, and cleaning.

VOCABULARY

Subsystem	Peeler
VCM	Reconstituting oven
Reel oven	Rack conveyor
Mechanical oven	Tilting skillet
Horizontal mixer	Buffalo Chopper
Pulper	Convection steamer
Belt conveyor	Radiation
Broiler	Upright mixer
Dollies	Compactor

Steam cooker	Microwave oven
Convection oven	Tank
Belt conveyor	Counter dishwasher

ANNOTATED REFERENCES

Avery, A. C. 1985. A Modern Guide to Foodservice Equipment. Rev. ed. New York: Van Nostrand Reinhold. (This text covers many equipment factors in detail.)

Beard, J. ed. 1975. *Cook's Catalogue.* New York: Harper & Row. (Small equipment and utensils are reviewed in this text.)

Campbell, S. 1980. *Cook's Tools: The Complete Manual of Kitchen Implements and How to Use Them.* New York: Morrow Publishing. (A thorough presentation of commonly used kitchen utensils and equipment.)

Douglas, P. 1979. *Kitchen Planning and Design: Case Studies.* Poole, England: Blanford Press. (Actual situations are presented to ensure common mistakes in kitchen design are not repeated.)

Dukas, P. 1973. *How to Plan and Operate a Restaurant.* 2d ed. pp. 109-132. Rochelle Park, N.J.: Hayden Book Company. (How to select foodservice equipment.)

Kazarian, E. A. 1979. *Work Analysis and Design for Hotels, Restaurants and Institutions.* Westport, Conn.: AVI Publishing. (Effective workflow patterns and work methods.)

————. 1983. *Foodservice Facilities Planning.* Westport, Conn.: AVI Publishing. (All aspects of kitchen layout and design are presented.)

Kotschevar, L. H., and Terrell, M. E. 1983. *Food Service Planning: Layout and Equipment.* New York: John Wiley & Sons. (Complete investigation of layout planning, equipment selection, implementation, and utilization.)

Wilkinson, J. 1981. *The Complete Book of Cooking Equipment.* Boston: CBI Publishing. (Extensive pictures of implemented equipment.)

Further materials on equipment may be requested from manufacturers or their representatives. Hobart Manufacturing, for example, has extensive materials on implementing equipment according to the systems approach.

CHAPTER 6

Purchasing, Receiving, Storing, and Issuing Food

OUTLINE

Once a menu is planned, a number of steps must be taken to bring it into reality. One of the first and most important steps is to purchase and receive the materials needed to produce the menu items. Skillful purchasing, coupled with good receiving, can do much to maximize the results of a good menu. In this regard, management must master six preliminary duties:

1. Know the market.
2. Determine the operation's purchasing needs, by department and category.
3. Establish and use specifications.
4. Design the purchasing procedure.
5. Design the receiving procedure.
6. Evaluate the purchasing task as a job description and fill the position.

KNOWING THE MARKET

Since markets vary considerably, a buyer must know the characteristics of the relevant local market. This requires some individual investigation of market suppliers of all types. In order to do a good job, the purchasing agent must also know a great deal about the products to be dealt with—for example, localities where the goods are grown or produced, the seasons of production, approximate costs of goods, conditions of supply and demand, laws and regulations governing the market, marketing agents and their services, processing stages, storage requirements, and grades. Since this means that the purchasing agent, or buyer, must maintain current information on changes in the market, it becomes important for this person to talk frequently with purveyors.

The Buyer

Buying demands integrity, maturity, bargaining skills, and a moderate disposition. Buyers are subject to bribes and other inducements from dishonest purveyors who want to get their business. Attempts are sometimes made to force a buyer to purchase from specific sources as well. A rule often quoted is, "Treat your boss's money as if it were your own"; and another is, "Be friendly, be courteous, and socialize if it means improving your buying, but always stop at the point at which you would lose your right to remain a free agent." Many professional societies of buyers have ethical codes (to which members subscribe) requiring high ethical standards in the relationship between buyer and purveyor.

A buyer also must know a lot about the internal organization for which buying takes place. The buyer must know what specific items an operation needs and must be able to obtain them at a desirable price. The procedures for production and the ways in which items are used in the operation must be known, and the right type of item must be bought to suit it. For example, the appropriate item for a particular use may not be first quality but third. Ground beef from the lower grades has more flavor than that from the higher ones. C-grade tomatoes are preferred over A-grade tomatoes for soups and sauces. It is senseless to purchase perfect walnut halves when they are to be chopped and used in bakery goods; a broken walnut meat serves just as well. Knowing these things can help an operation reduce costs, improve quality, and enhance customer satisfaction. A buyer must also know storage requirements, space available, the financial ability of the operation to make certain purchases, storage times and temperatures, yield-testing procedures, and the way to establish a specification so that the right item is obtained.

Because of the importance of this position, special care should be taken in selecting the correct person for the job. Following is a sample job description for the position, including a synopsis of the responsibilities involved.

POSITION DESCRIPTION
Position: Purchasing Agent
Reports to: General Manager
Supervises: Purchasing, Receiving, Storing, and Issuing

Basic Functions:

1. To supervise, train, and motivate storeroom employees.
2. To implement corporate purchasing policies and procedures.
3. To keep management informed of market conditions, price trends, product availability, and methods of reducing costs.
4. To maintain and upgrade the quality of items purchased.
5. To control purchase costs through competitive shopping for quality products.
6. To supervise all storeroom operations.

Responsibilities:

1. To carry out all administrative functions pertaining to payroll, scheduling, and recruiting. To maintain honest, reliable staff, and to promote personnel with potential.
2. To become a recognized "profit center" by recommending and implementing purchasing concepts that save money through contract purchasing, buying realistic quantities before price increases, and utilizing quantity purchase discounts and monthly liquor postoffs.
3. To maintain accurate written specifications on all products purchased, to understand these specifications, and to use them effectively in obtaining competitive price quotations and receiving products.
4. To have a written order and receiving schedule for all products. The appropriate forms should be used to prevent shortages and to minimize deliveries.
5. To maintain current market quotations on all products. Suppliers should be determined by the quality of their products, the dependability of their service, and the competitiveness of their pricing.
6. To set up a control system to ensure that all items being received are of designated quality, quantity, and price. Invoices and receiving records should be personally reviewed daily.
7. To supervise daily all issuing procedures, including ascertaining the following points: issuing hours are being enforced; requisitions are properly dated and signed, and products and quantities are clearly written; pricing (storeroom, direct, and meat tags) is accurate, and key controls are enforced.
8. To check storeroom procedures daily to ensure that stock is properly rotated, that items are properly priced, that sanitation standards are maintained, and that sufficient inventories are available for efficient operation.
9. To work closely with the chef with regard to items used, their amount, and when they will be required for food preparation. To constantly seek new or better products.
10. To work closely with the chef and the banquet department in recommending products that can be sold profitably, in discussing availability of seasonal items, and in estimating the time requirement necessary to obtain merchandise.
11. To visit local markets on a regularly scheduled basis, in order to be able to meet and select purveyors and to find and select the best-quality items available in the market.

Buying Methods

Buying methods depend both on the type of operation and on the buying market. Generally, buying methods can be grouped under two headings: formal buying methods, and informal buying methods. Formal methods are best and are most often used in large contracts for commodities purchased over time, while informal methods are more often used for casual purchasing when the amount involved is not large and when speed and simplicity are desirable. In formal buying, if a basic price has been established, prices do not vary much over the course of a year. Prices may vary to a great extent with informal buying, however, as both prices and supply may fluctuate widely.

Informal Buying

Informal buying methods, also called *open-type buying,* are the ones most often used by small foodservice operators. This type of buying usually involves oral negotiations. The buyer gets the price, based on the specifications of the operation, either over the phone or in person from a purveyor. Quality, price, and service are then weighed, and a decision is made to purchase or not. In using this system, buyers should obtain comparative prices from at least three to five different suppliers. While informal methods may vary from locale to locale, there are generally three types of methods used: the quotation-and-order-sheet method, the blank-check method, and the cost-plus method.

The Quotation-and-Order-Sheet Method. The quotation-and-order-sheet method uses a tabulation of particular commodities wanted, in the quantities and quality needed. These specifications are usually listed in a column on the left-hand side of a sheet. Additional columns are available to record the prices quoted by various purveyors (see fig. 6-1). Calls are made to the purveyors, and their prices are recorded in the column allowed for this. When as many prices as desired have been obtained, the prices are studied. A decision is then made to purchase something from a particular purveyor, and the price for that item is circled. Last, a secretary or clerk calls the purveyor to place the orders.

The Blank-Check Method. Blank-check buying can occur when there is an extreme shortage of a commodity on the market or when some other condi-

tion exists that necessitates buying an item (almost) regardless of its cost. By this method, a buyer orders something without knowing its price, and then pays whatever price is necessary to obtain the item. Only reputable vendors should be given a blank-check order. Often, upon obtaining a price on an item, a vendor checks with the buyer to see if the price is within an acceptable range.

The Cost-Plus Method. The cost-plus method is often used in situations where prices are not known or where the market is unstable. Many vendors prefer this arrangement, since they do not have to add a safety factor to avoid the risk of losing money on commodities that fluctuate considerably in price. Instead, purveyors are free to buy at the most favorable price and then add on an amount necessary to cover costs and give a profit. The amount charged to the buyer over and above the initial cost of the item is usually based on a standard percentage. Thus, a vendor may purchase fruits and vegetables and charge the buyer the original cost plus 20 percent.

Formal Buying

Formal methods, also known as *competitive buying,* involve giving vendors written specifications and quantity needs. Key stages of negotiations are done in writing; as the degree of formality increases, the proportion of negotiations reduced to writing increases, too. The invitation or request for bids may be made through newspaper advertising or by sending selected vendors a notice of buying needs.

Three formal methods are most common: the competitive-bid method, the negotiated method, and the futures-and-contract method. All are used to obtain the usual advantages of volume buying.

The Competitive-Bid Method. In competitive bidding, sellers are invited to submit bids through some type of written communication (see fig. 6-2). The vendors, in turn, send prices and other requested information on the commodities to the buyer. The cost-plus system is sometimes used in formal purchasing. Bids are opened at a specified time to determine awards. Only sellers that can meet the

Produce Quotation and Order Sheet

For use on _____   Delivery date _____

					Price Quotes			
	Specs	Amount needed	Amount on hand	Amount to order	Vendors			
					I	II	III	IV
Produce:								

Figure 6-1. Sample form for a produce quotation and order sheet.

INVITATION, BID, AND AWARD

| Issued by
Manager
Happy Haven Restaurent | Address
1122 Supply Street
Happy Haven, Maryland | Date _____ |

Sealed bids in duplicate will be received at the above office until _____.
19____ for the items and in the quantities indicated for delivery on the dates indicated. Quantities indicated are approximate may be reduced on instruction of the buyer. Increases up to 20 percent will be binding at the discretion of the buyer.

All items to be officially identified by the U. S. Department of Agriculture for class and quality. Costs of such service to be borne by vendor.

Items	Supplies	Quantity	Unit	Unit Price	Amount
1.	Chicken, fresh chilled fryer, 2-1/2-3 lb, ready-to-cook-U.S. Grade A To be delivered-----------	500	lb		
2.	Chicken, fresh chilled fowl, 3-1/2-4lb, ready-to-cook, U.S. Grade B To be delivered---------------	100	lb		
3.	Turkey, frozen, Young Tom 20-22 lb. ready-to-cook, U.S. Grade A. To be delivered---------------	100	lb		
4.	Ducks, frozen roaster duckling, 5 - 5-1/2 lb, ready-to-cook, U.S, Grade A To be delivered-------------------	50	lb		

Vendor _____

Figure 6-2. Sample competitive bid form.

established purchase conditions of the buyer are considered in awarding bids. The invitation to bid usually contains a set of general conditions, such as terms of payment, discounts, method of delivery, billing requirements, and payment arrangements. In addition, the particular requirements for each item are set forth in a specification.

The Negotiated Method. Negotiated buying is often used when vendors are hesitant to bid because of time restrictions, fluctuating market conditions, or high perishability of the product. In this case, negotiations may be conducted over the phone and confirmed later in writing. The negotiated method allows for quicker action because it is less rigidly structured than other formal methods. Several vendors may be approached to get a range of price, quality, availability, and other factors. This method is flexible yet still allows for competitive bidding.

The Futures-and-Contract Method. Futures-and-contract buying is often used by large businesses that have sufficient capital and staff to contract for future delivery of commodities at an established bid price. The advantage of this system is that an adequate supply at an established price can be arranged in advance. As a result, problems with shortfalls and price fluctuations that otherwise could affect the availability of items required for the menu can be avoided. This system is sometimes used for short periods of time—perhaps only a week or a month—when commodities such as meats or fresh fruits or vegetables may be in limited supply. Items of more stable price, such as canned goods or even mature potatoes, onions, or cabbage, are often placed on contract for longer periods of time.

In some cases, the quantity desired under contract may vary, so the contract may specify that the amount purchased depends on the amount used during the relevant period. A price may be agreed on, along with quality and other factors, but the specific quantity to be used is not set (although a range is noted). Deliveries then depend on the inventory on hand. The maximum stock of an item is set by the buyer; then, when the stock diminishes to a certain point, the buyer reorders so that the stock, on delivery, reaches its maximum once more. In some cases, the purveyor drops by the operation regularly to bring the inventory of the operation up to a preestablished level. Either arrangement is often called *par stock supplying.* It is important in par stock supplying to maintain a safety stock—a quantity of the item sufficient to tide the operation over between the time of reorder and the time of delivery. Even maintaining a reserve stock is worthwhile in case delivery is late. This system is often adopted to handle daily-order items, such as breads and dairy goods. All deliveries must be checked and all products rotated forward, leaving the newer stock to be used after the old stock is expended.

Selecting Purveyors

Selecting a purveyor is an important step in purchasing. One of the first considerations is how able a particular purveyor is to meet the needs of the foodservice—not only in price, but in meeting delivery times, maintaining quality standards, and upholding reliability in other areas. Information about various purveyors can be obtained from other buyers. Visits can be made to their establishments, and opinions can be gained by inspection and by discussion with them. The buyer must attempt to ascertain how reliable and stable a purveyor would be under competition and under varying market conditions. Normally, vendors fall into one of five categories:

Wholesalers stock many kinds of products and may be able to provide good service, maintain good quality, and meet special needs.

Direct sellers from manufacturers or packers may be able to provide some savings by eliminating marketing agents and services.

Local sellers, such as *farmers and processors* can supply perishable goods such as fruits, vegetables, milk, bread, and bakery goods, possibly from local rural areas.

Cooperative sellers may be able to supply commodities produced by local farmers or others who have joined together to market their products.

Retail food stores may be able to sell at very low prices because they can purchase in much larger lots than a foodservice can.

Purveyors are also selected on the basis of experience. Gradually, those who do not satisfy the needs of the operation are weeded out. New vendors may be tried and retained. Some of the considerations leading to a decision to deal on a continuing basis with a specific vendor have been detailed by Maizel (1971). These may be summarized as follows:

1. How well does the purveyor anticipate needs? A purveyor is a buyer for customers and must look ahead and anticipate their requirements. The purveyor should watch market conditions and notify customers when market changes may occur.
2. Can the purveyor offer adequate service in assembling the various items needed? Will the purveyor break quantities down to amounts the foodservice can use? Is the purveyor even willing to warehouse for preferred customers at times?
3. Will the purveyor maintain adequate stocks? If supplies run low, can the purveyor obtain replenishments quickly?
4. What credit terms does the purveyor offer? Are discounts available for prompt payment within a given time?
5. Will the purveyor be able to deliver the goods in good condition and at times required?
6. Will the purveyor use information about market conditions to protect customers or to make windfall profits?
7. Does the purveyor offer a wide range of services and a wide range of goods? Savings can often be made by consolidating services and products; many purveyors now may be able to offer frozen commodities, fresh fruits and vegetables, processed foods, meats, and even some dairy or specialty products. Some purveyors even feature such items as prepeeled potatoes and packaged meats. A purveyor offering many things a foodservice needs can simplify purchasing and reduce the number of contacts that must be made.
8. Does the purveyor understand customers' operations? Can the purveyor recommend items that suit customers' needs, or are its services limited to merely taking orders?

The relative importance of these considerations varies from operation to operation. According to a study presented in the *Hospitality Education and Research Journal* in 1984, however, buyers consider the following factors most important in evaluating potential suppliers:

Supplier dependability
Quality of delivery facilities
A.M. delivery
Absence of back orders
Quantity discounts
Cooperation in bid procedures
Turn-around time
Varieties of qualities carried
Price ranges carried
Varieties of products carried

In contrast, the least important factors, according to respondents to this survey, were the following:

Coupon refund offered by supplier
Reciprocal buying
Size of the supplier firm
Free samples offered by supplier
Weekend delivery

In some localities, the number of purveyors available to supply needs is very limited. Competitive bidding may not be possible, and the quality of service rendered may be poor. A difficult situation can develop, since there is no other practical source of supply, and since discontinuing buying would hurt both the seller and the buyer. Sometimes arrangements can be made for other purveyors not too far away to ship goods; when this is managed successfully, it may cause some nearby purveyors to shape up.

DETERMINING PURCHASING NEEDS

A menu dictates an operation's needs, and a buyer searches for a market that can supply those needs. After the right market is located, the various products available that meet the need are investigated. The proper product must be obtained to meet the production need and to yield the right kind of meal. Factors that affect purchasing requirements include the following:

Type and image of the establishment
Style of operation and system of service
Occasion for which the item is needed
Amount of storage available—dry, refrigerated, and frozen
Financial resources and buying policies of the organization
Availability, seasonality, price trends, and supply

In determining the right food item to meet a particular production need, the buyer should consider the skill of the employees, the processing method to be used, the suitability of the product for the required menu item, the storage life of the raw product, and other factors. The buyer weighs these factors and then searches the market to find a product that will best satisfy them. Usually, three general kinds of markets will be found to meet three principal foodservice needs: perishable, staple, and daily use or contract items.

Perishable Needs

The perishable market can supply fresh fruits, vegetables, meats, frozen foods, and dairy products. Prices vary, and so may supplies at times. It is wise to visit this market to inspect goods and ascertain market conditions. Phone calls may be helpful when an actual visit cannot take place. Informal methods of buying are used most often in this market. Perishables should be purchased to meet menu needs for a short period only.

Staple Needs

The staple food market can supply canned, bottled, and packaged products to be stored in dry storage without refrigeration. Formal or informal purchasing may be used. Because items are staples and can be stored, bid buying is frequent to take advantage of quantity prices. Staples packaged for foodservice use are generally in larger units than those packaged for the retail market. Because only 25 percent

of this market goes to foodservices, however, packaging may favor the retail market. Sometimes purchases may have to be made of smaller, retail-size units.

Daily Use Needs

Daily use or contract items are delivered frequently on a par stock basis: stocks are kept up to a desired level, and supply is almost automatic. Milk, bread, coffee, and ice cream are among the items supplied in this manner. Deliveries may be made daily, several times a week, or somewhat less often. Most items are perishable, and the supply kept on hand should be designed to last only until the next delivery time. The amounts remaining should be checked.

Quantity and Quality

Determining the quantity and quality of items to purchase is an important aspect of gauging the needs of an operation. The buyer should be informed by the chef or other members of the operation as to the quantity and quality of items needed. Management may establish quality guidelines and often may wish to supervise the ordering of quantities as well. After receiving this information, the buyer identifies the market and looks for the best possible item for the production need available at a good price. Delivery arrangements and other factors are usually handled by the buyer. Buying is not, therefore, the result of actions or decisions made by a single person, but is often the work of many. Buyers must act within the policies established by management in many matters relating to finance and delivery arrangements.

When considering the quantity needed, the buyer must keep certain factors in mind. First, the number of people to be served in a given period must be determined. Sales history data can provide this information. Portion sizes must also be known; these can be obtained from yield tests or standard portion lists (see appendix I). Knowing the weights and sizes of the various products helps the buyer estimate quantities needed within fairly precise limits (see table 6-1). Buyers need to know production results to be able to predict accurately how many portions a given amount of purchased goods will yield. They must also know the range of variability in yields. A purchase of veal may give one percentage of clear meat on one occasion and quite a different percentage on another. Cooking shrinkage may vary, too, causing predicted quantities to differ considerably from reality.

The desired quality of every product must be indicated to vendors so that the right product can be purchased. Grades, styles, appearance, composition, varieties, color, texture, size, relative absence of defects, and maturity should be specified. Quality standards should be established by management when the menu is first planned. Buying should then be a matter of following through to obtain products of the particular quality identified.

ESTABLISHING AND USING SPECIFICATIONS

Specifications describe the precise factors sought in an item in order for it to satisfy the production need. Specifications are usually given in writing and are filed in an easily accessible place. They present a constant reference point and are constantly

Table 6-1. Weights and Sizes of Common Cans and Jars

Can Size (industry term)	Average Net Weight or Fluid Measure per Can	Average Cups per Can	Cans per Case	Principal Products
No. 10	6 lb 3 oz (99 oz) to 7 lb 5 oz (117 oz)	12-13	6	Institution size—fruits, vegetables, and some other foods.
No. 3 cyl	51 oz (3 lb 3 oz) or 46 fl oz (1 qt 14 fl oz)	5¾	12	Institution size—condensed soups, some vegetables, and meat and poultry products. Economy family size—fruit and vegetable juices.
No. 2½	27 oz (1 lb 11 oz) to 29 oz (1 lb 13 oz)	3½	24	Family size—fruits and some vegetables.
No. 2 cyl	21 fl oz	3	24	Family size—juices and soups.
No. 2	20 oz (1 lb 4 oz) or 18 fl oz (1 pt 2 fl oz)	2½	24	Family size—juices, ready-to-serve soups, and some fruits.
No. 303	16 oz (1 lb) to 17 oz (1 lb 1 oz)		24 or 36	Small cans—fruits and vegetables, some meat and poultry products, and ready-to-serve soups.
No. 300	11 oz to 16 oz (1 lb)	1¾	24	Small cans—some fruits and meat products.
No. 2 (vacuum)	12 oz	1½	24	Principally for vacuum-pack corn.
No. 1 (picnic)	10½ to 12 oz	1¼	48	Small cans—condensed soups, some fruits, vegetables, meat, and fish.
8 oz	8 oz	1	48 or 72	Small cans—ready-to-serve soups, fruits, and vegetables.

NOTE: The net weight on can or jar labels differs among foods because of different densities of foods. For example, a No. 10 can contains 6 lb 3 oz sauerkraut or 7 lb 5 oz cranberry sauce. Meats, fish, and shellfish are known and sold by weight of contents of can.

being revised. If costs are given, their purpose is only to inform the buyer about what might have to be paid to get the desired quality. A maximum price allowable may be indicated.

Operations and management should define exactly what factors contribute to the overall adequacy of an ingredient to be used in a menu item. These factors can then be summarized to produce the specification. Size, grade, appearance factors, packaging, locality of production, and other elements may need to be defined. Trade and government specifications and standards relating to commodities should also be considered. Grade standards established by the federal government are the measures most often used, but at times trade or other standards may be used instead. Brands may be named to guarantee a certain quality. Good specifications simplify purchasing. The buyer and seller both know what is wanted when the specifications give all relevant facts. Better quality and lower prices follow when well-written specifications are used.

Standards of Quality

A quality standard indicates things such as maturity, flavor, and texture that contribute to eating satisfaction. A standard is a measure or benchmark used to evaluate quality, weight, value, or quantity. Standards have been established for many foods by the U.S. Department of Agriculture (USDA), the Department of Interior's Bureau of Fisheries, the Food and Drug Administration, and others.

Quality standards indicate the various characteristics of a specific grade of item. Three or more grades may be named, and in each the quality characteristics (for instance, maturity or texture) will differ to some extent. Not all items are graded on the basis of the same factors. Grades can be certified by federal graders; many meats, for instance, move on the market under federal grades. Eggs, butter, poultry, fresh and processed fruits, and vegetables are often graded. The purpose of quality standards is to make buying and selling more efficient by providing a means by which buyers and sellers can assess the quality of the items for sale

without having to examine them. When the grade of an item is known, it is easier to agree on a selling price.

Different grades are used on the market. Federal grades consist of Manufacturing or Processing, Wholesale, and Consumer. Foodservices usually use the Wholesale grades but sometimes may move into the Consumer ones. Trade grades also exist on the market—for example, the butter scores of 93, 92, 90, and 89. Some trade grades have been taken over by the government, such as Fancy, Choice (Extra Standard), and Standard for processed foods. Trade grade names are gradually being dropped; thus, the grades Fancy, Choice (Extra Standard), and Standard are being dropped for processed foods, and the grades A, B, and C are only used for first, second, and third quality. Butter trade scores are fast disappearing as the market focuses exclusively on AA, A, B, and C grades. Egg trade grades are seldom used. Only meat grades seem to be secure, although perhaps in the future these too will be subject to replacement by a different grade set, such as A, B, and C or No. 1, No. 2, and No. 3.

Voluntary and Mandatory Standards

Most grade standards are voluntary, which means that the item is not required to carry a grade. In fact, most processed fruits and vegetables, processed meats, and fresh fruits and vegetables do not carry a grade. Other items are graded, but only because the producer or packer wishes them to be—not because regulations require it. A shield is often used to indicate a grade stamp, and within the shield appears the grade of the item (see fig. 6-3). Both the USDA and the Bureau of Fisheries in the Department of Interior are responsible for assigning grades. The latter grades fish products only; the USDA has divisions that grade meats, poultry, fresh fruits and vegetables, cereals, processed fruits and vegetables, and other food items.

Because some items vary in quality more than others, a different number of grades may have to be used. Thus, some canned juice standards have only two grades, whereas beer standards have eight. The number of grades depends on what it takes to move items on the market. Federal standards define

This USDA grade shield may be on the wrapper or on a wing tag on chickens, turkeys, ducks, and geese.

This is the USDA grade shield used on butter. It is printed on the carton and on the wrappers of ¼-lb sticks of butter.

Prime beef is the best and most expensive grade. Not many stores sell it. Most cuts graded Prime are very tender, juicy, and flavorful.

This U.S. grade shield may be used on canned, frozen, or dried fruits or vegetables. It is also used on a few related products, such as frozen concentrated juices, jams, and jellies.

Steaks and roasts of Choice grade are tender and juicy and have a good flavor.

Beef graded Select is not as juicy and flavorful as Prime or Choice, but it is fairly tender and has less fat than either of the higher grades.

The U.S. Extra Grade shield may be used on instant nonfat dry milk. It means that the milk has a sweet and pleasing flavor, and dissolves immediately when mixed with water.

Beef graded Standard has very little fat and a mild flavor. It lacks juiciness but is fairly tender because it comes from young animals.

This is the USDA grade shield for eggs. It may be found on the carton.

Beef graded Commercial comes from older cattle and is not very tender. It needs long, slow cooking with moist heat (pot-roasting or braising). If cooked properly, it has a good, rich flavor.

Although most fresh fruits and vegetables are sold at wholesale on the basis of U.S. grades, not many are marked with the grade in the grocery store.

Figure 6-3. USDA grades used as standards in buying food.

factors that differentiate the quality levels in market products. Grade standards must be general enough to cover all kinds of products that may appear on the market. Thus, the grade standards for apples vary between apples grown in the state of Washington and those grown elsewhere, since the apples of the west take on more color. Peaches from Washington, California, Georgia, and Michigan differ significantly, and the standard must be broad enough to cover them all. Because a rather wide variation exists in the quality factors of citrus fruit, there are three standards: Florida, Texas, and California (including Arizona).

A brand often is specified to identify quality. Thus, many restaurants insist on Heinz catsup because of the product's known quality and because many customers recognize this quality and approve it. A brand is not based on minimum standards for tenderness, color, freedom from defects, maturity, and so forth as the government grades are: a brand is only the quality the manufacturer says it is. For this reason customers must sample the product often to see if it supplies the grade or quality they want. Brands are usually higher in price than unbranded items. Food buyers should accept only brands of reliable and established vendors.

There is a difference between a quality grade, which the producer or packer voluntarily chooses to have appear, and the mark of inspection for wholesomeness, which often must appear under the terms of mandatory standards set by the USDA and other agencies.

Meat and poultry carry a circular stamp in which is written "Inspected and Passed." A number within the circle indicates where the inspection occurred. This means that the item is fit for human consumption. Some meats and poultry cannot be graded until they have been inspected and passed for wholesomeness. The USDA largely administers certification for wholesomeness, on authority given it under the (recently revised) Meat Act.

All meat and poultry (including processed products) that move across state lines must be inspected and passed. The products must come from healthy birds or animals that have been handled and processed under strictly sanitary conditions. The products cannot be adulterated and must be truthfully packaged and labeled.

Other Standards

Two other standards have been established by federal agencies. One, the "standard of identity," indicates exactly what a food is. If a food does not conform to the established standard, it cannot be called by the common name. Thus, if a mixture of meat and vegetables does not contain 25 percent beef, it cannot be called beef stew. Minimum (and sometimes maximum) quantities of various ingredients are specified in the standard, and the food must satisfy the stated requirements. The Food and Drug Administration, part of the Department of Health and Human Services, has jurisdiction over the establishment of the standards of identity.

The second standard established by federal agency relates to standards of fill and weight. The term *fill* refers to the quantity that must be in packaged goods, which varies according to the product and its form of packaging. Official weights have been established for different containers. Thus, a barrel used to package flour must contain 196 lb (two 98-lb sacks). A cranberry barrel is smaller and must hold 100 lb. Bushels of various items must weigh no less than a stated number of pounds, and other measures must also conform. Various agencies administer standards of fill, but most such standards come under the jurisdiction of the USDA. The Department of Commerce regulates standards of weight and size.

The Treasury Department has jurisdiction over the various standards established for alcoholic beverages. Originally this administrative department was charged only with collecting taxes and enforcing laws relating to alcoholic beverages, but from there it moved on to establish standards for such things as quality, packaging, and identity.

If a product does not meet a standard established by the government, the label must say so. For example, if a can of fruit does not meet the standard of fill, the label must inform the buyer of this. Similarly, a product that does not meet the standard weight must carry a notice of this fact on the label. Foods that do not meet the standard of quality must carry a statement such as "Below standard in quality." This does not mean the food is unwholesome, only that it fails to meet established quality standards. Although many foods need not carry a statement of grade, a food that does not achieve the minimum standard of quality established for it must indicate this failure on its label.

Specification Writing

As was noted earlier, specifications describe in writing and in standard terms the ingredients needed to produce the item on the menu. Only after the operation's needs and the market offerings are known can the specification for an item be written. The specification should state exactly what is required to produce an item of the quality desired. Federal or trade standards of quality may be used, but these should only serve as models; usually, a foodservice has more specific needs than are named in these specifications. Thus, for example, the quality standard for fresh peaches may be too broad, raising the need for a narrower definition of quality. Since operations want items that meet special merchandising and quality needs, they write specifications that spell out these needs. For example, the Nut Tree Restaurant in California had a requirement for fresh pineapple that fell within a very narrow range of quality and, in fact, had to come from one specific area of Oahu in the Hawaiian Islands. The quality definition became so famous that it is now known as Nut Tree grade.

Writing the Specification

There are two major steps in writing a good specification: ascertaining the quality factors needed to give the right product and setting up the specification.

When the menu is planned, the quality of the items on it is established. For instance, suppose that a particular chicken breast dish of fine quality is planned. To obtain proper-size chicken breasts for the dish, the operation may need a 4-lb fryer of Grade A quality. Since only a few purveyors market a bird that is fed solely on milk mash (which pro-duces the very white, delicate meat needed for the item), the specification would also have to specify that only milk-mash-fed fryers are acceptable. The product also must be extremely fresh, so the specification should state that the birds must be fresh-killed. This means that delivery must be made within three days of slaughter, during which time the breasts must be held at 35°F (2°C). All details are covered in the specification so that the right product is obtained and no chances for error are introduced.

At times, a buyer or others concerned with defining the quality of the item needed may have to perform special tests to gain information. Four such tests can be used: raw food tests, canned food tests, butchering tests, and cooking tests.

Raw Food Tests. These tests determine the best count, weight, or quality of the product (usually a fruit or vegetable).

Canned Food Tests. These tests check the yields and costs of different canned or processed foods. They consider quality, drained weight, count density, clearness of syrup, and other quality or physical factors.

Butchering Tests. These cutting tests of meat, fish, and poultry determine portion costs after waste, trim, and by-products have been removed. The size of the portion and its appearance can also be judged. By preparing the item, the tester can judge its finished quality.

Cooking Tests. These tests determine final portion costs as served. The product should be taken as purchased and given the required pre-preparation treatment, then cooked, and then judged for portion size, appearance, quality, and any other factors (color, texture, form, and so on) that are considered important.

Once the characteristics required of the product are enumerated, the specification can be written. Usually food specifications include the following information:

Name of the item-this should be the name used for the item in the standard of identity; in meats, this would include the name of the cut plus the institutional meat purchase specification number; the name used should indicate clearly what is wanted.

Quantity of the item needed-this should be based on the factors previously discussed for deciding quantities.

Grade or brand wanted-this should to be stated in accordance with applicable standards; if a finer demarcation of quality is needed, appropriate details of this can be added.

Size of the item or number of items per package-this may be expressed, for example, as a 12- to 14-lb ham or as twenty-four No. 2 cans per case.

Unit size on which the seller's price is to be based-this may be a pound, a sack, a package, a case, or any other clearly defined unit.

Additional factors needed to get the exact item wanted-these may refer to geographical area of production, count size, drained weight, sieve size, packing medium, syrup density, color, style, or other relevant characteristics.

Figure 6-4 gives a sample specification for canned asparagus.

In writing a specification, some people like to add descriptive details such as "tender, succulent, dark red, and free from blemishes, broken slices, or end cuts." All of these factors, however, are included

---

Asparagus, canned, all green stalks or spears

10 cases

U.S. Fancy or Grade A

24/2's

Quote price per case.

Style shall be stalks not more than $3\frac{3}{4}$ inches in length; minimum drained weight shall be not less than 12 ounces; size of spears shall be extra large (mammoth). The product shall score 90 points or more. Pack shall be from current stocks. Inspector's certification of grade shall accompany invoice; all cases shall be marked with the certificate number.

Figure 6-4. Sample specification for canned asparagus.

---

in the standard for the grade; if the grade is stated, these characteristics must be present, since otherwise the product could not have obtained the grade named. Thus, it is superfluous to put such details in the specification—although some buyers like to add these just to remind vendors that they will be looking for these characteristics in the products they get. Specifications should be as brief and simple as possible, but they should not omit any essential factor needed to get the right item.

Using the Specification

The specification must be used properly to achieve the desired results. Having the specifications on file without using them accomplishes nothing. When specifications are used properly, the buyer, the receiving clerk, management, the storeroom personnel, and the purveyor all have copies and use them regularly in their daily jobs.

Copies of the specifications should be made available to all responsible personnel in written, printed, or computerized form. Copies filed alphabetically by food group can be kept in looseleaf notebooks, on 3×5 cards, or on computer disks. Today many of the best-run purchasing and receiving departments prefer to use computerized specifications.

Acceptance buying is used by some food services to purchase fresh, processed, or other foods. In particular, large buyers—state agencies, veterans' hospitals and federal agencies—tend to use this method. It requires that the vendor receive the specification and send the specified item to a federal inspector, who also has a copy of the specification, for approval. If the item meets the specification, the inspector stamps the invoice and package with a shield; if it does not, the inspector rejects it, and the vendor must send a replacement that does meet the specification.

Specifications should be subject to constant revision and scrutiny. Information about products purchased should flow back to the buyer and make clear where changes are necessary. New products regularly appear on the market, and these should be investigated to see if they offer improved quality or lower cost. As these are tested and approved, they should be used in place of the other product, and the specification should be revised to indicate the new preference.

DESIGNING PURCHASING PROCEDURES

Proper buying requires a great deal of communication among buyer, receiving clerks, accounting personnel, and others. Management should take care to establish fluid lines of communication in this sphere to ensure that good products reach the consumer. It is usually the buyer's responsibility to establish purchasing process procedures as well as to monitor the procurement process.

The purchasing process involves a considerable amount of detail, including the exact item needed, the specifications for it, and the delivery requirements. The principal function, ordering, is most often accomplished through what is called a *purchase order,* which may be a handwritten or computer-generated document. On this form, the number, size, weight, and other pertinent information about the item are listed. Each form is numbered for reasons of security and consistency, and a proper signature is always required prior to purchase authorization. Generally, four copies of the form are produced: one for retention by the purchasing department; one for the accounting department; one for the purveyor; and one for the receiving department, to advise it of the order prior to delivery of the product. In some cases, a signed vendor's copy is returned in advance of delivery; at other times, the copy accompanies the delivery. Regular purchase orders cover a single delivery on a specified date, while open-delivery purchase orders arrange for the purchase of items over a period of time (see fig. 6-5). Weekly and daily items are often purchased by open-delivery purchase orders.

A purchase record should also be maintained, listing each item ordered, its price, its purveyor, and any other information needed (see fig. 6-6). This purchase price record is often kept on index cards, but increased use of microcomputers has allowed it to be kept on computer files as well. Various computer software packages are available

that make recording purchasing information both fast and efficient.

RECEIVING*

All too often, the benefits of an excellent purchasing plan are lost because of poor receiving. It does little good to perform careful calculations of quantities required or to specify the exact quality needed, and then order from a purveyor who should be able to supply your needs, if the receiving clerk takes any amount and any quality of goods that come to the door. Food cannot be sold profitably if it arrives in short weight or poor condition, or if it does not arrive at all.

Receiving Practices

Receiving practices may vary with different foodservice companies, but the following general principles governing the process are standard:

1. Check the invoice to see whether or not the products delivered agree with it.
2. Inspect the merchandise to determine whether or not it conforms with the purchase order and specifications.
3. Tag all meats with the date of receipt, the weight, and any other information needed to properly identify the delivery.
4. List all items received on the daily receiving report.
5. Accept the merchandise by signing the invoice and returning a copy to the deliverer.
6. Store or deliver the items received properly.

In large foodservices, receiving is a highly specialized, full-time job that should be supervised by the accounting department. In some foodservices, however, a full-time receiving clerk may not be needed, in which case the job may be combined with one in the storeroom. Proper authority and

*This section is adapted from Lukowski, *Receiving Food in Foodservice Establishments.*

PURCHASE ORDER

No. 1124

HAPPY COW DAIRY COMPANY
(NAME OF PURVEYOR)
123 Milk Can Lane
(ADDRESS OF PURVEYOR)
New Haven, Connecticut 06511
(PURVEYOR'S CITY AND STATE)

TO PURVEYOR: OUR PURCHASE ORDER NUMBER (ABOVE) MUST BE SHOWN ON ALL YOUR INVOICES AND PACKAGES.

DELIVERY DATE (S):
    May 1-31,1987

DELIVERY INSTRUCTIONS: Deliver fresh Mon. thru Fri. no later than 6 A.M. to storeroom receiving area.

TERMS: 1% 10-Net 30 days

FOR OFFICE USE ONLY:

AUTHORIZED SIGNATURE

CHARGE TO (ACCOUNT):	TOTAL TO DATE:	BALANCE:

SERIAL MODEL, OR CIR SPEC. NUMBER	ITEM	QUANTITY ORDERED	QUANTITY RECEIVED	UNIT PRICE	EXTENSION
300.1	Milk Fresh Homo. 1 gal. Norris	2100 Gal	2250 Gal	$1.04	$2340.00

Date Received for Payment: 6/4/87
Prices, Extensions and Total Verified by: RC 6/4/87
Date Paid: 26.43
Check Number: W. a. H.
Bursar's Initials:

SUB TOTAL:	$2340.00
LESS DISCOUNT:	$23.40
PURCHASE ORDER TOTAL:	$2316.60

SHIPMENT RECEIVED AND VERIFIED BY: 5/31/87	SHIPMENT RECEIVED AND VERIFIED BY:
CULINARY INSTITUTE REPRESENTATIVE (DATE)	PURCHASE REQUEST ORIGINATOR (DATE)

Figure 6-5. Sample purchase order, with line-by-line explanation of blanks.

Name and Address: Used for the name, address, city, state, and zip code of the purveyor.

Delivery Date (s): Filled in as required for regular or open-delivery purchase orders.

Delivery Instructions: The specific building, section, or address where delivery is desired.

For Office Use Only: For operations maintaining separate cost accounts.

Terms: Used to record applicable discount or other terms, as specified by the vendor.

Authorizing Signature: Signature of the person authorized to approve purchase orders.

Serial, Model, or Specification Number: On purchase orders for equipment, filled in with the serial, model, or catalog number; on purchase orders for food, filled in with the specification number.

Item: An accurate, complete description of the item desired; if a specification number is used, the description may be shortened, since the specification itself gives complete details.

Quantity Ordered: The quantity needed and the correct unit of sale (such as 50 lbs, 25 doz, 4 gal).

Quantity Received: The exact quantity received; on open-delivery purchase orders, all delivery slips for the period must be added, and the *total quantity received* must be recorded.

Unit Price: The dollar and cents figure *per unit.*

Extension: The number of units received multiplied by the unit price.

Subtotal: The figures in the Extension column summed.

Less Discount: The amount of discount (if any), entered in red ink or in parentheses.

Purchase Order Total: Remainder when discount is subtracted from Subtotal.

Shipment Received and Verified by (Culinary Institute Representative): The signature, in ink, of the person actually receiving the merchandise.

Shipment Received and Verified by (Purchase Request Originator): Some establishments, when purchasing equipment and certain other items, require a purchase order request as authorization to prepare a purchase order. If a purchase order request is required, this section would be signed by the originator of the request. This would relieve the actual receiver from responsibility for having received the merchandise. This section would not be used on food purchase orders.

---

* Fixed space is required for constant needs and does not vary in any operation. Janitorial storage areas, employee toilets, restrooms, lounge area, and so on would be found in this space.

responsibility must be given to the individual in charge of receiving, including jurisdiction over those who help receive and store delivered items.

At least seven practices can be identified as essential to good receiving:

1. *Be ready for the delivery.* The foodservice, the customer, and food quality (especially that of perishables) all benefit if receiving is efficient and moves with dispatch and order. Being ready helps to make this occur.

2. *Check the merchandise thoroughly.* Check all merchandise to determine whether it meets the criteria named in the purchase order, specification, or other receiving document. Open cases if they are discolored or damaged or appear to have been tampered with. Date canned goods before storing them, or date them as they are placed on shelves. Arrange goods so as to ensure first-in first-out (FIFO) use. Many systems have been devised for checking produce quality, but careful exami-

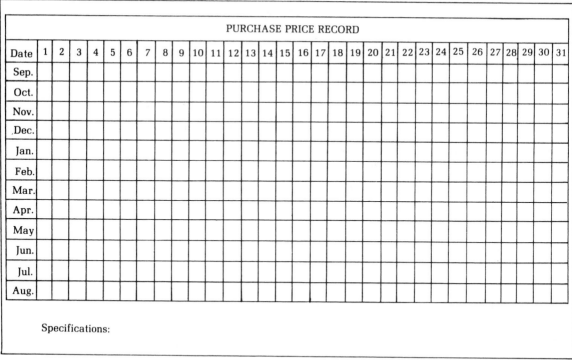

Figure 6-6. Sample form for a purchase-price record.

nation is at the core of every one. Many receivers select a typical fruit or vegetable and cut it in half to check such characteristics as juice, absence of rust, and taste. If quality cannot be thoroughly checked because of insufficient time at the receiving dock or for other reasons, a thorough check for quality should follow soon thereafter. The supplier should agree ahead of time to this and should make good any deficiency.

3. *Weigh items separately.* When receiving bulk items, remove excess paper, cheesecloth, or ice. A scale weighs anything and everything placed on it. Excessive wrapping or ice adds superfluous weight. A good practice in checking the net weight of items packed in ice is to weigh them just before preparation. But in any case, all iced items should be unpacked at least once a week and checked for net weight.

4. *Weigh meat items separately, never together.* Meat is the most costly item received, and weighing each item separately can catch errors that could significantly increase food cost. Items should not be weighed together because 10 lb of missing tenderloins (for example) are not offset by 10 lb of ground beef.

5. *Tag meats on delivery.* This practice prevents disputes over weights with the supplier, the kitchen staff, or the butcher. Tagging meats also reduces the chance of spoilage or excessive weight loss, since the tag can be dated for FIFO (see fig. 6-7). It also simplifies calculations of food costs, since a good record of meat withdrawals can be obtained from the tags taken from meat as it comes from inventory.

6. *Check for quality.* Checking for quality is often neglected by the receiving clerk. It is important to see that the grade and quality of the

Figure 6-7. Sample meat tag.

merchandise agree with those shown on the invoice, purchase order, or other receiving document. Care is especially necessary when there are grades within grades.

7. *Store items promptly.* Check and store perishable items first. Exposure to high room temperatures can lead to serious loss of quality or rapid spoilage. The quicker all merchandise is stored, the less chance it has to spoil, deteriorate, or get lost.

Because of large orders or the press of other duties, the receiving clerk does not always have time to make a complete check for quality; moreover, the clerk may not be capable of performing such a check. Meat, for example, is extremely difficult to judge and requires checking by a person who is

trained in meats. Quality checks can often be made on the basis of tests of random samples. For example, if ten cases of lettuce are received, the clerk could inspect several of the cases. It is wise to ensure that receiving clerks get training in quality determination so that they will be able to tell whether the quality of received items meets the operation's specifications or purchase order criteria.

Invoice Receiving

The most frequently used receiving method is called *invoice receiving*. In this method, the invoice accompanying the delivery is checked against the merchandise, along with the specifications, the purchase order, the quotation and order sheet, or other relevant document. Any discrepancies are noted and brought to the attention of the delivery-person, and action is taken immediately to correct the invoice. The quantity and quality of the products delivered should be checked against the purchase order and other receiving documents. This method is quick and economical; if correctly carried out, it is a fairly sure way of receiving goods properly.

Blind-Check Receiving

A blind receiving method involves giving the clerk a blank invoice or purchase order listing the incoming merchandise but omitting the quantities, quality, weights, and prices. The receiving clerk must insert these numbers into the order on the basis of a check of the delivery. This approach forces the receiving clerk to make a serious check of the delivery and not merely to glance at it to affirm that the goods probably agree with the figures on the invoice. If no weight is on the invoice, the receiving clerk must weigh the items to get an accurate figure. A count is also required, as is a quality check. Another invoice with quantities, weights, quality, and prices is mailed to the accounting office. This invoice is checked against the one from the receiving clerk, and the figures in both are verified. Blind receiving is an accurate method of checking merchandise and verifying deliveries, but it takes longer and costs more, since it requires the clerk to prepare a careful and complete record of all incoming merchandise.

Partial-Blind Receiving

A hybrid of the invoice receiving and blind receiving methods is called *partial-blind receiving*. In this method, the receiving clerk is furnished itemized purchase orders, invoices, or other receiving documents with only the quantities omitted. When the merchandise is checked, the receiving clerk lists the quantity of each item in the space provided. This method is slower but more accurate than invoice receiving, and it is faster but less accurate than blind receiving. It is essential in blind receiving and partial-blind receiving either that the supplier's invoice does not accompany the merchandise or that the information on quantities be omitted or made invisible by a black area where such information would appear. Otherwise, there is no guarantee that the receiving clerk's numbers represent independent research.

Detailed purchase specifications should be available for all merchandise received. These should be duplicates of the ones used for purchasing. If tomatoes are ordered from a specification that reads: "Tomatoes, US No. 1, fresh, 5×6, pink, 20 lb minimum to the lug," the receiving clerk should be able to check grade, ripeness, and number in the case as well as weight. There are usually three layers of tomatoes in a lug, and if there are five tomatoes per row and six rows, there will be ninety tomatoes in the lug at an anticipated net weight of 20 lb. Good specifications permit good checking. It also is helpful to show minimum weights of packing containers in a chart or on some other form. The net weight of spinach and other greens should not be less than 18 lb, and the container weight should be added to this. Florida oranges should have a net weight of 45 pounds per $\frac{4}{5}$ bushel carton, plus the weight of the container. Having such information can help make receiving easier and quicker. Catching discrepancies is also favored by such a system. A case of whiskey that is missing one bottle, for example, can quickly be detected if it is weighed and the total contained weight is about 3 lb less than it should be.

Forms and Records

Recording incoming deliveries is as important as checking their quality and quantity. The form or style of doing this may vary. The three forms most commonly used for this purpose are the daily receiving report, the substitution invoice, and the request-for-credit memorandum.

Receiving Clerk's Daily Report

The receiving clerk's daily report lists the merchandise received in a form suitable for checking against the supplier's invoice (see fig. 6-8). The daily report should list the following items:

Date of delivery
Invoice or purchase order number
Supplier
Number of units
Quantity received
Article
Unit price (omitted in blind receiving)
Total amount extension (omitted in blind receiving)
Distribution of the delivery

Deliveries of food are divided into two groups: food direct and food stores. Many purchases are sent directly to the kitchen for use, which saves time by omitting the steps of storage and withdrawal. It also helps the foods involved retain their freshness. This is charged out on the receiving report as a food direct delivery, and it goes immediately into the cost of food for the day. Purchases sent to the storeroom or to meat or produce refrigerators are classed as food stores and become a part of inventory. If the receiving record is used as a consolidation of food direct and food stores for each day's deliveries, the consolidated amount must be equal to the total amount for the day's deliveries.

Substitution Invoice

A substitution invoice is primarily used when merchandise arrives without an invoice. It contains practically the same information as the receiving record (see fig. 6-9). Indeed, some operations

RECEIVING CLERK'S DAILY REPORT

INVOICE NO.	FROM WHOM PURCHASED	UNIT	AMT.	ARTICLE	UNIT PRICE	TOTAL AMT.	FOOD DIRECT	FOOD STORES
				TOTAL FOOD RECEIVED				

SIGNATURE

Figure 6-8. Sample form for a receiving clerk's daily report.

consider it a duplication of effort and as a result do not use it. When the supplier's invoice reaches the accounting office, the substitution invoice is compared with it as a basis for verifying and approving the delivery.

Request-for-Credit Memorandum

The request-for-credit memorandum, which is usually made in triplicate, lists discrepancies such as shortages in quantity or failure of the quality to conform to specification (see fig. 6-10). The original is sent to the supplier, usually with the signed delivery invoice. A copy is retained by the receiving clerk and another is sent to the accounting office. If a credit memorandum is submitted because

of unsatisfactory merchandise, the following steps are usually taken by the receiving clerk:

1. Write up the request-for-credit memorandum, listing the reason why it is being made out.
2. Return the merchandise immediately.
3. Note on the invoice the reason for returning the merchandise.
4. Notify proper authorities so that menu changes can be made, if needed.

A good practice, when possible, is to have the delivery person sign the invoice for deficient merchandise. This can save explanations, telephone calls, and disputes.

SUBSTITUTE INVOICE

FROM: Farmer Joe's Meats   DATE: 3/20/88

QUANTITY	UNIT	DESCRIPTION	AMOUNT	
25	lbs.	Ground Round @ $.84	21	00

RECEIVED BY:_____John Black_____

Figure 6-9. Sample form for a substitute invoice.

Purchase Invoice Stamp

In some operations, a purchase invoice stamp is used on all incoming invoices (see fig. 6-11). The receiving clerk stamps and dates the invoice, indicating receipt, and signs or initials the line "Quantity O.K.," showing that the correct quantity has been received. This invoice usually goes to purchasing for approval of prices and other factors, and it is then sent to accounting, where the invoice is compared with the receiving clerk's daily report. Then, if all checks pass, the invoice is approved for final payment.

EVALUATING THE PURCHASING TASK

Even after the food is served and the profit is made, the purchasing task is not over. How well was the purchasing done? Could something better have been used? What was the yield? Could quality be improved? Were values purchased that were not necessary? Were other values needed? Every purchasing system should include a good feedback arrangement so that the purchasing task can be improved. Just as recipes and specifications are constantly under revision, so should the entire purchasing procedure be. New products come onto the market, and new purveyors appear who may give better service, prices, or quality than their competitors. Many markets are highly dynamic, and planners must constantly be on the alert to note changes and modify the purchasing system used.

Operations often do value analysis—an analysis of what is needed against what is obtained. Value represents quality divided by price, or $V = Q \div P$. If the quality of a purchase is given a score of 4 and the price is $2, the value in this case is 2 ($4 \div 2 = 2$). If a search of the market shows that a product of

OPERATION'S NAME AND ADDRESS

TO: _____   No. _____

ADDRESS: _____

CITY, STATE: _____   DATE: _____

GENTLEMEN: Please send Credit Memorandum for the following:

INVOICE NO.	ITEM	QUAN.	UNIT OF SALE	UNIT PRICE	EXTENSION
				Total	

REASON:

BY: _____

TITLE: _____

Figure 6-10. Sample form for a request for credit memorandum.

equal quality can be obtained for 50¢ less, the value of the latter product is 2.67 (4 ÷ 1.5 = 2.67).

Large factories set up value analysis departments. The personnel in these departments scrutinize what is purchased to see if a better product might be available, if some items are included that need not be, and if a better price might be obtained. The tendency of organizations to add such a department indicates that value analysis does help. It is not necessary, however, to set up a whole department. Buyers and others in the operation can practice value analysis themselves. By constantly seeking to improve the products purchased, they constantly upgrade purchasing performance.

PURCHASING AND RECEIVING BY COMPUTER

Today more and more foodservice operations have become computerized, through the use of microcomputers or through outside services. In

| Order No.   Rec'g No. |
| Date Rec'd _____ |
| Quantity O.K. _____ |
| Quality & Price O.K. ____ |
| Ext. & Footing O.K. _____ |
| Entered _____ |
| O.K. for Payment_____ |

| DATE REC'D_____ |
| QUANTITY O.K. _____ |
| PRICES O.K._____ |
| EXTENSIONS O.K. _____ |
| APPROVED BY_____ |

Figure 6-11. Sample purchase invoice stamps.

purchasing and receiving departments, great strides have been made in the last ten years toward reducing labor costs through computer automation. In the most sophisticated, high-volume operations, lasers scan the UPC numbers of incoming boxed orders and automatically record the entries into the data bank of the computer for comparison with the purchase order and for inclusion in the inventory. While such devices may be beyond the means of all but the largest operations, computerization by keyboard entry of the products received is not.

Perhaps the principal use of the computer in purchasing and receiving is in inventory control, verification of purchase orders, and par stock monitoring. Inventory control is achieved through connecting point-of-sale (cash register) data with storage files. Each time an item is purchased (or upon verification at the end of the shift, if so desired), a corresponding item is deleted from the inventory. Thus, the current inventory levels are monitored perpetually, and at any time the purchasing agent can ascertain the need for replenishment in any area by examining that area's inventory level.

Using the computer to process purchase and receiving orders has also become fairly widespread. In this system, each time a delivery is made, the delivery receipt is matched against the purchase order form on the computer for verification of size, weight, price, number of units, and so on. If the items do not match, the operator is alerted to the discrepancy. Once the delivery receipt is matched to a purchase order, the items are entered into the computer, and the inventory is immediately upgraded.

Using the computer for par stock ordering fol-

lows the same pattern, except that, as products drop below par levels in the inventory, a note is added on the printout or screen to alert the purchasing agent of the depleted stores, thus ensuring prompt reordering and maintenance of the needed par stock. Many programs have been devised that also provide for an automatic printout of needed items, by quantity, to create an immediate order form. Permanent records of the purchasing department, such as names of purveyors, purchase prices, and dates products were ordered and received, are also easily kept on file by means of the computer.

Another advantage of the computer in purchasing and receiving is its ability to perform rapid comparisons. By designing a program to store prices by purveyor, for example, a buyer can rapidly access information that can be used to identify the pricing trends of various purveyors. The same is true with respect to such information as timeliness of delivery, quality, and product omissions—all keys to making decisions on which purveyors to use.

STORING FOODS

Once food has been received, it must be properly handled to prevent waste and deterioration. While in many cases the responsibility for storing and issuing food is assigned to the same person who handles receiving and purchasing, in larger operations these may be separate jobs.

The task of properly storing and issuing food can pay for itself if it is conscientiously carried out by staff and management. While most manufacturing firms have recognized the importance of proper storage, many foodservices have not yet done so. Many storerooms in the industry are poorly planned and organized, poorly lit, and improperly secured— all of which contribute to lost time and money. In the worst cases, food products get stored in places where they are not found for months, by which time they are completely deteriorated. In many cases, the storerooms represent design afterthoughts and are put in inconvenient areas that would otherwise be surplus space. The main storage area often turns out to be the basement, where conduits, hot-water pipes, and other items offer both physical obstacles and high heat levels. Since the temperature in dry storage areas should not exceed 80°F (27°C) at any time, the placement of storage in relation to boilers, condensers, and heating units is an important issue. A storeroom should also be planned to promote smooth workflow, ease of maintenance, good security, and the preservation of value.

The correct storage temperature and storage humidity vary for different foods. If these are not kept at correct levels, an operator is inviting the outbreak of a food-borne disease. At the same time, a climate that is too dry in refrigerated or freezer storage can dehydrate the food and diminish its quality. Each of the three types of storage—dry, refrigerated, and frozen or low-temperature—has its own requirements for proper maintenance.

Dry Storage

A well-lighted, well-ventilated, dry, cool area is needed for good dry storage. It should be free of insects and rodents and should be clean, orderly, and well-managed. The dry storeroom usually holds canned goods, flour, cereals, spices, sugar, and even some oils and shortenings (in sealed cans). The best location for it is near the receiving station and the kitchen, so that long hauls are not required and security supervision can be maintained.

Temperatures in the dry storage area should be between 50° and 75°F (10° and 24°C), with a minimum of 40°F (7°C) and a maximum of 80°F (27°C). Proper temperatures preserve flavor and nutritive value and reduce waste and food spoilage.

Perishables such as potatoes, onions, fruits, and some vegetables need good ventilation and a temperature within the range from 40° to 55°F (4.5° to 13°C). They should be stored off the floor and away from the wall. Proper stacking and good arrangement on racks or skids can help facilitate movement of food items in and out. Bottom shelving levels should be at least 10 inches off the floor to ensure adequate ventilation and freedom from contamination by floor soil or water, as well as to

allow for cleaning underneath. For adequate ventilation, all shelving should be at least 2 inches away from the wall, giving air room to circulate in the back. Such procedures offer the best chance for temperature control and for the elimination of odor transfers, moisture buildup, and rapid food deterioration.

Rodents and insects can cause heavy damage. Because these pests carry disease, all shipments should be inspected for their presence, and infested shipments should be refused. Vigilance and constant effort are necessary to keep the storeroom free of vermin.

Cartons should be stacked so as to prevent creating spaces that might serve as nesting places for mice or rats. Insecticides or rodenticides should be used only by qualified personnel, and poisonous materials should never be stored where food is stored or prepared. Poisons should be stored in a custodian's closet, in the furnace room, or in a locked cabinet; containers should be clearly marked and handled only when necessary. Poisonous materials include drain cleaners, lye, acids, insecticides, rat poisons, bug bombs, fly sprays, and roach powders.

Managing dry storage properly requires planning and time. The responsibility for such management should be given to one individual who has complete control. No unauthorized personnel should be admitted to the dry storage area. Among the duties of the person in charge of dry storage are the following:

1. Keep the storeroom clean. At least once a week, the floor, tables, platforms, and shelves should be thoroughly cleaned. The floor should be swept and mopped according to schedule. A floor that slants toward drains facilitates mopping and drainage.

2. Inspect all shipments for damage, rodent or insect infestation, and spoilage, and take appropriate action if any is found. For example, the receiving station should be told to inspect items received more thoroughly. In addition, the purveyor might be warned, or the goods returned.

3. Place food in the storeroom as quickly as possible.
4. Date all packages.
5. Stack foods of a kind together to ensure good storeroom organization.
6. Place oldest stock in front and issue it first (FIFO). If the food items are stored in bulk, the bin containing them should be cleaned, and the new stock should be placed at the bottom of the bin. (This applies to drawers and bins in cooks' and bakers' tables, as well.)
7. Take frequent inventories.
8. Check frequently for evidence of damage, spoilage, broken or torn packages, and bulging or leaking cans. If any are found, they should be removed immediately, and the area should be cleaned thoroughly to prevent contamination of other foods.

Nonfood items that are stored in dry storage places include paper goods and reserve supplies of utensils and dishes. Cleaning supplies should have a separate storage place. Clean towels and uniforms should be neatly stored in metal cabinets, drawers, or other protected areas, away from dust and insects. Soiled linens and uniforms should be kept in hampers, laundry nets, or bags at appropriate points throughout the operation. They should be transported frequently to the laundry or to the place from which laundry trucks can take them away. Workers' personal belongings should be stored in spaces set aside especially for them, such as locker rooms—but not in the food storage area.

Refrigerated Storage

Sufficient and proper refrigeration is very important. Many sanitary codes require that the local health department approve all new refrigeration equipment prior to its use in a foodservice. The health department should be consulted before purchase is made of refrigerators or walk-ins to see if they meet required standards. The following perishable foods should be held under refrigeration until needed:

FRESH FOODS	PROCESSED FOODS
Meat	Vegetable or fruit salads
Fish	Custards
Poultry	Gravies
Vegetables	Sauces such as hollandaise
Fruits (except	Sweet dessert sauces that
tropical ones)	can ferment
Eggs	Condiments that are
Dairy foods	perishable
	Cooked foods
	(especially meats)
	Foods prepared in advance
	Carry-over foods

Walk-in refrigerators provide most of an operation's refrigerated storage because they typically have more permanent storage space than do reach-in units. Reach-in units are often used when refrigeration is needed in a local area near a work center. Six factors usually dictate refrigeration needs: space needed, sanitation, air circulation, temperature, placement, and general practices and procedures.

Space Needed

The space needed for refrigerated storage depends on the number of meals served, the type of service, merchandising practices, the food itself, and delivery schedules. Table 6-2 lists recommended minimum refrigeration space requirements for an average-size full-menu restaurant (not including beverage cooling or frozen foods).

Sanitation

Many foods will deteriorate, spoil, or become contaminated if they are not kept refrigerated. Clean

Table 6-2. Minimum Refrigeration Space Needed, Not Including Beverage Cooling or Frozen Foods

Number of Meals Served Daily	Recommended Capacity
75 to 150	20 cubic feet
150 to 250	45 cubic feet
250 to 350	60 cubic feet
350 to 500	90 cubic feet

refrigerated areas also help reduce the risk of food loss. Good cleaning habits include the following:

1. Wipe up any spilled food immediately.
2. Remove shelves, drip pans, meat hooks, ice trays, and containers, and wash them frequently with warm water containing a good detergent. Rinse and dry.
3. Defrost when any buildup occurs on coils or cooling surfaces. This improves efficiency and reduces operating costs.
4. Wash refrigerated area interiors often with warm water and a good detergent.
5. Wash rubber gaskets on doors (if present) with warm water and a good detergent or mild soap. This increases their life.
6. Wash the exterior of refrigerators with warm water and a good detergent.
7. Flush drainpipes with hot water and baking soda.
8. Retain a reliable service to clean, lubricate, and check mechanical refrigeration equipment periodically.
9. Check hinges, latches, gaskets, and other parts frequently.

Air Circulation

Air circulation is a must if the refrigerator unit is to work properly. Food items should not be overcrowded in the unit, and adequate space should be left between each product. Shelves should not be covered with paper in the reach-in unit, and no products should be stored against the wall or on the floor of a walk-in unit. Cold air should reach all items at all times.

Temperature

Temperatures in different parts of a refrigerated area may vary. The most perishable foods should be stored in the coldest areas, which are near the bottom (since cold air settles). Another cold area is located close to the coils. A thermometer should be located in the warmest area and checked frequently.

In some operations, separate refrigerators are used for various food groups. When this is the case, the ideal storage temperatures for each refrigerator are as indicated in table 6-3. A refrigerator-temperature record book may be maintained if needed (see fig. 6-12). Some refrigeration equipment has automatic temperature recorders. Unnec-

Table 6-3. Ideal Temperatures for Various Foods

Food Group	Temperature Range
Fruits	45° to 50°F
Vegetables, eggs, processed foods, pastries	40° to 45°F
Dairy products	38° to 40°F
Fresh meats	34° to 38°F
Fresh poultry, fish, seafood	32° to 36°F
Frozen foods	−10° to 0°F

Date	4/15/88		4/16		4/17		4/18		4/19		4/20	
Time	9	3	9	3	9	3	9	3	9	3	9	3
Freezer	0	−1	0	−1	+1	0	−1	0	0	+1	−1	−1
Fresh fish	33	34	34	36	33	35	33	32	35	33	32	34
Vegetables	43	41	43	42	41	41	40	40	42	43	42	42
Dairy	38	39	38	40	40	39	40	38	38	39	38	40

Figure 6-12. Sample refrigerator temperature record that has been completed twice daily for six days.

essary door opening should be avoided, since this warms the refrigerator and increases power consumption. Walk-ins may be equipped with reach-in doors to reduce the amount of travel in and out. To save energy, some foodservices may find it desirable to schedule all entries for purposes of storing and withdrawing foods. Most foodservice operations have successfully attached door closures to refrigerator doors to ensure that they close upon exit.

Placement

The location of refrigeration units is extremely important. Since the amount of time spent fetching items for use in foodservice kitchens has been estimated to consume 50 percent of total labor hours, any design that brings the refrigeration units closer to the user is a great labor-saver.

The location of the compressors and condensers is also important. These units should have good ventilation to ensure the necessary airflow for cool operation, and they should be as close to the refrigeration units as possible. Many foodservice operations have chosen to place the compressors and condensers on the roof of the building—perhaps a good location except from the point of view of serviceability—or at another outside location. If this is done, winterization controls must be installed to keep the units from freezing in cold weather, and housings must be constructed to protect the equipment from rain and snow. A long run from the compressor to refrigerated areas consumes energy and should be avoided. Most health departments require drains for refrigeration units to be trapped, rather than be run direct into sewer lines, to prevent backup into the water supply. Free-standing refrigerators should be at least 6 inches from the wall for cleanability and air circulation, unless they are mounted on casters for moving. All units should be either sealed to the floor or mounted 6 to 10 inches off the floor for cleaning. Refrigerators should not be located near cooking equipment, and all hot pipes nearby should be well-insulated.

General Practices and Procedures

The following practices and procedures should be among those set up for the use and care of refrigeration units:

1. Inspect deliveries before putting them into refrigeration units. Do not put spoiled, dirty, or vermin-infested products into the refrigerator.
2. Put food in as quickly as possible.
3. Shelves nearest the cooling unit or at the bottom are coolest. Use them for milk, meats, poultry, fish, and prepared dishes that contain these food items.
4. Use the refrigerator for perishable foods only. Jellies and tropical fruits such as bananas, pineapples, papayas, and avocados may not require refrigeration. The same is true for many root vegetables such as potatoes and onions.
5. Remove outside wrappings, which may contain soil or harmful bacteria. Packaged luncheon meats, butter, and cheese should be placed in airtight containers to prevent drying and discoloration.
6. Keep processed food and carry-overs covered to prevent them from drying out or transferring odors. This practice also prevents contamination from things dropping into them.
7. Be careful when placing warm food into the refrigerator. Food at the unit's center may retain enough heat to spoil. Warm food raises the interior temperature and may cause other foods to spoil. To cool food quickly, place the container in cold water or crushed ice, and stir frequently until it has cooled. Then cover the container, and place it under refrigeration. If a quantity of hot food must be refrigerated, make sure that it is stirred frequently while cooling. Such food should be poured into pans no deeper than 2 to 4 inches.
8. Store foods that have strong odors in tight containers.

Frozen Storage

Frozen storage needs have been increasing over the pasty thirty years, most recently because of the large number of new products that are prepared and packaged in advance and require freezer storage. Jule Wilkinson (1969) summed up the trends and the processes as follows:

The increase in frozen food items on the menu means more frozen food cabinet and walk-in space in foodservice layouts. More equipment for holding is in evidence in operations generally; in many instances equipment for on-premise blast freezing has also been installed.

The rising curve in use of frozen food is traceable to these factors: improved scheduling of production, portion control, labor costs, consistent quality, advantages in limited menus. Operators must have the frozen food storage space to buy advantageously and to provide needed variety.

Aware of the dollars that can be made through use of convenience foods, many operators are pre-preparing foods in their own kitchens on slow days for use on busier days, a practice that can level the work load and help hold the line on labor costs.

It is now agreed that the faster food freezes, the better it turns out, since sharp freezing keeps ice crystals small and undetectable. Actually, food freezing should be a 3-step process: (1) refrigeration to cool; (2) sharp freezing; (3) holding at low temperature.

When foods are frozen in areas which also contain stored frozen foods, variations can occur in the held foods which lead to deterioration. These facts underwrite the recommendation for enough engineered freezing capacity, located separately and distinguished from storage capacity, to freeze food items in quantities necessary to meet menu requirements.

To make the need for separate equipment clear, new emphasis is being put on correct terminology. Equipment designed to store frozen food is referred to as *frozen food storage,* or *low-temperature reach-in* or *walk-in space.* Such equipment is kept at 0° to −10°F. A 0° to −10°F temperature capability is urged by some designers who feel it offers greater safeguards for stored frozen foods.

Equipment designed to do the actual freezing job is referred to as a *food freezer* or *processing freezer* or, as is sometimes done, as a *blast freezer, plate freezer, tunnel freezer,* etc. This equipment operates below −20°F.

New types and varieties of frozen food are continually being introduced by processors. Tailored to a wide range of operating requirements, frozen foods are being welcomed as problem solvers. They are successfully replacing a sizable portion of on-premise food production.

More frozen food cabinets are appearing, and they're showing up in unexpected places in the operation. The cook, the baker, the salad maker, and counter workers for some time have been using frozen raw ingredients in preparing some dishes. Current use of these ingredients as well as frozen entrées is being stepped up to the point where efficiency requires the placement of low-temperature storage in all of these work areas.

Increasing acceptance of on-premise freezing as a way to make slack-time production pay, or as an offset for unexpected dropoffs in volume, has also put new emphasis on the value of adequate space in which to freeze-process foods.

The following guidelines should be observed in work with frozen foods:

1. Keep frozen foods stored at a temperature of 0°F (−18°C) or less. The lower the temperature is and the less it varies, the better.
2. Cook thawed foods promptly. Ground meat or moist meat provides an ideal place for spoilage organisms to develop rapidly.
3. Never refreeze foods that have thawed. Nutritive value, flavor, and appearance suffer as a result of refreezing.
4. Insist that frozen items be frozen when delivered. Store only clean packages that have been inspected carefully. Products to be frozen should be packaged in a commercial freezer wrap to protect them while they are being stored.
5. Place old stock in front to be used first. Rotate stock and purchase new items frequently.
6. Bear in mind that frozen food will not keep indefinitely. Over time, it gradually loses nutrients, flavor, texture, and color (see table 6-4).

Storage Controls

The use of correct storage controls ensures that food is appropriately handled before and during

Table 6-4. Maximum Frozen Food Storage Periods at 0°F

Product	Storage Period
Sausage, ground meat, fish	1 to 3 months
Fresh pork (not ground)	3 to 6 months
Lamb, veal	6 to 9 months
Beef, poultry, eggs	6 to 12 months
Fruits, vegetables	One growing season to another

Table 6-5. Maximum Storage Times and Temperatures for Items in Dry or Refrigerated Storage

Food	Suggested Maximum Temperature	Recommended Maximum Storage Life	Remarks
Candy (chocolate)	70	3 months	Wrapped or in original carton; may be frozen
Canned goods	70	12 months	In original containers
Cereals	70	6 months	In original packages
Beans, flour, rice	70	6 months	In original container or covered galvanized can
Cream-filled pastries, custards	36	serve day prepared	Spoil readily; must be served the day prepared
Dairy products			
Milk—fluid	40	5 days	In original container, tightly covered
Milk—dried	70	3 months	In original package. If open, 38° in tight can
Milk—evaporated	70	12 months	In cans; invert every 30 days
Butter	40	2 weeks	In waxed cartons
Cheese (hard)	40	6 months	Tightly wrapped
Cheese (soft)	40	7 days	In tightly covered container
Ice cream and ices	10	3 months	In original container, covered
Eggs	45	7 days	In original carton
Eggs (dried)	70	6 months	In original carton. If open, 45° in tight can
Egg whites	45	2 days	In tight container
Egg yolks	45	2 days	In tight container; cover with water
Fish (fresh)	36	5 days	Wrap loosely
Shellfish	36	5 days	In covered container
Fruits			
Peaches, plums, berries	45	7 days	Unwashed (wash before using)
Apples, pears, citrus	70	2 weeks	In original containers
Dried	70	3 months	In original containers
Gravies, sauces	36	2 days	In covered containers
Leftovers	36	2 days	In covered containers
Meat			
Ground	38	2 days	Loosely wrapped
Fresh meat cuts	38	5 days	Loosely wrapped
Liver & variety meats	38	2 days	Loosely wrapped
Cold cuts (sliced)	38	5 days	Wrap in semi-moisture-proof waxed paper
Cured bacon (sliced)	38	1 to 2 weeks	May wrap tightly
Ham (tender cured)	38	1 to 2 weeks	May wrap tightly
Ham (canned)	38	6 weeks	In original container, unopened
Tongue (smoked)	38	7 weeks	May wrap tightly
Dried beef	38	6 weeks	May wrap tightly
Poultry	36	3 days	Wrap loosely
Processed foods made with eggs, meat, milk, fish, or poultry	36	serve day prepared	In covered container. Spoil rapidly; must be served day prepared
Sugar—Spices	70	3 to 6 months	In original package or covered galvanized can
Vegetables			
Leafy	45	5 days	Unwashed
Potatoes, onions, and root vegetables	70	7 to 30 days	Dry in ventilated container or bags

NOTE: *Tightly wrapped* means that the wrapping material is placed as tightly as possible against the product. *Loosely wrapped* means that the wrapping material does not have to touch the product.

storage. One person should be given responsibility for seeing that good controls are instituted. This may be the receiving clerk, the storeroom clerk, or another person. Since good controls usually affect the storeroom most, the individual in charge of it should see that the controls are implemented. Duties of the storeroom clerk include the following:

- Receiving deliveries, checking them into storage, and tagging or marking them with the date received and the price paid
- Maintaining orderly arrangement and cleanliness in storage areas
- Informing the supervisor when stocks are low or when they need attention
- Assisting in food pricing and in the taking of inventory
- Ensuring that stocks are rotated and that foods are used promptly (see table 6-5)

Stock Record Cards

Stock record cards are used to indicate the quantity of stock that exists on inventory (see fig. 6-13). These cards are used for all items on hand and indicate how much has been received from purveyors, how much has been issued, and how much remains. The responsibility for maintaining stock record cards may be that of the storeroom, the accounting department, or some other department of the operation. Frequent spot checks to verify quantities on hand should be made.

Inventory Methods

Various inventory methods may be used. Overall, they serve to indicate the rate of stock usage, the amounts of replacement units needed, the types and sizes of stock on hand, and the dollar value of stock on hand. Two inventory methods are used most commonly: the perpetual inventory and the physical inventory. Stock record cards are perpetual inventories if they are properly maintained, since they provide a perpetually accurate record of the amount of items on hand; as a result, they can help considerably in reducing losses in stock. In some operations, computers maintain the perpetual inventory. An actual count of what is on the

NAME OF ITEM TOMATO PASTE						UNIT CAN	
LOCATION MAIN STOREROOM						UNIT PRICE	
REMARKS 1 co = 6/10 106 S.G.					ITEM NUMBER	HIGH LIMIT 24	
						LOW LIMIT 6	
DATE	REC'D	ISSUED	BALANCE	DATE	REC'D	ISSUED	BALANCE
4/28/81	8F		9				
4/29		2	7				
4/30	INV		7				
5/3		2	5				
5/5	18	1	22				
5/7		2	20				
5/9		1	19				
5/11		2	17				
5/13		2	15				
5/15		1	14				
5/17		2	12				

Figure 6-13. Sample stock record card.

shelves is called a physical inventory and is usually taken about once every month. A physical inventory is also taken periodically in operations that use a perpetual inventory, to verify the latter's figures.

A physical inventory is best taken by two people, one of whom should not be from the storeroom. If the outside person is from the accounting department or from another area, it is more difficult for the storeroom person to juggle figures during the count to cover or set up pilferage. The outside person counts the items on hand, and the other individual records the count on an inventory form (see fig. 6-14). This procedure can also be reversed. Rechecks may be made on spot items to verify the figures obtained by the two people who conducted the full inventory.

Minor differences arising between a physical inventory and a perpetual one can be adjusted, but major differences should be investigated. The number of items on hand multiplied by the value of the item is called the *extended cost* or *extension* of the item. All extensions are totaled to give the value of the inventory. Different pricing formulas may be

Figure 6-14. Sample physical inventory form.

used. An average price may be used if prices have changed. Some operations use the actual price paid for goods, while others use the most recent price paid. Deciding what system of pricing to use is up to management.

ISSUING FOOD

Issuing is the controlled process of transferring foods from storage to a place where they can be processed. At the end of the day or recording period, the total value of goods issued should be known. This value plus the value of direct deliveries (foods that were delivered from receiving to processing for immediate preparation, without going to storage) gives the value of foods used during the period. Most operations give responsibility for food issuing to the accounting department; thus, the storeroom personnel who issue food are on the accounting department's staff. An accounting clerk may issue from inventories, and it is best not to combine such a job with the job of purchasing, receiving, or maintaining other accounts. If specific hours are established for issuing, individuals who work elsewhere may do the job.

Mechanics of Issuing

Issuing hours should be maintained according to a strict schedule. Personnel should know their daily needs in advance, since running back and forth to and from storage only wastes time and money. The issuing of foods should be a planned event that is carried out in an orderly fashion. This implies that, when an attendant is not on duty to issue food, the storage area is locked and only certain designated individuals have keys. The orderly issuance of all goods is enhanced by tagging merchandise appropriately and by using requisitions properly.

Tagging Merchandise Appropriately

Tagging merchandise appropriately simply means recording the date of receipt and the price paid on the goods themselves whenever goods arrive for storage. Taking time to tag items when they arrive for storage ensures that they will be stored in accordance with the rule of FIFO (first-in, first-out) and that they will be costed out correctly during inventory. All meats should already have been tagged with their weight and price by the receiving clerk when they first arrived at the operation. Such tagging emphasizes to personnel that the items in storage represent money and that this money is their responsibility.

Using Requisitions Properly

Using requisitions properly is similar to using checks properly at the local bank. Goods in stor-

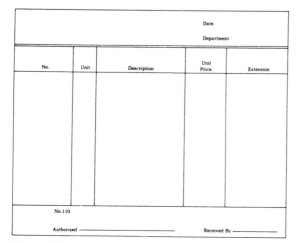

Figure 6-15. Sample food requisition form.

age represent money, so submitting a requisition form should be a mandatory step to take in order to obtain the goods, just as writing a check is a prerequisite for obtaining money from the bank. The requisition form contains space for the date, the name of the item issued, the weight and amount of the item, the price, and the signature of the person authorized to make the requisition (see fig. 6-15). Pricing the requisition is done by the individual responsible for issuing the food (someone from the accounting department). This task can be completed easily from the prices tagged on the products themselves in storage. Requisition forms are extremely important and should be handled carefully, just as checks are. One copy of the form returns to its maker, along with the issued merchandise; the other copy remains with the issuing clerk and is used to adjust stock record cards and to figure the daily food costs for the operation. Stock record cards, inventory procedures, and requisition forms constitute issuing controls as well as storage controls.

Issuing Controls

Good controls are necessary to prepare a meaningful daily food cost form (see fig. 6-16). When this form is completed, a fairly accurate computation of food and supply use can be performed with a minimum expenditure of time and labor. Comput-

ing costs only once a month, for purposes of developing a profit-and-loss statement, often renders the information too out-of-date to be of practical use; as a result, the daily food cost computation becomes a very important tool. Any measure designed to correct an undesirable situation is too late to have much effect on the original problem after a month's time. Frequent checks are costly but may pay for themselves. Management must decide how often food cost reports and other cost reports should be made. Computers are often used to calculate food costs daily or even by the meal.

The calculation of daily food cost produces an estimate rather than the actual cost. Kitchen carry-overs are not included, nor are items that make up daily supplies. If the bakeshop orders 1 lb of cinnamon and 1 gallon of vanilla extract, they are charged out as issues, but only a small part of each may actually be used. In the long run, however, the figures average out, and a fairly accurate cost computation is obtained. The omissions do not decrease values to any extent, for several reasons:

1. Most operations have roughly the same amount of carry-overs and daily-use supplies on hand from day to day. The variation is not great in either case.
2. The running or to-date daily costs average out over an extended period.
3. High cost figures result when poor forecasting occurs and there are high carry-overs. If proper recovery is made or if food issues are lowered, the figures adjust.

COMPUTER USE IN STORING AND ISSUING FOOD

The computer has been used in large foodservice operations for several years to keep track of food storage and inventory information. With the advent of the microcomputer, even the smallest foodservice operation can now successfully attain the same high degree of efficiency and economy as those larger operations.

Whereas in the past, products were tagged for storage by hand, today many foodservices utilize

	SUMMARY OF DAILY FOOD COST										MONTH TO DATE		
DATE	(1) BEGINNING STOREROOM INVENTORY	(2) STOREROOM PURCHASES	(3) TOTAL	(4) STOREROOM ISSUES	(5) DIRECT PURCHASES	(6) GROSS COST	(7) LESS TRANSFERS	(8) NET COST	(9) SALES	(10) FOOD COST PER CENT	NET COST	SALES	PER CENT
1/1	3500 00	310 00	3810 00	225 00	150 00	375 00	25 00	350 00	1050 00	33.3	350 00	1050 00	33.3
1/2	3585 00	400 00	3985 00	195 00	115 00	300 00	10 00	290 00	850 00	34.1	640 00	1900 00	33.7
1/3	3800 00												

*INFORMATION FOR COLUMN 2 AND COLUMN 5 COMES DIRECTLY FROM THE RECEIVING RECORD

Figure 6-16. Sample daily food cost form.

microcomputers to print out labels at the same time that they create a data bank of information regarding the incoming order. These labels often include not only date and price (the principal requirements of tagging by hand) but the purveyor, the unit price, and other information valuable to the operation. The storage function has also been substantially aided by the development of recipe files on disk, which include the exact quantities needed for each menu item. Using these files, a chef or clerk can print out the needed requisition items for each meal—by recipe or in bulk—and the printout can serve as the requisition form. At the same time, more sophisticated programs can automatically delete these items from the storage inventory as they are electronically selected on the computer for use.

Because a principal attribute of the computer is its ability to perform repetitive tasks with a high degree of consistency and speed, such required functions as extending inventories (multiplying price times number of items) are easily accomplished by setting up a spreadsheet format on the microcomputer. Most programs allow spreadsheet entries to be arranged in seconds alphabetically, numerically, by category, by date of purchase, or in any other format, simply by issuing a single command. Discrepancies can readily and rapidly be uncovered and traced by the computer as well.

SUMMARY

The storing and issuing of food are very important functions in the foodservice operation. Each provides, among other benefits, the essentials of control necessary for attaining a consistently profitable operation. But each must be performed step by step to attain the required end result. In dry storage, for example, cleanliness, ventilation, temperature control, and good organization are essential because contamination, deterioration, and waste can occur if the storage is improperly carried out.

Refrigerated or low-temperature storage is used

to protect foods that are relatively perishable. Refrigeration slows down the growth of bacteria and microorganisms, while freezing suspends their growth. Good air circulation, proper temperatures, efficient location, and observance of general practices and procedures all contribute to the maximum protection of refrigerated foods.

If proper storage controls are instituted, lower costs will be achieved. This is especially true if only one person is responsible for both storage and control.

Inventory methods vary, but generally a combination of perpetual and physical inventory methods is used. A perpetual inventory provides, at a glance, the current status of any product. It is obtained by entering into the record books each addition to and deletion from inventory. The same result can be achieved through the use of computers at a much faster and more economical rate. A physical inventory is used to verify the perpetual record through an actual count performed by an inventory team, usually involving at least one person not from the storage department.

Food issuance procedures should give one responsible person control of assets on both a daily and a continuing basis. Control is usually assigned to the accounting department. Deliveries and issues need accurate tabulation to give the proper information concerning food cost and supply cost. Deliveries must be properly recorded, and a distinction must be made between direct purchases and storeroom purchases. Requisitions from the storeroom provide a measure of control and accuracy in the distribution to the various departments. Meat and some other high-cost items should be tagged immediately to help maintain proper control. The requisition forms used may vary, but they should give an accurate account of the quantity and value of goods issued. Stock record cards, inventory records, requisition forms, and other forms and procedures are all part of issuing and storage controls. From these records, the daily food cost is calculated. Precosting, immediate costing, or other methods for indicating costs before or immediately after they occur are better methods of management than working out those costs long after the fact. It is better to compute an estimated cost frequently than to calculate the actual cost precisely but infrequently.

Through the use of microcomputers, many of the repetitious functions required in food storing and issuing can be carried out rapidly and without error. Such computers are used today in all types of foodservice operations, from the largest to the smallest.

CHAPTER REVIEW QUESTIONS

1. Good Food Restaurants of Memphis has been in operation for nearly ten years. During that time their operations have expanded from the original location on Lewis Street to a total of five operations in the Memphis metropolitan market. Purchasing and receiving have been carried out, to date, by each individual restaurant.

   Until about six months ago, this system seemed to be working well. Around that time, however, a new manager who had been hired to operate the restaurant on Third Avenue stopped buying from the purveyor that had been supplying fruits and produce to the unit for several years. The new manager told the corporate office that the move had been made because another purveyor offered better service at competitive prices.

   Fresh Daily, the purveyor with the long-term relationship to Good Foods, had called the switch to the attention of the company office at the time. The corporate office told Fresh Daily that selection of purveyors was a decision it had always allowed the restaurant managers to make. The office suggested that Fresh Daily continue to bid for the business of the restaurant in question, however, and Fresh Daily continued to serve the other restaurants in the chain.

   Now, six months later, the corporate office has noticed that the food cost at the Third Avenue unit has risen slightly and is now almost 1 percent higher than that of the other restaurants. The menus at all units are the same, and traditionally the menu mix has been quite similar as well. Upon further inspection of the purchasing pattern over the last six months, the accounting department has established that most of the additional food cost could be attributed to higher expenditures in fruits and produce at the Third Avenue unit. The Third Avenue unit manager's response is that "service with the new purveyor is much better, and it's well worth the extra 1 percent in food cost." The accounting office suspects that there may be other reasons for the switch in purveyors and the resulting increase in food costs, however—including the possibility of collusion and kickbacks to the manager of the Third Avenue unit. Since the purchasing has been left entirely to the restaurant manager's discretion in the past, without incident, the accounting office is at a loss to determine what steps to take to begin an investigation of the purchasing irregularity at the Third Avenue store.

As the supervisor of the five restaurants in the Memphis area, you are responsible for determining why the food cost at the Third Avenue store is higher than that at the other units and for devising a system to prevent future problems. Give details of both the plan of investigation and the program for prevention.

2. Businessmen's Hotels, Inc., of Tulsa, Oklahoma, began operations in the oil boom years of the 1970s and rapidly grew to ten operations within the next few years. The hotels are all located in the oil-producing region of the Southwest—in cities such as Tulsa, Oklahoma City, Midland, Houston, and Denver. As oil prices went up, so did the occupancy rates at Businessmen's Hotels. Through 1984, the company enjoyed occupancy rates company-wide in the mid-80 percent range annually. Their foodservice operations, designed to cater to the oil-industry businessmen who stayed in the hotels, boomed as well.

At the beginning of the summer of 1985, however, oil prices began to fall; by the autumn of 1985, oil prices had dropped to one-half of their previous level. By the spring of 1986, per barrel prices of oil had dropped to $10 to $12, and the industry as a whole was in a deep slump. Many oil companies laid off substantial numbers of employees and, as one way to reduce costs, eliminated most travel expenses. The Businessmen's Hotel chain's occupancy rates dropped to below 50 percent, as travel by people in their principal market was reduced. In some cases, room sales were as low as 30 percent of the total available space during peak weekday periods. The foodservice operations suffered along with the dwindling room occupancies, since much of the former food and beverage business had been linked to businessmen staying in the hotels.

During the boom years, the food and beverage operations had been thought of as an amenity to the hotels, since the real profits were coming from room sales. As a result, little attention had been paid to the profitability of the foodservice operations. Each hotel had designed its own system for foodservice purchasing, receiving, storing, and issuing; each operated independently from the other hotels in the chain. With the dwindling room occupancy rates, however, has come a need to redesign the foodservice systems to make them more nearly self-supporting.

The president of Businessmen's Hotels issued a memorandum on Monday that calls for the institution of strict storing and issuing functions, centralized in one location for cost savings (although he is not sure how this will help). As part of the program, the president also wants to use the hotel computer systems to detail the activities of the storing and issuing department more accurately and to eliminate unnecessary personnel from the payroll. Detail the steps you would take to begin to turn the foodservice storing and issuing department around. Explain the advantages and disadvantages of centralizing the departments, and respond to the president's request to computerize the department by outlining which functions are most readily convertible to computerization.

3. Study five nearby markets that sell food or other supplies used in foodservices. List them

indicating what they sell. How do supply and demand affect these markets? Select five different foods or supply items and indicate the channels through which they pass before arriving at the foodservice.

4. What should a food specification contain? What is the use of a specification? Who uses it? What is acceptance buying?

5. Study the buying routine and procedures used in a foodservice. Who decides quantity and quality required? Who actually searches the market and makes the purchase? Set up in an organized manner the various forms and records used. Explain them in detail. Could a simpler procedure be used? Could any of these forms be simplified?

6. Discuss the three types of receiving methods for advantages and disadvantages. Suppose you were a consultant and found receiving procedures almost non-existent, with cooks, busboys, and others signing for goods delivered and no inspection being made. How would you approach management for correction and what would you suggest?

7. What are the six considerations to be viewed in judging refrigerated storage systems? Are there others? Judge a refrigeration system of your choice according to these six factors or any others that may be appropriate.

8. What is meant by perpetual and physical inventories? What control system must be used to make either work?

9. What does the daily food cost form indicate besides the cost of food used? Why is this form the overall information sheet for management? Is dependence on this report emphasized too much in view of increasing labor and other costs? Do you think the cost of labor and energy or other important cost factors should be included as well? In Figure 6-16, complete the form for items 1 to 10 if the following were true:

Storeroom purchases	$ 350
Storeroom issues	250
Direct purchases	175

Transfers	12
Food sales	1175

VOCABULARY

Primary market	Direct seller
Secondary market	Purveyor
Retail	Staple food
Buyer	Brand
Grade	Substitution invoice
Informal buying	Value analysis
Blank check	Issuing
Specification	Low-temperature
Invoice	storage
Purchasing invoice	Physical inventory
stamp	Dry storage
Negotiation	Quotation and order
Purchase order	sheet
Cost plus	Shield-grade stamp
Ventilation	Futures-and-contract
Requisitions	buying
FIFO	Acceptance buying
Perpetual inventory	Partial-blind receiving
Direct deliveries	Invoice receiving
Vendor	Request-for-credit
Competitive bid	memorandum
Commodity	Daily receiving report
Wholesomeness	Stock record card
Interstate	Estimated versus
Blind receiving	actual food cost
Formal buying	Temperature record
Par stock	book

ANNOTATED REFERENCES

Axler, B. 1974. *Buying and Issuing Convenience Foods.* Indianapolis: Educational Publishers. (All aspects of controlling convenience products are reviewed here.)

Broadner, J.; Carlson, H. M.; and Maschal, H. T. 1962. *Profitable Food and Beverage Operations,* pp. 111-30. Rochelle Park, N.J.: Ahrens Publishing. (Discusses the storing and issuing of food.)

Coffman, J. P. 1977. *Introduction to Professional Food Service,* pp. 101-17. Boston: CBI Publishing. (How

storing and issuing of foods take place at the Culinary
Institute of America.)

Devel, W. 1975. *Quantity Cookery: Kitchen Management for Institutions.* Rochelle Park, N.J.: Hayden
Book. (Cost controls are described that enable restaurant operators to ensure the proper purchasing, receiving,
storing, and issuing of foods.)

Dukas, P., and Lundberg, D. E. 1973. *How to Operate a
Restaurant,* pp. 202-5. Rochelle Park, N.J.: Ahrens
Publishing. (Storing and issuing food.)

Kahrl, W. L. 1973. *Planning and Operating a Successful
Food Service Operation,* pp. 111-25. New York: Chain
Store Age Books. (Storage and management methods,
storage equipment, food-handling techniques, and issuing procedures.)

Keister, D. C. 1972. *How to Increase Profits with Portion
Control,* pp. 30-34. Chicago: National Restaurant
Association. (Storeroom control.)

Kelly, H. J. 1976. *Food Service Purchasing: Principles
and Practices.* New York: Chain Store Publishing.
(Valuable information on purchasing controls.)

Kotschevar, L. H. 1987. *Quantity Food Purchasing.* 3d
ed. New York: Macmillan. (How to identify quality
products for purchase.)

Lukowski, R. E. *Receiving Food in Foodservice Establishments.* Cooperative Extension Service, College of
Agriculture, University of Massachusetts. (Good coverage of receiving issues.)

Maizel, B. 1971. *Food and Beverage Purchasing.* New
York: ITT Educational Services. (A complete guide
to purchasing, receiving, storing, and issuing food and
beverage products).

Morgan, W. J. 1981. *Supervision and Management of
Quantity Food Preparation.* 2d ed. Berkeley, Cal.:
McCutchan. (Purchasing convenience foods.)

Peddersen, R. B. 1981. *Foodservice and Hotel Purchasing.*
New York: Van Nostrand Reinhold. (Specifications
for the purchase of all commodities.)

Steffanelli, J. 1985. *Purchasing and Procurement for the
Hospitality Industry,* pp. 180-215. 2d ed. New York:
John Wiley & Sons. (Excellent information on ordering
and receiving procedures.)

Stokes, J. W. 1973. *Food Service in Industry and Institutions,*
pp. 105-12. Dubuque, Iowa: Wm. C. Brown. (Dry and
cold storage, as well as essential controls.)

West, B. B., Wood L., and Harger, V. B. 1977. *Food
Service in Institutions,* pp. 84-90. New York: John
Wiley & Sons. (Dry and refrigerated storage.)

Wilkinson, J. 1969. *Storage Specifics.* Boston: CBI
Publishing. (All aspects of storing food, from dry stores
to freezer space.)

CHAPTER 7

Serving Food

OUTLINE

If all other functions in an operation are correctly done, but service—even service behind a cafeteria counter—is neglected, the establishment will fail. This is because service, more than any other single attribute of a foodservice operation, is identified by customers as the reason for frequenting a foodservice. In a national poll in 1985, for instance, 85 percent of the participants identified service as the main reason they go to a certain foodservice. While in many cases customers blame poor service on individual employees, service is fundamentally the responsibility of the manager. The staff meets the customers one on one and delivers the service that customers remember, but management defines what form of service will be used throughout its system: how food is to be served, by whom, and in what manner. Commercial foodservices attain high standards not only with good food but with excellent service. Therefore, management must take the blame for failures in service as well as in food. Management is responsible for training personnel and for setting the standards of service. Even though these standards vary from one foodservice to another, certain principles must be observed if proper service is to be performed.

SEATED SERVICE

Seated service occurs when a guest remains seated throughout the meal. The amount of personal service given can range from the level maintained in fine-dining establishments, where service personnel attend to every need, to that offered in fast-service outlets, where service, consumption, and payment are rapidly accomplished. The principle types of seated service used in foodservice establishments are American, English, French, Russian, banquet, counter, and tray. The type of service delivered depends to some extent on the menu, the desired atmosphere, the availability and skill of workers, and the desired market.

American Service

An inexpensive and fairly fast form of service is called *American.* It is easily learned by service personnel. The food is portioned in the kitchen and brought to the guests on plates or dishes, from which the guest eats. Side dishes such as bread and butter plates are used only when the main plate cannot accommodate the additional food. To add a bit more finesse to the service, personnel may include the bread and butter plates on the place setting and may serve rolls in a basket or plate covered with a napkin. The butter may be served separately, or it may already be present on the bread and butter plate. The coffee cup and saucer may be on the table from the outset, or they may be brought to the guest on request.

The service is simple. All solids are served from the guest's left with the server's left hand. Beverages are served from the guest's right with the right hand. When guests are a mixed group of men and women, service begins to the host's right with women (the oldest being served first), and then proceeds to elderly men, children, and finally men. When there are only men or only women, service begins at the

host's right and moves counterclockwise around the table.

Placemats or tablecloths are used. Tablecloths should hang at least 12 inches over the table edge but not so far as to pose an obstruction to the guests. Silence cloths of felt, foam rubber, or other material are used under the tablecloth. Figure 7-1 shows a typical setting.

Operators may wish to vary the American setting by combining other types of service with it. Each operation must suit its own needs, and management must decide the service most appropriate for its customers. Simplifying the service makes it easier to introduce personnel who lack training in service.

English Service

English service is also known as *family, host,* or *holiday* service. It is an adaptation of the service found in English country homes. English service differs from other types of service in that the food is served on large platters or in bowls that are placed on the table for service throughout the meal. Of course, if they become empty, they may be refilled or removed to the kitchen. English service is not used often, but it may be found in clubs and in some other types of foodservices. Meats are carved by the host, while guests dish their own vegetables and side dishes.

Figure 7-1. American service setting.

The Canadian adaptation of English service does not include a waiter, so the host and hostess must be thoroughly adept and organized. When English service is informal, it is known as family service. Whatever the precise form of English service used, all items are served from the right and cleared from the left.

French Service

French service at one time was extremely elaborate. Because of the high cost of labor, however, the service has grown less popular. The equipment used is also expensive: a table-high rolling cart (guéridon) from which food is served; a chafing dish (*réchaud*) typically mounted on the guéridon and designed to prepare special dishes and keep food warm; and silver platters and trays used to bring food from the kitchen.

Two people wait on the tables, supervised by a captain who may oversee four tables. The principal waiter is called the *chef de rang,* and the assistant is known as the *commis de rang.* Both must be highly trained. The dress frequently includes white gloves. Duties of the *chef de rang* include the following:

1. Seat the guests, if no headwaiter or captain does.
2. Take guests' orders.
3. Serve all apéritifs, if no cocktail waiter does it.
4. Finish preparing the food at the table before the guests.
5. Present the check and collect the money.

Duties of *commis de rang* include the following:

1. Receive orders from the *chef de rang,* take them to the kitchen, and order food from the kitchen.
2. Pick up food in the kitchen, bring it on a tray, and place it on the guéridon.
3. Serve food after the *chef de rang* prepares it.
4. Stand ready to help the *chef de rang* whenever necessary.

The *réchaud* is used to prepare food or keep it warm. If the *chef de rang* does not carve the meat,

bone the chicken, or debone the fish, the captain may do it. All sauces or garnishes are prepared by the *chef de rang.* The wine steward, or *sommelier,* comes to the table to discuss the various wines to be served. This individual takes the order and fetches the wine, after telling the *chef de rang* which glasses will be needed. The *commis de rang* secures the glasses and puts them in their proper places on the table.

The *chef de rang* uses a serving fork in one hand and a spoon in the other to transfer food from the platters or *réchaud.* The *commis* holds the guest's plate below the silver platter or *réchaud,* ready to receive food and catch spills. When there is only one waiter, the *chef de rang* must do all functions. The fork and spoon are then used in one hand to transfer the food to the plates. The rule in French service is usually that all food is served from the right, except butter. Bread plates, salad plates, and silver used on the left are placed from the guest's left. A left-handed waiter may have to serve completely from the left, which is difficult.

The setting for French service is a silence cloth, tablecloth, and top. The top is another tablecloth, easily removed after a meal and replaced for the next guests. A service plate about 10 inches in diameter is placed directly in front of the guest. An hors d'oeuvre plate may be placed on this, and then the folded napkin. To the left of the service plate is the dinner fork. Above this is the butter plate and butter knife; in very formal French service, no bread is served, so the plate is not used. To the right of the service plate is the dinner knife, with the cutting edge toward the plate. A soup spoon may be next to the knife, or it may be brought with the soup, if ordered. Above the service plate, parallel to the table's edge is a dessert fork and spoon, but this can be omitted. Figure 7-2 illustrates a typical service setting. Knives and spoons are always put on the right, with the spoons to the right of the knives; forks go on the left. Guests use the silver from the outer edge in, as the courses proceed. Silverware also can be brought with the respective courses, such as the soup spoon with soup or the cocktail fork with the shrimp cocktail.

Wine glasses may be preset on the table or placed just before the wine is served. Sometimes, if more

Figure 7-2. French service setting.

than three wines are served, three glasses may be arranged at the place setting and others added later after the used glasses are removed. Water is usually not served; if it is, as is true in the United States, the water glass is at the tip of the knife. Wine glasses are arranged next to this, and the progression is to move through the glasses from right to left for the various wines.

Coffee is served after dessert, and the coffee spoon may come with it. Fresh napkins may be given during the meal or immediately after finger bowls are used. Finger bowls—small containers holding liquid for cleaning the hands—may also be used during the meal, with fresh napkins. It is not considered proper to have ashtrays on the table, since smoking during the meal in French service is disapproved. Salt and pepper shakers are not on the table either, because the seasoning is supposed to be correct as served. Dining should proceed in a leisurely manner.

Russian Service

Russian service differs from French in that all food is dished onto platters or serving dishes in the kitchen and brought to the table for service. Hotels use this service much more than any other for their higher-quality service. It is simple yet elegant.

One waiter takes the orders, gives them to the kitchen, and does all serving. If a party of six is dining and there are three identical orders, these will be placed on one serving dish. A busperson

may bring food to the table if there are a number of dishes, but this person does not take part in the service. The various trays are set on a serving stand. Empty plates for service are distributed in a clockwise fashion around the table by the waiter, at the guest's right, using the right hand. The service is reversed when all plates are down: food is put on the plates counterclockwise. The food dish is held in the left hand at the guest's left, and the waiter, using the right hand to hold a spoon and fork, places portions on the guest's plate. If it is soup, the soup is dished from a tureen into the soup bowl at the guest's place, using a soup ladle. Guests may direct the waiter on the size portions they want. Any unused foods go back to the kitchen.

Clearing is the same as for French service. Coffee is served from the right, following dessert, and a finger bowl and fresh napkin are presented to the guest at the close of the meal.

Russian service is best in an operation offering relatively few entrées, because problems arise in attempting to arrange different orders attractively on one tray. Another problem involves keeping food hot after leaving the kitchen and before service. Russian service is excellent for banquets, since all foods are the same.

The table setup for Russian service may be very much like French service, or it may be unique to the menu offered (see fig. 7-3). A fairly large inventory of silver service is needed, as is true in French

Figure 7-3. Typical Russian service setting.

Figure 7-4. Banquet covers fitted on plates to allow stacking.

service. In both French and Russian service, there is a trend toward simpler table settings, with the necessary silver and glassware placed on the table only as needed for each course, rather than the entire setting being used.

Banquet Service

Banquet service may be American, French, Russian, or a blend of these. Organization and speed are important, so foods are served at every table at the same time. The service should be based on this need, plus that of giving the guest the feeling of elegance and luxury.

American service is most commonly used, with a slight variation in that plates portioned in the kitchen are covered with banquet covers to keep the food warm and to allow stacking of many plates to a tray (see fig. 7-4). If English service is used, the Canadian adaptation is most usual. Some caterers use family service for popular-priced banquets, bringing the food in on platters to be passed around the table. Russian service is often used for the nicest banquets. On such occasions, the waiter serves the entrée from a silver platter. Care must be taken to see that the platter is attractive and not messy, even down to the last portion served. The type of item being served is important. Good training can also help to make the service attractive. One problem is that much part-time help may be necessary. A short but informative training session can be given by the banquet manager before service begins. The banquet function sheet also can help inform personnel and ensure a smooth-running function (see fig. 7-5).

NAME OF ORGANIZATION   DATE   TIME

TYPE OF FUNCTION   ROOM OR LOCATION

NUMBER OF GUESTS   IN CHARGE

RESERVATION MADE ON   CONFIRMED

DEPOSIT RECEIVED   BALANCE

HEAD TABLE SEATING   TABLES SEATING

TABLE PLAN AND SET UP

SEATING ARRANGEMENTS   SPACE FOR DANCING

TYPE OF LINEN, CUTLERY, GLASSWARE

FLOWERS SUPPLIED BY

DECORATIONS (candles, favors, programs, place cards)

MUSIC   LECTERN   DAIS   MICROPHONE

CHECKROOMS   CASHER   LOCATED

MENU

SERVERS REQUIRED AND TABLE POSITION

TABLE 1   TABLE 2   TABLE 3

TABLE 4   TABLE 5   TABLE 6

PERSON IN CHARGE OF STAFF

GRATUITIES

Figure 7-5. Sample Form for a banquet function sheet.

Counter Service

Counter service is economical in labor cost, quick, and efficient. It appeals to guests who are in a hurry and will be found in fast-service operations— coffee shops, drugstore fountains, department stores, and others featuring convenience, low prices, and generally good food with fast, efficient service.

Guests are served at a counter. The menu is presented with a glass of water at the right hand side of the cover. The place setting known as the cover may or may not be preset. Service personnel take the order as soon as the guest has selected the food, and this should be transferred at once to the preparation departments. If the cover is not set, it can be set while the guest is deciding what to order. Speed and dispatch are desirable. Typically, a knife (with the cutting edge facing the space where the plate will be placed) and a spoon are set on the customer's right. A fork, with a napkin under or on top, is placed at the customer's left. The order is placed in the center of the cover. When service is over, the check is presented face down. Soiled dishes and tableware should be removed promptly. Dirty dishes are unappetizing to view while eating a meal, and other guests' appetites may be disturbed by them. They also can cause confusion, in that a guest sitting down while they are still there may be thought to have just finished eating and may not receive prompt attention.

Counter service is often coupled with table or booth service. Usually, special service personnel serve guests at these, while the counter service people serve only guests at the counter. The various counter shapes are important to speed and efficiency of service. The straight line counter is least efficient and takes the most labor. Rectangular or U-shaped counters are more efficient, since service personnel can work the front and both sides easily from one position.

Tray Service

Tray service is used in health facilities or in places where food must be delivered. A meals-on-wheels program furnishes such delivery service to elderly people. Some boarding houses and homes also use the service. Hotel room service is a variation of tray service (see fig. 7-6). Food is dished onto plates, placed on trays, and then distributed to recipients, either from a cental kitchen or from pantries located on each floor or wing (see fig. 7-7). If the food comes from the kitchen, the service is said to be *centralized.* If it comes from pantries, it is said to be *decentralized.*

Centralized Service

In the recent past, centralized service has been favored; but with the development of individual frozen food portions and many convenience foods that are easily portioned, decentralized service has taken on new importance. In centralized ser-

Figure 7-6. Hotels use tray service when serving food to guests in their rooms.

Dispensator

MOBILE EQUIPMENT AND
SYSTEM FOR HOSPITAL FOOD
SERVICE

1. Carrier and dispenser for trays
2. Mobile table for food requisitions
3. Hot food unit, dispenser for hot foods and heated dishes
4. Ditto 5-ditto
5. Ditto
6. Urn stand with urns for coffee and hot water
7. Dispenser for heated pots for coffee, tea, etc.
8. Dispenser for cups and saucers
9. Table for supervisor
10. Starting platform for trays
11. Conveyor belts for trays
12. Elevators
13. Carrier and dispenser for silverware, napkins, tray covers, setups
14. Dispenser for bread and butter
15. Dispenser for salads
16. Dispenser for pies or desserts
17. Dispenser for milk
18. Dispenser for ice cream
19. Dispenser for glasses
20. Dispenser for glasses
21. Dispenser for heated food covers
22. Dispenser for cooled food covers
23. Wagon for food trays being loaded
24. Wagon with food trays being unloaded

Figure 7-7. Tray service system.

vice, all trays are prepared in the serving section of the main kitchen. Here, under the supervision of the dietary department, proper controls, food temperatures, correct diet, and attractive food arrangement can be maintained. The trays may be distributed by conveyors to various floor levels, or they may be loaded onto carts and transported there. Either dietary personnel or nursing personnel distribute the trays to patients in health facilities. In some institutions, trays may be brought to a central dining room and given to patients or others as they come in to eat.

Decentralized Service

In decentralized service, food prepared in a central kitchen may be sent in bulk or in convenience food portions to service pantries, where it is placed onto dishes, trayed, and sent to those who must eat. Usually some type of mobile transport equipment is used to get the trays to where they are needed. In decentralized service, supervising all areas where food is being dished is difficult. Additional food handling is often required in decentralized service— once in the kitchen, and again in the pantries. Maintaining food quality may also be a problem.

Some decentralized services require more labor-hours to do the same job than do centralized service units.

SELF-SERVICE

Self-service is called *informal service,* and it is becoming more popular. The guest often dishes up the food and either eats it in a place provided or takes it elsewhere to eat. Depending on where the food is eaten and the rules of the establishment, guests may or may not return dishes to a central area. If not, busing personnel do this. The different types of informal service are buffet, cafeteria, drive-in or take-out, and vending.

Buffet Service

In buffet service, food is put out for guests to select. Frequently, a long table is provided on which a quantity of food is displayed. Good merchandising effects are possible by presenting a mass of varied food types in a colorful display. Often, cold foods are first and hot foods last. Salads, sandwiches, seafood, soups, meats, vegetables, casserole dishes, and others are featured. The garde manger section of the kitchen often prepares many of the display pieces. Although buffet service is largely self-service, on some buffets a cook carves the meats or otherwise assists guests—particularly if service must be rapid. The price of the meal covers the entire meal, although some operations may charge extra for beverages or dessert.

Showmanship is the key to a successful buffet. Themes such as holiday, a luau in Hawaii, Polynesian in the South Pacific, and Creole in New Orleans should be used. Centerpieces can be flowers, ice carvings, or decorated cakes. Lighting is important and can emphasize food. Spotlights on special foods can add much. Tables may be straight, L-shaped, U-shaped, or V-shaped. To speed service, some tables may be separate from others. For instance, the table where beverages are dispensed may be separate from the one where foods are served.

Figure 7-8. Continental breakfast buffet.

Many operations today are combining buffet with seated service. Guests are allowed to select cold foods (which are largely salad materials) from a buffet. They then order the rest of what they want from a menu. Not all buffets are elaborate or stress showmanship. Many operations today use buffets to get a lot of people served in a short time. A salad bar is a good example. Others use buffets because they lack proper facilities to care for guests in another way. Thus, breakfast buffets may range from one in which guests can get only hot beverages, juice, and sweet bread products (continental breakfast) to one in which they can get scrambled eggs and other products as well (see fig. 7-8). A hotel that caters to tours may find that one tour coming down to the regular dining room will swamp service and disappoint other guests. Therefore, the tour may be taken care of at one time in a separate dining room, using buffet service.

A *smorgasbord* is a buffet featuring Scandinavian foods, but a true one must have pickled herring, rye bread, and mysost or gjetost cheese. A hot entrée may be ordered from a menu. The entrée is served by service personnel after buffet foods are eaten. Russian buffets are used at receptions. These feature hors d'oeuvre foods. Caviar in an ice bowl, rye bread, and butter are typical foods, along with many other tangy types. Often, if a buffet is used to serve the main foods, waiters later pass among seated guests with trays of food and beverages. This helps reduce congestion at the buffet.

The location of the buffet is important. It should be near the entrance and close to where guests will be seated. A central position allows service to be achieved from either side, although this complicates reservicing the buffet because of cross-traffic between servers and guests. It should not be located far back in a corner of the room.

Cafeteria Service

Cafeteria service may not be entirely self-service because the food is dispensed to guests, who carry it to a cashier or checker and then to a table where the food is eaten. Some cafeterias have service personnel carry the tray to the table. Often busing personnel remove the soiled dishes. Some cafeterias have a system in which people get a check from a checker and then pay as they go out. The most usual system is to pay at the end of the cafeteria line. Cafeteria service is popular because it reduces labor costs, thus allowing more food to be given for the money. It also is speedy service, and guests can see what they are getting. Quality of food is an important factor in the success of a cafeteria. It must usually be moderate in price but should not in any way be low in quality.

Cafeteria service is most frequently used in mass-feeding situations, such as at schools and military installations. Commercial cafeterias catering to the public are gaining in popularity, however, principally as a response to the demand for faster service. Today, many large corporations provide in-house cafeteria-style service for their employees, either on a contract basis with an outside foodservice operator or through their own foodservice department.

Normally, guests pick up a tray and their silver and napkin at the start of the cafeteria line. They then select the foods they wish. Usually cold foods are first and hot foods last, but this can vary. A menu board plainly indicates the foods available and their price. Two basic cafeteria systems are used: the line, and the scramble.

The Line System

The line system has people form a line and then move through, selecting foods. Service personnel serve and also replenish the counter. Emphasis is placed on standardized portions and speedy service. Colleges, in-plant foodservices, school lunchrooms, and even downtown eating places use such service. Counters may be L-shaped, straight, U-shaped, or even circular. Some line systems break up service into a speed line, where the foods offered can be quickly selected and served so that the line moves quickly, and a slower line where foods requiring slower service are offered. One of the problems with the line system is that a person who stands and ponders what to choose slows the entire line down. In some systems, by-passing is encouraged.

The Scramble System

The scramble system has counters where specific kinds of foods can be obtained. They are not joined together in a line, so an individual goes where a certain desired food can be obtained, gets it, and then goes to another area. This system is sometimes called the *shopping center system,* since it resembles the organization of an enclosed shopping area. It is also called the *hollow-square system.* Once the guests have collected their food, they go to the exit of the square, where they pay the cashier.

Today modifications of this system are also referred to as *food fairs* or *food bars.* Combinations of food categories can be arranged together so that the customers spread out somewhat to alleviate line crowding. For instance, cold foods could be found at one station, salads at another, beverages at a third, and hot entrées at still another. This eliminates the need for customers to file past each selection whether or not they are interested in those foods.

Originally it was feared that customers would find such a system confusing, but studies indicate that the customer quickly adapts to the spread-out stations offering different foods. Signage indicating the location of different products is the key to directing traffic and educating customers when using a scramble system.

A fairly recent offshoot of the scramble system is

the *food court.* First popularized in the World Trade Center in New York City, this system involves the establishment of several small satellite operations offering different food products. Each satellite prepares or finishes the products it offers on site. Emphasis is on menu variety provided by the myriad different choices. In many instances, these operations are backed by a central commissary or food preparation center for processing foods prior to their delivery to the satellites for finishing. This system may also appear under a variety of names. In Canada, for instance, it is referred to as a *village concept,* in reference to the cottage-industry production period in history, when different villages often produced separate foods. A good example of this type of system can be found in Boston's Faneuil Hall.

There are three definite advantages to the scramble system. First, there is no waiting line, so more people can be served in a given time than with the line system. Second, the system has greater flexibility. During low-volume times some sections can be closed; this would not work as well in a line system. A scramble system can also be enlarged more easily. Third, improved labor utilization occurs, particularly in the dispensing of hot and cold beverages at a central square and with foods guests can pick up themselves, such as prepackaged items.

Drive-in or Take-out Service

Drive-in or take-out service is largely self-service in that guests usually pick up their own food after ordering it. Variations include ordering and then driving to a pick-up window, where service personnel give out the food, and ordering in place and receiving car-hop service. Guests may be expected to eat in their cars, or a small dining area may be provided. The menu is limited and specializes usually in one particular item such as chicken, hamburgers, tacos, or roast beef sandwiches. Because of the speedy service and low price range, this type of operation is popular. According to an article in *Food Management,* take-out foodservice has

increased its dollar sales by 13.9 percent since 1980 (*Food Management* 1985).

Vending Service

Vending service utilizes machines to dispense food. Some vending systems dispense complete meals. Specific machines often dispense foods in a kind of shopping center arrangement. The fact that service from the machine is impersonal keeps many patrons from visiting such an operation. On the other hand, many industrial and institutional employees find them acceptable. Vending reduces costs. There are some disadvantages. The offerings must be limited, and some foods do not hold up well in the machines. Sanitation can be another problem. Some vending services dispense food that can be reheated in microwave, infrared, or quartz units.

Convenience Service

Convenience service has grown from a practically nonexistent segment to a healthy participant in foodservice in only a few years. It is characterized by the use of ready-prepared and ready-to-eat foods that the customer chooses and finishes preparing. The ready-prepared foods, such as sandwiches and popcorn, require cooking, which is usually done by a customer-operated microwave oven. The ready-to-eat foods, such as doughnuts, sandwiches, and salad items, can be heated in a microwave or eaten as they are. In either case, the system is essentially self-service. The growth in this industry has been tied to that of convenience food stores, which cater to neighborhood and passerby traffic. In some cases, the demand for food products in these stores has been so great that fastfood companies have placed miniunits in convenience food stores to capture the market.

In convenience purchasing, food products are either consumed on the premises or taken out. In many convenience stores, small seating areas have been set aside to accommodate the demand. The popularity of this system in convenience stores has led to the establishment of similar operations in supermarkets and office buildings. As more and more innovative methods of sustaining the shelf-life of foods are perfected, this system will grow further.

THE SERVICE EMPLOYEE

The service employee is the person with whom the customer is most likely to have regular contact. Whether waiter or waitress, busser, maître d', *sommelier,* cafeteria server, or any other employee, this person is responsible for delivering not only the products but also the image of the establishment. Therefore the value of the service employee cannot be overstated. This person is also the chief sales agent for the business. In a full-service restaurant, for example, each server may be responsible for as much as $150,000 to $300,000 per year in sales. A considerable amount of time and money may be required to train these employees properly. The *NRA News* recently estimated that the cost of training each server may amount to between $500 and $2,500, depending on the type of service involved (*NRA News* 1986). Therefore, good food-service establishments take great care in devising systems for the proper training and continuing motivation of service employees.

The service employee may be responsible for a variety of different tasks, depending on the type of foodservice. These may include delivering the food, taking orders, promoting products, removing dishes, and selling and opening wines or other beverages. In many cases, service employees are tipped by the customer for these services and derive a substantial portion of their wages from this source. In others, such as the cafeteria system, tips are often not involved, and the employees depend on the business for their entire remuneration.

In large foodservice operations, the responsibilities of hiring, training, and retraining service employees may be conducted by a human resources department. In smaller operations, the unit manager usually takes on these responsibilities. In either case, communication is the principal tool used. This communication may be primarily verbal, or it may involve pictures, photographs, charts, video presentations, interactive computer video, or a wide range of other methods.

COMPUTERS IN SERVICE

Electronic Cash Registers (ECRs) have, in recent years, revolutionized the service aspects of the foodservice industry. Though the trend toward automated systems began in the fastfood segment, table-service restaurants have moved rapidly to capitalize on the advances in ECR technology. This has enabled many restaurants to enhance both the speed and quality of their service.

Most modern ECRs have either *preset* keys for each menu item or a *price look-up* (PLU) feature (or both). Under either system, menu items and prices are programmed into the ECR and accessed by either an item key (preset) or a code number (PLU). The server taking the guest's order presses either the preset key or the proper code number on the ECR keyboard. The item is then automatically printed on the guest check or receipt. The price of the item is also recorded, and the bill is totaled. In many systems the order is also printed or displayed in the kitchen. When the order is ready, the server is notified to pick up the order and proceed with the service.

The improvement in speed is a result of two factors. First, the server does not have to enter the kitchen in order to place the order. This is done by the system, and many steps are saved thereby. Second, the server does not have to add up the check manually, since this is done automatically as the order is placed.

The improvement in quality of service is related to the development of ECRs. Because of the time saved, service personnel are able to spend more time with the customers. In addition, fewer errors are made in the totaling of a guest's check.

The consequences of these improvements in service are higher table turnover, greater guest satisfaction, and higher staff morale. While no definitive studies have yet been made, many operators claim to have achieved higher check averages and better tips for their employees as a result of the improved service. Clearly, the installation and full utilization of an ECR system would benefit virtually every foodservice facility.

SUMMARY

It is the responsibility of management to establish the type of service and the standard of excellence for the foodservice. The service should suit the operation and the type of food served. There are basically two types of service: seated and self-service. At times these may be mixed, but whichever type predominates determines the classification.

In seated service, customers are served by service personnel. There are several kinds. American service is a fast means of distributing food, as food is plated and portioned in the kitchen. The table setting also is simple. American service is inexpensive and easily learned by nonprofessional personnel. English service involves having the host and hostess participate in the plating of food at the table. Depending on the operation, service personnel may be used to assist. If they do not, the type of service may be called *Canadian.* French service is one of the most luxurious and expensive. It uses a great deal of expensive equipment and two waiters per station. The table setup is elegant but practical. In French service, food is prepared in front of guests.

Russian service differs from French in that portions of food are placed onto serving dishes in the kitchen, and waiters then serve the guests from these at the table. Russian service is next to French in elegance but it also is simple and works well for large groups.

Banquet service may use American, French, English, or Russian service, or blends of these. American service is often used because of its speed and simplicity. French service is used less frequently than Russian because of the cost and time. Russian service is used when the service must be elegant

but must still meet the needs of banquet arrangements that reserve time for a speaker or for entertainment. Counter service occurs behind a counter and is much like American in the table setting. Speed is essential. Tray service may be centralized or decentralized. Centralized service has dish-up occurring in the main kitchen, whereas decentralized service sends foods to smaller service units for final preparation and dish-up.

Informal service and self-service are synonymous. It is used to simplify service requirements, give speed, and reduce costs. Buffet service is service from a table, where people help themselves. Some waiter service may be combined with this, such as the service of beverages and desserts by service personnel. Cafeteria service involves having customers pass in front of counters and select foods from them. Two types of cafeteria dispensing systems are used. One is the line system, in which customers stand in line and move along single-file, selecting foods. The other is the scramble system, in which required foods are dispensed from specific separate stations. The scramble system can be called the *shopping-center system* or the *hollow-square system.* Drive-in or take-out service is an informal type suited to the fast pace of modern living. Some service may be given by car-hops or personnel who assist in removing trays. A vending service uses machines to dispense food. Although impersonal, it does answer the need of reducing service personnel costs and allowing food to be dispensed from remote locations away from production centers.

Convenience service has grown rapidly in the past few years. It is notable for its use of ready-prepared and ready-to-eat foods that the consumer gives final production. The ECR (electronic cash register) has made a significant difference in foodservices by providing the ability to speed service to the customer. Using this system, the server does not need to go to the kitchen to turn in orders, and fewer errors are made in accounting. The results of the introduction of ECRs to foodservice are greater customer satisfaction, faster customer turnover, and perhaps higher check averages.

CHAPTER REVIEW QUESTIONS

1. The Good Food Restaurant has been in operation since 1965 at the same location. From a small eatery utilizing only counter service, the operation has been expanded to include table service as well. At present, the operation has twenty-four counter stools and six $24'' \times 24''$ tables. The menu of Good Food has always highlighted the "homecooked goodness" of the foods prepared by the owner's wife, Erma, and has been moderately priced. The restaurant has been open six days a week (closed on Mondays) for breakfast and lunch, and it has closed daily at 3:00 P.M. Sam, the owner, has been the waiter for Good Food; when business was brisk, his daughter and son-in-law pitched in to help. Good Food has provided the necessary income for Sam and Erma for twenty years.

   Recently, however, the area where Good Food is located has undergone a transformation and is now the new "hot spot" part of town. A number of new restaurants have entered the market, mostly offering fine dining, full service, and bar operations. Sam has decided that, rather than change with the market, he would rather sell out now and retire.

   A group of young lawyers has purchased the building, equipment, and business from Sam and has hired you to manage the revised restaurant. As part of your job, they want you to devise the concept for the restaurant. The lawyers think the new restaurant should be more upscale than Good Food in order to meet the needs of the new market and its new owners. The new owners also would like to change the decor somewhat, but they are not interested in major renovation of the physical plant. Describe the types of operation possible for the new restuarant and how you would design the service system for the new concept.

2. Outline the essential features of American, French, Russian, English, and Canadian services. What are the advantages and disadvantages of each?

3. Demonstrate these five services before a group. Use dishes, trays, tables, or whatever is necessary to make the service as realistic as possible.

4. What are the advantages and disadvantages of centralized and decentralized foodservice? What are the trends today? Compare also line-type cafeteria operation with that of the scramble system. What are the advantages and disadvantages?

5. Discuss merchandising and the factors that can be used to promote business. Differentiate among the six factors discussed in this chapter.

6. How does an operation's atmosphere merchandise food? What is meant by external and internal factors in atmosphere? Find pictures of outside and inside areas of operations and indicate good and bad features as far as external and internal factors in atmosphere are concerned.

VOCABULARY

French service	Finger bowl
Russian service	Function sheet
American service	Centralized service
English service	Decentralized service
Canadian service	Straight-line cafeteria
Banquet service	Scramble system
Counter service	Vending service
Tray service	Convenience service
Réchaud	Human resources
Guéridon	ECR (electronic cash
Chef de rang	register)
Commis de rang	Price look-up keys
Tureen	Preset keys

ANNOTATED REFERENCES

Axler, B. 1974. *Showmanship in the Dining Room.* New York: ITT Educational Publications. (This text discusses merchandising in the dining room.)

Coffman, J. P. 1974. *Introduction to Professional Food Service,* pp. 219-38. Boston: CBI Publishing. (Serving methods as taught at the Culinary Institute of America.)

Dukas, P. 1973. *How to Plan and Operate a Restaurant.* 2d ed., pp. 175-86. Rochelle Park, N.J.: Hayden Book. (Restaurant promotion as a means to build a thriving business.)

Food Management. 1985. *Food Management* 20(12): 33-34. (Results of a survey on changes in the food-service market.)

Goodman, R. J. 1979. *The Management of Service for the Restaurant Manager.* Dubuque, Iowa: Wm. C. Brown. (Useful chapters on types of service, equipment used in service, and wine and beverage service.)

Kahrl, W. L. 1973. *Planning and Operating a Successful Food Service Operation,* pp. 138-51. New York: Chain Store Age Books. (Some points on achieving proper service within the operation are stressed in this text.)

Kinder, F. 1968. *Meal Management.* 3d ed., pp. 345-508. New York: Macmillan. (Styles of meal service, procedures at the table, and serving information about both formal and informal occasions.)

Knight, J., and Salter, C. 1985. (Use of Video Tapes in Training.) *Cornell Hotel and Restaurant Quarterly* (August 1985): 54-55. (Using videos as a training tool in the military.)

Martin, W. 1971. *The Essentials of Good Tableservice.* Ithaca, N.Y.: School of Hotel Administration, Cornell University. (This text presents step-by-step procedures for good table service.)

NRA News. 1986. *NRA News* (March 1986):17-19. (Cost of training service personnel.)

Stokes, J. W. 1973. *Food Service in Industry and Institutions,* pp. 153-75. Dubuque, Iowa: Wm. C. Brown. (Service and distribution of food in industrial and institutional operations.)

———. 1982. *How to Manage a Restaurant or Institutional Food Service,* pp. 66-107, 288-98. Dubuque, Iowa: Wm. C. Brown. (Merchandising, public relations, and styles of food service.)

West, B. B.; Wood, L.; and Harger, V. F. 1977. *Food Service in Institutions,* pp. 62-68. New York: John Wiley & Sons. (Serving food.)

PART II

Quantity Food Preparation and Management

CHAPTER 8

Cooking Principles and Methods

OUTLINE

Cooking is basically the application of heat to food to make it more appetizing, digestible, palatable, and safe to eat. Heat has been applied to food for centuries, but only recently have new methods and equipment been developed to aid cooks in producing quality food in a short period of time.

To prepare food properly, a person must have knowledge of basic cooking principles and methods. Food reacts or changes when heat is applied to it.

Thus, in cooking, a roast not only changes color but changes texture and flavor as well. A rare steak is best when it is still fairly red inside but no longer has the soft, jellylike consistency of raw meat. A cake is the product of a delicate balance of the gelatinization of starch, the coagulation of protein, and the action of a leavening agent. A soup depends on the solubility and flavor development of the ingredients used. The ability to produce a wide

165

variety of fine food takes years of training and learning.

COOKING PRINCIPLES

Cooking is a science, as are chemistry, microbiology, physics, and geology. Of these, cooking is most closely related to chemistry and physics. The properties of many ingredients used in cooking resemble those of chemical substances, since they react under certain conditions. For example, baking powder and baking soda react to give off carbon dioxide gas. Mayonnaise is an emulsion made by using egg to bring tiny globules of oil into a state of suspension. Heat causes many reactions to occur and is the focus of the discussion in this chapter.

Heat

Heat is measured by a unit called the *calorie,* defined as the amount of heat required to raise the temperature of 1 gram of water by 1 Celsius degree. It is a one-thousandth part of the Calorie (or Kcal) which is the amount of heat required to raise the temperature of 1 kg of water by 1 Celsius degree. Our present American system uses the Btu (British thermal unit) to measure heat. This is the amount of heat needed to raise the temperature of 1 lb of water by 1 Fahrenheit degree. About 4 Btu equals 1 calorie, since 1 Btu equals 0.252 calories; 1 Calorie or Kcal equals 3,968 Btu.

The Celsius method of measuring heat uses a scale based on the range between the temperature at which water freezes (0°C) and the temperature at which water boils at one atmosphere of pressure (100°C). The distance between freezing and boiling is then divided into 100 equal units—the Celsius degree. In contrast to this, the Fahrenheit scale identifies 32°F as the freezing point of water and 212°F as the boiling point of water. Thus there are 180 Fahrenheit degrees between boiling and freezing (212 − 32 = 180). This means that a Fahrenheit degree is 100/180 of a Celsius degree, and that a Celsius degree is 180/100 of a Fahrenheit degree.

These work out to the fractions $\frac{5}{9}$ (0.55) and $\frac{9}{5}$ (1.80), respectively.

To convert temperature readings from Fahrenheit to Celsius, subtract 32 from the Fahrenheit reading and multiply the remainder by $\frac{5}{9}$ or 0.55. For example, 50°F equals 10°C ($50 - 32 = 18 \times \frac{5}{9} = 10$). To convert temperature readings from Celsius to Fahrenheit, multiply the Celsius value by $\frac{9}{5}$ or 1.80 and add 32. For example, 40°C equals 104°F ($\frac{9}{5} \times 40 = 72 + 32 = 104$).

When we speak of Btu or calories, we are talking about a quantity of heat. When we say that it takes 30,000 Btu (about 7,500 calories) for an electric range to bring a stockpot containing 10 gallons of soup from 50°F (10°C) to boiling (212°F), we are indicating the quantity of heat needed to do this job. Only about 13,500 Btu actually perform the heating; the rest of the heat is lost from the range top. A kilowatt of electricity produces 3,412 Btu. Thus, it takes nearly 10 kilowatts or 34,120 Btu of energy to do the job.

Comparing Fuel Heat Values

A gas range is about as efficient as an electric range, if the usable heat of the gas range is considered. The gas range must produce more actual heat than the electric range to do the same job, however, because it must exhaust some heat with its combustion gases. Electricity is said to be 100 percent efficient, while gas is said to have an efficiency of from 75 to 80 percent.

Competitive pricing makes the cost of electricity and gas about the same in many localities. A kilowatt-hour of electricity often sells for about 4.5 times more than a cubic foot of gas, if prices are competitive. For example, if electricity sells for $0.03 per kilowatt-hour, natural gas must sell for around $0.007 per cubic foot to be competitive ($0.03 ÷ 4.5 = $0.00694).

Suppose that a kitchen needed 20,000,000 Btu in one period. If electricity sold for $0.03 per kilowatt-hour and gas for $6.94 per Therm (1 Therm equals 100 cubic feet of gas or 1,052,000 Btu), what is the cost of electricity and of natural gas to furnish 20,000,000 Btu?

$$\frac{\text{ELECTRICITY:}}{100\% \text{ efficiency} \times 3{,}412 \text{ Btu/kilowatt-}} = \$175.84$$
$$\text{hour} \times \$0.03$$

$$\frac{\text{GAS:}}{75\% \text{ efficiency} \times 1{,}052{,}000 \text{ Btu/Therm}} = \$175.07$$
$$\times \$6.94$$

In terms of usable heat, steam equipment has a slightly higher efficiency than gas-fueled or electrical equipment. As an energy source, steam has an efficiency of 100 percent, compared to electricity at 100 percent and natural gas at 75 to 80 percent. Steam is sold on the basis of 1,000-lb lots; thus, 1,000 lb of steam must sell for nearly the same price as a Therm of gas to be competitive with it, and it must cost approximately 290 times more than a kilowatt-hour of electricity.

Sometimes steam is rated on the basis of horsepower. For instance, a kitchen's demand might be said to be 5 horsepower per hour. A horsepower of steam equals 34,000 Btu, so the requirement in this example would be $5 \times 34{,}000 = 170{,}000$ Btu.

As we move into the future and energy becomes more scarce and costly, we will have to become more knowledgeable about the energy efficiency of various kinds of equipment—as well as about the efficiency of the various kinds of fuel available to us—so that we can compare their costs and determine which provides the maximum yield for the energy and money expended.

Heat Transfer

Heat moves by conduction, by convection, or by radiation. In cooking, all three means are used, although the first is perhaps the most commonly used. Heat flows from relatively warm portions or areas to relatively cool ones. When two substances reach the same temperature, there is no flow of heat between them.

Conduction. Conduction is the movement of heat through material by passing from one molecule of matter to the next, spreading eventually through the whole substance. An electrical element buried in an iron griddle top becomes hot; and since the element is touching the iron, the heat flows to it and then spreads throughout the griddle. If a match is lit and held at the end of a metal rod, the heat will flow along the metal until it is felt at the other end of the rod. In cooking, we transfer heat through a burner into the pot, from there into the water or fat, and from there into the food. Thus, several layers of conducting media are involved. Copper and aluminum are very good conductors of heat, and iron is not bad. Because stainless steel is a relatively poor conductor, stainless steel frying pans and other equipment made of this metal usually have copper-clad bottoms; the copper readily picks up the heat, and then transfers it evenly through the pan.

Convection. Convection is the movement of heat in liquid or gas. Hot air expands, making it lighter than cold air and causing it to rise. Cold air descends, where it in turn becomes heated. The result in an enclosed space is a circular motion of air picking up heat, carrying it upward, cooling, and then sinking back down to get more heat. In the convection oven, heat is moved by a fan that distributes or convects the hot air throughout the oven. A convection oven works more efficiently than a regular oven, which depends on the natural convection of hot air. Natural convection does not spread the heat out as well. Convection can also occur with hot liquids such as water or fat. A refrigerator works because a liquid (the refrigerant) picks up heat from inside the refrigerated chamber and moves it away.

Radiation. Radiation is the transfer of heat by wave energy. Radiated heat travels about 186,000 miles per second, so it takes the sun's heat about 8.3 minutes to reach the earth from the moment it is radiated. Radiated heat is tiny particles of energy that flow from a hot body to a cooler one. One person who is warmer than another in a room will radiate heat to the other person.

Broilers and toasters cook largely by radiation.

To get the highest amount of radiation from the heating element, the level of white heat should be reached. An object glowing with red heat gives off some radiation in the infrared wave-energy range, but an object glowing with white heat gives off considerably more radiant energy. This is why some broilers contain ceramic particles that reach white heat when heated up—a temperature about 6,000°F (3,316°C).

A dark object absorbs more heat than a lighter one does. This is why aluminum pans containing frozen foods are colored black on the outside. Because a shiny object reflects radiated heat away, heat reflectors are used in ovens to bounce radiant energy back at the food being cooked. By the same token, a shiny, bright aluminum pan will not bake a pie as well as a duller pan will. If we want to wrap something in a way that helps hold the heat in, we put the shiny aluminum side of the wrapper inside, so that it bounces the heat back. Conversely, if we want to keep heat from getting in, we put the shiny aluminum side of the wrapper on the outside.

Time and Temperature

Time and temperature must be controlled to get the desired cooking results. If a food is cooked at a lower temperature, the cooking time must be extended. Raising the temperature may shorten the cooking time. Through the manipulation of the relationship between temperature and time, food can be cooked to the proper doneness. Too high a temperature cooks a cake on the outside before the leavening gas has fully developed inside. The cake eventually cracks on the top because the gases expanding inside, after the top has become firm, break through all at once. A steak can be overcooked on the outside and undercooked on the inside because of too much heat. On the other hand, many foods come out soft and pasty when insufficient heat is used to cook them.

Large pieces of meat are best cooked for longer periods of time at lower temperatures. This results in better flavor, more juiciness, and a better texture. Smaller pieces of meat should be cooked at slightly higher temperatures, because the longer cooking times associated with lower temperatures can lead to dried-out meat. Tougher cuts of meat and vegetables are best cooked for longer periods of time, in order to tenderize or soften them. Extended, low-temperature cooking dissolves the connective tissues in meat, while high heat can make meat less tender by causing excessive shrinkage and a toughening of some of the protein.

Overcooking can destroy nutrients, as can too much heat. Steam destroys nutrients faster than cooking in water because it is higher in temperature; however, since steam does not leach away or dissolve as many of the nutrients as cooking in water does, the overall nutrient loss is usually less. Temperatures must be adjusted to the particular food being cooked (see fig. 8-1). A potato baked at 350°F (177°C) is soggy and has a poorer flavor than one baked at 425°F (218°C). Some people prefer a fairly high heat for broiling a steak, since this improves the outside flavor as a result of caramelization of some of the substances.

Energy

For a long time, this country took its supply of energy for granted: it was there, and that it could possibly run out was never considered. In 1972, American oil and gas production peaked; ever since then, the production of these two energies has decreased. Today, the United States imports about half of its oil needs from OPEC nations and others. We are also beginning to make substantial shipments of frozen liquid natural gas, and this import of gas should increase substantially in coming years. Since 1973, energy prices have more than doubled. Energy prices are expected to continue to rise by between 5 and 10 percent annually in the future.

Coal and nuclear fission seem to be the best present answers to our future fuel needs. We have enough coal to last for over 500 years and enough uranium to last for about 200 years. Thorium, plutonium, and other heavy molecular substances can also be used to produce energy. If a way to fuse molecules together (as in the fusion of two atoms of hydrogen to make helium) can be found, our sup-

Figure 8-1. Oven temperatures for different cooking purposes.

°C	°F	
232-246	450-475	Very hot (quick) oven
232	450 and up	Grilling heat at heat source
204-218	400-425	Hot oven
177-190.5	350-375	Moderate oven
149-190.5	300-375	Usual for shallow frying, deep-frying, and griddling
149-163	300-325	Slow oven
128	250	Steam at a pressure of 103-4 kN/m^2 (15 pounds)
109	228	Steam at a pressure of 34-5 kN/m^2 (5 pounds)
100	212	Water boils at a sea level
95	203	Flour and cornflour are thickened
		Simmering, poaching, braising
85-91	185-195	Good for dissolving gelatine
		Holding coffee and hot chocolate
85	185	Maximum for egg custards
		Hollandaise sauce
82	180	Final rinse in dish machine (10 seconds)
		Well-cooked meat
71	160	Medium-cooked meat
69	156	Eggs coagulate (yolks (76°C) whites (74°C))
65	150	Thermotainers
		Most food for serving
60	140	Hot fudge and similar sauces
		Rare meat
		Wash water for tableware
51	125	Roll warmers
7.5-60	45-140	Danger range within which food bacteria thrive in moist nonacid food materials
7.5	45	Holding fountain syrups and sauces
4.5	40	Holding most fruits, vegetables, and dairy products
	34-36	Meat storage
0	32	Water freezes
-4.5--3.30	24-26	Service of milk shakes
-13.5--11	8-12	Holding ice cream for dipping
-29--18	-20-0	Holding frozen foods

(not to scale)

ply of nuclear energy may be inexhaustible. Solar energy, the manufacture of gas and other combustible products from organic materials, the extraction of oil from shale or tar sands, the use of geothermal energies, wind energy, tidal energy, and energy from the heat of the seas are all possibilities. All will undoubtedly contribute to our energy needs in the future. While we will probably not run out of energy, the energies we use in the future will differ from those we used in the past. Energy is also going to be much more expensive.

We have been an energy-wasteful nation because we have had so much of it, and because energy was so cheap. Often, it was less expensive to use energy than to add insulation or build better buildings. We could overspecify needs in lighting, in heating, and in cooling because the cost of doing so was not great and the additional benefits were desirable. Now, this must stop. In addition to finding new sources of energy to supply our ever-increasing needs, we have to start saving energy and obtaining maximum yields from energy use. We can no longer afford to waste energy, and our government will see that we do not, by monitoring our use of energy in the future. We will have to learn to make do with less, because the supply will be limited.

Programs to save energy have been established by the National Restaurant Association, the American Hotel-Motel Association, and others. Many foodservices, hotels, and motels set up energy-saving programs. It is not unusual to achieve a 25 percent savings without too much effort. Both employer and employee must bear some responsibility for reducing energy use. The program for practicing this joint responsibility will have to be carefully planned and implemented, if energy is to be saved.

Responsibility of Management

Management must originate, plan, and implement energy-saving programs. To do so, it must have an overall grasp of what is involved and what is possible. No program will be successful it it does not pay off within a reasonable amount of time, and management should focus first on conservation steps that give the biggest payoff.

Most of the energy used in a foodservice is expended on heating and air-conditioning the facility, cooking food, and heating water. Much less energy is used for lighting, refrigeration, and other purposes. Producing savings in areas where large amounts of energy are used is therefore going to pay off more than producing proportionate savings in areas where small amounts of energy are used. Nonetheless, the small areas of use should not be omitted from attack. For example, reducing the number of lights or changing their wattage is a simple energy-saving step; and in any program of attack, the ease with which a program can be implemented should be a significant factor to consider.

Management should take time to study the problem and develop an overview of the whole establishment's use of energy. In some cases, an energy reduction in one area would simply require an energy increase of the same size in another. The advice of the utility companies serving the operation should be sought, since they are knowledgeable about how energy balance can be used to achieve savings. Management should also consult with the engineering division (if there is one) and should allow engineering to help plan and assess any energy-saving programs.

Ideas on how to save energy should be invited. Perhaps installing a solar heater would reduce the cost of heating water enough to allow long-term savings; installing curtains to stop airflow through doorways of walk-in refrigerators or freezers might likewise be desirable. A computer might be used to shut down some equipment during peak energy-use periods, in order to reduce the demand rate. Many operations pay not only a basic charge for the amount of electricity they use, but also a charge based on the maximum demand made for electricity at any one time during a period. Thus, reducing this maximum demand can often save money. It may be feasible, without creating any hardship for personnel, to make the building slightly less warm in winter and slightly less cool in the summer, thus saving energy. For every Fahrenheit degree in temperature saved in building heating or cooling, about a 3 percent saving in energy occurs. Cold-water detergents coupled with a sanitizing rinse in iodoform may provide an energy-efficient alternative to washing dishes in hot water. There are many possibilities that management should seek out and evaluate. When an idea seems to warrant implementation, management should see that a plan for accomplishing this is established.

A good program of preventive maintenance and repair can save energy. Employees of the engineering department should set up a schedule to see that such regular procedures as frequent defrosting of refrigeration coils, removal of lint and soil from around refrigeration condensers, testing limit switches for proper working order, ensuring the presence of a bluish white flame on gas burners, and checking to see that good gaskets are in use on refrigerators and steam equipment so that a complete seal is created (a paper put into a closed refrigerator or steamer door should be held firmly and should not be able to be pulled out) are maintained. Lights lose efficiency very quickly when they gather dust and soil. Consequently, lights and fixtures should be cleaned periodically to save energy. A light that is old uses a lot of energy but does not produce much light. This lowered efficiency can be ascertained when a light globe shows an inside darkening. It is better to throw such a light away and install a new one than to wait for it to burn out. Some operations now have a program in which lights are all changed at a specific time, regardless of whether they are still burning. The saving in labor of going around one time to change all lights in a facility—rather than spasmodically changing them one at a time—and the saving in energy previously discussed make such a program pay off.

It is management's responsibility to set up a program to instruct employees on the need, the ways, and the means of saving energy. No program will be successful if employees are merely told that they should save energy. They need instruction, guidance, and supervision.

After management has surveyed the situation and decided on a course of action, it sets the plan up and instructs employees to implement it. But management's job is not yet done. Employees need counsel and attention, and management must check to see that the plan is being followed.

It is wise to set up a chart that shows how many Btu of energy have been used during a month and what the cost of this energy is. This information can be put on a graph and placed prominently where employees can see it. This helps keep employees interested in the conservation program and lets them see how well they are doing.

Responsibility of the Employee

The focal point of any energy-saving program must be the employees, since it is primarily they who use the energy. Much energy is lost because employees turn equipment on too far in advance of use. The heat-up times of equipment should be ascertained, and employees should be instructed not to turn equipment on until only a period equal to the heat-up time remains before the equipment will be needed. Employees also often fail to plan production properly. As a result, they frequently use equipment when only a partial load is inside it. Scheduling the use of a grill, oven, or other unit can save energy by holding back production until a full batch is processed. One study found that the use of electricity in a bakeshop could be reduced by 27 percent simply by replanning the use of ovens, baker's stoves, and other heating equipment. Too often, energy-consuming equipment stands idle, waiting for items from some other part of production to be readied for it.

Employees often turn equipment on with the thermostat set extra high, thinking that this will make the unit heat faster. It will not. Then the employee goes on working and often forgets to turn down the heat, letting the equipment overheat and forcing workers to turn it off so it can cool down to the proper temperature. This is both wasteful of energy and hard on the equipment. Also, if an operation has its electric bill figured on a demand basis, employees should not turn all electrical equipment on at once. Turning on one or two units that are needed first is the correct procedure. When these heat up, several other units can be turned on next, and so on until all needed equipment is ready.

This avoids setting a high peak demand at the start and saves money as well as energy.

Energy can be wasted by careless employees in a number of ways. An employee should know that when water boils, it is as hot as it will ever get. Keeping the heat up and letting the boiling continue does not cook the food any faster: it only wastes energy. Over three times as much energy is needed to keep something on full boil as to keep it on simmer, and yet the cooking time is about the same for both. When an item boils, the excess heat goes through the product and is lost. No extra heat goes into the food. Then, extra energy must be used to operate fans to move this lost heat so that it does not become a problem for the employee.

Employees should be taught how to maintain equipment and do simple repairs on it. It should not be necessary for an engineer to fix a gas burner to ensure a proper flame; it is a simple enough task, requiring only proper adjustment. Many times equipment wastes energy because it is dirty or because it is improperly handled and maintained. Operational and maintenance manuals should be available for employee use. Supervisors should see that they are used and should instruct employees on the proper handling of equipment.

Employees should be taught to organize ahead for withdrawals of food from walk-in refrigerator and freezer units and even for withdrawals from reach-ins. Open doors can let a lot of cool air escape. Similarly, opening an oven door leads to a reduction in oven temperature of about 30 Fahrenheit degrees for every 5 seconds the door remains open.

More heat is needed to raise the temperature of water 1 Fahrenheit degree than to raise the temperature of almost any other substance an equal amount; yet employees run it freely, thinking little of the energy going down the drain. Much energy is saved if water temperatures in the boiler are reduced; 160°F (71°C) is much too hot to put one's hand into; 140°F (60°C) water serves just as well for many kitchen uses.

Employees should be aware of how costly it is to operate equipment. The energy needed to run a high-power fan can cost over $3 per day; furnishing the hot water for a pot-and-pan sink costs about $11 per day; energy for ranges and ovens can run as high as $9 per unit per day. Compiling a list of costs and publishing these may bring about increased awareness of the cost of energy. Perhaps then a dishwasher will not be left running when nothing is going through it, and other units may be shut down when they are not needed.

Employees should feel that they have an obligation to see that maximum yield is obtained for the energy used, and they should realize that energy-saving steps can occur only through their actions. Saving energy benefits not only the operation but also the country and, ultimately, the employees themselves.

Responsibility of the Manufacturer

In the future, manufacturers undoubtedly will pay a lot more attention to the energy efficiency of their equipment than they have in the past. A small gas pilot left on for 24 hours, 365 days a year, can cost as much as $70 each year in some high-energy-cost areas. Automatic-lighting pilots are needed. Temperature sensors should be installed so that, when foods reach a specific temperature, the heat shuts off or shuts down to a continuing temperature. Better conducting materials and better insulation are also needed. More efficient burners than are produced by drilling holes into pipe are possible. Some refrigerators have automatic defrosters that rely on electric heat to remove the ice on coils, while at the same time heat that could be used from the condensers is allowed to dissipate into the area.

More attention should be paid to ensuring that energy in equipment reaches the items to be cooked rather than go out freely into space. Heat reflectors or other heat-directing equipment could help. Better thermostats are needed, too. A solid-state thermostat is currently available, but few manufacturers put it on equipment, since it is more expensive than conventional thermostats. Manufacturers should alert buyers to the fact that, by paying slightly more for equipment, they can obtain a substantially better payoff in energy saving. In the past, the low cost of energy did not make it practical for businesses to invest more in energy-saving devices and controls; now, however, with the higher cost of energy, buyers are more willing to pay the extra initial cost if they are aware of the benefits.

COOKING METHODS

A good chef or cook knows that *mise en place* is one of the most important things to learn in the profession. The term means "put in place," and it refers to organizing the job beforehand, getting all the materials needed, and then keeping things in order, cleaned up, and moving toward the final goal of production. Items needing no cooking—such as chopped onions, carrots, and grated cheese—should be ready and easily accessible. All materials to be used should be on hand, as should all necessary tools and utensils. Tools should be sharp and in good condition.

Another important thing to know is which cooking method is best to use for a particular menu item. Many times recipes indicate which method to use, but professional cooks and bakers have learned that specific products are best produced through certain special cooking methods. These methods can be separated into two general categories: cooking with liquid, and cooking without liquid.

Cooking with Liquid

Liquids used in cooking may be water, milk, tomato juice, wine, broth, or stock. Cooking in liquid is called *moist-heat cookery.* Meats contain a fibrous substance called *collagen* that holds them together and makes them tough. Because collagen can be dissolved by moist heat, many tough cuts, such as beef chuck, are cooked in liquid. The connective tissue in vegetables is called *cellulose,* and this too must be softened by moist heat. Most other foods can also be cooked in liquid. Even tender items such as fish may be cooked in this way to give them special moistness or to develop their flavor. Some vegetables are baked—but only those

containing enough moisture to produce the effect of a moist heat in baking.

The most common methods of cooking in liquid are boiling, blanching, braising, poaching, simmering, steaming, and stewing. Some of these involve only slight differences in cooking methods.

Boiling

Boiling involves cooking substances by submerging them in water that is maintained at a sea-level temperature of 212°F (100°C) (see table 8-1). A disadvantage of this method is that cooking in water leaches out valuable nutrients, which may be lost if the cooking water is discarded. Such nutrients can be saved, however, by using the cooking liquid for a stock, soup, or sauce. Usually foods are boiled for a minimum time only. Vegetables, for instance, may not be completely cooked when removed from the boiling water; instead, they are sent to the steam table, where they finish cooking while being held. Many items are cooked in part by being dropped into boiling water, which shortens their overall cook-

Table 8-1. Boiling Temperatures at Various Altitudes

Altitude above Sea Level (ft)	Boiling Point of Water	
	°F	°C
0	212.0	100.0
500	211.1	99.6
1,000	210.2	99.0
2,000	208.4	98.0
3,000	206.6	97.0
4,000	204.8	96.0
5,000	203.0	95.0
6,000	201.2	94.0
7,000	199.4	93.0
7,500	198.5	92.5
8,000	197.6	92.0
9,000	195.8	91.0
10,000	194.0	90.0
12,000	190.4	88.0
15,000	185.0	85.0

Source: Nichols 1971.

ing time. Spaghetti, other pastas, and cereals are cooked by being dropped into boiling water and stirred so that they avoid sticking together. Hard boiling is never recommended because it wastes fuel and can toughen some items and break up others (such as soft vegetables). Meats are seldom boiled, but many are simmered instead. Eggs, poultry, and fish are not boiled, either, because the high boiling temperature harms the proteins they contain.

Blanching

Blanching involves subjecting an item to boiling water for only a short time. It may be called *scalding,* although this term usually refers to dipping a food into water or allowing a hot water bath to strike the food for a very short time. Scalded milk is milk brought just to boiling and then taken off the flame to reduce its temperature rapidly. Kidneys and chicory may be blanched to remove some of their strong flavor, and liver and sweetbreads may be blanched to remove the external membrances. Some fruits and vegetables, such as peaches and tomatoes, may be blanched or scalded to remove the outer skins. Because blanching can stop enzymatic action, some fruits and vegetables that are to be frozen are blanched first.

Blanching also commonly refers to the nearly complete cooking of vegetables in deep oil, after which the cooking of the blanched vegetables is completed in a second step just before service. Parboiling is another form of blanching, but in this case the item remains in the water for a longer period of time. Again the purpose is to cook the item partially before giving it other treatment. Thus, squash may be parboiled before it is baked. Parboiling may also be done to firm a food before it is handled further. Even though blanching, scalding, and parboiling do not usually produce completely cooked food, they are special methods of liquid cooking that are classed as separate cooking techniques.

Braising

Braising involves cooking food in a small quantity of liquid. Fowl (old chickens), meat, vegetables, and other foods that must be cooked for a long time are often braised.

There are two methods of braising: *brun* (brown), or *blanc* (blond). *Brun* involves first searing the meat to give it color. It is erroneously thought that searing seals in a meat's juices; studies show that this is not true. Searing is usually done in a small quantity of fat, and the meat is turned frequently until it is well-browned on all sides. Some foods may be dredged in flour before being seared. A blond product is braised in the same way as a browned one is, except that it is not seared, that is, it is not placed in a small quantity of hot fat to gain color first. After searing, if it is done at all, the product is put into a covered pan, known as a brazier, and liquid (water, stock, thin sauce, or a combination of these) is added to the level of one-third of the height of a roast or two-thirds of the height of smaller food products. Often, a mirepoix (50 percent chopped onion, 25 percent chopped carrots, and 25 percent chopped celery) is added, along with seasonings. The mixture is then brought to a simmer, on top of the range, after which the brazier is tightly covered and placed in a 300° to 325°F (149° to 163°C) oven until the product is well done or tender. The leftover liquid may be used to make a sauce or pan gravy, if meat is being cooked.

Pot-roasting, swissing, fricasséeing, and jugging all are forms of braising. Pot-roasting is usually a *brun* product, and a smaller quantity of liquid may be used for it than for some other braised items. Swissing is very similar to pot-roasting but is done to smaller meats. A fricassée is often a braised product, although sometimes it refers to a stewed product. Jugging is a form of cooking that takes place in a covered pot. It is often used with game meats, especially hare.

Poaching

Poaching is cooking in liquid at a temperature below the boiling point of water. It amounts to a low simmer. The food may or may not be covered with liquid, although the liquid should be at least halfway up the food. Poaching is usually done in a shallow pan in stock, court bouillon (for fish), milk, or some other liquid. Food may be basted with the liquid. Fish, eggs, and certain other foods that require gentle handling and low-temperature cooking are often poached. Poaching poultry increases its flavor, moistness, tenderness, and yield over roasting, particularly in larger birds. This method takes only half the time of roasting and requires less cooking space. Turkeys may be poach-roasted with excellent results. For this, turkey cut into parts is placed skin-side-down in pans, partially covered with water or stock, and poached in an oven.

Simmering

Simmering involves immersing food in a liquid and cooking it at a temperature of between 185° and 205°F (85° and 96°C). Often, the liquid is brought to a boil, the food is added, and the product is then held at the simmering temperature until cooked. At other times, the liquid and the product are brought slowly up from room temperature to simmering and then held there. This is the procedure used in making a clarified consommé or bouillon. Meat placed in cool water and brought from the cold stage to a simmering temperature gives slightly more flavor to stock than does meat added to already hot water and cooked. Simmering is usually described by a chef as "let the liquid smile, not laugh out loud." "Laughing out loud" is thought of as hard boiling. In simmering tiny bubbles appear from time to time and only some slow motion is apparent. Meat, poultry, and some other items are more tender, juicier, and more flavorful when simmered. The cooking liquid may be used to add flavor. Since braising is also cooking below a boil, it can be considered a simmering method.

Steaming

Steaming involves cooking foods in boiling-hot water vapor. This method favors the retention of nutrients. In free-vent steaming the food is placed over or in live steam and allowed to cook. Many vegetables, potatoes, and other foods cook well this way. Free-vent steaming can also be done in a waterless cooker—a very heavy kettle fitted with a

tight lid. No water is added to the cooker, but the food generates enough of its own liquid to produce steam. Carrots, cabbage, and some other high-moisture vegetables cook well by this method.

Special equipment may be used for steaming vegetables. For example, steam can be introduced under pressure, to raise the temperature and cook the food more quickly (see table 8-2). High-pressure steamers of this type cook with a pressure of around 15 psi; lower-pressure steamers cook at around 6 psi; in the former type, some vegetables cook in a matter of seconds. Food cooked in the lower-pressure units reach doneness a bit more slowly, but still much faster than when boiled.

Cooking can also be accomplished with forced steam convection, which feeds steam in around food with great turbulence, increasing the speed of heat transfer to the food without requiring the heat to exceed 212°F (100°C). The theory underlying this method is that the force of the steam convection breaks a naturally formed barrier that exists between the steam and the food in a more static steamer.

Steaming may reduce shrinkage, as well as preserve form, flavor, and nutrients. There is no burning or boiling over, which reduces the amount of cleaning required. The same-size pans can be used for steaming as are used during holding in the steam-table; thus the number of pots that have to be washed is reduced. Almost any kind of food can be steamed, but foods that pack and some doughs

Table 8-2. Steam Temperatures at Different Pressures

Gauge Pressure (psi)	Temperature	
	°F	°C
0	212.0	100.0
2	218.3	103.5
4	224.6	107.0
6	229.8	109.9
8	235.0	112.8
10	239.4	115.2
15	249.6	120.9

and batters do not respond as well to steaming as to other methods. Steam can also be used to reheat foods quickly, and it is a good way to thaw foods prior to giving them other treatment.

Stewing

Stewing involves simmering small cuts of meat, disjointed fowl, or cut-up meat in liquid. It is distinguished from braising in that braising typically involves whole or sliced food, whereas stews are made up of chopped or cubed food. Another difference between stewing and braising is that, in stewing, the item being cooked is completely covered with water, stock, broth, or other liquid, whereas in braising only the amount of liquid needed for service (2 ounces per person, typically) is used. Stewing usually involves thickening the liquid with starch and serving it, together with its cubed, cut, or chopped contents, as a one-dish course. Braised foods, on the other hand, are served with garnishes and vegetables.

Stewing is done in a heavy pot to ensure even cooking, and it usually takes place on top of the range or in a steam-jacketed kettle. Depending on the color desired in the stew, the food to be cooked may or may not be browned first. Thus, stews are either *brun* or *blanc*. Browning results in a darker-colored stew such as a brown ragoût. The light-colored Irish lamb stew, on the other hand, requires no browning of ingredients. Whether or not the cooking vessel is covered is another variable that affects the end product. Greater reduction (through evaporation) of the liquid takes place in a stew that is allowed to vent freely, and the result is a thicker, heavier stew.

Meats, poultry, seafoods, fruits, vegetables, and various combinations of these are stewed. Stews may be seasoned in different ways, and usually an operation develops its own stew of distinctive flavor. Many stews are low in cost and yet highly popular with customers.

Cooking without Liquid

Methods of dry-heat cooking (cooking without moisture) are usually employed for tender meats,

fish, and poultry, for some less-tender products of these, and for moist food products. Meats high in connective tissue do not cook well in dry heat. Low temperatures are usually used, although broilers may generate temperatures of up to 6,000°F (3,316°C). Overcooking or excessive heat can dry products out and toughen them; lower-temperature cooking allows some of the connective tissues to soften before the item is done. Tough products that must be cooked a long time in dry heat come out tough, dry, and unpalatable.

Major methods of cooking without liquid include baking, barbecuing, broiling, grilling, ovenizing, roasting, and frying (both deep-frying and sautéing). Frying and sautéing use no liquid other than hot fat, which may be viewed as presenting a special case of dry-heat cooking because of its particular traits as a cooking medium.

Baking

Baking involves cooking in dry heat in an oven. Vegetables, meats, doughs, batters, fish, and poultry are often baked. Baking temperatures normally range from 250° to 475°F (121° to 246°C), although higher temperatures can be used (see table 8-3).

Some hard-crusted breads and other products must be baked with steam. This keeps the crust soft during part of the baking so that a heavier, crisper crust is formed later when the steam is turned off.

Table 8-3. Oven Temperatures

Description	Temperature		Gas No.
	°F	°C	
Very slow	250	121	½
Slow	300	149	1
Medium slow	325	163	2½
Medium (moderate)	350	177	4
Medium hot (moderate)	375	191	5½
Hot (moderately hot)	400	204	7
Hot	425	218	8½
Very hot	450–475	232–246	10–11½

Source: Adapted from Nichols 1971 and Harmond 1964.

Some ovens are heated in stacks, with the heat rising from the bottom level to the top stack. The temperature difference may be 5 to 10 Fahrenheit degrees (2.7 to 5.6 Celsius degrees) between the bottom level and the top level of the stack. Foods requiring relatively high baking temperatures are baked in the lower stacks, and foods requiring relatively low baking temperatures are baked in the upper ones. The heat in baking is transferred mostly by natural convection, except in convection ovens. Some radiation can be obtained, as well, by using metal reflectors. A casserole is said to be baked, but it is actually cooked by a form of braising in the oven. Baking and roasting may be the same thing.

Barbecuing

The term *barbecuing* is often applied to a method of broiling foods while basting them with a special sauce. Real barbecuing, however, involves roasting foods in a covered pit. Some barbecue ovens duplicate this, introducing a smoke that gives special flavor to the product. The sauce added is usually quite tangy. In oven- and pit-barbecuing, cooking temperatures are kept quite low; but in barbecuing over a grill or in a broiler, the temperatures are higher. Barbecued food is normally very popular.

Broiling

Broiling involves cooking by radiant heat. Food is placed on a rack above, below, or between the heat source(s), which may use gas, electricity, or charcoal. The proper temperature to maintain is governed by the fattiness, tenderness, and size of the food. Broilers should be preheated but should not be left on constantly unless used constantly. Food is usually dipped into oil or brushed with oil to prevent it from sticking and to reduce evaporative loss. Depending on the thickness of the food and the intensity of the heat, food is placed 3 to 6 inches from the heat source. Frozen foods and very thick pieces are cooked even farther from the heat source, so the heat will not be too great. Flames should be controlled. Charring (the burning of fat from broiling) is suspected by some authorities of causing cancer.

Meats, poultry, seafood, fish, many vegetables, and some fruits are prepared by broiling. A 2-inch-thick steak requires about 10 minutes of broiling on each side. Some cooks prefer to use a higher temperature at the end to develop a rich, brown color. Broiling takes skill; creativity and expertise are required to produce a good broiled product. Pan-broiling is a method of cooking food on the hot, dry surface of a pan in which conduction, not radiation, is the process of heat transfer. Any fat present during pan-broiling is discarded before it can accumulate.

Grilling

In its broadest sense, the term *grilling* refers to cooking on a fat-coated surface or griddle at fairly high temperatures of 325° to 400°F (163° to 204°C). The French consider grilling to be synonymous with broiling, and we hear the word used in this sense also. The term *mixed grill* is often used for broiled meats. Grilling and frying or sautéing are very similar. For grilling, food is put on a lightly greased griddle and fried. Additional fat may be added. Griddle-broiling involves cooking foods on a hot, dry surface, as in pan-broiling. The fat is removed as it forms around the product; similarly, in pan broiling, the fat is poured from the pan as it forms.

In both grilling and griddle-broiling, the product is cooked or browned on one side and then turned and cooked or browned on the other. The item should not be punctured, covered, or cooked in any liquid. Eggs are grilled at 325°F (163°C); French toast, at 350°F (177°C); and pancakes, potatoes, fish, and meat, at 400°F (204°C).

Ovenizing

Ovenizing involves placing food on greased pans, frequently dribbling fat over it, and baking it in an oven. Fairly high temperatures are used—325° to 425°F (163° to 218°C). Some smaller foods may be cooked at even higher temperatures. The finished food looks much like fried or sautéed food. Ovenizing is used in quantity cookery to produce large amounts of food with relatively little labor. Breaded foods need more fat added than nonbreaded ones do. In either case, however, the total amount of fat used is less in ovenizing than in sautéing (frying) or deep-frying.

Roasting

The term *roasting* originally meant cooking on a spit over an open fire—a practice that would be called *broiling* or *barbecuing* today. Today it means cooking food with dry, indirect heat in an oven. The term *baking* is frequently used to mean roasting, but it may also be used differently: we bake a ham, but we roast a sirloin; bread and other bakery products are baked, but nuts are roasted. For roasting, meat is placed, fat side up, on a rack or trivet (perforated underliner) in an uncovered pan that contains no liquid. As the meat cooks, the fat bastes it. Because the meat is raised above the bottom of the pan by the rack or trivet, it avoids braising in its own juices and fat. The meat should be fitted to the pan. Leaving too much bottom surface exposed allows the drippings to char and burn.

Using a temperature as low as 300°F (149°C) gives the highest yield and the best flavor. Some chefs start roasts at 450°F (232°C) to sear the meat and give it a nicely browned outer surface; they then drop the heat to the desired roasting temperature. Smaller pieces of meat may be roasted at higher temperatures to limit their drying out.

Meat is considered well done when it has an internal temperature of around 170°F (77°C) or more, medium done at around 160°F (71°C), and rare at 140°F (60°C). Aged meat may have to be cooked to lower internal temperatures for rare and medium, since the color change in such meat occurs at a lower temperature than in unripened meat. A large roast should be removed from the oven when its internal temperature is about 15 to 25 Fahrenheit degrees (8.3 to 13.9 Celsius degrees) away from the desired degree of doneness, since a temperature rise in the meat's interior occurs after removal from the oven. Pork, rabbit, and some other meats should always be cooked to well done to ensure that trichinae are destroyed.

Frying

Frying involves cooking foods in a fat or an oil. It adds a rather nutty, pleasing flavor to the food, as well as crisp texture and good appearance. Over- or underfrying is easily possible. A fry cook possessing considerable skill makes a delicious and wholesome product; a poor fry cook produces greasy, dry, hard, tasteless products. The term *frying* may indicate either deep-frying or sautéing. In this text and in the trade, however, the word *fry* most often means sauté; if deep-frying is meant, the term *deep-frying* is usually used.

Deep-Frying. Deep-frying involves cooking foods by immersing them in hot fat. If properly done, this method produces tasty, attractive products. Fat is kept from penetrating the food either by a coating of flour, batter, or dough that forms an impenetrable crust when the item begins to fry, or by the use of sufficiently high fat temperatures to cause the product itself to create a barrier of steam that prevents grease penetration. Problems arise if the temperature of the fat drops below the level required to keep the vapor barrier around the food: the result is a soggy, greasy product. To deep-fry successfully, a cook should know something about fats and oils, cooking temperatures, and the proper techniques to obtain high-quality products.

A cooking fat and a cooking oil are very similar chemically. They differ in that a cooking fat has a higher percentage of saturated fatty acids, while a cooking oil contains a higher proportion of polyunsaturated and monounsaturated fatty acids. In terms of cooking there are differences as well. Products deep-fried in cooking fats have a slightly different flavor—one that is preferred by several fastfood companies for cooking french fries—than products deep-fried in cooking oil. An oil can be made to approximate a cooking fat through the process of hydrogenation, whereby the unsaturated portion of the oil accepts additional hydrogen atoms and, therefore, increases the proportion of saturated fat in the oil. The higher the proportion of saturated fat in a cooking oil or fat, the more solid it will appear. For instance, at room temperature butter is relatively solid and opaque, a cooking fat is soft and cloudy, and an oil is liquid and translucent.

An oil is made into a solid fat by being heated under pressure, having ground nickel added to it, and then having hydrogen gas bubbled through it.

An atom of nickel picks up a hydrogen atom and fixes it at an unsaturated point. It then leaves, picks up another hydrogen atom, and fixes it at another unsaturated point. Thus, the nickel does not join the fat permanently but acts as a carrier to help the reaction along. We call this type of chemical agent a *catalyst* and we call this process *hydrogenation.*

Oils and fats are called *saturated* (if all places are filled on the carbon chain), *monounsaturated* (if one place is not filled), or *polyunsaturated* (if more than one place is unfilled). Hard fats from meat, coconut oil, and cacao (chocolate) oil are usually saturated. Some vegetable oils, lard, poultry fat, and a few others may contain combinations of saturated and unsaturated fats and oils in varying ratios. Fish and some vegetable oils are quite unsaturated. A monounsaturated or polyunsaturated oil does not perform as well in frying as does a saturated one.

Other factors also are important for frying. A good frying oil should not have a smoking point (the temperature at which decomposition occurs and fumes are given off) below 425°F (218°C). Satisfying this condition requires starting with a good oil or fat that contains a large proportion of saturated particles. Stabilizers are also added. One of the best frying oils on the market contains a silicone compound that helps prevent the oil from breaking down and thus keeps it in good condition for frying. Most frying fats and oils contain antioxidants to reduce the chances of oxidative rancidity (or chemical deterioration) of the fat.

To produce a fat or oil, three fatty acids must react with one glycerol molecule to form a triglyceride. Basically, fats and oils are mixtures of triglycerides. Any fatty acid that is not linked to a glycerol molecule in a fat or oil is referred to as a *free* fatty acid. Removing free fatty acids from a fat gives it a higher smoking point and makes it a more durable cooking medium. Butter, lard, fish oils, and other fats contain many free fatty acids, which is why they smoke at relatively low temperatures and do not make good frying products. If pork, fish, and some other products are fried in a good frying fat, their fat with its free fatty acids gradually mingles with the good oil and lowers its quality.

When a fat or oil breaks down, its fatty acid chains break away from the glycerol molecules and become free fatty acids. When a fat breaks down extensively and smokes, acrolein—a white vapor that causes the nose, eyes, and throat to smart—is formed. A fat that is badly broken down assumes a dark color, smokes at a fairly low temperature, and gives food a sharp, acidic flavor. If breakdown is allowed to continue further, the fat begins to foam, and pale yellow bubbles crawl up and over the fryer.

Fats may not always break down; instead, they may join together to form waxes or resins. Resinous products may form on griddles or in deep fryers for this reason. Fats or oils that join together are called polymers. The formation of polymers is considered harmful to fat. Using fats properly and following recommended techniques helps prevent fat breakdown and the formation of polymers. Deteriorated fat should be discarded, since good foods cannot be produced in it.

Allowing foreign matter such as charred particles or crumbs to accumulate in a frying fat speeds the fat's deterioration, so the rule is to filter fat frequently. Fry kettles and equipment should be kept very clean, as well. Fat in a deep, narrow fryer will not break down as quickly as fat in a shallow, broad one with a much greater exposed area. Because metals such as copper, brass, and iron speed deterioration, fryer surfaces are usually made of nickel, chrome, or stainless steel. Salts such as common table salt and the curing salts used in cured meats also speed deterioration. Therefore, salt must be kept away from the fryer, and cured meats should not be fried in the deep fryer. Fat should be stored in a cool, dry, dark location in airtight containers. New oil or fat should never be put into uncleaned containers. Rancidity or other undesirable reactions are likely to occur if these frying products do not receive good care.

At the time a fryer is being loaded with fat, the thermostat should be set at 250°F (121°C) or lower. Fats will melt first around the heating elements and, if the temperature is too high, will scorch there. Once a fat breaks down, it quickly causes other good fat to go through the same process. Even though only a small amount is scorched, the breakdown of the entire mass of fat will be more rapid. A 15-lb fry kettle holds 15 lb of frying oil or fat, and this is the correct quantity to use for frying in that particular kettle. The ratio of fat to food is usually 6 to 10 lb of fat to 1 lb of food. French-fried potatoes and a few other foods can be fried at the lower ratios, while some others must be fried at the higher ones. A good fry kettle holding 15 lb of fat can fry about 2 to 2.5 lb of french-fried potatoes at one time, but only about 1.5 lb of chicken.

If about 15 to 20 percent of the fat or oil in the fryer is used up each day and new fat is added—along with good filtering, proper frying techniques, and correct temperatures—no fat need ever be discarded. The new added fat is sufficient to keep the whole mass of fat fresh and in good condition. This daily addition of fat without discarding the old is called *turnover.* Obtaining the right turnover and using proper frying methods will produce good fried products and save money.

Foods to be fried must be prepared differently according to the food and the final product desired. Some require little final preparation. For example, potatoes for french-frying are often soaked in cold water to prevent them from darkening. They are then drained well and fried, with no further treatment. Other foods may have to be breaded, dipped in batter, or wrapped in dough before being fried. High-moisture foods need a heavier, tighter cover than do drier products. Firm foods need less cover than do soft foods. Foods to be covered should be properly cleaned and dried first.

For breading, five trays or containers need to be set in a row: the first contains the product to be breaded; the second contains flour; the third contains a moistening mixture of egg wash (eggs plus liquid, usually milk), plain egg, or plain liquid; the fourth contains bread crumbs, cracker crumbs, corn meal, flour, or a prepared mix or some mixture of these; and the fifth (which may be a rack) holds the breaded product. Uniformity of crumb size in the fourth container is necessary. The finer the crumbs, the finer the coating will be. Breaded products should be allowed to dry for at least fifteen minutes

in the final pan or rack to give a coating that adheres best and puts as little moisture as possible into the fat. The fat bubbles less when drying has taken place (see fig. 8-2).

Batters need to be thick to adhere properly to food and give a good cover on the end product. Mixes are often used that only require the addition of water. Batters can also be made from scratch. Dough wraps must be done tightly to seal the product in and to prevent excessive fat penetration. The deep-fried apple turnover and the Chinese egg roll are examples of dough-wrapped products.

The temperature to use for deep-frying is dictated by the quantity of food to be fried in each batch, the temperature of the food, and the kind of food. The lowest frying temperatures are around 325°F (163°C), and the highest are around 425°F (218°C)—the latter being unusual but desirable for making puffed (souffléed) potatoes. A large quantity of cold food added all at once to the fryer drops the temperature, so original temperatures may have to be higher to prevent the food from cooling the fat so much that the food becomes soaked with grease and is poorly cooked. Large pieces of food are usually cooked at lower temperatures to prevent them from being overfried on the outside by the time the inside is done. Some thin items may be fried at high temperatures because they would dry out with extended cooking in fat. Food fried at the

Figure 8-2. Breading.

right temperature is golden brown, crisp on the outside, and low in retained fat. Foods fried at too high a temperature develop a dark brown, hard crust and a burned taste, and often have an uncooked center. Foods fried at too low a temperature become fat-soaked, unattractive, and unpalatable.

Fats subjected to heat should not remain unattended, since they might burst into flames. The flashpoint of a fat or oil is around 600°F (316°C). The melting point of most cooking fats is about 120°F (49°C). The smoking points for suet, butter, lard, and cottonseed oil are 235°F (113°C), 325°F (163°C), 345°F (174°C), and 420°F (216°C), respectively.

Deep-fry baskets should be loaded away from the fryer to prevent moisture or food particles from dropping into the fat. The baskets should not be overloaded. The lowering of the food into the fat must be done slowly so that the fat can adjust. If done too quickly, the fat may flow out of the kettle. After it is fully immersed, the basket is given a slight shake to loosen food that might be sticking together and to adjust it into the available space. The food may be lifted out during cooking and given another shake to distribute portions to cook all areas. When the food turns a golden brown, the basket is lifted. At this point, the food may be given a slight shake and the basket left to drain momentarily above the fat. Food should never be held in the basket over the fryer for prolonged periods of time, as this will lead to excessive fat absorption by the food and a greasy taste. Batter-dipped items should be put into the fryer after the basket has been lowered, in order to prevent the food from cooking onto the basket. The finished product should be held in a dry, warm place or under an infrared lamp. Products should only be salted immediately before service. Salting ahead reduces the crispness of the product. The following summary of proper deep-frying procedures was put together by Market Forge.

ACCEPTABLE FRIED FOODS RESULT FROM PROPER FRYING PROCEDURES

1. For good color and flavor, use only good- to excellent-quality fat.
2. Room temperature foods fry more uniformly than chilled or frozen foods.
3. Keep thermostat temperatures below 400°F for good products and minimum fat breakdown.
4. Thick foods require lower frying temperatures and longer cooking times.
5. Breaded products usually provide a crisper, longer lasting crust than do batter-treated products.
6. Reasonable workloads aid in producing high-quality foods and prolonging the life of the fat.
7. Fry pieces of similar size at the same time, to ensure evenly cooked pieces of uniform color.
8. Lower battered foods into fat slowly, to prevent splattering.
9. Turn doughnuts and fritters just once.
10. Fill frying baskets to only one-half to two-thirds of capacity—no more.
11. Always cover fat that is not in use.
12. Refrigerate fat that is to be held for more than a few hours. This helps lengthen the life of the fat.
13. Do not mix foods in a fryer, as there will be a flavor transfer.
14. Foods of high sugar content absorb more fat.
15. Foods high in moisture absorb more fat.
16. The greater the surface area of food exposed, the greater the amount of fat absorbed.

PROPER OPERATION OF THE FRY KETTLE PROLONGS THE LIFE OF THE FAT

1. Never melt fat at a temperature higher than 250°F. Otherwise, scorching will occur.
2. To revitalize fat, add 15 percent new fat every frying day.
3. The food-to-fat ratio can be a minimum of 1 lb food to 10 lb fat and a maximum of 1 lb food to 6 lb fat.
4. Reduce the kettle temperature to 250°F, if the kettle is to stand idle for ½ hour or more.
5. Never allow elements or burners to be exposed while melting fat.

A CLEAN FRY KETTLE IS ESSENTIAL TO AVOID
EXCESSIVE FAT BREAKDOWN

1. Strain and clean fat once every 8 hours or once a day.
2. Thoroughly clean kettle, elements, and burners once a week.
3. Never salt food over fat.
4. Always skim off floating particles between batches.

MISCELLANEOUS FRYER AND FAT INFORMATION

1. Always operate a fry kettle under an exhaust fan.
2. Shortenings that are liquid at room temperature are more digestible than ones that are solid at room temperature.
3. Hydrogenated fats and oils are treated with hydrogen and therefore keep longer. They are solid at room temperature.
4. Vegetable shortenings can be used for frying or baking, and also have a higher smoke point than fats.
5. Fat that is in the process of decomposing does not maintain necessary frying temperatures.
6. Fat should be checked daily for foreign flavors.
7. Fryers should recover temperature within the first third of total cooking time.
8. Thermostat calibration should be checked at least once every six months.
9. When checking the temperature of fat in a fryer, place the fat thermometer's bulb approximately 1 inch below the fat's surface for a proper reading.
10. A fat that has a low smoke point will decompose quickly at frying temperatures.

A form of cooking that combines steam-pressure cooking and frying is called *pressure frying.* In this method, food is immersed in hot fat, a lid is tightly screwed down on the kettle, and the steam released during cooking builds up a pressure that helps cook the food and make it more tender. At a certain point, the pressure of moisture trying to leave the food equals the pressure buildup inside the kettle, resulting in an equilibrium of pressures and the retention of more moisture in the food. Since the moisture cannot leave the food, 75 percent of the item's natural juices remain inside it, as compared to 50 percent in conventional deep-frying. Pressure frying can also reduce fuel costs.

Sautéing. Sautéing is cooking in shallow fat at a temperature of from 335°F (168°C) to 425°F (218°C). The fat is usually about ⅛ inch deep in the pan. Sautéing is a quick cooking method; indeed, the word *sauté* comes from the French infinitive *sauter,* which means "to jump." A *sauteuse* or sauté pan is straight-sided to keep fat from getting out too easily. The pan can be covered so that the food can also be braised in it. Foods that are sautéed and then braised are often only seared briefly in fairly hot fat before braising begins. A pan with slanting sides called a *poêle,* or frying pan, is used when the item is to be flipped (as potatoes or an omelet may be) or turned with a spatula.

Many sautéed foods leave a crusty deposit on the bottom of the pan. This is deglazed by adding wine, stock, or other liquid and reheating the pan while removing the encrusted materials with a fork. They then go into solution with the liquid and make what is technically called a *fond* but is more often termed a *sauce* or *au jus.* An already-prepared sauce or thickening agent may be added at this stage, or the fond may be naturally reduced. Reducing the fond involves lessening its volume by boiling it. The reduced sauce is then served with the sautéed food. Deglazing is also done after roasting to save and use drippings that might otherwise be washed down the drain. Many foods are sautéed, including fish, meat, potatoes, vegetables, and poultry.

Pan-frying is another word meaning the same thing as sautéing. It usually refers only to food cooked completely by the process—that is, with no subsequent braising.

HEAT SOURCES FOR COOKING

The first heat used for cooking may have come from burning wood. Gas and oil escaping from the earth and accidentally lit by some means—as well as escaping steam and hot water—were also available sources of heat from the earliest times. Coal undoubtedly became available near the beginning of civilization and was known for its heat-giving properties. Thousands of years ago, the Chinese drilled into the earth to capture natural gas and piped it in bamboo tubes to locales where it could be used. Today oil, gas, wood, coal, and some other combustible substances are available for heat; and energy from electricity can be used in different forms for heating, as well.

Combustible fuels must have oxygen from the air in order to burn. The gases formed during combustion must be exhausted to keep the air pure for humans to breathe. The loss of heat resulting from this necessary venting has been previously noted, but many combustible fuels are still used and will perhaps be used for a long time to come, although they will be in shorter and shorter supply.

Because electricity can be converted to different forms of energy, it is much used in foodservice work. New ways to use electricity have made it possible to improve some cooking methods and to speed others up. Three such advanced forms of cooking based on electricity are infrared, microwave, and quartz cooking.

Infrared Cooking

If a beam of sunlight falls on a prism, it separates into a spectrum of different colors. The shortest visible wavelengths of light appear as violet, and the longest as red. If a sensitive thermometer is moved across the spectrum, greater heat is found in the red band. But when light is broken up, most of its energy goes into the area just beyond the red band, where no color at all appears. This is known as the *infrared band* of the spectrum.

Infrared heat is used considerably in foodservices. The heat penetrates food directly as a form of radiant energy that does not rely on a carrying or transporting medium (as conducted and convected heat do). The amount of radiant energy reaching the food is directly related to the food's distance from the heat source. Ovens for reconditioning frozen foods, broilers, and modern bake ovens all use infrared energy. Infrared lamps are good for keeping cooked food warm in foodservices, because they maintain a constant temperature and can keep foods warm and tender for up to twenty-four hours with good moisture retention.

Microwave Cooking

Longer waves than light waves also carry energy. Radio and TV waves are quite long waves of electromagnetic energy; some radio waves, in fact, are as long as a football field. We can produce an energy wave with an amplitude (wavelength) of several inches or more in a magnetron tube. Once generated, the wave travels just as radio or light waves do, strikes hard objects such as metals, and bounces back. This discovery led to the use of these waves in detecting distant objects during World War II. Later it was found that, when these waves penetrated soft food, they disturbed the food's molecular structure, causing the molecules to vibrate at a frequency comparable to that of the waves—915 to 2,450 million times per second. This intense activity creates friction within the food, producing heat. We call this process of vibration *kinetic action,* and it is what happens during microwave cooking. Because water molecules become most active, foods high in moisture cook most rapidly by microwave. A potato, for example, may burst during microwave cooking because of the violent boiling going on within it. Foods also tend to dry out quickly because the hard boiling evaporates moisture rapidly. Cooking times must be measured very precisely in working with a microwave oven, since the heating occurs at so much faster a rate than in conventional cooking.

Microwaves do not brown food, and it is also not possible to give food a fried or broiled appearance or texture in a microwave oven. Steaming more closely resembles microwave cooking in its results. Cooking with microwaves begins at the food's center or about 2 inches deep inside. Small foods such as potatoes, fish, and some vegetables cook better in microwave ovens than larger foods such as roasts.

Larger foods need more attention because of this. Bakery goods cook too fast to rise properly when subjected to microwaves.

For various reasons, therefore, microwave cooking cannot replace conventional cooking; still, it is excellent for defrosting foods, warming them, boosting liquid temperatures, heating rolls, and finishing foods during rush hours. Many frozen prepared foods are handled nicely by microwave cooking. Cooking times increase in direct proportion to food quantities. If a single potato takes four minutes, two take eight minutes. Some foods have a higher yield in portions when cooked by microwave, while others have a lower yield. The determining factors are the composition and size of the item, and (of course) the time in the oven. Thinner slices of meat seem to come out juicier, since they are cooked for a shorter period of time than roasts (which tend to dry out). Metal cooking containers cannot be used in microwave ovens, as the metal disrupts the flow of the microwaves within the oven and can result in damage to the magnetrons in the unit.

Figure 8-3. Quartz broiler.

Quartz Cooking

Quartz cooking may be considered a variation on infrared cooking, since the heat wave is very similar. The quartz tube diffuses infrared energy waves evenly, giving a steady, consistent source of heat. This infrared heat is developed by running an electrical charge through a quartz filament in a vacuum tube. Such tubes used in a broiler can produce up to twenty times the energy concentration possible from other infrared sources, such as glass or metal. A quartz tube can tolerate very high temperatures, and it can withstand a greater thermal shock (a quick extreme change in temperature) without cracking or breaking than can glass. There are now quartz ovens, quartz broilers, and other heating units using the quartz tube (see fig. 8-3). The quartz oven was originally designed to thaw bulk frozen foods, and its success in this regard made possible the cooking-to-order revolution in volume feeding.

SUMMARY

Cooking basically involves the application of heat to make food more appetizing, more digestible, safer to eat, and more palatable. Although heat has been used to cook food for centuries, only recently have new methods been developed to improve and hasten the process.

To cook food well, a person must know a lot about what happens to food when it is cooked. Heat changes food. Starches gelatinize or absorb water, thickening foods. Proteins coagulate, changing color and becoming more firm. Other chemical and physical reactions occur, as well. Knowing these principles is an important prerequisite for producing good food.

Standard measures of heat are the calorie and the Btu. The amount of heat available in calories or Btu helps determine whether satisfactory cooking performance can be obtained from a particular piece of equipment. Heat transfer is also important.

To cook well, heat must be quickly and evenly transferred to cooking vessels, cooking media, and the food itself. Heat frequently gets into food by conduction—the direct transfer of heat from one particle to another. Another way heat gets into food is by convection: air or a liquid such as fat or water move through an enclosed space, carrying heat with them. Food can also be cooked by means of a form of heat energy called *radiation,* which transfers heat by electromagnetic waves. The amount of heat and the length of time it is applied to food must be controlled if good cooking is to occur.

Cooking usually occurs in one of two ways: cooking with liquid, or cooking without liquid. Boiling is a method of cooking in water or other liquid at a temperature of 212°F (100°C). Blanching (sometimes called scalding) is another way of heating food in water; the food is only partially cooked, but the heat treatment is sufficient to produce the desired result. Parboiling is another method of partial cooking; afterward, the food is usually cooked to completion by another method. Braising is a method of cooking in small amounts of liquid. Pot-roasting, swissing, fricasséeing, and jugging are all forms of braising. Poaching involves cooking in liquid below the simmering point of water—about 195°F (91°C). The liquid should at least half cover the food. Simmering involves cooking food in liquid at a temperature of between 185° and 205°F (85° and 96°C), so that the water is sufficiently hot to cook but does not boil. Stewing is a method of cooking in water or other liquid whereby small cuts, disjointed fowl, cut-up meat, and other products are submerged in liquid and cooked at simmering temperature.

Steaming may be free-vent, pressure, or forced convection. Free-vent cooking uses steam at normal boiling pressure to cook food. Sometimes waterless cooking uses such steam for cooking; in this case, the food itself furnishes the moisture to produce the steam. Pressure steaming may occur in conventional steamers at around 6 or 7 psi of pressure or in high-pressure steamers at around 15 psi. The time of cooking is very short in the latter instance. Forced-steam convection is a relatively recent idea in steam cooking. Steam at a temperature of 212°F (100°C) and under considerable forced convection strikes food. The cooking is very rapid, as occurs under steam pressure.

Baking is a method of cooking by dry heat in an oven. No liquid is used. Barbecuing is a method of cooking over coals or in a pit; a tangy sauce is used to baste the product. Broiling involves cooking food by means of radiated energy. Grilling involves cooking food on a flat, heated surface at moderate temperatures; it sometimes is called griddle-frying, and it is closely akin to sautéing and pan-frying. Griddle-broiling and pan-broiling are two other forms of cooking that resemble sautéing, except that in these the fat is not allowed to accumulate around the item as it cooks. Ovenizing is a process by which items are given a fried or sautéed appearance by being cooked in the oven. Roasting involves cooking by dry, indirect heat in an oven. Baking is a term used interchangeably with roasting, although each describes the cooking of certain distinct (and different) kinds of foods. Both baking and roasting are done in an oven with dry, indirect heat.

Frying includes both deep-frying and sautéing. Deep-frying is a type of frying in which the product is completely immersed in hot fat. Foods for deep-frying are often breaded, batter-dipped, or dough-covered. Pressure frying is a form of frying under pressure. Sautéing involves frying food in shallow fat; the food may be braised after such sautéing. Pan-frying is a form of sautéing.

Three new kinds of electrical energy are being used to create heat for cooking: infrared, microwave, and quartz. They have special advantages but also some disadvantages.

CHAPTER REVIEW QUESTIONS

1. Janet Joplin is the kitchen manager for the Spinnaker Bar and Grill, a restaurant specializing in the simple preparation of fresh seafood. She has been working closely with the owner/manager, Chris Cristopherson, on developing a wide-ranging new menu. Their goal has been

to come up with a well-balanced menu that exhibits a variety of cooking styles and presentations. In the past, the restaurant has had a standard range and a deep-fat fryer in the kitchen. The operation is in the process of installing a broiler and a steamer, as well, which will give Janet and Chris considerably more freedom in planning the menu.

Janet has taken particular pride in being able to hire people with little previous cooking experience and train them in a short time to produce a high-quality product. She knows that the new menu will require that her staff be trained in the new types of cooking becoming available to them with the addition of the new equipment. She also wants to strengthen their knowledge of the cooking procedures they have been using heretofore. Janet wants to be able to do this in a short (not more than two pages), concise guide to exactly what each cooking technique is and what its strengths and weaknesses are—particularly with regard to seafood.

Since she knows that you are covering this material in a class you are now taking, she has approached you for help in designing this manual. In return, you get a candlelit dinner for two at the Spinnaker. Draw up a document for her that covers all the major cooking techniques available to her. Bear in mind that she has an oven, range top, deep-fat fryer, broiler, and steamer at her disposal, as well as a wide variety of pots and pans.

2. Compare and contrast the three forms of heat transfer. Give examples of each, noting which pieces of equipment transfer heat by which form.

3. Describe the step-by-step procedure for braising. What do the terms *blanc* and *brun* mean? What foods are braised?

4. Discuss the methods of cooking by steam. What are the advantages or disadvantages of each method? What is pressure-fryer cooking?

5. Discuss several new ways in which electricity is being used to cook foods in quantity kitchens.

VOCABULARY

Celsius	Baking
Fahrenheit	Ovenizing
Calorie	Frying
Btu	Sautéing
Conduction	Deep-frying
Convection	Free fatty acid
Radiation	Smoking point
Mise en place	Hydrogenation
Boiling	Catalyst
Braising	Scalding
Simmering	Griddle-broiling
Steaming	Infrared
Brun	Microwave
Blond	Broiling
Mirepoix	Barbecuing
Poaching	Pan-broiling
Blanching	Grilling
Parboiling	Acrolein
Free-vent	Turnover (fat)
Stewing	Spectrum
Roasting	Fricassée

ANNOTATED REFERENCES

Axler, B. H. 1969. *Methods and Manners of Cooking.* New York: Funk & Wagnalls. (All facets of cooking.)

Casola, M. 1969. *Successful Mass Cookery and Volume Feeding,* pp. 1-10. Rochelle Park, N.J.: Ahrens Publishing. (Basic principles of cooking.)

Fowler, S. F.; West, B. B.; and Shugart, G. S. 1971. *Food for 50,* pp. 66-75. New York: John Wiley & Sons. (Baking temperatures, deep-fat frying, and other cooking processes.)

Griswold, R. M. 1962. *The Experimental Study of Foods,* pp. 249-83. Boston: Houghton Mifflin. (Fats.)

Haines, R. G. 1973. *Food Preparation for Hotels, Restaurants, and Cafeterias,* pp. 48-70. Chicago: American Technical Society. (Cooking methods and techniques.)

Harmond, B. 1964. *Cooking Explained,* pp. 3-30. New York: Longmans. (The main methods of cooking.)

Johnson, R. J. 1965. *Food and Cookery,* pp. 59-70. London: J. M. Dent & Sons. (Methods of cooking are presented in one chapter of this text.)

Kaplan, A. 1971. *Elements of Food Production and Baking,* pp. 44-51. New York: ITT Educational Services. (Certain cooking methods.)

Kotschevar, L. H., and McWilliams, M. 1969. *Understanding Foods,* pp. 57-76. New York: John Wiley & Sons. (The cooking process.)

Lundberg, D. E., and Kotschevar, L. H. 1970. *Understanding Cooking,* pp. 1-59. London: Edward Arnold. (In-depth chapter on the cooking process.)

Mott-Smith, M. 1962. *The Concept of Heat and Its Workings Simply Explained.* New York: Dover Publications. (All aspects of heat.)

Nichols, H. L., Jr. 1971. *Cooking with Understanding,* pp. 1-96. Greenwich, Conn.: North Castle Books. (Various cooking principles and methods, in depth.)

Paul, P. C., and Palmer, H. H. 1972. *Food Theory and Applications,* pp. 213-50. New York: John Wiley & Sons. (Fats and oils.)

Pauli, E. 1979. *Classical Cooking the Modern Way,* pp. 217-78. New York: Van Nostrand Reinhold. (Cooking principles, methods, and convenience foods.)

Pyke, M. 1974. *Catering Science and Technology,* pp. 66-94. London: John Murray Publishers. (The use of heat and various cooking methods.)

Smith, E. E., and Crusius, V. C. 1970. *Quantity Food Management,* pp. 53-60. Minneapolis: Burgess Publishing. (Quantity cooking techniques in summary form.)

Smith, L. L., and Minor, L. J. 1974. *Food Service Science,* pp. 465-511. Westport, Conn.: AVI Publishing. (An in-depth study of fats and oils.)

Terrell, M. E. 1971. *Professional Food Preparation,* pp. 3-89. New York: John Wiley & Sons. (General aspects of cooking methods and production.)

CHAPTER 9

Pantry Products

OUTLINE

A number of occasional or partial meal foods are prepared in the pantry, including appetizers, sandwiches, salads and salad dressings, beverages, and fountain items. Desserts may also be dished here. In some operations, the pantry prepares breakfast items. In a large continental kitchen, much of this work is taken over by the garde manger section, and the pantry may be a part of it. In this chapter, however, only appetizers, sandwiches, salads and their dressings, and beverages are considered.

Pantry work is distinguished by the wide variety of foods prepared there. Much preparation is required to get foods ready for final service. Vegetables, fillings for sandwiches, butters and toppings for appetizers, syrups and dessert toppings, garnishes, and a host of other items must be readied for service, and handling this takes advance preparation. In addition, work must be fast, neat, and accurate. A salad—even one with everything ready for assembly—can take twenty or more manipulations, and a sandwich can take just as many. Foods must be very attractive. Since many cold foods are served from the pantry, sanitation there must be very good. Workers must be dexterous and skilled and must be able to work under pressure. Keeping a clean and organized work area is paramount to good-quality products and fast production. The pantry is often a place where workers get their first job, before moving up to more sophisticated sections and more responsible positions. It is excellent training for the exacting work required for more complex tasks in the kitchen.

APPETIZERS

An appetizer is a food used to whet the appetite. Appetizers should be zesty, often tangy food that encourages hunger by stimulating the taste buds and salivary glands, starting the flow of gastric juices in the stomach. Because of their fairly high salt content and piquant flavor, they go well with alcoholic cocktails. This description may not seem to fit all items classed as appetizers (such as salads and soups), but they all are served to help whet the appetite.

Appetizers should look appealing. Contrasts in color and shape are important; attractive service also enhances their appeal. If well-prepared, appetizers can be an extremely important drawing card for an operation.

Appetizers usually require a lot of labor, so good organization and planning in their production are essential. Ingredients used include seafoods, meats, poultry, fruits, vegetables, juices, and dairy products. Finished products include canapés, cocktails, dips, hors d'oeuvres, relishes, salads, and soups. A soup or salad may also be considered a course in a meal or a food proper, rather than an appetizer.

Canapés

Canapés are small finger foods often served as tiny open-face sandwiches cut into fancy shapes and served either hot or cold. Size and thickness depend on the items used. A base of crackers, toasted bread, rye bread, pumpernickel, pastry shells, puffs, or something similar can be topped with a rich, savory paste or seasoned butter and artistically decorated. Imaginative shapes can be made with a variety of tools, but special decorative equipment is needed, including the following items:

Pastry bags and small pastry tubes
Vegetable cutters
French knives
Serrated bread knife
Small pair of scissors
Large and small cookie cutters
Channel knife
Decorating tools
Oval food cutters and vegetable cutters
Shallow oval vegetable timbales
Small and large parisienne cutters
Small timbales with high sides for aspics and the like
Apple (rose) cutter
Special design cutters
Small vegetable knives and other knives

Canapés can be topped with good-quality carry-over foods such as meat, fish, hard-cooked eggs, and seafoods. Many foods can be made into pastes and worked into butters. A tiny shrimp with a caper nestling inside it, resting on top of a small round of bread spread with a tangy shrimp butter is but one example of an attractive canapé. The garnish is important, although it can be simple or ornate. Possible garnishes include slices of stuffed olives, mushrooms, caviar, parsley, pimiento, or truffles. Labor costs must be contained, since labor can be intensive. Mixing a few fancy canapés with relatively many simple ones reduces labor costs.

To mass-produce canapés with a minimum of labor, slice trimmed two-day-old bread loaves lengthwise, ¼-inch thick, and arrange them in rows so that they cover a flat surface; then apply spreads with a spatula or pastry bag. Arrange the toppings for each canapé, garnish, and then cut for service. Refrigerating (to give more firmness) may help cutting. A layer of seasoned butter can prevent the garnish or other food on top from soaking into the base of the canapé. Wrapping to prevent drying before service and refrigerating to reduce deterioration are recommended practices.

When other appetizers are to be served alongside canapés, it is advisable to plan to run out of canapés and let the guests switch to eating dips and other more simply prepared foods toward the end of the function. The nature of the product allows prices to be set rather high, with a good markup on food and labor.

Cocktails

Cocktails may be alcoholic or nonalcoholic. At most occasions, both should be offered. Patrons are beginning to prefer wines or light alcoholic drinks to the heavier ones. Too much alcohol dulls the taste buds, but a small amount stimulates the flow of gastric juices in the stomach.

Cocktails should be tangy, highly palatable, and not too sweet, since sweetness dulls the appetite. Sweet cocktails are usually served with light foods; light, tart, stimulating cocktails best complement heavy or rich meals. Alcoholic cocktails consumed as apéritifs include martinis, manhattans, and other mixed drinks. Light dry wines, Dubonnet, sherry, and Madeira are usually offered as well.

Nonalcoholic cocktails served as a first course may include shrimp, crab, oysters or clams on the half shell, fruit cups, lobster, fish, and fruit or vegetable juice. Meat or fish cocktails are usually served with a tangy sauce. An unusual cocktail could be made with fruit juice and a bit of soda water, with a small ball of sherbet swimming in the center.

All cocktails should be ready to eat when served. Fruits should be free of seeds, inedible pulp, and membranes. Seafoods should be shell-free, except for oysters or clams in the half shell and minced lobster in its shell. About 10 lb of seafood is needed for 100 1½-oz portions; about 18 lb of fruit or other solid food is needed for 100 3-oz servings (about ⅓ cup each). Creative use of garnishes can increase the appeal of a cocktail.

Dips

Dips are appetizers that can be scooped up with a chip, cracker, vegetable stick, or other crisp food. They are low in labor cost and can be made from many carry-over foods. The variety of dips is almost unlimited. Bacon and onions, clams, shrimp, or brown beans stirred into sour cream or cream cheese or blended with tiny-curd cottage cheese can be offered. Fondues and other hot dips can also be used.

A dip's consistency is as important as its flavor. If the dip is too thick, the dipping food item may break; if it is too thin, the patron will be unable to scoop enough onto the dipper, and what is scooped may dribble onto the patron's chin or clothes. Refrigerating cold dips until about 15 minutes before service helps keep them thickened to the right consistency. Hot dips are usually served in chafing dishes. The amount of dip required depends on what else is served and on the duration of the function. If each dip occupies a volume of 1 tsp, it follows that 1 qt holds about 200 dips. At a rate of 5 dips per person, 1 qt of dip serves about forty people. This can vary. A popular dip can run out very quickly, and a less popular one may receive scant attention.

Hors d'Oeuvres

Once hors d'oeuvres were small portions of food served during a multiple-course meal and eaten with a fork. Today, they are bite-size morsels that are often picked up with the fingers. For this reason, they should be small. Toothpicks can be used to facilitate picking them up. Hors d'oeuvres should be tangy and stimulating to the appetite. They are often placed on trays (as are canapés) and passed to guests or left on a buffet to be picked up as desired (see fig 9-1). Hot hors d'oeuvres are usually served in a chafing dish on a buffet table. Tiny plates and napkins may be provided there so that several of these foods can be picked up at one time. Hors d'oeuvres may also be placed on a small dish and served as a first course to a seated guest. Oblong or square glass dishes, china, earthenware, wood, or plastic service can be used. If the food is highly acidic, some metals should not be used. Silver and copper resist most normal food action, but copper may form a poisonous compound when it reacts with some acids.

Like dips, hors d'oeuvres come in almost endless varieties. The type used should be suited to the other foods served with the meal. Usually about five or six selections are sufficient. Some hors d'oeuvres can be easily made for fifteen to twenty people but not for several hundred. Labor cost can be a big factor in the selections and quantities made.

Typical hors d'oeuvres include shellfish (especially oysters, clams, and mussels); fish such as trout, eel, herring, whitefish, and sturgeon; caviar; meats such as veal tongue, smoked beef, sausages, and various hams and pickled meats; vegetables

Figure 9-1. Seafood hors d'oeuvres.

that have been stuffed, marinated, pickled, or cooked; and poultry and dairy products such as chicken wings, turkey, deviled eggs, and cheese tidbits.

Carry-over foods can be used. Color and flavor contrasts, along with attractive presentation, are desirable. Simplicity reduces cost and improves the product, since overgarnished hors d'oeuvres do not look appetizing.

The number of hors d'oeuvres needed depends on the time of day, duration, and nature of the function. Some foodservices prefer to use premade products that are purchased frozen.

Relishes

Relishes are either crisp, fresh vegetables or pickled items. Many may be purchased ready to serve. They should be attractively arranged and presented.

Fresh vegetable relishes include radish roses, celery hearts, carrot curls, cauliflower buds, turnip or green pepper strips, and small scallions. Pickled items include pickles, corn, sweet onions, cranberries, watermelon rind, green tomatoes, spiced fruits, and stuffed olives. Crushed ice is often served over relishes when they accompany a meal.

Salads

Some salads, such as a seafood salad, are offered as appetizers. Many operations serve a small chilled tossed salad as a first course; this is called *California service* — usually on a glass plate or wooden bowl. Pâté, chopped chicken livers, pickled herring, and other items are also frequently served in this way and thus are considered appetizer salads.

Soups

Most soups can be appetizers, except the heavy ones that are almost meals in themselves. A consommé, bouillon, turtle soup, light cream soup or bisque, split-pea or lentil soup, or delicate French onion soup can be a good appetizer. The meat juices in meat soups stimulate the taste buds and start the flow of gastric juices.

SANDWICHES

A sandwich consists of bread, a spread, a filling, and a garnish; the garnish may be omitted. Sandwiches can be close- or open-face, and they can be broiled, grilled, deep-fried, baked, or toasted. A sandwich can be a simple snack, a main entrée, or a hearty meal in itself. A toasted open-face sandwich with a filling of butter, brown sugar, and pecans and topped with a scoop of ice cream is a dessert; a toasted open-face tangy cheese sandwich can be served as an appetizer. Sandwiches can be simple or elaborate, hot or cold, big or as small as finger foods. They can account for a significant portion of an operation's income—especially for lunch. Some operations specialize in sandwiches and serve nothing else.

Planning Production

Sandwiches require much labor. All items to be used should be ready at final assembly. Tools and dishes must be close at hand, and simplification of motions is essential.

Each kind of sandwich requires special equipment and tools. The work center should be comfortable for the worker. Short workers may prefer a surface that is 34 inches high, while taller ones may be best-served by a surface that is 36 to 42 inches high. A worker should have about 16 inches of free space (measured from the elbow) on either side to move about in. Containers for fillings and spreads should be tilted toward the worker for easy access.

A free work area in front can act as a cutting board. A scrap opening or chute should be located on the right for right-handed workers. Plate and bread dispensers can help a worker reach what is needed. A toaster, grill, or microwave oven may be needed; a sink is essential. Necessary tools include a sharp knife, a two-tine fork for picking up small items, scoops for fillings, a short spatula (about 1½ inches wide and 4 inches long) for spreading, and tongs for picking up items. An electric knife is good for cutting sandwiches after they have been made. A portion scale may be needed to check fillings.

Each tool should have its own storage area within easy reach.

Supplies

Sandwich supplies include breads, spreads, fillings, and garnishes. All should be of high quality.

Breads

Fit the kind of bread to the sandwich; a Reuben sandwich, for example, needs good pumpernickel or rye bread. Breads used may be cracked wheat, whole wheat graham, white, rye, pumpernickel, French, Italian, Boston brown, or the various quick breads such as nut, date, or banana. Buns, hard or soft rolls, and specially shaped breads are used for special kinds of sandwiches. All bread should be fresh and firm enough to take spreads easily.

Rolled sandwiches are made using moist, freshly baked bread no older than one day. The loaf is sliced lengthwise about ¼ inch thick and then the slice is lightly flattened with a rolling pin to give it firmness. The spread is applied and the bread is rolled up and stored in a refrigerator, tightly wrapped in a damp cloth or plastic wrap. Later, the wrap is removed and the roll is sliced so the rounds show the roll. Carry-over bread makes good toasted or grilled sandwiches. Sandwich bread is sliced from ⅛ to ¾ inch thick. The number of slices per loaf for different types of bread is given in table 9-1.

Spreads

Butter and margarine are the usual sandwich spreads. They add richness and keep moist fillings from soaking into the bread. They should be softened for easy spreading, but no extra moisture should be added. Spices, prepared mustard, chopped chives, parsley, or pimiento can be added to give special flavor. Melted spreads do not prevent soaking as well as unmelted ones do. Other spreads include peanut butter, cream cheese, and some types of whipped cheese. Jelly, mayonnaise, and salad dressings are apt to soak.

About 1 tsp of spread is usually sufficient for 1 slice of bread; 100 sandwiches (200 slices) are spread with about 2 lb of butter, which equals 1 qt or 192 tsp of spread. (See the Appendix for information on how to translate these quantities into metric units.) With peanut butter, 1 lb is 1¾ cups; so if 1½ Tbsp are used per sandwich, 5⅓ lb (2⅓ qt) are used for 100 sandwiches. Many other spreads, such as cream cheese, take the same quantity as butter.

Table 9-1. Bread Slices per Loaf, Excluding End Crusts

Bread Type	Weight of Loaf	Thickness of Slice	Number of Slices
white	1¼ lb	⅝ inch	19
white	1½ lb	⅝ inch	24
sandwich white	2 lb	½ inch	28
sandwich white	2 lb	⅜ inch	36
sandwich white	3 lb	½ inch	44
sandwich white	3 lb	⅜ inch	56
whole wheat	1 lb	⅝ inch	16
whole wheat	2 lb	½ inch	28
whole wheat	3 lb	½ inch	44
whole wheat	3 lb	⅜ inch	56
rye	1 lb	¾ inch	23
rye	2 lb	¾ inch	33

Source: Adapted from American Institute of Baking 1964, p. 8.

Fillings

Sandwich fillings may be spreads, or they may be cuts of cheese, meat, poultry, or sausage. A thinly sliced or well-chopped filling makes the sandwich easier to eat; 1 to 2 oz of thinly sliced meat gives greater production volume per lb and may be more tender than a thick slice. Chopping should not be so fine that it results in a paste.

Portion control is important. Appropriate scoops should be used to ensure uniform measures of spreadable fillings, and a close check should be made of sliced portion size. If a No. 20 scoop (1½ oz) of spreadable filling is used, 100 sandwiches take 5 qt of filling.

The average weight of sliced filling used per sandwich is 1½ to 2 oz. Table 9-2 lists equivalent measures of various fillings.

Garnishes

Garnishes should be planned to complement sandwiches. They should be edible and eye-appealing. Lettuce or other salad greens, relishes, cheese, peppers, pickles, pimiento, and olives are commonly used garnishes. Other possible garnishes include potato chips, nuts, and shoestring potatoes.

Table 9-2. Equivalent Measures of Various Fillings

Food Item	Quantity	Equivalent Volume	Other Measure
Bacon	1 lb	1½ c, cooked and chopped	25 strips
Celery	1 lb	1 qt, chopped	
Cheese, grated	1 lb	1 qt	
Chicken	1 lb	1 qt, cooked and diced	
Cottage cheese	1 lb	1 pt	
Eggs, hard-cooked	1 dozen	3½ c, chopped	
Jelly	1 pt		16 sandwiches
Lettuce	1 head		16 leaves
Mayonnaise	1 pt		50 bread slices
Meat, ground	1 lb	3 c, cooked	
Nut meats	1 lb	3¾ c, chopped	
Olives, drained	1 qt	3 c, chopped	
Onions	1 lb	1 pt, chopped	
Pickles, drained	1 qt	3 c, chopped	
Salmon	1 lb	1 pt, flaked	
Tunafish	1 lb	1 pt, flaked	
Tomatoes	1 lb		3-4 fruits

Source: American Institute of Baking 1964, p. 8.

Sandwich Care

Sandwiches are quite perishable and must be stored properly if they are being held for service. To prevent bread from becoming stale or developing mold, store it at 75° to 85°F (24° to 29°C). Bread stales most quickly under refrigeration and least quickly when frozen. In a warm, moist climate, bread may have to be refrigerated to prevent mold. The bread storage area should be situated well above floor level and should be dry. Fresh bread easily absorbs flavors, so it should not be kept near fish, onions, cabbage, garlic or other strong-smelling foods. To avoid crushing breads, stack them properly.

Storage for fillings and other sandwich products is also necessary. Usually a refrigerator is set aside for such supplies, but a lower part of the work area can be refrigerated to keep them there.

If sandwiches are to stand for several hours, they should be refrigerated. Place them on trays not more than two deep, and cover the tray with plastic or other wrap to prevent drying. Most sandwiches should not be stored for more than 12 hours at 40°F (4.5°C). Some fairly dry sandwiches with cheese or meat fillings can be stored for 24 hours. Depending on their fillings, some sandwiches can be frozen for from several days to several weeks at 0°F (−18°C) or lower. Filling ingredients that freeze well include the following:

Canned, ready-to-serve, or cooked meat
Chopped and sliced cooked or canned poultry and fish
Dried or ground cooked beef and ham
Cooked egg yolk but not egg white
Baked beans
Peanut butter
Butter or margarine
Applesauce
Canned crushed or tidbit pineapple
Mashed apricots
Grapefruit, lemon, orange, or pineapple juice
Dairy sour cream
Milk or cream
Horseradish
Chopped parsley, chives, or onions

Filling ingredients that do not freeze well include the following:

Chopped, sliced, or grated raw vegetables and fruit
Meats such as bacon, frankfurters, and liver-sausage
Cooked egg white
Nuts
Jelly, jam, or preserves
Honey
Olives
Pickles (dill or sweet)
Piccalilli
Chili sauce or catsup
Pimiento
Prepared mustard
Mayonnaise or salad dressing
Strong spices such as garlic, cloves, and cinnamon

Sandwiches to be frozen should be individually wrapped. Frozen sandwiches thaw in about 1 to 2 hours at room temperature; they should be consumed soon after thawing.

Sandwich Presentation

Sandwiches should be presented in good arrangement with suitable garnishes. The plate should fit the size of the sandwich and garnish. If other foods (such as a cup of soup) are served with the sandwich, a larger plate should be used. Crowding is not recommended. Figure 9-2 shows different ways to cut and arrange sandwiches.

The sandwich and its size should fit the occasion. For an outdoor picnic, sandwiches can be larger to suit hearty appetites; but at a tea, sandwiches should be much smaller. At such functions, contrasts in fillings, shapes, and garnishes add interest.

Sandwich Preparation

Unorganized sandwich production wastes time, causes confusion, and yields a poor product. A

SANDWICH ARRANGEMENTS

The following illustrations suggest possible sandwich arrangements from cutting cues given on preceding page. Garnishes, relishes, salad or soup accompaniments can be arranged in open spaces.

Figure 9-2. Sandwich cuts and arrangements.

completed sandwich reflects the skill of its creator and the character of the work center. Sandwiches are prepared in three different ways: by order, in quantity, or in advance.

By Order

The freshest sandwich is the one prepared to order. A well-planned sandwich center should be able to fill each individual order as it comes in. Figure 9-3 identifies manipulations to use in producing such sandwiches.

In Quantity

When many sandwiches are to be made at one time, all fillings, spreads, breads, and garnishes should be prepared and assembled. To produce from thirty-two to forty-eight sandwiches at one time, pick up four slices of bread with each hand and place them on the work counter. Repeating this process creates a 4-by-4 square (16 slices). Place the spread on the individual slices with one motion of the spatula across each surface. Then measure and deposit the filling on each piece of bread with

JOB: board method for sandwiches made to order (1 operator)	
What to do	How to do it
1. Place 2 matching slices of bread on board.	**1.** Use left hand. **2.** Place bread slices in front of you. **3.** Open them as you lay them down.
2. Spread softened butter or margarine on bread slices.	**1.** Use right hand. **2.** Use spatula to spread butter to edges of both bread slices.
3. Place filling on one slice of buttered bread.	**1.** Use right hand. **2.** Transfer sandwich filling portion with scoop or spatula to center of bread. If filling is sliced cheese, tomatoes or meat, transfer with fork. **3.** Use one stroke of the spatula away from you and one stroke toward you to spread filling evenly to edges of bread.
4. Place lettuce for sandwich.	**1.** Use left hand. **2.** Place 1 portion of lettuce on sandwich filling.
5. Close sandwich.	**1.** Use left hand. **2.** Place other slice of buttered bread over lettuce leaf lining up edges of bread.
6. Cut sandwich.	**1.** Use both hands. **2.** Hold sandwich together with thumb and first finger of left hand. **3.** Cut sandwich into desired sections with a sharp knife held in right hand in a straight downward motion.
7. Serve sandwich.	**1.** Use both hands. **2.** Transfer completed cut sandwich to cold plate by sliding cutting knife under it and supporting sandwich with other hand. Don't push completed sandwich from the board to the plate. **3.** Garnish as desired. **4.** Place check with order after completion.

Figure 9-3. Step-by-step method for sandwich preparation by the order.

a scoop, or place a sliced filling on each piece of bread by hand. Using a short spatula, distribute the spreadable filling evenly, moving from the upper right to the upper left and continuing in an S motion to the lower right and finally the lower left portion of the bread. Garnishes may be placed on each slice at this point. With four slices of bread in each hand once again, place two on each sandwich—one to finish a layer of sandwiches (16 total) and another to begin a second layer (32 total) on top of the first. To make 48 sandwiches, repeat the process a third time. After filling, cut the two or three layers of sandwiches, wrap them, and store them in a refrigerator, if they are to be held. Figure 9-4 lays out an alternative, assembly-line approach to making sandwiches in quantity.

Advance Preparation

Sandwiches sometimes must be made ahead. If so, they must be properly made and stored to retain their quality. Their ingredients should be ones that do not deteriorate during refrigerated or frozen storage. Do not prepare in advance sandwiches that are apt to soak badly.

Management's Responsibility

To produce good sandwiches, management must provide well-planned work centers equipped with the proper tools and equipment and the right kind and quality of ingredients. Workers should be trained to use these tools and ingredients correctly to make good sandwiches. Sanitation must be carefully watched. Management must also guide workers in how to present products. Pricing is a special management concern. Since the labor cost is high in relation to food cost, inappropriate pricing can result if the amount of labor involved is not considered. Sandwiches should carry a good markup.

SALADS AND SALAD DRESSINGS

A salad should be made creatively so that its various parts contrast in color, texture, flavor, and form (see fig. 9-5). Originality must be employed

to ensure that salads are different from the competition's. In total, eye appeal, arrangement, simplicity, and variety in the end product are keys to successful salads. Dressings should complement the salad. A fruit salad is improved when a slightly tart, honey-fruit dressing is used with it. Bland salads require relatively tangy dressings, while zesty ones may use milder dressings.

Salad Planning

Salads generally consist of chilled ingredients placed on an underliner and topped with a dressing and garnish, but other foods are called salads that do not fit this definition, including hot salads, frozen salads, salads without underliners, and salads without garnishes. Salads are especially popular because of today's emphasis on healthful foods. People realize that salads are low in calories and high in nutrition for the calories they carry. Salad bars have become so popular that even fastfood operations feature them. Nonetheless, some people find that salad bars get very boring when they endlessly repeat the same offerings. Giving a salad bar special distinction by accenting it with different offerings or with a slightly different manner of presentation can do much to heighten patron approval of the salad bar.

The Salad Menu

A wide variety of salads can be offered on a menu. They should suit the taste of patrons, meet cost restraints, and be planned around items that will be available. They are often high in labor cost compared to material cost. A salad may be used as an appetizer, as an accompaniment to a meal, as a main dish, or as a dessert.

Appetizer Salads

The appetizer salad selections should be light and small and should be designed to stimulate the appetite.

Accompaniment Salads

Accompaniment salads, whether served with the main course or offered as a separate course, should

JOB: assembly line method for uncut sandwiches

What to do	How to do it
1. Station workers.	**1.** Station 6 workers in a sitting or standing position along one side of a long work table, forming a single assembly line that flows toward the left.
2. Number 1 worker cuts wrapping material and places 2 matching slices of bread.	**1.** Use both hands. **2.** Cut sandwich wrapping material to proper size (8-inch × 12-inch). **3.** Place 2 matching slices of bread, side by side, on cut wrapper, sliding it along to number 2 worker.
3. Number 2 worker spreads softened butter or margarine on bread slices.	**1.** Use both hands. **2.** Use spatula to spread butter to edges of both bread slices, sliding it along to number 3 worker.
4. Number 3 worker places filling on one slice of buttered bread.	**1.** Use both hands. **2.** Transfer sandwich filling portion with scoop to center of bread. If filling is sliced cheese, tomatoes, or meat, transfer with fork, sliding it along to number 4 worker.
5. Number 4 worker spreads filling and closes sandwich.	**1.** Use both hands. **2.** Use one stroke of spatula away from you and one stroke towards you to spread filling evenly to edges of bread. **3.** Place lettuce on filling if it is used. **4.** Place other slice of buttered bread over lettuce or filling, lining up edges of bread. **5.** Slide closed sandwich along to number 5 worker.
6. Number 5 worker wraps sandwich.	**1.** Use both hands. **2.** Bring long ends of wrapping paper together in a pharmacist's fold onto center of sandwich. **3.** Follow fold with both hands, running left hand to left edge of sandwich and right hand to right edge of sandwich. **4.** Tuck paper in securely at each end with left and right hands, folding top edge in first, then bottom edge. **5.** Slide wrapped sandwich along to number 6 worker.
7. Number 6 worker stacks wrapped sandwiches and transfers them to refrigerator.	**1.** Use both hands. **2.** Stack wrapped sandwiches in wire baskets, on bun pans or trays; allow some space for air circulation between each row for quick chilling. **3.** Label sandwich containers with variety they contain. **4.** Place filled sandwich containers in refrigerator on shelves or a movable rack during the entire holding period.

Figure 9-4. Step-by-step method for sandwich preparation in quantity.

Figure 9-5. Salads are becoming increasingly popular as main dishes.

provide a contrast in flavor, texture, color, form, and temperature with the main course food. Moderate portions are served. Hearts of lettuce, cabbage, pickled beets, savory vegetables, fruits, fruits with cottage cheese, and molded or frozen salads are proper. A heavy meal calls for a lighter salad, and vice versa. A salad featuring meats, beans, potatoes, macaroni, or other heavy items should accompany a light meal, such as a sandwich or a soup and a glass of milk. A lighter, more delicate salad should be offered with a meal consisting of roast beef, potatoes, and vegetables.

Main-dish Salads

Some salads are served as entrées. They often have a base of meat, fish, seafood, or cottage cheese, extended by chopped celery or other vegetables. Cooked macaroni products, rice, potatoes, or other starchy items can be used as well. The pasta salad, for example, is quite popular. A main-dish salad—such as a chicken salad with pineapple and tomatoes, or a tomato stuffed with tunafish salad—can be served as the main dish for a luncheon or even for a dinner.

Dessert Salads

A dessert salad is usually sweet and can be quite rich. It may be served as a single item accompanied by a beverage at parties, or it may be served as a complete meal. After a bridge or club session, a dessert salad can be served with finger sandwiches. Fresh salads made of nuts, fruits, or dairy products, gelatin salads, and frozen salads can all be used as dessert salads. A small salad of some sweet mixture served in a bite-size creampuff shell or in a small lettuce cup, a strawberry mousse, and jellied fruit are other dessert salads. The dressing is usually sweet.

Salad Equipment

Mise en place—organizing beforehand, getting all materials needed, and then keeping things organized, cleaned up, and moving toward the final goal—is vital to efficient salad production. It must be accompanied by the use of good tools and equipment. The work center must be planned thoughtfully and arranged for proper placement of foods, tools, and equipment, to save time and motion. Sanitation is important, since many foods are perishable and cold. Storage is another important consideration, since so many items are prepared ahead of service.

Small tools include sharp knives, zesters (often used to peel orange or lemon rind), parisienne scoops (used in making melon balls), peelers, corers, wire whips, appropriate cutting tools, and suitable trays and containers. A good cutting board is needed— preferably of plastic, for better sanitation. Larger equipment includes a vertical cutter/mixer (used to prepare both salads and salad dressings), a food slicer, a vegetable peeler, a food cutter (with an attachment hub for grating, dicing, and slicing), and a food mixer. The tools and equipment should be sufficient to enable the pantry section to produce high-quality products with a minimum expenditure of labor. Adequate refrigeration space should be available, providing a constant 40°F (4.5°C) holding temperature.

Salad Ingredients

Salads are often considerably more than greens, sliced tomatoes, or other simple products served with a dressing; they can be complex combinations of many ingredients. Salad greens are, however, the base of most salads. They can serve as both the underliner and the body. Fruits, vegetables, and other ingredients are also used.

Salad Greens

Salad greens contribute body and bulk to a salad, as well as variety in color, texture, and flavor. Only fresh young greens that are free of blemishes should be used. These should be trimmed, washed, and chilled before using to ensure that they are well-drained, cold, and crisp at service. Salad greens are best dipped into water, shaken free of excess moisture, and then placed into wet cloths, plastic sacks with holes in them, or some other suitable container in which they can cool and crisp. *Do not use sodium sulfite to keep the greens fresh in appearance.* This chemical sometimes produces severe allergic reactions in people who ingest it. Do not put greens into water for holding, since air and water are both needed to crisp. Soaking also causes a loss in nutrients.

Fruits and Vegetables

Fruits and vegetables are the main ingredients of salads. They augment the greens by adding flavor, texture, and color. Such a salad may use (for example) the greens of torn romaine and spinach, mixed with fresh, crisp bean sprouts, chopped hard-cooked egg, and fresh bacon bits, and topped with a sweet-and-sour dressing. Some fruit salads may contain only celery or one other crisp item for flavor and texture contrasts to the fruit. The blend of fruits and vegetables with greens should be suitable. It is also important to use ingredients that are available year-round. A number of fresh, frozen, or canned fruits are available for salads throughout the year, including the following:

Apples	Lemons
Apricots	Nuts
Avocados	Oranges
Bananas	Peaches
Cantaloupe	Pears
Cherries	Persimmons
Cranberries	Pineapple
Dates	Raisins
Figs	Raspberries
Grapefruit	Strawberries
Grapes	Tangerines
Honeydew melon	Watermelon
Kumquats	

Many vegetables for salads are plentiful throughout the year, as well, including the following:

Artichoke	Olives
Asparagus	Onions
Beans, green	Parsley
Beets	Parsnips
Broccoli	Peppers
Brussels sprouts	Peas
Cabbage	Potatoes
Celery	Radishes
Corn	Squash
Cucumbers	Swiss chard
Garbanzo beans	Tomatoes
Garlic	Turnips
Mushrooms	Watercress

Other Salad Ingredients

Other items such as croutons, nuts, and seeds, plus seasonings such as basil, chives, chervil, rosemary, tarragon, and thyme, can be used to give salads special texture, body, or flavor. Crisp foods such as crackers or even rolls or hot breads may be served as an accompaniment. A chapon (a dry piece of bread flavored with garlic) can be added to the salad for flavor.

Salad Presentation

Not all salads are served as individual units. Salads may be dished into bowls and served from a buffet, or salad materials can be put into containers on a salad bar where patrons are invited to make their own combinations. As little handling as possible is usually best. Salads served immediately after preparation or after chilling look and taste the best.

Individually Served Salads

Small or appetizer salads are usually served on a plate about 5½ inches in diameter. A regular dinner salad is served on a 7-inch plate. The salad should not come to the plate's edge; instead, some space should appear between the margin of the salad and the edge of the plate, so that the food is framed by the plate. Salad height is important. A flat salad appears small and insignificant. By using chopped greens, chunks of firm lettuce, and similar items, preparers can give a salad the appearance of having better form and of being lighter. Colors in a salad should be mixed; various greens can give a good color contrast. Messiness is to be avoided. Salads made of soft materials should be mixed as little as possible. Garnishes should be appropriate, selected to suit the flavor, texture, and appearance of other salad components. Showmanship can be exercised by using form and color to give striking effects; salads should not, however, present garish contrasts; they should look good through careful attention to the principles of proportion and color matching.

Preparing and presenting individual salads at the tableside can do much to merchandise salads. This can be done from a mobile cart on which various salad materials are assembled, including the dressings and garnishes. The server doing the preparation should be deft and should set up attractive salads with good proportions and form. Good measurement should be achieved by eye and practice, just as it is when a good bartender mixes a drink.

Buffet Salads and Salad Bars

Salads can be prepared in large bowls, attractively garnished, and placed on buffets, from which guests serve themselves or are served. Simplicity makes salads attractive and reduces labor costs. Salads can be served from attractive ceramic bowls, silver platters or other platters, or ice bowls; a fruit salad can be placed in a half scooped-out watermelon. It is important to offer different kinds of salads on a buffet. Thus, a fruit salad, a potato or pasta salad, a seafood salad, and a vegetable salad could be there.

Salad bars, too, should hold a variety of salad materials in containers set on a refrigerated counter. Chopped greens, sliced or sectioned tomatoes, chopped sweet onion or thinly sliced onion rings, green and red pepper strips, carrot cubes, crisp green vegetables, olives, celery, sliced mushrooms, cottage cheese, spinach leaves, garlic-seasoned crou-

tons, chopped chives, and other items can be offered. At a slightly greater cost, marinated quartered artichoke hearts, pickled pepperoncini, molded fruit, thinly sliced sausage, and chopped cheese can be offered. Four to six dressings should be presented.

Salads and the plates onto which they are dished should be chilled. Some localities require that sneeze guards be installed and other sanitary precautions be taken when customers are allowed to dish their own foods.

Salad Preparation

Fresh, crisp ingredients, skillfully and imaginatively prepared, make good salads. Eye appeal plays a large part in salad acceptance.

Base or Underliner

The salad base usually is a salad green that holds the salad and leaves a border in the bowl or plate on which it is served. Limp lettuce hanging over the plate's edge can ruin appearance. The base may contribute to color, texture, or both. It should be clean and edible, even though guests usually do not eat it. To encourage consumption, the base can be sliced or chopped.

When the salad is made of large, loose particles of food, a cup or good base helps hold the salad's shape. A base can also help give the salad height. The base should be in proportion to the salad, with its highest point at the back of the plate, away from the guest.

Bibb, boston, iceberg, leaf, or romaine lettuce, as well as chicory, curly endive, escarole, and other greens such as spinach leaves, may be used for underliners. Large outside lettuce leaves do not cup well, but they can be used flat on trays or in bowls for buffet salad underliners. Unusual underliners might include thinly sliced apple latticed under a molded fruit salad or sliced tomatoes laid under a mixed bean salad. Cabbage is not used as a base because of its tough texture.

Body

The body of a salad comprises its main ingredients and usually gives the salad its name. The arrangement of the body on the base or in the serving dish should be neat and appealing. Simplicity can enhance the salad's attractiveness. Individual ingredients (particularly main ones) should remain distinct; they should not be chopped, minced, or mashed to the point where desirable appearance and crispness are lost. Variety of form produced when cutting or tearing salad materials adds interest. Many kinds of foods may be used as the main body, and all require different treatment.

Fruits and Vegetables. The size of the fruits or vegetables in salads should be established in purchase specifications. Thus, tomatoes or artichokes of a specific size may be needed.

Fresh, dried, frozen, and canned fruits and vegetables are used effectively. All inedible parts—including seeds, skins, and stems on fresh items—should be removed. Particle size can be varied for interest, and contrasts in color, flavor, and texture should be sought. Soft-textured items such as bananas, pastas and artichoke hearts combine well with crunchy items such as apples, celery, nuts, and crisp greens. Some fruits darken when cut and exposed to air. Cutting these with a stainless steel or nonmetal knife and dipping the pieces into an acid such as pineapple or lemon juice, a special oxidizing solution, or even salted water helps prevent darkening.

Firm vegetables such as cucumbers and radishes should be cut thin enough to be easily chewed. Cutting vegetables into julienne, diced, sliced, or round shapes adds to their interest, as can random chopping, cutting, or grating. Cooked items should be firm, not mushy. Carry-overs can be used, but they should not be inferior products.

Gelatin Mixtures. Gelatin is often used for salads—either plain or as a prepared, sweetened, and flavored mixture. Gelatin adds a different flavor, texture, and color to salads. Soak dry gelatin in cold water and then bring it into solution at 170°F (77°C) or higher in more liquid. As it cools, it absorbs water or liquid, forming a soft gel. A good gelatin makes a strong yet tender gel; a poor gelatin produces a weak and watery gel or a tough and leathery one with poor flavor. Gelatin has no grades; it should be purchased on the basis of the quality of the product or brand.

Gelatin strength is decided by the following six factors: the gelatin's quality; the amount of liquid; the amount of sugar and acid (sugar strengthens and acid weakens); the amount of added materials; the temperature at which the gelatin sets; and the temperature of the gelatin mixture. Typically, $3\frac{1}{2}$ oz of unflavored gelatin forms a good gel in 1 gallon of liquid; $1\frac{1}{2}$ lb of powdered gelatin dessert mix is required per gallon. Fruit or vegetable juices add flavor, as do syrups from canned fruits, meat stocks, and even carbonated beverages. Sweetness in plain gelatin mixtures can come from the ingredients or from added sugar. Solid materials can be added as soon as the gelatin is put into solution. Ingredients that tend to float to the top should be stirred in just before the mixture sets. If a lot of ingredients are to be added, less liquid should be added.

Gelatin powders are added to hot liquid to bring them into solution; water is usually the liquid used, but drained juice or other liquids also work well. The sweetness of canned fruit juice can produce too sweet a mixture, however. Gelatin products usually hold their quality for several days under good refrigeration. A number of gelatin products can be produced.

Basic Gelatins. Whether unflavored or flavored, basic gelatin is a simple combination of gelatin and liquid, with the possible addition of seasonings, solids, or a sweetener. Sugar increases the firmness of a gel, as does milk, while acids and any solids added tend to weaken the gel. Gelatin in any form is derived from the hides, skins, connective tissues, and bones of all types of animals.

Cubed and Flaked Gelatins. Variations in the cutting of basic gelatins result in interesting salads. Cubed gelatin is made by cutting gelatin $\frac{1}{2}$ to $\frac{3}{4}$ inch deep into cubes and serving it alone, with different-flavored cubes, or with mixed fruit. Flaked gelatin is prepared by running firmly set gelatin through a food grinder at high speed and serving it with other flaked gelatins (for color contrast), with coconut, with fruit, or with ice cream.

Gelatin Foams. Because gelatins have a high protein content, they retain air well and easily foam when beaten. *Whips* are basic gelatins blended or beaten until they double in volume. Such whipping occurs when the gelatin mixture has the consistency of thick, raw egg white. Foaming takes place best if the partially thickened gelatin is whipped in a chilled bowl or over ice water at high speed. *Snows* or *sponges* are similar to whips, except that they have egg white blended in at the point of whipping. The result is a gelatin product whose volume is tripled.

Layered Gelatins. Two or more basic gelatins can be layered on top of another, creating different colors and flavors for each layer. The first layer must be completely jelled when the second layer is poured—already partially thickened—on top of it. Each succeeding layer is then poured, partially thickened, after the preceding layer poured has completely gelled.

Gelatin Molds. Decorative molds offer attractive shapes to gelatin salads. The mold may be lightly oiled first to prevent gelatin adhesion. If oil is not used, the jelled mold must be dipped in warm water up to its edge and then inverted, allowing it to slip onto a serving platter. Molds frequently have arranged fruit in them. This is accomplished by taking a chilled mold, coating a section with partially thickened gelatin, arranging the fruit as desired on the gelatin, allowing this area to jell quickly, and proceeding one section at a time until the mold is done. Of course, many times the fruit or solid food is simply stirred into partially thickened gelatin, the mixture is poured into a mold, and the salad is unmolded when it has jelled, with food particles suspended throughout the mold. (NOTE: Raw pineapple, papaya, figs, and some other fruits containing certain enzymes cannot be used in gelatin production because the enzymes they contain break down the gelatin's structure and do not allow the gelatin to jel.)

Other Gelatin Products. By adding various ingredients and performing certain preparations, other gelatin products as popular as salads are created.

Aspics - are similar to basic gelatins and may be clear or seasoned with meat stock, tomato, spices, or other foods.

Bavarian creams - combine basic gelatin and egg yolks cooked a few minutes to form a custard;

when chilled, the mixture is folded into a stiff meringue, and whipped cream is added.

Mousses - are rich desserts made by combining cream thickened with gelatin and whipped cream.

Chiffons and spanish creams - are basically the same as bavarian creams, except that whipped cream is not added.

Charlottes - are mousses enclosed in or trimmed with sponge cake or ladyfingers.

Quick Gelatin Preparation. Dissolve the gelatin in up to one-half of the liquid called for, and measure the rest of the required liquid as crushed ice, covered with cold water, in the measuring container. Combine the crushed ice and water with the gelatin mixture, and stir until the ice melts and the gelatin thickens. A quickly formed gel is more likely to lose its structure when removed to higher temperatures than is one that solidifies at higher temperatures.

Protein Foods. Main-dish salads usually contain meats, fish, or poultry as the major ingredient—roast beef, ham, tongue, crab, lobster, shrimp, salmon, tunafish, chicken, or turkey—along with cheese or eggs. The pieces should be bite-size. Protein foods can be cut in a food chopper or mechanical cutter. Meats and poultry are usually diced or cut into julienne strips; fish is often coarsely flaked with a fork. It is difficult to cut some foods into pieces of the proper size. Do not mince foods, as this often gives them a pasty consistency when mixed with a salad dressing.

Rice and Macaroni. Rice and macaroni products are frequently used in salad bodies because they are neutral in color and taste and because they accept seasoning and garnish well. Rice and macaroni products should be cooked *al dente* (firm and chewy), rather than mushy or overcooked. Rice must be dry and fluffy, and pastas must be thoroughly drained. Rice and pastas can replace vegetables in some salads, or they can be mixed with protein foods.

Salad Greens. Salad greens give a variety of textures, flavors, and shapes to a salad. When they are used as the main ingredient and garnished with vegetables and other foods, the result is a tossed or green salad. To prepare, simply toss the salad greens with other ingredients or by themselves to make the body. Wash all of the greens thoroughly. The core in an iceberg lettuce should be pushed in with the palm of the hand or be removed by being pressed on a hard surface. The head should be placed in cold water and then thoroughly drained, with the open-end surface down. Other greens should be washed in cold water rather than in a colander under running water. Colander washing does not free dirt as well as does putting the greens into a cold-water bath and letting soil sink to the bottom. A small bit of salt added to the water draws out worms and insects, but delicate greens may wilt from such treatment. For such greens, carefully scrutinize the leaves instead of using salt. Place washed clean greens in plastic bags or covered containers, and allow them to crisp under refrigeration.

To use, shake the greens free of water, and cut them with a sharp knife or tear them to avoid bruising. When time allows, tearing is preferred. Pieces should be bite-size. Heads of solid materials may be quartered, their cores removed, and the heads roughly chopped or evenly sliced or grated.

Salad Dressings

Salad dressings are flavorful sauces applied to salads to enhance their flavor or appearance and sometimes to add moistness. They are usually emulsions—mixtures containing two liquids that do not combine. Thus, when oil and vinegar (two common salad dressing ingredients) are shaken together, they mix for a few minutes, but the oil soon rises to the top of the vinegar. Such a mixture is known as an *unstable* or *temporary emulsion*. If as a third ingredient an emulsifying agent is added, the mixture can become a *stable* or *permanent emulsion*. One such emulsifying agent is egg, as in mayonnaise, which coats the droplets of oil and holds them in a water-oil emulsion. French dressing is a temporary emulsion, while mayonnaise and cooked or boiled dressings are permanent emulsions. A relative few basic dressings provide the foundation from which most dressings are prepared.

French Dressing. French dressing is a 3:1 blend of oil to an acid such as lemon juice or vinegar. Seasonings such as salt, pepper, paprika, mustard, sugar, honey, and garlic are added for flavor and to help stabilize the emulsion and give some thickness. Tomato paste also can be added. The oils most commonly used are corn, cottonseed, olive, peanut, safflower, or soybean. Vinegars may be cider (apple), distilled (white or brown), malt, or wine.

Mayonnaise. Mayonnaise is a permanent emulsion of acidic liquid (such as vinegar or lemon juice), oil, and egg yolk or whole eggs, with added seasonings. Usually the acidic liquid, seasonings, and egg are mixed together, and the oil is then added very slowly while the mixture is beaten. Gradually, a thickened emulsion forms.

Cooked or Boiled Dressings. Cooked or boiled dressings are thickened with starch and perhaps eggs; they contain less oil than French dressing or mayonnaise. Flour is often the thickener, although cornstarch, arrowroot, or another starch can be used. The liquid is milk, water, vinegar, juice, or some blend of these. When the mixture is cooked and thickened, eggs are added—as in making a pudding or sauce. The oil, margarine, butter, or other fat is then added; and vinegar or lemon juice and seasonings are added last. Acids tend to break down starch pastes, so they are added last to minimize this possibility. Care must be taken to ensure that the dressing does not become lumpy or get scorched.

Other Basic Dressings. Other popular dressings are based on sour cream, cream cheese, whipped sweet cream, and other liquids and semisolids. These are often seasoned with vinegar, herbs, spices and salt. Among the variations on these are sour cream with chives, cream cheese dressing with chopped Spanish olives and honey, and sour cream with fruit and nuts. A hot dressing used for wilted salads is a French dressing variation that sometimes is lightly thickened.

A marinade is a mixture, such as oil and vinegar plus seasonings, in which foods are soaked or marinated to gain flavor. A five-bean salad is often marinated. Other marinades are used to flavor meats, fish, and some vegetables before they are used in a salad. Leafy vegetables are not marinated because they wilt. Any excess marinade should be drained off when the salad is dished for service.

The Garnish

The garnish of a salad corresponds to the icing on a cake; it should offer contrasts in color, flavor, and texture, as well as harmony with the salad and dressing. Garnishes should be edible, eye-appealing, and simple. The following garnishes are among the many possibilities:

Anchovies
Apple—slices, balls, sticks
Aspic cubes
Bananas—scored with fork and sliced
Beet—rings, shreds
Cabbage—shredded, slaw
Carrots
Celery—curls, hearts, stuffed
Cherries (green and red) stuffed with almonds or cheese, cut into petals, or whole with stem
Cheese—grated, balls, slivers
Chives—chopped
Coconut—white or faintly tinted
Cucumber—slices, fingers, rings, sticks, boats, curls, fluted
Dates, figs, or prunes—stuffed with peanut butter, cheese, or nuts
Eggs—hard-cooked, sliced, chopped, riced, deviled
Endive
Fruits—glazed, candied
Grapes—plain, frosted, in clusters
Jelly cubes
Kumquats—fresh or preserved
Lettuce—edges dipped in paprika
Melon—balls, cubes, pickled, rings, sticks
Mint—fresh sprigs or chopped
Nut meats
Olives—ripe or green, stuffed, sliced, or whole
Onion—rings
Oranges or grapefruit—segments, slices
Paprika
Parsley—fresh sprigs or chopped

Peppers—green or red, rings, chopped, or strips
Pickles—dill or sweet, sliced, stuffed, fans, strips
Pimiento—strips, stars, chopped
Pineapple—fingers, cones, fans, dipped in paprika or edge rolled in finely chopped parsley or nuts
Pomegranate seeds
Preserved or spiced fruit
Radishes—slices, roses, fans
Raisins
Relish—raw fruit and vegetables
Rhubarb—curls, raw
Scallions
Sherbet
Spinach—small leaves
Strawberries—sliced, dipped in sugar, whole
Tomatoes—sliced, diced, quartered
Truffles—fancy shapes
Turnip—strips, thin slices
Watercress

Management Controls

Management must plan to coordinate salads and salad dressings into the total production picture. Standards must be set and followed, and costs must be controlled. Quality can be controlled by proper purchasing and handling procedures; quantities must be controlled by good recipes and portion control.

Standards for Salads

Production standards can be established by using good recipes, by referring to pictures of salads, and by good training. Employees should understand that good salads are light, appetizing blends of ingredients with a proper dressing. They must be arranged with symmetry and uniformity of design. Creative blends of salad ingredients with dressings and artistic presentation should be incorporated into the recipe to achieve consistency in how products are served. Fresh, high-quality ingredients that offer complementary contrasts of textures, colors, and flavors should be used. Salads should not appear tired from having been overhandled. No inedible portions or wilted or rusted particles should appear. Portions should fit the plate.

Cost Controls

Labor can be significant in making salads and dressings because much of the preparation is by hand. Purchasing pre-prepared materials, such as diced vegetables, chopped lettuce, and salad dressings, reduces costs and still can maintain high standards.

Food costs can be controlled by controlling portions. Tossed or green salads served as meal accompaniments should be approximately 1 cup (2½ oz) each; about 16 lb European plan or 20 lb American plan of greens is needed for 100 salads. A 3-oz scoop (No. 12) is used for potato, pasta, and fruit salads. A good portion of gelatin salad is ½ cup; thus, slightly more than 3 gal gives 100 portions. Comparing portion costs between convenience items and items made from scratch can indicate which should be used, provided that quality is equal.

Labor is an important consideration in salad making. Space should be provided so that many salads can be prepared at one time. Plates can be spread out on 18″ × 26″ sheets, filled, and then loaded into refrigerators to be held until needed. Enough refrigerator space must be planned. Making one set of motions for many salads reduces labor time. Thus, all bases can be set down for twenty-four salads, followed by the body, the garnish, and perhaps the dressing. Sometimes, however, it is preferable to have serving personnel add the dressing and garnish just before serving.

The salad buffet and salad bar are labor savers and customer pleasers. The hand labor required to place underliner, body, garnish, and dressing on each individual plate is saved. Even though larger servings may be taken, which raises costs, they take the edge off appetites with relatively inexpensive food, which again saves the operation money.

BEVERAGES

Beverages are an important part of meals, partial meals, and snacks, and may even be taken on their own. Many foodservice operators feel that coffee, for example, is something guests remember and come back especially to have. It is commonplace in the foodservice industry that a good cup of coffee or tea draws customers. While seemingly simple to make, beverages must be made with care. Proper attention must be paid to see that ingredient proportions are correct, that equipment is clean, that the making is right, and that the service ensures preservation of the care taken in making the beverage.

Coffee

Coffee has been a symbol of hospitality for generations. The Arabs use it to greet guests and start business meetings. The coffee break is an important part of a worker's day.

Coffee Equipment

The right size of coffee maker must be used. The equipment must be flexible enough to meet coffee needs at both peak and slow periods. A cup of coffee is 6 oz; if free refills are offered, every patron can drink 1 pint or more of coffee. Small units are used during low-demand periods, and often the number of units in service is increased or larger equipment is used when demand is high.

The coffee brewer should be constructed of glass, porcelain, or stainless steel. Bitterness, astringency, or metallic taste results if the equipment contains tin plate, aluminum, copper, or nickel.

Another concern is whether an automatic or a manual brewer is best. Labor costs, skilled workers, and the availability of service personnel for maintenance and repair are factors that must be considered. Manual brewers are less expensive and have fewer mechanical devices that fail, but they require more attention from personnel and may, therefore, increase costs. Semiautomatic brewers are also available (see fig. 9-6). The filtering devices and the water feed into the grinds are also important to the purchase decision. Their design should provide adequate waterflow over and around the grinds, sufficient capacity to prevent backup and overflow, sufficient support of the grounds so that they do not touch the beverage, and easy and the correct amount of very hot water flows through the coffee. The old cartridge is then replaced with a new one to make a fresh batch. Coffee is also made by boiling, although this is seldom done in today's foodservices. Special coffee makers such as the espresso machine are also used. An *ibrik* is used to make Turkish coffee.

The Product

Coffee is a small bean that comes from a red, cherry-like fruit. Many different kinds exist. The Arabica plant is the one most often grown. It makes a rich mellow coffee if grown under the right conditions. Coffee flavor and quality vary with the season of the year, the processing method, and the growing area. Colombian coffee is rich and aromatic in flavor, with a bouquet quite different from the full and mellow flavor of the Santos coffee of Brazil. The Robusta plant is also grown and is the primary source of African coffee. Its flavor is stronger than the Arabica's but not quite as full. It is often blended with the Arabica.

Before roasting, coffee is a whitish green bean. The raw beans are often blended to produce a coffee of particular flavor. Rio coffee is coffee grown in the lowlands; it has a somewhat harsh and bitter flavor. It is blended into coffees to give them more bitterness or acidity. Coffee beans are roasted to develop their flavor and color. After roasting, coffee beans are highly perishable. Roasting can be light, medium, or dark. The Italians and the French like a dark or heavily roasted coffee.

The next step in the coffee-making process is the grinding of the beans. The grind may range from coarse to very fine, but it must be suited to the type of equipment on hand. A drip machine needs a fine drip grind. An urn coffee is ground more coarsely. The contact time with the water and the size of the grind are related: fine grinds stay in contact with the water for less time (see table 9-3). If the grounds and water are in contact too long, overextraction occurs, and bitter flavors are released. If the water is not in contact with the grounds long enough, the coffee is underextracted and weak in flavor.

Coffee loses flavor less rapidly in the whole bean than when ground. After grinding, flavor loss is

Figure 9-6. Semiautomatic coffee maker.

access to all areas for cleaning. The mechanical reliability of each unit also should be evaluated before the final selection is made. Automatic brewers can save labor and simplify the process so that inexperienced workers can make good coffee.

Urns are large units that make coffee by the drip method. The coffee is placed evenly in a basket and boiling or very hot water is put over it to drip through. Vacuum coffee makers work by forcing boiling water (by steam) into an upper chamber, where it comes in contact with finely ground coffee. The water stays in contact with the grounds for a short time, and then the steam pressure is released—often by removing the boiling lower part from the heat. When the steam condenses in the lower part of the coffee maker, a vacuum is formed that sucks the liquid in the top down through a filter, leaving the grounds in the upper chamber to be removed and discarded.

New types of drip equipment can make 9-cup, 12-cup, or larger batches. The coffee is put into a small cartridge or container, a button is pressed,

Table 9-3. Proper Exposure Times of Different Grinds to Water

Type of Grind	Use	Exposure Time
Fine	Vacuum coffee maker	1-3 minutes
Drip	Urn brewer	4-6 minutes
Regular	Electric percolator	6-8 minutes

very rapid; in three days, the loss can be 20 percent. Coffee held over a week should be either vacuum- or gas-packed. It should be stored at room temperature only when necessary. A cool, dry place is needed. Coffee that is not to be used within a day should be stored in a freezer, since freezing or refrigerating delays deterioration.

Coffee stocks should be rotated so that the oldest coffee is used first. Packaging should be the exact size needed to produce the desired amount. Some operations purchase bean coffee and grind it as needed to get the freshest coffee possible.

Coffee best releases its flavors in water heated to about 205°F (96°C). The contact time is controlled to suit the grind. Tastes or odors in some water spoil coffee. Some waters that are high in iron make a very dark coffee that turns green when cream is added. Odors, flavors, and iron content can be filtered out. Hard water makes acceptable coffee, provided that it is not too hard. Water containing too many bicarbonates or other hard materials may cause a sediment to form that delays water flow through the grounds, resulting in overextraction. Hard water salts or lime can build up in the equipment, destroying temperature controls or otherwise interfering with proper water delivery and ultimately reducing the life of the equipment. Using water softeners under these circumstances is recommended, but they must not be allowed to deliver too many bicarbonates. Polyphosphate substances can be introduced to reduce bicarbonates. The water used should be freshly boiled, since overheated water can be stale and can lack vitality.

The right amount of coffee of the right grind and blend should be used. The correct ratio is usually 2½ gal of water to 1 lb of coffee. Some experts recommend 3 gal of water per lb. Management must decide on the strength of the brew it wants to serve and should set standards accordingly.

Home measurements are 2 Tbsp per 6 oz or ¾ c of water. For a strong demitasse, however, 4 oz of water are used. Coffee purveyors usually indicate the correct proportions for their product. Coffees designed for the home do not hold up well in commercial use.

Brewing Coffee

The right amount of water heated to the right temperature and added to the right amount of properly ground coffee for the right contact time gives a good coffee brew. In an urn, the grounds are usually spread evenly on the filter to a depth of 1 to 2 inches. Evenly spread coffee promotes uniform extraction. Paper or cloth filters are most commonly used, although filters can also be made of woven wire screens, perforated plates, or metal disks, which allow only the finest particles of coffee to pass through. The water should thoroughly saturate the coffee. If only a part of the desirable flavor is extracted, a weak coffee results; too much saturation produces an overextracted coffee that is strong and bitter.

If all of the water does not pass through in the prescribed time, it may be necessary to run less water through the grounds and to add hot water directly to the new brew or to place some water in the urn before brewing. Coffee should not be extended by pouring too much water through it, since this extracts bitter and unflavorful products. An acceptable brew extension only results if the flavorful and good fractions alone are extracted; then these are diluted to the smallest extent possible.

The filtering device should be removed immediately after the water passes through. Leaving the grounds over the brewed coffee harms the brew. Pouring fresh coffee through extracted grounds increases its bitterness. In an urn, most of the flavor comes off first; bitterness and less flavor come off last. For this reason, it is wise to mix the coffee in the urn by removing the grounds and then repouring some of the coffee from the bottom of the urn back in at the top, to give a more balanced strength and flavor. The coffee can also be mixed by stirring. In some new urns, automatic agitation does this.

Brewed coffee should be held at 185° to 190°F (85° to 88°C) for up to an hour. Coffee cannot be reheated without a distinct flavor and color loss. Each category of coffee maker—vacuum, urn, semiautomatic, and automatic—has its own brewing procedure. The guidelines that follow were drawn up by the Coffee Brewing Center.

Vacuum. Accurate measurement is the most important step. Use 1 oz. of coffee to each 16 to 20 fl oz of water. Measure cold, fresh water into the lower bowl, leaving at least 1 inch at the top for water expansion. Place the coffee maker on heat and bring to a boil.

Place a clean filter in the upper bowl. If a cloth filter is used, rinse it in hot water.

When the water boils, reduce the heat or turn off the electricity.

Measure fine-grind coffee into the upper bowl, and insert the upper bowl with a slight twist to ensure a tight seal. Return the maker to reduced heat.

Let water rise into the upper bowl, and allow it to mix with the ground coffee for 1 minute, stirring thoroughly in a zigzag motion for the first 20 seconds.

Remove the maker from the heat. The brew should return to the lower bowl in no more than 2 minutes.

Remove the upper bowl, rinse it and the filter with hot water, and place the rinsed filter cloth in cold water until next use.

Hold the coffee at 185° to 190°F (85° to 88°C), and never allow it to boil. Never reheat coffee, and always serve it fresh. Brewed coffee should be discarded after 1 hour.

Urn. Accurate measurement is the most important step. Use 2 (never more than 2½) gallons of water to 1 lb of coffee.

Spread fresh drip-grind coffee evenly in the filter. To obtain good extraction, spread the layer of coffee evenly (1 to 2 inches in depth). If a new urn bag is to be used, rinse it thoroughly in hot water before placing it on the urn bag ring. If the urn is not equipped with a brewing basket, use a gridded riser to ensure proper support of the urn bag.

Use fresh boiling water. The urn should be attached only to a cold-water line. Be sure that the water temperature is 200°F (93.5°C) when it comes into contact with the coffee.

Pour the water in a slow, circular motion. This helps ensure even extraction. Make sure that you wet all the grounds evenly. Total contact time must be between 4 and 6 minutes. Brewing time starts when the first water touches the coffee and ends when the last water has passed through the grounds and the brewing device is removed. Replace the urn cover between pours, to preserve the aroma.

Remove the filter device as soon as the water has dripped through. If the brewing device is left in the urn, steam from the coffee rises, condenses into water, and passes back through the grounds, releasing astringent and bitter materials. Rinse the cloth filter in clear hot water, and then store it in cold water until next use.

If all of the water cannot be passed through the grounds within the prescribed brewing time, it may be necessary to place some of the water (up to 40 percent) in the bottom of the urn before brewing. This prevents overextraction and bitterness.

Mix the brew. Draw off the heavy coffee from the bottom of the urn and pour it back into the brew to ensure uniform mixing. Mix at least 1 gallon for each 1 lb of coffee used.

Never repour brewed coffee back through spent grounds. It only makes the coffee bitter, and is a waste of time.

Semiautomatic. Accurate measurement is the most important step. Use 1 oz of coffee to each 16 to 20 oz of water. For 48 oz of water (8 cups), use from 2.4 to 3 oz of coffee. For 60 oz of water (10 cups), use from 3 to 3.75 oz of coffee.

Place filter paper in the brewing cartridge. Spread fresh fine-grind coffee evenly in the filter paper; an even coffee bed is important for even extraction.

Check the water temperature. The coffee coming from the brewing cartridge must be at least 190°F (88°C) to ensure that water was 200°F (93.5°C) when it was filtered through the grounds.

Check the brewing time. All pour-over brewers should deliver a bowl of coffee in from 3 minutes 20 seconds to 4 minutes 20 seconds. Remove the grounds as soon as the water has dripped through. Rinse the cartridge; wipe the underside of the spray head area on the coffeemaker at least once a day.

Automatic. Use 4 oz (never less than $3\frac{1}{5}$ oz) of coffee to each $\frac{1}{2}$ gallon of water. If a 3-oz package is used, reduce the beverage yield to 54 oz or less.

Place a filter in the brewing chamber. If a cloth filter is to be used, rinse it thoroughly in hot water before its first use.

Spread fresh coffee grounds evenly in the brewing chamber. An even coffee bed is important for even extraction. Use either a drip grind or a fine grind, depending on the machine's brewing cycle.

Check the water temperature. The coffee coming from the brewing chamber must be at least 190°F (88°C) to ensure that the water was 200°F (93.5°C) when it filtered through the grounds.

Remove the grounds immediately after the water has dripped through. If a cloth filter was used, rinse it in clear hot water, and then store it in cold water until next use.

Sanitation and Quality Control

Coffee flavors are carried in volatile or essential oils that can break down easily, become rancid, or otherwise react unfavorably with substances. Long holding or improper making leads to major flavor loss. Coffee that smells good may not taste good because much of what is good is escaping into the air. High temperatures encourage rapid flavor loss, and yet for best flavor coffee must be served hot.

A rancid odor or taste in coffee can be caused by a dirty filter, uncleaned equipment, or a clogged gridded riser that contains old grounds. Urn bags absorb coffee flavors that deteriorate and unpleasantly flavor new brew. It is best to use paper filters and discard these after each use. A new cloth bag should be rinsed well, since starch fillers can give off-flavors to the brew. All surfaces should be thoroughly cleaned; rinsing is not enough. Serving cups should also be clean.

Urns should be rinsed after each use and a brush should be used to clear away sediment or coffee oils. Before a new batch is made, clear water should be run through the urn to rinse it. At the end of the day, equipment should be disassembled and

thoroughly cleaned. The urn is reassembled and partly filled with water, which remains in it overnight. Leave the urn top ajar so air can circulate through. Twice a week, the urn should be filled with water and an urn-cleaning compound added, in accordance with the manufacturer's directions. The compound is left in the water overnight, and the following morning the unit is thoroughly cleaned. If this overnight standing is not possible, allow the urn to soak for at least 30 minutes before cleaning. Check to see that all parts are working. Do not use bleaches, soaps, or detergents on coffee equipment unless these are thoroughly rinsed off before use. Small coffee equipment can be soaked frequently in cleaning compound, thoroughly scrubbed, and rinsed. Good sanitation is one essential step in producing good coffee.

A cup of coffee should be judged for its flavor, odor, color, body, and clarity. The flavor should be sweet (but not too sweet) and slightly bitter. No saltiness should be evident. Some acidity should be present, but the effect should be mellow, not sharp. Coffee odors should be fragrant and aromatic, with a rich, true coffee smell; harsh or strong odors indicate poor quality. The color should be a blackish brown, not pale or weak. Coffee should have some body or density, since good making extracts about 22 percent solids from the grounds. Body is judged by using 18 percent milkfat cream (not half-and-half or whipping cream): the cream should flow into the coffee and feather; that is, it should stay in a separate layer and not mix. Cream or milk quickly blend with tea because tea has no body. Clarity is essential. A cloudy cup of coffee almost always has a poor flavor. When the coffee is consumed, no sediment or grittiness should be evident. A silver spoon lowered into the coffee shows up clearly until it is hidden on the bottom.

Serving and Merchandising Coffee

A good cup of coffee sells itself by exuding the characteristic rich odor of coffee so many people find appealing. Coffee tastes best right after it is made. In formal service, coffee is served after all dishes are removed and the table is crumbed. The coffee is poured from the container into a cup sitting on a saucer directly in front of the patron. The handle of the cup should be to the right and at an angle toward the patron. Less formal service allows the cup to be lifted with the saucer for pouring and then replaced in front of the patron.

Special coffees can add interest to a menu. Espresso is made by using steam pressure to force water over very finely ground coffee that has a dark roast. The brew has a heavy flavor with some bitterness and a heavy body. Cappuccino consists of espresso and hot milk poured simultaneously from two different pots into a cup containing nutmeg, cinnamon, powdered chocolate, or whipped cream. Turkish coffee is made from sugar and heavily roasted, finely powdered fresh coffee; it is boiled at tableside in a small brass pot called an *ibrik*. Café diablo is espresso poured into a silver bowl at the table and heated (usually over a guéridon), liqueurs are added, and the drink is flamed. Demitasse coffee is strong dark-roasted coffee often served with liqueurs, lemon, or spices in small cups; sugar should be offered with it. Viennese coffee is similar to demitasse coffee, but it is always topped with whipped cream; hot milk may be used to thin it. French coffee (also called *café au lait*) is a combination of strong, dark-roasted coffee and milk. Irish coffee is a blend of black coffee, Irish whiskey, and heavy cream. By mixing coffee and liqueurs of its own choosing, an operation can create its own specialty coffee.

Few operations today offer instant coffee. The delicate nature of coffee flavors and their high volatility make it difficult to capture them, and much escapes during processing. Instant coffee processed by the freeze-dry method has the most flavor of the instant types, and some brands do a good job of approaching good coffee flavors.

Tea

Tea is a popular beverage that is less expensive than coffee. The stimulant (theine) in a cup of tea contains about half the caffeine contained in a cup of coffee. Tea can be served hot or cold. If hot, it should be very hot; if cold, it should be iced. A good tea is brisk in flavor. Black tea produces a beverage the color of a bright new copper penny.

Tea prepared with hard water is dark, and a slight film may cover the surface because of tannin precipitates. Using soft water corrects this. Lemon juice also lightens tea.

Tea comes from the young leaves of a tropical bush. Normally, two leaves and a bud are picked from the end of each stem. The highest-grade teas come from the tiniest leaves. Tea grown at high elevations and picked at the start of the season is best. Climate and the making of tea influence quality, too.

After being picked, tea is withered, rolled, and fired. Black tea is fully fermented between the rolling and firing processes; fermentation consists of an oxidation of the tannins. Oolong tea is partially fermented, and green tea is not fermented at all. Firing stops fermentation and preserves the tea.

Preparing Tea

Teas may be blended from as many as thirty different varieties of tea. Oolong tea is a somewhat tan-colored beverage, and green tea brew is a yellowish green. Green tea contains the most tannins, oolong has less, and black tea has the least. Tea should be made by what is called *wet service*. The tea is put into a preheated pot (1 tsp for every 2 cups of water), and boiling water is poured over it and left to steep for about 3 to 5 minutes. A poor cup of tea results when boiling water is put into a cup or pot and the tea bag is put on the saucer beside it, for the patron to immerse. Tea is not as perishable as coffee, but it can deteriorate, so fresh supplies should be maintained.

Tea also clouds easily, particularly under refrigeration. This clouding is caused by the precipitation of tannins. The Tea Council suggests making iced tea in quantity by the 1, 2, 3 method:

1 qt of boiling water over
2 oz of tea; steep for 6 minutes; stir; pour off the brew into
3 qt of cold tap water

This tea is then added to ice cubes as needed. Finished tea can be held for about 4 hours for making iced tea. Mint or lemon is usually served with iced tea. The best sugar to use is fine or fruit sugar, because it goes into solution more quickly than regular granulated sugar. Often, tea for icing is made quite strong, and the hot brew is poured over ice cubes. Some operations use instant tea for iced tea.

To make tea in quantity, use 5 to 8 oz of tea and 4 to 7 gallons of water for 100 to 150 cups. One cup (1 oz) of dry loose tea, makes 50 cups, or a little more than 2 gallons of beverage. Freshly boiling water makes the best tea. Tea can be made in a large pot on the range or in a steam-jacketed kettle. The water is brought to a boil, the tea added, the heat shut off, and the tea allowed to steep for about 3 to 5 minutes. Leaving tea leaves in the brew longer than this extracts too much tannin, giving a bitter flavor and an excessively dark tea.

Tea can be served with milk, but cream masks its delicate flavor. Lemon adds a bit of briskness to tea; sometimes a clove is served.

Some teas contain special flavors. Jasmine tea contains jasmine flowers, which give the tea a fruity flavor and a highly perfumed aroma. Teas can be blended with fruit juices and other liquids for special occasions. A spiced tea is made by steeping tea with orange or lemon rind, whole cloves, cinnamon sticks, and sugar. The Russians make a tea that is sweetened and seasoned with orange, lemon, pineapple juice, and a bit of cinnamon.

Tea Quality

A good cup of tea should be judged by its flavor, strength, clarity, and color. Body is not a factor, since tea has little or no body. The tea should have a slightly bitter flavor. Green tea is the most bitter (again, because of its tannin content), oolong next, and black tea least. Some teas have a distinct sweetness, and others have a distinct acidity; still others have blends that fall in between these. The taster should know what to look for in the particular tea. Teas should be aromatic with a fruity, fragrant odor. Flavor and odor are best obtained by swishing the tea inside the mouth, and then breathing in to catch the aroma. The mouth is then opened so that the taste buds can give their signal on what they find. A brisk tea should have a zesty stimulating

quality. Weak teas are described as thin or weathery. All teas should be clear and have no oiliness.

Cocoa

Where cocoa service is infrequent, it is best to use individually packaged mixes of good quality. When service is regular or large, cocoa can be made from dry cocoa, sugar, and either liquid milk or dry milk and water. Breakfast cocoa is 22 percent cocoa butter. Some cocoas contain less fat. Cocoa that is too high in fat solidifies. Butter or margarine can be added if nonfat dry milk is used. Richer cocoas can be made by adding chocolate and by using half-and-half or cream in place of some of the milk.

Cocoa should have a rich, chocolate color. A gray or muddy color indicates poor quality. A definite chocolate flavor should be discernible. A poor cocoa powder makes a cocoa that has a flat flavor and produces much sediment. Wateriness or syrupy quality is undesirable.

There should be no scum on top or in the cocoa. Putting foam on the cocoa by whipping it or by adding marshmallows or whipped cream stops scum formation. Covering the kettle also accomplishes this. Cocoa contains starch, so some slight thickening occurs when it is heated, giving it some body. Adding starch to improve body is not recommended.

SUMMARY

The pantry is responsible for the production of a number of food items that require a lot of labor and are often served cold. These include appetizers, sandwiches, salads, salad dressings, and beverages. Because of the number of motions they must perform, employees should be skilled and well-trained, and their work centers should be efficiently planned.

Appetizers and sandwiches are related products requiring somewhat similar production techniques. Sanitation is important. Appetizers are foods designed to whet the appetite, such as canapés, cocktails, dips, hors d'oeuvres, relishes, salads, and soups. A sandwich is a food item made of bread, a spread, a filling, and a garnish. Sandwiches may be double, open-face, or even tiered, and they may be hot or cold. Sandwiches can be served as snacks, entrées, desserts, and luncheon offerings.

A salad is usually a crisp green, vegetable, or fruit medley combined with other foods and served either hot or cold. Salads may be used as appetizers, meal accompaniments, full meals, or desserts. A salad usually consists of a base or underliner, a body, a garnish, and a dressing. Salad greens are the most common ingredient and contribute color, texture, and flavor. Fruits and vegetables are used to accent the greens and form a major portion of the body. Other salad ingredients are added for interest, variety, and flavor. The success of a salad depends on its freshness, on its crispness, and on the adequacy of the various parts. The body of a salad may consist of greens, meat, fish, poultry, gelatin mixtures, cheese, pastas, or combinations of these.

A dressing is a flavorful sauce used to add flavor, texture, and perhaps even color to a salad. The two basic types are French dressing and mayonnaise or stable-emulsion dressing. French dressing separates into vinegar and oil components, so it is called an *unstable emulsion.* Mayonnaise and boiled dressings form a fixed phase of oil in water and are called *stable* or *permanent emulsions.*

Garnishes for salads should be edible and should offer contrasts in color, flavor, texture, and form.

Beverages are liquids served before, during, or after meals to provide a flavorful, stimulating drink. Coffee, tea, and cocoa all contain stimulants related to caffeine. Coffee should be made with special care for the product, the equipment, and the brewing method used to produce it. A fresh product, scrupulously clean equipment, and the right production method can yield a desirable cup of coffee. The right roast and right grind are also crucial. Coffee water should remain in contact with the grounds for a set time and be of the right temperature— around 205°F (96°C). Some alkalinity in the water is acceptable, but if the water contains too many bicarbonates, the contact time may have to be increased because a sediment will form that delays passage of the water through the grounds. Approxi-mately 2½ gallons of water should be used for each 1 lb of coffee.

Tea comes from the last new leaves on the stems of a tropical bush. Quality also depends on the variety of tea, on growing conditions (including elevation and climate), on processing, and on brewing technique. Black tea is fully fermented, a process that removes tannin. Oolong tea is partially fermented, and green tea is not fermented. After plucking, tea is withered, rolled, fermented (or not), and then dried.

Iced tea can be made by the 1, 2, 3 method recommended by the Tea Council. Iced tea is best made from freshly brewed tea that is poured over ice. Storing tea in refrigerators encourages clouding.

Cocoa is made from cacao beans, which are also the source of chocolate. In processing, more than half the cocoa butter is removed, and the remainder of the bean is ground. Breakfast cocoa is high in cocoa butter, containing 22 percent or more. When service is infrequent, cocoa should be made from packaged mixes. There are several ways to prepare cocoa in quantity from cocoa powder and other ingredients.

CHAPTER REVIEW QUESTIONS

1. You have been retained as an instructor in a junior college to teach a quantity food preparation course along with two other food-related courses. The junior college lacks a good quantity food preparation kitchen but does have a space in which most of the major pieces of quantity production equipment are available. You are able to set up a pantry work center; but lacking a real production center, you decide to put together a set of slides that demonstrate the production of appetizers, sandwiches, salads, salad dressings, and beverages. Set up a list of the slides that will be shown, and write a commentary to accompany each slide as it is shown.

2. Compare the different kinds of appetizers, and indicate the nature of each. Why are

color, contrast, and arrangement important in preparing these?

3. What are some of the methods workers should use in making sandwiches?
4. Identify the amount of finished salad, by weight or measure, that is required for 100 portions of the following salads:
   a. Potato salad
   b. Salad of mixed greens
   c. Gelatin salad
5. What are the four parts of a salad?
6. What factors strengthen gelatin mixtures, and what factors weaken them?
7. How is French dressing prepared? What is a stable emulsion? What is an unstable emulsion? How is mayonnaise made?

VOCABULARY

Tannin	Rio coffee
Oolong tea	Rancidity
Bicarbonate	Wet service
Appetizer	*Ibrik*
Canapé	Robusta
Arabica	Salad dressing
Urn	Espresso
Boston lettuce	Salad body
Mayonnaise	Bibb lettuce
Salad bar	Iceberg lettuce
Sodium sulfite	*Mise en place*
Hors d'oeuvres	Appetizer salad
Work center	Temporary emulsion
Garde manger	Garnish
S motion	Sandwich
Sandwich filling	Sandwich spread
Salad body	Main-dish salad
Stable emulsion	Open-face
Cocktail	Romaine
Pasta	1, 2, 3 method
Salad	Accompaniment salad
Escarole	Black tea
Gel	Salad greens
Dessert salad	Boiled dressing

Base or underliner	Brisk flavor
Curly endive	Chapon
Green tea	Breakfast cocoa
Permanent emulsion	Relish
Automatic brewer	

ANNOTATED REFERENCES

Axler, B. 1969. *Methods and Manners of Cooking,* pp. 99-102. New York: Funk & Wagnalls. (A wide variety of hors d'oeuvres, but no recipes.)

Blair, E. 1974. *Salads and Salad Dressings.* Boston: CBI Publishing. (Salad and salad dressing recipes.)

Casola, M. 1969. *Successful Mass Cookery and Volume-Feeding,* pp. 184-213. Rochelle Park, N.J.: Ahrens Publishing. (Information and recipes for salad and salad dressing.)

Castle, C., and Lawrence, B. 1973. *Hors d'Oeuvre, Etc.* San Francisco, Cal.: 101 Productions. (All aspects of appetizer production and service.)

Coffee Brewing Center. "There is No Substitute for Good Coffee. Here's What You Need to Make It." Pub. No. 14. New York: Coffee Brewing Center. (Many such informative booklets available.)

Crosby, J. and Bateman, R. C. 1969. *Serve It Cold,* pp. 18-40. New York: Doubleday. (Appetizers served cold.)

Fowler, S. F.; West, B. B.; and Shugart, G. S. 1971. *Food for 50,* pp. 81-85, 355-72. New York: John Wiley & Sons. (Appetizer and sandwich production in quantity, with recipes.)

Gates, J. C. 1976. *Basic Foods,* pp. 100-07, 173-95. New York: Holt, Rinehart & Winston. (Emulsions, salad dressings, and salads.)

Haines, R. G. 1973. *Food Preparation for Hotels, Restaurants, and Cafeterias,* pp. 67-91, 124-64. Chicago: American Technical Society. (Recipes of salads, salad dressings, and appetizers.)

Huebener, P. O. 1968. *Gourmet Table Service.* Rochelle Park, N.J.: Hayden Book. (Beverage service and merchandising.)

Kaplan, A. 1971. *Elements of Food Production and Baking,* pp. 155-68. New York: ITT Educational Services. (Salads and salad dressings.)

Kansas State University. 1966. *Practical Cookery,* pp. 63-69, 139-49. New York: John Wiley & Sons. (Salad, salad dressing, sandwich, and canapé recipes.)

Lundberg, D. E., and Kotschevar, L. H. 1968. *Understanding Cooking,* pp. 320-40. Amherst, Mass.: University of Massachusetts. (Salads and salad dressings.)

Middleton, E.; Carter, M. R.; and Vierin, A. 1968. *100 to Dinner,* pp. 275-82. Buffalo, N.Y.: University of Toronto Press. (Quantity sandwich production.)

Sonnenschmidt, F. H., and Nicolas, J. F. 1988. *Art of Garde Manger,* 4th ed., pp. 185-212. New York: Van Nostrand Reinhold. (Recipes and ideas for a variety of appetizers.)

Tea Council. "Two Leaves and a Bud." New York: Tea Council of the USA. (One of many publications offered by the Tea Council.)

Terrell, M. E. 1971. *Professional Food Preparation,* pp. 222-46. New York: John Wiley & Sons. (Various aspects of salad and salad dressing preparation.)

Thorner, M. E., and Herzberg, R. J. 1970. *Food Beverage Service Book.* Westport, Conn.: AVI Publishing. (Complete beverage systems.)

Treat, N., and Richards, L. 1966. *Quantity Cookery,* pp. 370-400. Boston: Little, Brown. (Quantity recipes for salads and salad dressings.)

Waldner, G. K., and Mitterhauser, K. 1971. *Book of Buffets,* pp. 17-44. Boston: CBI Publishing. (Canapés and hors d'oeuvres.)

CHAPTER 10

Stocks, Soups, and Sauces

OUTLINE

Stocks form the base of many soups, sauces, and prepared dishes. The difference among individual soups and sauces is often a matter of seasoning, ingredients, and consistency.

STOCKS

Stocks are thin, flavored liquids made from simmered meat, fish, or poultry flesh or bones, vegetables, seasonings, and a liquid such as water, milk, or tomato juice. Simmering extracts flavors, making a rich, flavorful stock. Proper ingredients, preparation methods, and care after preparation are necessary to make a good stock.

Ingredients

Quality stocks result only when clean, wholesome ingredients in the right quantities are used (see fig. 10-1). The right equipment must also be available. A gallon of stock is made from 4 lb of

216

Figure 10-1. Quality ingredients help ensure a fine stock.

bones, 5 qt of water, 1 lb of mirepoix (8 oz of leeks or onions, 4 oz of celery, and 4 oz of carrots), and seasonings. The best bones to use are knuckle, shank, or neck bones, in that order. Chicken carcasses and parts make an excellent stock. The bones, head, and skin of lean white fish make a light, delicate fish stock. Veal bones may be added to produce gelatin; beef for a rich flavor; and pork or ham for special flavor. Bones should be cut into 4-inch lengths and cracked. Meat may be simmered with the stock, and then removed for other uses.

A mirepoix is a mixture of roughly cut vegetables of high quality. Besides the primary ingredients (leeks or onions, celery, and carrots), mirepoix mixtures can contain parsley, turnips, cabbage, and other vegetables. Kitchens save vegetable parts such as the tops of fresh tomatoes, pieces of parsley, and water from canned vegetables; however, the stock pot is not a garbage can for disposing of undesirable wastes. Seasonings and spices such as bay leaf, thyme, clove, peppercorns, garlic, and parsley stems are added to stocks. The spices are usually wrapped in a small cloth or bag called a *sachet* or *bouquet garni.* Stocks should only be lightly salted because they are often concentrated or combined with other foods, and too much salt here may oversalt the finished product.

Equipment for making stock can be very simple. Bones are cut and cracked in the meat section, where the band saw, cleavers, and meat blocks are found. A stock pot for top-of-the-range cooking or a steam-jacketed kettle can be used to cook the stock. The stock pot should have a spigot so that stock can be withdrawn from the bottom. A cutting board, a French knife for preparing vegetables, a ladle, a skimmer, and a china cap are necessary tools.

Preparation Methods

Most stocks are simmered for 4 to 8 hours, but fish stocks should not be simmered for more than forty-five minutes and chicken stocks for more than 3 hours, to prevent clouding.

Some operations maintain continuous stock kettles; the French call them *pots-au-feu.* Stock is taken as needed, and additional bones, water, vegetables and vegetable water are added. After four or five days, the stock becomes weak or cloudy and must be started anew. Recent evidence indicates that adding a bit of vinegar (not enough to flavor the stock) helps dissolve calcium from the bones, producing stock that is a richer source of calcium than milk.

Procedures

Certain common procedures must be followed to prepare good stocks. Place the bones in a stock pot, add cold water to cover them, and bring the liquid to a boil, skimming off scum as it rises. When the stock begins to boil, lower the heat to a simmer. Some chefs start stocks from hot water, saying that it produces a clearer, more flavorful stock. Cold water dissolves some proteins in bones, which then coagulate to form a cloudy scum. Some chefs discard the first water just as it comes to a boil, to get a clearer stock, but some flavor and nutrition are lost thereby.

Mirepoix and seasonings may be added to the bones at the start or later, depending on the type of stock to be made. When the stock is done, it is drawn or poured from the pot through a china cap lined with cheesecloth. It is then ready to use or store. Four major types of stock are made: brown, white, chicken, and fish.

Brown Stock. A brown stock is usually made with beef and veal bones. The beef bones give the stock a rich flavor, and the veal bones provide gelatin that give it body. To prepare, oil the bones lightly, place them in a roasting pan, and brown well in an oven. Overbrowning results in a bitter stock; underbrowning gives a weak flavor and a poorly colored stock. After browning, put the bones into a stock pot. Pour off the fat, and, over heat, deglaze the roasting pan by removing the fond (browned portion) with water. Add this to the pot, and cover the bones with water. Bring to a complete boil, skim, and simmer until the stock is full-flavored. Add the mirepoix and sachet about midway through the cooking. Some chefs add tomatoes to enrich the stock's color and add flavor; others say this should not be done to a base stock.

White Stock. White stock is more delicately flavored than brown. Veal bones are best for it, but a combination of beef and veal bones is usually used. Do not brown the bones. Instead, cut them, wash them, and place them in cold water; then bring the liquid to a boil. Change the water if the stock appears cloudy at the start. Simmer for from 4 to 6 hours. Add the mirepoix and sachet about halfway through. Strain the finished stock, and use or store it.

Chicken Stock. Chicken stock is sometimes also called *white stock*. Prepare it as you would white stock, but simmer it for only 2½ to 3 hours. Add the mirepoix and seasonings after the first hour of simmering. Some chefs omit carrots from the mirepoix for this stock, but the decision is a matter of personal preference. End by straining the chicken stock.

Fish Stock. Bones, heads, skins, and trimmings from lean, white deep-sea fish are often used for fish stock. Rich, fatty fish such as salmon, mackerel, and trout give a strongly flavored and slightly dark stock. Do not wash the bones before cooking. Start with cold water; bring the liquid to a boil, skim, and then simmer. Add the mirepoix and spices immediately after skimming. An acid such as lemon juice may be added. Simmer for 45 minutes.

Adding vinegar, lemon juice, or some other acid to a stock helps give it clarity and adds flavor. It also helps to leach calcium out of the bones in the stock pot. Add only a small amount of acid; most of it boils away in the cooking, so little flavor is left.

Stock Products

Many items made from stocks are used to enrich foods. A glaze is stock reduced by one-fourth in volume. The mixture is syrupy and coats a spoon when warm; it produces a solid gel when cold. A stock simmered to one-half its original volume is called a *demiglaze.* Stocks reduced to a paste consistency are called *glacés;* thus we have *glacé de poulet* or *glacé de volaille* (chicken), *glacé de viande* (from brown or white stock), and *glacé de poisson* (fish). Essences are rich stocks simmered with wine, vegetables, and herbs. They are used to flavor and enrich items. After simmering, essences are strained and reduced to the desired consistency—usually that of a demiglaze. A fumet is a rich essence reduced almost to a glacé and thinned with sherry or Madeira wine.

Care After Preparation

Cool stocks rapidly to below 45°F (7°C), to prevent them from souring, as they are an excellent medium for microorganism growth. This is best managed by dividing the stock into 2-gallon lots, placing the containers in a sink, and circulating cold water around them. Then refrigerate or freeze each lot. Leave the congealed fat on top to prevent things from falling into the stock. When reheating a stock, bring it to a boil as quickly as possible. Continual recooling and reheating lowers a stock's quality.

Prepared Bases

Many operations today use prepared bases to make stocks because they lack the bones and meat required to make their own or because they find the prepared bases' labor-saving aspects desirable and their product quality adequate. These bases may also be used to enrich existing stock and other items. To ascertain the ingredients in a prepared base, read the list of ingredients; these are listed by quantity, from greatest to least. A base that reads "Salt, monosodium glutamate, fat, sugar, flavoring, spices, and coloring" contains no meat product and is probably not a high-quality product. Poor-quality bases make poor products. One base prized by many chefs has a label listing "Chicken meat including natural chicken juices, salt, monosodium glutamate, chicken fat, sugar, flavoring, and turmeric," indicating that chicken meat is greatest in quantity, and turmeric least.

SOUPS

One way of classifying soups is to separate them by their consistency, which reflects their ingredients and indicates their use. Thus, one simple classification has three categories: thin soups, thick soups, and national or specialty soups.

Thin soups are generally clear—such as broths, bouillons, and consommés—or begin with clear stocks that are made opaque by only a few ingredients. A broth is a rich, flavorful stock. A bouillon is a soup made from stock, extra meat, and seasonings; it may or may not have been clarified. A bouillon is often a rich broth that carries the flavor of beef. A consommé is a rich, delicate, clear soup made by clarifying a rich stock or broth after enriching it by simmering it with meat and other flavoring ingredients. Thin opaque soups may include cream soups, bisques, purées, light vegetable soups, and some cold soups such as vichyssoise.

The borderline between thin and thick soups is difficult to draw. A purée can be thin or quite heavy and thick. Some vegetable soups are very heavy because they contain a lot of ingredients, while others are almost clear. Many heavy soups are thickened with rice, potatoes, pastas, starch, or eggs. A chowder or gumbo is thick because of its many ingredients.

A thick purée is made from vegetables such as potatoes, tomatoes, and asparagus; from legumes such as lentils, split peas, and lima beans; or from fruit such as prunes and apples that are pulped, strained, and added to the desired base—either plain or thickened stock. Starch may be added to thicken the mixture and hold the ingredients evenly in the soup. Neither milk nor cream is added to a purée, since that would make the product a cream soup.

The word *chowder* comes from the French word *chaudron* which was the name of a large cooking kettle used by French Canadian fishermen of the Maritime Provinces. Chowders originally contained seafood or fish as their main ingredient, but they may now be made primarily from corn, lima beans, or mushrooms. Diced potato, chopped onion, and bacon fat or salt pork are added after the vegetables have been sautéed in fat. Manhattan (Philadelphia or Long Island) chowder contains fish stock and tomatoes; Boston or New England chowder contains milk or cream.

Bisques can be thin or thick. The base is usually some type of shellfish, such as lobster or abalone. A gumbo is quite heavy and often contains seafood, chicken, vegetables, and rice; it must contain okra—a vegetable of distinct flavor and some thickening power. Gumbo can be thickened with cornstarch. Potato soups are heavy soups.

National or specialty soups may be thick or thin. They fall into this category because of their ingredients, their method of making, or their origin. French onion soup, mulligatawny from India, Scotch mutton broth with its typical barley, olla podrida of Spain, borsch from Russia, and minestrone from Italy fall into this category. Many specialty soups are served cold, including a delicate avocado soup seasoned with lemon and sherry, a jellied madrilène, a gazpacho, and many chilled fruit soups.

Soup Preparation

High-quality ingredients, the right production techniques, and proper service are all important in soup preparation. Attention must also be given to the soup's consistency, seasoning, and garnish, and to special production needs.

Consistency

Many thin soups are watery because the stock lacks suitable body. Good body results from using a fairly large amount of gelatin that occurs naturally in the bones of young animals. Additional body can come from thickening agents, meat, fish, poultry, and vegetables. When a roux (equal parts fat and flour, by weight, cooked together) is added to a stock, a velouté results. The amount of roux used determines whether the velouté is thin or thick. Adding the velouté to a soup such as a bisque or a cream soup determines its thickness.

When cream soups are made using a velouté, 1 pint of the vegetable purée (for flavoring) is added for each gallon to be prepared. A small portion of this hot soup is then gradually added to warmed milk or cream, and the milk or cream mixture is stirred vigorously back into the hot soup. Such precautions must be taken to prevent curdling. This method is often called the *velouté method* of making a cream soup. High temperatures and excessive salting, as well as the presence of any acid, may cause curdling. A cream soup that is too thick for service can be thinned with warmed milk or cream. The consistency desired in cream soups and most thick soups is similar to that of moderately heavy cream.

Seasoning and Garnish

Seasoning a soup successfully involves achieving a blend of flavors, with no one flavor predominating. Adding spices and other seasonings toward the end of preparation ensures maximum flavor. Delicacy of seasoning should be sought. Just a tiny pinch of ground cloves added to a cream of tomato soup can make a great difference in its flavor. A touch of sage has a similarly beneficial effect on clam chowder. Monosodium glutamate may help to smooth out and elicit delicate flavors. Subtlety in flavoring can add much to a soup's quality.

Many thin soups are enhanced by an appropriately chosen garnish. A cream of asparagus soup with a tiny asparagus spear floating in it, lobster bisque graced with chopped lobster, cream of corn soup with popcorn croutons, and other garnishes of this kind make soups stand out. Croutons made from toast or pastry, small-grained cereals such as rice or barley, grated cheese, or a daub of sour cream add a distinctive touch when used sensitively. Garnishes used for consommés and bouillons sometimes give the soup its name. Thus, a consommé Florentine has a few tiny cooked leaves of spinach in it, and a bouillon vermicelli has a few cooked vermicelli in it and a tiny slice of truffle.

Special Procedures

The following procedures for making a good soup are standard:

1. Skim the surface of the stock to remove fat and scum. This gives a clearer stock and a better soup.
2. Strain stocks and soups. All stocks should be strained after completion to remove impurities and give a clearer soup. Particularly thin soups should be strained through a china cap covered with cheesecloth. Bouillons, consommés, and other clear soups should be so clear that they sparkle.
3. Add spices with care. Subtle seasoning is the key. A stock and a soup should be a blend of flavors. Some chefs remove the little round part of a clove because it can give a slight bitterness. Others crack whole peppercorns to extract more flavor. Spices should not be added except in a sachet bag, and they should be kept in only long enough to contribute the flavor they should.
4. Sauté some vegetable garnishes to improve their flavor.

Cream soups often have problems with curdling. Asparagus, potatoes, tomatoes, and other vegetables or ingredients may contain tannins, acids, or other substances that cause curdling. Small curds separate out as a result of curdling, damaging the soup's appearance. One precaution that can be taken is to blend a small quantity of the curdling product *into* some milk or cream to temper it. This mixture can then be blended back into the soup. If all of the soup is to be added at once, take two precautions: add the curdling product *into* the milk or cream slowly; simultaneously, give the mixture rapid agitation with a wire whip. Do not add cold milk or cream; warm them first. If the velouté method is used, the curdling product is bound in with the starch, which lessens chances for curdling. Reducing the heat and cutting back on salt help reduce curdling as well. An old stock of cream soup should never be mixed with a new one. Preparing only the quantity of soup needed for a short serving time is a good practice.

Some cream soups (and others) may get extra flavor, smoothness, and body from a liaison. This is a mixture of one part egg yolk and three parts rich cream. Some of the hot soup is blended into the liaison, and then this blended mixture is stirred carefully into the hot soup mixture. The heat is raised as the soup is stirred well, and cooking proceeds only until thickening occurs. The soup should be served shortly after it thickens.

Some soups evaporate when they stand in the steam table. As this occurs, the soup may become too salty or the seasonings too heavy. To counteract this, watch the soup closely, and add liquid to replace any lost to evaporation.

Soup Service

Soup temperatures at service should be 160°F (71°C) or more. Many soups are held at 190°F (88°C). Chilled soups should be served at between 40° and 45°F (4.5° and 7°C). Containers into which hot soup is to be served should be preheated. Menus should offer both thin and heavy soups, plus others. The soups served should contrast in appearance, presentation, and accompaniments (such as bread or crackers). A kettle of bouillabaise can be served with garlic toast, and a hearty bowl of clam chowder with the traditional oyster crackers. Fat globules should not be visible, as a good sheen is important (see fig. 10-2).

Soup Care

Carry-over soups have many uses. They can be added to the stock pot, if they are of the right kind, or they can be used as a base for other dishes. Often they can be combined with other soups to make new soups. For example, cream of tomato soup blended with split-pea soup makes a Mongole soup. Most soups sour easily and must be handled as stocks are. Cool them quickly in 2-gallon (or smaller) containers in a sink, and refrigerate them as soon as possible. Thick soups cool more quickly when they are stirred.

Figure 10-2. Fat globules as seen in this cup of soup are a disgrace to any foodservice operation.

A run-out time for soups can be planned, to reduce carry-overs. For backup, you can use a convenience soup, many of which are of good quality.

Portion Control

The right quantity of soup must be served to meet management's cost estimates. A standard portion for a first-course soup is about 6 oz (¾ c or 160 cc). A big bowl holds about 10 oz (1¼ cups or 300 cc) and often suffices for a light meal. Because soups are not high-cost items, a tureen or crock of soup may be put on the table, and guests invited to help themselves. Alternatively, a soup bar may be offered, along the lines of a salad bar.

SAUCES

Sauces are used to enhance the flavor, appearance, nutritional value, and moistness of food. They were originally created to increase foods' flavor and palatability. Sauces should not be designed to hide poor food quality but to complement the flavor of items served. A sauce's flavor should never overwhelm the flavor of the food. Sauces should be of correct consistency so that they flow readily but are not soupy. All sauces must be based on a rich stock or liquid to enhance the end product. Good planning, careful preparation, and proper handling result in good-quality sauces.

Planning

Planning for sauce production includes obtaining good-quality ingredients and using proper production agents.

Thickening Agents

Sauces can be thickened with roux, eggs, butter and flour (beurre manié), and starches. A sauce's consistency is important to its function (see table 10-1).

Roux. Roux is often used to thicken sauces. A slack roux has more fat than flour, by weight; a lean roux has more flour than fat. Cooking roux is done to give sauces color and to remove any starchy flavor that might be present. A white roux is cooked just long enough to blend the fat and flavor properly. A blond roux is cooked slowly until a fawn color is

Table 10-1. Items to Add to Different Sauces to Achieve a Desired Consistency

Sauce Prepared	Purée Added	Liquid to Finish With
Velouté sauce (stock thickened with roux)	Vegetable purée	Milk or cream
Béchamel sauce (stock thickened with roux and thinned with milk or cream)	Thickened vegetable purée	Milk or cream (if the sauce is too thick)
White or cream sauce (milk or cream thickened with roux)	Vegetable purée	Milk or cream (if the sauce is too thick)

obtained; this type of roux is used to make velouté sauce. A brown roux is cooked to a rich brown color.

Stir all roux while cooking them. Brown roux is often finished slowly in an oven; slow browning gives a finer product. To speed browning, the flour may be prebrowned in an oven. Browning destroys some thickening power: a heavily browned roux has one-third of white roux's thickening ability.

Add cool roux to hot liquids, and add warm or hot roux to cool liquids. Continue stirring until the mixture boils, and then cook for 10 minutes.

Roux can be refrigerated and held. A roux makes a smooth sauce, if properly handled, by separating starch granules with fat. The starch swells or gelatinizes in the presence of hot liquid, and these granules then crowd each other and thicken the entire mixture. Acids such as vinegar and tomato juice reduce the thickening power of starch granules by reducing their swelling.

Eggs. Eggs—both whites and yolks—can be used to thicken. Their proteins hold moisture loosely, giving the sauce a creamy consistency. Yolks have more thickening power than whites and produce a more stable thickened mixture. When eggs coagulate with liquid, they bind it in and thicken it. If the mixture is stirred and not heated too fast, a smooth thickening occurs. Thickening occurs in most mixtures at about 185°F (85°C).

The use of liaisons has already been mentioned. In this process, eggs are blended with milk, cream, or stocks before being added to a sauce. To add the eggs, first remove the sauce from the heat; next add a ladleful of hot sauce into well-bended eggs, stirring rapidly with a wire whip; then stir this back into the sauce, and continue stirring until thickening occurs. Use low heat, and cook only until thickening occurs. Curdling can occur if too much heat is used. A slightly curdled mixture can be saved by being strained through a cheesecloth.

Eggs are often used to thicken blanquettes, white ragoûts, fricassées and some special soups. A hollandaise sauce is thickened with eggs, but the result is more an emulsion than a cooked product.

Beurre Manié. Beurre manié consists of butter and

flour that have been kneaded together to form a soft paste. It is usually composed of equal parts butter and flour. Small portions are added to hot sauces to thicken them. Vigorous stirring is necessary. The butter melts as heat is applied, and the flour thickens the mixture. No lumping occurs. Kneaded butter and flour are sometimes used in place of roux, but they may leave a slight taste of uncooked flour if overused.

Starches. Many starches are used as sauce thickeners. Each has a different thickening power, clarity, and viscosity (resistance to flow). Waxy maize or converted starch is the most powerful thickener. Corn, potato, rice, and arrowroot starches come next and thicken about equally. Tapioca and wheat flours are weakest. Cake and pastry flours thicken better than bread flour because they contain more starch. Waxy maize or converted starch has the most clarity, followed by arrowroot, tapioca, and cornstarch; rice starch, potato starch, and wheat flours are the least clear. Cornstarch, wheat flours, and rice starch are the most viscous; each makes a firm gel. Potato starch, arrowroot, and tapioca have low viscosity and form somewhat fluid gels. Waxy maize or converted starch forms the least viscous gel of all. A firm gel is desirable for puddings and cream pies, because it allows a piece of cream pie to hold its shape when cut. Waxy maize or converted starch is used for fruit pie fillings since it has good clarity and is not too viscous when cool, giving a soft, pasty texture that is desirable in such a pie. Arrowroot, tapioca, and waxy maize or converted starch can be frozen without breaking (curdling) upon thawing.

Starch in very hot water swells and absorbs moisture; maximum thickness is attained at 194°F (90°C). This process is called *gelatinization.* The swelled starch granules begin to crowd each other, and soon the mixture becomes thick. Overlong exposure to high temperatures or excessive stirring can cause a starch to lose some of its thickening power. Acids break down starches. Even the slight amount of acid contained in meat juices necessitates using a bit more flour to get thickening equal to what would be achieved in milk or water. For this rea-son, acidic ingredients are sometimes withheld until cooking is complete and the product is about to be cooled, since the action of the acid is less at lower temperatures.

A starch blended with a liquid and then added for thickening is called a *slurry.* To add a slurry, take a bit of the hot mixture to be thickened, add it to the slurry, and blend well; then add this mixture to the hot mixture, giving good agitation to work the starch in quickly. Use a heavy pan that gives good heat distribution.

Other Ingredients

Other ingredients used in sauces are wines, spices, seasonings, vinegar, butter, fats and oils, mirepoix, and sachet bags. To *finish* a sauce means to add the final, completing touch. An ingredient such as heavy cream, butter, or liaison is added to give a smoother, mellower, and subtler flavor. Wines may be used. Many sauces take a garnish such as chopped mushrooms, truffles, the grated rind (zest) of a lemon or orange, raisins, or pineapple.

Preparation

The sauce cook is called a *saucier.* Sauce making is an art that must be carefully learned and practiced. Most sauces are derived from one of a few basic sauces that are called *major, grand,* or *mother* sauces. The sauces derived from them are called *small* or *secondary* sauces.

The major sauces are brown (Spanish or Espagnole), Béchamel, velouté, tomato, and hollandaise. The first three have a meat base; tomato sauce may or may not have a meat base; and hollandaise sauce does not have a meat base. Sauces that lack a meat base are called *neutral.*

Brown (Spanish or Espagnole) Sauce

The most commonly used sauce is brown sauce. A common preparation is to sauté 2 lb of mirepoix in ½ lb of fat until the onions are transparent. Then ½ lb of flour is added, and the mixture is cooked for 10 minutes, until it acquires a tan color. Then 1 gal of cold brown stock is stirred into the hot roux. The cook then adds ½ cup of tomato purée, a bay leaf, and salt and pepper to taste, and simmers the mixture for 1½ hours. When strained, the mixture yields 1 gal of sauce. Some cooks add a ham bone or lean bacon during simmering to give a distinctive flavor, although others say this is not a true brown sauce. Brown sauce is the base of many small sauces.

Velouté Sauce

A velouté is neither a white nor a cream sauce. To make it, add 1 gal of white stock to 20 oz of blond roux, and simmer until proper thickness occurs. Fish sauce *(vin blanc)* is a velouté with a white fish stock and dry white wine as an addition; this might also be used for a Newburg sauce. Small sauces based on velouté include *allemande, bonne femme* caper, homard, horseradish, and *suprême.*

Béchamel Sauce

Count Béchamel was a famous French gourmet whose chef invented the Béchamel sauce. Some chefs say a Béchamel sauce is a velouté sauce because it is made from a meat base and is a white sauce. Foodservice professionals feel that a white or cream sauce should be called a Béchamel. A white sauce has a milk base thickened with a white roux; a cream sauce is made of rich milk or is a white sauce to which cream is added. In this text Béchamel is considered a basic sauce and white and cream sauces are considered variations of Béchamel. The great chef Escoffier's recipe for Béchamel calls for veal poached in milk as the basic liquid, with white roux added. Today, we use a rich veal or chicken stock, thicken it with roux, and add rich milk or cream. This way of making the thickened stock actually produces a velouté.

To make 1 gal of Béchamel, reduce 3 qts of white stock to 2 qts. Add ½ cup of chopped onions, ½ cup of carrots, two bay leaves, and 1 Tbsp of crushed peppercorns. Blend 1 lb of white roux with the stock. Strain, and then add 2 qt of coffee cream. Béchamel is an excellent sauce for chicken, cheese, white fish, or other delicate preparations that need a light, white sauce. Small sauces based on Béchamel include Albert, à la king, cardinal, cheese, egg, mornay, mustard, and Newburg.

Tomato Sauce

Stock, a tomato source (tomatoes, tomato purée, or tomato paste), seasonings, and roux make tomato sauce. It is served with many fried items, such as breaded veal cutlets, pork chops, and fish. It is the base of many other sauces, as well. To make 1 gal of tomato sauce, sauté 1 Tbsp of minced garlic in 12 oz of butter. Add 1 lb of finely chopped onions and 8 oz of finely chopped celery, and sauté until soft. Then add 6 oz of flour and cook for 5 minutes. Add 3 qt of hot stock (brown, white, or ham), and stir until thickened and smooth. Next add 1 qt of tomatoes, 2 qt of tomato purée, 1 tsp of ground thyme, two bay leaves, 1 tsp of crushed peppercorns, and three whole cloves. Reduce the mixture's volume by a third, and strain through a china cap. Check for seasoning, and serve.

Hollandaise Sauce

Hollandaise is often called the queen of sauces. It is an emulsion of egg yolks and melted butter. One yolk can absorb about 3 oz of butter. Melted butter is gradually beaten into the yolks, which have been placed in a pan over hot water. Adding butter too fast does not result in a good emulsion. If overcooked, the sauce curdles.

Hollandaise is not difficult to make if the proper techniques are used. To make 2 qt, melt 2 lb of butter, and clarify it (melt the butter, and remove the scum on top and the milk solids on the bottom, leaving clear butter). In a separate stainless steel bowl, whip sixteen egg yolks and 3 oz of water. Place the bowl above simmering water, and whip the mixture steadily over slow heat until it is thick and creamy. Remove the bowl, and add the clarified butter very slowly to the yolks while whipping. When all the butter has been added, season with the juice of two small lemons, with cayenne pepper, and with salt to taste. Serve with a vegetable such as broccoli or asparagus, with eggs, or with fish, or use as a base for other sauces. It is the sauce used for eggs Benedict.

Miscellaneous Sauces

Butter sauces can be made from butter or margarine. The basic butter sauce is butter blended with lemon juice and cayenne pepper. From this, compounded butters are made by adding minced or pulped ingredients. Compounded butter sauces include anchovy, caper, garlic, and mustard, maître d'hôtel butter, beurre meunière, noisette beurre, and beurre noir. The last four butters mentioned are melted with a bit of lemon juice and chopped parsley. The first is served just that way; the second is lightly browned (with almonds, it makes amandine sauce); the third is browned to a nut-brown color; and the last is almost blackened, but not burned. Burned butter tastes bitter.

Basic and compounded butters are made into fancy shapes with a pastry tube, and then are chilled before being served. Butters are used for canapés and can also be served on hot foods. For example, a rosette of anchovy butter might be served on top of a broiled steak; it finally melts but makes a nice presentation. Melted butters are served over fish, steaks, chops, vegetables, and other foods. *Beurre noir* is often served over sautéed calves' brains.

Cold sauces include cocktail sauce, tartar sauce, and dill sauce. A sauce used to decorate cold meats, called *chaudfroid,* is made by hydrating 12 oz of unflavored, granulated gelatin in cold water and dissolving it into 2 cups of boiling water. This is then added to 1 gal of warm velouté sauce or mayonnaise. Next, 1 qt of coffee cream is added, and the whole mixture is seasoned with salt and white pepper. This is cooled until syrupy, and then ladled over a meat item to give it a white cover. The item is chilled to allow the sauce to set, and the pouring of the sauce over the meat is repeated until a thick white coating covers the meat. The item can then be decorated and glazed.

Simple sauces are gravies or sauces made from meat drippings. *Au jus* is an unthickened browned meat juice made by deglazing a pan in which meat has cooked. After extraction, this fond is strained through a cheesecloth. Rich brown stock may be added, if needed. *Jus lié* is very slightly thickened *au jus* and is used in much the same way.

Gravy differs from other sauces in that its flavor is dominated by the flavor of the meat from which it came. Gravy is usually made from meat drippings to which some good stock is added. The mixture is usually thickened with a roux. Different gravies include country, giblet, roast beef, and roast lamb.

Sweet sauces include sweet butters, sweet purées, and creams. The consistency may range from fluid to quite stiff. Starch and eggs frequently are used as thickening agents. Some sweet sauces may consist of fruits in their own juice. Sweet sauces served with meat include raisin sauce (with ham) and pineapple sauce (with Hawaiian chicken). Many flavored syrups are served over desserts. Sweet sauces may be hot or cold.

Care After Preparation

Some sauces take great skill to produce. They also require proper handling after preparation. A good sauce cook can resort to many tricks to save a sauce if something goes wrong. If a sauce is too thick, a liquid such as stock, wine, milk, or water can be blended in, with a wire whip. If the sauce is too thin, a bit of beurre manié, roux, or slurry may be added. A lumpy sauce can be strained or even vigorously whipped to remove lumps. A curdled sauce from a broken emulsion can be repaired by adding a small amount of liquid to a bowl and then vigorously whipping the broken emulsion into the liquid. If the emulsion is mayonnaise or hollandaise sauce, egg or egg yolk is used in place of liquid. Since too much heat can cause a rich gravy or sauce to break, these are only given moderate heat.

To avoid having a crust or skin form on sauces, cover a hot sauce with a tight lid, or put a thin film of melted fat or butter over the top. Buttered paper can also be put over the surface and kept on the sauce until it is to be used. Whenever a crust does form, do not stir it into the sauce; instead, remove it, or strain the sauce to remove it.

Sauces should be carefully cooled and then stored. The same procedures and precautions should be taken for sauces as for stocks and soups. Some sauces do not store as well as soups and stocks. These should be used at once. Sauces can be frozen only if thickened with specific kinds of starches.

A good sauce should have a high sheen from the

fat and should be rich in color—whether creamy white or dark brown. Many sauces should have a varnishlike brilliance. A dull, heavy, pasty product gives evidence of poor quality. Consistency should be very thin to thick, depending on the particular sauce. Thin sauces flow readily; thicker sauces cling to the product. In a sauce, the many flavors should blend subtly and agreeably, with no particular flavor predominating. A standard portion of sauce or gravy is 2 to 3 oz.

SUMMARY

Stocks are thin, flavored liquids made by simmering meat, bones, vegetables, spices, and other substances. Some stocks can be just a plain liquid. The equipment required is simple and includes a stock pot, cutting board, French knife, ladle, skimmer, and china cap. Scrap ingredients can be used to make a stock, if they are of good quality. Seasonings include bay leaf, thyme, cloves, peppercorns, garlic, parsley, and bouquet garni. Stocks are lightly salted and may be started in either cold or hot water.

Major stocks are classified according to their ingredients and color. Brown stock is made from well-browned beef and veal bones. White stock ideally is made from veal or chicken bones, but often is based on unbrowned beef and veal bones. Chicken stock is made from chicken carcasses or chickens that are cooked and then used for other purposes. Fish stock is made from the bones, heads, skins, and trimmings of white, lean, deep-sea fish.

Stocks can be used to make a glaze, a demiglaze, a glacé, an essence, or a fumet. Stock care is important. Stocks should be cooled rapidly, kept refrigerated, and used soon after making. Convenience stocks are widely used today. Buyers should read the ingredient list to see what they contain, before buying.

Soup categories include thin, thick, and national or special. Thin soups are served with hearty meals.

The meat flavor in a consommé, bouillon, or similar soup aids in stimulating the appetite. Thick soups are used with lighter meals or constitute meals in themselves. There are many national or special soups. Soups to be carried over should be cooled immediately and refrigerated.

Sauces are used with other foods to enhance their flavor, appearance, nutritional value, and moistness. Thickening agents include roux, eggs, *beurre manié,* and starches. They give body and consistency. Other ingredients are stock, seasonings, wine, and sometimes a garnish. Grand sauces are the foundation of many small sauces; they include brown or Espagnole sauce, velouté, Béchamel, tomato sauce, and hollandaise sauce. Miscellaneous sauces and their derivatives include butter sauces, cold sauces, simple sauces, and sweet sauces. Achieving proper consistency, preventing curdling, and obtaining proper flavor blends take skill on the part of the *saucier.* Standards in sauce preparation dictate the appearance, consistency, flavor, and overall eating quality of the finished product.

CHAPTER REVIEW QUESTIONS

1. You have been hired as the manager of a new club that is still in the planning stage. A meeting is to be held with the house-building committee on planning the kitchen. No menu has been set. The club is not intended to appeal to a deluxe membership but to individuals of above-average income; therefore, the food must be very good but not elaborate. Some members of the committee feel that in keeping with the *nouvelle cuisine,* the menu should not feature sauces and other rich foods. Other members do not agree. Opinion is also divided as to whether cooks are needed who have the ability to produce a wide variety of sauces or whether some of the modern food bases could be used instead for what is needed in stocks, soups, and sauces.

    You do not want to take sides and want the members to make the final decision, but you feel personally that making stocks, soups, and sauces from scratch is the better policy. You jot down some pros and cons that you will present to the members when they meet on this matter. Set up this list, covering such things as product quality, variety, equipment needs, personnel needs, and cost differences. What about *nouvelle cuisine?* Are stocks, soups, and sauces eliminated, or are they merely changed in nature?

2. You are the manager of a restaurant catering to a fairly good clientele. You are not satisfied with the soups and sauces being produced and are planning to talk with the chef and steward about the matter. You want to go into this discussion well-prepared to deal with these two professionals, so you set up a list of questions you want to ask, inquiring into why these products are not meeting a sufficiently high standard. What are these questions, and how should you handle this discussion?

3. What are the ingredients of a good stock? What are the reasons for starting a stock in cold water versus hot water? Why would only a small amount of salt be used? Describe the preparation of a standard mirepoix and of a sachet bag?

4. How are brown, white, fish, and chicken stocks made? Name at least one soup and one sauce derived from each stock. Describe what a high-quality stock should be like.

5. Name the different classes of soups, and identify the consistency of each. What seasonings and garnishes are used for soups?

6. List the common thickening agents, and explain in detail how each is used. Give examples of products in which each agent might be used.

7. Identify the grand sauces, and describe how each is prepared. What ingredients are used for each? Give some major points in the care of sauces. Are these points also applicable to stocks and soups? List at least two small sauces derived from each grand sauce.

VOCABULARY

Stock	Velouté
Bouquet garni	Liaison
Sachet	Roux
Mirepoix	Lean roux
Brown stock	White roux
White stock	Brown roux
Chicken stock	Blond roux
Fish stock	Slack roux
Glaze	*Beurre manié*
Demiglaze	Arrowroot
Glacé de viande	Waxy maize starch
Glacé de poulet	Slurry
Glacé de volaille	*Saucier*
Glacé de poisson	Brown sauce
Fumet	Espagnole sauce
Essence	Spanish sauce
Convenience stock	Neutral sauce
Bouillon	Béchamel sauce
Consommé	Escoffier
Bisque	Hollandaise
Chowder	Butter sauce
Gumbo	Maître d'hôtel butter
Purée	*Beurre noisette*
Boston chowder	*Beurre meunière*
Coney Island chowder	*Beurre noir*
Olla podrida	*Chaudfroid*
Borsch	*Au jus*
Mulligatawny	*Jus lié*

ANNOTATED REFERENCES

Axler, B. H. 1969. *Methods and Manners of Cooking*, pp. 67-91, 103-8. New York: Funk & Wagnalls. (Detailed attention to various sauces, and general coverage of soups.)

Casola, M. 1969. *Successful Mass Cookery and Volume Feeding*, pp. 11-50. Rochelle Park, N.J.: Hayden Book. (Soups, sauces, and gravies, their preparation, and some recipes.)

Folsom, L. A. 1974. *The Professional Chef*, pp. 263-324. Boston: CBI Publishing. (Soups, stocks, sauces, and thickening agents, with recipes.)

Foods and Nutrition Department, Kansas State University. 1966. *Practicing Cookery,* pp. 71-76, 93-104. New York: John Wiley & Sons. (Soups and sauces.)

Haines, R. G. 1970. *Food Preparation for Hotels, Restaurants, and Cafeterias,* pp. 164-205, 259-303. Chicago: American Technical Society. (Stocks, soups, sauces, and gravies, with recipes for each.)

Kotschevar, L. H. 1988. *Quantity Food Production.* 4th ed., pp. 193-213. New York: Van Nostrand Reinhold. (Stocks, soups, sauces, and gravies.)

Terrell, M. E. 1971. *Professional Food Preparation,* pp. 159-93. New York: John Wiley & Sons. (Soups, sauces, and stocks explained in detail.)

CHAPTER 11

Fruits, Vegetables, and Cereals

OUTLINE

FRUITS AND VEGETABLES

Fruits and vegetables are good sources of vitamins and minerals, while often contributing a fairly low number of calories. They are also important sources of bulk in the diet and enhance many meals with their color, flavor, and texture.

Planning Production

Public interest in healthful foods has made fruits and vegetables more popular on the menu. At one time, many menus stinted on these food items, but the popularity of salad bars and the addition of vegetables and fruits with main entrées have brought them back. Proper planning for service demands a knowledge of the seasonal availability and cost of various fruits and vegetables, plus a knowledge of how best to merchandise and prepare them. Properly prepared fruits and vegetables can be as good as any other food in a delectable meal.

The menu should offer a variety of fruits and vegetables. Fresh fruits can be featured as cocktails, fruit juices, breakfast items, and (with or without cheese) as desserts. Similar presentation opportunities at lunch and dinner exist for raw and cooked vegetables.

Fruits are the seed-bearing part of a plant. Thus,

229

cucumbers, squash, green beans, snow peas, and tomatoes are fruits although we class them as vegetables. In food preparation, fruits are usually fleshy or pulpy, often juicy, and usually sweet, with aromatic flavors. Cereal grains and nuts are dry seeds and thus are prepared differently for various dishes. Vegetables come from various parts of a plant—the bulb, part of the root, the flower, the fruit, the leaves, the seeds, the stems, or even part of the stalk (see table 11-1).

Improved handling, packaging, and processing have extended the season in which fruits and vegetables are available. Menus should be planned with a view toward seasonality, since prices tend to be high during the off-season (see table 11-2). Canned, frozen, and dried fruits and vegetables can add variety and compensate for a lack of fresh items during some periods of the year. Some fruits and vegetables store very well and so are available for much longer periods than others are.

Purchasing

Many fruits and vegetables are highly perishable, and their quality and cost can vary. Thus,

Table 11-1. Classification of Vegetables by Part of Plant

Category	Vegetable
Bulb	Garlic, leeks, onions, shallots
Flower	Broccoli, cauliflower, artichoke (French or global)
Fruit	Cucumbers, eggplant, okra, peppers, squash, tomatoes
Leaf	Brussels sprouts, cabbage, greens
Root	Beets, carrots, radishes, potatoes (sweet), turnips
Seed	Beans, corn, peas
Stem	Asparagus, celery
Tuber	Jerusalem artichokes, potatoes (white)

purchasing must be done with care. The market can fluctuate quickly. Prices must be balanced against freshness, tenderness, shape, appearance, trim loss, total weight, and cooking loss. Best buys do not always involve the lowest-cost item. Specifications should be made in such a way as to ensure that the right vegetable or fruit is purchased for the production need.

Grades

Most fruits and vegetables are sold by grades that indicate their quality. When grades are not available, brands may give a quality clue. Grades are set by the USDA on the basis of color, shape, uniformity of size, ripeness, and freedom from defects. U.S. Grade No. 1 is a high-quality grade suitable for use in foodservices. It represents most of the crop. U.S. No. 2 is marketable but is generally lower in quality. A few U.S. No. 3 grades exist; and combination and field-run grades are sometimes found. U.S. Fancy and Extra Fancy are grades above U.S. No. 1 and represent better-than-average quality. Some fruits and vegetables may be available for only part of the year; off-season, the above-average grade must be purchased at times. Sometimes buyers have to purchase in consumer grades, which are U.S. A, B, and C. The grades for processed vegetables and fruits (canned, frozen, and dried) are as follows: U.S. Grade A or Fancy (first grade), U.S. Grade B or Extra Standard or Choice (second grade), and U.S. Grade C or Standard.

Other Purchase Factors

The product's size, trim, variety, ripeness, packaging, and place of origin, among other factors, should be considered. Production needs dictate which factors are especially important.

The amount to purchase depends on storage available, product perishability, and amount needed. Potatoes, cabbages, yams, and some other items keep well, whereas others keep poorly. Processed items can be purchased in quantities suitable to a foodservice's needs and available storage. Dried fruits and vegetables can spoil quickly and become infested with weevils and other insects.

Purchase quantities should be calculated on the

Table 11-2. Availability of Fruits and Vegetables, by Month

Monthly Availability of Fruits, Expressed as a Percentage of Total Annual Supply

COMMODITY	% Jan	% Feb	% Mar	% Apr	% May	% June	% July	% Aug	% Sept	% Oct	% Nov	% Dec
Apples	11	10	10	8	6	3	2	3	10	15	11	11
Apricots					5	62	31	2				
Avocados	11	11	11	11	9	7	6	6	5	6	8	9
Bananas	7	8	9	9	10	10	8	8	7	8	8	8
Blackberries						13	56	19	12			
Blueberries					2	32	39	23	4			
Cantaloupes	*	1	1	3	8	24	24	22	12	4	1	
Casabas						1	5	16	29	29	18	2
Cherries	*				14	39	42	4				1
Coconuts	8	6	8	5	3	3	4	4	11	14	18	16
Cranberries	1	1							6	21	49	22
Crenshaws			*	3	8	17	27	27	15	2	*	
Figs, Fresh					1	15	8	29	24	19	4	*
Grapefruit	12	12	13	12	10	6	3	2	2	8	10	10
Grapes	3	3	3	3	2	6	10	18	19	15	11	7
Honeydews	2	5	7	6	3	7	14	22	21	12	1	*
Lemons	7	6	7	8	10	11	11	10	8	7	7	8
Limes	6	4	4	4	6	15	16	13	10	7	6	9
Mangoes				2	19	39	29	10	1			
Nectarines	2	5				16	35	34	8			
Oranges, all	12	11	11	10	9	7	5	5	5	6	8	11
Oranges, West	9	9	10	10	9	7	7	7	7	8	6	11
Oranges, Fla.	15	15	14	11	10	6	2	1	*	3	10	13
Peaches	*	*	*		2	26	31	27	13	1		
Pears	6	6	7	6	4	1	6	15	16	15	10	8
Persians					*	5	15	29	31	19	1	*
Persimmons	1								2	41	39	17
Pineapples	8	9	12	14	15	17	7	4	2	3	4	5
Plums-Prunes	1	1	1	2	18	25	25	24	3			
Pomegranates									20	63	15	2
Raspberries					1	21	55	5	6	7	4	1
Strawberries	1	2	5	15	31	26	10	5	3	1	*	*
Tangelos	10									7	46	37
Tangerines	24	8	3	1							20	44
Watermelons		*	1	2	11	27	33	21	5	*		

*Less than 0.5 of 1% of annual total
The table is based on unloads of fresh fruits in 41 cities as reported by the U.S. Department of Agriculture, and on import figures.

Monthly Availability of Vegetables, Expressed as a Percentage of Total Annual Supply

COMMODITY	Jan %	Feb %	Mar %	Apr %	May %	June %	July %	Aug %	Sept %	Oct %	Nov %	Dec %
Artichokes	6	7	12	23	15	5	4	3	4	6	9	8
Asparagus	*	2	20	33	28	15	1	*	*	1	*	*
Beans, Snap	5	5	6	8	9	13	12	11	10	8	7	6
Beets	4	4	5	5	7	13	15	13	12	11	7	4
Broccoli	10	10	12	11	9	5	4	3	6	10	11	9
Brussels Sprouts	14	9	5	2	1	1	1	2	11	19	20	16
Cabbage	9	8	10	9	9	10	8	7	8	8	8	8
Carrots	10	8	10	9	8	8	8	7	8	8	8	8
Cauliflower	9	7	7	7	5	5	4	5	11	19	14	8
Celery	9	8	9	9	8	7	7	7	8	9	10	9
Chinese Cabbage	9	8	7	7	6	8	9	8	9	10	11	10
Corn, Sweet	1	1	2	6	15	16	20	18	11	4	3	2
Cucumbers	4	4	5	9	12	14	14	10	8	8	8	6
Eggplant	8	6	7	8	7	8	9	12	12	8	8	8
Escarole-Endive	7	7	9	8	7	9	9	9	9	9	10	8
Endive, Belgian	5	15	15	14	11	4			4	10	9	15
Greens (misc.)	10	10	11	11	8	7	6	6	6	8	8	10
Lettuce	8	7	8	9	9	9	9	9	9	8	8	8
Mushrooms	10	9	10	10	8	7	5	5	6	8	10	11
Okra	*	*	1	4	11	19	23	21	12	7	3	1
Onions, dry, all	8	7	8	9	9	10	9	8	9	8	8	8
Onions, dry, Texas	*	*	6	32	30	14	11	6	1	*	*	*
Onions, dry, New York	10	9	10	6	2	1	2	12	14	13	11	11
Onions, dry, California	2	2	1	1	9	21	23	14	9	8	7	3
Onions, Green	6	6	8	10	10	11	11	10	8	7	7	7
Parsley and Herbs	6	6	8	8	7	8	8	8	8	10	13	11
Parsnips	13	11	11	9	6	5	3	3	8	14	11	9
Peas, Green	7	8	9	15	13	15	13	9	5	3	2	2
Peppers, Sweet	7	6	7	7	8	10	10	10	10	9	9	7
Potatoes, All	9	7	9	9	9	9	8	8	8	8	8	8
Potatoes, California	4	4	4	3	10	26	24	11	5	3	3	4
Potatoes, Maine	11	11	16	19	16	9	2	*	*	1	5	9
Potatoes, Idaho	14	12	14	14	9	2	*	2	3	8	12	12
Radishes	6	6	8	9	11	12	11	9	8	7	7	7
Rhubarb	6	12	15	22	27	13	3	1	*	*	*	1
Spinach	9	8	10	10	10	8	6	5	7	9	9	8
Squash	7	5	6	7	8	9	10	9	10	11	11	8
Sweetpotatoes	9	8	9	7	4	2	3	6	10	12	17	13
Tomatoes, All	6	6	8	8	11	11	12	10	8	8	6	6
Tomatoes, Florida	12	10	14	16	23	8	*				4	13
Tomatoes, California	2	1	*	*	2	8	19	17	16	19	12	4
Tomatoes, Mexico	13	20	24	22	13	3	*	*	*	*	1	4
Turnips-Rutabagas	12	11	10	6	4	4	4	4	9	12	13	11

*Less than 0.5 of 1% of annual total
The table is based on unloads of vegetables in 41 cities in 1963-65 inclusive as reported by the U.S. Department of Agriculture.

basis of the number of times within a purchase period that the item will be served multiplied by the number of portions per service day multiplied by the portion size. Thus, if frozen peas are offered five times in a three-week period, with eighty 3-oz portions needed each time, the purchase amount is $5 \times 80 \times 3 \div 16$ oz $= 75$ lb. If an additional reserve of 25 lb is desired, the purchase amount should be 100 lb.

Quantities needed should be stated precisely. Thus, if fresh spinach by the bushel is to be purchased, the specification should say "Spinach, bushel, minimum net weight 18 lb"; other appropriately precise specifications might say "32-size grapefruit, minimum weight per carton 42 lb" or "50-lb carton Idaho baking potato, 100 count." Grade and other quantity and quality factors should be added as necessary.

Storage and Handling Care

Fruits and vegetables are living things, and even after harvest they can change quality. Refrigeration and proper humidity retard the natural processes of deterioration and drying out. All items should be inspected on delivery to ensure that they meet specifications.

Management should establish procedures for handling and storing fruits and vegetables. Crates and packages should never be dropped, thrown, or pushed roughly. Many products bruise easily, and some crates of produce are as delicate as a crate of eggs.

Suitable handling during pre-preparation can avoid damage. Do not allow food to stand in unfavorable temperatures. Do not stack items so high that items underneath are crushed. Rotate stock, using older items first; dating may be desirable. Fruits and vegetables need air to hold well. Piling them up without access to air can harm them. Items that give off odors should be stored separately. Canned fruits and vegetables with a high acid content (such as plums, sauerkraut, and tomatoes) are best held for a maximum of six months.

Proper temperature, humidity, and ventilation are important for fresh items as well as for frozen, dried, and canned foods. Hold fresh produce under refrigeration at 45°F (7°C) or lower, but do not freeze it. Store frozen products at 0°F (−18°C) or lower. Most canned foods keep for about a year. Optimal storage for all forms of food should be known and adopted.

Cooking Methods

Cooking can change the texture, color, flavor, and nutritional value of fruits and vegetables. Personnel should be informed about what these changes are and how best to control them to obtain only desirable changes.

Baking

Baked potatoes are common on many menus. Numerous other fruits and vegetables can be baked with equally favorable results, including apples, carrots, cucumbers, eggplant, green peppers, onions, stuffed mushrooms, squash, tomatoes, turnips, and parsnips.

Sufficient moisture must be present to soften the cellulose of the baking item. Low-moisture items can be parboiled before being baked; covering items while they bake also helps. Baking may act to caramelize sugar and to brown items, producing a desirable flavor. Nutrients are retained well in baking, since there is no water-leaching. Baking in covered casseroles that contain only a small amount of water also reduces nutrient loss.

Baking temperatures range from 350° to 450°F (177° to 232°C); squash and potatoes should be baked at the higher temperatures. A baking time of 30 to 60 minutes is usually sufficient. Overbaking high-starch products or failing to prick and open the skin immediately after baking can result in a soggy product.

Boiling

Fruits and vegetables should not be boiled at a hard boil, since this can break them up. Bring the cooking liquid to a rapid boil, then add the product, and bring the liquid back to a boil as fast as possible; then reduce the heat to a simmer. Water is never hotter than 212°F (100°C), regardless of the size of the bubbles in it. Cook delicate vegetables and fruits for as short a time as possible. It is common today to serve vegetables with some crunch still in them. Some vegetables, such as onions, must be cooked for a long time to remove their strong flavor. Others, such as members of the cabbage family, develop strong flavors with long cooking. Cooking in a small amount of water is often recommended for delicate vegetables; but if they are dropped into a large amount of boiling water, the cooking proceeds faster. It is also desirable to cook strongly flavored vegetables in plenty of water, to reduce the flavor somewhat. Water should be salted at the rate of 1 tsp of salt for every 1 qt of water.

Fruit cooked in plain water breaks up more easily than fruit cooked in a syrup, because sugar strengthens the fruit's fiber. The higher the sugar content of the boiling liquid, the less the breakup of the fruit.

Covering the cooking pot saves heat, but some vegetables and fruits should be cooked uncovered (see table 11-3). Most fruits can be cooked covered; but delicate green vegetables should be cooked uncovered for at least the first 5 minutes of boiling so that they retain their greenness.

Batch-cooking is recommended for vegetables and some fruits. In each batch, cook about the quantity needed for 20 minutes of serving. Never mix old and new batches. If demand suddenly increases, use a high-pressure steamer to get a batch to service quickly. Vegetables can be parboiled in advance, plunged into cold water, and refrigerated.

When needed, they can be cooked to doneness in their original cooking water.

Metals and some chemicals can change the texture, color, and flavor of fruits and vegetables as they cook. Hard water preserves the green color in vegetables; very hard water destroys thiamine and ascorbic acid. Acids destroy the green color. An alkaline reaction (from hard water or soda added to water) helps green vegetables retain their green color but also softens the product. Legumes cook more quickly if soda is added to the cooking water. Soda destroys thiamine and ascorbic acid, however, and gives some vegetables a poor texture. Iron reacts with red vegetables and fruits, causing them to turn a muddy color. Acids make red fruits and vegetables redder, while alkalies turn them a muddy red. Acids preserve the color of white vegetables and fruits (see table 11-4).

Braising

Vegetables are braised more frequently than are fruits. Celery, onions, cabbage, lettuce, and Belgian (French) endive are among the vegetables that can be braised. To braise a vegetable, sauté it in a small amount of fat until it is almost tender. Then toss, with quick stirring, and serve partially cooked (this is the stir-fry method). Other vegetables should continue cooking while a thickening agent (usually starch or flour slurry) is added. If more moisture is desired, add hot stock to the pot, and simmer it. Continue cooking the product until it is tender, turning and stirring it.

Broiling

Fruits and vegetables are usually not broiled, since a lot of moisture evaporates in broiling. Only very tender, moist produce broils well. For example, some fruits that are first topped with butter, sugar, and seasonings can be broiled successfully.

Many items are parboiled first to make them tender and moist. An eggplant that has been parboiled almost to tenderness can be covered with mayonnaise and broiled. Tomatoes, because of their high moisture, can be broiled. Other items put onto shish-kebabs broil well after parboiling. The lack of moisture in many broiled items leaves them crisp

Table 11-3. Preferability of Boiling Various Vegetables Covered or Uncovered

Vegetable	Covered or Uncovered	Exceptions
Bulb	Uncovered	
Flower	Uncovered	
Fruit	Covered	Okras, Pepper
Leaf	Uncovered	
Root	Covered	Rutabagas, Turnips
Seed	Uncovered	Corn
Stem	Uncovered	
Tuber	Covered	

Table 11-4. Effect of Boiling Pigments in Acidic or Alkaline Liquid

Name of Pigment	Color	Example Where Pigment Is Found	Effect of an Acid on Product	Effect of Alkali on Product
Anthoxanthins[†]	White	Onion	White	Creamy white to yellow with more alkalinity
Chlorophyll*	Green	Green vegetables	Olive green	Intensified green, loss of nutrients, slimy texture
Carotenoids*				
Carotenes	Orange	Carrots	Little effect	Little effect
Lycopene	Red	Tomatoes	Little effect	Little effect
Xanthophylls	Yellow	Corn	Little effect	Little effect
Flavonoids[†]				
Anthocyanins	Red to blue/ purple	Red cabbage	Little effect or intensified red	Bluish green

[†]This pigment dissolves in water.
*This pigment dissolves in fat.

and slightly charred, which may add flavor but may also leave a tough texture. Many broiled items are served with sauces or butters, for added moistness.

Deep-frying

Fried foods have rich flavor and good texture. Potatoes deep-fry well. A one- or two-step process can be used. Potatoes cut into strips fry crisply in 5½ to 7 minutes in fat heated to 350°F (177°C). The two-step method fries potatoes at 260°F (127°C) for 6 minutes, and then finishes them at 325°F (163°C) for 2½ minutes. Shake the strips well after the first step of frying, and set them aside until orders come in. The potatoes can then be finished quickly. Refrigerate the strips if they are to be held for any length of time. Frozen strips are prefried in this manner, so only a short cooking time is needed to prepare them fully.

Vegetables such as parsnips and some fruits can be parboiled and then deep-fried. Breaded bananas and other fruits can be deep-fried without requiring any previous cooking. Some breaded vegetables such as eggplant and mushrooms deep-fry well. Even slices of dill pickles, batter-dipped and deep-

fried, make a delicious accompaniment to roast ham, corned beef, or a pastrami sandwich. Table 11-5 lists ways to deep-fry selected items.

Sautéing

A shallow sauté pan, a griddle, or a well-greased baking sheet can be used to sauté vegetables. Proper cooking temperatures range from 350° to 400°F (177° to 204°C). Most vegetables and a few fruits sauté well, including apple rings, tomato slices, mushrooms, zucchini, eggplant, onions, and all forms of potatoes.

Steaming

Vegetables that do not pack tightly around each other tend to steam well. Vegetables that must be put into water to steam are usually better when boiled. Spinach, peas, and some other vegetables pack so tightly that the centers undercook. Steaming retains nutrients well because of the absence of water-leaching, but the high temperatures can destroy some vitamins.

Few fruits are steamed. They are better when stewed or boiled with sugar added, except in cer-

Table 11-5. Deep-frying Methods for Various Vegetables

Vegetable	Blanch*	Breading	Batter	325°F (163°C)	350°F (177.5°C)	375°F (191°C)
Asparagus tips	X	X				1 min
Broccoli flowers	X		X			1½ min
Brussels sprouts	X	X			1½ min	
Carrots (peeled halves)				1½ min		
Cauliflowerettes, plain				1½ min		
Cauliflowerettes	X	X				1 min
Corn (whole ears)				1½ min		
Cucumbers (thin slice)			X		1½ min	
Eggplant (¼″ slices, peeled)					1 min	
Eggplant (thin slice)			X		1½ min	
Snap Beans (whole)					1½ min	
Squash (2″ strips)	X		X			1½ min
Sweet potato (¼″ slices)					2 min	
Zucchini (2″ slices)				4 min		

*Items to be blanched are pre-cooked, breaded, or battered, and finished at the indicated fryer temperature just before service.

tain special preparations. Vegetables that are usually covered when boiled come out better when steamed. Steaming (especially pressure steaming) reduces cooking time. Timing must be watched closely, since temperatures are much higher, and cooking is consequently faster. Pressure at 15 psi cooks vegetables very rapidly. If a pressure of 5 to 7 psi is used, quantity production is best. Pressure cookers, unlike convection steamers, cannot be opened at any time during cooking without releasing steam—sometimes very dangerously.

Many vegetables and some fruits can be steamed in perforated pans that allow the steam to filter around the product. Tough parts such as asparagus or broccoli stalks may come out best when cooked first in hot water with only the stalk immersed and then tipped over with the entire vegetable (including the tender head) immersed. When steaming vegetables in pans of water or in perforated pans, do not fill the pans with water to a height of more than 2 inches.

Stewing

Fruits and some vegetables stew well. Fruits to be stewed should be fresh, sound, and not overripe; they should be stewed in water, if a sauce is desired, or in sugar or a sugar syrup, if the fruit is to retain its shape or if a fruit compote is desired. To obtain a good compote syrup, add 1 cup of sugar for every 2 cups of water. Adding more sugar results in a preserve or a jam. Too much sugar causes fruit to shrink and harden.

Preparing Fruits and Vegetables

Fruits and vegetables are often prepared according to whether they are fresh, frozen, canned, or dried. Each kind of food takes a different kind of preparation.

Canned Fruits and Vegetables

Canned fruits are often used because of their nature or because fresh fruits are not available. A canned pear or pineapple and cottage cheese salad is not at all inferior to a fresh fruit served in the same way. Because fresh Kadota figs are seldom on the market, the canned product usually must be used. Canned ready-to-use pie fillings are labor-saving good-quality items.

Selecting a canned product should be based on the production need. Higher-grade fruits are more uniform in size and color, are free from defects, and have a heavier syrup than lower grades have. On the other hand, the lower grades are suitable for many purposes. High-grade peaches can be served as a sauce; a lower water-pack grade can be used for pies.

When purchasing canned items, the buyer should distinguish between styles offered. Fruits may be whole, halved, sliced, cut, diced, chunks, spears, tidbits, or crushed. Can sizes vary from the large No. 10 (3-qt and larger) size to No. 303 (16 oz) or even smaller. Smaller cans may be used at the end of a serving period, when a smaller quantity is needed.

Canned items should be stored at temperatures lower than 70°F (21°C) but above freezing. Good ventilation is important. Rusted, leaking, bulging, or badly dented cans should be discarded. Often they can be sent back to purveyors for credit.

When fresh items are not available, or when high labor costs militate against the daily preparation of fresh items, many operations rely on canned fruits and vegetables. The nutritive value of canned items is nearly the same as that of any fresh produce, there is little waste, and the cost per serving is easy to calculate.

The syrup accompanying canned or frozen fruit can be used to make fruit drinks, sweetened juices, or molded salads, or it can be used as the base for cold fruit soups or served with the fruit. Carry-over fruits can be used in salads, in fruit soups, and in puddings.

Fruit drinks or juices made from natural or synthetic fruit juices are served as breakfast beverages, as appetizers for lunch, or as cool drinks in the afternoon. A 4- or 5-oz glass is an adequate portion. A No. 3 (46-oz) cylinder can yields from 9 to 11 portions.

About two-thirds of a can of vegetables consists of the drained item, and the remainder is juice. Pour the brine from the vegetables into a pot, and heat it until it is reduced by about half. Then return the vegetables to it, season, and serve. Unused brine can go into the stock pot. Vegetables served with some of their brine have added nutritional value. Canned vegetables should be served as soon as possible after reheating.

No. 10, No. 2½, No. 2, and No. 303 cans are used for vegetables. They hold, respectively, 106 oz, 24 oz, 20 oz, and 16 oz. Vegetables may be garnished at service with fried bacon, pimiento, browned almonds, cooked chopped green pepper, cubed carrot bits, chopped parsley, or various cream or cheese sauces.

Dried Fruits and Vegetables

A dried fruit such as a prune contains about 25 percent moisture. Dried vegetables contain much less. Fruit may be dried naturally or vacuum-dried. The latter method reduces moisture to about 2 to 5 percent. Some vegetables such as beans, peas, and other legumes dry naturally. In vacuum-drying, the product is placed into a chamber and warmed, and the air is evacuated, creating a partial vacuum into which the moisture in the vegetable is quickly drawn. Most products dried in this way have a rather porous texture and rehydrate well. Vegetables are rarely freeze-dried, although a few items such as mushrooms and chives might be. In freeze-drying, the item is frozen and placed into a chamber where a vacuum is created. A small amount of heat is applied and the moisture goes from ice to water vapor without ever turning to water—a process called *sublimation.*

Apples, apricots, figs, dates, peaches, pears, prunes, and raisins are the most commonly used dried fruits. They go into breads, pies, puddings, cookies, cakes, candies, and desserts. Some are eaten in their dried form.

Dried fruits should be washed well before using. To rehydrate a fruit, place it into water; the dried fruit absorbs liquid and plumps up. Just 1 lb of dried prunes yields 3 lb of cooked prunes. Some types of dried fruit should be soaked for a short time, while others can be simmered immediately. Use 1 qt of water for each 1 lb of fruit. Add sugar as necessary, depending on fruit sweetness.

Dehydrated potatoes are the most commonly used dried vegetable, with dried onions following. Just 1 lb of dried onions equals about 8 lb of fresh EP. Dried parsley, peppers, tomatoes, and others are used occasionally.

Legumes are dried beans, peas, and other seeds of leguminous plants. Chick-peas (garbanzos), cow-peas (black-eyed peas), split peas, and lentils belong to this family. Legumes are used in soups, salads, and main dishes. All foreign matter should be removed from the legumes. Small rocks of about the same weight as a legume can cause a patron to break a tooth. After sorting, the legumes are washed. They may be soaked in cold water, although split peas and lentils need no soaking. After soaking, the legumes are simmered for several hours until tender; water is added as needed. About 2 tsp of salt are added for every 1 lb of legumes. Cooking legumes in steamers after soaking them requires less time and less water.

A quantity of 5 to 6 lb of dried legumes yields 100 3-oz portions—or more, if other ingredients are added. Because acid interferes with the softening of legumes, brown sugar (slightly acidic), molasses, catsup, and tomatoes should not be added until the legumes are tender.

Fresh Fruits and Vegetables

Fresh fruits can be served raw and eaten in hand. They also can be cut up for salads, appetizers, prepared dishes, and desserts. All fruits should be washed thoroughly before being used, since chemicals and sprays may be on them. Many fresh fruits are pared, cored, pitted, or trimmed before serving. Table 11-6 describes ways to prepare different fruits.

Fruits such as peaches, pears, and apples tarnish (turn brown) when their cut surface is exposed to air. Dipping the cut pieces into acidic juices (such as lemon or pineapple juice) or into an antioxidant solution retards or eliminates the browning. Putting cut fruit into a gelatin mixture also stops browning to some extent.

Fresh fruit can be stewed or baked and served in the form of fruit sauces, compotes, preserves, or baked fruit. Some fruits, including apples, bananas, and pineapple, can be sautéed. Grapefruit halves, bananas, pineapple slices, and some others can be broiled. Fresh fruit can be seasoned with brown or maple sugar, nuts, raisins, nutmeg, cinnamon, or cloves.

Fresh vegetables are served raw or cooked. Many raw vegetables are served as relishes or in salads. Some are used raw as garnishes. Vegetables may be cooked by boiling, simmering, steaming, baking, or broiling. Table 11-7 describes ways to prepare different vegetables.

Clean vegetables thoroughly before using them. Lukewarm water cleans better than cold water does. Some thin-skinned vegetables, such as potatoes, can be cooked and then peeled. Others, such as turnips and rutabagas, should be pared. Thin paring or peeling after cooking saves nutrients. Some vegetables tend to discolor when pared or cut. Dipping them in an antioxidant or holding them in water can prevent discoloration. Dipping leaches fewer nutrients from the product; any soaking should be minimal. All personnel who prepare vegetables should know cooking procedures and times.

Frozen Fruits and Vegetables

Freezing can retain the nutrients, flavor, color, and texture of many fruits and vegetables and can reduce spoilage and storage space. Frozen items can be purchased in 5-, 10-, 20-, or 30-lb packages. Some 2- and 2½-lb packages are also available. Store frozen foods at $0°$ to $-10°F$ ($-18°$ to $-23°C$). Items are best thawed under refrigeration.

Cook vegetables directly from the frozen state by dropping them into salted boiling water. Frozen vegetables cook in less time than fresh ones do because they have been blanched before freezing to hold their color and flavor; they may also contain salt. Do not refreeze items once they have been thawed.

Management Responsibility

Management is responsible for establishing and maintaining proper standards for vegetables and

Table 11-6. Preparation Techniques for Fresh Fruit

Fruit[†]	Preparation Techniques	Trim Loss Percent	Quantity Needed for 100 4-oz Portions	
			(AP) lb	*(EP) lb*
Apples*	Wash under running water; peel and core as required; cut as desired.	10 peeled 25 peeled & cored	28 33.5	25 25
Apricots*	Wash under running water; cut in two; remove pit; slice as desired.	6 pitted	27	25
Avocados*	Peel; cut in two lengthwise; remove pit; cut as desired.	25 pitted	33.5	25
Bananas*	Peel and cut as desired.	30 peeled	36	25
Berries (except strawberries)	Sort and remove stems; wash under spray; drain; cut as desired.	5 topped	26.5	25
Cherries*	Sort; remove stems and pits; wash under spray.	12 topped & pitted	28.5	25
Citrus fruit	Peel and cut into sections. (Grapefruit sections may be replaced into the peel.)	40 pared	42	25
Grapes	Remove stems; wash grapes; cut in halves; remove seeds.	10 seeded	28	25
Melons	Cut in half; remove seeds before or while preparing.	50 pared	50	25
Peaches*	Blanch to remove skin; cut to remove pit; serve as desired.	15 pitted	29.5	25
Pears	Wash under running water; peel and core as required; cut as desired.	10 peeled 25 peeled & cored	28 33.5	25 25
Pineapples	Remove tops and bottoms; pare; cut as desired.	45 pared	45.5	25
Plums	Wash thoroughly in containers of water; cut in two to pit.	5 pitted	26.5	25
Rhubarb	Remove leaf and hard area at base of stem; wash; cut across stem into desired width.	10 prepared	28	25
Strawberries	Remove stem; wash under spray; cut if desired.	10 topped	28	25

[†]All fruit listed is of medium size.
*Place in solution to retard browning.

Table 11-7. Preparation Techniques for Fresh Vegetables

Vegetable†	Approximate Quantities Needed for 100 3-oz Portions				Preparation and Possible Seasonings‡	Boiling* 212°F 100°C	Baking 350°F 177°C	Baking 450°F 232°C	Steaming 0psi 212°F 100°C	Steaming 6psi 230°F 110°C	Steaming 15psi 250°F 121°C
	AP (lb)	Trim Loss (%)	Cooking Weight Gain (+) or Loss (−)	EP (lb)							
Artichokes French	50	20	0	8⅓ doz	Wash; cut top and tips; cook with lemon; serve whole (6.5 oz).	40	—	—	—	20	10
Jerusalem	25	25	0	19	Pare thin; serve whole, quartered, or sliced.	30	45	—	35	25	15
Asparagus	38	35	−10	21	Wash, removing sand, dirt, and scales from stem; break woody base from stem and tip; cook & season with 17, 24, or 25.	15 stems in water	—	—	18	13	1½
Beans lima	50	60	−5	20	Shell; wash; drain; cook & season with 15, 19, 22, 23, 25, or 26.	20	—	—	30	12	1½

†All vegetables listed are of medium size.
‡The numbers listed in this column correspond to the following:

1. Allspice	6. Celery seed	11. Dill	16. Mint	21. Rosemary
2. Basil	7. Chives	12. Fennel	17. Mustard seed	22. Sage
3. Bay leaves	8. Cinnamon	13. Ginger	18. Nutmeg	23. Savory
4. Cardamom	9. Clove	14. Mace	19. Oregano	24. Sesame seed
5. Caraway seed	10. Curry powder	15. Marjoram	20. Poppy seed	25. Tarragon
				26. Thyme

*Boiling times indicated are from the point after the vegetables are added and the water has returned to a boil.

Table 11-7. *(cont.)*

Vegetable[†]	Approximate Quantities Needed for 100 3-oz Portions				Preparation and Possible Seasonings[‡]	Approximate Average Time (min) and Temperature (in 10-lb lots)					
			Cooking Weight			*Boiling**	*Baking*		*Steaming*		
		Trim Loss (%)	*Gain (+) or Loss (−)*	*EP (lb)*					*0psi*	*6psi*	*15psi*
	AP (lb)					*212°F 100°C*	*350°F 177°C*	*450°F 232°C*	*212°F 100°C*	*230°F 110°C*	*250°F 121°C*
Beans *(cont.)* snap	23.5	15	−5	20	Wash, remove ends; cut as desired; cook & season with 2, 14, 15, 16, 17, 19, 23, 25, or 26.	20	—	—	25	20	2½
Beets new	27	25	−5	20	Remove roots & tops; wash; cook; peel; cut as desired & season with 1, 3, 5, 9, 11, 13, 17, 23, or 26.	35	50	—	50	40	7
old	27	25	−5	20	Same as for new.	70	60	—	75	65	14
Broccoli	35	40	−10	21	Remove woody stems and coarse leaves; wash; drain; split stem for uniformity; cook & season with 5, 11, 17, or 25.	9	—	—	15	8	2
Brussels sprouts	22	17	+5	18	Remove leaves and stalks; wash; soak briefly in salt water; cook & season with 2, 5, 11, 17, 22, or 26.	13	—	—	15	11	2

Table 11-7. *(cont.)*

Vegetable[†]	Approximate Quantities Needed for 100 3-oz Portions				Preparation and Possible Seasonings[‡]	Approximate Average Time (min) and Temperature (in 10-lb lots)					
			Cooking Weight Gain (+) or Loss (−)			Boiling*	Baking		Steaming		
	AP (lb)	Trim Loss (%)		EP (lb)		212°F 100°C	350°F 177°C	450°F 232°C	0psi 212°F 100°C	6psi 230°F 110°C	15psi 250°F 121°C
Cabbage**	25	20	−5	20	Trim as needed; wash; quarter; cook & season with 5, 6, 11, 16, 17, 18, 23, or 25.	12	—	—	15	10	2
Carrots	27	22	−10	21	Remove tops; peel; cut as desired; cook & season with 1, 3, 6, 11, 12, 13, 14, 15, 16, 18, or 26.	15	35	—	20	13	3
Cauliflower	45	50	−15	22.5	Remove outer leaves and stalk; wash; break into flowerets; cook & season with 5, 6, 11, 14, 15, or 25.	9	—	—	11	8	2½
Corn-on-the-cob	60	15	+2	8½ doz	Husk, removing all silk; cook & season with butter and salt.	10	30	—	13	9	3½
Eggplant	24	20	0	19	Pare; cut before cooking; cook & season with 15 or 19.	14	45	—	15	7	1

**Shredded cabbage is cooked in approximately half the time of quartered cabbage.

Table 11-7. *(cont.)*

Vegetable[†]	Approximate Quantities Needed for 100 3-oz Portions				Preparation and Possible Seasonings[‡]	Approximate Average Time (min) and Temperature (in 10-lb lots)					
			Cooking Weight			*Boiling**	*Baking*		*Steaming*		
	AP (lb)	*Trim Loss (%)*	*Gain (+) or Loss (−)*	*EP (lb)*		*212°F 100°C*	*350°F 177°C*	*450°F 232°C*	*0psi 212°F 100°C*	*6psi 230°F 110°C*	*15psi 250°F 121°C*
Onions	26	12	−15	22.5	Pare; cook & season with 5, 17, 18, 19, 22, or 26.	25	45	−	30	20	5
Peas	50	60	−5	20	Shell; wash; cook & season with 2, 11, 15, 16, 19, 21, 22, or 23.	7	−	−	10	4	1
Potatoes white	25.5	25	0	19	Scrub and wash; cook; pare (unless baked); cut; season with 2, 3, 5, 6, 7, 11, 17, 19, or 26.	25	−	50	35	20	8
sweet	25	23	0	19	Scrub and wash; cook; pare; cut (unless baked); season with 1, 4, 8, 9, or 18.	20	−	50	25	15	6
Spinach	25.5	27	−5	20	Remove coarse stems; wash; cook & season with 2, 14, 15, 18, or 19.	5	−	−	8	4	1

Table 11-7. *(cont.)*

Vegetable[†]	Approximate Quantities Needed for 100 3-oz Portions				Preparation and Possible Seasonings[‡]	Approximate Average Time (min) and Temperature (in 10-lb lots)					
			Cooking Weight			*Boiling**	*Baking*		*Steaming*		
									0psi	*6psi*	*15psi*
	AP (lb)	*Trim Loss (%)*	*Gain (+) or Loss (−)*	*EP (lb)*		*212°F 100°C*	*350°F 177°C*	*450°F 232°C*	*212°F 100°C*	*230°F 110°C*	*250°F 121°C*
Squash summer (zucchini)	25	15	−10	21	Wash; remove ends; cut; cook; pare if desired; season with 1, 2, 8, 9, 12, 13, 17, 18, or 21.	13	30	—	17	10	2
winter (hubbard)	32	20	−25	25.5	Wash; cut; remove seeds and fiber; cook; pare; season with 1, 2, 8, 9, 12, 13, 17, 18, or 21.	25	50	—	30	17	9
Tomatoes	22.5	10	−5	20	Cook; skin if desired; remove stem core; cut; season with 2, 3, 6, 19, 22, 24, 25, or 26.	10	15	—	12	5	1½

fruits. Grading can be used to help select good-quality products. Yield and comparative tests are used to check quality and select the best items. Standards should cover flavor, color, texture, form, and other relevant attributes. Flavors should be natural to the product and should blend with the flavors of other foods. Colors should be bright and natural. Shape and size should favor easy eating and should contrast with other foods. Textures should complement those of other foods.

The choice among canned, dried, fresh, or frozen fruits or vegetables should be based on availability, storage space, labor, and cost. Fresh items should be used if they are available at a good price and if labor is available to process them at a satisfactory cost. Menus should feature fresh or processed fruits and vegetables because of the variety they give and because they carry a good markup.

Vegetables and fruits should be served in ways that bring out their true flavors. Good seasoning and buttering are important in serving vegetables. Fruits should be plump and well-filled.

Fruits and vegetables should be merchandised by having menus emphasize an interesting range of cooking styles, such as scalloped, au gratin, souffléed, glazed, and stuffed. Offering an attractive salad bar can also encourage produce consumption and patron satisfaction.

CEREALS

Over 50 percent of our calories should normally come from carbohydrates. Foods such as potatoes, rice, wheat, legumes, sugars, and syrups contain a liberal supply of carbohydrates, and these are frequently included as one of the foods in a meal. People commonly eat a cooked or dry cereal for breakfast, and rice, potatoes, pasta, hominy, or even couscous may be eaten at lunch or dinner.

Cereals require special treatment in cooking. The starch swells and absorbs considerable moisture. Usually, about 1 gal of lightly salted water is used for every 1 lb of cereal or pasta (noodles or spaghetti). Fine breakfast cereals such as cornmeal, farina, and grits make a desirable thickened mixture in these ratios, but coarser ones such as oatmeal and cracked wheat require about 1¼ lb for each 1 gal. Yields of various cereal products are identified in table 11-8. The salted water is brought to a boil, and the cereal is added while stirring. Some items (pasta and rice, for example) have enough water to obviate the need for further stirring, but breakfast cereals do require some stirring while cooking to a thick paste. Fine cereals can be mixed

with a bit of water and then added to the main volume of water, to prevent lumping. The more a cereal is stirred during thickening, the more slick and pasty it becomes.

Pasta, rice, and other such products should be *just* cooked; cooks describe the resulting product as *al dente,* which means "to the tooth" or still having some firmness. Selecting a good-quality long-grain rice or a pasta that is made from semolina paste gives a firmer product and one that holds up better in the steam table. Poorer-quality products get flabby and soft and are less pleasant to eat. Breakfast cereals are cooked to complete doneness but should not be overcooked. After cooking rice, noodles, or pastas in a large quantity of water, drain, blanch in cold water, drain, and then use.

Some people cook pasta items with 3 qt of water and 2 Tbsp of salt for each 1 lb of product. The water should be boiling when the product is added. Stir, cover tightly, remove from direct heat, and let stand for 10 minutes or until the product is tender. Then drain and blanch in cold water. Some thick-walled pasta products must be left on low heat to cook properly by this method. If cooking is done in a steam-jacketed kettle, add the cereal products to the boiling water, stir, cover, turn off the steam, and allow to stand until cooked.

In the Orient, rice is cooked in less water than it is in America, but the result is still a flaky product. The Oriental method has the advantage of yielding a more nutritious product, since the process of cooking in a lot of water, draining this cooking water off, blanching in cold water, and then draining again results in a loss of nutrients. In the Oriental method, all the cooking water is absorbed. Some people, however, advocate washing the rice several times before cooking it, to get rid of excess starch. The following formula is used:

Table 11-8. Yields in Weight and Volume of 1-lb Batches of Dry Cereal Products

Cereal Product	Cooked Weight	Cooked Volume
Rice	3–4 lb	1½–1¾ qt
Pasta	4 lb	2¼–2½ qt
Noodles	3 lb	2 qt
Fine cereals	9 lb	1⅛ gal
Coarse cereals	9¼ lb	1¼ gal

1 lb long-grain rice 2 Tbsp (1 oz) oil	1. Wash the rice, if desired; drain well, and add the oil. Mix the oil in well to coat the rice.
1¾ qt cold water 2 Tbsp salt	2. Add the water and the salt; cover tightly, and bring to a boil. Stir once,

cover, and lower heat to a very low level. Cook tightly covered for about 20 minutes. During the last 5 minutes uncover so that the rice steams dry. If the rice absorbs all the water but is still uncooked, add more water and cover again tightly and cook until tender. Too much water gives too soft a product.

A steam-jacketed kettle or heavy pot on the fire can be used for this method. Often the cooked rice is fluffed up with a fork just after the cover is lifted and the rice is cooked. This allows steam to escape and gives the grains more separation.

Beans and other legumes are usually presoaked in 1½ gal of water for each 1 lb of product. After soaking (usually overnight), the product is put into plenty of lightly salted boiling water and allowed to cook until tender. Press between the fingers or against the side of the cooking vessel to check for doneness. Breaking of the legume's skin indicates overcooking. If legumes, rice, or pastas are to be cooked further after boiling in water, the product is usually slightly undercooked at boiling.

SUMMARY

Fruits, vegetables, and cereals add variety and appeal to menus. Production procedures should protect nutritive values and produce the best-quality product. Fruits and vegetables furnish minerals and vitamins. Fruits are low in protein and fat, and some contain substantial amounts of carbohydrate. Vegetables are good sources of minerals and vitamins and are also low in fat, and some contain significant quantities of protein and carbohydrate. Cereals are an important source of carbohydrates, plus other nutrients. These items should be placed on menus for their nutritive yield and also because of their appeal to patrons.

Classification of fruits and vegetables for culinary purposes usually follows the cooking method used and the use of the product in the menu. Thus, some fruits are treated as vegetables in cookery, and vice versa.

To ensure quality, specify a grade or brand when purchasing fruits and vegetables. Variety should also be considered, since different varieties have different flavors or other qualities. Size or count should be specified, and the amount ordered should be based on storage facilities, quantity needed, and product perishability. Temperature, humidity, and ventilation are important factors in the care of fruits and vegetables.

Cooking methods vary according to the final product desired and according to how particular fruits or vegetables respond to handling, preparation, cooking, and service. Boiling and steaming are two often-used methods. Braising is used more for vegetables than for fruits. Some fruits and vegetables can be broiled to give a different presentation. Frying fruits and vegetables can also add distinction. Frying methods include sautéing, stir-frying, and deep-frying. Stewing is normally used for fruits.

Canned fruits and vegetables have been processed by being sterilized in their moisture- and vapor-proof containers. Fruits are usually packed in syrup, and vegetables are usually packed in a lightly salted brine. The syrup or brine can be used in other foods. Canned vegetables need only reheating and seasoning before service.

Dried fruits are used in breads, pies, puddings, cookies, cakes, and other desserts. Legumes are the seeds of leguminous plants. Other dried vegetables that may be used are potatoes, onions, and peppers. Fruits and vegetables should be soaked, usually before being cooked.

Fresh fruit can be served whole to be eaten in-hand, such as in a fruit basket, or can be cut and served. Fresh berries are popular. Fresh vegetables are served either raw or cooked. Frozen fruits and vegetables are handled in much the same manner as their fresh counterparts. Cooking frozen vegetables takes less time because they have already been blanched during first processing. Special care must be taken to prepare and cook vegetables and fruits so as to gain maximum nutrients, flavor, color, texture, and form. Processed fruits and vegetables save storage space and labor and reduce the chances of spoilage.

Management must set good standards for the production of fruit and vegetable items on the menu. Costs must be controlled, since preparing these products involves considerable labor. Perishable items can deteriorate or spoil and thus cause monetary loss. Only the quantities needed for a limited time should be purchased. Fruits and vegetables should be properly stored and handled.

Cereals require special cookery because of their high content of starch, which swells on cooking and absorbs moisture. About 1 lb of rice, cornmeal, pasta, or the like is added to 1 gal of boiling water and cooked to tenderness. Coarse breakfast cereals require just a bit more product per gallon. Rice, pastas, and other such foods are blanched after cooking and before use. If the product is to receive further cooking, it may be undercooked to allow for the further cooking.

would a cook parboil an item such as winter squash before baking it?

6. Correctly fill in the spaces left blank in the following table:

Color Pigment	Reaction to Heat	Reaction in Acid	Reaction in Alkali
Green (spinach)	Turns olive green	Turns olive green	
Red (beet)	None		
White (onion)	None		
Orange (carrot)	None		

7. What does *al dente* mean?
8. What are the approximate amounts of salt and water used to cook 1 lb of rice the regular way (in which the rice is blanched after cooking)?
9. If a 5-oz portion of noodles is served, how many pounds of noodles must be cooked to give 100 such portions?

CHAPTER REVIEW QUESTIONS

1. You are the manager of a good restaurant and want to feature fruits and vegetables on the menu. What will you do?
2. Customers say that most of the food in a foodservice is good but that the fruits and vegetables are flavorless and lack good color and texture. What should be done by management to improve the quality of the produce they serve?
3. What factors must be considered in purchasing fruits and vegetables? What are the grades for fresh, frozen, and canned fruits and vegetables? How does a buyer compute the quantity needed?
4. Summarize the various cooking methods for cooking fruits and vegetables, giving times, temperatures, cooking methods, and cooking procedures.
5. What kind of vegetables can be baked? Why

VOCABULARY

Drained weight	Batch cooking
Fine grain	Braising
Coarse grain	Sautéing
U.S. No. 1	Long-grain rice
U.S. Fancy or Extra	Portion
Fancy	Sublimation
Semolina	Vacuum-dry
U.S. Grades A, B,	Freeze-dry
and C	Garbanzo
Stir-fry	Stewing
Legumes	Compote

ANNOTATED REFERENCES

American Home Economics Association. 1975. *Handbook of Food Preparation,* pp. 47-59, 85-105. Washington, D.C.: American Home Economics Association. (Fresh and processed fruits and vegetables.)

Casola, M. 1969. *Successful Mass Cookery and Volume Feeding,* pp. 148-83, 247-51. Rochelle Park, N.J.: Ahrens Publishing. (Vegetable recipes, and information on fruits.)

Haines, R. G. 1973. *Food Preparation for Hotels, Restaurants, and Cafeterias,* pp. 225-62. Chicago: American Technical Society. (Vegetable preparation, with numerous recipes).

Kansas State University. 1966. *Practical Cookery,* pp. 35-42, 77-92. New York: John Wiley & Sons. (Preparation of and general information about fruits and vegetables.)

Kaplan, A. 1971. *Elements of Food Production and Baking,* pp. 125-40. New York: ITT Educational Services. (Vegetables.)

Kotschevar, L. H. 1975. *Quantity Food Purchasing,* pp. 40-250. New York: John Wiley & Sons. (Complete purchasing information on both fresh and processed fruits and vegetables.)

Lundberg, D. E., and Kotschevar, L. H. 1968. *Understanding Cooking,* pp. 200-42. Amherst, Mass.: University of Massachusetts. (Extensive instruction on vegetable cookery.)

Peckham, G. G. 1974. *Foundations of Food Preparation,* pp. 62-81, 149-96. New York: Macmillan. (Cereals, fruits, and vegetables.)

Terrell, M. E. 1971. *Professional Food Preparation,* pp. 93-158. New York: John Wiley & Sons. (Fruit and vegetable preparation.)

Treat, N., and Richards, L. 1966. *Quantity Cookery,* pp. 303-69. Boston: Little, Brown. (Quantity vegetable recipes.)

Vail, G. E.; Phillips, J. A.; Rust, L.; Griswold, R.; and Justin, M. 1973. *Foods,* pp. 35-81, 100-31. Boston: Houghton Mifflin. (All aspects of fruits, vegetables, and cereals.)

West, B. B.; Wood, L.; and Harger, V. F. 1966. *Food Service in Institutions,* pp. 240-60, 268-72. New York: John Wiley & Sons. (The physical and chemical attributes, nutritive value, and cookery of fruits and vegetables, plus cereal cookery.)

CHAPTER 12

Meat, Poultry, and Seafood

OUTLINE

I. Nutrition
II. Purchasing
   A. Market Forms
   B. Grading
   C. Cuts and Parts
   D. Inspection for Wholesomeness
III. Receiving, Storing, and Issuing
IV. Cooking Principles
   A. Color

   B. Doneness
   C. Flesh Composition
   D. Tenderness
   E. Flavor
   F. Cooking Methods
   G. Frozen Meat Cookery
   H. Poultry
   I. Seafood
V. Management Controls

Meat, poultry, or seafood often constitutes the main item of a meal, as well as being the item prominently featured on a menu. Because these foods are the center of most meals, the other foods served revolve around them.

The term *meat* commonly refers to the edible portions of cattle, swine, and sheep. Beef is the most popular variety of meat in this country, followed by pork, veal, lamb, and mutton, in that order. Poultry comprises chickens, turkeys, ducks, geese, guineas, and squabs. Game birds include grouse, pheasants, partridges, quail, peacocks, wild duck,

and wild turkey. Poultry is relatively cheap and has good menu appeal because of its inexpensiveness and low content of fat and saturated fat. Chicken is the most popular type of poultry, with turkey far behind in second place. The approximate age of a bird is told by moving the keel bone; if this bone is flexible, it indicates a relatively gelatinous content, signifying that the bird is still growing. In this chapter, the word *fish* refers to gilled animals with fins, while *shellfish* refers to crustaceans, mollusks, and other shelled water creatures. The word *seafood* includes both. Seafood is popular today because of its nutritional qualities and its low levels of fat and saturated fat. Most shellfish contain higher levels of cholesterol than meat or poultry.

NUTRITION

Meats, poultry, and seafood are highly nutritious. They contain complete proteins and are highly digestible. Lean meat, poultry, and seafood are about 20 percent protein. All are low in carbohydrate. Lean flesh often contains about 10 to 13 percent fat. Meat or poultry containing heavily marbled or layered fat has a substantially higher fat percentage. Lean pork has no more fat than other lean meats. All are an excellent source of the B vitamins—especially organ meats. Lean pork is high in thiamine. Most of the fat on poultry is found along the back. Geese and ducks are quite fat, but much of their fat is cooked off. Both meat and poultry liver is high in Vitamin A. Seafood items (especially fish liver) are high in vitamins A and D. Meat contributes some potassium, sodium, zinc, and other minerals to the diet; in fact, minerals constitute about 1 percent of the total composition of lean meat. Poultry furnishes good phosphorus, some potassium, zinc, and some trace minerals. Seafood supplies good quantities of minerals and is especially high in iodine, if it comes from saltwater.

PURCHASING

Flesh foods are delicate substances that must be properly selected, handled, and cooked to end up as acceptable items. It is necessary to know what each item offered on the market is, because each kind requires special preparation. Following is a short summary of the types of animals whose flesh can be selected on the market.

BEEF

Steer	Young male cattle castrated before sexual maturity
Heifer	Young female cattle that has had no calf
Cow	Older female cattle that has had a calf
Bull	Sexually mature male cattle
Stag	Sexually mature male cattle that has been castrated
Bullock	Young uncastrated bull

VEAL AND CALF

Veal	Young calf 4 to 14 weeks old
Calf	Young calf 14 to 52 weeks old

PORK

Barrow	Young male hog that has been castrated
Gilt	Young female hog that has not had a litter
Sow	Older female hog that has had a litter
Boar	Mature sexually active male hog

LAMB AND MUTTON

Lamb	Young sheep under a year old
Yearling	Young sheep about a year old
Mutton	Sheep over a year old, usually castrated
Ewe	Mature female sheep
Ram	Mature sexually active male sheep

CHICKEN

Broiler	Young chicken of either sex under 9 weeks old
Fryer	Chicken of either sex 8 to 12 weeks old
Roaster	Chicken about 12 weeks old weighing around 5 lb
Capon	Desexed male chicken weighing 4 to 7 lb
Hen (fôwl)	Older female chicken
Rooster	Mature male chicken

Rock Cornish hen	Classed as a chicken but smaller than one and usually purchased quite young, weighing 1 to 2 lb

TURKEYS

Fryer-Roaster	Turkey about 16 weeks old weighing 4 to 8 lb
Hen, young	Female turkey under a year old weighing 12 to 16 lb
Tom, young	Male turkey under a year old weighing 12 to 30 lb
Hen, mature	Female turkey over a year old
Tom, mature	Male turkey over a year old

DUCKS

Broiler-fryer	Duck less than 8 weeks old weighing about 2½ lb
Duckling	Young duck about 16 weeks old, weighing 3 to 7 lb
Mature duck	Older duck of either sex

GEESE

Young	Goose under 6 months old, weighing 4 to 10 lb
Mature	Over 6 months old, weighing 10 to 18 lb

PIGEON

Squab	Pigeon 3 to 4 weeks old, weighing 8 to 14 oz
Pigeon	Older bird

FISH

Salmon	Little Atlantic salmon is available and most goes into lox; purchase Pacific salmon, 8 to 12 lb, for slicing or baking
Cod	The best weigh 5 to 8 lb; scrod is a young cod weighing 1½ to 2½ lb; many fish, including haddock, and cusk, are classed as cod; finnan haddie is lightly smoked and salted cod
Sole	Member of the flounder family; lemon sole, petrale, and Dover sole (from the Pacific—not true Dover sole) are all sold as sole
Mackerel	Fish weighing ¾ to 1½ lb; quite fat and often broiled
Snapper	Red snapper comes from the Gulf and southern waters; other species are caught in the Atlantic and Pacific; should weigh 1½ to 4 lb
Trout	Purchase Idaho trout; should weigh about ¾ lb
Halibut	Delicate, lean, white-fleshed fish; best ones come from small fish weighing 12 to 20 lb
Yellow perch	Freshwater fish caught in considerable numbers in Canada and shipped to this country; fillets weigh 2 to 3 oz
Whitefish	Fat fish caught in the Great Lakes; prized as a delicacy
Bullhead	Fish now grown in considerable quantities in some southern states

SHELLFISH

Crab	Blue crab comes from north Atlantic and Gulf waters, dungeness from Puget Sound and Pacific waters, king from Alaskan waters, and stone from southern waters of the Atlantic; the body of blue crab is eaten (soft shell crab are blue crab that are molting); only the legs of king

Crayfish	Small lobsterlike shellfish; they run about 8 to 12 per lb
Clams	Mollusks; littleneck and cherrystone clams are eaten raw; most others are eaten cooked, either deep-fried or in chowders
Lobster	True lobster have claws; most come from New England and Maritime Province waters; laguna lobster caught off California is a spiny lobster without claws; chicken lobster weighs just under 1 lb
Lobster tails	Spiny lobster with the head removed; most are imported
Oysters	Bluepoints and Chincoteagues from Maryland and Chesapeake Bay waters are well-known; Pacific oysters are the large Japanese variety and the tiny prized Olympias
Scallops	Mollusks whose inner muscle only is eaten; bay scallops are considered superior to sea scallops; New Bedford scallops are sea scallops of high quality
Shrimp	A small crustacean of the lagoste family; the best come from Gulf and Caribbean waters; sold by count per lb; pink and white shrimp varieties are considered best, but brown and red are marketed; some aquaculture shrimp are available from Taiwan; if purchased glazed, glazing should be only 6 percent of total weight, but

and stone crab are eaten; and the legs and body of the dungeness are eaten

it can run 20 percent or more, raising the cost considerably

Market Forms

Meats are available in carcass, wholesale-cut, or portion-cut form. Much beef is sold in boxed form, which is meat that has been boned and wrapped in air-exhausted plastic. Much beef is also now aged in air-exhausted plastic rather than by dry aging. Pork is seldom purchased in the carcass. Most operations purchase legs (hams) and loins as wholesale cuts, but most pork is actually used in the portion-cut form. Cooked and canned products are also available. Most foodservices prefer to buy unfrozen meat, but occasionally it may be desirable to purchase it frozen.

Poultry is available whole, cut up, in steaks, or in cutlets. Some rolls (flesh that is boned, rolled, and tied) are available. Some turkey and chicken today are processed so as to imitate ham or to fill wieners or other sausages.

Market forms of fish are given in table 12-1. Most foodservices prefer to purchase fresh fish, but the quality of frozen fish has improved so much that more operations are purchasing fish in this form. For purposes of recognition, whole fresh fish may be categorized as either flat or round (see fig. 12-1). The process of preparing a fresh fish for cooking is outlined in figure 12-2.

Shellfish such as crab, lobster, mussels, oysters, and clams are often sold alive. Live mollusks can be identified by their tightly closed shells; if the shell is gaping open, the animal is dead. Crab and lobster show more active signs of life. A *weak* is a lobster that is dying. A *chicken lobster* is one that weighs about 1 lb. Clams, mussels, and oysters may be sold shucked. Shucked clams and oysters should not have more than 8 percent free liquid on them. Some shrimp is marketed alive but most is frozen—often, headless but unshelled. PDQ (peeled, deveined, and quick-frozen) shrimp are available. Cooked shrimp, either in the shell or peeled and deveined can be purchased as well. King crab legs

Table 12-1. Market Forms of Fish

Form	Definition	Edible Portion	Best Ways To Cook
Fin fish (whole or round, fresh)	Fish just as they were caught. They must be cleaned (by taking the insides out), and the scales must be taken off before they can be cooked. The head, tail, and fins may also be cut off before cooking.	45%	Bake, poach, broil, fry, steam
Drawn (fresh or frozen)	A drawn fish has been cleaned. It must be scaled and have the fins cut off before it can be cooked.	48%	Bake, poach, broil, fry, steam
Dressed or pan-dressed* (fresh or frozen)	A dressed fish has been cleaned and scaled. The head, tail, and fins are usually cut off too.	67%	Bake, poach, broil, fry, steam
Steaks (fresh or frozen)	Steaks are slices of fish about ¾ to 1 inch thick. They have been cut across the fish. A part of the backbone is the only bone in a fish steak. Steaks are ready to cook.	84%	Bake, poach, broil, fry, steam
Fillets (fresh or frozen)	Fillets are the sides of a fish. They have been cut away from the backbone and are ready to cook.	100%	Bake, poach, broil, fry, steam
Butterfly fillets (fresh or frozen)	Butterfly fillets are the two sides of the fish cut lengthwise away from the backbone and held together by the uncut flesh and skin of the belly.	100%	Bake, poach, broil, fry, steam
Single fillets (fresh or frozen)	A fillet cut from one side of a fish is called a *single fillet.* This is the type most generally available on the market. The fillets may or may not be skinless.	100%	Bake, poach, broil, fry, steam
Chunks (fresh or frozen)	Chunks are pieces cut across the fish. They are larger than steaks and are ready to cook.	100%	Bake, poach, broil, fry, steam

*Pan-dressed is smaller size to fit pan for cooking.
Source: U.S. Department of Agriculture, U.S. Department of the Interior, National Fisheries Institute.

Table 12-1. *(cont.)*

Form	Definition	Edible Portion	Best Ways To Cook
Breaded portions (frozen)	Portions are pieces of fish that have been cut from blocks of frozen fillets. They are covered with batter and all of the portions in a package are the same size. Portions sold raw must be cooked. Precooked portions are cooked only a little bit more before being served. The package label should be read for cooking instructions.	100%	Ovenize, deep-fry
Fish sticks (frozen)	Sticks are made the same way portions are, but sticks are smaller. All sticks are cooked a little bit before being frozen, cooking must be completed before they can be served.	100%	Ovenize, deep-fry

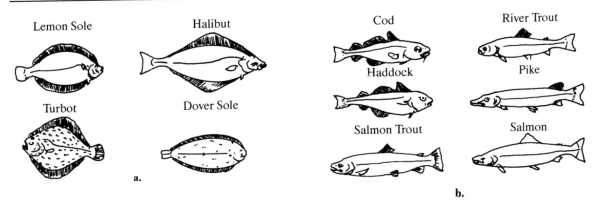

Figure 12-1. Categories of fish: (a) flat fish; (b) round fish.

are often cooked and frozen before sale, and picked crab meat is also available.

Grading

Quality grading of beef, veal, calf, lamb, and mutton is much the same. Grades are Prime, Choice, Select, Standard, and Commercial for beef; they are Prime, Choice, and Select for calf, veal, lamb, and mutton (see fig. 12-3). Other grades are available, but foodservices seldom purchase these (see table

12-2). Pork is graded U.S. No. 1, 2, or 3. Bulls and cows cannot make the Prime grade; bullocks can, but they are graded on a slightly different basis from the one on which steers and heifers make Prime grade. Mutton cannot make Prime. Sows cannot make U.S. No. 1 for pork. Some foodservices find that pork graded U.S. No. 2 is as satisfactory as pork graded U.S. No. 1.

Poultry is graded U.S. Grade A, B, or C. Few operations purchase anything other than U.S. Grade A in this area. Fish and shellfish are not graded

Figure 12-2. Preparing whole fresh fish for cooking.

Scaling

Wash the fish. Place the fish on a cutting board and hold the fish firmly by the head with one hand. Holding a knife almost vertical, scrape off the scales, starting at the tail and scraping toward the head. Be sure to remove all the scales around the fins and head.

Cleaning

With a sharp knife, cut the entire length of the belly, from the vent to the head. Remove the intestines. Next, cut around the pelvic fins, and remove them.

Removing the pectoral fin

Remove the pectoral fins by cutting just in back of the collarbone. If the backbone is large, cut down to it on each side of the fish.

Removing the head and tail

Then place the fish on the edge of the cutting board so that the head hangs over, and snap the backbone by bending the head down. Cut any remaining flesh that holds the head to the body. Cut off the tail.

Removing the dorsal fin

Next remove the dorsal fin (the large fin on the back of the fish) by cutting along each side of the fin. Then give a quick pull forward toward the head, and remove the fin with the root bones attached. Never trim the fins off with shears or a knife because this will leave the root bones at the base of the fins in the fish. Wash the fish thoroughly in cold running water. The fish is now dressed or pan-dressed, depending on its size.

Cutting steaks

Large-size dressed fish may be cut crosswise into steaks, about 1 inch thick each.

Figure 12-2. *(cont.)*

Filleting

With a sharp knife cut along the back of the fish from the tail to the head. Then cut down to the backbone just in back of the collarbone.

Filleting

Turn the knife flat and cut the flesh away from the backbone and the rib bones.

Filleting

Lift off the whole side of the fish (the fillet) in one piece. Turn the fish over and cut the fillet from the other side.

Figure 12-3. USDA grade mark for highest-quality meats.

except in some processed forms. The grades for the processed product are U.S. Grade A, B, and C. Buyers must therefore rely on their own judgment to identify high-quality seafood. The best insurance for obtaining good seafood is to pick a good, honest purveyor. Most of the quality characteristics of fish depend on freshness. To check quality, look for the following characteristics:

Flesh - Firm, not separating from the bones.
Odor - Fresh and mild. Fish from the water has practically no fishy odor, but the odor is more pronounced with time. Fish and shellfish should not have a strong odor nor any ammonia smell. Open fish that has been eviscerated should not have a fishy smell.
Eyes - Bright, clear, and full. As fish stales, the eyes cloud and turn pink. Eyes protrude on fresh fish, but sink as the fish ages.
Gills - Red, bright, and free from slime. Gill color fades with age to a light pink, to gray, and then to a brownish or greenish color.
Skin - Shiny, with color unfaded. Iridescence may be present when fish are first caught. Look for pronounced markings and colors. Fresh fish have scales that are tight and difficult to remove.

Frozen fish should be solidly frozen when received. Some may be water-sprayed to prevent dehydration.

Table 12-2. USDA Quality Grading for Meats

Beef	Veal and Calf	Lamb and Yearling Mutton	Mutton
Prime	Prime	Prime	Choice
Choice	Choice	Choice	Good
Select	Good	Good	Utility
Standard	Standard	Utility	Cull
Commercial	Utility	Cull	
Utility	Cull		
Cutter			
Canner			

Such spray should not be over 6 percent of total weight. Good storage temperatures for fish are 0°F (−18°C) or below. Frozen fish should have the following charactertistics:

Flesh - No discoloration or freezer burn. If fish is thawed and refrozen, quality is diminished. Brownish edges indicate thawing and refreezing.
Odor - Little or no odor. A strong odor usually signals poor quality.

Most frozen fish is wrapped, either individually or in pieces or packages of various weights. Wrappings are composed of moisture- and vapor-proof material, air-exhausted.

Beef, veal, and calf are given yield grades based on the ratio of flesh to bone and fat. No. 1 yield indicates highest yield, while No. 5 represents lowest (see fig. 12-4). Each yield grade gives approximately 4.6 percent more edible retail cuts than the next lower grade. Prime grades cannot qualify for highest yield grades, since too much fat is required in achieving so high a quality. Foodservices do not find yield grades as helpful as do supermarket and other buyers. Consequently, purchase is usually by IMPS (Institutional Meat Purchase Specifications) number, which limits the amount of surface fat, specifies the cut size, and so on. The IMPS also allow a foodservice to specify the range from which it wants the carcass

or cut to come. For example, there are five ranges for beef, covering carcass weights of 500 lb to 1,000 lb and over. Indicating the desired range of the cut—say, of a No. 109 oven-ready rib—thus indicates the desired weight, as well.

IMPS numbers are standard specifications used nationally to indicate what portion of the carcass is wanted. A No. 103 rib, for example, is a full rib just as it is cut from the carcass; but a No. 109 rib excludes the lower parts of the rib (shortribs), the chine bone, the upper muscle over the chine bone, and other parts, and the remaining rib must be ready to be put into the oven. Purchasing by IMPS number simplifies ordering and ensures getting what is needed. Beef cuts have numbers in the 100 range; lamb and mutton, the 200 range; veal and calf, the 300 range; and pork, the 400 range. Portion cuts are numbers in the 1000s. Thus, a lamb loin chop would be No. 1232.

Quality meat grades for beef, veal, calf, lamb, and mutton are based on the conformation or yield of the meat as judged by the size of the rib eye and other conformation factors, the amount of flesh marbling, the color of the lean, the texture and appearance of the flesh, age, and so on. Hog grades are based on carcass weight, depth of fat back, fullness of muscles, and carcass length. Table 12-3 lists quality factors related to color and texture. Poultry is graded on the basis of conformation, fat cover, freedom from defects, freedom from pin or vestigial feathers, and so on. Again, seafood is usually ungraded, except for certain processed items.

Cuts and Parts

Beef is available in carcass, side, quarter, wholesale, or portion cuts. Wholesale cuts include round sirloin (loin end), short loin, rib, flank, plate, brisket shank, chuck, and neck (see fig. 12-5). Calf, veal lamb, and mutton are sold by carcass or by breast shoulder, rib, leg, or portion cuts (see figs. 12-6 and 12-7). If ribs, legs, or other cuts of these meats are purchased, they may come double; that is, they may be joined by the spine (chine) bone into left and right units. Large calves are sometimes cut

Figure 12-4. Yield grades for gauging the relative amount of edible meat on a cut or carcass.

much as beef is. Pork is purchased as picnics, shoulders (Boston butts), loins, spareribs, side pork (bacon), legs, and portion cuts (see fig. 12-8). Some few operations may purchase pork jowls, heads, ears, tails, or hocks. Variety meats such as kidney, liver, and sweetbreads from all animals are available.

Poultry is available whole, by sides, in quarters, or in parts; ground turkey or chicken is also available. Chicken parts are breasts (boneless or bone-in, and skinless or skin on), legs (drumsticks and thighs), drumsticks, thighs, wings, and backs. Livers, hearts, gizzards, and necks are also available.

Table 12-3. Meat Quality Factors: Color and Texture

Animal	High Quality	Poor Quality
Beef		
Lean	Bright red after cutting, and smooth-grained	Darker red, rough-grained
Fat	Creamy white, firm, and brittle	Yellow or orange, scant, and unevenly distributed
Bone (backbone)	Red, soft, and spongy, with abundant cartilage	White, hard, and brittle
Veal		
Lean	Grayish pink, fine-grained, and smooth	Pale or dark
Fat	Grayish or pinkish white, firm, and brittle	Little or none present
Bone	Red, soft, and spongy, with abundant cartilage	———
Lamb		
Lean	Pinkish red, fine-grained, and smooth	Darker and stronger-flavored
Fat	White or pinkish, firm, flaky, and brittle	Heavier layers
Bone	Red, soft, and spongy, with abundant cartilage	———
Pork		
Lean	Grayish pink and fine-grained	Darker and coarser
Fat	White, very firm, but not brittle	Excess both internally in lean and externally
Bone	Red, soft, and spongy	Less red

Inspection for Wholesomeness

Inspection considers the fitness of meat and poultry for human consumption; grading considers its palatability and yield. Meat and poultry inspection is required under law in every plant. Animals must be inspected before and after slaughter. The packinghouse or processing plant must be sanitary and must meet rigid standards in equipment, procedures, and other categories. Inspection is carried out under municipal, state, or federal auspices. Local standards must equal or exceed federal ones.

Grading is not mandatory, but inspection for wholesomeness is. Some operations purchase meats and poultry by brand name. Pork is especially often purchased in nongraded form. Meat quality and yield grades are indicated by the grade appearing in the shield. The stamp indicating wholesomeness is a circle in which the words "Inspected and Passed, USDA" appear. A number is also included to identify the particular processing plant. By this means the place where the meat was inspected and passed can be traced. Under the shield on a grade stamp, the initials of the individual who graded the meat may appear.

RECEIVING, STORING, AND ISSUING

Flesh products are usually the most expensive food items purchased by a foodservice, and receiv-

Figure 12-5. Wholesale and retail cuts of beef.

Figure 12-6. Wholesale and retail cuts of veal.

Figure 12-7. Wholesale and retail cuts of lamb.

Figure 12-8. Wholesale and retail cuts of pork.

ers must make sure that the proper quantity and quality are delivered. Temperatures of refrigerated items should not be higher than 40°F (4.5°C), and frozen items should be solidly frozen. All items should be clean, sanitary, and well-packaged or well-wrapped. If a receiver is unable to identify

grade or other quality factors, someone in the organization should be called to assess these factors on what has been delivered.

After delivery, items must be stored in such a way as to prevent waste through pilferage, deterioration, or infestation. Older stocks should be moved to the front, so new deliveries can be stored behind and used last. Refrigerated products should be held at about 35°F (1.6°C) and frozen items at −10°F (−23°C) or lower. Storage areas should be clean, with all stock stored off the floor. Table 12-4 gives some recommended holding times for meat storage. Poultry can be refrigerated for about three days and held frozen about six months. Fish may be held refrigerated for about three days. Fat fish (such as mackerel, salmon, and tuna) may be held frozen for about three months, while lean fish (such as haddock, cod, and swordfish) may be held frozen for about six months.

The issuing of meats and expensive fish is simplified if they are tagged when received. Tagged items need not be reweighed or otherwise identified when they are issued, and tags are also helpful in reordering. The bottom half of the tag is returned to the purchasing agent when the item is issued, thus facilitating inventory control. All items issued should be recorded on properly signed requisitions that are sent to food and beverage accounting (along with records of direct deliveries) for compilation of the food cost of the day.

COOKING PRINCIPLES

Cooking meat, poultry, or fish makes it more palatable to most people, changing its texture, flavor, and appearance. Cooking also sterilizes the product.

Color

The red color of flesh comes from a red pigment called myoglobin. Beef, lamb, and mutton flesh are high in it; veal and pork have very little. Chicken has some, especially in the legs, but fish has almost none. Myoglobin changes to hematin when heat strikes it. This accounts for the color change we see in meat when it goes from uncooked to well done. Some red meats become quite red when exposed to air because the myoglobin oxidizes and changes into oxymyoglobin. If myoglobin joins with nitrogen to form nitrosomyoglobin, it will not change to a done color when cooked but will remain red, as happens with cured ham or in cured brisket of beef. A ham loaf containing ham, veal, and pork is

Table 12-4. Holding Times for Meat Storage

Meat	Holding Period
Chilled	
Solid, fresh cuts of beef, pork, lamb, and veal	2 to 4 days
Ground items and variety meats (liver, etc.)	1 to 2 days
Most cooked, processed meat items, and cooked leftovers	3 to 7 days
Frozen	
Beef	6 to 12 months
Lamb and veal	6 to 9 months
Pork	3 to 6 months
Ground Beef	3 to 4 months
Ground lamb, ground veal, and variety meats	3 to 4 months
Ground pork	1 to 3 months

red because of the nitrogen in the salts used to cure the ham. Onions dried in inert nitrogen gas or root vegetables grown in a highly nitrogenized soil may contain enough nitrogen to turn meat red. Sometimes, enough nitrogen curing salts get rubbed onto a cutting block to contaminate meat and make it look red. This can happen if ham steaks are cut, and then the meat block is not cleaned before some braising steaks are cut. The braising steaks become red permanently and do not look done when cooked. The color change to a brownish color when meat spoils is due to a change of myoglobin into metamyoglobin.

Doneness

When flesh reaches about 160°F (71°C), its color begins to change and the protein coagulates; coagulation is complete at around 175°F (78.6°C). Just before coagulation, denaturation (a moisture loss) occurs. The higher the cooking temperature is and the longer the flesh is exposed to it, the greater the moisture loss is. This loss is called *shrinkage*. The degree of doneness often dictates the amount of shrinkage (see table 12-5). Thus, flesh cooked rare may shrink 10 percent; flesh cooked medium done, 15 percent; and flesh cooked well done, 25 percent.

Table 12-5. Stages of Doneness in Flesh

Temperature	Doneness	Description
140°F (60°C)	Rare	Flesh is quite red; there is a good brown color on the outside, with some pink next to it, and then redness. Appearance is full and plump, and the flesh yields under pressure; juices are red but not bloody.
160°F (71°C)	Medium	Interior is a modified rose; pink juices are apparent but less plentiful than in rare; exterior is well-browned; surface is not as plump or full; there is definite resistance to pressure.
175°F (78.6°C)	Well done	Meat is completely cooked; little or no juice appears; flesh is hard and flinty to the touch and has a shrunken appearance; surface is brown and dry.

High heat does not seal in the juices and reduce shrinkage. A constant low temperature is best for cooking flesh foods.

High heat develops browning in meat and an accompanying flavor change—a sort of caramelization. Salt delays browning; and since its penetration is small (from ¼ to ½ inch) it is frequently omitted until service.

Flesh Composition

Flesh is about 25 percent solids and 75 percent moisture. Of the solids, 20 percent consists of fat, fatlike compounds, ash, and other substances; the remaining 80 percent is protein. Fatty tissue is from 15 to 50 percent moisture. This is why we lay fatty meat over meat during cooking to help baste it or add moisture. We also lard meat to add moisture. Rib and strip sirloin roasts are roasted fat-side-up so that, when the fat melts in cooking, the released moisture bastes the meat.

Flesh is bound together by connective tissue that winds through the meat fibers and holds them together. They also join together and make a tendon that attaches to the bone, holding a muscle in place. There are two kinds of connective tissue: collagen, or white connective tissue; and elastin, or yellow connective tissue. Collagen changes into gelatin and water when exposed to moist heat. Acids speed the transformation, and that is why we add tomato juice or other acidic liquids to some meat that is to be braised. Elastin is not changed by

heat. It must be broken up by grinding, pounding, cubing, or some other mechanical treatment.

The lean flesh of meat largely consists of meat fibers—thin, long, tiny rods that contain moisture, salts, vitamins, fats, and flavor. Fine, silky fibers are a sign of tender, moist meat. Coarse, dry ones indicate meat that may be tough when cooked. As meat cooks and loses moisture, the fibers pack closer together, and this results in a drier, tougher piece of meat. We can see this happen when we compare the tenderness of a rare or medium-done steak with that of a well-done steak.

Most meat proteins are soluble in cold water, but coagulation makes them insoluble. We can see soluble proteins coagulating when scum floats to the surface of boiling meat.

Tenderness

Age is perhaps the greatest factor in making meat tough. As an animal ages, its connective tissue content increases, the fibers get coarser, and the moisture content of the flesh decreases. Muscles that receive a lot of exercise are tougher than ones that receive little exercise. Thus, in beef, the flesh of the leg is tougher than the flesh of the rib or loin area. Flesh from the rarely exercised muscles of a young animal is apt to be exceedingly tender. The composition of poultry flesh is much like that of meat, but fish contains little connective tissue and therefore is not tough.

Flesh can be tenderized by breaking up the connective tissue or by cooking it in moist heat. Actually, flesh is most tender when it is uncooked; rare flesh is next in tenderness, medium done is next, and well done is least tender. We can also use an enzyme such as papain to digest connective tissue and make the flesh more tender. This is frequently accomplished by injecting an animal with a papain solution just before slaughter, allowing the heart to pump the papain throughout the tissues, and then slaughtering the animal. When the meat from such an animal is cooked, the papain goes to work digesting some of the connective tissue. We can also dip a cut of meat into a papain product, but this is not as effective. Making meat into what are called *formed products* is another way to tenderize meat. First the meat is frozen and thinly shaved; then it is thawed and mixed well for about 8 minutes with a bit of salt to draw out collagen from the meat. The meat can then be shaped—into steak form, for example— frozen in this shape, and cut into steak cuts. The shaving of the meat cuts through the connective tissue so that it is no longer tendinous, making the flesh tender. Putting meat into a marinade can make the meat tenderer, but only slightly so. Heavy electric shocks on flesh can shatter connective tissue and thereby tenderize it.

Aging flesh increases its tenderness, as well as adding moistness and flavor. Enzymes in flesh work slowly to break down connective tissue. Flesh is dry-aged by being held at 35° to 45°F (1.6° to 4.4°C). Aging can also occur when meat is placed into air-exhausted plastic wraps and left to stand at a temperature of about 35°F (1.6°C). Flesh aged in this way needs no fat cover to protect it from molds and bacteria. Aging for about 14 days is usual, but flesh can be aged for 21 days with good results. After 21 days, the aging benefits drop significantly. Sometimes the process of aging meat is called *ripening*.

Flavor

The flavor of flesh comes from nitrogenous and nonnitrogenous extractives and waste products, plus aromatic, essential oils. The oils are extremely important in giving meat flavor. Flavor develops in flesh during cooking for up to about 3 hours; then it declines.

The animal's diet influences its flavor because many essential oils the fat contains come from the foods it eats. A milk-mash diet for chickens produces mildly flavored flesh. Cattle fattened on distiller's mash have a sharply acidic fermented-flavored meat. Hogs fed on peanuts—as is done with some Virginia pork—yield flesh that has a slightly peanutty flavor. Wild ducks feeding in sea marshes acquire a fishy flavor, but those feeding on wild rice and on grains from farmers' fields in the Midwest develop a marvelous flavor.

A large proportion of the essential oils in flesh can be found in the fat. This is because these oils are soluble in fat but not in water. Fat appears as surface fat, as marbling (tiny flecks of fat between fibers), and as fats or fatlike substances in meat juices. Thus, the most flavorful meat is that having some fat.

Poultry—except, at times, duck—is usually cooked well done. Pork is always cooked well done to destroy any trichinae that may be present. Seafood is *just* cooked to doneness; overcooking leaves it dry and toughened.

Cooking Methods

Meat, poultry, and seafood are cooked by the following dry-heat and moist-heat methods:

DRY-HEAT
Broiling
Roasting or baking
Barbecuing
Sautéing, pan-frying, or grilling
Deep-frying
Ovenizing

MOIST-HEAT
Braising (pot-roasting, fricasséeing, casseroling, swissing, or stewing)
Simmering (poaching or stewing)
Steaming
Blanching

The cuts of meat for which each of these cooking methods is appropriate are listed in table 12-6.

Table 12-6. Preferred Cooking Methods for Various Cuts of Meat

Beef	Lamb	Fresh Pork	Smoked Pork	Veal	Variety Meats
Roasting					

Rib
Sirloin butt
Loin strip
Tenderloin
Rump butt*
Round*
  Inside (top)
  Outside (bottom)
  Knuckle (tip)
Inside chuck*
Shoulder clod*
Loaf (ground beef)
	Leg
	Loin
	Rack
	Rolled shoulder
	Cushion shoulder
	Loaf (ground lamb)
		Ham (leg)
		Loin
		Boston butt
		Picnic
		Rolled shoulder
		Cushion shoulder
		Spareribs
			Ham
			Picnic
			Shoulder butt
			Canadian-style bacon
			Loaf (ground ham)
				Leg (round)
				Loin
				Rib
				Rolled shoulder
				Loaf (ground veal)
					Liver

Broiling, Griddle-broiling, or Pan-broiling					
Rib steak Club steak T-bone steak Porterhouse steak Sirloin steak (cut from loin strip) Butt steak Tip steak (knuckle) Inside chuck steak* Top round steak* Beef patties (hamburger) Flank*	Shoulder chops Rib chops Loin chops Leg steaks Lamb patties (ground lamb)	Fresh pork is not broiled or griddle-broiled.	Sliced ham Sliced bacon Sliced Canadian-style bacon Shoulder butt	Veal is not broiled unless it is fairly mature and well-fatted, and then only loin chops or steaks.	Sliced veal or lamb liver Lamb kidneys Brains Sweetbreads

Braising

Chuck (all cuts) Brisket Plate Flank Neck Outside (bottom) round Heel of round Rump butt Shank Short ribs Skirt steak Ox tails (joints)	Breast Chops Loin Rib Shoulder Cutlets (leg) Neck Shoulder Shank	Breast Neck Shank Shoulder	Chops Loin Rib Shoulder Feet Hocks Spareribs Fresh ham steaks Tenderloin	Heart (all kinds) Liver Beef Pork Kidney Tripe

Simmering

Fresh
Chuck (all cuts)
Rump butt
Shank
Heel of round
Brisket
Plate
Flank
Short ribs
 	
Corned
Brisket
Rump
Plate
Round
	Neck
	Shank
	Breast
	Flank
	(Large cuts of veal are usually not cooked in water.)
		Neck
		Breast
		Flank
		Shanks
		(Large cuts of lamb are usually not cooked in water)
			Spareribs
			Backbones
			Pigs feet
			Hocks
			
			Ham
			Shoulder
			Picnic
			Shoulder butt
			Hocks
				Kidney
				Heart
				Tongue
				For precooking:
				   Brains
				   Sweetbreads

*Usually only prime to choice quality in these should be cooked in this manner.

Cooking by radiant heat is called *broiling.* The term *grilling* once meant the same thing as *broiling,* but now it means sautéing or frying. Only tender flesh is broiled. To broil well, the flesh should have some fat content. Lean sole or veal does not broil well. Leaner items should be broiled a bit faster and basted with butter or other fat. Thin pieces should be positioned close to the broiler. The broiler temperature should be lowered for cooking thicker items such as turkey breasts and chateaubriands. Too high a temperature produces a hard, dry crust that slows heat penetration, giving a charred outside and an undercooked inside.

To broil, dip the item into oil and place it gently on the grid. Cook to half doneness, and then turn and season. For larger pieces, two turns may be needed. Otherwise, the two sides can be completely cooked with one turn. Do not allow drippings to flame; the smoke and soot can harm flavor. Grease fires are dangerous. Put fires out with water. Place fish, shellfish, and small pieces of meat or poultry onto grids that hold the product firmly and allow turning without requiring the product itself to be lifted up and flipped.

Pan-broiling is done in fairly heavy skillets suited to the quantity, so drippings do not burn. Rub the pan bottom lightly with fat. Preheat the pan almost to smoking. Cook the item on one side and then on the other. Pour off fat as it gathers. Do not cover and do not add water. To griddle-broil, place the item onto a lightly greased 325°F (161°C) griddle, and cook with no fat.

Items for roasting should fill the pan and leave no space for drippings to burn. A trivet or perforated underliner is placed under the roast so that drippings can collect underneath, away from the flesh. A mirepoix may be introduced to give added flavor. Salt is not added until browning is complete. Do not pierce the flesh of a roasting or broiling item; instead, roll it over or insert the fork into fatty tissue. Use no liquids. Place the fat side of the item up; this means that poultry should be roasted with its breast side down until the last stage of roasting. Among seafood, only fat fish roasts or bakes well. Use thermometers to monitor the temperature for correctness. Low-heat roasting gives a tenderer and more flavorful product. Cook large pieces to just under their doneness temperature (about 10 to 25 Fahrenheit degrees under it), because the heat inside the item will continue to cook it after withdrawal from the oven. Foodservices commonly have special ovens for roasting.

Barbecuing involves roasting or broiling meat while basting it with a tangy sauce. The sauce is more clearly the indicator of the method than the cooking technique. Barbecued items are often cooked before, under, or beside an open fire or in a covered pit.

Frying is cooking in a thin layer of fat—the same technique that is used in sautéing. Pan-frying involves cooking in shallow fat, and grilling is the same except that the item is cooked on a griddle.

Deep-fat cooking is a method of cooking foods by immersing them in hot fat. The quality of the finished product depends on the frying temperature, the quality of the fat, and the quality of the food item itself. Many breaded or battered meat, poultry, or fish items are deep-fried. Fish responds especially well to deep-frying because it lacks fat, so the enriching by fat during frying helps give it palatability.

Ovenizing consists of placing items onto well-greased baking sheets or pans and then putting them into an oven to fry or sauté. The items should be drizzled with fat after being placed on well-greased pans. Oven temperatures should be 325° to 425°F (161° to 212°C). Ovenizing is most appropriate when large quantities are needed.

Flesh foods can be cooked by any of a number of moist-heat methods in which the quantity of moistness is controlled. Sometimes just enough moisture is used to tenderize the collagen, while in other cases the amount of moisture is almost enough to constitute stewing. Braising may also be called *stewing, pot-roasting, fricasséeing,* or *swissing.* Often a product is sautéed before it is braised. If this occurs, the product is called *brun;* if not, the product is called *blond.* Alternatively, marinating may occur before braising. If a flesh food is served in an earthenware casserole without vegetables, it is listed on the menu as *en casserole.* If it is served with vegetables, it is described as *en cocotte. Jugged* means braised in a pot. The word *poêler* means to brown well and then to braise in juices while basting with butter; the temperatures used in this process are high.

Containers should be well filled with meat so that moisture is built up inside. Add fat to cover the bottom, and heat; then add the product. Brown if the item is to be *brun*. Add moisture if needed, and add vegetables if desired. Simmer. When it is done, remove the meat and thicken the gravy. Put all together again, heat, and serve.

Many items in quantity are best braised in shallow steamed-jacketed kettles. To do this, heat the kettle with its cover down and steam on full; add some melted fat, and drop in evenly sized pieces of the meat or poultry (fish breaks up too much when treated this way). Turn the pieces every 15 to 25 minutes. Then add a small quantity of water or liquid, cover, reduce heat, and simmer.

Cooking items in water at just below the boiling point is called *simmering* or *poaching*. Few flesh foods are boiled, since this tends to toughen them. Simmering gives a more tender, moist, and flavorful product. To simmer, bring the water to a boil, add the product, and maintain the temperature at between 185° and 205°F (85° and 94.6°C). Test for doneness by inserting a fork about ½ inch deep and twisting. Do not overcook, as this gives a dry, shreddy meat. Skim and add liquid as necessary. Add vegetables 30 minutes before serving, or cook them separately and add at service. Meat may be sliced and kept warm in stock.

Meats, poultry, or fish may be steamed over rich stock—a process called *free-venting*. Steam pressure cooking reduces steaming time, making it easy to overcook products. Many items are given preliminary prebrowning and then are finished in a steam chamber. A court bouillon (flavored fish stock) is used for steaming fish; the aromatic steam rises and flavors the fish.

Dropping products momentarily into boiling or simmering water to give them partial cooking is called *blanching*. It is more a preparation than a method of cooking. Some cooks presoak items in cold, salted water before blanching them. Thus, sweetbreads would be soaked in this manner, and then their outer membranes would be removed,

before the actual cooking began. Brains and sweetbreads are blanched in slightly acidulated water to whiten them.

Frozen Meat Cookery

Meats, fish, and poultry are frozen rapidly to produce small crystal growth and to protect the meat fibers from rupture. Slow freezing causes a breakdown of the fibers and a greater loss of drip upon thawing. Frozen items can generally be cooked in the same ways as nonfrozen ones. Better flavor and higher nutrient values result if meat is cooked directly from the frozen or partially frozen state rather than from the thawed state, but sometimes this is not possible. Partial thawing, followed by cooking, reduces cooking time. Hard-frozen products take about three times longer to roast than refrigerated products do.

For roasting, put frozen roasts fat-side-up and roast in a 325°F (161°C) oven. Cook until thawed; then insert a thermometer, and roast at 300°F (147°C) until done. Thin frozen items take only slightly longer to cook than do regular unfrozen ones, but thicker frozen items need two to three times as much cooking time.

To broil, place thin or medium-thick frozen pieces 4 inches from the heat source; place thicker pieces 8 to 12 inches from the heat. Reduce the heat to thaw, and then cook as for regular items. To pan-broil, place frozen items in an ungreased pan on fairly low heat, and cover until thawed or almost thawed; then cook them in the same way as regular items are cooked. If thick frozen items are dropped into 325°F (161°C) fat, the fat speeds thawing without overcooking the outside. Sautéing may be preferred to pan-broiling because it thaws foods more rapidly, but lower temperatures must be used at the start. To sauté frozen breaded items, partially thaw them first. Braising small frozen pieces is done the same as with unfrozen items. If frozen pieces can be separated, they may be dredged with flour before being browned. Otherwise they must be thawed first. Simmering frozen items differs little from simmering unfrozen items.

To thaw frozen food, leave it wrapped under

refrigeration; thawing takes 1½ hours per lb. Thawing at room temperature takes about 1 hour per lb. If the food is put in front of an electric fan, time is reduced. Items in waterproof wraps can be thawed in a basin of cold water or under running cold water, but this cannot be done if the food is unwrapped. Thawing in water takes about 1 hour per lb.

Poultry

Unfrozen poultry should be received at a temperature below 40°F (4.4°C) and stored at a temperature below 34°F (1.2°C). Hold frozen poultry at 0°F (−17.6°C); it holds well for about 8 months at this temperature, but at 20°F (−6.6°C) it holds for only 2 to 4 months. To thaw, place the frozen poultry in a 40°F (4.4°C) area. Small birds thaw in 1 to 2 days, but larger ones take 2 to 4 days. Thaw poultry in moisture-proof wraps under water—1 to 2 hours for chickens, and 2 to 6 hours for turkeys. To speed thawing, remove the giblets and neck as soon as possible, and spread the legs and wings. Cut-up poultry can be separated as soon as it is crinkly. Wash thawed birds in cold water, drain, and prepare them for cooking. Avoid refreezing.

Poultry should be cooked in the same ways as meat. Low-temperature cooking at 250°F (120°C) results in less shrinkage and a moister, better-looking finished bird. Cook old birds in moist heat and young ones in dry heat. Most poultry is cooked to well done except (sometimes) duck. Small birds such as squab and quail are best baked at tempera-tures around 400°F (202.4°C), to reduce drying out. Rabbit should be cooked just as poultry is.

Turkeys weighing over 18 lb have a skeletal structure that accounts for 9 percent of their weight, and they have about the same size abdominal cavity as 18-lb birds, so purchasing birds weighing more than 18 lb gives a greater yield of servable meat per lb purchased (see table 12-7). Four portions, with bone and skin, are obtained from a 3½-lb duckling. A 2½-lb chicken, without neck or giblets, gives four cooked portions of 6 to 7 oz each. About 12 oz AP of turkey provides a good portion.

To roast poultry, truss the legs and wings of small birds, but not of large ones. Season the birds inside and out. Place the birds breast-side-down until they are almost done; then turn them and brown the breasts, if they are to be carved in front of guests. Geese and ducks can be roasted breast up. Place chickens and ducks in a preheated 325°F (161°C) oven. When they are done enough to allow it, break away the legs so that heat can penetrate around the thighs; this speeds roasting. Roasting times in an oven heated to 325°F (161°C) are listed in table 12-8. Roast large birds at 250°F (120°C). Doneness is signaled by a temperature of about 180°F (81.4°C) in the thigh or breast center. Some cooks roast large, tender birds until only slightly underdone, and then cool and slice them. The slices are placed over mounds of dressing—dark meat first, covered with broad slices of white meat. The platter is covered with a moist cloth and refrigerated. When ordered, the sliced meat is warmed in an oven or

Table 12-7. Portion Yields of Turkeys of Different Weights

Dressed Weight (lb)	Loss to Ready-to-Cook	Ready-to-Cook Weight (lb)	Sliceable Meat Cooked (lb)	Number of Portions		
				2-oz	3-oz	4-oz
12 to 14	15%	10 to 12	4½	36	22	12
14 to 16	15%	12 to 14	4½	42	26	15
16 to 18	15%	14 to 16	6	48	30	18
18 to 20	15%	16 to 17	6⅔	54	32	20
20 to 22	15%	17 to 18	7⅓	59	37	23
22 to 24	15%	18 to 20	8	64	40	25
30 to 35	13%	26 to 30	13½	108	67	40

steamer and served, one mound per plate, covered with very hot gravy. Roasting and then chilling before carving gives a greater yield. Figure 12-9 illustrates how to cut up a cooked bird.

Poach-roasting is a method in which poultry parts are placed into pans skin-side-up and then covered with water to about two-thirds of their height. The procedure for cutting up a turkey for poach-roasting is illustrated in figure 12-10. Bones are left in. The parts are seasoned lightly and roasted in a 325°F (161°C) oven until tender. The product is allowed to cool in the stock. Alternatively, poultry may be

a.

b.

c.

Figure 12-9. Basic chicken cuts: (a) wing cut; (b) leg cut; (c) breast cut.

Table 12-8. Timetable for Roasting Poultry in a 325°F Oven

Ready-to-Cook Weight (lb)	Approximate Minutes (per lb)	Total (hr)
1⅓ to 2½	30 to 40	1 to 1¾
2½ to 3½	30 to 40	1½ to 2½
3½ to 4¾	30 to 40	2 to 3
4¾ to 6	30 to 40	3 to 3½
6 to 8	30 to 40	3½ to 4
8 to 10	25 to 30	4 to 4½
10 to 14	18 to 20	3½ to 4
14 to 18	15 to 18	4 to 4½
20 to 30	12 to 15	5 to 6

NOTE: Ready-to-cook weights are for unstuffed birds.

poached in water sufficient to cover it. Large birds are sectioned and boned before poaching. To poach poultry, place parts in a stock pot, roasting pan, or steam-jacketed kettle, and cover with hot, salted water or stock, using 1 Tbsp of salt and 1 tsp of white pepper for every 6 lb of bird. Simmer at low heat for about 2 to 2½ hours, or until fork tender. Let it cool in the stock. Remove, and chill covered. Then slice (on a machine, preferably). Use the meat and stock within three days. If desired, add some vegetables for seasoning.

Older birds may be steamed. The bird, whole or in parts, is placed into a pan with a small quantity of water and steamed until tender. Like red meat, poultry can also be braised. Fricasséed or stewed poultry is braised poultry. Both tender and tough birds can be prepared in this way. Frying or sautéing poultry proceeds in much the same way as for meat.

Seafood

The flesh of seafood contains little connective tissue, so it cooks to tenderness quickly. Extended cooking toughens some shellfish, such as clams, oysters, and shrimp. Overcooked fish is dry and breaks up easily.

Seafood is a highly perishable product. It keeps well under refrigeration for about three to five days. Use it as soon as possible after thawing. Sometimes products can be cooked directly from the frozen state, which saves nutrients by avoiding drip loss and also retains more flavor.

About 4 to 5 oz of fish is enough for a portion, if clear meat is used (see table 12-9); but if there is much bone and skin, larger portions are required. Fish flesh contains from 1 to 20 percent oil, which is spread throughout. Fat fish such as salmon, mackerel, shad, and trout bake, broil, or poach well. Lean fish such as flounder, halibut, and cod are best poached, deep-fried, sautéed, or simmered; sauces are often added to these to increase their richness and moistness. Lean fish is frequently breaded or batter-dipped for sautéing or deep-frying. Higher baking temperatures help keep small fish from drying out. If lean fish is baked, either it or the baking pan must be covered with fat. Lean fish can be broiled if dipped into flour and basted frequently. Cooking in a grid helps keep the fish from breaking up. Seafood is sautéed in slightly more fat than are meats and poultry—especially lean fish, which is often floured lightly. Serve sautéed fish as soon as possible, since quality is lost in standing. To simmer or poach, barely cover the fish with liquid and cook gently.

Any large fish should be cooked in a cloth so that it can be raised easily; a lightly greased trivet with handles can also be used for this purpose. If the fish is to be served cold or decorated, allow it to cool in its own stock. This means removing the fish from the heat before cooking is complete, because otherwise overcooking will occur during standing. Large

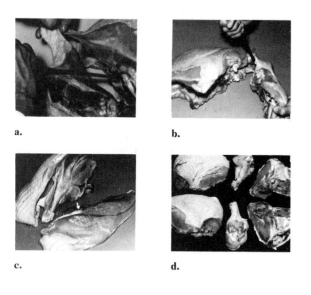

a.

b.

c.

d.

Figure 12-10. Preparing a turkey for poach-roasting: (a) remove the legs and wings; (b) remove the back; (c) separate the breast from the breastbone; (d) retain legs, thighs, and breast for poach-roasting.

Table 12-9(a). Portion Size and Amounts for 100 Portions of Seafood

Species	Serving Size (EP)	Approximate Weight for 100 Portions (EP)
Fish		
Dressed	8 oz	50 lb
Pan-dressed	8 oz	50 lb
Steaks	6½ oz	40 lb
Fillets	5 oz	32 lb
Portions	5 oz	32 lb
Sticks	5 oz	32 lb
Shellfish		
Clams—live, shucked	3 oz	19 lb
Crabs—live, soft-shell	5 oz	32 lb
Lobsters—live	1½ lb	100 lobsters
Spiny lobster tails—frozen	6 oz	100 tails
Oysters—live, shucked	3 oz	19 lb
Scallops—shucked	4 oz	25 lb
Shrimp—headless, raw; headless, raw, peeled	5 oz	32 lb

Table 12-9(b). Time and Temperature for Various Methods of Cooking Seafood

Baking		Broiling		Boiling, Poaching or Steaming	
Temperature	*Minutes*	*Distance From Heat*	*Minutes*	*Method*	*Minutes*
350°F	40 to 60			Poach	10/lb
350°F	25 to 30	3 in	10 to 15	Poach	10
350°F	25 to 35	3 in	10 to 15	Poach	10
350°F	25 to 35	3 in	8 to 15	Poach	10
350°F	30 to 40				
400°F	15 to 20				
450°F	12 to 15	4 in	5 to 8	Steam	5 to 10
		4 in	8 to 10	Boil	10 to 15
400°F	15 to 20	4 in	12 to 15	Boil	15 to 20
450°F	20 to 30	4 in	8 to 12	Boil	10 to 15
450°F	12 to 15	4 in	5 to 8	Steam	5 to 10
350°F	25 to 30	3 in	6 to 8	Boil	3 to 4
				Boil	3 to 5
350°F	20 to 25	3 in	8 to 10	Boil	3 to 5

Table 12-9(b). *(cont.)*

Deep-fat Frying		Pan Frying		Ovenizing	
Temperature	*Minutes*	*Temperature*	*Minutes*	*Temperature*	*Minutes*
325 to 350°F	4 to 6				
350 to 375°F	2 to 4	Moderate	10 to 15	500°	15-20
350 to 375°F	2 to 4	Moderate	10 to 15	500°	10-15
350 to 375°F	2 to 4	Moderate	8 to 10	500°	10-15
350°F	4	Moderate	8 to 10		
350°F	3	Moderate	8 to 10		
350°F	2 to 3	Moderate	4 to 5		
375°F	2 to 4	Moderate	8 to 10		
350°F	2 to 4	Moderate	8 to 10		
350°F	3 to 5	Moderate	8 to 10		
350°F	2 to 3	Moderate	4 to 5		
350°F	2 to 3	Moderate	4 to 6		
350°F	2 to 3	Moderate	8 to 10		

To convert to degrees Celsius, remember
350°F = 177°C
375°F = 191°C
400°F = 204°C
450°F = 232°C
500°F = 260°C

fish and pieces are best started in cold water. Strong-flavored fish is also best started cold. Put small pieces into barely boiling liquid, reduce the heat to a simmer, and cook until done—about 8 to 10 minutes. Some types of white-fleshed fish are baked in milk. Fish is steamed until just done, usually over a court bouillon. Steamed, simmered, or poached fish is good served cold—especially a fat fish such as salmon.

A *matelote* is a fish braised with vegetables and lightly thickened stock. *Bouillabaisse* and *chioppino* are fish stews served with the stock, together or in separate bowls. Few seafoods are braised, since fish are so tender that they break up under this treatment, and since shellfish get tough with the longer cooking given in braising. When seafood is braised, wine, court bouillon, or some other liquid is added to it. Because of the short cooking time,

the cover is left off so that as much evaporation as possible takes place.

Shellfish can be cooked in a number of ways with good results (see table 12-10). If cooked at too high a temperature or for too long, however, they become tough and rubbery. Simmering at 190°F (87°C) is preferable to boiling; a temperature of 140°F (59.4°C) immediately kills shellfish. Simmer lobsters in 205°F (95.2°C) water to get a tender and flavorful item. *Do not overcook.*

Shrimp can be cooked either shelled or unshelled. Prepare unshelled cooked shrimp by peeling off the shell and cutting along the back to remove the vein; then wash. To cook shrimp, use ¼ cup of salt to 1 gal of water and 5 lb of raw, headless shrimp. The yield after cooking, peeling, and deveining is 50 percent. *PDQ* shrimp stands for *peeled, deveined,* and *quick-cooked* shrimp. They may be purchased

Table 12-10. Preferred Ways to Cook Shellfish

	Form	Description	Best Ways to Cook
	Clams, shucked (fresh or frozen)	Removed from shell	Bake, deep-fry, pan-fry, poach, steam
	Crabs, in-shell (fresh or frozen)	Raw or cooked	Pan-fry, poach, steam
	Crabs, out-of-shell (fresh, frozen, or canned)	Raw or cooked	Pan-fry, poach, steam (thaw for cooking)
	Lobster tail (fresh or frozen)	Meat from the tail of the lobster; usually sold in shell	Bake, broil, poach, steam
	Mussels, shucked (fresh or frozen)	Removed from shell	Deep-fry, pan-fry, poach, steam
	Oysters, shucked (fresh or frozen)	Removed from shell	Bake, deep-fry, pan-fry, steam
	Scallops, shucked (fresh or frozen)	Removed from shell	Bake, deep-fry, pan-fry, poach, steam
	Shrimp, head-less (fresh or frozen)	Raw, in-shell shrimps	Bake, broil, deep-fry, ovenize, pan-fry, poach
	Shrimp, peeled (fresh or frozen)	Used to describe shrimp from which shell has been removed	Bake, broil, deep-fry, ovenize, pan-fry, poach
	Shrimp, deveined (fresh or frozen)	Peeled shrimp from which the black sand vein has been removed	Bake, broil, deep-fry, ovenize, pan-fry, steam
	Shrimp, cooked, peeled, and deveined (fresh or frozen)	Cooked	Thaw for cocktail

fresh or frozen; the federal government allows a 6 percent water glaze to be added, but no more should be present.

Wash clams and oysters in the shell thoroughly, using a stiff brush. To rid clams of sand, add ⅓ cup of salt per gallon of tap water; soak for an hour or so, and wash. Repeat until they are sand-free. Some cooks put clams into salted water, add cornmeal, and leave them overnight under refrigeration. The live clams eat the cornmeal and disgorge the sand. To steam clams, use six to eight clams (¾ lb) per portion. Place them into a container with a perforated bottom containing ½ cup of water per lb of clams. Steam for 5 to 10 minutes or until partially opened. Serve on a plate, with the clam nectar in a cup and a side dish of melted clarified butter. To roast clams or oysters, place them in a 450°F (230°C) oven for 15 minutes or until they are open. Bake or barbecue in the half-shell. Poach lobster tails for 5 minutes in salted water; then split them and broil for 5 to 6 minutes. To reduce curling of the tail, thaw and split; then remove the thin undershell, and bend the tail back firmly, breaking the connective tissue that causes curling.

MANAGEMENT CONTROLS

Since meat, seafood, and poultry items make up the most important part of menu offerings, much care must be given to their selection, handling, storage, preparation, service, and merchandising. It is management's responsibility to see that the desired standards are achieved in these areas. Management should select competent workers to bring the goals to a satisfactory conclusion. It should recognize and select items popular with patrons, as well as those it can produce well and profitably. Specifications should follow through on management's thinking, and receiving procedures should ensure that the right goods are obtained and that management's interests are protected. Storage, handling, and issuing accountability must be present. Good recipes should be used and properly executed. Portion control must be established. Forecasts of quantities needed should be accurately calculated

so that waste or carry-over is minimized. Service should be in keeping with the high standards established in the other areas. Good sanitation is essential and should be carried to a point where patrons and employees are assured of adequate protection. Meat, seafood, and poultry are highly perishable products and require special attention if they are to be good and safe to eat.

Pricing should be based on good recipe yields or yield tests (see fig. 12-11). Good accounting procedures should give management knowledge of the cost and profitability of items. Menu offerings should be properly balanced among meat, seafood, and poultry items. The program designed to offer these items should extend year-round. They are too important to the success of an operation for the program to be any less comprehensive.

Poultry is an item that is growing in popularity. It is low in cost and provides good protein, vitamins, and minerals. It is usually low in calories, cholesterol, and saturated fats. Ways should be found to serve the item in a manner that differs from those usually presented in the home, since poultry is today a frequent item on the family menu. Seafood is also popular, for reasons of health and taste. Fish is low in saturated fats and cholesterol. Shellfish is low in saturated fats but has fairly large amounts of cholesterol. The caloric yield is not high if the

ITEM:	DATE:	CARD NO.
		%
	Quantity	100
Gross Weight		
Preparation Loss (Trimming Waste)		
Cooking Loss (Shrinkage)		
Serving Loss (Slicing Loss & Tasting)		
Net Yield		

Figure 12-11. Sample yield test card.

seafood is prepared in a manner that does not add a lot of calories. Many high-quality frozen items are now on the market, so foodservices far from fresh supplies can still serve high-quality items. Meats are still the most frequently selected menu items. They provide an excellent source of protein and yield a good supply of important minerals and vitamins. In the future, while patrons may avoid red meats in general in their diets, they may throw their dietary restrictions out the window when they go out to eat, and select what they miss; thus, meat may still continue to be the most selected item on the menu.

SUMMARY

Meat, seafood, and poultry are prepared and cooked by similar methods. All are usually the center of a meal and supply valuable nutrients. Meat and poultry animals are separated by age and sex. Selection by class is necessary to suit the cooking process. Fish and shellfish are only selected by kind, except some few such as littlenecks, cherrystones, or chowder (quahog) clams of the New England variety; their classification is by size. Cod is sometimes separated by size, too, into scrod and cod; and lobsters are as well. A chicken lobster weighs around 1 lb and makes a good portion.

Meats and poultry are graded. Some meats are graded both for quality and for yield. It is important to know the cuts of meat in order to cook them properly. Some meats from the less extensively used muscles are especially tender; meat from young animals is also apt to be more tender. Tenderness depends on the cooking method, the age and cut of the animal, the tenderizer used (such as papain), and the mechanical treatment of the item (if any), such as grinding, cubing, or pounding. Meats and poultry must be inspected for wholesomeness. Grading for quality or yield is not mandatory, but inspection for wholesomeness is.

Meat, seafood, and poultry are highly perishable products and need care in handling, storage, and cooking. Cooking makes these items more palatable by causing flavor, texture, and color changes.

The color of flesh changes in cooking. Myoglobin, the pigment in red meat, changes into hematin; other flesh—such as the breast of chicken or the flesh of fish—also changes color, but not from red to the gray color seen in cooked meat. Cooking can tenderize flesh but it can also toughen it, especially if the item is cooked too long or at too high a temperature. Myoglobin reacts differently depending on handling and cooking, so some color changes in meat may not follow the pattern of cooking to a gray doneness. Flesh heated to 160°F (71°C) changes color, and the protein it contains coagulates and denatures. Coagulation is a firming process, and denaturation is the loss of water. High cooking temperatures cause greater denaturation than lower ones.

Connective tissue in flesh is the major cause of toughness. Flesh that has little connective tissue (such as that in young animals, birds, and fish) is more tender. Older animals and muscles that get quite a bit of exercise contain more connective tissue and therefore are apt to be more tough, requiring a cooking method that tenderizes. The connective tissue known as *collagen* is tenderized by long, moist cooking. The connective tissue called *elastin* is not affected by cooking and must be broken down by mechanical means or by using a tenderizer. Flesh gets more tender with aging. The flavor of meat comes from nitrogenous and nonnitrogenous fractions. The fat in flesh also carries much flavor, since flavor esters are absorbed into it. Fat contains from 15 to 50 percent moisture, which helps it keep meat moist in cooking.

Stages of doneness in most flesh are as follows: rare, 140°F (59.4°C); medium, 160°F (70.4°C); and well done, 175°F (78.6°C). Poultry and pork are usually cooked to well done. Seafood is just cooked to doneness. Some meats are cooked rare or medium.

Meat and poultry are cooked by dry-heat and moist-heat methods. Dry-heat methods include broiling, roasting or baking, barbecuing, sautéing, pan-frying or grilling, deep-frying, and ovenizing. Moist-heat methods include braising (pot-roasting, fricasséeing, casseroling, swissing, or stewing), simmering (poaching or stewing), steaming, and blanching. Moist-heat methods usually require a long cooking time to allow the moisture and heat to break down connective tissue. Frozen meat may be cooked from either the frozen state or the thawed state. If flesh is cooked after thawing, the cooking procedure is much the same as for regular products.

Meat is broiled by radiant heat. Only tender and fairly well-marbled meats broil well. Lean meats must be basted well during broiling to prevent them from drying out. Pan-broiling is a method of frying in a hot pan or griddle without any fat. Sautéing involves cooking in shallow fat. Deep-fat-fried meats are usually breaded or batter-dipped. Roasting or baking is done in dry heat. Some products such as veal can be roasted covered to help retain moistness (since veal is quite lean). Barbecuing often consists of broiling over coals or a flame while basting with a tangy sauce. It can also be done in an oven. Ovenizing is a method in which items are placed onto well-greased pans, drizzled with fat, and then baked in an oven at fairly high heat. The product comes out much as if it had been sautéed. The method can be used to produce a lot of items at one time.

Meat may be prebrowned before braising, or it may be braised without browning. The meat is allowed to form its own juices, and liquid may also be added. The item is cooked for a long time covered. Pot-roasting, fricasséeing, casseroling, swissing, and stewing are all forms of braising. Blanching, poaching, and stewing all involve cooking in a small quantity of water. The difference is that blanching occurs for a very short time, stewing occurs for a long time, and poaching is cooking only to doneness. To boil is to cook in boiling water—a method infrequently used in meat cookery. Steaming is just what it says: cooking in steam.

Poultry is cooked in much the same way as meat. Poach-roasting is often used for turkey. The bird is divided into pieces, placed into water that nearly covers it, and cooked in an oven. Turkey can also be simmered, sliced, and served as roasted turkey. Birds cooked in water are often allowed to cool in the stock to prevent them from drying out. Tough poultry is cooked by moist-heat methods.

The methods used to cook seafood depend on the amount of oil in the flesh. Fatty fish broil, steam, poach, or bake well. Lean fish are often sautéed, deep-fried, poached, or steamed. Steaming is done over a court bouillon. All fish are cooked only to doneness. Shellfish are toughened by extended cooking, especially at high heat.

Meat, poultry, and seafood must be well merchandized to meet patron favor. Good merchandising must be backed up with good menu planning and presentation, good purchasing and storage methods, good preparation, and good service.

CHAPTER REVIEW QUESTIONS

1. You are the owner of a very popular restaurant. You have a chef who is well known for his excellent food. The instructor of the quantity food class at the local university has invited you and the chef to come to the school and tell the class how you achieve such high standards in the preparation of meats, seafood, and poultry. The talk is to be for two school class hours (100 minutes), and you and the chef decide to split the time, leaving some time after each talk for questions. Make an outline of what management presents as its way of achieving high standards in the production and service of these foods, and make another outline of what the chef feels are the essentials in achieving high standards. Since time is limited, there can be little or no demonstration—just a straight lecture.
2. Why are seafoods considered healthful? Can a person on a low-saturated-fat diet eat both shellfish and fish? Can one on a low-cholesterol diet?
3. What quality factors should be checked when receiving fish and shellfish? What are the various market forms of fish? What are the various market forms of shellfish? Are all seafood products inspected and passed for wholesomeness?
4. What are the different cooking methods suited to lean fish? to fat fish?

5. Why are cooking times and temperatures so important in cooking fish and shellfish?
6. Why should meat be in a person's diet? Name some of the important nutrients meat supplies.
7. Define what each of the following is on the market: veal, calf, steer, heifer, cow, lamb, barrow, gilt, yearling, mutton, and ewe.
8. Should a foodservice heart of the house today be designed with a complete butcher shop? Explain.
9. Where are the most tender cuts on an animal? Are muscles that get a lot of exercise apt to be tougher or tenderer than those that get little exercise? What steps can be taken to make meat tender in handling or cooking?
10. What is meant by *moist-heat methods*? Name four of them. What is meant by *dry-heat cookery*? Name five dry-heat methods.
11. What are the interior temperatures when meat is rare, medium done, and well done?
12. What is aged or ripened meat?
13. What are some of the guidelines for handling and cooking frozen meat? frozen poultry?
14. How can portion control be achieved in the production and service of meat, seafoods, and poultry?
15. A steak dinner costs $9.80, and a chicken dinner costs $7.50. The food costs are, respectively, $3.10 and $2.00. If the desired food cost is 30 percent of menu price, why has management priced these foods as it has? Which item offers the best gross profit, in dollars? Would management wish to sell steaks or chicken, based on this difference in gross profit?
16. How do meat, seafoods, and poultry compare in nutritive value?
17. What are the kinds and classes of poultry?
18. What type of chicken should be used to make a roast chicken?
19. What is the top grade for poultry?
20. What are the various methods used in foodservices to cook poultry? How should an old tom turkey be prepared?
21. What are the market forms of fresh poultry?
22. What is management's responsibility in seeing that good meat, seafoods, and poultry are put before patrons?

VOCABULARY

Cholesterol
Saturated fat
Complete protein
Seafood
Shellfish
Fish
Crustacean
Mollusk
Chicken lobster
Fillet
PDQ
Flounder
Sole
Salmon
Fat fish
Lean fish
Round (whole) fish
Steak
Butterfly
Deveined
Cherrystone
Littleneck
Bluepoint
Rooster
Tom
Ready-to-cook
Eviscerated
U.S. Grade A
Chincoteague
Olympia
Bay scallop
Sea scallop
Snapper
Court bouillon
Trivet
Double grid
Dungeness
Blue crab

Yearling
Mutton
Ram
Ewe
Barrow
Gilt
Sow
Boar
Prime
Choice
Select
Standard
Yield grading
Quality grading
Rib
Round
Sirloin
Flank
Chuck
Shank
Short loin
Plate
Strip (loin eye)
Braise
Simmer
Boil
Steam
Blanch
Breast
Leg
Ham
Jowl
Spareribs
Ripening (aging)
Connective tissue
Elastin
Collagen
Papain

King (Alaskan) crab
Stone crab
Glazing
IMPS
Marbling
Variety meats
Bullock
Steer
Heifer
Veal
Calf
Stag
Cow
Lamb
Roast
Sauté
Deep-fry
Barbecue
Ovenize

Marinating
Shrinkage
Myoglobin
Nitrosomyoglobin
Oxymyoglobin
Metamyoglobin
Duckling
Squab
Rock Cornish hen
Fryer
Roaster
Capon
Hen (fowl)
Broil
Poach-roast
Dry-heat cooking
Moist-heat cooking
Conformation

Annotated References

American Home Economics Association. 1975. *Handbook of Food Preparation,* pp. 39-46, 68-75. Washington, D.C.: American Home Economics Association. (Market forms and grades of fish and meats, plus some cooking methods.)

Casola, M. 1969. *Successful Mass Cookery and Volume Feeding.* pp. 96-111. Rochelle Park, N.J.: Ahrens Publishing. (Recipes and information on poultry preparation.)

Chemical Publishing. 1967. *Fish Handling & Processing.* New York: Chemical Publishing. (Fish handling, processing, and marketing.)

Folsom, L. A., 1974. *The Professional Chef,* pp. 29-170. Boston: CBI Publishing. (Preparation techniques and cooking methods for meats, poultry, and fish, with recipes.)

Haines, R. G. 1973. *Food Preparation for Hotels, Restaurants, and Cafeterias,* pp. 324-519. Chicago: American Technical Society. (Recipes and illustrated preparation techniques for meats and fish.)

Howe, R. 1970. *Poultry and Game.* New York: Drake Publishers. (General instructions and recipes for poultry.)

Kotschevar, L. H. 1988. *Quantity Food Production.* 4th ed, pp. 270-303. New York: Van Nostrand Reinhold. (Meats, fish, and poultry.)

Lawrie, R. A., 1974. *Meat Science,* pp. 190-357. Elmsford, N.Y.: Pergamon Press. (The storage and preservation of meat, its eating quality, and meat and human nutrition.)

Levie, A. 1967. *The Meat Handbook.* Westport, Conn.: AVI Publishing. (Total investigation of meat for the foodservice industry, locker plant, and meat retailers.)

Lundberg, D. E., and Kotschevar, L. H., 1986. *Understanding Cooking,* 4th ed. pp. 80-153. Holyoke, Mass.: Marcus Publishing. (Meat, poultry, fish, and shellfish cookery.)

Miloradovich, M. 1970. *The Art of Fish Cookery.* New York: Doubleday. (Instruction and recipes for the proper cooking of various fish.)

Mountney, G. J., 1966. *Poultry Products Technology,* pp. 228-45. Westport, Conn.: AVI Publishing. (Barbecuing poultry, as well as other cooking methods.)

National Association of Meat Purveyors. 1973. *Meat Buyer's Guide to Standardized Meat Cuts.* Tucson, Ariz.: National Association of Meat Purveyors. (Specific cuts of meat, pictured and described.)

National Live Stock and Meat Board. 1974. *Lessons on Meat.* Chicago: National Live Stock and Meat Board. (Charts, tables, figures, and other information on meats.)

———. 1975. *Meat in the Foodservice Industry.* Chicago: National Live Stock and Meat Board. (Presents a systematic approach to all facets of meat preparation.)

Simms, A. E. 1973. *Fish and Shellfish.* Surrey, England: Virtue & Company. (Preparation techniques, recipes, and pictures of many fish and shellfish.)

Terrell, M. E., 1971. *Professional Food Preparation,* pp. 372-459. New York: John Wiley & Sons. (Selection and preparation of beef, veal, lamb, pork, and variety meats.)

Treat, N., and Richards, L. 1966. *Quantity Cookery,* pp. 232-62. Boston: Little, Brown. (Recipes for cooking poultry in quantity.)

West, B. B.; Wood, L.; and Harger, V. F. 1966. *Food Service in Institutions,* pp. 109-18, 218-26. New York: John Wiley & Sons. (Many different aspects of poultry preparation.)

Ziegler, P. T. 1968. *The Meat We Eat.* Danville, Ill: Interstate. (The processing and handling of meats.)

CHAPTER 13

The Bakery

OUTLINE

I. Ingredients
   A. Flour
      1. Gluten
      2. Bread (Hard-wheat) Flour
      3. Pastry (Soft-wheat) Flour
      4. All-purpose flour
   B. Shortening
   C. Sugar
   D. Leavening Agents
      1. Air
      2. Steam
      3. Chemical Leaveners
      4. Yeast
   E. Eggs
   F. Liquids
   G. Flavorings and Spices

II. Breads
   A. Yeast Breads
   B. Quick Breads
III. Desserts
   A. Cakes
   B. Cookies
   C. Egg-thickened Desserts
   D. Fried Desserts
   E. Frozen Desserts
   F. Fruit Desserts
   G. Gelatin Desserts
   H. Pies and Pastries
      1. Pie Crust
      2. Production Methods
      3. Pie Fillings
      4. Pastries
   I. Puddings
      1. Steamed (Boiled) Puddings
      2. Starch-thickened Puddings

Good hot breads and desserts are appreciated by patrons and can do much to draw business. Sweet breads, muffins, or rolls enhance a breakfast; and a baked dessert provides an excellent conclusion to a meal. Many operations try to emphasize bakery products because of their appeal and profitability.

INGREDIENTS

The ingredients used in baking are critical to product quality. Bakers must know what ingredients do and how they interact to produce high-quality goods. Handling the proper ingredients in the proper manner brings baking success.

Flour

For baking purposes, *flour* can be defined as a ground starch product that is used to give structure and body to bakery products. Different flours are needed to make the many products produced, and different wheats are blended to produce the kind of flour needed. Regular flour contains from 63 to 73 percent starch and from 7 to 15 percent protein. The rest consists of moisture and small amounts of fat, sugar, and ash (minerals). Varying the relative amounts of starch and protein dramatically affects how flour acts in baking.

When wheat is milled to make flour, patent flours come off first, then middlings, and then clears. Patent flours are of the highest quality, middlings are next, and clears are the poorest. Straight flour is all the flour from the kernel. Whole-wheat (graham) flour is straight flour plus some of the bran. Good patents are mixed with rye, straight flour, or poor flours to make them work properly.

Gluten

Flour protein is called *gluten*. It can absorb twice its own weight in moisture. Moistened gluten is sticky, and in a batter of dough it forms a thin, gummy, stringy mass that can stretch out, giving elasticity to the mixture. Working a dough or batter forms a network of gluten throughout the mixture. Baking firms this network and helps support the baked item. Some products, such as yeast bread, need a strong network; others, such as cake, need a weaker one. Mixing a dough or batter helps gluten develop, which is desirable in bread but not in muffins. Bread or hard-wheat flour is called *strong* because it forms strong structures. Pastry or soft-wheat flour is called *weak* because it produces more tender and delicate structures.

Bread (Hard-wheat) Flour

Hard or spring wheat contains from 65 to 70 percent starch and from 12 to 16 percent gluten. The high protein content (plus good-quality protein) allows it to make strong structures that yeast breads and some pastry products need. Most bread flours contain from 12.5 to 12.8 percent gluten. Hard-crusted breads and hearth breads need a 13 percent gluten flour; a strong patent flour containing about 15.5 percent protein is blended with rye and other flours that need gluten.

Pastry (Soft-wheat) Flour

Wheat that is planted in the fall and matures in early summer is called *winter wheat*. It develops less gluten and more starch than hard wheat, and its gluten is not as strong as that of spring or hard wheat. Cake flour contains from 7 to 8 percent protein. The patents of soft wheat make the best pastry and cake flours. A weaker gluten is desirable for making cakes, cookies, hot breads, and pies. A cake flour contains enough gluten to give a weak structure that suffices to support the sugar, fat, and other ingredients blended with it. A fine cake flour gives a tender, velvety crumb.

A soft flour holds together when squeezed in the hand, but hard-wheat flour crumbles. Hard-wheat flour is yellowish because gluten is a faintly yellow color. If 2½ oz of cornstarch is added to 14 oz of hard-wheat flour, the mixture approximates a soft wheat flour in its structural characteristics.

All-purpose Flour

All-purpose flour falls between soft- and hard-wheat flour in gluten content. It makes fair bread, cakes, and pastries but is not really suited to quantity work. It is designed for use in the home.

Shortening

Shortening is a fat used in baking to lubricate ingredients and prevent products from sticking. Shortening interferes with gluten particles' sticking together and thus makes a short dough. It also provides slip, which is needed so that batters or doughs can move when leavening gases start to push them. Different shortenings are used in baking: a short one makes pie crusts and other products tender, while an elastic fat makes a good puff paste. Cakes need a fat that spreads easily and quickly in a batter; emulsifiers such as monoglycerides and diglycerides are used to do this in cake shortenings. Special margarines or shortenings are used for frostings, icings, and special products needing butter.

The development of hydrogenation was an important step in shortening development, since it made oils solid, thus increasing their plasticity and firmness and giving them moldability and workability over a wider range of temperatures. A plastic shortening should be medium firm—not brittle or oily—and must hold texture over a 55° to 90°F (13° to 32.2°C) range. Most hydrogenated shortenings have a relatively short plastic range but are especially made to be of superb plasticity. A waxy, tough, extensible, plastic, firm fat is needed to produce a flaky pie crust so that, when the dough is rolled out, layers of fat remain between layers of the dough (see fig. 13-1). Lard is an excellent fat to use for making pie crusts; its waxiness and plasticity spread it out in pieces or layers, giving good shortness. It remains sufficiently firm at mixing temperature so that it does not work completely into the dough. Icings need a flavorless, plastic fat that creams (aerates) well, has no greasiness, and holds a lot of sugar. For some cakes, plasticity and waxiness are needed so that air is incorporated, increasing volume and creating a light batter. Plasticity and shortness are related, since fats lacking plasticity may not spread well and therefore may not shorten the gluten. Tallow (beef suet) and oleo are too firm and brittle to spread well. Chicken fat has excellent shortening power but is too soft to use in many products.

Sugar

Sugar is used to sweeten and also to tenderize products. It gives color and texture to baked goods and adds calories. The bakeshop uses many different sugars. Powdered sugar (ground sugar) is used for dusting, icing, or coating items. The "X" on a sugar label indicates the grind fineness, with 4X to 10X sugars being the ones most often used; 10X is the finest. Coarse sanding sugars are used for coating doughnuts, candies, orange peel, and so on. Regular granulated sugar has a moderate-size crystal. Fruit sugar is fine granulated sugar used for making cakes, meringues, and other bakery products; it goes into solution rapidly. Angel and sponge cakes are best made with fruit sugar. Fondants and other products high in sugar content are also available on the market.

Brown sugar is less refined than white sugar. It ranges in color from very light to very dark and is used in different ways to achieve different results. The darker brown sugars give a stronger, richer flavor and a moister product. Molasses is a syrup that is a by-product of white cane sugar. Like brown sugar, molasses may range from light to dark; a darker molasses gives a moister product with a rich, heavy flavor. Honey and some other sweeteners are sometimes used for special needs.

Leavening Agents

A leavening agent aerates bakery goods, giving them an open, light texture and greater volume. The kind used, the amount, and the other ingredients in the product all influence how much rise occurs. Insufficient amounts of leavening in a product give a poor, heavy, coarse crumb and poor volume. As a result, the finished product is too compact to be of good eating quality. Too much leavening gives an open, loose, crumbly grain; the flavor is poor, and the product may fall because the excess gas has broken down the gluten structure.

Getting the right leavening action to accomplish proper aeration takes skill. A leavening agent creates gas in a product, which is captured when protein coagulates and starch gelatinizes, firming the product. The texture is then light and open. Steam alone is the only leavening agent used in popovers and cream puffs; the shell of these baked items is strong enough to hold the gas inside, creating a large cavity. Yeast feeding on sugars and other

a.   b.

Figure 13-1. Pie crusts: (a) flaky pie crust, produced by using a fat:flour ratio of 1:2; (b) mealy pie crust, produced by using a fat:flour ratio of 1:1.

carbohydrates creates carbon dioxide gas, which leavens breads. Soda, ammonia, and baking powder spread in doughs or batters and, during baking, create carbon dioxide, which leavens the mixture. Sometimes, as in overdeveloped muffins, the gas collects and forms tunnels that work up to the top as the gas tries to escape. Thus, many products cannot be worked too much and remain tender enough to allow the leavening to work. The sugar and shortening in cakes and cookies counteract such toughening, so these batters and doughs can be worked more. A double-acting baking powder is one that makes a small quantity of gas in the cold stage but makes a far greater quantity of gas in the hot stage. Single-acting baking powders, which work completely in the cold stage or in the hot stage, are little used in quantity work.

Air

Air is incorporated into products when eggs are whipped to a foam, as in angel cake. Air is also worked into a batter in creaming. Air leavens a pound cake. When heated, air swells, causing the product to rise and develop a fine texture. Once air is in a batter or dough, it must not be lost. Thus, a sponge cake should be folded only until the dry ingredients are incorporated into the egg foam; overmixing loses the air in the foam.

Steam

Water swells to 1,600 times its liquid volume when it converts into steam; thus, it can be a powerful leavening agent. Steam leavens many bakery products. A cake is leavened one-third by air incorporated during creaming, one-third by steam, and one-third by baking powder. Cream puffs, éclairs, popovers, crackers, and pie crust depend entirely on steam for leavening. About 1 qt of liquid per lb of flour gives adequate leavening by steam.

Chemical Leaveners

Soda was perhaps the first chemical leavener used. It produces carbon dioxide gas. If the product contains an acid ingredient, such as sour milk, vinegar, or chocolate, the acid reacts with the soda, releasing carbon dioxide (see table 13-1). Heat also causes this reaction; thus, when a product is baked, the soda gives off the necessary gas for leavening. Cream of tartar can be used with soda to make a single-acting baking powder, with the cream of tartar acting as an acid. If too much soda is added, a slightly disagreeable flavor results. Soda also causes the pigments in some foods to darken. Bananas, spices, chocolate, and other ingredients change color when soda is used, the excess soda causing an alkaline reaction. Such a product may fall because alkalines tenderize gluten. This sometimes happens to gingerbread.

Two dry ingredients can be combined to make a leavening agent. The first baking powder was cream of tartar and soda, but it reacted entirely in the cold stage, so products had to be completely mixed, the baking powder added, and the mixture *immediately* panned and baked; otherwise, the gas would be

Table 13-1. Soda/Liquid Combinations for Leavening

	Liquid Required for Complete Reaction		Soda Required for Complete Reaction	
Type	Weight	Measure	Weight	Measure
Sour milk or buttermilk	8.3 lb	1 gal	¼ oz	2⅔ T
Molasses	11.5 lb	1 gal	1¾ oz	3 to 4 T
Sorghum	11.3 lb	1 gal	1 oz	2¼ T
Honey	11.3 lb	1 gal	½ to 1 oz	1 to 2¼ T
Vinegar, 40 to 50 grain	3 oz	⅓ c	1¼ oz	2⅔ T
Orange juice	4 oz	½ c	1¼ oz	2⅔ T
Cream of tartar	5 oz	1 c	2 oz	4½ T

lost in standing. Then other acids were found that could be combined with soda and that reacted only in the hot stage. Thus, double-acting baking powders became possible. A popular one today contains two acid reactors—one that reacts in the cold stage, and another that reacts in the hot stage. Another popular baking powder in quantity work contains only one reactor, but it reacts very slowly in the cold stage and releases most of its gas in the hot stage. The federal government requires a baking powder to yield not less than 12 percent of its weight in carbon dioxide; most commercial powders yield 17 percent. All baking powders contain a small quantity of cornstarch, which helps absorb moisture and prevents the powders from reacting in their containers.

Baking ammonia gives off carbon dioxide and ammonia gas when heat strikes it in a batter or in a dough. If all of the gas works off during baking, there is no aftertaste, although a distinct odor of ammonia is evident during baking. Thick products such as cakes capture some of the ammonia, so it is not used for them. For thin-shelled products such as cookies or cream puffs, however, baking ammonia works well. It gives good spread to cookies; that is, it causes them to spread out in baking.

The leavening powers of ammonia, soda, double-acting baking powder, and single-acting baking powder are, respectively, 1:0.75:2.5:5. Thus, if a recipe called for 1 oz of soda, you could probably substitute $1\frac{1}{3}$ oz of ammonia ($1.00/0.75 \times 1$), or $3\frac{1}{3}$ oz of double-acting powder ($2.5/0.75 \times 1$), or $6\frac{2}{3}$ oz ($5/0.75 \times 1$) of single-acting baking powder. If the recipe called for 3 oz of double-acting baking powder, the equivalent amount of ammonia, soda, or single-acting powder would be, respectively, 2 oz ($1/2.5 \times 5$), 0.90 oz ($0.75/2.5 \times 3$), and 6 oz ($5/2.5 \times 3$). The rule is to divide the ratio of the leavening agent in the recipe into the ratio of the substitute leavening agent and then to multiply the result by the amount of the first leavening agent (the one called for in the recipe).

Yeast

Yeast is a tiny fungus that thrives on carbohydrates and creates, as by-products, carbon dioxide gas and alcohol. The gas acts as a leavener. Yeast grows best at temperatures of 78° to 90°F (25.5° to 32°C). Its growth slows at around 98°F (37°C), and it is killed at 140°F (60°C). Yeast needs warmth, moisture, and carbohydrate in order to grow. Salt slows its growth. Yeast grows best when certain other substances are present, and bakers add conditioners to provide these in a dough. They also add malt, which contains glucose—the ideal food for yeasts.

Compressed, dry regular, or instant dry yeast is used in foodservices. Compressed yeast should be held at 45°F (7°C). Freezing may do some harm to compressed yeast, but not much. Thaw it at 40°F (4.5°C). Add compressed yeast crumbled into 110°F (43°C) water. Sift dry regular yeast into water heated to the same temperature, and allow the particles of yeast to hydrate thoroughly. Instant dry yeast is mixed with the dry ingredients. Bakers weigh yeast, rather than measure it. The amount of yeast required is less in warm weather than in cold weather (see table 13-2).

Eggs

Eggs coagulate and give bakery goods body; they also add flavor, color, moisture, nutrients, volume, and tenderness. Eggs help bind ingredients together and also emulsify fats. Bakers treat eggs as moisture, so they count them as a part of the liquid. Thus, a cake should contain about 170 percent liquid to 100 percent flour, with other liquids accounting for 100 percent and eggs 70 percent. Actually, egg whites contribute about three-fourths of their weight in liquid, yolks one-half, and whole eggs about two-thirds.

Liquids

Liquid can act as a leavening agent by turning to steam. It also provides the base into which many ingredients are dissolved, bringing them together in the batter or dough. Liquids contribute moistness, flavor, and tenderness and help retard staling. Moisture is absorbed by starch and gluten, which give

Table 13-2. Yeast/Water Combinations for Proper Mixing

Compressed Yeast	Active Dry Yeast	Water*	
		Weight**	Approximate Measure
1 oz	½ oz	2 oz	¼ c
2 oz	¾ oz	3 oz	½ c
4 oz	1½ oz	6 oz	1 c
8 oz	3¼ oz	13 oz	1 pt
12 oz	4¾ oz	1 lb 3 oz	1¼ pt
1 lb	6½ oz	1 lb 10 oz	1¾ pt
2 lb	12¾ oz	3 lb 3 oz	1 qt 1¼ pt
3 lb	1 lb 3¼ oz	4 lb 14 oz	2 qt 1 pt
4 lb	1 lb 9½ oz	6 lb 6 oz	3 qt 1 c
5 lb	2 lb	8 lb	4 qt

*Water temperatures should be 90° to 100°F for compressed yeast and 5 to 10 Fahrenheit degrees higher for dry active yeast.
**Corrected to nearest ¼ oz.

the product structure. If moisture were not present leavening agents would not work.

Flavorings and Spices

Spices and flavorings add flavor. Natural oils or esters used as flavorings include lemon oil, clove oil, and vanilla. Other flavorings may be imitation. Some flavorings are best when they come from the natural product, while others are better in the imitation product. High-quality spices should be used, since the quantity is small but the flavor contribution is large. Spices should be stored in tight containers, away from heat and moisture. Only enough to last about a month should be purchased. Spices are usually weighed in baking; flavorings are measured, if they are liquid.

BREADS

Most operations today buy their loaf breads but bake their own rolls and hot breads to ensure top-quality products. The prepared mixes on the market produce a variety of yeast and quick breads. The cost and quality of the mix must be evaluated against the merits of making the product from scratch.

Yeast Breads

Yeast breads are evaluated on the basis of their volume, crust, symmetry, evenness of baking, grain (internal appearance), texture, and flavor. White bread is made from good-quality white (bleached) hard flour. Whole-wheat (graham) bread is usually 40 to 60 percent whole-wheat flour, with the rest being a good patent white flour. Whole-wheat bread dough is mixed less because of the weaker gluten in the whole-wheat flour.

Regular rye bread consists of 20 percent rye and 80 percent strong white patent; the ratio can go up to 100 percent rye. Pumpernickel uses all of the rye kernel; it is somewhat heavy and compact because it lacks gluten. Rye bread is mixed less and is made with less moisture because rye flour cannot absorb as much moisture as hard-wheat flour can. A loaf of rye bread can burst in baking because of its weak gluten.

Hard, French, Italian, and hearth breads are made from quite lean (nonrich) doughs. The heavy crust develops because steam remains in the oven during the early stages of baking. Sourdough bread is made by adding a fermented starter or old dough to a new one. Sweet doughs vary in richness and may have shortening rolled into them, as puff paste does. Rich doughs can be retarded (refrigerated) or frozen better than lean ones can.

Table 13-3. Bread Ingredients and Proportions

Ingredients	Lean	Rich
Flour, bread	100%	65 to 100%
Flour, cake	—	0 to 35%
Sugar, granulated	2 to 3%	6 to 25%
Shortening	1 to 12%	8 to 40%*
Eggs, whole	—	10 to 45%
Yeast, compressed	2 to 3%	2 to 8%
Liquid	58 to 60%	40 to 60%
Milk, nonfat, dry	0 to 6%	3 to 8%
Salt	1 to 2½%	1½ to 2½%
Spices	—	¼ to ½%
Flavoring	—	¼ to ½%
Conditioner	¼ to ½%	¼ to ½%

*Use additional shortening (20% to 50% of the flour) for rolling in.

Basic yeast bread requires flour, yeast, liquid, and salt. Fat can also be added. Sweet doughs and other rich types contain sugar, eggs, more fat, and added flavoring. Ingredient proportions for breads and many other bakery products are always given in their percentage relative to flour. Thus, a bread recipe may list the liquid as 60 percent, which means it is present in a weight equivalent to 60 percent of the flour (see table 13-3). Graham breads, rye breads, and those high in milk and shortening need more salt. Salt controls yeast growth; thus, more salt must be used in summer than in winter. Salt should be added with the flour rather than mixed directly with the yeast.

The straight-dough method of making dough combines all ingredients at one time. The following steps (and the approximate time required for each) are involved in the straight-dough method:

1. Weighing and mixing (12 minutes)
2. Fermentation (45 to 60 minutes)
3. Punching (3 minutes)
4. Benching and resting (10 to 15 minutes)
5. Makeup (20 minutes)
6. Proofing (15 to 20 minutes)
7. Baking (Rolls, 20 minutes; loaves, 60 minutes)
8. Cooling
9. Storing

Thus, the total preparation time in the straight-dough method is from 2 to 4 hours. The actual work time is about 45 minutes for 100 portions or 11 lb of dough.

A sponge yeast is made by mixing all of the ingredients except for about 20 to 40 percent of the flour. The dough is fermented, and then the rest of the flour added. Best-quality bread results from this method.

A no-time yeast bread is made by the straight-dough method, with an increase in the amount of sugar and yeast and a higher baking temperature. The bread often remains in the mixer for its rapid fermentation rise. Makeup and proof times are shortened, and baking times are normal. The bread is quick to produce, but it lacks something in quality, being slightly yeasty and staling quickly.

Weigh all ingredients before starting. Most operations use an upright or vertical mixer with a dough hook; small batches can be made by hand. Rehydrate the yeast in a small bit of liquid, and then add the remaining liquid and fat at proper temperature for good yeast growth. Add dry ingredients and mix until a soft, sticky ball is formed and the gluten is well-developed (see fig. 13-2). When properly mixed, the dough should stretch out into a thin sheet, indicating good gluten development. Doughs should come from the mixer at 74° to 84°F (23° to 29°C). A relative humidity of 75 percent is desirable. If the humidity is lower, cover the dough with a damp cloth or brush the top of it with oil or shortening. When the dough doubles in volume or when fingers can be inserted easily about 3 inches into the dough, with it reacting by puckering or receding, the fermentation period is over. During fermentation, the dough ripens and develops into a soft, smooth, and silky mass with good elasticity. Extended fermentation or too high temperatures cause the dough to develop too much acid, giving a sour bread of poor texture when baked. The most desirable fermentation temperature is 81°F (27°C).

Punching is a technique of folding a dough over from its sides into the middle, and then turning the dough completely over in its container. This remixes food that the yeast needs so that it can start working again. Some strong doughs may be allowed to ferment a second time. Benching and resting are

a.   b.

c.   d.

e.

Figure 13-2. Dough mixing: (a) crumble the yeast into warmed liquid, and allow to stand; (b) add the eggs, remaining liquid, and melted or liquid fat; (c) add the sugar; (d) add the flour, and mix; (e) at the end of mixing, the dough is smooth and leaves the sides of the bowl.

done to let the dough recover from punching. Rich doughs and doughs containing a lot of yeast need a shorter rest. If the makeup time is extended, the rest is shortened. Makeup involves shaping the dough into the form needed for baking. Dinner rolls are portioned at about 1 lb per dozen; breakfast rolls are made into 1 oz (strong) if two are served, and 2 oz if only one is served. Baking loss is about 12 percent. If 1 lb per pan is desired, the scaling weight at makeup is 18 oz. After being weighed (scaled), the dough is rounded into smooth, round

shapes (see fig. 13-3). A rough surface allows carbon dioxide to escape and gives a poor-looking product. A short bench rest, called *bench proofing,* of 8 to 12 minutes allows the dough to recover from the effects of rounding. This helps to relax the dough and let it shape up better in the pan. Similar shaping techniques are used with bread loaves (see fig. 13-4).

Proofing is the final stage of conditioning before baking. The relative humidity for proofing is from 80 to 85 percent or more, at a temperature of from 90° to 100°F (32° to 38°C). This gives a soft, delicate product with maximum increase in volume. Too much proofing results is an open-grained, gray-colored bread, as well as a loss of flavor and lower volume. Some breads are docked just after proofing and before baking. Docking is gashing the top to allow the bread to rise without breaking or bursting. This procedure is done on hard-crusted, rye, and other breads.

When proper procedures are followed, baking yields a product with maximum volume, good texture and flavor, and good appearance. Bake loaves at 425°F (218°C) for 15 minutes and then at 375°F (191°C) for 45 minutes. Larger loaves may need slightly lower temperatures and longer baking. Rolls that are separated should be baked for 15 to 30 minutes at 425°F (218°C); pan rolls and other rolls that touch must be baked nearly as long as loaf breads. Rich doughs are baked at lower temperatures because they tend to burn or scorch at bread-baking temperatures (see table 13-4). Bread rises rapidly during the first period of baking, and a slight tan develops on the top. This rise is called *oven spring.* A well-baked bread gives a hollow sound when it is tapped. Appendix F lists reasons that should be checked to ascertain why bread fails.

After baking, loaves, large rolls, and other products that touch in the pans are dumped for cooling. This allows the steam and alcohol to escape, resulting in a less soggy bread. Breads should not be placed in drafts because these might cause them to crack or shrink. Hard-crusted bread and some others are not wrapped or stored in tight containers; instead they are put into open boxes and left at room temperature. Other breads may be stored in good containers or put into moisture- and vapor-proof

Figure 13-3. Rolls and techniques for making them: (a) pan rolls; (b) twin rolls; (c) cloverleaf rolls; (d) fantans or butter rolls; (e) Parker House rolls; (f) single or bow-knot rolls; (g) double or rosette rolls; (h) kaiser-knot rolls; (i) triple or braided rolls.

wraps. Hard-crusted breads should be used as soon as possible. Carry-over bread can be made into crumbs, croutons, or stuffings.

Quick Breads

Quick breads are made from batters and doughs. They are prepared much more rapidly than yeast breads, since they can be baked as soon as mixed.

Leavening may be obtained from chemicals, air, steam, or yeast. A slight variation in method, ingredients, or timing can yield a completely different product, even though the same procedures are followed (see table 13-5, page 292).

Biscuits are the closest things to yeast bread. Shortening is worked into the flour, leavening agent, and salt until the mixture looks like cornmeal. Liquid is then added. The dough is worked on a

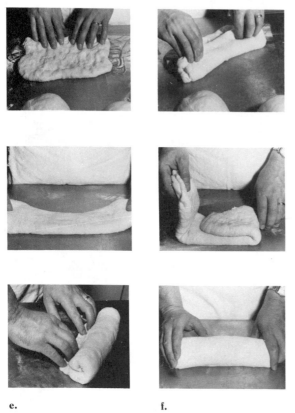

e.   f.

Figure 13-4. Dough shaping: (a) stretch the dough double the pan length; (b) fold the dough in thirds; (c) pat the dough out; (d) fold; (e) seal the edge; (f) pan the loaf with the seam down.

floured board for several minutes until smooth. It is then rolled out and cut into biscuits. Flakier biscuits are made by using slightly more shortening and cutting it only to the size of a small pea. Good kneading is also required; however, overmixing results in a tough biscuit. A good biscuit has an attractive shape, with straight sides and a level top (see table 13-6, page 293).

Dropped biscuits are not shaped like other biscuits because they are not kneaded. The dough is simply dropped onto greased pans after mixing. Beaten biscuits are like baking powder biscuits without the baking powder; they are popular in the South. Scones are a type of baking powder

biscuit. Shortcakes are made from a rich biscuit dough containing extra sugar and shortening. Dumplings are a variation of biscuits and may contain eggs. All biscuit items are baked at 425°F (218°C) for 15 to 20 minutes. Dumplings are steamed or cooked over boiling liquid with a tight cover on the container.

Muffins are made from a rather thick batter that is produced by blending flour, salt, sugar, and baking powder with a liquid (eggs, milk, melted fat, or oil). Very little mixing is given to the batter, which is kept cold to prevent gluten from forming. In a mixer, the batter is mixed for only 15 to 20 seconds, at low speed. The flour mixture should just disappear, and the mixture should seem pebbly (see fig. 13-5). Muffin pans should be conditioned and only lightly greased. A light dusting of flour over the greased tins reduces sticking. Muffins should be panned and baked immediately after mixing; they are not as good if allowed to stand before being baked. Portioning into tins for baking should be done by taking batter from the outside edge in, to eliminate working the batter. Normally, 6 to 7 lb of flour (14 to 16 lb of batter) yields 100 portions (150 muffins).

Overmixing, mixing too slowly, putting too much flour or liquid into the batter, using insufficient leavening, or setting too low an oven temperature gives a poor muffin. A good-quality muffin is large for its weight. The crust is crisp, shiny, pebbly, and golden brown. The top is rounded, free from knobs, and quite rough. A moist, light, and tender crumb is evident on breaking. No tunneling should be evident. The flavor should not be bready or too sweet. In taste, a muffin is midway between a cake and bread. Loaf breads, quick coffee cakes, and other variety breads are based on muffin mixtures.

Griddle cakes, pancakes, and hotcakes are different names for the same food item, made with the same batter. Waffle batter is richer and slightly sweeter and thicker. Both batters are mixed very much as muffins are, but more mixing can be given because the additional liquid helps separate the gluten particles and lessens the danger of gluten development. Thick waffle batters, however, should not be mixed too much. For 100 portions of hotcakes (two cakes

Table 13-4. Baking Temperatures for Various Bakery Items

Product	Pan Size	Units per Pan	Scaling Weight	Temperature (°F)	Temperature (°C)	Baking Time (min)
Rolls, small	8 in.*	12	1 to 1⅓ oz	400 to 425	204.5 to 218.0	15 to 20
	17 × 25 in.	72 to 100				
Rolls, medium	8 in.*	8 to 12	1½ to 1¾ oz	400 to 425	204.5 to 218.0	15 to 20
	17 × 25 in.	60 to 85				
Rolls, large	8 in.*	8	2 to 2⅓ oz	390 to 420	198.8 to 215.5	20 to 25
Cinnamon rolls	8 in.*	8 to 12	1 to 2 oz	375 to 385	190 to 196	25
	17 × 25 in.	72 to 100		375	190	30
Sweet rolls	17 × 25 in.	24	2 oz	380 to 400	193 to 204.5	25
Tea rings	8 in.*	1	10 to 12 oz each	375	190	30
	17 × 25 in.	4	with 2 oz filling			
Topped coffee cakes	8 in.*	1	10 to 12 oz each	375	190	30
	17 × 25 in.	8	with 2 oz topping			
Fancy coffee cakes	8 in.*	1	10 to 12 oz each	375	190	30
	17 × 25 in.	3 to 5	with 2 oz filling			
Bread, white	1¼ lb	1	26½ oz	400	204.5	60
Bread, rye	1 lb	1	18 oz	400	204.5	45

*Round or square pan.

per portion) or waffles, about 13 lb of flour or 30 lb (4 gal) of batter is required.

Hotcakes are baked on a well-greased griddle, allowing about 2 oz for a large cake. The cake cooks on the bottom and bubbles appear on top. When a slight dryness appears at the edge, the cake is turned and allowed to cook on the other side. The less turning, the better. If the top is pitted after baking, the cake was cooked too long on the first side or the heat was too high. A hotcake that has a raised middle may not be completely cooked. Good hotcakes have an even, good, brown color, and a good rounded shape. They should be tender and moist. The outside should be slightly crisp, and the flavor pleasing and slightly bready.

A waffle grid should be conditioned well. The batter should contain enough fat to make greasing unnecessary—about 4 oz per lb of flour (the same proportions work well for hotcakes). If the griddle sticks even though the recipe is correct, the grid may need conditioning or the temperature may be too low or too high. Put enough batter in so that when the top is lowered, the batter completely spreads over the iron, giving a waffle with an even

top and bottom. A large waffle needs about 4 oz of batter. A waffle is considered done when it stops steaming in the grid.

Good waffles are evenly browned with a crisp outer surface and only slight moistness inside. The grid markings are distinct. Flavor is sweet, nutty, and pleasant.

DESSERTS

Desserts are usually sweet and are used to conclude a meal. They should blend with the meal and complement it. Desserts are supposed to end the appetite, and for this reason they are sweet. They can be used to heighten meal interest and to add something extra to a meal.

Cakes

Cakes are low in cost, easy to prepare, and can be carried over without too much loss in quality. Cakes made from mixes hold less well than cakes made from scratch. High-quality ingredients, exact

Table 13-5. Comparative Analysis of Quick Breads

Part I. Approximate Ingredient Percentages

Ingredient	Biscuits (%)	Muffins (%)	Cornbread (%)	Griddle-cakes (%)	Waffles (%)
Flour, bread	0 to 50				
Flour, pastry	50 to 100	100*	100**	100	100*
Sugar	0 to 2	10 to 65	5 to 25	2 to 10	15 to 30
Shortening	20 to 30	20 to 40	6 to 20	5 to 15	50 to 40
Eggs	0 to 10	20 to 25	20 to 25	15 to 35	20 to 65
Liquid	60 to 70***	70 to 80	80 to 90	125 to 200	130 to 180
Milk, dry, nonfat	7	8	8	10 to 15	10 to 15
Baking powder, double-acting	6	6	8½	6 to 10	6 to 8
Salt	1 to 2	1 to 2	1 to 2	1 to 2	1 to 2

*For greater tenderness, cake flour may be used.
**About 50% of the flour is cornmeal.
***For shortcakes, reduce liquid to 50 to 60% and increase sugar to 15 to 20%.

Part II. Scaling Weights, Baking Temperatures, and Baking Times

Product	Pan Size	Units per Pan	Scaling Weight	Baking Temperature (°F)	(°C)	Time (min)
Brown bread, steamed	4 × 9 × 4 in.	1	1½ lb	Steam	Steam	60 to 90
Biscuit, 2¼ in.	17 × 25 in.	88	1¼ oz	425	218	15 to 20
Dumpling	8 in.*	12	1½ oz	Steam	Steam	20 to 30
Cornbread	17 × 25 in.	1	6 lb	425	218	30
Griddlecakes			4 oz	350 to 375	176.5 to 190	3 to 5
Muffins, plain			1⅓ to 1½ oz	425	218	15 to 20
Muffins, bran			1½ oz	425	218	20 to 25
Breads, quick	7½ × 3½ × 2¼ in.	1	18 oz	350	176.5	60
Breads, date and nut	7½ × 3½ × 2¼ in.	1	22 oz	350	176.5	60
Breads, quick	4 × 9 × 4 in.	1	1¾ lb	350	176.5	60 to 75

*Round or square pan.

measurement, good equipment, and skill are needed to make good cakes.

Three types of cakes exist: butter, pound, and foam. Butter cakes (the most popular type) are made from shortening (in the past, butter), sugar, eggs, liquid, flour, salt, leavening, and flavoring. Pound cakes contain, proportionally, 1 lb each of shorten-ing, eggs, flour, and sugar. The shortening, eggs, and sugar are creamed and then folded into the flour. Fruit cakes, nut cakes, and steamed puddings are made in this way. Angel foods, sponge cakes, and chiffon cakes are foam cakes. The leavening is contributed by air in the egg foam, although some sponges and chiffons may also contain some bak-

Table 13-6. Biscuit Defects and Their Causes

Defect	Possible Causes
Heavy or compact crumb	(1) Overmixed or overkneaded dough; (2) insuffficient baking powder or shortening; (3) too much liquid or flour; (4) oven not hot enough
Pale crust	(1) Oven not hot enough; (2) baked in too deep a pan; (3) too much flour
Poor volume	(1) Oven not hot enough; (2) insufficient baking powder
Light but not flaky	(1) Shortening cut too finely into flour; (2) insufficient kneading
Poor shape	(1) Dough too slack; (2) uneven rolling; (3) twisting the cutter; (4) careless cutting or panning

a.

b.

Figure 13-5. Muffin preparation: (a) ingredients are mixed until the dry ingredients barely disappear; (b) batter appears rough and pebbly, and for panning it is removed from the outside edge in.

ing powder. Foam cakes cannot be prepared in quantities greater than 100 portions per batch because they are so delicate.

Mixing methods vary, depending on the cake type. The prescribed method for making a butter, pound, or foam cake should be followed carefully.

Butter cakes can be made by creaming the shortening, eggs, and sugar until a light mass is achieved. Then a mixture of flour, salt, and baking powder is added alternately with the liquid to form a thick batter. Many butter cakes, however, are made by the blending method, which gives a tighter grain, a more velvety texture, and a better-keeping cake. The flour and shortening are mixed with a mixer paddle on low speed for 3 to 5 minutes, during which time the bowl is scraped frequently. If chocolate is to be used, it is added in melted form at this stage. Sugar, salt, baking powder, dry milk solids, and cocoa (if used) are sifted and added with one-third to one-fourth of the liquid in two parts to give a smooth batter. Spices are also added at this time. Mixing continues for another 3 to 5 minutes, again with frequent scraping down. Then the remaining liquid, flavoring, and eggs are added in about three parts, and mixing proceeds for 3 to 5 minutes at low speed with frequent scraping down. This method enables the fat to coat the flour, yielding a tenderer, more even-grained cake and reducing moisture loss. The batter is thin, but this is not a defect.

A third mixing method is the muffin method, in which all liquid ingredients (including oil or liquefied shortening) are blended into the dry ingredients. A cake mixed in this way must be served soon, since it keeps poorly. A conventional sponge cake is used in very hot climates. Because the shortening may be too soft to cream, half of the sugar is mixed into the shortening, after which dry ingredients are sifted together and then blended in, followed by liquids. Warm eggs beaten to a fluffy sponge are then folded into the mixture with the remaining sugar.

Pound cakes are made by creaming the shortening and then adding sugar and creaming these together well. The eggs are added and creaming is continued until the mass looks like thick whipped cream. Finally, flour is blended in carefully. Some pound cakes call for a bit of liquid and some baking powder. A good pound cake begins with having the ingredients at 75°F (24°C).

Foam cakes depend on egg foam for their lightness and texture. For angel cakes, egg whites at 110° to 125°F (44° to 52°C) are beaten until they reach a soft peak, at which time one-third to one-half of the sugar is beaten in. The remaining sugar is sifted into the flour to help blend the egg whites more easily. The egg whites are folded into the flour and salt with a down-and-under motion, with care being taken not to break the foam. Angel cakes are usually baked in regular tubular ungreased pans; greasing gives a lower volume because the batter cannot climb up the sides of the pan. Angel cakes can be baked in loaf pans or in sheets. A sponge cake is made of warm whole eggs or yolks (if only yolks are used, some other moisture is added). After a stable foam is made with salt, lemon juice, or cream of tartar, sugar is added; the flour is then folded in. A delicate hot butter or hot milk sponge cake is difficult to make. The butter must be melted and hot; the milk is usually added at 140°F (60°C). Chiffon cakes are made somewhat like sponges, except that they contain oil. The grain of chiffon cakes is tight but light, and they keep well.

Panning is important to cake quality. Butter and pound cake batter should evenly fill pans one-half to two-thirds full (see fig. 13-6). Straight-sided, ungreased sides give greater volume. Greased bottom paper liners are often used. Foam cake batter is placed in nongreased pans, filling them about three-fourths full. Since black metal absorbs heat, black pans are preferred. Butter cake batter fills pans at about 0.2 oz per square inch of pan. An 18″ × 26″ pan holds about 6 lb of batter. The scaling weights of cakes are usually specified (see table 13-7).

Cake baking occurs in four stages. Preheated ovens should be used. The first stage consists of a slight batter thinning accompanied by a rapid rise.

a.

b.

Figure 13-6. Panning cake batter; (a) butter cake batter should be too thick to spread itself out on the cake pan; (b) a spatula must be used to spread the batter out evenly.

Rising starts at the sides and moves in toward the center. In the second stage, the center starts to rise slightly higher than the sides. Coagulation and gelatinization are taking place. A slight darkening is seen on the surface of the batter, with some bubbles. The cake is in a critical state; any jarring will cause the cake to fall or lose volume. The process is now one of capturing maximum rise through structural firming. No further rise occurs in the third stage; but the crust now takes on color and the structure sets. At the end of this stage, the cake structure is firm enough to allow the pans to be moved gently. In the fourth stage, the cake shrinks slightly and moves away from the pan sides, and the aroma of baked cake is evident. Good bakers never look at a cake to see if it is done. Instead, they judge doneness

Table 13-7. Baking Procedures for Different Cakes

Type Cake	Scaling Weight	Baking Temperature (°F)	(°C)	Time (min)
Layer				
Butter or Pound (1½ to 2 in. deep)				
6 in. diameter	6 to 8 oz	375	191	18
7 in. diameter	9 to 11 oz	375	191	20
8 in. diameter	12 to 14 oz	375	191	25
10 in. diameter	20 oz	360	182.2	35
12 in. diameter	1½ to 2 lb	360	182.2	
14 in. diameter	2¼ to 3 lb	360	182.2	
Foam cakes				
6 in. diameter	4 to 5 oz	375	191	20
8 in. diameter	9 to 10 oz	375	191	
10 in. diameter	16 to 18 oz	360	182.2	
12 in. diameter	1½ to 1¾ lb	360	182.2	
Loaf				
Pound, 3¼ × 3½ × 8 in.	1 lb	355	179.4	50
Pound, 3¼ × 6 × 11 in.	3 lb	325	163	100
Fruit, 3¼ × 3½ × 8 in.	1½ lb	315	157.2	90
Angel, 3¼ × 3½ × 8 in.	7 to 10 oz	365	185	
Angel, tube, small	8 to 10 oz			
Angel, tube, 10 in.	1½ to 2 lb	360	182.2	50
Sheet				
Butter, 1 × 18 × 26 in.	6 to 7 lb	360	182.2	35
Butter, 3 × 18 × 26 in.	8 to 10 lb	350	177	
Sponge, 1 × 18 × 26 in.	3 lb	360	182.2	25

NOTE: Weights, times, and temperatures are average only; adjust for each cake. Butter cakes made by the blended method may be baked at slightly higher temperatures than those used for conventionally made cakes; temperatures given here are for the blended type.

by aroma. The cake will be firm to the touch, springing back and leaving no imprint; however, foam cakes and some rich butter cakes such as German chocolate cake may lack this spring. When a wire tester or toothpick that is inserted into the cake comes out clean, the cake is done.

Pans that touch the oven sides or each other do not produce good cakes as consistently as do pans that the air is free to circulate around. When baking is done in a convection oven, the fan should not be used during the first two stages, because the air flow will move the batter and cause a rippled effect on the top; volume will also be less. As with meat, small products are baked at higher temperatures than large ones, and thin products are baked at higher temperatures than thick ones. Some cakes require more than one temperature over the course of baking.

The final steps in cake production are cooling, storing, and makeup. Cool cakes in the pan for at least 15 minutes; loaf and pound cakes may take 30 minutes. Foam and pound cakes should cool upside down. Foam cakes are easier to remove from pans while they are still slightly warm. Depan the cakes, and store them when completely cool in a moisture- and vapor-proof wrap. Makeup includes cutting, shaping, filling, frosting, and decorating (see fig. 13-7). Cakes can be made up before being stored.

Cookies

Cookies use virtually the same ingredients as cakes, and some are made in exactly the same way as cakes. Cookies are usually richer than cakes, however, and contain the same ratio of flour to shortening as pie doughs do. Sugar, ice-box, and similar cookies are made by the creaming method. Foam-type cookies such as ladyfingers and meringues are related to the foam cake family. A chewy cookie is made with syrups containing a large amount of invert sugar (such as molasses, honey, or corn syrup), plus more eggs and less fat to flour. Crisp cookies contain high ratios of fat and sugar to liquid and are baked at a higher temperature. Soft cookies contain a lot of liquid and are baked at a lower temperature. Thickness and size affect crispness and softness. Better spread is obtained if

soda or ammonia is used as the leavener than if baking powder is used. Spread is also greater with cookies that are high in sugar; the coarser the sugar, the greater the spread. Cool cookies well, and store them in airtight containers.

Egg-thickened Desserts

Desserts prepared from eggs are quite delicate and can fail unless properly done. Such desserts include custards, soufflés, and meringues.

A good baked custard is firm and soft. When cut, it shows an even, glossy, cream-colored surface. The top should be even, not cheesy in texture, and golden brown. Doneness is indicated when a pointed knife inserted near the edge comes out clean (see fig. 13-8). Another test is to shake the custard and note its consistency. It can be removed when slightly underdone in the center since baking continues after oven removal. A stirred or soft custard is made in the same way as baked custards, except that the mixture is constantly stirred over simmering water.

Meringues are blends of whipped egg white foam and sugar. Pies are topped with soft meringues;

Figure 13-7. A well-presented piece of cake.

Figure 13-8. Testing a custard for doneness.

hard meringues are the base for meringue shells, which are filled with whipped cream or act as the base for a Schaum torte. Whip the whites, as described in chapter 5, and add the sugar gradually during whipping. Soft foams are made in a 1:1 ratio of egg whites to sugar (by weight). Hard meringues have a ratio of 1:1.75 or 1:2. Per lb of whites, use ¾ tsp of cream of tartar and a bit of salt. Hard meringues sometimes contain 1 oz of liquid per lb of whites. If the liquid is lemon juice, the cream of tartar is omitted.

Soft meringues are baked for from 12 to 18 minutes at 350°F (177°C); hard meringues are baked at 275°F (132°C) for 1½ hours or for 50 minutes at 325°F (163°C). Hard meringues are scaled at 1¼ oz each or 15 to 18 oz per dozen (see fig. 13-9). A 9-inch pie needs 4 to 5 oz of soft meringue to cover it well.

Fried Desserts

Doughnuts are popular for breakfast, snacks, or desserts. Cake doughnuts are made from a rich muffin dough that is handled as muffin dough would be—kept cold and not overworked. The doughnuts are cut from the rolled dough and dropped into hot fat. Yeast doughnuts are made from a rich (and usually sweet) yeast dough. They are cut from the dough, proofed, and deep fried. Some bakers cut simple circles instead of doughnuts with holes. After proofing, they lift the circle of dough up carefully and put their forefinger though it, making

Figure 13-9. Meringues being prepared for baking into hard shells.

a hole. The doughnut is then dropped from the fingers into the hot fat. Frying temperatures for doughnuts may be as high as 385°F (196°C). Doughnuts should be drained well on absorbent paper after frying. They can be coated with various frostings or glazes.

Two other popular fried desserts are fritters and crêpes. Fritters, which usually are deep-fried, are of two kinds: fruit that is dipped into batter and fried; and fruits or other items mixed into a muffin batter and deep-fried. Most fritters are served with syrup or a sweet sauce. Thin pancakes are called crêpes, *blini,* or some other name, depending on the type and on the culture from which they come. They are also popular filled with meat, poultry, or fish mixtures and served as entrées. The crêpe is a mixture of egg, a small bit of liquid, a bit of salt, and flour. The thin batter is poured into well-conditioned buttered pans, and moved quickly around by twisting the pan to distribute the batter evenly in all areas. It is browned well on one side, flipped over, and browned on the other. Special crêpe pans have been designed for producing crêpes. Crêpes Suzette contain a rich, sweet orange filling and are doused with liqueurs and flamed. Crêpes can be made ahead of time, then refrigerated or frozen, and made up for service later.

Frozen Desserts

Frozen desserts include ice cream, sherbet, ices, mousses, mallows, glacés, biscuits, parfaits, junkets, puddings, and whips. A slush, granite, or frappé is a coarse, granular product that is only partially frozen. Most frozen desserts are purchased ready-made. They usually are a low-cost product and require little labor.

Ice cream and sherbet contain a lot of air, which gives them volume and texture and enhances their flavor. Therefore, in dishing or scooping, it is important that the ice cream or sherbet be given maximum volume and not be packed firmly. Figure 13-10 shows a good way to scoop. These frozen items should be served at 8° to 15°F (−13.2° to −9.4°C). Table 13-8 gives the portion size in scoops.

a.   **b.**

c.   **d.**

Figure 13-10. Scooping ice cream: (a) insert the scoop about ½ inch deep into the frozen dessert, starting at the outer edge or wherever the last scoop left off; (b) draw the scoop lightly and evenly across the surface, rolling the dessert into a ball; (c) when the scoop is filled, turn it up with a twist of the wrist; (d) keep the surface smooth, working evenly across the top.

Table 13-8. Portion Size (in Scoops) of Various Ice Cream Desserts

Item	Scoop Size	Number of Scoops per Portion
Banana split	No. 30	3
Bowl of ice cream	No. 30	4
Parfait	No. 30	3
Ice cream soda, malt, or milkshake	No. 24	2
Pie, cake, or pudding à la mode	No. 20	1
Sundae	No. 20	2
Table d'hôte, plain	No. 16	1
Sundae, meal portion	No. 12	1
A la carte portion	No. 10	1

Figure 13-11. Desserts featuring fruits are highly popular.

Store frozen desserts at temperatures of from 8° to 15°F (−13.2° to −9.4°C).

Fruit Desserts

Fresh fruit makes one of the best and simplest desserts. Fruits are low in calories and high in nutrients (see fig. 13-11). Serve them cold. A crisp, cold, and sweet yet tart apple, a mellow peach or pear, a flavorful bunch of grapes, a spicy orange, delicious slices of pineapple, and a bowl of succulent berries all vie with the finest bakery creations for credit as the most popular of desserts. Many are served plain; others may be served with sugar and cream. Acidic or antioxidant solutions can be used to prevent tarnishing of freshly cut fruit.

Frozen fruits have a better texture if they are served while still slightly frozen. A 5-lb carton of frozen fruit at 0°F (−18°C) takes 2 to 3 hours to thaw at room temperature and 4 to 5 hours to thaw under refrigeration. A portion of such fruit is usually ½ cup, or 4 oz.

Fruits can also be cooked and served. Some dried fruits need no sugar. Others can be served in a syrup. Fruits in extra-heavy syrup are called preserves; fruits in heavy syrup are called *compotes,* and fruits in light or medium syrup are called *stewed fruits* or *fruit sauces.* About 15 lb EP of fruit cooked in 1½ gal of light or medium syrup yields 100 ½-cup portions of sauce; four No. 10 cans of fruit usually provide enough fruit to serve 100, but the count or size of the fruit must be appropriate for this purpose.

A crisp is a fruit mixture topped with a blend of flour, sugar, fat, and seasonings, and then baked. Oatmeal can be used in place of flour to give a crisper and more nut-flavored top. Betties are layers of fruit alternating with layers of bread or cake crumbs, sugar, and butter or margarine; after being properly layered, the betty is baked. Shortcakes are rich biscuits filled and topped with fruit and whipped cream. Cobblers are fruit dishes with biscuit dough or pie dough on top.

Apple or fruit dumplings are popular dessert items. They consist of rich biscuit dough rolled ⅛ in. thick and filled with fruit, which is then sealed inside the dough (see fig. 13-12). The dumplings are baked in sweetened water, which thickens slightly during baking and is served as a sauce over the dumplings.

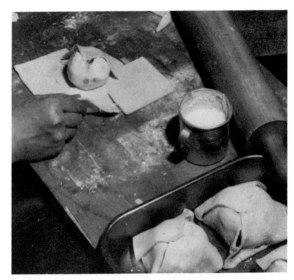

Figure 13-12. Preparing apple dumplings.

Gelatin Desserts

Gelatin desserts include plain gelatin mixtures, gelatin mixtures with fruit, whipped gelatin mixtures, bavarians, and Spanish creams. They are popular and usually fairly inexpensive to make. They lend themselves well to merchandising. Many fruits, fruit juices, and other products carried over can be used in gelatin desserts.

Pies and Pastries

Pies and pastries are popular, but they require considerable labor and expensive ingredients. Many operations purchase ready-made items because they do not have the specialized labor necessary to make them.

Single-crust pies have only a bottom crust. They can be prebaked, filled with various fillings, and topped with meringues or whipped cream. Unbaked single crusts are filled with custard, pumpkin filling, or a pecan filling. Double-crust pies are usually filled with fruit and covered with a top crust that is sealed around the edge to the bottom crust. Baked pie shells can be filled with ice cream, gelatin mixtures, whips, and other products. Tarts, dumplings, and other desserts are closely related to pies.

Pie Crust

Pie dough is usually made from flour, shortening, salt, and water. The fat shortens the dough and makes a tender crust. Flakiness is achieved by having fat particles separate layers of dough. The fat melts, creating a pool; then steam forms here and raises the dough, and (when coagulation and gelatinization occur) solid, flaky layers of crust are formed. Salt adds flavor but toughens the gluten, so minimal amounts of it are added. Working a dough also develops gluten. The ingredients and their amounts (in percentages based on 100 percent for flour) for different pie doughs are shown in table 13-9.

Bread flour is used in making puff paste, giving a firmer dough so that more flakiness results. About 10 percent gluten flour is used for the other crusts —although, to make a good flaky crust, some bread flour may be used. To give sufficient shortness when bread flour is used, the shortening is increased. Flaky and puff paste doughs contain as much shortening as they do flour. A weak flour can be mixed

Table 13-9. Relative Percentages of Ingredients in Various Pie Doughs (Flour = 100 Percent)

Ingredient	Mealy Crust	Semi-flaky Crust	Flaky Crust	Puff Paste
Bread flour				100%
Pastry flour	100%	100%	100%	
Shortening	50–60%	75%	100%	100%
Salt	2–3%	2–3%	2–3%	1%
Water	25–30%	30–35%	35–40%	35–40%

more and can contain less shortening than a stronger flour.

Specialty crusts are made from ground pecans, almonds, filberts, or other products, replacing 25 percent of the flour. Adding these ingredients weakens the flour and produces a shorter crust. Adding soy flour does the same. Graham cracker crusts are made by weight: 100 percent cracker crumbs, 30 percent sugar and 55 percent butter or margarine. Cinnamon, almond flour, powdered sugar, or other ingredients may be added. Ginger snaps, vanilla wafers, chocolate wafers, or other dried crumbs can be used for variety crusts. About 2 oz of the crumb mixture packed well on the bottom and sides are sufficient for a 9-inch pie. The crust can be baked in a 350°F (177°C) oven for 10 minutes. Some foodservices prefer to refrigerate such crusts overnight without baking them.

Production Methods

Mealy, semiflaky, and flaky crusts are made by varying the ingredients and method of mixing. Rubbing the shortening thoroughly into the flour produces a mealy crust. Mixing it in only to the size of peas gives a semiflaky crust, and leaving the grains the size of walnuts produces a flaky crust. The materials should be cold, to reduce gluten formation. Mixing should be limited to the amount needed to spread water around. A pie dough is better if it is left standing for at least 15 minutes after mixing. When this is done, the dough is easier to roll and the baking shrinkage of the dough is less. Mealy

crusts soak less than others, so they are used for custard pies, pumpkin pies, and other pies in which an uncooked filling is put into an unbaked crust. Semiflaky crusts have good tenderness and flakiness and make a good all-purpose crust. A flaky crust is used for baked pie shells that are to be filled later and for tops of double-crust pies. Since a flaky crust soaks easily, cream fillings and others that would soak are not put into the shell until just before needed. Puff paste is made by the rolled dough method (see fig. 13-13).

Regular pie crust doughs are usually made from 6 oz of dough for bottoms and 5 oz of dough for tops of 9-inch pies. The crust is rolled to about ⅛ inch thick. Machine rolling is used for quantity production. Hand-rolling with a rolling pin or roller that is about 1½ inches in diameter and about 18 inches long is common. A smooth surface, rolling cloth, or board is used, with only a small amount of rolling flour on it. Additional flour toughens dough. The piece of dough should be well-rounded and flat. The roller pushes out the dough gently, allowing the dough to move on its own and not be stretched; stretching causes shrinkage in baking. The gluten strands need to be relaxed in rolling. The dough is lifted and turned as often as is necessary to get a perfectly round dough. An experienced baker can do this and get the exact shape needed so that no trim is required. The pie crust is folded and laid gently into the pan without stretching. It is then shaped to the pan. Crusts may be baked docked (pierced with a fork all over) to keep the crust from blistering or bubbling on its surface. Double-panning — putting another pan tightly over the crust — also prevents blistering. The extra pan is removed shortly before the crust finishes baking so that the crust can take on a more even color. Many bakers turn the first pan upside down, put the dough over it, and then put the other pan down over this.

Single crusts should be baked at temperatures of from 425° to 450°F (218° to 232°C) for about 15 minutes. Double-crust pies should be baked at temperatures of from 425° to 450°F (218° to 232°C) for 10 minutes; then the temperature should be dropped to between 350° and 375°F (177° and

a.   b.   c.

d.   e.   f.

Figure 13-13. Making puff paste by the rolled dough method: (a) roll the dough paste out about three times longer than wide and about ½ inch thick, and cover two-thirds of the surface with a ½-inch-thick layer of puff paste shortening; (b) fold over the uncovered third; (c) fold the dough again to seal the shortening completely between layers of dough; (d) making a four-fold pastry dough is similar; (e) rest the dough for 15 to 20 minutes; (f) give the dough a turn, and roll it out to its original shape.

191°C) for the remainder of baking. A tough crust results from too low a temperature. High heat causes overbrowning and, in double-crust pies, an unbaked filling. Putting hot fillings into double-crust pies reduces their baking time.

Pie Fillings

Many different fillings are used for pies. Single-crust pies can be topped with meringues, whipped cream, toasted coconut, crumbs, nuts, or other products. Unbaked single crusts are filled with uncooked fillings, such as custards, chiffons, soufflés, or pecan custard. A 9-inch pie needs 3 to 4 cups of filling. A meringue or whipped cream topping takes up some space, so less filling is used. Management

should require that pie markers be used, to ensure that all crusts are the same. Some pies are of better quality if slightly warm at service.

Pastries

Tarts, tartlets, turnovers, fried pies, and other items may be made from pie doughs or puff pastes (see fig. 13-14). Tartlet tins are filled, and then dry beans or rice is poured in to keep the crust from blistering during baking. Double-panning can also be used when baking tartlet crusts. Docking after the dough is put on the outside of the small pan is also possible. For tartlets, bakers often use a very rich pastry dough that is more a cookie dough than a pie dough. Rings or hoops can be placed on greased baking sheets and filled in with dough for large tarts. The dough shapes are given a border and then docked and baked. Dumplings and turnovers can also be made in fancy shapes and baked. If they are deep-fried, the dough should be leaner; the results of this method are called *fried pies*.

Puddings

Most puddings can be made quickly in quantity at reduced labor cost. Material cost is often low. Every menu should offer some of the wide variety

Figure 13-14. Display trays of various finished puff pastries.

of puddings. An old-fashioned rice custard pudding or bread custard pudding commonly sells out before other desserts.

Steamed (Boiled) Puddings

Steamed puddings are usually heavy products served warm with a sauce. They are usually either steamed or boiled, although some cooks modify this and bake them. They often use suet as the shortening. Bread crumbs, eggs, and strong bread flour are used to hold heavy quantities of fruit and nuts. Some contain no added moisture, since the fruit furnishes all that is needed; this is the case with carrot pudding or apple pudding. The ratio of batter to fruit and nuts is the same one used in fruit cakes—from 1:1 to 1:2.5. Some steamed puddings are made from pound cake batters. Soda is usually the leavening agent, which results in a darkened product because the fruit, nuts, spices, and some other ingredients darken in the presence of alkalies. The texture is porous. A good steamed pudding is rich, delicate in texture, and flavorful. The puddings are steamed in large or individual-portion containers, which are greased and floured well. The batter swells and so the containers are filled to about two-thirds full; then they are covered. Steaming takes from 2½ to 3 hours. Baking is done with the puddings standing in water in a 325°F (163°C) oven. Steamed puddings usually keep well and can be reheated.

Table 13-10. Thickeners Needed for One Gallon of Pudding

Type of Starch Thickener	Amount of Thickener*	Whole Eggs
Cornstarch	4 to 5 oz (1c)	1½ lb (1½ pt or 16 eggs)
Flour	8 oz (1 pt)	1½ lb (1½ pt or 16 eggs)
Rice, uncooked	9 to 14 oz (1 to 1½ pt)	
Rice, cooked	1	
Tapioca, granular	6 to 9 oz (1½ to 2 c)	1½ lb (1½ pt or 16 eggs)
Tapioca, pearl	12 oz (3 c)	1½ lb (1½ pt or 16 eggs)
Cake or bread crumbs	1 to 2 lb (1 to 2 qt)**	
Cornmeal, farina, or other	1 lb (1 qt)	

*Increase thickener if eggs are omitted.
**Quantity depends on moistness of crumbs.

Starch-thickened Puddings

Starch thickens many fine puddings. Cornstarch, tapioca, or arrowroot may be used as the thickening agent. A blancmange is made by adding cornstarch, sugar, and vanilla to milk and cooking the mixture in a double boiler, steam-jacketed kettle, or steamer. A steamer is not the best piece of equipment to use, since the product should be stirred as it cooks.

The amount of cornstarch needed varies from 6 to 12 oz per gal of liquid. Molded puddings require more cornstarch, while cream puddings require less. A cream pudding is a blancmange with eggs added; it needs less cornstarch because the eggs act as thickeners (see table 13-10). Some margarine or butter may be added. Pearl, granular, or quick-cooking tapioca can also be used to thicken puddings. Indian pudding is thickened with cornmeal and contains molasses. A portion is ½ cup; about 3¼ gal per 100 portions are needed.

SUMMARY

Bakery products can do much to enhance a meal and to bring in added income in commercial operations.

Flour is a starchlike product used to give structure and body to bakery products. Hard-wheat or bread flour is used for yeast breads and other items needing strong structures. Pastry or soft-wheat flour is used for pastry, quick breads, cakes, and cookies. The gluten or protein in flour gives products their basic structure. It is elastic. If overworked, it can make some products tough. A yeast bread needs a strong structure, so the dough is worked considerably; pie dough is not, because a tender product is wanted.

Shortening adds richness, color, sheen, grain, and texture to bakery goods. It makes items tender by lubricating gluten.

Sugar adds sweetness and also tenderizes and gives color, texture, and moistness to products. Some sugars draw moisture and thus make products moister. Sugars are also used for frosting, sanding, and coating materials.

Leavening agents aerate, or make bakery goods light. They help to give volume, shape, and texture. Air, which is a good leavener, is brought into bakery goods by creaming, by beating, or by being incorporated into egg foams. Steam, another good leavener, expands 1,600 times in volume in changing from water to vapor. Steam is the only leavener in items such as cream puff shells and is also important in leavening cakes, breads, and other products. Baking soda, one of the oldest chemical leaveners, gives off carbon dioxide gas, which leavens the product. An acid reacts with soda to produce the gas; heat with moisture also produces the gas. Baking powders combine dry acid ingredients with soda. When they are moistened and heat is applied, they react to form carbon dioxide gas. Single-acting baking powders react completely when moistened in the cold stage. Heat is not necessary to produce carbon dioxide. Double-acting baking powders react partially when cold and more fully in the hot stage. Double-acting baking powders are usually used in foodservices. Baking ammonia, which gives off carbon dioxide and ammonia gas when moistened and heated, is used in cookies, cream puff shells, and other thin-shelled products.

Yeast is also a leavener. It feeds on carbohydrates, producing alcohol and carbon dioxide gas. Yeast is a plant and must be nurtured by favorable conditions to make good products.

Eggs are added to bakery products to add structure, tenderness, volume, nutritional value, flavor, color, and moisture. They coagulate and thus help to firm up bakery products. Spices and flavorings are used to give flavor, richness, and color to bakery goods.

Breads are either yeast or quick-type and can be made from scratch or from mixes. A straight yeast dough is made by mixing all ingredients at one time; a sponge yeast dough is made by withholding part of the flour and adding it after the first fermentation. A no-time dough is made in the same way as a straight dough but is richer in sugar and contains more yeast. This method is used to produce yeast breads in as short a time as possible. A rich or sweet yeast dough is used for Danish pastries, coffee cakes, rich breakfast rolls, and other products. Leaner yeast doughs are used for regular loaf bread, sandwich bread, rolls, and hard-crusted breads.

After mixing, a yeast dough is left to ferment in a warm area. After the dough reaches a stage in which it will pucker when a hand is put into it, it is punched. Punching distributes the food so that the yeast can get new energy-giving materials. The dough is then benched (given a rest) and afterward made up into the desired shapes. In the proofing stage, temperatures and relative humidity are higher than for fermentation, in order to get a fast rising action before baking. The bread is then baked, cooled, and stored. Hard-crusted breads are not wrapped.

Quick breads are leavened by chemical leaveners — usually baking powder. Biscuits are made from a fairly stiff dough and resemble bread. Muffins are made from a more slack dough; care must be taken to ensure that too much gluten does not develop and make them tough. Muffin dough is kept cold to reduce the chance for gluten development. The batter for griddlecakes and waffles is thinner than for muffins. They often are served for breakfast.

Desserts on a menu should be selected for their flavor, richness, color, variety, texture, form, appearance, and ability to lend themselves to quantity production. They need not be expensive and can do much to improve a meal.

Cakes are not difficult to prepare. Butter cakes (the most popular) are made by creaming shortening, sugar, and eggs, and then adding sifted dry ingredients and liquid; or they may be made by the blending method, which calls for blending first the fat and flour and then the other ingredients. A muffin method and a sponge method also are used occasionally to make butter cakes. Pound cakes are made by creaming equal quantities by weight of shortening, sugar, and eggs, and then folding in the same amount of flour. Foam cakes (chiffon, angel, and sponge) are leavened largely by the air in egg foams. These delicate cakes are difficult to make. Cookies are made with the same ingredients, mixing techniques, and other methods used for cakes.

Custards are liquids thickened with eggs. They can be baked or stirred over heat. Custards contain $1\frac{1}{2}$ to 2 lb of whole eggs to 1 gal of liquid. Soufflés are very light baked desserts thickened and leavened by eggs. Meringues are made of egg white and sugar, with cream of tartar and salt added. Soft meringue tops pies and desserts, and hard meringue is a base for ice creams or tortes.

Fried desserts include doughnuts, fritters, and crêpes. Cake doughnuts are made from a rich muffin batter-type dough. Yeast doughnuts are made from a sweet (rich) yeast dough. Fritters consist of fruit that is either batter-dipped and deep-fried or incorporated into a muffin batter and then deep-fried. Fritters usually are served hot with a syrup or sweet sauce. Crêpes are very thin pancakes that usually contain a sweet filling and often are flamed.

Frozen desserts, such as ice cream and sherbets, and fruits served as desserts are very popular in today's foodservice operations.

Pies and pastries can be made from various kinds of pie doughs and then filled. Pie dough is made from flour, shortening, salt, and water. The amount of fat and how it is incorporated are varied to produce a mealy crust, a semiflaky crust, or a flaky crust. Puff paste is made by a special method using pie dough ingredients. A mealy crust is used for unbaked single-crust pies that are filled with an uncooked filling, such as custard. A semiflaky, all-purpose crust can be used for all pies. A flaky crust is used for baked pie shells or for topping double-crust pies. Single-crust pies are frequently topped with meringue or whipped cream. Double-crust pies are usually filled with fruit.

Pie dough should not be worked too much and should not be stretched as it is being rolled. Baked shells are docked or double-panned for baking. Pastries made from pie doughs or puff pastes include tarts, tartlets, turnovers, and fried pies.

Most puddings are low in cost and can easily be made in quantity. Steamed (boiled) puddings are rich products containing fruit, nuts, spices, and other ingredients. The shortening is often suet. They can be boiled, steamed, or baked and are served warm with a sauce. Starch-thickened puddings include blancmanges, cream puddings, arrowroot puddings, and tapioca puddings.

CHAPTER REVIEW QUESTIONS

1. A large foodservice corporation with many multiple units has made a rather good merchandising program by serving its own home-

made breads, pastries, and desserts; but now it is having difficulty finding good bakers. Management is also wondering whether running its own bakery in individual units pays off. It calls in a consultant to review the operation's entire baking and dessert program. It wants to know if it can purchase adequate breads and dessert products to satisfy menu needs. Would it pay to have some units produce their own items or should the foodservice purchase entirely from outside, or should it set up a central commissary in its most heavily concentrated sales areas to provide the products for those areas and let the individual units outside make their own? In other words, which way should the operation go? With a limited background on the company and on relevant conditions, set up the pros and cons that you as a consultant should consider in assessing the situation. Why should a foodservice today make its own breads, pastries, desserts, and other bakery products? Why should it not? Why should a large foodservice chain depend on products from the outside? There are many other potential factors you should add to your summary to cover the problem thoroughly. Set up a summary of your ideas in outline form, since you are to present this account verbally before a meeting of executives of the company.

2. What two kinds of wheat flours are used in bakery goods? Why is each used? Why is a good patent flour added to whole-wheat flour or rye flour in making bread?

3. What is gluten? What does it do in flour and in bakery goods? What procedures should be followed to develop or retard development of gluten? Name some products that need a strong gluten and some products that need a weak gluten.

4. List some of the other more commonly used bakery ingredients, and list the job each does.

5. Name the four major types of leavening agents and the subtypes. How does each work?

6. What methods are used to make yeast breads? Give the steps used to make bread by the straight-dough method. Explain what is done in each step. List the proper temperatures that should be used in the various steps. How are hard-crusted breads handled in storage versus soft-crusted breads?

7. List the various kinds of quick breads and indicate how they are made. Give some of the standards that should be looked for in these products.

8. List the three major classifications of cakes. How are butter cakes made by various methods? What kind of foam cakes are common? Indicate the properties of each type of cake in the major classifications.

9. How do cookies differ from cakes in ingredients and methods of making?

10. Describe the making of a meringue. State the proportions of sugar and eggs in soft and hard meringues.

11. How are fruits used as desserts? List the ways fruits can be served cooked.

12. What is a crisp? a betty? a shortcake? a cobbler?

13. How are steamed puddings made and cooked? How are starch-thickened puddings made?

VOCABULARY

Gluten
Ash
Patent
Strong flour
Hard-wheat flour
Soft flour
Weak flour
Middlings
Clears
Cake flour
Pastry flour
Bread flour
Graham flour
Shortening
10X
Leavening
Carbon dioxide
Single-acting
Double-acting
Baking powder

Waffle
Hotcake
Pancake
Waffle griddle
Butter cake
Creaming method
Blending method
Foam cake
Angel cake
Sponge cake
Blistering
Single crust
Double crust
Fried pie
Chiffon cake
Pound cake
Conventional sponge method
Muffin method
Panning

Baking ammonia
Yeast
Natural flavoring
Pumpernickel
Sourdough bread
Graham cracker crust
Stretching
Rolling pin
Lean dough
Sweet dough
Fermentation
Punch
Bench
Rest
Makeup
Proof
Docking
Biscuit
Beaten biscuit
Dropped biscuit
Dumpling (steamed)
Muffin
Griddlecake

Scaling
Spread
Meringue (soft)
Meringue (hard)
Cake doughnut
Yeast doughnut
Fritter
Crêpe
Crêpes Suzette
Stewed fruit
Compote
Preserve
Crisp
Shortcake
Betty
Cobbler
Tartlets
Mealiness
Flakiness
Blancmange
Steamed pudding
Cornstarch pudding
Cream pudding

ANNOTATED REFERENCES

Amendola, J. 1972. *The Bakers' Manual,* Rochelle Park, N.J.: Hayden Book. (Quantity baking and pastry-making techniques.)

Amendola, J., and Lundberg, D. E. 1974. *Understanding Baking.* Boston: CBI Publishing. (Pies, cakes, cookies, rolls, and breads.)

Folsom, L. A. 1974. *The Professional Chef,* pp. 393-422. Boston: CBI Publishing. (Desserts pictured and described, with recipes.)

Haines, R. G. 1973. *Food Preparation for Hotels, Restaurants, and Cafeterias,* pp. 520-642. Chicago: American Technical Society. (Quick breads, cookies, rolls, pies, cakes, and desserts.)

Hardwick, G. B., and Kennedy, R. L. 1979. *Desserts & Beverages.* Boston: Cahners Books. (All desserts frequently found in foodservice operations.)

Kotschevar, L. H. 1988. *Quantity Food Production.* 4th ed., pp. 304-443. New York: Van Nostrand Reinhold. (Coverage of the items discussed in this chapter.)

Terrell, M. E. 1971. *Professional Food Preparation,* pp. 463-525. New York: John Wiley & Sons. (The bake shop and its production.)

CHAPTER 14

Eggs, Milk, and Cheese

OUTLINE

High temperatures toughen proteins of the type found in flesh foods. Eggs, milk, and cheese contain more delicate and unstable proteins than do flesh foods, so they require special care in cooking.

EGGS

Eggs are a versatile food. They can be a complete dish or entrée, or they can be served for breakfast or in a luncheon omelet. They can be stuffed and used as appetizers or chopped and used for sandwiches or in salads. They thicken and bind some products and cover others. When whipped to a foam, they bring air into items such as cakes, soufflés, and foamy omelets. Eggs, especially yolks, can emulsify, as in making mayonnaise or hollandaise sauce. They can clarify soups or give stability and texture to frozen desserts and candies. In fact, eggs are one of the kitchen's workhorses. They need special consideration in each different use.

Nutrition

Eggs contain the most digestible of proteins and supply good quantities of vitamins A and D, thiamine, riboflavin, niacin, fat, minerals, and calories. Eggs' iron is well used in the body. One large egg contains over 250 mg of cholesterol, and so people on low-cholesterol diets must restrict the number of eggs in their diet. The American Medical Association recommends that the total diet contain not more than 300 mg of cholesterol per day.

Quality

Eggs are at their highest quality immediately after laying. Unless chilled and held at low temperatures, they deteriorate rapidly. They are neutral or slightly acidic when laid but gradually become alkaline. Moisture is lost and the air sac gets larger as they age. A fresh egg has a high yolk and a white that clings to the yolk; there is little thin liquid. As aging occurs, the yolk's height drops, the white becomes thinner, and the yolk breaks easily when the egg is shelled. Older eggs whip to a better foam than fresh eggs do.

An egg's flavor changes as it ages. The white contains sulfur, and the yolk contains iron. When the iron and sulfur join, they make ferrous sulfide—an offensively strong-flavored and odoriferous product. Rotten eggs contain a lot of iron sulfide. Because iron sulfide is black, it also discolors eggs. Some off-flavors bake out in old eggs used in bakery goods, but this does not occur in breakfast eggs. Refrigerate eggs at 40°F (4.5°C). Remove only those that are to be used soon.

Processed eggs can be used in the bakeshop or in other production (see table 14-1). A high-quality frozen whole egg is available that can be used for French toast, omelets, and custards. Frozen whole eggs, frozen yolks, frozen whites, a sugared yolk (10

Table 14-1. Processed Dried Eggs and Their Fresh Egg Equivalents

	Part I. Processed to Fresh	
Processed Product	Egg to Water	Fresh Equivalent EP (Large Eggs)
No. 10 can (3 lb) dried whole		100 whole eggs
1 lb dry whole and 2½ pt water	1:2½	3½ lb whole eggs
1 lb dry yolks and 1½ pt water	1:1½	2½ lb yolks
6 oz dry whole and 1⅞ c water	3:7	dozen whole eggs
1 lb dried whole and 2½ pt water	1:2½	3 doz whole eggs (3½ lb)
1 lb dried whites and 5 pt water	1:5	100 whites (6 lb)
1 lb dried yolks and 1¾ c water	8:7	47 yolks

	Part II. Fresh to Processed			
	Quantity for 1 lb Equivalent			
Fresh Egg (and number to give 1 lb)	Dried Egg		Water	
	Ounces	*Measure*	*Ounces*	*Measure*
Whole egg (9)	4½	1 c 2 Tbsp	11¼	1 c 7 Tbsp
White (17 to 19)	2¼	½ c	13¾	1¾ c
Yolk* (20 to 24)	7¼	1 c	8¾	1 c 1 Tbsp
Yolk** (25 to 27)	7½	1 c	8½	1 c 1 Tbsp
Yolk*** (16 to 20)	6½	1 c	8	1 c

*43% solids
**45% solids
***Add 1.6 oz of sugar to give yolks with 10% sugar as used in the bakeshop for frozen sugared yolks.

percent sugar), and whole eggs containing added yolks (proprietary eggs) are used. All processed eggs must be pasteurized. Never use bakeshop-quality eggs for breakfast eggs or for regular cooked items.

Grades

Eggs are graded for quality on the following scale (from highest to lowest grade): AA, A, B, and C. C grade cannot be sold on the market, but instead must go into processed eggs. Few grade B eggs are used. Shell color is not a grade factor. Eggs are sized as shown in figure 14-1. Foodservices usually use large eggs.

Principles

When heat strikes eggs, the protein changes color, becoming firmer as it does in meats, fish, and poultry. The following coagulation temperatures are useful to know: whole eggs, 156°F (69°C); yolks, 144° to 158°F (62° to 70°C); whites, 140° to 149°F (60 to 65°C). When eggs are mixed with sugar or liquids, the coagulation temperature rises to around 175° to 185°F (79° to 85°C). If the temperature is raised quickly, a higher coagulation temperature is needed than if the temperature is raised slowly. Coagulation can also occur when eggs are mixed with strong acids or alcoholic drinks. High temperatures cause egg protein to toughen and develop a strong flavor. Adding an acid such as cream of tartar, lemon juice, or tomato juice makes them tenderer, retards undesirable flavor development, lowers the coagulation temperature, and increases the eggs' thickening power. Eggs beat to a foam better when they are slightly acidic.

Uncooked egg protein can combine with moisture. When heat strikes this mixture, the water binds tightly to the protein, causing the firmness seen in custards. Too much moisture or too high a heat can cause the protein to lose moisture—a process called *syneresis.* Gentle temperatures and a slightly acidic condition help to avoid it.

Beating air into eggs develops foam in whole eggs, yolks, or whites. Egg white does not foam if fat is present. Thus, whole eggs are harder to whip to a foam because of the fat in the yolk. Yolks whip well alone, however, older eggs foam better than fresh ones do. Dried or frozen egg products also whip well into foams. Eggs that have warmed to about 60°F (16°C) separate best into yolks and whites; they whip best if they are warmed to 75° to 110°F (24° to 43°C) and if they are slightly acidic. Some cooks think adding salt also helps. Acid also lightens the eggs. The amount of acid to use varies; about ¼ oz of cream of tartar to 1 lb of eggs is normal. Sugar gives egg foam stability. Eggs containing sugar can be whipped more without danger of being overwhipped. Some sugar is usually added soon after a good foam is obtained. Table 14-2 identifies the four different foam stages.

Cooking

Eggs for breakfast can be prepared in quantity, but it is difficult to do so. Custards and soufflés, however, pose no problem in quantity.

Boiled Eggs

Table 14-3 gives cooking times for soft-, medium- and hard-boiled eggs. The texture ranges from a soft, almost runny white and only warmed yolk for soft-boiled eggs to a completely coagulated egg for hard-boiled eggs. The latter should have no dark ring around the yolk; such a ring contains iron sulfide, which gives poor appearance and flavor. Good eggs cook to clear, shiny colors; poor ones are dull and have off-colors. Overcooking turns a good egg into a bad one. Overcooked eggs are tough, rubbery, or puffy.

Eggs to be stuffed or sliced should be boiled fairly hard, to give them enough toughness to handle.

Figure 14-1. Egg sizes and weights per dozen.

Table 14-2. Stages of Egg Foams

	First Stage	Second Stage	Third Stage	Fourth Stage
Foam appearance	Liquid, but well blended; foam is in large bubbles	Medium-size air cells throughout mass; foam is shiny, moist, and fluid; tips fold over into rounded peaks; liquid separates out in standing	Stiff foam; small air cells; no longer fluid, especially whites; still moist, smooth, and glossy; points stand when peaked	Dry, dull, brittle foam; flakes off and can be cut into rigid parts; curds may appear indicating coagulation; it is difficult to beat whole eggs or yolks to this stage
Foam use	Clarifying soups; French toast; coating foods; blending into mixtures as liquid	Sponge or angel cakes; soufflés; foamy omelets	Cooked frostings; divinity; soft or hard meringues; tortes; sponge cakes	Has no use in food work; eggs are so overextended that they will not extend further in baking, causing a failure in the product

Table 14-3. Cooking Times for Boiled Eggs

	Simmering		Steam Pressure (7 psi)
Boiling Style	212°F* (100°C)	190° to 195°F* (88° to 91°C)	
Soft-cooked	3 min	6 min	1 min 25 sec
Medium-cooked	4 min	8 min	
Hard-cooked	12 to 15 min	20 to 25 min	3 min 10 sec

*These times vary at elevations above 3,000 feet.

Simmer-cooking gives a tender egg that is delicate to eat but breaks in handling. Very cold eggs added to hot water can crack. Therefore eggs may be prewarmed or added to cooler water for cooking. To boil eggs in quantity, put them into a perforated basket, lower this into tepid water, and bring the water quickly to a boil. After cooking, plunge the eggs into cold water and send them immediately—as hot as possible—to service. The quick blanch stops the cooking. Eggs can also be steamed in the shell, but it takes skill to tell time and to get correct doneness.

To peel eggs, plunge the hot eggs into cold water and let them stand for 5 to 10 minutes. Then crack well and start to peel at the large end, where the air sac is. If they peel with difficulty, peel them under cold running water. The water helps lift the shell from the egg. If chopped eggs are needed, break eggs into lightly greased pans to a depth of about 2 inches, and steam them until hard-cooked. Then turn them out of the pan, and chop.

Coddled eggs are eggs put into boiling water — 1 pt per egg. After they have been added, the pot is covered, and the eggs are allowed to cook, without further heat, to desired doneness.

Fried Eggs

Eggs can be fried *over easy, sunny-side-up,* or *basted.* Over easy is frying until the egg is almost done, and then turning it over in the hot fat only to coagulate the top. A sunny-side-up egg is fried without being turned. Basted eggs are also called *country-style* eggs. They are fried with a tight cover on the pan so that steam cooks the tops. Alternatively, they can be basted with hot fat during frying. Some cooks fry sunny-side-up and then add a bit of water and cover tightly until a coating is formed over the eggs by the steam.

To fry, heat about ⅛ inch of fat in a pan to a temperature of from 350° to 375°F (182° to 190°C). Slide the egg into the hot fat, and quickly lower the heat; the hot fat helps keep the egg from spreading. Too hot a fat toughens the bottom of the egg, browning it and giving it a poorer flavor. Egg pans should be conditioned for frying. Eggs can also be fried on a grill. They are not as attractive as pan-cooked eggs, but more can be produced. Use good-quality fat or clarified butter. Set the grill's thermostat at from 300° to 325°F (149° to 163°C). Start some eggs at one place on the grill, and add more while the first batch is frying. Add more grease as necessary. Remove the eggs in the order they have been put onto the grill.

To baste, cover the eggs with a small pan. Often eggs are only partially fried before being put into pans and sent to the service area, where the pans are placed in the steam table and the eggs finish cooking.

Omelets

Omelets are made from whole eggs. Cook them at a higher temperature than most egg products, giving them a brown or delicate tan outside. They

a. b.

c. d.

Figure 14-2. Making an omelet: (a) have the fat fairly hot, and pour the beaten whole eggs into the pan; (b) lift until the entire mass is well-coagulated, and then fill and fold; (c) shape, if desired; (d) if the filling is sweet, dust with powdered sugar, and burn with a poker.

should be moist, tender, and delicate in flavor. Omelets should be rolled neatly and have a good shape. A ragged, separated omelet lacks proper appearance. A French omelet is made by beating whole eggs to a stage-one foam and adding them to a pan covered with about ⅛ inch of hot fat. Stir lightly to lift cooked portions and allow uncooked portions to flow underneath, but stop before the eggs become dry, so a *whole* mass can be obtained. Cheese, creamed fillings, marmalade, or other items can be placed at the center, and the omelet is then folded over. This is done while some moist egg remains on the interior, and this then cooks to seal the filling inside. The omelet can be flipped to cook on the other side, if desired. To unpan, tip the pan and let the omelet slide down. Place a plate under the pan, and let the omelet fall gently onto it. Omelets with sweetened centers can be "burned" as shown in Figure 14-2. Omelets can be made on a grill, but this is a difficult procedure.

Poaching

Shelled eggs cooked in water are called *poached.* The water should be 2 to 2½ inches deep in a

4-inch-deep pan. Use 1 Tbsp of salt and 2 Tbsp of vinegar per gal of water. Have the water gently boiling, and slide the eggs (already broken) from a plate or platter into the water. Sliding rather than dropping the eggs helps reduce flattening the egg. Poach 8 to 16 eggs per gal of water. The same water can be used for 3 to 4 batches before it must be discarded. Cooking time varies from 3 to 5 minutes.

Scrambling

Scrambled eggs are the easiest type to prepare in quantity. Stage-one mixed whole eggs (salted lightly) can be added to a steam-table pan and scrambled there. Finished scrambled eggs should be in fairly large segments, so stirring should be limited while they cook. Let the eggs cook on the bottom, and then lift them up and allow the liquid eggs to flow under to cook. Using too much heat during holding or holding for too long can cause a dark, tough bottom and a poor flavor. The eggs should be tender, moist, and delicate in flavor. Liquid such as milk or cream can be added in a ratio of 1:4 to eggs. Medium cream or white sauce can also be used. Scrambled eggs hold well for about 30 minutes. In the kitchen, they are cooked in large skillets, steamers, double boilers, steam-jacketed kettles, grills, or in bain-maries. Scrambled eggs to order are cooked in regular egg pans.

Shirred Eggs

Shirring is a method of baking an egg. Eggs are put into shallow ceramic dishes that are liberally buttered. These are placed over heat until a trace of coagulation appears on the bottom. They are then finished under a broiler or in an oven. The whites should be cooked, but not the yolks. Excessive heat makes them rubbery. Good shirred eggs have a bright, solid appearance; poorly made ones are dull and puffy. Sometimes ham or several cooked strips of bacon are placed on the dish bottom, and the eggs are put over them and shirred. Cream and cheese can be put over the eggs before they go into the oven. Creamed chicken, seafood Newburg, chicken livers, tomato quarters, mushrooms, diced ham, or other mixtures are placed over shirred eggs after cooking.

Soufflés

A soufflé can be an entrée or a dessert. It is a mixture of well-beaten egg whites folded into a starch base containing the yolks and a seasoning mixture. Thus, the paste for a cheese soufflé contains milk, roux, and seasonings, along with cheese. This paste is cooked, and the yolks are added. Then the stage-three beaten egg whites are folded in, and the mixture is baked in a greased casserole or other dish. The oven is set at about 300°F (149°C), or at 375°F (190°C) if the baking dish is placed in a pan of water.

Soufflés are delicate and can fall when they are removed from the oven. Some cooks pull soufflés to the edge of the oven when they are done and leave the door open for a few minutes to allow them to adjust. A good soufflé should have a slightly rounded top that is puffy and slightly cracked. The crust should be a delicate brown (see fig. 14-3). Chopped meat, seafood, poultry, and other foods can be added to the paste. As a dessert, soufflés may be flavored with chocolate, strawberry, vanilla, or other flavors.

Custards

A custard is a combination of milk and eggs. Custards can be sweet and used as a dessert, or they can be unsweetened and combined with vegetables for service as a timbale. A fondue (different from a Swiss fondue) is a light custard-like entrée resembling a soufflé. It combines milk and eggs and may

Figure 14-3. Freshly baked soufflé.

be baked with cheese, poultry, or seafood. The fondue is then served with a sauce. Soft bread cubes are usually added to give it a light texture. Swiss fondue is a melted mixture of white wine, garlic, Swiss (Emmentaler) and Gruyère cheese that is served in a chafing dish. People at the table dip cubes of hard-crusted bread into the mixture. The Swiss also have a fondue that uses hot oil in a chafing dish to deep-fry meat items.

A stirred custard is a sweetened mixture of milk, eggs, and seasoning that is cooked while being stirred over hot water, until it coats a spoon. Constant, thorough stirring and gentle heat must be used to prevent curdling. Stirred custard is used as a sauce over desserts. Sabayon (French) and zabaglione (Italian) are stirred custards composed of eggs and a wine such as Marsala; they are cooked until slightly thickened and then served over desserts. Often only egg yolks are used because they are less likely to curdle than whole eggs.

The proportion of eggs to liquid for a custard is 1½ to 2 lb of whole eggs to each 1 gal of liquid. If yolks are used or if cereals are combined with the custard, the quantity of eggs may be reduced. Thus, fewer eggs are used to make a bread or rice custard pudding. A custard bakes better if the milk is already heated to about 140°F (60°C) when it is added to the eggs. Custards often are baked in pans of water, to protect them from the heat. Too much heat

causes syneresis. Baking temperatures usually range from 325° to 340°F (164° to 171°C), with the custard baked in a pan of water.

DAIRY PRODUCTS

Milk and its products are among our most nutritious foods. They are an excellent source of calcium and phosphorus, and they also provide a limited amount of iron. They are a good source of some B vitamins, especially riboflavin. The protein in milk is complete and very digestible. Milk fat is fairly saturated. Table 14-4 gives the percentage makeup of different milks. Available grades of milks, creams, butter, and cheese include the following (from best to worst): AA, A, B, and C.

Milk and Cream

Coffee or table cream is 18 percent milkfat; light whipping cream is 30 to 34 percent milkfat; heavy cream is 34 to 36 percent milkfat; half-and-half is about 10.5 percent milkfat; and regular milk is 3¼ to 4 percent milkfat. The milkfat of yogurt, buttermilk, and other dairy products varies. Sour cream is 18 percent milkfat. Evaporated and condensed milk are fairly high in milkfat, since they are concentrated from regular milk.

Table 14-4. Approximate Composition of Different Milks

Type of Milk	Fat (Butterfat)	Nonfat Solids (Protein, Milk Sugar, Minerals)	Water	Sucrose (Sugar)
Fresh whole milk	3.5%	8.5%	88%	
Fresh nonfat milk	trace	9%	91%	
Evaporated whole milk	8%	18%	74%	
Evaporated nonfat milk	trace	20 to 30%	70 to 80%	
Sweetened condensed whole milk	8%	20%	30%	42%
Dry whole milk	27%	70%	3%	
Nonfat dry milk	trace	96%	4%	

Milk and its products are used in many foods as a liquid base in which other ingredients are brought together. It contributes flavor, color, texture, and richness. A cake baked with milk keeps better. Dry milk is satisfactory for much cooking and baking. Butter is made from cream and is 80 percent fat; the remainder is salt and liquid. Margarines are also 80 percent fat. Most contain milk solids for flavoring. Low-saturated-fat margarines are available. The fat in butter is fairly saturated. Butter may be made from either sour or sweet cream. Sweet cream butter is very mild in flavor and can be ordered unsalted. Grades for butter are the same as for other dairy products, except that it can also be ordered by grade score: AA is 93 score, A is 92 score, B is 89 score, and C is 88 score. Foodservices normally order AA (93 score) or A (92 score). Cooking butter may be A or B. Little or no grade C butter is used. Butter is usually available in pats, in wrapped quarters, half-pounds, or pounds, or in cubes of pound bricks stacked $4 \times 4 \times 4$ or 64 pounds. Cooking butter is often ordered in cubes. Pats come usually in 5-lb boxes, layered between sheets of parchment, wax, or polyethylene paper, with seventy-two to ninety pats per lb.

Principles

Milk is a delicate substance that can curdle and scorch easily. Fresh milk is almost neutral, but bacteria that produce lactic acid can sour it. With a pH of about 4.6, milk becomes unstable and curdles, separating into casein and whey. Wine, lemon juice, tomato juice, vinegar, or other acids easily curdle milk. Curdling is a problem since these are often blended with milk in cooking. Milk can also be curdled by salts such as nitrites or nitrates in cured meat, by tannins in potatoes, asparagus, and other products, by very hard water, and by coffee. Heat and salt speed curdling. Evaporated milk is the most stable form of milk, with fresh milk next and dry milk last.

To prevent curdling, cook at low heat and withhold salt until just before service. Any acid should be withheld until it must be added. Adding soda to milk makes it more alkaline and helps it resist curdling, but it also destroys vitamin C and thiamine and has a bad effect on flavor and (sometimes) color. Curdling substances, such as a tomato velouté for tomato soup, must be handled in a special manner. First pour a small bit of the curdling product into the warmed milk; stir vigorously to blend, and then add this tempered mixture into the tomato sauce.

Some milk proteins coagulate when heated. As a result, a scum forms over the top or milk solids collect on the bottom, which leads to scorching. Putting a bit of fat over the milk top prevents the scum from forming. To prevent scorching, heat milk in a double boiler, a steam-jacketed kettle, or a steamer. It also can be heated over a hot surface in a very heavy pan, if it is stirred well. Milk heated for a long time acquires a darker color and a flatter, caramelized flavor.

Pasteurization and Homogenization

Dairy products are pasteurized to destroy pathogens. Milk is pasteurized by being heated for 30 minutes at 143°F (62°C). It can also be flash-pasteurized by being heated for 15 seconds at 160°F (71°C); even higher temperatures and shorter times are now common. Ultrapasteurized products are subjected to the highest temperatures of all. Homogenization divides fat globules so that they remain suspended in the product instead of rising to the top. Milk to be homogenized is forced under very high pressure through tiny holes; this breaks up the fat into a fine emulsion. Whipping cream is usually not homogenized, since homogenization reduces its whipping ability.

Foams

Milk and its products have the ability to foam because they contain protein and fat. The more fat present, the stabler the foam.

Whipping cream and the container in which it is whipped should both be cold. Warmth destroys whipping ability. Using a deep bowl helps develop foam. The increase in volume is about two to three times; recipes usually state the amount of unwhipped cream to use. Using powdered sugar as a sweetener instead of granulated gives a more stable foam.

Whipping cream turns into sweet butter if over-whipped.

To whip evaporated milk, scald it first and then cool it down. (Cans may be put into boiling water for 5 to 10 minutes). Adding a bit of hydrated gelatin (½ tsp unhydrated gelatin per pt) aids in giving a more stable foam. When the milk is at 40°F (4.5°C), it can be whipped. When the foam has almost developed, add 3 Tbsp of lemon juice per pt (with sugar and flavorings) and finish beating. Then refrigerate.

Although it is difficult to get a stable foam with a product that is less than 30 percent milkfat, whole or nonfat dry milk can be used to make a low-calorie whipped product. The increase is to four times the original volume, but the foam is not stable. Use 1 qt of instant dry milk or ¾ qt of regular dry milk per qt of ice water to make a foam. Whip this until a soft peak forms, and then add a cup of lemon juice. The resulting foam has a lemony flavor. Whip until the product is stiff, and add 2 cups of sugar and other flavorings. Then refrigerate.

Uses of Milk Products

Dry milk is milk evaporated until only the solids remain. It becomes like regular milk when this moisture is replaced; 1 lb of dry milk per gal of water makes a slightly more concentrated milk than natural milk (see table 14-5). Dry milk made a day before use tastes better than newly reconstituted milk, since the lactose takes time to go into solution. Dry milks may curdle with hard or extended boiling. Add 5 oz of butter or other fat per gal of nonfat milk to give the milk a fat content equivalent to that of regular milk.

Adding extra milk solids to baked products and frozen desserts improves their quality, texture, and flavor. They also keep better. Frozen desserts with extra milk solids are smoother. Some recipe adjustment may be necessary.

Instant dry milk has been processed to go into solution easily. Regular dry milk does not, so it must be mixed more carefully. In baking, add dry milk with the sifted dry ingredients, and add the extra liquid with the liquid used in the recipe. Weigh dry milk, rather than measuring it. This allows easy interchange of instant and regular dry milk. The best way to blend regular dry milk into water is to sift it over the top and use a wire whip to blend it in.

Evaporated milk is milk that has had a lot (about 55 percent) of its water extracted. If the evaporated milk is from whole milk, multiply the quantity of evaporated milk by 2.2 to get the equivalent amount of whole milk. Thus, 1 pt of evaporated milk (16 oz) equals 35.2 oz of whole milk ($2.2 \times 16 = 35.2$). The regular No. 1 can holds 14.5 oz, which is equivalent to 1 qt of whole milk ($2.2 \times 14.5 = 31.9$). Sweetened condensed milk is evaporated milk that contains 45 percent added sugar. It is seldom used in foodservices.

Cream is made from milk. It is lighter than milk and so can be centrifuged out of it. Customers add cream to coffee until they see a desired color. The higher the milkfat content, the better the color. About 1 Tbsp (½ oz) is a portion. Cream is often portioned. An individual portion is usually calculated to have a 6 percent loss. Homogenized cream has a smoother flavor in coffee than nonhomogenized. Many operations use synthetic products rather than true cream.

Table 14-5. Processed Milk Equivalents of 1 Gallon of Milk

For 1 gal whole liquid milk use:	For 1 gal nonfat liquid milk use:
18 oz dry whole milk	13 oz dry nonfat milk
7½ lb or 3¾ qt water	7¾ or 3 qt 2½ c water
or	*or*
13 oz nonfat dry milk	4½ lb nonfat evaporated milk
5 oz melted fat	
7½ lb or 3¾ qt water	4¼ lb or 2 qt ½ c water
or	*or*
4¼ lb evaporated whole milk	3 lb condensed nonfat milk
4½ lb or 2¼ qt water	7 lb or 3½ qt water**
or	
4 lb condensed whole milk	
6¼ lb or 3¼ qt water*	

*Will also contain 1 lb 10 oz sugar.
**Will also contain 1 lb 5 oz sugar.

Cheese

Cheese is primarily composed of milkfat and casein. It is separated from milk by adding bacteria that develop lactic acid, by adding acid, or by adding rennet (an enzyme that solidifies milk into a clabber so that it can be separated into curds, which are solids, and whey, which is liquid). There are many kinds of cheese, and each type is made by a slightly different technique. Most cheese is made from cows' milk; others are made from the milk of goats, sheep, reindeer, or buffalo.

The aging of cheese is divided into three periods, called *current, medium,* and *aged* or *ripened;* American current is aged up to 30 days; medium, 30 to 90 days; and aged or ripened, over 90 days. Swiss current is aged up to 60 days; medium, 60 days to 6 months; and aged, over 6 months. Most foodservices purchase their American cheese in daisies weighing about 25 lb, but they can get cheese in other size units as well. Swiss cheese comes in different-sized units, too. Large wheels of Swiss can weigh 50 to 100 lb. Processed cheese usually comes in 5-lb bricks. Stages of cheese processing are identified in figure 14-14.

Aged (ripened) cheese has a relatively tart, sharp flavor and is softer and more mellow than fresh cheese. Fresh cheese is rubbery and more difficult to blend into sauces. Moisten dry cheeses such as Parmesan before trying to blend them with other ingredients.

Cheese is a delicate product. High heat hardens it. In a sauce or rarebit, high heat causes curdling. Cheese is blended into sauces at temperatures below the boiling point. Cheese can curdle milk, as sometimes happens in cheese sauces. To avoid this, first thicken the milk with starch, binding the casein in, and then add the cheese.

Enzymes and bacteria aid in cheese development. Limburger is ripened by having bacteria work their way into the cheese, making it softer and giving it a ripe, mellow flavor. Brie, Camembert, brick, and other cheeses ripen in the same way. Others, such as Swiss, ripen by having bacteria work from within them; for this to happen, bacteria must be added to the cheese as it is being made. While the cheese is aging, these bacteria are at work; the large bubbles or eyes in Swiss cheese come from bacteria-developed gas in the cheese. Other cheeses are ripened with molds, including Roquefort, blue, Gorgonzola, and Stilton.

Some cheeses are quite dry because the temper-

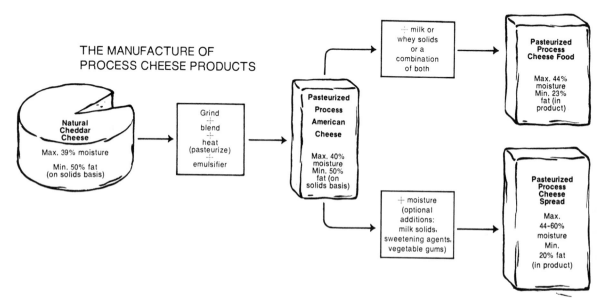

Figure 14-4. Manufacturing cheese and process cheese products.

ature was raised while they were being made, driving out moisture and hardening the curd. Other cheeses, such as mozzarella used for pizza, are tacky and stringy. These are pulled and worked so that the casein joins together into a sticky mass. Some cheeses become very smooth as they age; their flavor gets richer and also more tart. Selecting the right cheese for a particular cooking need is not difficult if a proper study has been made of cheese and its properties.

Natural cheese is a product made by coagulating milk and then separating the solid curd from the whey. Some natural cheeses are ripened to develop flavor and textures, while others are used unripened. Ripened cheeses often are labeled as to their degree of ripening. Cheddar cheese, for example, may be labeled "mild," "medium," or "aged (ripened)." Some connoisseurs prefer natural cheese to others because of its flavor and texture. Cheese flavors range from bland (cottage cheese) to tangy (blue) to pungent (Limburger). Textures vary from the smooth creaminess of cream cheese to the firm elasticity of Swiss.

A processed cheese does not age because, after being brought to the proper flavor and texture, it is pasteurized (which prevents further changes). Processed cheese is 98 percent cheese. It can be flavored with other items. It goes into solution very easily in sauces because it contains an emulsifier that helps blend it in. It does not have a rind, so there is little waste. Processed cheese is available in blocks, slices, or spreads.

Pasteurized cheese food is a blend of fresh and aged natural cheese, processed cheese, and other substances such as dry whey, dry milk solids, and fillers. It may lack the milkfat content that is required to be in regular cheese. It is usually pasteurized, and it is often made into spreads.

SUMMARY

Eggs and milk products are high-protein foods that require similar treatment in cooking and baking.

Eggs contain excellent protein and other important nutrients. They add color, richness, and flavor to food.

Egg quality is important. A very fresh egg with a high yolk and a firm white is desired for breakfast purposes. High-quality frozen processed eggs also can be used for breakfast. All processed eggs are pasteurized to destroy harmful bacteria. Processed eggs include dried whole, dried whites, dried yolks, frozen whole, frozen whites, frozen yolks, and other specialty frozen products. They are used primarily in baking.

Eggs coagulate when heat strikes them. The protein changes color and firms. If the egg has a lot of liquid added to it and the heat is too high, the liquid can separate out, causing a curdling called *syneresis*. Eggs will foam. Eggs separate best at around 60°F (16°C) and whip best at about 110°F (43°C). Whites do not whip well if any grease is present.

Egg yolks contain iron, and the whites contain sulfur. When iron joins with sulfur, it makes ferrous sulfide, which is an offensively odorous, bad-tasting, dark product. Overcooked and old eggs easily develop this substance. As fresh eggs age, they become more alkaline, which favors the development of ferrous sulfide. Adding acid ingredients to eggs discourages the formation of this chemical.

Eggs can be boiled, coddled, fried, poached, shirred, scrambled, and made into omelets and soufflés. Eggs also are used to make baked or stirred custards. The grades of eggs used in foodservices are AA, A, and B. The sizes are jumbo, extra large, large, medium, small, and peewee.

Milk, which is an excellent food nutritionally, is used in cooking to blend substances together. Acids, tannins, salts, and some other substances cause milk to curdle, as will heat. Curdling is the separation of the casein in the milk from the liquid whey. Milk has proteins that will coagulate, as seen in the scum that forms on heated milk or collects on the side of the pan. The collected protein on the bottom of a pan causes milk to scorch easily, so milk usually is cooked over water, in a steamer, or in a steam-jacketed kettle.

Milk and its products are pasteurized to destroy harmful bacteria. They may also be homogenized to separate the milkfat into tiny globules so that it does not rise to the top. Milk can be made into foams. Dry milks will foam if properly handled, as will evaporated milk. Whipping cream comes from a cream that contains more than 30 percent milkfat. To whip properly, the milk or cream and the utensils used in whipping should be very cold.

Milk products used in production are creams, half-and-half, soured products, buttermilk, yogurt, dry whole or nonfat milk, evaporated milk, and condensed milk.

Cheese is made from milk by separating the casein and milkfat from the whey. Ripened cheese is sharper and stronger in flavor than unripened cheese. It is also softer and goes into solution in sauces and other foods more easily. A processed cheese is a natural cheese that has been pasteurized to stop ripening. It contains an emulsifier, which makes it go into solution more easily. Fruits, vegetables, meats, and other products are added to processed cheese. Some processed cheese is made into spreads.

Chapter Review Questions

1. A cook has curdled a batch of cream of mushroom soup. Set up an outline of what a chef should tell the cook about preparing such products.
2. You want to present a lecture to a group of trainees on how to cook eggs. Set up an outline on what should be covered.
3. Name five ways eggs are used in food production, and indicate the procedure used. For instance, if you say that eggs are used to make emulsions, state how the egg is used to form an emulsion.
4. Why are eggs and milk products nutritious foods?
5. Describe a fresh egg, and indicate what happens when an egg ages. Are fresh eggs *always* best to use in cooking and baking? Explain.
6. What is coagulation in an egg? What is ferrous sulfide, and how does it form in eggs? What does heat do in the formation of ferrous sulfide?
7. Name the types of processed eggs. Why must they now be pasteurized? What are the

grades and sizes of eggs? How are eggs sized?

8. What would you tell an employee about how to make a good egg foam?
9. Describe how eggs are cooked. Prepare some of these products in the laboratory, and critique them for quality.
10. List some of the products that come from milk, and identify how they can be used in food production.
11. What makes milk curdle? How can milk's tendency to curdle be reduced?
12. Certain phenomena occur when milk is used in cooking. Why do coagulation, scum formation, and scorching happen? What are pasteurization and homogenization, as applied to milk and its products?
13. What kinds of foams can be made from milk products? Describe how each foam should be made.
14. How should the various milk products be handled in food production?
15. What is cheese? processed cheese? cheese food? How do they differ? State several principles that should be observed in handling cheese in food preparation.

Vocabulary

Fresh egg	Shirred egg
Ferrous sulfide	Soufflé
Proprietary eggs	Half-and-half
Pasteurization	Coffee cream
Coagulation	Light whipping cream
Grade AA	Heavy whipping cream
Curdling	Dry whole milk
Hard-cooked	Dry nonfat milk
Medium-cooked	Evaporated milk
Soft-cooked	Condensed milk
Sunny-side-up	Butter
Over easy	Margarine
Basted	Homogenization
Country-style	Natural cheese
Coddled	Processed cheese

French omelet

Foamy omelet

Burned omelet

Poached egg

Cheese food

Ripened cheese

Syneresis

ANNOTATED REFERENCES

Gates, J. C., 1976. *Basic Foods,* pp. 334-80. New York: Holt, Rinehart & Winston. (Eggs, milk, and cheese in food preparation.)

Hughes, O., and Bennion, M. 1970. *Introductory Foods,* pp. 196-255. New York: Macmillan. (Eggs and egg cookery and milk and milk products.)

Lundberg, D. E., and Kotschevar, L. H. 1986. *Understanding Cooking,* pp. 176-99. Holyoke, Mass: Marcus Printing. (Egg cookery.)

Peckham, G. G. 1974. *Foundations of Food Preparation,* pp. 213-50. New York: Macmillan. (Eggs, milk, and cheese.)

Vail, G. E.; Phillips, J. A.; Rust, L. O.; Griswold, R. M.; and Justin, M. M. 1973. *Foods,* pp. 147-94. Boston: Houghton Mifflin. (Eggs, milk, and milk products.)

PART III

Quantity Food Management— The Five P's

CHAPTER 15

Management of People

OUTLINE

Foodservice is a very people-oriented and people-intensive industry. Unlike manufacturing, where many repetitive tasks can be completed by machines, foodservice depends on the productivity of human beings for customer satisfaction and industry growth. Although it was once assumed in management circles that the proper way to increase productivity was to break each task down into the smallest possible repetitive tasks, today we realize that in many instances this system does not work (except for purposes of training). For whatever reasons, today's worker does not share the same attitudes and reactions held by workers in the past. Workers who lived and worked through the Depression regarded job security as their principal motivation for working. But today's baby boomers, who make up a large portion of the work force, may be more motivated by job satisfaction and opportunity than by security. Just providing a job to today's workers may not be enough; there must also be a reason for work.

Experts believe that job satisfaction will become an even more important issue in the future. While today's work force has been inflated to accommodate the largest bulge in population ever known to this country, the work force of the future will be different. Instead of there being too many workers, there will likely be too many jobs. In a labor-intensive industry such as foodservice, this may become especially true. If a future trend toward labor shortage is combined with the already people-intensive criteria of the foodservice industry, a real problem could develop. Therefore, good foodservice managers today are learning not only the basics of personnel management, but also the finer points of what has come to be called *human resources development.*

THE HUMAN RESOURCES CYCLE

At one time American management assessed the skill of workers on the basis of their technical expertise. Yet this is not always true today—especially in the case of foodservice. Proficiency in foodservice depends on a combination of the ability to complete tasks and appropriate behavior. The most obvious example is the waiter or waitress who delivers service to a customer. But it is also true for heart-of-the house personnel. For instance, a cook combines behavior with task in preparing a meal. While the task portion of the cook's job seems most obvious, each meal is made slightly differently; therefore, even with strict guidelines for preparation, each meal varies somewhat. This variance raises the behavioral aspect of service because, unless the differences in task are handled with dedication and sincerity, the meal will not be acceptable. Without a balance of the two requirements, a foodservice staff can become either technically perfect but hostile or very friendly but incompetent. The human resources cycle offers steps that, if properly followed, can help eliminate both potential problems. Both competence and proper behavior should be viewed as crucial to successful staff development.

The first step is selection. Without a properly implemented plan for selecting personnel as a foundation, all other steps will fail. The second step is performance—the establishment of criteria for determining whether or not a job is being done correctly. The third step is appraisal—the evaluation of performance standards, including the operation's rewards system and its method of development or training.

LEVELS OF PEOPLE MANAGEMENT

In almost every business, there are three levels of personnel management: corporate, general, and operational. Managers at the corporate level are interested in, among other things, the strategic planning (or anticipation) of human resources needs. At this level, the primary goal is to develop policies to determine where people fit over time. At the second level (usually handled in foodservices by general managers), the main objective is the proper allocation of human resources. Questions such as what kind of human resources are needed, where the needs are, and what arrangement will handle them most efficiently are addressed by this level of management. The manager at this level is interested in determining where each employee fits in, how well each can perform the duties required, how many duties each can handle, and so on. This is also the level at which skills development for personnel management takes place. In foodservice operations, however, all three levels can become the responsibility of the foodservice manager.

Strategic Human Resources Needs

Sometimes foodservices neglect to plan adequately for personnel management. We have all seen the results of failure at this level—such as a hastily trained server whose first day on the floor came too soon.

One of the best ways to anticipate the personnel needs of a business is to use a variation of the G. E. matrix, which was developed in the 1950s. In this system, a foodservice manager determines both the needs and the skills required in the operation by plotting them on a matrix.

Human Resources at the General Managerial Level

At the managerial level, the objectives are to find individuals who can fill the jobs, establish pay scales, and so on. The goal is to determine how to fit the employees' needs into those of the operation. While many managers feel that the key consideration for all employees is money, several other factors are at least as important to most employees. The reward systems involved in personnel management are determined at the managerial level, as are the requirements for and methods of promotion, incentives, recognition, and respect. Since in many cases an employee can choose from several job opportunities (in the worst case) or produce only half-heartedly (in the best case), this level of human resources management is very important.

Objectives at the Operational Level

The human resources objectives of management at the operational level are often inadequately carried out, perhaps because management commonly regards the supervisory activities these objectives demand as time-consuming and distasteful. Yet their importance can be measured in direct on-the-job performance. If, for instance, performance appraisals of employees are conducted fairly and equitably, the staff will be more satisfied and will produce better. If only half-hearted attempts are made, however, or if the system is biased for any reason, the staff will respond with lower productivity. The operational level is also where training programs are instituted to develop more competent and productive employees. If the training is designed in such a way that management and employees both benefit from it, the program will achieve its aims.

NEEDS ANALYSIS

The first step in determining an appropriate human resources program for a foodservice is to perform a needs analysis. Here, the objective is to seek information about the operation and its personnel, in order to determine discrepancies between desired and actual performance levels.

The task goals of a foodservice staff are generally included in the mission statement of the organization. In a fastfood operation, for example, the company might establish as its principal objective the need to serve customers within 3 minutes of receiving their orders. All other activities then revolve around or depend on the initial goal of fast service. Production of food, type of service, training, and so on all reflect the priority of 3-minute service as the operation's mission. An objective evaluation of how often this primary goal is achieved determines in the most general terms the human resources needs.

SKILLS ANALYSIS AND JOB DESCRIPTION

In order to anticipate the personnel needs of a foodservice organization, management must clearly delineate the skills required for each job and must analyze the skills that the organization already possesses through its present human resources. In both cases, management's undertaking is often called a *skills analysis.* The skills analysis for the job itself often takes the shape of a job description, while analysis of individuals within the company is performed by means of various methods that evaluate personnel skills in different job tasks and behaviors.

Too often foodservice managers feel that, if they could only get the job description down on paper, employees would perform correctly. Nothing is farther from the truth. While writing a good job description is a necessary step in human resources development, it is not a be-all and end-all. Properly set down, the job description simply establishes the criteria by which performance will be evaluated.

Job descriptions vary from company to company; however, most include a description of the tasks to be performed, requirements for personnel hired to fill the position, the form of work evaluation to be used, and such specific items as the time when and place where work is to be done.

JOB DESIGN

A job may be performed incorrectly by an employee for many reasons. While many foodservice managers attribute such poor performance to a problem with employee behavior, the fault more frequently rests with the job itself. How jobs are designed often determines how well they will be performed. Consequently, a considerable degree of thought should be given to designing each job correctly. There are four principal aspects to any job design: the content of the job; the methods of doing the job; the performance level of the people doing the job; and the relationship of the people doing the job with other people on the staff. Many foodservice managers have found that involving the employees in job design is beneficial, for two important reasons. First, the employees know the most about the requirements of the jobs they do. Second, by involving employees in job design, management enlists employee support for the resulting design description, thereby introducing a higher degree of job satisfaction. Workers are more likely to support a job whose requirements they had a role in determining.

ASSESSING THE PERFORMANCE OF MANAGEMENT AND STAFF

As part of its regular human resources plan, every foodservice should have a method for evaluating the performance of management. In addition to supplying the company with valuable information about the progress of personnel, these evaluations also provide a responsible basis for establishing criteria for raises and promotions. Various types of performance evaluations have been successfully used in foodservices. Among the most prevalent types are skills audits, performance appraisals, and assessment centers. Once it has established standards for the level of job performance expected, management should measure performance, compare it to the standards, and then make an evaluation.

Skills Audits

Skills audits are a qualitative method often used to assess the abilities of management. First, a workshop of managers and supervisors is organized, and participants are divided into peer groups. Then, aided by facilitators, these groups brainstorm the performance standards, skills, priorities, behaviors,

and task resolutions for each job description. By working in groups, people in management are challenged to define what their roles should be in the foodservice.

Performance Appraisals

The performance appraisal is perhaps the most widely used method of evaluating both workers and management. Performance appraisals are based on progress toward a clear set of goals, which can be established for three principal reasons: compensation, promotion, and career development. The goals should be established by management in consultation with the staff—not by management alone. In the case of a foodservice, the goals should be both procedural and behavioral.

After the goals to be accomplished have been set, specific methods of measuring progress toward the goals should be established. Like the goals themselves, the measurement scale should be determined jointly by management and staff, and the measurement itself can be performed by either of the two. Various performance appraisals have been successfully conducted, including management appraisals of staff, staff self-appraisals, staff evaluations of management, group evaluations, and management self-evaluations. Often it is beneficial to combine two or more of these methods in order to eliminate any bias that may otherwise skew the appraisal. One method often used in foodservice is for the staff members to evaluate themselves individually at the same time that management is evaluating them. An open discussion of both the consistencies and the inconsistencies that exist between the two evaluations has often fostered future employee growth and development, as well as better communication between employees and management. After the goals and measurement methods are established, regular evaluations are performed to determine the progress of each person involved.

Several negative factors can influence the performance appraisal system, and a manager should be aware of the threat by each. Among the most likely errors in an evaluation is to note the most recent act as typical, when in reality it may be isolated. Favoritism can also play a distorting role in performance appraisals unless closely monitored, as can the "halo effect," in which the evaluator recognizes only performance levels in a favorite portion of the job. To eliminate these pitfalls, many managers utilize a system of spot-checking appraisals at random to determine their reliability. While the system is not foolproof, it has proved valuable to many foodservice operators.

Assessment Centers

Assessment centers were originally designed by the military during World War II for training agents. Since then, various businesses, including many foodservice organizations, have adopted such centers as an effective means of evaluating personnel. To date, the assessment center format has been used primarily to test the ability of management to make decisions, yet the process can also be used to evaluate employees as potential managerial candidates.

In using the assessment center system, small groups of six to eight managers (or prospective managers) are formed, and each group is asked to perform in a variety of situations that either simulate on-the-job management or call for role playing by the participants. While participating, the members of each group are evaluated by an observer on the basis of various attributes displayed.

One of the greatest strengths of the assessment center is the opportunity it affords to evaluate the interpersonal skills of each participant. Since the test situations call for the development of group decisions, observers are able to determine how management personnel will interact with other members of management or with the staff.

EMPLOYEE RECRUITMENT AND SELECTION

Even though employees account for thousands of dollars in wages each year to the foodservices for which they work, many managers spend very little time on the procedures by which these employees are recruited or selected. Too often, the workers are hired only on the basis of last-minute newspaper advertisements. When this is done, the future of the foodservice depends on whoever answers the ads.

To recruit and select employees properly, the foodservice manager should establish both long- and short-term employee needs goals. In addition, a pool of available potential employees should be kept on file so that they can be reached at need. To provide for an orderly recruitment and selection process, the foodservice manager should design and have ready the proper type of recruiting material to be used for each job position. Many foodservices, for instance, design advertisements for schools, newspapers, magazines, bulletin boards, and in-house memos well in advance of their actual need. In addition to creating specific advertisements for recruiting, however, a foodservice manager must also maintain an adequate supply of applications, orientation booklets, policy statements, and procedural outlines for each job description, in order to be able to respond to demand as needed.

Too often, management assesses the people working in the organization only in terms of dollars and cents. This is wrong. The people in a foodservice can represent money in the bank, if properly managed, and a positive attitude toward staff will become even more important in the future.

The first step in developing a responsible attitude toward workers is for management to establish a commitment to the personnel in the organization. For many foodservice companies, this means thinking of employees in terms of the opportunity costs associated with them. An employee who is properly selected, oriented, trained, and managed with integrity will become an asset to the firm. If these steps are bypassed, on the other hand, or if shortcuts are taken, the opposite result is likely. One method of effectively displaying a commitment to employees is through a policy of internal recruitment and selection. Under this policy, prior to any external recruitment for job vacancies, a foodservice will post the jobs internally. By doing this and promoting deserving candidates, a manager can build the type of respect for integrity with the staff that is essential in a good operation. In addition, many foodservices have found that the current staff is a good source of recommendations for potential employees from the outside. Hiring people on the recommendation of other staff members can build a rapport in much the same manner as hiring internally.

For hiring from the outside, a foodservice should maintain records showing the degree of effectiveness of each type of advertisement used. This will help identify, over time, the most effective methods of recruitment, which can then be developed and reused. The outside sources of employees most often used by foodservices are newspaper, radio, and billboard advertisements, other foodservices (which may have a surplus of good applicants), schools, colleges, temporary help agencies, employment agencies, and former employees.

Employee selection can be effectively accomplished through various methods. In many cases, the methods used depend on the size of the staff available to accommodate the process. If the foodservice has a personnel department, for instance, the process can be lengthy; but if the manager in charge of operating the foodservice is also the person responsible for all of the hiring, quicker methods may be appropriate. Many foodservices have found that personal interviews combined with questionnaires are a good way to handle selection. Other foodservices use psychometric tests that analyze attitudes, values, personality, and beliefs to identify desirable personnel. Still others use skills tests or organizational records in selecting personnel. Today, many foodservices also use preemployment polygraph tests to determine the desirability of potential employees. At all times, the method used should be accompanied by reference checks of the individuals applying for the position. In addition, a foodservice manager must scrupulously follow the guidelines established by the EEOC and other government agencies for fair hiring practices.

ORIENTATION

Although orientation is often dismissed by foodservice management as being a time-consuming and insignificant portion of the human resources process, it can provide employees with a solid understanding of the job to be done. If the orientation clearly sets out the requirements and responsibilities of the job, the employee will know from the start what is expected. A good orientation should also include a complete tour of the facility, introductions to all personnel with whom the new staff member will be working, and a description of all company policies and procedures that are pertinent to the job.

Orientation should never be left entirely to another employee. While it may be necessary or even wise for an employee to lead the tour or handle the introductions, well-run foodservices always involve management in the orientation process. In such foodservices, one manager is often designated as the training manager and bears managerial responsibility for orientation.

TRAINING

Training is one of the most effective methods of eliciting good performance on the job. As such, it should not be left up to other employees to perform. Training should be thought of as an educational process whose specific goal is to teach job competence.

The first step in designing an effective training program is to determine the critical incidents (most important aspects) of the job. The next step is to determine the exact criteria on which performance during training should be evaluated. This, of course, varies from one foodservice to another, as well as from job to job. In most cases, the criteria should address both behavioral and procedural objectives. The procedural objectives might include such points as how to perform a certain task properly and how much time to allow for the task. These objectives should be broken down into the smallest identifiable tasks, before being used for training. Each task should require no more than a single sentence to describe, and each should always begin with an action verb—such as "pick up the cup by the handle." This part of the training is often carried out in simulation before it is actually performed in situations involving customers or products of the foodservice; it should always be directed by a manager or supervisor in charge of training.

Several different methods of directing the employee during the first part of the training program have been successful. In some, all training is done at the work station; in others, training is conducted in classrooms or mock work environments.

After the stage of initial training is complete, most foodservices have found it advantageous to turn the new employee over to a current employee for apprenticeship training, which may last from a few hours to a few days. By observing the actions of a more experienced employee, the trainee can get a hands-on feel for the job before being called on to produce independently.

Training Tools

In addition to providing direct training by management and other personnel, foodservices use various audiovisual and classroom training tools. Depending on the position and the company, training may include classroom meetings in which the objectives of each job are described in detail. In addition, many foodservices today use videotapes to show how to perform tasks effectively. Others use computers, audio tapes, pictures, or presentations to describe task completion techniques. When designing a training program, management should investigate each method to determine how well it might work for its own foodservice.

Behavioral Training

Foodservices sell both products and service. Therefore, training in foodservices is not limited to the issue of task completion. Because the industry depends on delivering service to customers, behavioral training is an essential part of the training process. This is especially important for the front-of-the house personnel in a foodservice, but it is also important for the heart-of-the house staff.

Behavioral training is not as easily accomplished as task training. And since most foodservice managers are themselves trained by a process of on-the-job training in each position, they may not be well-informed in behavioral training goals either. As a result, many foodservice managers find it difficult to determine the behavioral attributes needed for each foodservice job.

Behavioral training, like task training, depends on the introduction of clear objectives to each employee. Only after specific attributes are described in detail can the employee's possession and development of them be adequately measured. To identify these objectives, many foodservice managers must place themselves in the position of a customer or of another employee. By doing so, they can better recognize what is desirable behavior and, by extension, can determine what the objectives of the behavioral training process should be.

Part of successfully conducting behavioral training involves maintaining a concise record of progress and referring to it often. This allows the employee to get a sense of what kind of progress is being made. Taking note of specific progress also helps define areas that are in need of improvement. In this type of training, it is important for the manager to give immediate feedback on both progress and shortcomings. The immediacy of the appraisals tends to confirm the employee's objectives and enables the employee to adopt additional goals throughout the training process.

The final step in behavioral training for foodservice work is a complete evaluation of the employee's progress. Most managers have found that this is best accomplished one-on-one with the employee, in an open environment that invites discussion. This approach encourages self-analysis of training progress by the employee, including a determination of what additional goals need to be met. From this evaluation meeting, clearly stated objectives should be established to serve as the basis for future assessments of progress. Records of these meetings should be made a part of the employee's permanent file. This "final" evaluation should not be the last that the employee receives, however; many foodservices have found that reevaluations every three to six months help spur the employee to achieve progressively higher goals.

COMPENSATION AND BENEFITS

How a foodservice manager compensates workers can obviously have a great bearing on the overall performance level they attain. While to many managers compensation may mean only dollars and cents, this is not the only aspect of a good compensation policy. Such steps as establishing management integrity, encouraging staff participation in decision-making, and offering fair evaluations of performance play a major role in the compensation package. Indeed, employees who feel unfairly treated by management often want more in the way of direct monetary compensations than do employees who experience job satisfaction.

The basic rules of compensation in the foodservice industry are set forth in federal and state statutes and sometimes in local ordinances. These regulations change periodically, and a good foodservice manager should be aware of those changes. Just to be aware of the existence and overall effect of regulations such as the Fair Labor Standards Act of 1938 and the Equal Pay Act of 1963 may not be enough, since many of the provisions that apply to foodservice employees differ in important respects from those that apply to other industries. Information concerning the most recent legal statutes governing pay can be obtained from federal and state wage-and-hour offices and from other government agencies.

The critical points to remember in establishing compensation packages for employees of a foodservice is that compensation is possible at three levels: wages, incentives, and benefits. Wages are dollars earned for completing the tasks assigned. In many cases, these are insufficient to generate the type of production required for foodservices, since so many foodservices have developed programs that offer incentives and benefits. Incentives—rewards for performance—often supply the motivational basis for employees to attain the standards required in foodservices. In some cases, bonuses and profit-sharing in return for excellent work are offered as incentives by foodservices.

In many cases, foodservices have also developed benefit programs to enhance the level of job satisfaction felt by employees. Benefit packages vary greatly from company to company and from position to position. In some foodservices, the principal benefits offered are those required by state and federal regulations, such as workmen's compensation and unemployment compensation. In others, a long list of benefits can be found. Today, many foodservices are discovering that, to attract the type of employee who will stay with the company and be productive for a long time, more benefits must be offered. The most common benefit packages are insurance-related. Whether directed toward health insurance, life insurance, or retirement payments, benefits have proved to be a strong attraction in foodservices—especially with the cost of hospitalization rising as it is. Other benefits that may be offered by foodservices include health maintenance organizations (HMOs), fitness and conditioning programs, drug- and alcohol-dependency programs, pensions, low-cost short-term loans, tuition assistance programs, education assistance, flexitime positions, and part-time positions.

SUMMARY

Foodservices are people-oriented businesses that require skill in knowledge of various methods of human resource development. The goals and objectives of the baby boomer work force differ in some ways from those of earlier work forces; therefore, new personnel practices are required to fulfill the needs of foodservices.

The human resources cycle involves selection, performance, and appraisal. Each step is critical to the development of a good foodservice staff, and each must be considered on both procedural and behavioral levels.

The three levels of personnel management are strategic (corporate) management, general management, and operational management. Each has different objectives. Strategic management focuses on planning for the future; general management is involved with filling the job, designing compensation programs, and so on; and operational management is primarily concerned with training and with evaluating on-the-job performance.

Before beginning a personnel management program, a foodservice should develop a needs analysis to determine what types of personnel and skills are needed. During this process, the most important objectives of the organization should also be set down. After the needs analysis is complete, the company should evaluate personnel on the basis of the skills they possess. This is called a *skills analysis.*

A job description sets out the specific requirements of a job and describes how it is to be completed. Job design is often overlooked (with unfortunate consequences) by foodservice managers. It is important to get workers to participate in designing jobs, as this tends to increase the level of job satisfaction among employees and to encourage their involvement in the decision-making process.

Skills audits, performance appraisals, and assessment centers are all methods of evaluating performance. A performance appraisal, the most common of these, identifies the specific goals that a job was designed to achieve and evaluates the progress of the employee in attaining those goals. Management and personnel should both be involved in the analysis process.

Even though employee recruitment and selection strongly influence how the job is completed, recruitment is often treated as a last-minute task. A good recruitment program should include establishing the integrity of the company in the community and among employees, adopting a policy of internal hiring, and seeking potential employees by the most effective means available. Selection can be based on interviews, questionnaires, psychometric testing, skills analysis, skills tests, or various other methods. Many foodservices combine several selection methods in an effort to obtain the best employees.

Orientation of new employees to the foodservice is a critical task that should be carried out by management. Included in the orientation are a tour of the facility, introduction to the other employees, and a discussion of all relevant policies and procedures of the company.

Training is one of the most important aspects of developing a good foodservice organization. It should be performed by management rather than by staff. The training supervisor should establish specific goals to accomplish in the course of training, and these goals should have both procedural and behavioral components. Numerous training tools are available to foodservice managers, including videotapes, audio tapes, computers, pictures, classrooms, and guest lectures.

Compensation packages consist not only of wages, but also of incentives and benefits of various kinds. Today, many foodservices are finding that they must develop more and better compensation packages to attract desirable personnel to their companies.

CHAPTER REVIEW QUESTION

Dianne Ross has taken over a foodservice operation that is known throughout the company as a problem. The operation has among the highest rates of absenteeism and turnover of any in the organization. In addition, the unit's sales and productivity have been declining of late.

On her first day on the job, Dianne immediately notices that the employees are reluctant to talk to her. In fact, they avoid Dianne. After investigation, she finds out that this is due to the management tactics of her predecessor, who often singled out employees and publicly berated them for their poor performance on the job. Moreover, the former manager virtually was unapproachable with any problems concerning either the operation or personnel.

Since Dianne has graduated from a hospitality school in which she was required to take a few courses in personnel management, she knows the answer: she must begin to develop a sense of faith and fair play with the staff. Since Dianne is so busy with the day-to-day operations (which were left in a shambles), she has asked you to help her design a program to turn the personnel policies of the operation around. Dianne has asked you to make an outline describing the key elements in a human resources program for her foodservice. Because she will have to introduce this program to junior management in the organization, she has also asked that you give some details on the importance of each step. How would you begin to develop such a program for Dianne?

VOCABULARY

Human resources	Recruitment
Human resources cycle	Internal recruitment
Orientation	Skills tests
Performance appraisals	EEOC
Job design	Critical incidents
Skills audits	Simulation
Assessment centers	Behavioral training
Job descriptions	Benefits
Employee selection	Equal Pay Act of 1963
Needs analysis	Fair Labor Standards Act of 1938
Job design	Profit-sharing
Compensation	Benefit packages

REFERENCES

Bowers, D. 1977. *Systems of Organization: Management of Human Resources.* Ann Arbor, Mich.: University of Michigan Press.

Craig, R. L. 1976. *Training and Development Handbook: A Guide to Human Resources Development.* 2d ed. New York: McGraw-Hill.

Funosch, G., and Kvitka, E. F. 1978. *Meal Management: Concepts and Applications,* pp. 201-27. San Francisco: Canfield Press.

Heaton, H. 1975. *Productivity in Service Organizations: Organizing for People.* New York: McGraw-Hill.

Pigors, P., and Myers, C. 1977. *A Personnel Administration: A Point of View and a Method.* 8th ed. New York: McGraw-Hill.

Staton, E. 1977. *Successful Personnel Recruiting and Selection.* New York: American Management Association.

Steinmetz, L. 1971. *Interviewing Skills for Supervisory Personnel.* Reading, Mass.: Addison-Wesley.

Sussman, L., and Deep, S. 1984. *Comex: The Communication Experience in Human Relations.* Cincinnati: South-Western Publishing.

West, B. B.; Wood, L.; and Harger, V. B. 1983. *Food Service in Institutions.* 6th ed. New York: John Wiley & Sons.

Management of Products

OUTLINE

CONTROL OF FOOD COST

The best-planned menu in the world will do an operation little good if it is not produced as intended. Failure to follow through on an excellent menu is a common fault in foodservices today. The food must come into the dining room with the proper quality, while yielding the right profit.

Management must see that proper controls are instituted to obtain production efficiency, to minimize waste, and to reduce costs. Standardized recipes, tests for yield, quality controls, precosting methods for menu items, production schedules, security procedures, and the right selling price are all necessary for proper managing of products.

Standardized Recipes

A standard is a measure used to evaluate a quantity, quality, or volume. We obtain a value of something and then compare this value to the standard to see whether it is equal to, exceeds, or falls below the value of the standard. These results tell us that the item measured is, respectively, equal to, better than, or worse than the standard.

A standardized recipe is a formula established by management that yields a known quantity of product of a known quality. In quality and quantity, it meets standards that have been established by management as desirable for the foodservice. The calculation of food cost and selling price cannot be made with any accuracy unless recipes are standardized to use only specific ingredients in known amounts, resulting in a known yield of portions. Using a standardized recipe reduces the risk of poor food handling and preparation failure. Such a recipe should establish standards of presentation and service, as well as of quality and quantity. A well-standardized recipe also can help train employees in good work methods and in basic food production principles. It also is a safeguard against the dominance of a chef or cook who keeps the recipe used a secret and leaves management to guess at costs and yields. Using the standardized recipe allows others to fill in for the chef and produce successful foods.

Standardizing any recipe begins with analyzing it thoroughly. Certain standard proportions in food production must be observed. For example, the proper ratio of sugar to flour in a butter cake is 1.25:1. A recipe in which the amounts of sugar and flour

---

Preparation time: ¾ hour   Cooking time: 2½ hours
Major utensils used: covered $12'' \times 20'' \times 4''$ pan, scale, steam cooker, oven
Proper method of serving: serve on dinner plate
Nutritional facts: 470 calories per portion; protein 33 g; fat 23 g; carbohydrate 33 g; calcium 87 mg; iron 6.1 mg;
    Vitamin A 3700 I.U.; thiamine 0.3 mg; riboflavin 0.46 mg; niacin 8.96 mg; ascorbic acid 63 mg

Yield Count: 24 servings   Portion Measurement: 1 cup   Total Yield: 5½ qt

Ingredients	Weights	Measures	Counts	Method
Beef cubes, cut in 1-to 1½-inch pieces	7½ lb			Combine flour, salt, pepper, and paprika. Dredge beef cubes in seasoned flour and save remaining flour.
Flour		2 cups		
Salt		3 Tbsp		
Pepper		½ tsp		
Paprika		2 tsp		
Cooking fat		¼ cup		Heat cooking fat in a $12'' \times 20'' \times 4''$ pan. Add floured beef cubes and brown at 375°F (moderate oven) for approximately 1 hour. Stir once during browning; add remaining flour just before stirring.
Whole cloves			12	Place 1 clove each in the end of 12 of the onions.
Onions, small whole			24	
Water, hot		2 qt		Add water to browed meat mixture. Stir thoroughly. Add onions, potatoes, carrots, and bay leaf.
Potatoes, small	4 lb, E.P.			
Carrots, cut lengthwise, then into thirds		16	16	
				Cover tightly and cook in oven 1½ hours or until meat and vegetables are done.
Bay leaf			1	
Brussels sprouts	2½ lb			Cook Brussels sprouts, drain, and fold into stew.

Figure 16-1. Standardized recipe card for beef and brussels sprout stew.

vary too much from this ratio probably will not produce a good item. Checking a recipe against these standard proportions can thus give a good clue as to whether it is properly balanced or needs revision.

After analysis, the recipe should be tested. For this step, all ingredients must be carefully weighed or measured, production time should be carefully noted, and the condition of the item as it goes through production should be described. Taking notes during testing allows the testers to work back later to see exactly what happened. Mixing procedures, preparation and cooking times, temperatures, major utensils used, and the method of serving should be precisely recorded, as well as yield and portion size (see fig. 16-1). Dividing portion size into total yield gives the number of portions obtained. Nutritional facts may be stated on the standardized recipe. If possible, a picture of the finished product should be taken and perhaps also a picture of a portion, so employees will know how both are supposed to look. The whole recipe is then critiqued, changes are made if necessary, and the item may be retested.

If the people performing the tests know food production, they usually need not do more than three tests, and often one or two tests are sufficient. To perfect some recipes, however, many tests are needed. For example, more than thirty tests were needed to develop the 100-portion Navy recipe for chiffon cake. The recipe worked well in small quantities, but increasing the ingredients to give 100 portions in the same ratios yielded an unsuccessful product. Consequently, a completely different recipe, varying in ingredient ratios from the small-quantity one, had to be developed by trial and error. It often is desirable to submit a recipe for evaluation to people other than those doing the testing—even customers.

A recipe that is properly standardized can be modified to give more or fewer servings. The method for modifying the quantity of ingredients to increase or decrease portions appears in the conversion charts in appendix E. No recipe is ever finished; each time it is used, it should be reevaluated. Whenever a recipe is improved, food standards rise. Recipes can also become outdated as new materials appear on the market. For example, many recipes still in use today call for the addition of soda to a liquid before adding it to the product. This step was specified because many years ago soda was more coarsely ground than it is now, and dissolving before adding was necessary to get it properly distributed in the product. The soda of today is fine enough to be sifted in with the flour. Yet people still go on dissolving the soda, just as others did fifty years ago, not realizing that the practice is no longer necessary.

In scoring a product, analysts must evaluate the factors of flavor, texture, color, tenderness, appearance, form, and temperature. Score sheets are usually used (see fig. 16-2). Some testing facilities have tasting rooms; judges are carefully selected for their abilities to taste, see, and evaluate. The committee that accepts the final recipe also accepts the standard of presentation it establishes. Testing is the backbone of all standardized recipes. When the entire menu has been translated into standardized recipes, all recipes should assume the same form and contain the same information (see fig. 16-3).

Yield and Quality Tests

If costs are not known, potential profit cannot be known. To identify costs, it may be necessary to run yield tests so that the cost per portion can be determined. Yields recorded should reflect those obtained under actual operating conditions.

A yield test is often done to determine the number of usable products obtained from a recipe, as compared with the total amount of materials purchased to make the product. If the item cost is not at or below a desired maximum, it must be removed from the menu. Information gained from yield tests may include the extended cost, the portion cost, the unit cost, and the cost factor. These are defined as follows:

Extended cost - total cost of the material tested (for example, 5 gal of ice cream)

Portion cost - cost per serving; total yield divided by portion size gives the number of portions, and the extended cost divided by the number of portions gives the portion cost

Score System Grade Quality	Directions:				
A Excellent B Good C Fair D Poor F Unacceptable	1. Place the grade in the upper left hand corner. 2. Comments should justify the grade. 3. Evaluation of the food products must be on an *individual* basis. PRODUCTS				
Characteristics	I	II	III	IV	V
Appearance					
Consistency or Texture					
Tenderness					
Flavor					
Overall Quality					

Figure 16-2. Sample evaluation form for scoring products.

Unit cost - cost per unit as purchased, usually stated on the purchase invoice (for example, 1 gal of ice cream)

Cost factor - the ratio of portion cost (the computed cost per serving after the yield test is done) to unit cost (the original cost per unit as produced or purchased), obtained by dividing the portion cost by the unit cost; the cost factor allows analysts to determine the new cost per portion when the item's price increases or decreases, without having to redo yield tests

Figure 16-4 shows a sample yield test card recording the results of a yield test involving chocolate ice cream. A 5-gal container gives approximately 145 portions, if a No. 16 scoop is used. It is wise in making yield tests to check to see if the actual yield matches the computed yield. Once the extended cost has been obtained, analysts can calculate the portion cost by dividing the extended cost by the number of portions. In the present example, $5.45 ÷ 145 portions = $0.038. It also is sometimes desirable to obtain a cost factor, which is equal to the

a. Ingredients	Measures	Method
Mayonnaise	3 cups	Preheat broiler. Combine mayonnaise, Parmesan cheese, and Worcestershire sauce.
Parmesan cheese, grated	1 cup	Blend well and place ½ tsp of mixture on small crackers. Brown lightly
Worcestershire sauce	2 Tbsp	under broiler.

b. Action	Measures	Ingredients
Preheat broiler. Combine and blend well	3 cups 1 cup 2 Tbsp	mayonnaise, grated Parmesan cheese, and Worcestershire sauce.
Place Brown	½ tsp	mixture on small crackers. lightly under broiler.

c. Ingredients	Measures	Method
Mayonnaise	3 cups	1. Preheat broiler. 2. Combine mayonnaise, Parmesan cheese, and Worcestershire sauce.
Grated Parmesan cheese	1 cup	3. Blend mixture well.
Worcestershire sauce	2 Tbsp	4. Place ½ tsp of mixture on small crackers. 5. Brown lightly under broiler.

d. While the broiler is preheating,
   combine 3 cups mayonnaise,
   1 cup grated Parmesan cheese,
   and 2 Tbsp Worcestershire sauce.
   Blend well, and place ½ tsp of the
   mixture on small crackers.
   Brown lightly under the broiler.

Figure 16-3. Forms of recipe presentation: (a) *descriptive form* - giving ingredients followed by modification, then measures, and then method; (b) *action form* - giving narrative action with listed measures and ingredients; (c) *standard form* - giving modified ingredients first, measures second, and method third; (d) *narrative form* - giving ingredients and methods together.

portion cost divided by the unit cost. In figure 16-4, this is shown as $0.038 ÷ $1.09 = 0.035. If the price of ice cream increased to $2.18 per gal (unit cost), management could immediately ascertain the new cost per portion by multiplying the new unit cost by the cost factor of 0.035. In the example illustrated in figure 16-4, the new portion cost would be $0.0763.

The important formulas to remember in yield testing are the following two:

Cost per portion = Extended cost ÷ Portion yield
Cost factor = Cost per portion ÷ Unit cost

A selling price can be calculated from this information. If the portion cost is divided by the desired

Product: Chocolate Ice Cream

	Quantity 5 gal	Unit Cost $1.09	Extended Cost $5.45
Size of Portion	No. 16 scoop		
Average Portion Yield	145		
Cost per Portion	$\dfrac{\$5.45}{145} = \$0.038$	$\dfrac{\text{Extended Cost}}{\text{Portion Yield}}$	
Cost Factor	$\dfrac{\$0.038}{\$1.09} = \$0.035$	$\dfrac{\text{Cost per Portion}}{\text{Unit Cost}}$	

Figure 16-4. Sample yield test card.

percentage of food cost, the selling price is obtained. In the example illustrated in figure 16-4, the selling price at a food cost percentage of 25 percent would be 15 cents ($0.038 ÷ 25% = $0.15 or 15¢).

Sometimes a selling price factor is obtained, and the selling price is computed from this. The selling price factor is calculated by dividing 100 percent by the desired food cost percentage. When this factor is multiplied by the portion cost, the result is the selling price. Thus, if a food cost percentage of 25 percent were desired and the portion cost were $0.038, the calculation would be (100% ÷ 25% = 4; 4 × $0.038 = 15.2¢).

Besides yield tests, patron acceptance tests should continually be made on food items. There are a number of ways to ascertain customer acceptance of menu items. One of the simplest is to keep track of the number of portions that are sold, by checking sales slips. The totals can be recorded daily; then the total monthly sales of each item can be compiled from the daily records. Such records are often kept on a filed copy of the menu. The daily sales record sheet should also give the price of items, the combination of items offered, and such general information as customer count, serving time, run-out time, amount of carry-overs, weather, and special events that might have affected sales (see fig. 16-5). If an item is not selling, it may lack customer appeal, it may be of poor quality, or its price may

be too high. Keeping the daily sales record gives management information on items that sell well and on those that do not.

A good sales record also helps management to forecast amounts that will probably be sold and to estimate the number of personnel and the amounts of materials and supplies that will be required to meet production needs. Running out of items too early may indicate poor forecasting, while a large carry-over may signify overforecasting, lack of patronage appeal, an excessively high price, or poor quality. The projection of sales on any one day should be based on the sales of the item on that day of the week in the past, modified by the other factors maintained on the sales record that management believes may be influential. For example, on Saturday night many steaks might be sold, whereas on Sunday fried chicken might be the big seller. Suppose that a big convention center is located across the street from the foodservice and that a big boxing event is to occur there on Saturday night and a gospel revival meeting (which many elderly people are expected to attend) on Sunday. These two events alone would cause management to stock up for bigger steak sales on Saturday night and for extra chicken sales on Sunday.

Management also can perform other tests to determine correct portion sizes, the most pleasing color and flavor combinations of food, and good

```
┌─────────────────────────────────────────┐   ┌──────────────────────────────────────┐
│              Coffee Shop                  │   │ ○  ○  ○  ○  ○  ○  ○  ○              │
│ Day and Date: Tuesday,      Weather: Raining │ │  Coffee Shop        No. 000624       │
│               April 1, 1988               │   │ ┌────┬──────────┬──────────┬───────┐ │
│ Customer Count: 160    Events in Town: Parade │ │ DATE│NO. GUESTS│TABLE NO.│WAITER│ │
│ Meal: Dinner, 5-8 PM                      │   │ │4/1/88│   3    │   14   │  HJ  │ │
└─────────────────────────────────────────┘   └──────────────────────────────────────┘
```

		Coffee Shop			
		No. 000624			

DATE	NO. GUESTS	TABLE NO.	WAITER
4/1/88	3	14	HJ

NO	ITEM	FOOD	LIQUOR
2	Filet of sole	×× ×	
1	Chef salad	××	
2	Banana Cream Pie	×	

Food				
Tax				
Liquor				
Total				

Coffee Shop

Day and Date: Tuesday, April 1, 1988   **Weather:** Raining

Customer Count: 160   **Events in Town:** Parade

Meal: Dinner, 5–8 PM

Menu Item	Price	Sales (portions)	Run-out Time	Carry-overs (portions)
Filet of Sole	XXX	35	7 PM	- - -
Chef Salads	XX	45	- - -	- - -
(etc.)				
Banana Cream Pie	X	30	- - -	12

Comments: Promote desserts on Tuesdays to match sales during rest of week.

Figure 16-5. Sample sales record sheet and sales slip.

food arrangement. Good testing gives information that can lead to better management decisions, without guesswork.

Precosting Menus

Precosting is a procedure used to determine costs and establish production quotas before actual food production begins. It is important to know this information before food is purchased so that any necessary changes can be made. Some useful data for precosting can be obtained from accurate yield tests. The cost of a portion multiplied by the number of portions sold gives the dollar food cost for all portions sold. The same number of portions sold multiplied by the selling price gives the dollars in sales that the item brings in. The food cost divided by the total sales then gives the food cost percentage of this item. Often precosting is done to obtain just such information. The following example illustrates the procedure for obtaining a food cost percentage:

40 portions of soup at a cost of $0.15/portion = $6.00 food cost
40 portions of soup sold at $0.60 each = $24.00 in sales
$6.00 ÷ 24.00 = 0.25 or 25% food cost percentage

Most foodservices know their costs and establish a desirable food cost percentage so that the expected costs will be obtained and a predictable profit will result. Again, knowing the food cost percentage of an item enables management to determine whether the item's price meets the standard of the desired food cost percentage. If it does not meet this standard, management must determine which price is better for the operation. No menu ever consists of items that all have the same food cost percentage. Some are higher than the desired standard, and others are lower. Management expects by a proper sales mix to achieve the desired percentage. If this does not happen, management is in trouble. This explains why achieving a correct sales mix is important in producing a menu.

Here is an example of how sales mix and various food costs work out. Item 1 has a food cost of $0.25 and sells for $1.00, giving a food cost percentage of 25 percent. Ten units are expected to be sold, for a sales yield of $10 and a total food cost of $2.50. Item 2 costs $1.50 and sells for $4.50, giving a food cost percentage of 33.3 percent. Twenty units are expected to be sold, for a $90 sales yield and a total food cost of $30. The total sales are now $100, and the total food cost is $32.50, for an overall food cost percentage of 32.5 percent. The rule, then, is to find the food cost of an item and to multiply this by the number expected to be sold, and then to multiply the selling price by the number expected to be sold. The results of these computations give both the food cost and the sales for each item. Next, all food costs and all sales should be totaled. By dividing total food costs by total sales, the ana-lyst can calculate the expected overall food cost percentage.

In a typical operation, total food costs for a day are forecasted, and so are sales. Management estimates the expected overall food cost percentage. Thus, if sales were forecast (estimated) to be $1,000 and food costs to be $430, the estimated overall food cost would be 43 percent ($430 ÷ $1,000 = 0.43) (see table 16-1). If this forecast of food cost is unacceptably high, management must either replan the menu to achieve a lower overall food cost percentage or alter the menu to achieve a different sales mix. To accomplish the latter purpose, more higher-gross-profit items must be sold to increase sales dollars and fewer lower-gross-profit items must be sold to decrease food costs.

Precosting of daily menus and *du jour* menus should occur before the individual menu is written, but cycle menus must be precosted before the entire cycle begins—a considerably more difficult job. Menus used continuously should be precosted every thirty days, or whenever food costs change considerably. Precosting employees' menus is also necessary, regardless of whether the food comes from the regular menu or is prepared especially for the employees. Computers today can simplify the job of precosting.

A failure to sell all items that were forecast to be sold can raise havoc with precosting calculations. Suppose that in the previous example, only ten (instead of the predicted twenty) $4.50 items were sold. Now the food cost remains at $32.50 but sales

Table 16-1. Precosting the Menu, Item by Item

Menu Item	Portions to Be Sold	Food Cost per Portion	Extended Cost	Sales per Portion	Extended Sales	Food Cost Percentage
Item 1	10	$0.25	$ 2.50	$1.00	$10.00	25%
Item 2	20	$1.50	$ 30.00	$4.50	$90.00	33%
Item 3						
•						
•						
•						
GRAND TOTAL			$430.00		$1,000	43%

are only $55. Table 16-2 compares the two situations: The expected food cost in Situation A is 32.5 percent, but in Situation B (omitting consideration of the value of ten carry-overs of the $4.50 item) it is about 59 percent. In cases in which sales are not achieved, management can find itself in trouble with few remedial options. The bottom line is that forecasting must be accurate. The only benefit to be salvaged from early detection of a radically off-the-mark forecast is that management is advised of the problem much sooner than if it were to wait until the end of the month to see what happened.

The Production Sheet

The production sheet is a final control needed before the menu begins to govern kitchen production. It tells the purchasing department and the kitchen what food items to purchase and prepare for any particular day. Because overpurchasing and overproducing are the chief causes of high food costs, the production sheet is an extremely important control device. By promoting proper purchasing and production, the production sheet reduces waste and, thus, reduces the food cost percentage.

The production sheet must name the item to be prepared, the portion size, the number of portions, the mass of portions (by weight or measure), the time and place of service, and the recipe number for each item. Employees' meals, banquets, luncheons, and in fact every meal served must have a separate production sheet. Only through such organizing can purchases be planned ahead and materials made available when needed. Overloading refrigerators, using excessive labor, producing too much food, and wasting food through poor planning are all eliminated when the production sheet is used properly (see fig. 16-6).

Table 16-2. Comparison of Food Cost and Sales Totals

	Situation A		Situation B	
	Food Cost	Sales	Food Cost	Sales
Item 1	$ 2.50	$ 10.00	$ 2.50	$10.00
Item 2	$30.00	$ 90.00	$30.00	$45.00
Total	$32.50	$100.00	$32.50	$55.00

Selling Price

The determination of selling price is based on information gained from a yield test. Such a determination is necessary in menu planning for sales made to customers. It is not necessary if customers'

Figure 16-6. Sample production sheet.

Name of Operation _____   Time of Service _____   Date of Service _____

Menu Item	Size of Portion	Number of Portions	Quantity of Portions	Recipe Number
Beef and Brussels stew	8-oz ladle	24	5½ qt	XX
_____				
_____				
_____				
_____				
_____				
_____				

meals are included with lodging for a single price, as in the American Plan or in hospitals. Nonetheless, management in such institutions must have much the same information to arrive at an overall selling price as is needed to calculate selling prices on menus. Selling prices vary with the quantity of food served, the type of service, and other factors. The selling price must cover costs in these operations, as well as giving the needed profit. If it does not, the operation does not last long. Different methods are used by foodservices to determine selling price. Among the most common of these are the multiplier method, the pricing factor method, and the planned profit method.

The Multiplier Method

The multiplier method is a handy rule-of-thumb technique, but it is of dubious value because it bases selling price on food cost alone. Based on what the food costs, the menu sets the price at three or four times this, or any of various other multiples of the cost. There are two approaches to using the multiplier method: actually multiply food cost by a factor derived from dividing the desired food cost percentage into 100 percent; or divide the food cost by the desired food cost percentage. For example, if a food cost percentage of 40 percent were sought, the analyst could compute the desired food cost factor (100% ÷ 40% = 2.5), and multiply this by the food cost of an item to get its selling price. Thus, if the food cost is $1.20, the calculated cost is $1.20 × 2.5 = $3.00. Using the same example, the second approach to the multiplier method gives $1.20 ÷ 0.40 = $3.00 as the selling price.

The problem with this method is that not all food items involve the same amount of labor or other costs for their production, although the assumption in using food cost as the sole criterion is that they do. Thus, an operation's management might not know that it is losing money on certain items that have much higher than normal nonfood costs associated with them. Even if proper cost calculations were made, management would still not know. Too many operations depend on the multiplier method. This may lead the management astray, as well as price items unfairly to customers.

The Pricing Factor Method

The pricing factor method offers a solution to some of the problems posed by the multiplier method (Dukas 1973). For this method, each food item is placed into one of two categories: foods needing little or no preparation (Nonprep); and foods needing a significant amount of preparation (Prep). Thus, milk would be classed as Nonprep, and beef stew would be classed as Prep. The raw food cost is recorded and summed for both Nonprep foods and Prep foods (see table 16-3). In the situation represented in table 16-3, the operation has budgeted

Table 16-3. Pricing Factor Method

	Nonprep (Foods)	Prep (Foods)	Total	Percentage of Sales
Raw food cost	$ 60	$140	$200	40%
Labor			$150	30%
Prep employees		$ 60		
Nonprep employees	$ 27	$ 63		
Other expenses	$ 30	$ 70	$100	20%
Profit	$ 15	$ 35	$ 50	10%
Total	$132	$368	$500	100%
Pricing factors	2.2	2.6		

$200 for all food—30 percent (or $60) for Nonprep, and 70 percent (or $140) for Prep food. Total raw food cost accounts for 40 percent of sales.

Next, labor cost is placed into Nonprep and Prep categories. The labor cost of pantry workers, fry cooks, bakers, and others doing actual preparation is charge to Prep only. This is logical, since these workers are paid only to prepare foods. The costs of employees such as busboys, waiters and waitresses, dishwashers, and others responsible for all food (Prep and Nonprep) served in the operation are charged in proper proportions to both Nonprep and Prep categories. This, too, is logical, since these workers are paid to see that both Nonprep and Prep foods are served. If total labor costs account for 30 percent of sales (or $150 in this case), and if the operator notes that 40 percent of the total labor expense is found to be incurred in preparing foods, then $60 (40 percent of $150) should be charged to Prep only. The rest of the expense ($150 − $60 = $90) should be allocated to both Nonprep and Prep, in the same proportions used for the total raw food cost—30 percent to Nonprep foods, and 70 percent to Prep foods. This is logical, since each food category should reflect Nonprep labor expenses proportionate to the cost of the food allocated to that category. Thus, the remaining labor expense is noted as $27 (30 percent of $90) in Nonprep, and $63 (70 percent of $90) in Prep.

Other expenses (accounting for 20 percent of sales in this example) are $100 and are allocated to the two food categories according to the 30:70 raw food cost ratio. Other expenses include $30 (30 percent of the $100) under Nonprep and $70 (70 percent of the $100) under Prep. Finally, in this example, profit is distributed, as 10 percent of sales, according to the same 30:70 ratio. On this basis, the Nonprep category receives $15.00, and the Prep category gets $35.00.

Different steps must be taken to arrive at selling prices for the Prep and Nonprep foods. For any Nonprep food, the operator would divide the total sales for this food group (which is $132) by the total cost of food not requiring preparation ($60, in this case). The $132 is the sum of raw food cost, labor cost, other expenses, and profit. The pricing factor thus becomes 2.2 ($132 ÷ $60 = 2.2). In a similar manner, the pricing factor for food requiring extensive preparation can be determined by dividing $368 by $140. This gives a pricing factor of 2.6 ($368 ÷ 140 = 2.6).

Peter Dukas appropriately concludes his discussion of the pricing factor method with the following comments:

> From this point on, if this food service operator wished to change prices of his existing menu, he could simply multiply food cost of the prepared portion by the appropriate factor. For example, if he purchased a half-pint of milk in a disposable carton for 4½ cents, he could multiply his cost by the factor of 2.2 and establish a selling price of 10 cents. On the other hand, if a chicken pot pie, requiring a great deal of preparation labor, cost $.50, the sale price of $1.30 would be determined by multiplying $.50 by 2.6.
>
> Once these factors have been determined for any single operation, they may be used to update menu prices, until a significant change occurs in either the ratio of one food group to the other or in the proportion of direct preparation expense to the total labor expense.
>
> The immediate results of using this simplified, yet much more effective, method of pricing menu items are:

1. A predetermined food cost percentage [in this example 40 percent] can still be achieved even though two or more price factors are used.
2. Because of the use of two or more price factors [2.2 and 2.6], menu prices will be uniquely different from other foodservice operations, enabling the operator to compete very effectively for his share of the total market.
3. The allocation of food into categories to which can be added direct labor expenses enables the user to immediately identify menu items that are being sold for a loss or that are not carrying their fair share of expense.
4. The elimination of loss items and the inherent fairness of prices charged to the customer invariably increase sales volume and profits of the operation.

The Planned Profit Method

The planned profit method of the Texas Restaurant Association is a third method of setting a selling price. The basics of this system involve creating a well-planned budget that gives a preview of expected financial operations over a given period in terms of operating (overhead) costs, actual raw food costs, labor costs, and planned profit. Operating costs include expenses such as advertising, telephone and utilities, laundry, insurance, rent, taxes, employee meals and uniforms, office supplies, linens, and china. Actual raw food costs are determined from standardized recipes, with the cost of all extra trimmings included. Labor cost includes wages and salaries paid to employees. Finally, profit is figured as an expense. Profit must be included if it is desired.

After establishing the budget, the operator determines the menu prices needed to meet the expenses by calculating—per volume dollar of business—the operating cost percentage (operating costs ÷ total sales), the labor cost percentage (labor cost ÷ total sales), and the planned profit percentage (planned profit ÷ total sales). These three percentages are then summed and subtracted from 100 percent to give the desired raw food cost percentage per dollar volume of business. By adding together operating costs, labor costs, planned profit, and desired raw food cost, the operator obtains a figure for total sales. By dividing the actual raw food cost (figured from the standardized recipe of a menu item) by the desired raw food cost percentage, the operator can compute the selling price of the menu item. For example, suppose that the following percentages have been computed:

Operating cost percentage (operating cost ÷ total sales)	= 37.4%
Labor cost percentage (labor cost ÷ total sales)	= 17.0%
Planned profit percentage (planned profit ÷ total sales)	= 15.0%
	69.4%

The sum of these percentages is 69.4 percent. The desired raw food cost percentage is therefore 30.6 percent ($100\% - 69.4\% = 30.6\%$).

To arrive at the selling price of an item, the ingredients' costs are summed. Suppose that for Item C the following ingredient costs are identified:

Ingredient I	$0.12
Ingredient II	0.05
Ingredient III	0.09
Ingredient IV	0.11
Ingredient V	0.01
	$0.38

The total ingredient cost of Item C is therefore $0.38. This is divided by the desired raw food cost percentage (which is 30.6 percent) to arrive at an indicated selling price of $1.24 ($0.38 ÷ 30.6% = 1.24).

If this method of calculating selling price is used, the operator is sure of making 15 percent profit—as long as the costs have been accurately calculated and do not change. Because in reality expenses continually change, however, the operator must review selling prices carefully and frequently in order to make this system work.

Three rules may be helpful in setting menu prices:

1. Maintain a realistic price spread between the highest- and lowest-priced items. Receiving a smaller profit percentage on a high-priced item may still result in a higher check average and more income, although the raw food cost percentage is relatively high. A saying in the foodservice business is, "You don't operate a business to make percentages, but to make dollars."
2. An item sold at or below cost to attract customers is a loss leader. Such an approach is good for a drugstore where other items may be purchased. It is not good for a restaurant or other profit-oriented foodservice, where nothing else is purchased to give a profit.
3. Control costs and review menu prices, but do not neglect sales volume. A 10 percent increase in sales will add more to profit than is often expected. This is because fixed costs remain unchanged, and little more labor is

needed to handle the extra volume; relatively few additional expenses are incurred, too. Consequently, profit can rise as a proportion of sales. Fair menu pricing, with good merchandising techniques, builds volume.

Menu Engineering

A fourth method of pricing takes into account the popularity of individual items and their respective contribution to profits. This method was popularized by Don Smith and Michael Kasavana. First, overall cost of the product is calculated. This would include the cost of the item from the standard recipe, plus the cost of any garnishes and any other food included in the price of the meal, such as bread and butter or a salad. This figure represents the potential cost if no food were wasted, incorrectly proportioned, or stolen. It is subtracted from the price being charged on the menu, providing a contribution margin. The contribution margin represents funds that pay labor and overhead costs and contribute to profit. In some cases, a food item may have a high cost on a percentage basis, but its contribution margin will still be higher than that of other items. The menu items are then classified by whether they have high or low contribution margins.

Next the popularity of the item is judged. This is done in terms of the menu mix—the proportion of items sold in each category. An item with a high contribution margin and high sales has more of an impact on profit than does an item with a low contribution margin and high sales. The menu mix average is determined by dividing the number of sales of each item by the total number of items sold. Any item that has a menu mix percentage of below 70 percent of the average is deemed to have low popularity. Any menu mix percentage above that level is considered to indicate high popularity.

At this point, each item is judged to have either a high or low contribution margin and either a high or low popularity. On the basis of these two classifications, items can be separated into four different groups:

High contribution margin-High popularity "Stars"
Low contribution margin-High popularity "Plowhorses"

High contribution margin-Low popularity "Puzzles"
Low contribution margin-Low popularity "Dogs"

Specific menu items can then be evaluated with respect to their performance on the menu and their ability to contribute to the overall objectives of the operation. Stars are the real performers on a menu, contributing significantly to the bottom line. Plowhorses sell well but do not contribute a lot. These items may be attracting customers because they are seen as good values; increasing their price should only be done very carefully. They can be turned into Stars, but only if people value them enough to pay a higher price. The Puzzles are not selling, but if they did they would contribute substantially to profits. These are items that may merit some experimentation in price, placement on the menu, or sales effort from the staff. The Dogs are not selling well and do not contribute either. Serious thought should be given to replacing them on the menu with something more promising. Ideally, all items would be either Stars or Plowhorses, and food cost and profitability would be excellent. Because of ever-changing customer tastes and preferences, however, menu engineering must remain an ongoing process. It is a process that can provide insight into customers' buying patterns as well as into controlling production costs.

QUALITY CONTROL

Quality control in a foodservice facility relies on the establishment of standards. To be meaningful, these standards must apply to all aspects of an operation—from the moment the purchase decision is made to the moment the finished product is presented to the customer. The standards should apply to all edible products and their contact points. An effective quality-control program results in better overall control of the product and increased customer satisfaction.

Perception of quality is affected by a consumer's background and life-style as well as by the surroundings in which the meal takes place. In addition to psychological influences, tangible attributes of the product such as taste, texture, color, appearance, and nutritional value all contribute to the perception of quality. Quality guidelines have been defined to some extent by the Food and Drug Administration and the U.S. Department of Agriculture, which have established standards (for determining whether a product is safe for consumption) and grades (for defining the composition of the product).

Comparisons of various products provide a useful technique for determining whether a product meets the standards of a particular establishment. It is not unusual for purveyors to offer samples for exactly this purpose. Once the product is in the foodservice establishment, it is up to the employees to maintain the quality of the product.

Receiving and Storage

The product may go through any number of processes once it is inside the doors of an establishment. Inspection during receiving is the first step in any quality-control program. Purchasing specifications establish standards for the ordering and receiving of goods. At receiving, the product must be inspected to ensure that it matches what was ordered in number, weight, and quality. The packaging should be examined for breaks or leaks. Frozen goods should be checked for signs of thawing or freezer burn.

During storage, a number of factors can influence the quality of the product. The shelf-lives of foods vary, and this must be taken into consideration in arranging and maintaining storage. Fresh foods tend to have very short shelf-lives—in some cases as brief as 24 hours—so ordering exactly the amount needed is essential. Frozen foods have longer shelf-lives, but they deteriorate over time as well. Maintaining proper storage temperatures for frozen or refrigerated foods is imperative. Carefully watching temperatures during thawing is important also. For the most part, products should be allowed to thaw under refrigeration, unless they can begin cooking while still frozen. Dry goods and groceries tend to last indefinitely; however, poor storage conditions (such as exposure to moisture or high temperatures) can have a negative impact on

the quality of dry foods and can shorten their storage life. In many cases, proper observance of the first in, first out (FIFO) inventory system helps keep inventories fresh.

Production and Holding

Once the product has entered the preparation phase of production, various elements work together to ensure its continued high quality. Here again the standardized recipe plays an important role by outlining the correct procedures, timing, and use of equipment for proper presentation of an item. To ensure consistency of quality standards, the recipe should be followed scrupulously. Sanitation standards establish a basis for maintaining quality during preparation as well. Proper handling of the product and rigorous observance of sanitary procedures are necessary. In this respect, the equipment, too, must be kept sanitary and in good working condition. Tools and utensils must be properly cleaned to avoid contamination of food during preparation; equipment should be subject to a regular maintenance and cleaning schedule and should be repaired immediately in the event of breakdown. A cook who does not possess the correct tools in proper condition cannot be expected to produce a high-quality product.

Once cooking has begun, control of temperatures and timing becomes important. Ovens need to be checked on a regular basis for the accuracy of their thermostats. Even if the oven is gauged properly, loss of heat from a bad seal or from cold spots can have a negative effect. In any event, cooks should be encouraged to carry and use thermometers to check internal cooking temperatures and holding temperatures. Temperatures of deep-fat fryers need to be monitored closely. High temperatures, along with exposure to air, contribute to the deterioration of fat, resulting in soggy and discolored deep-fried products. The fat should be filtered after each shift and covered when not in use. The use of timers is extremely helpful. In a busy kitchen, it is not unusual to lose track of how long something has been cooking. The timer serves as a reminder that helps avoid costly overcooking or burning of the food.

Observing proper temperatures during holding is necessary not only for sanitary reasons but to maintain quality. Foods, whether they are to be served hot or cold, must be held at the proper temperature. It is not unusual for lettuce to wilt or for sauces to separate if their temperatures are not controlled. Products have a holding life that must not be exceeded. Some foods hold much better than others, without diminishing in quality. This can be a function of the preparation technique used or of the actual contents of an item. In many cases, recipes can be modified to facilitate holding.

SECURITY

Unfortunately, theft is a fact of life in the food-service industry. Ignoring the possibility of its existence can wreak havoc on food costs and prove disastrous for an operation. The best approach is to foster prevention by removing temptation and opportunity. Many managers may be aware that theft exists in an operation without being aware of its extent. Considering the number of failures in the industry, controlling theft should be a major goal of any organization. Any effective effort to control it will translate directly into profits.

There are multitudinous opportunities for theft in purchasing and receiving, if proper controls are not maintained. The thief can be an employee or a purveyor; in some cases, they may be working together. One major danger arises when the purchasing agent is also in charge of receiving. Common types of thievery include kickbacks, fictitious companies, credit memo games, invoice "errors," weight shortages, and quality substitutions. Separation of functions can help avoid many of these problems. Many of the systems and procedures described in chapter 6 were designed to eliminate opportunities for theft.

Storage areas can be prime targets for dishonest activity. In many operations, they are located close to a door, and long periods of time may elapse during which other people are not in a position to observe activity there. Storage areas are the bank vault of a foodservice establishment and should be secured accordingly. Limited access and keeping storage areas under lock and key can help considerably. Assigning keys to only those who need them and changing locks when they leave the operation are good preventive measures. Imagining the position of a thief and pondering opportunities can bring lax areas to the manager's attention. Maintaining perpetual inventories can help alert management to and pinpoint theft problems in storage.

Food in process can be particularly difficult to safeguard. Management should have a pretty good idea of raw product requirements for daily preparation. Overproduction should be discouraged. Eating policies should be made clear and enforced for all personnel. Theft is theft, whether it is being done by management or staff; double standards only set a bad example. Food should be given to servers only with the proper documentation. Supervisors must be vigilant against cooks' providing food for their or others' personal consumption. Following standardized recipes, adhering to production schedules, and observing correct menu ordering procedures will go a long way toward preventing theft.

COMPUTERIZATION

Computers are beginning to take a larger role in controlling and managing the product. Purchasing databases provide information on market costs and item availability. In the near future, a purchasing agent may be able to access information directly from the computer of the purveyor to allow for direct ordering. This information will aid the foodservice operator in forecasting and should cut down on the transit time of fresh products from the grower to the consumer.

Once the product is received, quantity and price information can be fed into the foodservice's system and placed in an ingredient file. This makes it considerably easier to maintain a perpetual inventory (a time-consuming process when done by hand). The food production supervisor thus has immediate access to current information on in-house item availability, without having to take a walk through the storage facilities. This information is also available for precosting menu items and determining food costs. Recipes are pulled from a database containing standardized recipes, and then the recipes are exploded to the proper quantities. The product cost of a menu item is then determined individually, as well as on a gross production basis, through integration of data from the ingredient and recipe files. And all of this is done on the basis of yesterday's or today's prices — not those from six months ago. Armed with this information, the supervisor can modify recipes, change a menu plan, adjust production schedules, or change purchasing decisions in an informed and timely manner. Computerization of these functions will improve overall control over the product, contribute to product quality, and further limit opportunities for theft.

SUMMARY

Such factors as reducing waste, increasing productivity, and using food efficiently should be considered in planning a menu. The standardized recipe, which gives a known quantity of food of a known quality, can be used to maintain standards and control production. Using such recipes also gives an operation greater flexibility. Other important factors influencing what may be put on a menu are yield, quantity, and quality tests. These indicate the yield of the items from quantities purchased and give an accurate cost estimate. The quality of items can also be checked to see if it meets the operation's standards.

Menus should be precosted. This can come both from costing standardized recipes into portions and from yield tests. Knowing the cost of an item allows an analyst to calculate a selling price and then the food cost percentage — the percentage of sales that the food represents. By precosting and knowing ahead the cost of items, management can remove or add food items in order to increase or decrease the food cost percentage until it reaches a desired level. The production sheet is a control needed before the menu becomes a reality; it instructs the purchasing department and the kitchen to pur-

chase and prepare specific food items for a particular day.

Another factor to consider in managing the product is the determination of the selling price of menu items. Among the different methods used to determine selling price are the multiplier method, the pricing factor method, the planned profit method, and the menu engineering method of Kasavana and Smith.

Quality control depends on the establishment of and adherence to standards. These standards need to be followed from the moment the product arrives at the foodservice until the moment it is placed in front of the customer. In purchasing and receiving, arriving products must be inspected, and then proper storage must be provided. In production and holding, standardized recipes, sanitation guidelines, equipment maintenance, and temperature controls all help maintain quality.

Security has become an area of major concern as it becomes more difficult for foodservices to make a profit. Prevention — through the removal of opportunity and temptation — is the best approach. Theft is most likely to occur during purchasing, receiving, or storage. A comprehensive security program can virtually eliminate the problem of theft.

Computers are being used more frequently to control and manage the product. Through the use of databases, the food item can be tracked from purchasing to receiving to production to service. Computer advances will make it much easier to integrate many of the other important procedures into the operation.

CHAPTER REVIEW QUESTIONS

1. Eric Burton has just retired from his job as an airline pilot. He has spent a number of years in a service industry and would like to pursue a second career as a restaurant owner. He finds the idea of playing host to all his old friends very appealing. He admits that he doesn't have a detailed knowledge of the restaurant business, so he has hired you to be his manager. He will still be your boss, and he intends to

play a major role in making decisions, although he will trust your judgment.

Eric realizes that proper management of food production is crucial to the success of his operation. Consequently, he is very interested in the process of costing and setting menu prices. Eric would like you to give him a brief explanation of the methods you are familiar with, identify which one would be your choice, and tell why. Draw up an outline of your explanation and your advice.

2. Standardize a recipe that needs it. Include nutrition information on it. Set the recipe up to give five, ten, twenty-five, and fifty portions. Include temperatures, planning instructions, yield, portion size, file number, and other required information.

3. Give the advantages and disadvantages of the three methods discussed for setting selling prices.

VOCABULARY

Profit	Raw food cost
Yield test	Food cost percentage
Standardized recipe	Precosting
Extended cost	Portion cost
Unit cost	Cost factor
Multiplier method	Planned profit method
Pricing factor method	Contribution margin

Menu mix	Quality control
Security	Database

ANNOTATED REFERENCES

Dukas, P. 1973. *How to Plan and Operate a Restaurant.* 2d ed. Rochelle Park, N.J.: Hayden Book.

Levinson, C. 1976. *Food and Beverage Operation: Cost Control and Systems Management.* Englewood Cliffs, N.J.: Prentice-Hall. (All aspects of tracking and controlling the flow of production.)

Ninemeier, J. D. 1982. *Food and Beverage Security: A Manual for Restaurants, Hotels, and Clubs.* Boston: CBI Publishing. (Theory and concepts of foodservice security, as well as a specific plan for security.)

————. 1982. *Planning and Control for Food and Beverage Operations.* East Lansing, Mich.: Educational Institute of the American Hotel & Motel Association. (Detailed information on all food and beverage controls.)

Powers, T. F., and Powers, J. M. 1984. *Food Service Operations: Planning and Control.* New York: John Wiley & Sons. (All aspects of planning and control of a foodservice establishment.)

Spears, M. C., and Vaden, A. G. 1985. *Foodservice Organizations: A Managerial and Systems Approach,* pp. 125-306. New York: John Wiley & Sons. (An excellent overview of managerial aspects of controlling the product.)

Thorner, M. E., and Manning, P. B. 1983. *Quality Control in Foodservice.* Westport, Conn.: AVI Publishing. (Detailed information on controlling the quality of the product.)

CHAPTER 17

Management of Plant/Property

OUTLINE

PLANT/PROPERTY COSTS

The costs associated with physical space occupied by a foodservice establishment have probably risen faster than any other in the last fifteen years. Yet most foodservice operators remain largely uninformed about this topic. While most foodservice operators can readily recall the ups and downs of the energy industry for the past decade or more, and the effects on customer counts of the long gas lines of 1974 or the tumbling oil prices of 1985-86, few associate those turbulent changes with dramatic cost fluctuations in their own businesses. Fewer still have any idea of what to do to control those costs. Yet the foodservice manager can and must learn the basics of energy management and conservation, of building management, and of maintenance management in order to ensure a profitable operation in the future.

In most foodservice operations, the manager is the chief engineer and energy specialist. While this is not true, of course, in large properties such as hotels, resorts, military installations, and some institutional operations or mixed-use facilities, most foodservice managers do not have the luxury of organizational structures that managers in those operations enjoy. In addition, the foodservice manager in most operations is also responsible for building and grounds maintenance. In many establishments, this alone can be an awesome task. In many older buildings that provide an attractive ambiance for restaurants, for instance, managers must be aware of and able to solve problems ranging from leaks in the plumbing, roof, or walls to whether or not the structural loads associated with equipment additions can be maintained.

At one time the costs associated with plant/ property engineering and maintenance were viewed as fixed, since they varied little from year to year. Now the costs associated with these duties can range from 2 or 3 percent of total sales to 10 percent or more. In addition, these annual expenses may represent up to 30 percent of the original investment for the operation; in fastfood operations, this average is about 24 percent (Borsenik 1979). In other words, the costs associated with engineering and maintenance could equal the original costs of establishing the business every five years or so. Utility costs average another 2 to 4 percent of sales per year, and indications are that these will continue to rise dramatically. In more remote locations where maintenance and utilities cost more, the level of cost increases may be even higher.

FOODSERVICE DESIGN

The type of foodservice establishment is a major factor in planning the design of the facility. Each market demands a different physical layout emphasizing the operation's particular attributes of type and style. A commercial fine-dining foodservice design, for instance, would differ significantly from a university cafeteria design. Each type also calls for specific variations in the amount of space devoted to various functions in the design. This means that, while the heuristic (or rule-of-thumb) assumption that 33 percent of the total foodservice space should be devoted to the kitchen may be valid in many instances, it is not always so. Most variations in kitchen design, however, can be roughly categorized into two principal types: the straight-line flow, and the functional flow.

Flow of Work in the Kitchen

Establishing a manageable flow of work through the kitchen helps speed production and reduce labor. Since much of the actual labor time in kitchens is spent fetching or retrieving items for use, an efficient design is important. Each facility requires a different specific pattern based on the anticipated production level of each menu item, the types of equipment used, and the expertise of the staff. Although the details of each pattern will differ, Kotschevar and Terrell (1985) have identified eight basic rules to follow in establishing flow in work centers, sections, and the entire layout:

1. Functions should proceed in proper sequence directly, with a minimum of crisscrossing and backtracking.
2. Smooth, rapid production and service should be sought, with minimum expenditure of worker time and energy.
3. Delay and storage of materials in processing and serving should be eliminated as much as possible.
4. Workers and materials should travel minimum distances.
5. Materials and tools should receive minimum handling, and equipment should receive minimum worker attention.

6. Maximum utilization of space and equipment should be achieved.
7. Quality control must be sought at all critical points.
8. Minimum cost of production should be sought.

Straight-line Flow for Kitchen Design

The straight-line flow for kitchen design is most efficient when adopted by an operation producing a restricted number of similar products; it is often referred to as the *assembly-line flow method*. The word *straight-line* refers more to the type of production than to the actual design layout (which may be in any of various shapes). In terms of production, however, products proceed in a line from one area of the kitchen to their final stop in another area. Interruptions are short-term, and there is no stop-and-stare. This system can be found in fastfood operations, in military and institutional foodservice settings, and in large cafeteria operations.

Functional Flow for Kitchen Design

Also called the *process* method of design, functional flow system is used most often when many and various products are made to order. The functional design system assumes that numerous unrelated products are being prepared simultaneously in different areas of the work center, with concurrent peaks and valleys of workloads in each area. This method is most commonly found in commercial kitchens that produce from menus.

Kitchen Design Space Allocations

The exact amount of space needed to complete any specific function in a foodservice varies, depending on volume, type of service, number of workers, type of supplies, storage requirements (especially in remote areas that receive limited deliveries), and so on. Still, a good rule of thumb for allocating space for the kitchen has been devised by Rutes and Penner for hotel foodservice operations and is convertible to most other types. It calls for the following allocations of space:

6 square feet of kitchen space for each foodservice seat

2 square feet for each banquet seat

1 square foot for each cocktail lounge seat

Table 17-1. Storage Areas as a Percentage of Total Storage

Type of Storage	Percentage of Total Storage
Dry storage	30%
Refrigerated storage	25%
Frozen storage	10%
Beverage storage	15%
Refrigerated beverage storage	5%
Nonfood (china, linen, paper, silver, etc.) storage	15%

According to this formula, storage can be allocated on the basis of the total kitchen space multiplied by 3 to 5 square feet, and storage areas can be broken down as shown in table 17-1.

Receiving, Storing, and Issuing Requirements of the Plant Property

In the amount of space they devote to the functions of receiving, issuing, and storing, foodservices differ considerably. In each case, however, the location of storage space should be close to receiving and production (if possible). In larger operations, the receiving area has a receiving dock large enough to accommodate the trucks that are used to deliver products to the foodservice. In most locations this means having a dock that is 40 to 44 inches above the driveway. The receiving area should be sufficiently large to accommodate the number of products likely to be received in a day. In most climates, accommodations should be made at the dock to protect deliveries from inclement weather conditions. It is also important to install a door at the receiving dock that is sufficiently large to allow a hand truck or four-wheel dolly to pass through it easily. In most cases, this means a door at least 3½ feet wide, although 4-foot-wide doors or double doors with no center post are suggested.

The receiving, storing, and issuing areas should be large enough to contain not only the products but also the equipment used in those departments. For many foodservices, the receiving area should contain bulk weighing scales, food-testing equipment (such as fat analyzers), and hanging scales. In larger foodservices, a separate office is provided for receiving and contains a variety of modern equipment used in the process. For example, computers may be used to scan incoming deliveries and add the products immediately to inventory totals. The personnel working in this department must be well-versed in the grades and types of products available in the foodservice industry today and must maintain specific standards established by the operation.

Foodservice Offices

The types of offices used in the industry are almost as numerous as the types of foodservices themselves. In many small foodservices, there may be no formal office at all; while in larger operations, offices may be provided for each department. There may, for instance, be receiving department offices, personnel offices, service management offices, and maintenance offices. The amount of space allocated for office use depends on the style and type of operation, as well as on the available space.

As computers are used more and more in foodservices, the amount of space used for offices has changed. Today, even small convenience foodservices use computers for various aspects of the operation and thus require additional office space. In most operations, cash and receipts are stored in the foodservice office, and this function determines the size of space needed. A small, one-person office may only require a $6' \times 8'$ space.

In many foodservices, the location of the office is determined by the function it performs. The office should provide ample working space for the personnel involved, allow access to the workplace, and satisfy any special requirements of the foodservice (such as including space for conferences or file storage). In foodservices where only one office is used, the location should be such that the office is central to as many aspects of the operation as possible. If the public is meant to frequent the office, it should not be located in the kitchen.

The equipment needs of a foodservice office vary with the other facets of the business. In some cases, only a wall shelf, a calculator, and a small desk with drawers are needed. In others, the office must accommodate several filing cabinets, computers, printers, copiers, and so on. With the growing use of personal computers in foodservices, each operation should carefully consider adopting this resource in order to remain competitive. Certainly, the management located in the office should be supplied with all the equipment needed for a smooth and efficient operation.

Kitchen Equipment Space Allocations

The size and configuration of the kitchen depends on the style of service, the equipment space requirements, and the size of the operation. Choosing commercial kitchen equipment and designing the configuration of work areas around the equipment can require a great deal of expertise and experience. Often the design is worked out by a contract architect or by a designer on the staff of an equipment supplier. In some smaller foodservices, however, the owner or manager may be responsible for designing the kitchen equipment configurations.

Commercial kitchen equipment comes in various sizes. A range/oven combination, for instance, can be purchased in widths of anywhere from 24 inches to several feet, depending on the number of burners and/or flat grills associated with the item. The same is true (although with a lesser degree of variation) of equipment depths. The height—at least in terms of the working surface—remains fairly standard. Most equipment can be set either on legs or on casters, depending on the foodservice's needs. Many operators prefer that equipment be placed on casters, to ensure ease of cleaning.

The varieties of equipment required in an operation depend on the type of cooking to be performed. In foodservices that specialize in making sautéed foods to order, for instance, there is a greater-than-average need for open burners for skillets and sauté pans. In institutional foodservice operations, where large quantities of foods are prepared together, a minimum number of open burners may be required, thanks to the reliance on such bulk production equipment as tilting braising pans. An inexperienced operator should consult with other foodservice operators and with experts in the field (either consultants or reputable equipment suppliers) prior to making decisions about equipment purchases.

Dishwashing

Several plant/property considerations must be included in space allocation planning for dishwashing equipment. The most important of these considerations are the type of system to be employed, the location of the system, and the issue of sound pollution.

While dishwashing was at one time performed mostly by hand, most foodservice operations today use automated dishwashing equipment. Since one of the principal requirements of a dishwashing system is that it be able to handle the load during peak hours, the load for that period should be used as the basis for comparing the adequacy of various dishwashers to meet the foodservice's needs. The operator must also decide whether an electrical or gas-fired unit would be best for the operation, and whether the dishwasher should be conveyorized (primarily of value in larger operations) or hand-propelled. The number of stainless-steel dish tables to have available on either side of the unit (dirty dishes on one side, clean dishes on the opposite) must also be determined after an investigation of the number of dishes handled during peak load periods. To conserve energy, an operator must consider the various new low-temperature dishwashers on the market today that utilize both temperature and chemicals for cleaning.

The location of the dishwasher is important to the flow of the entire kitchen. Servers or clearers who remove dishes from tables should be able to drop dishes off at the dishwasher station without entering the main work area of the kitchen. In this way, traffic in the kitchen can be limited. Because the function of servicing the cook and service areas with clean dishes is essential, the dishwasher should be situated so as to reduce the amount of time spent carrying dishes to these areas. Locating the dishwashing system properly will also reduce breakage because of the improved flow of both dirty and clean dishes. Because the dishwashing area is noisy, the sound should be contained within the specific washing area. In many foodservices, separate dish rooms are designed as part of the kitchen operation, to prevent noise pollution of either the main kitchen or the dining areas.

Waste Disposal

Waste disposal is an essential function of every foodservice operation. Careful consideration should be given to the type of products served, the size of the operation, the location of the waste system, and the type of waste (food, paper, plastic, or cans) before any single system is implemented. In addition, the state and municipality in which the foodservice is located will likely have codes or laws regulating how waste may be handled. Among the possible disposal methods for foodservices are compaction, incineration, pulping, use of in-sink-erators (trough, sink, or cone), or use of garbage cans. Any of these systems (other than simply placing garbage in cans or dumpsters for pickup) will reduce the odor and bacterial contamination of waste.

In many instances, hybrid waste disposal systems are used. For example, large institutional, hospital, resort, and military foodservices often use dumpsters for nonfood products and pulping for food waste. In some states, pulping—a system that creates a liquefied waste by grinding foods with a recirculating water system—is now required by health departments. Other locales restrict the amount of pulping because of overloaded sewage disposal facilities. A foodservice operator who is unfamiliar with either the local codes for waste disposal or the availability of different systems can seek information from architects, consultants, or foodservice equipment companies. In many areas of the United States, a foodservice operator can find consultants who specialize in waste disposal.

Dining Room Space Requirements

Effective dining room design must take various needs into consideration. The amount of seating space required, traffic corridors, décor provisions, customer facilities, and service stations all affect the total amount of space needed. The two most important topics to be considered during allocation of dining room space are the comfort of the diner and the efficiency of the service personnel.

Seating Space Considerations

Space for dining room seating is generally calculated on the basis of square feet per diner.

The size of dining room tables can vary greatly. It is important to remember when choosing tables that both the size and the shape affect customer comfort and efficient dining room flow. Tables that are 24 to 30 inches square are often used in bar/lounge seating, but those sizes are generally too small for comfortable dining. In a dining room, $36'' \times 30''$, $36'' \times 36''$, $36'' \times 40''$, and $36'' \times 42''$ tables are commonly used. Square or rectangular tables, because of their straight edges, are preferable in cases where it may be necessary to move tables together to accommodate larger groups. Aisle space should be calculated on the basis of the types of equipment to be used in the dining area—taking into consideration, for instance, the specific dimensions of such items as rolling service carts. Adequate aisle space must be maintained, of course, whether or not dining room service carts are to be used. Most designers recommend setting aside a minimum of 24 inches between chairs to ensure adequate aisle space. That distance is, in fact, required by code in many states and municipalities for safety reasons.

Seating Arrangements

The seating arrangement to adopt for a foodservice facility depends on the type of operation and the desired capacity. In some facilities—fine dining rooms, for example—free-standing tables that seat four customers (called *four-tops*) are the norm. This arrangement may not be the best for other types of establishments, however. Wall-oriented booth seating, for example, accommodates more guests than do free-standing tables in a rectangular dining room. In cafeterias, institutional foodservices, and military installations, long tables accommodating eight to twelve (or more) guests may be the most common type used. In coffee shops and some other types of foodservices, counter seating may be the best choice, providing the style of comfort desired

by the customer and allowing optimum use of facility space. The average size of the party of anticipated customers should also be considered, as this varies greatly in different types of foodservice operations. Each type of seating arrangement requires different space allocations for table height, size, width, and so on; the operator is responsible for matching all the ingredients correctly to create the efficiency and ambiance desired.

ENVIRONMENTAL CONSIDERATIONS

Making customers physically comfortable during their visit to the foodservice operation may be as important to the operation's success as offering high-quality food and courteous service. While in the past foodservices were able to accomplish this goal with a minimum of expenditure, today such items as heating and air conditioning have a major impact on the bottom line. How each of these areas is handled in a foodservice depends on the type of operation, the climate, the locale, the building's construction, and other factors. In new foodservice operation construction, a great deal of thought is given to such features as heat loss or gain, automated or computer-controlled systems, energy-efficient equipment, and alternative sources of power. In most existing foodservices, however, major renovations to incorporate such attributes are not feasible, so other measures must be adopted to provide the highest possible comfort for the customer.

Structural Changes that Reduce Energy Costs

Many changes can be made in existing foodservices to reduce energy cost and increase comfort. For example, adequate insulation of walls, windows, ceilings, and doors can markedly improve the efficiency of existing HVAC (heating, ventilating, and air conditioning) systems. Double or revolving doors at entrances are another relatively minor alteration that can improve the internal environment. Adding doors to the kitchen to lessen airflow into the kitchen's exhaust system can greatly reduce energy costs.

The type and placement of air ducts in both the kitchen and dining areas should be given due consideration. It is important, for instance, that tables not be placed directly beneath fresh air ducts, since customers do not want a constant stream of hot or cold air rushing over them during dining. In the kitchen, air ducts should be placed in work areas in a layout designed to maximize comfort for the workers. In the kitchen, the air ducts must not be placed near the kitchen's outside exhaust system (designed to remove smoke from cooking areas); otherwise, a substantial waste of energy could occur from the exhausting of newly conditioned air. Similarly, if the thermostat is located in a particularly warm spot (in the sun, for example), the air conditioning system will overwork itself trying to compensate for the temperature at that spot rather than for the temperature in the room as a whole.

Using a heat recirculation system (to capture some of the heat produced by equipment for use elsewhere), solar energy, or conventional means of energy conservation can lower the size of the monthly energy bill. One of the first steps a foodservice operator should take is to inspect and correct the thickness of insulation in the floors, ceiling, and walls to reduce heating or cooling loss. The degree of seriousness with which conservation of energy is practiced can make the difference between success or failure in a foodservice operation today. If the foodservice operator is not well-versed in this area, specialists should be consulted for a thorough evaluation of all available options.

The Kitchen Exhaust System

In most instances where cooking is involved, foodservices are required to install and maintain kitchen exhaust systems to remove smoke, grease, and odors. These systems vary in size from small units with 1/4-hp motors to very large units with motors that have a capacity of several horsepower. In most states, foodservices are required to install exhaust systems that have no rough edges. In addition, new units must have welded seams, to satisfy established building codes. Operators should be aware of the specific requirements governing exhaust systems in their state or community. This information can usually be learned from a municipal building inspector or from the local health department.

An operator either can purchase a prefabricated exhaust system with motor and roof- or wall-mounted exhaust or can have a custom unit built for the foodservice. This decision should only be made after a thorough investigation of the variabilities of the operation, the costs of different exhaust units, and the opinions of specialists in the field. The type of metal to use in constructing the unit depends on the local and state codes governing the system. In some states, galvanized metal is allowed; in others, the unit must be made of stainless steel. Most foodservice equipment companies can provide the necessary answers concerning exhaust systems, as can independent experts.

The exhaust system should be mounted in such a way as to cover (usually with an additional 3 to 6 inches on either end) the cooking equipment completely. In many foodservices, units are secured to beams in the roof and suspended by cables or steel bands over the cooking line, where they penetrate the ceiling. In addition, they penetrate the roof, to exhaust the air and smoke outward. The area around the roof penetration (where the exhaust throws the air) can be a likely place for leaks to develop. Proper flashing must be mounted at this point, either by the exhaust firm or by a separate roofing contractor.

The size of fan to use in the exhaust system can be determined by evaluating the kitchen cooking equipment involved. This determination may involve the participation of an architect or engineer, especially in larger foodservices. Many smaller foodservices allow the equipment company to determine the airflow needs of the exhaust. In either case, the unit's construction and location can substantially affect the heating and air conditioning costs of the operation. If the exhaust is located near the dining room, for instance, or operates in a manner that causes it to draw air from the dining room, that room's conditioned environment can be disturbed, leading to energy waste.

Some of these problems can be overcome by designing a kitchen exhaust system that balances air intake with air outflow. In all exhaust systems, the air coming into the system (usually through hollow panels in the system's walls) should be balanced with the air outflow. In some locales, this incoming air must be tempered through installation of a heated makeup air (incoming air) system; in others, air directly from the outside can be used.

MAINTENANCE OF PLANT/PROPERTY

In order for a foodservice operation to function properly, the plant/property must be kept clean and in proper working order. This is best accomplished through a regular maintenance program. While many foodservices provide maintenance only after a problem develops, this approach to corrective maintenance is both expensive and nonproductive. Instead, operators should practice a system of preventive maintenance that stresses proper regular care and servicing of all aspects of the foodservice plant/property.

Equipment Maintenance

To institute a program of preventive maintenance, a foodservice manager must first make a list of all equipment to be included in the program. This list should include not only food-preparation items in the kitchen, but also all heating, air conditioning, plumbing, lighting, and other equipment. On the basis of this list, the foodservice manager should compile maintenance and repair data pertinent to the equipment listed. This data may include steps to be taken during maintenance, specific items to be checked or replaced, and descriptions of how service is to be performed (for example, "check grease level or exchange filters"). From the list of equipment and specifications, the foodservice manager can develop a checklist for regular use. This checklist should specify dates for inspections and make provision for signature of the parties who

provide service, whether a member of the staff or a representative of an outside agency.

The equipment maintenance checklist should be entered or otherwise developed on the basis of a calender of events. Many foodservice operators actually use a calendar for this purpose, writing directly on it the items to be serviced on the dates marked; others use separate dated files or even computerized reminders. On the checklist, the exact maintenance to be performed at different intervals must be specified, and each item should be discussed comprehensively in terms of which services can be performed as regular maintenance, which require additional service, and which involve replacement of parts. The form used to record service should also provide a space for listing the condition of the equipment when serviced, leaving ample room for comments that can be followed up on during the next servicing. Space should also be provided for listing service purchases and the costs associated with those purchases. This form should be kept as part of the permanent record file of the operation, as it provides a good record of the condition of each piece of equipment used in the foodservice.

Other Maintenance of Plant/Property

While the proper care of equipment may be the most easily recognizable need in a foodservice maintenance program, it is not the only one. The building (both inside and out), the parking lot, and the grounds should all be covered by regular maintenance programs as well. Indeed, since these are more likely to be visible to the public than the equipment is, maintenance of them may influence the profitability of a foodservice more quickly than would a program for equipment maintenance.

A foodservice manager should establish the same type of program for interior plant/property maintenance as is established for equipment. This means that prevention, rather than correction, is the goal. A calendar of maintenance items should be established that includes both daily and less frequent items. Like the equipment list, this list should specify the exact duties to be performed during maintenance. Items on the list should range from duties performed by the regular foodservice staff (such as after-shift cleanups) to work done by outside agencies (for example, carpet cleaning or window washing.) The list should also cover maintenance of all surfaces of the plant/property, including ceiling tiles, walls, floors, doors, glass, and any decor items used in the foodservice. In many foodservices, separate lists are maintained for each area of the facility. In such a case, one list may be kept for kitchen maintenance other than equipment (such as walk-in cleanups and wall washing), another for the dining room, and a third for public facilities.

The list for areas outside the building should include walls, sidewalks, the roof, ducts, windows, doors, and awnings, among the other items. Some tasks must be performed to maintain appearances (such as window washing, painting, and otherwise beautifying the property); others must be done to ensure customer safety (such as oiling door hinges and inspecting the roof). In the parking lot, a regular schedule of light-bulb changing, sweeping, and litter removal should be established. To a large extent, the maintenance of property grounds depends on the type of property. In some instances, lawns must be mowed and weeded; in others, trash dropped by passers-by must be picked up.

THE EXTERNAL ENVIRONMENT

Creating a pleasant external appearance can encourage customers to frequent the establishment. While many aspects of the external environment must be left to specialists (such as architects or designers with expertise in building construction appearance), others are within the province of the foodservice manager. One example is the creation of a proper environment around the trash-holding area of the foodservice. There is probably no quicker way to discourage customers from visiting than by improperly protecting the trash area. This portion of the facility should be kept away from the customers' view—either by location or by fencing or other means—and should be kept clean and neat,

with no small pieces of trash left littering the area and calling attention to it.

Parking and Parking Lot Lighting

The proper planning of parking lots is important to any foodservice operation. In order to design this portion of the property effectively, a foodservice operator must be able to appraise the external appearance of the establishment from the point of view of a customer. Curb appeal is especially important to foodservice operators in the commercial segment. For example, curb cuts (entrances to the parking lot) should be designed to offer ample turning space and minimal stacking of traffic in the street at the entrance. The parking lot must be adequate for the size of the establishment. In many locales, the amount of parking a foodservice establishment must provide is dictated by code—usually in terms of a formula based on the seating capacity of the operation. The external environment of the plant/property depends not only on regular maintenance of the grounds and building exterior, but also on the efficient construction of outside facilities.

Other considerations that are important in planning a parking lot for a foodservice are walkways, lighting, landscaping, accessibility to the building, and visibility of the trash removal and receiving areas. The most important aspect of walkway construction is that the walkways should clearly direct the customers to the main entrance of the foodservice establishment. The parking lot (and hence the walkways) should be located as close to the front door as possible. Steps (and ramps for the handicapped) should be carefully planned.

The arrangement of lighting in the parking lot is significant for both aesthetic and security reasons. For the safety of the customers, no portion of the lot should be improperly lighted. Several different types of adequate lighting are available today, including mercury, metal halide, and sodium. Each variety has advantages and disadvantages that the foodservice operator must weigh in the context of other variables in the operation. Lighting should be connected to timers or electronic activators so that it switches on when needed, in order to reduce energy consumption.

Many foodservices have found that well-landscaped parking areas and grounds can add considerably to the overall ambiance of the facility and thereby increase business. In the parking lot itself, the type of surface employed should be adjusted to the climate, season, and type of operation.

Signage and External Environment Merchandising

In many foodservice facilities, the external environment is shaped as an advertising aid to promote the restaurant. Theme-oriented commercial foodservices, for instance, might include in the design of the external building or grounds a continuation of the motif presented inside. In some cases, foodservices incorporate a lot of glass windows—in part to provide light and ambiance for the customers inside, but also to draw the attention of potential guests outside. In other operations, the outside of the building is illuminated with indirect floodlighting to call attention to the facility. The entrances to a foodservice represent another area of the external environment that requires substantial attention. The entrances should be designed to allow freedom of entry and egress as well as give a positive appearance to the property.

The external environment can be complemented by signage. In some instances, signage is required because of poor visibility of the plant/property itself; in others, the signage simply supports the impression made to the public by the building and grounds. Since the signage is such a visible advertisement for the foodservice, care should be taken in its design. Foodservice operators must also take into consideration the various city, county, and state signage codes in force in their area. These codes were created as a means of preserving the tone and integrity of the community, and they dictate in many instances the type, size, color, and construction materials for signage that can be used. Lighting of these signs can be accomplished in a variety of manners. Signs may be illuminated from the inside (with neon or internal light bulbs) or from the outside (with spotlights directed onto the signs). How illumination is achieved should be determined by how well each prospective method would promote the overall ambiance desired.

CODES AND OTHER REQUIREMENTS

Each locale has codes or other ordinances that apply to various aspects of foodservice operations. While these codes may seem restrictive and burdensome to many foodservice operators, they actually provide sound bases for management of the property. General codes affecting foodservices include building, construction, fire, and safety codes. Building codes, for instance, affect the types and locations of businesses that are permitted. Construction codes govern the materials that may be used. Fire codes (especially important from a customer safety standpoint) regulate the building size, number of entrances, types of materials, and manner in which foodservices are constructed.

In addition to these general codes, certain industry-specific codes dictate many of the plant/property requirements of the business. Probably the most important of these to a foodservice are health codes.

The maintenance practices discussed heretofore have two important goals: establishment of a clean and efficient operation and adherence to health codes. In most locales, health codes dictate the types of storage required for many foods and the temperatures of storage required. How often refrigeration units should be cleaned, for instance, may be based on health maintenance codes. For many foodservice operators, these codes offer a good basis or reason for instituting maintenance policies. Code provisions relating to employee hair length and restraints, for example, give the foodservice manager sound reasons for instituting hair hygiene rules for the staff. Codes can help the manager establish operating hours, quality of products, and customer adherence to sanitation as well. Requirements dictating that foodservices must use inspected products, for instance, provide safety for customers from various food-borne diseases. In each locale, foodservices are governed by codes that affect daily business. A good foodservice manager must be aware of and adhere to each relevant code provision. Generally, an outline of these requirements is available through the city, county, or town offices in which the facility is located.

SECURITY

A foodservice operation often constitutes a major investment. Therefore, the security system employed to protect the operation should be chosen with great care. And since operations vary greatly in their security needs, a system designed specifically for the foodservice should be implemented. For some foodservices, the operational needs might include internal security of a valuable china, art, or silver collection that must be counted and secured at the end of each shift. For other foodservices, the principal needs might only extend to security of the cash and the equipment. In all types, however, there is an overriding need for security of the customer.

External Security

The first line of external security for a foodservice and its customers is the outdoor lighting system. A foodservice that is well-illuminated is usually significantly protected against crime and vandalism. In addition, well-lighted external property reduces the possibility of accidents that can injure staff and customers.

The building's doors and windows provide the most likely points of attack for vandalism and burglary. In designing a foodservice with effective security built into these two areas, such measures as using metal instead of wooden frames should be adopted, and alarms should be mounted on the doors and windows. The locks on doors themselves can provide different degrees of security. For instance, a dead-bolt or frozen dead-bolt lock pro-

vides greater security than do many other types. The type of door is also a significant variable. A hard-core wooden door, for instance, provides more security than a hollow-core wooden door; and a metal door provides more security than a hard-core one.

Alarm systems have been used effectively to deter crimes during times when the foodservice operation is closed. Many different types are available, including microphoned premises, contact systems, and light beams. In choosing a particular alarm system, the foodservice operator must consider how the system is interfaced with the local police department or sheriff's office. A sensible alarm system should contact the authorities—or the alarm company headquarters—prior to notifying the foodservice manager.

Internal Security

Most foodservice operations employ internal security systems to protect valuables. In many operations, for instance, a safe for storing cash and other valuables at night is located in the manager's office. Some properties have gone a step further and effectively installed safes that require two keys to open, can only be opened during certain times of the day, or can only be opened by armored car services.

While cash receipts have the most obvious need for security, other aspects of a foodservice operation require a great deal of security as well. The inventory of a foodservice, for instance, is generally a very valuable asset of the operation, and without a well-designed plan to secure it, it can be lost at great potential cost. Locks on walk-in refrigerators, food storage rooms, reach-ins, liquor storage areas, and supply storage areas should form an integral part of a foodservice's security system. In addition, regular maintenance and spot inventories of each of these areas should provide a double-check for security. Even maintaining the proper level of inventory can help prevent loss, since keeping too much on hand tends to create the impression that a small quantity will not be missed. The foodservice operator should strive to diminish the likelihood of internal theft by employees by eliminating opportunities for it.

Fire Security

Protection of both the customers and the plant/property from fire is another area of great concern to the foodservice operator. All foodservices should be equipped with fire alarm systems to detect fires as early as possible—both in the public areas and in the kitchen. In addition, since the kitchen is the most likely area in a foodservice for a fire to start in, the operator should install a fire-extinguishing system there. In many locales, such a system is now required by law.

Various fire-extinguishing systems can be installed, depending on the needs of the foodservice. In some cases, a fire-extinguishing system is mounted in the kitchen exhaust system, over the cooking equipment. This system can detect higher-than-normal heat levels and automatically release an extinguishing agent such as CO_2 (carbon dioxide) or halon gas. A CO_2 unit extinguishes fire by discharging a foam or powder containing CO_2 over the area to smother the flames, while a halon unit draws away and consumes the oxygen in the area, thereby eliminating the fire. In an efficiently designed exhaust-hood system, the filters in the system help prevent the possible spread of fire as well as remove grease and dirt from the air being exhausted. To operate efficiently, these filters should be regularly cleaned to reduce grease buildup, and the entire duct system should be included in the maintenance program of the property, so that the interior is thoroughly cleansed periodically of potentially hazardous buildup.

For the safety of both employees and customers, a foodservice facility should provide ample fire exits. In most locales, the number, location, and size of these exits are dictated by codes or laws that base their requirements on the size of the building and the type of construction used in the property. These exits should always be kept clear of obstructions such as tables and chairs and should be clearly designated by appropriate signage. For illumination during electrical outages, battery-operated emergency lighting systems are usually located near exits.

PLANT/PROPERTY CONSTRUCTION

Constructing a foodservice facility of any size can be a major undertaking. To carry out this process properly, operators who lack significant experience in construction should solicit the aid of a licensed architect at least, and probably also a designer, a construction supervisor, and several other specialists. The number of specialists to engage depends on the complexity and size of the project. A large foodservice construction project might include—in addition to the architect—an interior decorator, a sign contractor, an interior designer, a foodservice equipment consultant, a site surveyor, a construction manager, a structural engineer, a mechanical engineer, an electrical engineer, a fire protection consultant, a parking consultant, a landscape architect, a lighting consultant, and various suppliers of products. Moreover, any project will call for the involvement of a number of subcontractors, working under the general contractor or construction manager, to build different facets of the facility. In smaller foodservices, these various consultants are often eliminated in favor of a triumvirate of the architect, the designer, and the construction manager or contractor. The number and degree of involvement of outside experts in each foodservice construction project will depend on the operation.

Construction Planning

The planning of a foodservice operation can (and probably should) take several months to complete. During this time, the architect and the owner, with perhaps a designer and a construction specialist acting either as an outside general contractor or as an in-house manager, will meet to develop the property. The architect is generally the project team leader, and the ultimate responsibility for the development rests with this specialist. It is the architect who must take the ideas developed in group meetings and put them on paper to give the project visual definition. While many of the subcontractors may draw up additional plans and submit these to the architect for review or revision, and while the designer may develop plans for specific aspects of the property, the architect oversees the operation in general. For this, the architect receives a fee ranging from 1 to 5 percent of the total project cost. The percentage tends to be higher on smaller projects, as the total costs are less.

During the process of creating the project on paper, the development team goes through several identifiable phases. The first phase is called *schematic design*. During this stage the architect, designer, and owner develop the general scheme of the foodservice. The drawings are generally single-line and limited in definition, and they concentrate on perspectives rather than specifics. It is important that a feasibility study, a menu, and other operating information be available to guide the planning. The second phase (called *design development)* is characterized by detailed drawings that indicate specific aspects of the mechanical, plumbing, equipment, structural, electrical, and fire protection systems. Building materials are also selected during this phase.

After the design documents (drawings produced during the design development stage) are approved, the construction documents (or construction drawings) are made. These detailed drawings identify all aspects of the facility exactly as it is to be built. They must be extremely detailed in most cases, since the workers who build the facility will depend on these drawings for their understanding of what is to be built.

Site Analysis

Many foodservices fail because of the site chosen for them to occupy. The old axiom of "location, location, location" regarding real estate fully applies to foodservice facilities. This means that, unless the location is right, the facility will probably fail, regardless of all other conditions. To identify a desirable foodservice site, an operator should take into consideration the visibility of the site from the vantage point of potential customers. For a commercial facility, this usually means visibility from the streets or highways that pass the site; for an institutional operator providing foodservices to a college student clientele, it may mean visibility to the greatest volume of walking traffic; and so on. The operator should also consider the accessibility of the site. Far too often, a good site is located and built on, without providing adequate access for the proposed users. This may mean, in the case of a commercial facility, that potential customers passing by on the street find it difficult to drive to the plant/property. To a military foodservice operation, inaccessibility may be a matter of the distance that the majority of troops must walk to get to the facility, and the obstacles they may encounter along the way. To an industrial plant foodservice, inadequate access may involve difficulties workers experience with getting up or down flights of stairs, elevator congestion, and so on.

Careful site analysis should include a visual plan of the site prior to development of the project. Temporary drawings should be made that convey the general impression of the planned facility on the site, to foster discussion and analysis of various issues associated with the venture. Consideration of the natural dimensions of the property, water, sewer, and gas connections, and various other characteristics of the site is essential to this process. In addition, the steepness of slope (slope can be determined by dividing the rise, or elevation, by the run, or distance), wind exposure, and type of ground surface (swamp, rock, clay, sand, or other) should be considered when planning a foodservice. Many operators who are inexperienced with foodservice construction and planning have to engage a site analysis firm to test these various aspects of the proposed location. This should be done prior to land purchase, if possible.

The Construction Process

The length of the construction process for a foodservice facility depends on the type of facility, the materials used, climatic conditions, and other factors. In some parts of the country, for instance, the short outside building season considerably prolongs construction time. The entire process should take from eighteen months to three years, depending on the project's size and complexity. Of that total, the planning process averages from six months (for smaller foodservices) to two years (for large operations).

In most construction projects, a construction schedule is necessary to ensure that adequate progress is made. This schedule should outline the specific times—in days, weeks, or months, depending on the size of the project—by which various elements will be constructed. A good construction schedule will ensure, for instance, that someone will not be trying to lay a floor at the same time that the ceiling contractor is trying to install the ceiling. The schedule should also develop overall guidelines to enable each of the separate subcontractors to plan their work schedules on different jobs.

Construction Materials

The materials used in foodservice construction vary widely. Among the criteria used to determine the selection of materials are needs, climate, availability, cost, and energy efficiency. During the planning process, decisions about which type of materials to employ should be carefully considered and evaluated by the architect, the owner, the designer, the construction manager and other interested parties. In some cases, the city or state has imposed restrictions on what types of materials may be used and on how each may be employed.

The type of materials used can have a great bearing on the cost of the foodservice construction project. This is true not only of the exterior or structural elements of the project but also of the details of interior construction. For example, choosing a floor surface to use in the kitchen could involve selecting from among several different options, each at a different cost. The kitchen floor could consist of poured concrete with sealant, quarry tile, vinyl asbestos tile, a poured acrylic floor cover, or some other type. Each option presents a different cost factor to consider. Because of the high number of

variables involved, many architects and contractors have developed computer programs to analyze them. The resulting rapid and efficient analysis of such options is one good reason for a foodservice operator to consult specialists when planning a facility.

During the planning process, a foodservice operator must consider the wear and tear on the materials used in construction. It may be cheaper overall, in some cases, to use more expensive materials from the outset than to replace less costly materials regularly as they wear out. Because of the many decisions that must be made in planning the materials to use in constructing or renovating a foodservice operation, the careful planner will seek and value professional assistance.

SUMMARY

At one time, the cost of energy was a relatively small, fixed expense for foodservices, but this is no longer the case. Today, energy costs can represent a substantial portion of overall foodservice expenditures. In most smaller foodservice operations, the manager must be well-versed in plant/property energy and maintenance costs as well as in procedures that can be used to reduce these.

The design of a foodservice facility can largely determine its viability. Both labor and food costs can be affected by the foodservice facility's design. The design should follow a functional pattern, especially in the kitchen area. The type and purpose of the operation will point toward making this design either straight-line or functional flow, depending on the type of operation.

The space devoted to specific aspects of the foodservice is important to the future success of the foodservice. A heuristic approach suggests how foodservice space should be divided in the kitchen and the public areas to achieve maximum efficiency and comfort.

Among the more important environmental decisions facing a foodservice operation are the choice of the type of HVAC system, the location of air ducts, and the manner in which kitchen fumes are exhausted.

Proper maintenance of a foodservice facility must

be done on a preventive rather than corrective basis. This approach allows maintenance personnel to identify and correct possible problems with the plant/property before the operation suffers any significant inconvenience. Developing a preventive maintenance checklist is the first step in establishing such a system.

The external environment of a foodservice— including such elements as the outside appearance of the building, the garbage-holding areas, the parking lot, lighting, signage, and security—can significantly affect the viability of the operation.

Plant/property construction may vary a great deal, depending on the foodservice's type and function. Architects, designers, contractors, and other specialists should be employed in the analysis of such decisions. The site and materials to be used in construction help determine the costs and needs of the project as well. During construction, a schedule should be set up that clearly identifies when different parts of the construction must be performed.

CHAPTER REVIEW QUESTION

Smokey's Restaurant is located in an old historic mansion near the downtown market in Charlotte, North Carolina. Smokey's specializes in sautéed items, most of them cooked personally by the owner, Smokey Robertson; consequently, the restaurant uses a lot of open gas burners in the kitchen. The restaurant has been open about fifteen years, and Smokey and his family have always made a good living from the business. Over the past four or five years, however, Smokey's profits have dropped by about 30 percent annually, despite the fact that sales have held their own.

The drop in profits is due to the increased costs of energy and maintenance in the old building, which was built in 1846. Originally, Smokey compensated for the increased costs by raising prices. After three price increases, however, Smokey feels that he can no longer pass the costs on to his customers without doing serious harm to his business. Already, while his sales have remained about the same, his customer counts have dropped following the last two price increases; Smokey knows that, if he increases prices again, he risks alienating his customer base further. Instead, he must begin to address the problem of high energy costs directly.

The building is made principally of brick and stone. The roof was newly installed only three years ago. The parking lot represents a continual drain on funds because the gravel used for it tends to wash away with heavy rains, so that Smokey has to regravel the lot at least once (and sometimes twice) per year. Smokey has avoided paving the lot because of the cost involved, rationalizing that a few dollars spent on gravel now beats the major cost of paving. The floors in the building are old oak plank and have formed a major part of the décor since Smokey opened for business. Floors in the kitchen are the same. For part of the year, Smokey can use the outdoor patio attached to the rear dining room for additional seating, and during those months his volume increases dramatically. He would like to figure out a way to use it year-round without destroying the ambiance of the setting.

The restaurant seats 100 during cold weather and 145 in warm months because of the patio. It is a full-service operation with a small bar. There are lots of windows in the facility, as you might imagine in an old house. Service is offered on both the first and second floors.

Smokey feels that he does not know how to go about renovating for energy savings. Other than putting more insulation in the walls and maybe the roof (things he has read about in the newspaper), he simply does not know what to do. His banker (a regular customer) has promised to lend Smokey the money required to complete the upgrade, if sound reasons for changes can be offered to the bank's loan committee.

Outline a program of maintenance and renovation that would help reduce and control Smokey's energy expenses. Include an equipment maintenance program, based on what you assume Smokey would be using in the kitchen given the menu items mentioned. In describing the program, justify the expense of both loan money and labor hours.

VOCABULARY

Heuristic
Straight-line design
Functional flow
  design
Four-tops
Waste compaction
Waste incineration
Waste pulping
Curb appeal
HVAC
Kitchen exhaust
Makeup air
Preventive
  maintenance
External
  environment
Curb cuts

Codes
Dead-bolt lock
Internal security
  system
External security
  system
Halon gas
CO_2
Schematic design
  phase
Design development
  phase
Construction
  documents
Site analysis
Slope
Construction schedule

ANNOTATED REFERENCES

Borsenik, F. 1977. *Maintenance and Engineering for Lodging and Foodservice Facilities.* East Lansing, Mich.: Educational Institute of the American Hotel and Motel Association. (Terminology and technical aspects of energy, engineering, and maintenance management.)
————. 1979. *The Management of Maintenance and Engineering Systems in Hospitality Industries.* New York: John Wiley & Sons.

Burstein, H. 1985. *Hotel Security Management.* 2d ed. New York: Praeger.

Douglas P. 1979. *Kitchen Planning and Design: Case Studies.* Dorset, U.K.: Blandford Press.

Jernigan, A. K., and Ross L. N. 1980. *Food Service Equipment.* 2d ed. Ames, Iowa: Iowa State University Press. (All aspects of foodservice equipment, including cleaning and sanitizing equipment.)

Kazarian, E. 1983. *Foodservice Facilities and Planning.* 2d ed. Westport, Conn.: AVI Publishing. (The entire planning process of foodservice establishments.)

Kotschevar, L., and Terrell, M. E. 1985. *Foodservice Planning: Layout and Equipment.* 3d ed. New York: Macmillan.

Powers, T. F., and Powers, J. M. 1984. *Foodservice Operations: Planning and Control.* New York: John Wiley & Sons.

Scriven, C., and Stevens, J. 1980. *Food Equipment Facts.* Troy, N.Y.: Conceptual Design. (In-depth section on security systems.)

Woods, C. 1978. *The Anatomy of Foodservice Design 2.* Boston: CBI Publishing. (Sample plans of dining rooms, kitchens, and equipment systems.)

CHAPTER 18

Management of Profits

OUTLINE

In the simplest terms, profits are the excess of income over expenditures during a given period of time. If income has exceeded expenditures over that period, a profit is realized. If expenditures are not properly managed, however, a net loss may result—regardless of the amount of income realized. In the foodservice industry, which is notable for the failure within the first few years of operation of three-fourths of the new businesses that enter the field, learning how to manage income and expenditures can make the difference between success and failure. For the foodservice manager who wishes not only to be among the surviving entrants in the field, but also to be among the successful ones, management of profits is mandatory.

The foodservice manager must begin the task of managing profits by becoming proficient with some basic accounting tools, including profit-and-loss (or

income) statements, balance sheets, break-even analysis, and budgeting. In addition, the foodservice manager must learn how to calculate and control labor, food, and beverage costs.

PRINCIPAL ASPECTS OF ACCOUNTING

For ease of communication and comparison, some basic assumptions of accounting are generally accepted. The most important of these for the foodservice manager to learn relate to the business as an entity, the fundamental accounting equation, the theory of the going concern, the use of cost and money as bases for measurement, the concept of consistency, and the concept of conservatism. The following descriptions offer working definitions of these terms:

Business entity - is the concept of separation of the business from the person who provides the assets. For a foodservice manager, this means that purchases or sales made on behalf of the business should always be kept separate from those of a personal nature. No business funds should be used for personal purchases and no personal funds should be used for business, unless the transaction is listed as a loan or other capital source to the firm.

Fundamental accounting equation - has three components: assets, liabilities, and capital. Assets are the resources of the business; liabilities are the debts; and capital is the amount invested in the firm. All transactions recorded in accounting can be stated in terms of how these three components are affected. Any increase in a business's assets, for instance, must be balanced by a corresponding decrease in another asset account or by an offsetting increase in liabilities or capital.

Going concern - is a concept based on the assumption that a business will continue to operate for an indefinite period of time. This assumption provides the basis for recording assets at acquisition cost, rather than at market value, because the purchase is assumed to be intended for continued operations.

Money and cost - are closely related concepts. All items are recorded at cost, based on the assumption that items recorded at their cost value are less subjectively valued than items recorded at a relative value such as a market appraisal value. All money entries are made in terms of today's dollars, rather than in terms of some reference-year value of the dollar. While we know that the dollar has less buying power now than it had in 1956 or 1978, we still record the value of a dollar today as $1 — just as we did in those years.

Consistency - is a theoretical basis for using the same methods for all accounting transactions. For instance, if straight-line depreciation has been used in the past, it should also be used in the future; any change in accounting methods should be properly noted at the time it is made, and a sound business should refrain from introducing repeated changes.

Conservatism - is a concept based on the theory that the values of transactions should not be overstated. Instead, moderation and restraint should be used in estimates and appraisals of all accounting transactions.

The Profit-and-Loss Statement and Its Preparation

The profit-and-loss statement is a record of the activity of a business covering an entire specific period of time. In some nonprofit organizations, profit-and-loss statements are called *statements of revenues and expenses.* The profit-and-loss statement reflects each transaction—whether a cost or a sale—that took place during that period of time. For a foodservice manager who is experienced with the profit-and-loss statement, the record can provide a window through which to see the past, in order to prepare for the future.

A profit-and-loss statement is prepared by entering each item of income or expenditure in an appropriately labeled category. The major categories used in foodservice operations include sales (or income), cost of sales, controllable and capital expenses, and fixed costs. To make the profit-and-loss statement more meaningful, many foodservices break these major categories down into subcategories such as food income, beverage income, cigarette income, laundry costs, insurance costs, and payroll costs.

The first step in preparing a profit-and-loss statement is to enter the sales or income figures for the period, followed by the cost of goods for the period. To allow computation of the cost of goods for the period, two inventories must be taken. The opening (or beginning) inventory is taken at the start of the period (which often covers one month), and the second (or ending) inventory is taken at the end of the period. In each case, the items are first counted and then multiplied (or extended) by the price paid for them. When all items have been extended, a total dollar value for the inventory is complete.

To complete the computation of the cost of goods sold during a period, the accountant must add all purchases to the beginning inventory, and then deduct the ending inventory (which has been computed in the same manner as the beginning inventory). The result is the cost of goods consumed during the specified time period. This total should then be listed in the appropriate columns on the profit-and-loss statement as the cost of goods sold (or consumed).

The following simple equation illustrates this calculation:

Beginning inventory (+$)
+ Purchases (+$)
− Ending inventory (−$)
Cost of goods sold

Deducting the cost of goods sold from income leaves the gross profit.

The next step in preparing a profit-and-loss statement is to list all controllable expenses that are not products, including operating wages, payroll taxes, utilities, supplies, and laundry. These items are often referred to as *controllable* expenses because the amount of each is to some extent under the control of the foodservice manager. After controllable expenses are deducted from gross profit, all fixed costs are then deducted from this total. In the profit-and-loss statement, fixed costs comprise items that are present at a set cost each month, regardless of the volume of business done. Deducting fixed costs from income after controllable expenses provides a figure called *operating profit*. In some foodservices, additional items are then deducted; in others, these items are treated as either controllable expenses or income (as appropriate). After all of these steps have been completed, the bottom-line figure is called the *net profit* for the period.

The Balance Sheet

Unlike the profit-and-loss statement, the balance sheet is a statement of assets, liabilities, and owners' equity at a particular point in time. The balance sheet is often completed for a foodservice on the last day of the month, quarter, or year (depending on the accounting cycle used). As its name implies, the balance sheet must balance; therefore, the total amount of assets must equal the combined total amount of liabilities and owners' equity. The assets are listed on the left-hand side of the sheet, and the liabilities and equity are listed on the right-hand side. If the two sides of a balance sheet are not equal to one another, there is an error somewhere in the calculation.

The assets on a balance sheet are divided into four categories: current assets, fixed (or long-term) assets, other assets, and funded reserves. The current assets include all cash and all assets that can be converted readily into cash within a short period of time—generally one year. Current assets thus include cash on hand, cash in savings and demand deposit bank accounts, and marketable investments, but not receivables or inventories. The fixed assets include capital improvements, furniture, fixtures, equipment, land, and building structures. Items listed as other assets on a balance sheet include such items as prepaid expenses, escrow accounts, and prepaid fees. Funded reserves listed on a balance sheet include depreciations and other amortized items.

The liabilities listed on the right-hand side of the balance sheet include both short- and long-term obligations to pay. Current liabilities include such items as accounts payable, accrued expenses, and the current portion of any fixed liabilities (such as mortgages). Long-term liabilities are debts such as the amount of total mortgage owed, capital leases, and deferred income taxes.

The owners' equity portion of the balance sheet reflects the difference between total assets and total liabilities. If the assets outweigh the liabilities, the equity is a positive figure. The reverse is true if the liabilities are larger. In many new businesses, the liabilities may be larger for some period of time; but in ongoing businesses, the assets should always outweigh the liabilities. Included in the equity portion of the balance sheet are such items as capital stock, capital surplus, reserves for replacement, and income over the previous time period.

Break-even Analysis and Its Calculation

Good foodservice managers work out strategic operating plans for their businesses. For most foodservice managers, the plan includes a determination of the operation's break-even point. The term *break-even analysis* refers to a determination of the point at which the operation will break even (with no profit, but also no loss). The break-even is not difficult to determine, if the correct steps are followed.

The first step in determining a break-even point is to decide in the case of each cost whether it is either fixed or variable. By definition, fixed costs are costs that remain constant from month to month. Variable costs are costs that change every month in response to the amount of business done during the period. For instance, a mortgage payment is a fixed cost, whereas the amount of money used to purchase food supplies varies with the volume of business. In some cases, a cost category may contain both fixed and variable components, and these must be separated before a break-even point is computed. For instance before a calculation of the break-even point is attempted, labor costs that would exist whether or not any customers come in should be separated from those that depend on the volume of business.

There are two methods of calculating the break-even point for a foodservice. The first is algebraic and can be expressed as the following formula:

$$\text{Break-even point} =$$
$$\text{Fixed costs} \div \left(1 - \frac{\text{Variable costs}}{\text{Sales}}\right)$$

As an example, consider the ABC restaurant, which had the following relevant costs and sales last period:

Fixed costs = $25,000
Variable costs = $60,000
Sales = $100,000

If these figures are inserted into the formula for break-even analysis, the result reads as follows:

$$\text{Break-even point} = \$25,000 \div \left(1 - \frac{\$60,000}{\$100,000}\right)$$
$$= \$25,000 \div (1 - 0.60)$$
$$= \$25,000 \div 0.40$$
$$= \$62,500$$

The second method of calculating the break-even point is by means of a graph. This involves first establishing costs on one axis and sales on the other. The costs should be graded in realistic form from a point below the lowest potential costs to a point above the highest possible costs. Once these have been determined, the next step is to enter the fixed costs. For this example, the figures used in the preceding formula will be used again. Therefore, the fixed costs are $25,000, so a straight line is drawn across the graph at that point. Then sales are recorded by drawing a diagonal line from the origin of the graph (at 0) to the actual sales figure (here, $100,000). The final step in this method of determining the foodservice break-even point is to draw a diagonal line from the point at which fixed costs intersect the cost axis (here, $25,000) until it crosses the sales line. This intersection point represents the break-even point for the foodservice. As this line is extended forward toward $100,000 in sales, the gap between costs and sales widens, reflecting the progressively greater profit that can be made as sales increase.

Budgeting

Budgeting is one of the principal procedures used to manage profits in a foodservice. The primary purpose of budgeting is to establish the goals of a business in written form. Budgets also provide one of the most often-used frames of reference for analyzing the performance of a foodservice.

The following rules are observed by most foodservice managers in establishing their budgets:

1. Involve everyone who is responsible for achieving the results of the budget in the process of establishing goals through the budget.
2. Base the budget on appraisals of potential performance—not on unachievable goals.
3. Develop a budget that effectively assigns responsibility to individuals who possess a considerable degree of influence over the budget's success, rather than to people who have little bearing on the outcome.

4. Plan to make the budget valid over a range of levels, rather than appropriate for achieving a single goal.
5. Review and update the budget periodically, and revise it when necessary.
6. Break the budget down into periods of coverage that are short enough to allow timely appraisals of progress toward the goals.
7. Include information systems — for accurate and timely input on how the foodservice is living up to the budget — as part of the system.

Many foodservice managers have found that the process of establishing the budget can be as valuable as the budget itself. This is true because, by analyzing alternative courses of action in the process of establishing a budget, foodservice managers develop a keener awareness of the needs of their operation. At the same time, establishing a budget forces the foodservice manager to examine what is necessary to achieve the profit levels being forecast in the budgets and establishes a basis for future comparisons. If used properly, the budgeting process can also act as a self-evaluating tool for a foodservice organization. In fact, many foodservices have found that an optimal method of using budgets is to create them monthly as part of the process of closing the operation's books. In this way, the performance of the past month can act as a guide in determining how to budget the next month; at the same time, it can provide the occasion for the self-evaluation and goal-setting needed to spur management to accomplish higher goals.

LABOR COSTS

Labor costs are among the most volatile expenditures that must be managed by a foodservice operator. This has become especially obvious in recent years in foodservice because of increased wage and salary rates, increased unionization, increased fringe benefits, and increased levels of mandated minimum wage. Therefore, learning how to manage labor costs properly represents a big step toward ensuring a profitable foodservice operation. In the final analysis, managers who effectively utilize their labor force are in many cases the same managers who operate the most successful food services. The basic tools for effectively managing labor costs are the schedule, staffing guides, and employee participation in job design.

Scheduling

The first tool a foodservice manager should master in order to begin to control labor costs is the schedule. The object of proper scheduling is to have the correct number of employees at work at any given time. Having too many employees on the clock results in a labor cost that is too high, while having too few leads to inadequate service of the clientele. In order to plan for the correct number of employees, the manager must make a schedule for each shift. Sometimes weekly schedules are used; in other cases, monthly or even permanent schedules are created. While arguments can be made in support of each method, most foodservice managers will find that the shorter the schedule is, the more flexibility the manager has in controlling labor costs.

For each job description (or employee category), a separate schedule should be prepared. To be most effective, the schedule should be easy to read and conspicuously posted. In addition, it should be posted early enough to allow for changes; in the case of weekly schedules, many foodservice managers post the schedule for the following week on Thursday — in plenty of time for all employees to see the schedule and arrange to make any necessary changes prior to the start of the schedule week.

Foodservices differ in their staffing needs, depending on the type of operation involved. In a foodservice where the level of customers can be predicted from day to day, the schedule may require little flexibility. On the other hand, in a commercial foodservice where the number of customers is less predictable, a labor force that can be adjusted to accommodate increases or decreases in customer volume is highly desirable. Many foodservice managers have found that the use of relief and part-time personnel provides the level of flexibility sought in such cases. Relief personnel are workers whose employment is intermittent, depending on the volume of business, and who are willing to be called on short notice when business or employee absences raise the need for extra personnel. Part-time personnel are those who work regularly, but only a few days per week or a few hours per day.

The use of part-time personnel has become especially widespread in fastfood operations. In some parts of the country, for instance, fastfood operations hire men and women to work only during the lunch hour, while their children are in school. In other cases, part-timers are employed after school or in the evening for short periods of time. While this tactic is certainly not limited to the fastfood segment of our industry—since part-timers also make up a large portion of the staff at many other types of foodservices—it is most prevalent there. A variation on part-time work that has evolved is called the *split shift*. Under this method, employees work the peak periods of lunch and dinner only, and are not employed during the hours in between. This approach is only possible, of course, when employees are willing to work such hours.

The Staffing Guide

The first step in utilizing a schedule is to prepare a staffing guide for the foodservice. The purpose of this guide is to present an outline of basic personnel needs for a given period of time. Because the staffing guide varies from one foodservice to the next, it is wise for the manager to be in charge of developing this instrument. For the novice manager, however, various industry-standard staffing guides are available from a wide range of sources. For advice on predicting the number of employees that will be necessary for each job category, for instance, an inexperienced manager would be wise to consult the National Restaurant Association, the state restaurant association, or perhaps an accountant or other consultant.

To prepare a staffing guide, a foodservice manager must first determine the business's hours of operation and service. Once this is done, the number of employees required, by position, for each

hour of operation must be determined. In staffing terms, these employees are referred to as *FTEs*, or *full-time equivalents*. One FTE represents one full-time employee needed. Because the number of personnel required varies from day to day, a typical staffing guide is often constructed to portray the FTEs needed per week, thus taking into account both slow and busy periods. Once the total staff requirements are outlined, the foodservice manager can begin to use the scheduling method previously outlined.

Job Descriptions

A job description is a written account of the responsibilities involved in a job. In addition, it formally describes the tasks, duties, and performance requirements of each job. In order for a foodservice to operate at its highest level of effectiveness, emphasis must be placed both on creating these descriptions and on making certain that each employee knows the requirements of the job. Each job description should include the following items:

The title of the job and its classification in the organizational hierarchy
A complete description of all tasks and duties associated with the job
Performance requirements of the job
Standards of measurement used in appraising performance on the job

It is important that the job description reflect the real job; too often, foodservice job descriptions are outdated or ambiguous.

Job Design

The way in which a job is designed is often the single most important factor affecting how well the task is done. This can be especially true in the case of service operations. If the jobs in a foodservice are properly designed, the work is more likely to be completed successfully within an allotted time period. If, on the other hand, jobs are designed without consideration of how tasks interrelate, the opposite result can be expected. The first step in designing a job accurately and effectively is to analyze the task. Recently, many foodservice managers have discovered that one of the best ways to ensure high-quality job performance is to involve employees in designing the task.

FOOD AND BEVERAGE COSTS

Food and beverage costs are a major area of concern in the management of profits. The most important element in such management—the calculation of selling prices—is discussed in detail in chapter 16.

SUMMARY

Profits are the excess of sales over costs. In order to make a profit, an operation must carefully manage both sales and costs.

Understanding several principles of accounting is mandatory for knowing how to manage profits. Among these principles are the business entity concept, the fundamental accounting equation, the theory of business as a going concern, money and cost at constant values, consistency in accounting methods, and conservatism.

The profit-and-loss statement is a record of business activity for a *specific period of time;* the balance sheet is a record of business at a particular point *in time.* Break-even analysis is important for determining the amount of sales a company must make to reach a point of no profit and no loss—the break-even point. This can be determined in two ways: through an equation, or through a graph.

Budgeting is any method of planning for sales and expenses. A budget constitutes the written goals of a foodservice.

Labor costs are very volatile in foodservices, and among the basic management tools that must be mastered to deal with these costs are scheduling, staffing guides, and employee participation in job design. The schedule provides an operational budget for labor costs over a period of time. A staffing guide indicates how to plan for scheduling. Job descriptions are written outlines of job responsibilities that are used as the basis for evaluating job performance and for identifying training needs.

Food and beverage cost management is another essential area of financial management.

CHAPTER REVIEW QUESTION

Lydia Lunchcounter has just taken over a branch restaurant with a problem. While some years ago the operation was one of the most consistent performers in the entire company, recently the profits have dipped to the point where the restaurant is now losing money. Lydia, known throughout the chain as a turnaround specialist, has been sent in to make the operation profitable again.

After observing and analyzing the operation for a week, Lydia is ready to begin the turnaround. She has separated the task into several different categories, including upgrading and retraining of service personnel, revitalization of the décor and physical plant, and profit management. As a new member of Lydia's management team, you have been given the responsibility of overseeing the management of profits. It is an opportunity to shine and to establish yourself with Lydia for the future.

Outline the steps you would take to determine how the foodservice is currently performing and how you would begin to establish workable goals for the future. Because the last management team seemed to operate pretty much from the seat of their pants, your agenda will include establishing budgets, a break-even point, and a profit-and-loss statement based on the current month. The list that follows contains the pertinent figures you will need. You should not only complete the analysis called for in each step, but also provide a short description of how the figures were arrived at, which members of the staff you consulted for information, and how you plan to monitor progress. Include a break-even graph in your work.

Sales; $80,000 (food, $60,000; beverage, $20,000)

Fixed costs: $26,000

Variable costs: $43,000

Prior month inventory total: $35,000

Inventory this month: $41,000

Purchases during month: $23,000 (food, $19,000; beverage, $4,000)

Expenses

  Operating wages: $12,000

  Payroll taxes: $3,000

  Insurance: $800

  Utilities: $1,400

  Laundry: $400

  Repairs: $600

  Travel: $300

  Rent: $1,800

  Depreciation: $2,000

VOCABULARY

Profits	Concept of consistency
Profit-and-loss	in accounting
statement	Conservatism
Balance sheet	Inventory extension
Break-even analysis	Beginning inventory
Budget	Ending inventory
Food cost	Cost of goals
Beverage cost	Fixed costs
Labor cost	Variable costs
Business entity	Assets liabilities
Fundamental account-	Equity
ing equation	Break-even point

Going concern	Labor schedule
Money and cost con-	Staffing guide
cepts in accounting	

ANNOTATED REFERENCES

Axler, B. H. 1979. *Foodservice: A Managerial Approach,* pp. 265-371. Dubuque, Iowa: William C. Brown. (Chapters on financial control specific to the foodservice industry.)

Coltman, M. 1982. *Hospitality Management Accounting.* 2d ed. New York: Van Nostrand Reinhold.

Keiser, R. J., and Kallio, E. 1974. *Controlling and Analyzing Cost in Food Service Operations.* New York: John Wiley & Sons.

Lundberg, D. E. 1989. *The Hotel and Restaurant Business.* 5th ed. New York: Van Nostrand Reinhold.

Matthews, L. M. 1977. *Practical Operating Budgeting.* New York: McGraw-Hill.

Powers, T. F., and Powers, J. M. 1984. *Food Service Operations: Planning and Control,* pp. 224-324. New York: John Wiley & Sons. (Chapters on budgeting and control of food, beverage, and payroll costs.)

Sherry, J. H. 1972. *The Laws of Innkeepers for Hotel, Motel, Restaurants, and Clubs.* Ithaca, N.Y.: Cornell University Press.

Stokes, J. 1979. *Cost-Effective Quality Food Service: An Institutional Guide.* Md.: Aspen System Corporation.

West, B. B.; Wood, L.; and Harger, V. B. 1983. *Food Service in Institutions.* 6th ed. New York: John Wiley & Sons. (Chapters on administration and cost control, including helpful charts and checklist.)

CHAPTER 19

Management of Promotions

OUTLINE

In order to promote a foodservice professionally, the operator must carefully plan the enterprise's goals and how to meet them. This is especially true of foodservices in which both production and service aspects take place under one roof. In such a case, the foodservice operator is selling products *and* services—not just one, as a manufacturing concern might. The products are the foods and beverages offered on the menu. The services are the less tangible attributes of the operation: ambiance, lighting, sounds, smells, friendliness of the staff, manner of delivery, and so on. Like those of any other service operation, these attributes are perishable (cannot be stored for use when desired),

are simultaneously produced and consumed, and vary to the extent that each service person may deliver them in a different manner.

It is up to the foodservice operator to package the products and services in a manner that is most pleasing to customers. The first step here is to determine who the customers are and what they want. The process of answering these questions and devising a program to meet the needs identified is called *marketing*. While this text deals primarily with internal promotional concepts—and while marketing is mostly external—it is important to cover a few of the basic concepts of marketing as well.

FOODSERVICE MARKETING

Marketing is not the same as advertising. In fact, an advertising program is only one aspect of a good marketing plan. Marketing involves building in customers' minds the business image that management would like them to perceive, while advertising is simply one method of conveying that image to customers. Other marketing methods include the correct packaging of products and services to meet demand and the proper presentation of products and services.

Determining the likely customers of a foodservice —or the *market,* as it is often called—can be accomplished in several different ways. The most common is through a market research survey, which collects demographic information concerning the operation's locale. From this information, the foodservice operator can determine such critical factors as the educational levels of potential clientele, food taste preferences, age, income, number of persons per household, and average amount of money spent dining out. On the basis of this information, a marketing plan can be built. If the survey indicates, for example, that most potential patrons prefer steak dinners and full service, the operator would be wise to establish this type of operation. This rule about responding to market interest applies not only to commercial foodservices but to all other types of foodservices as well. It is just as important for a military foodservice to cater to the preferences of its clientele as it is for a commercial operation to do so.

In addition to the basic market research survey, more involved methods can be used to determine the market for a foodservice. One popular method used for foodservices is a focused group study, in which meetings are conducted with the potential patrons to identify specific likes and dislikes about an existing or planned foodservice. This can be especially beneficial for determining the attitudes and spending habits of members of the prospective market. Life-style analysis is another method of market research that has gained in popularity. It is based on the assumption that, by studying the life-style of the market—amounts of time spent on various leisure activities, preferences for life-style, and so on—an operator can better determine how to tailor the operation to fit those with that life-style.

Yet simply studying the market in which a foodservice will be located does not supply enough information to plan the foodservice properly. The operator must also plan to position the business in the market. Since the market in which a foodservice is located probably offers a variety of dining options to choose from, the foodservice operator should pinpoint the segment of the market for which it will compete. The public is likely to associate the operation with a few salient features such as price, type of foods sold, and ambiance; therefore, the operator should determine how to present these features before entering the market. This is at the heart of positioning a business. For instance, if several steak houses are already in the market offering moderately priced meals, the operator might consider positioning the operation to fill a segment where the competition is less heavy, such as by opening a gourmet burger business. While this type of fine-tuning may seem most appropriate to commercial foodservice operations, it is equally useful for all other types of foodservices.

Once the market and the positioning of the business in the customers' minds are established, the operator can begin to promote the business, both externally (through a marketing plan) and internally (through merchandising).

MERCHANDISING FOOD

If an operation is to succeed in pleasing customers and building sales, merchandising must occur. This is true not only for commercial operations that must attract customers, but also for institutions that serve a captive audience. Many operations fail to realize the importance of good merchandising and, as a result, have poor merchandising systems. The operation that does a little extra in merchandising often beats out the competition, even when the quality of its food and service may be slightly inferior.

The areas of chief importance to merchandising are the training of employees, the planning of special promotions, the featuring of menu items, the creation of atmosphere, the development of good public relations, and the use of promotional material.

Training Employees

The term *merchandising* may be narrowly defined as the selling of merchandise, but in a broader sense it is the presentation of factors that entice people to buy. Many operations could sell more food if they used better merchandising techniques. Employees can be invaluable in getting people to buy. They usually have the first contact with the customer and consequently have the best opportunity to sell. Suggestive selling has been found to be especially effective in foodservices (Solomon 1971). Solomon, who has made a specialty of suggestive selling in his McGarvey's Restaurant, describes the technique as follows.

Eighty percent of our customers (yours and mine) don't know what they are going to eat until they look at the menu. It's up to you to help them if they require help and suggest the "extras" which make their dinner an unforgettable treat.

When the average person dines at home or is a guest in someone's home, he is given little or no choice in the courses that will be served to him. The first thing we require of a customer before we can serve him is that he make a choice from the 70 or 90 items listed on the average menu. This is impossible for the vast majority of our customers, because of the mass of items which tempt him or his lack of knowledge about the products listed on the menu.

You are your customer's guide through the maze of decisions which he must make while selecting his meal. To do this effectively and promptly, we must have a plan of sales and carry it through with dispatch to insure customer satisfaction. Therefore we have . . .

Suggestive Selling

The key to suggestive selling is to do the thinking for the customer by recommending à la carte items as you lead him through the order.

It is our observation that many presold customers look quickly at the menu, order the main course, and hand the menu back to the waitress. She must then carry him through the rest of the order verbally.

If your guest is undecided, you will probably count

to 7 without receiving an order, or the count will be interrupted with a statement to show that the customer has turned his meal selection over to you. The most familiar lines are: "What's good today?" or "What would you suggest?"

Have ready for him at least two items from the menu. Every restaurant has its specials of the day. Use these first. If he hesitates, suggest the most popular items or your own particular preferences.

Write down the number or abbreviation of the main course your customer has selected. Never show personal distaste in his food selection. Everyone's taste isn't the same.

If steak is ordered, ask how he would like it prepared: rare, medium, or well done. "Would you like an order of fresh broiled mushrooms with your steak?" Offer the choice of french fries or baked whipped potato. If he hesitates, explain that the baked whipped potato is the specialty of the house and describe how it is prepared. Proceed to the salad and ask his preference for cole slaw or garden fresh salad. If he chooses garden fresh salad ask, "With Roquefort?" If he hesitates or asks whether you have French, say "I'll bring our dressing tray, which has a selection of dressings." Follow through with the beverage by asking, "Coffee with dinner or later?" He may want milk, hot tea, iced tea, or soft drink. Serve all cold drinks with dinner, including beer, if it has not been ordered as a cocktail before dinner.

Next, suggest the appetizer, putting the item you wish to sell last. (The last thing you hear is usually that which you remember.) Start by saying, "Would you like tomato juice, soup (be sure to say what kind), or a shrimp cocktail?"

Now try to sell an order of french-fried onion rings. Don't offend the customer by overselling. An order of french-fried onions will be sufficient for four.

The customer who orders cocktails before dinner and orders a steak is more easily sold than the one who orders the lowest-priced dinner and nothing before dinner. Don't be discouraged if you don't always make a sale. The best salesman (in any line of business) is not the one with the glibbest tongue, but the one who keeps plugging. We had a waitress whom we called "Little Annie." She was tops in sales and we asked her the secret of her success. Her reply was, "Use suggestive selling at every table."

We can teach you to sell, but it is up to you to do the selling. There's a world of difference between being an order taker or a super sales hostess. It can mean many, many dollars in your pocket over a period of time.

The job of service personnel is thus a lot more than order taking.* Personnel should be trained to make suggestions to customers highlighting the high-gross-profit items on the menu or the items that should be moved. Salesmanship, not "pushmanship," is desired. Good salesmanship can help please a customer more than is generally realized. A smart service person often can sense what might please a customer, or a few well-directed questions or comments may give enough information to know what the individual would be most pleased with.

Because service is the aspect of a foodservice that is most often recognized by customers as the determining factor in whether or not to return, care should be taken in the selection, training, and retraining of service personnel. It is certainly a good idea for a foodservice operator to devise a strategic plan for merchandising products and services, but unless that plan is carefully carried out by the service personnel it is doomed to failure. A proper merchandising training program, therefore, must take into account not only the products and services offered, but also the behavior of the personnel delivering those items to the public.

Planning Special Promotions

Business in a foodservice may fluctuate, and low-volume periods may cause a major loss of profit. Building business at these times can take up some of the slack and help meet overhead and labor costs that exist whether or not there is business. Three methods are used to build foodservice business with special promotions: personalizing service to include special events in customers' lives; developing special promotions around holidays; or capitalizing on local events that lend themselves to special promotions.

Special Day Celebrations

All customers have specially important days in their lives—birthdays, anniversaries, graduation days, or visits from friends or relatives. Some operations offer patrons cards to fill out identifying such spe-

*Suggestive selling can also occur behind a cafeteria counter, in a take-out operation, or even in a hospital room. It need not be confined to a waiter or waitress in a commercial operation.

cial days. These cards are then filed and used to remind the customers to come in to celebrate; some type of arrangement in keeping with the occasion is offered to make the proposal more attractive. This is all done through the mail, with a tickler file reminding the operator to notify the guest of the impending special event. Even if the guest does not come in, the reminder is good public relations.

Holiday Celebrations

Holiday promotions can be quite successful. Mother's Day, New Year's, Thanksgiving, and other holidays are special days on which many people want to eat out. Special menus can be printed and sent to customers or shown around the operation; they also can be put into newspapers or otherwise advertised. Suitable tags on service personnel, table tents, and verbal reminders are also effective. The event can be emphasized in advance by special decorations.

Local Happening Celebrations

Local events offer many opportunities for special promotions. A football game, a convention, or a community project may provide the occasion. A "winning-team special" can be used to feature the first event, and a "convention caper dinner" can be used to feature the second. Even offering special snacks after visits to theaters or nearby museums can help bring people in.

Other Special Promotions

Special events are not needed for special promotions. For instance, as the baby-boom generation has grown older, a small boomlet of children of these baby boomers has developed. This provides a perfect market for a foodservice operator to promote. Because the baby boomers themselves have grown up dining out, they are used to going out to eat; but because they now have children, their dining habits have changed. Now the boomers are looking for foodservices that cater to the special needs of parents and young children. A special promotion aimed at children—such as one offering balloons, toys, or coloring books—can be very effective in capturing this market.

A foodservice operator should plan both routine

and special events to promote the business internally through merchandising. Routine (or everyday) activities such as music or other entertainment have often been successfully used, as have the use of banquet or meeting-room facilities. Myriad possibilities for promotions can be discovered when planning a merchandising program. For information on activities that others have successfully used, an operator can contact such organizations as the National Restaurant Association or the American Hotel/Motel Association.

Featuring Special Menu Items

Operators at all levels of the foodservice industry feature food items in their merchandising programs. One secret of merchandising food is to develop several things that are especially distinctive and make the operation stand out. These may include certain foods, special service, or special uniforms. Cocktails served in a distinctive fashion or with a special flair can be enough to compel attention and bring business back. Special food combinations offered at a good price during low peak times can help. Women shoppers may be enticed to come in for a special combination of small pieces of cake and tea. Other foods that can be emphasized on the menu are hors d'oeuvres, salads, and desserts.

Hors d'Oeuvres

Hors d'oeuvres can attract customers and raise check averages. Instead of simply leaving a patron to eat a hard roll while waiting for the soup to be served, the operation may present a lazy susan jam-packed with hors d'oeuvres for sale. The popularity of hors d'oeuvres is especially high if a cocktail is offered with it. The price can be right for one or both. Even though the profit may not be as great as with some other items, the buildup of the check average can help greatly.

Salads

Salads have become a major product for many foodservices. This is especially true because of changes in American dining and health habits that emphasize more selective and healthful dining. For

Figure 19-1. A special feature: the "spinning salad bowl" used at Don Roth's Blackhawk Restaurant.

many diners today, the salad has become not just an addition to the meal, but the meal itself. In order to capture this market, foodservices have developed merchandising programs that emphasize salads. In fine dining, this may mean placing salads on a cart and wheeling it around the dining room in colorful display for guests to see, or carrying salads on a tray through the dining area. At other times, the salads are prepared at tableside with flair, to capture the attention of diners (see fig. 19-1). In other types of foodservices, salads are promoted through the use of salad bars that offer a wide range of products from which customers can make their own special salads. The degree of acceptance of such promotional tools can be seen in the regularity with which salad bars are offered today. Salad bars can now be found in fastfood establishments, in institutional settings, and even on jumbo airliners. Whether the salad is served at the table or through a bar, garnishes can give it color and texture. Pickles, anchovies, parsley, and many other items are offered for this reason (see fig. 19-2).

Desserts

Desserts can be high-profit items, but many people today avoid them, thinking of the calories. It is possible, however, to plan desserts that contain few

Figure 19-2. Salad garnishes.

calories but still satisfy the almost universal desire for something sweet, delicate, and pleasing to eat at the end of a meal. A group of different desserts can be placed on a cart and rolled to guests' tables for them to see and select from. The trays on which desserts are placed should be carried so that other patrons see them. A few special desserts can become so well known that customers come to the foodservice especially for them.

Creating Atmosphere

Service and atmosphere are important aids in selling a foodservice. Atmosphere is important in giving guests total satisfaction in their dining. Both external and internal atmospheres establish in patrons' minds an opinion about the operation that can strongly influence whether they will be pleased by the experience of eating there or not.

External

The external atmosphere of an operation is affected by the neighborhood in which the operation is located, as well as by the appearance of the building and grounds. In some foodservices, the interior approach to the dining area is treated as part of the external atmosphere. In a nursing home or institution, the interior approach might include the entrance to the building, the halls, the elevators, and other areas through which patrons must pass to get to the dining area.

Cleanliness and neatness are two very important factors in creating a good external atmosphere. There should be no debris or clutter in the surrounding yard. Drive-ins should be particularly careful to see that paper and other debris are quickly picked up. Waste receptacles where paper goods and other materials can be deposited should be located conveniently and in plain view. These receptacles should be neat and have a good cover. Parking lots should be kept orderly and should be plainly marked as to entrances, exits, and areas for parking. The building should be nicely landscaped and properly maintained. Colors should be inviting. The sign should be informative but also should carry the logo or emblem by which the operation is identified. Signs of franchise operations may remind guests of pleasant visits to other operations in that chain. If an operation is located in a poor neighborhood through which people must pass to get to it, it is extremely important for management to make the place stand out and give the external area a neat and inviting appearance. A good image is extremely important, and the contrast to close surroundings can help create such an image. Steven and Iris Laine (1972) offer the following description to show what might be done to establish an image that conveys a standing invitation to come in and dine.

Suppose you decide to open a moderate-priced family restaurant, one that you would like to have patronized by families with children. All you can find is a building that looks like an old Southern mansion with big white pillars and a circular drive with small formal garden in the center. There is nothing about this exterior to suggest a restaurant that will welcome children. In fact, when you look at the formal structure, children seem out of place. You have thus created a wrong image, and, unless you correct that image, you may discourage families from coming in.

Since you can't change the basic structure of the building, you must do something else so that it will create an image of the kind of restaurant this is. You might, for example, paint the pillars in red and white stripes to look like peppermint candy sticks. You could change the garden somewhat and put a red and white striped bench in it. Perhaps the building would lend itself to trim in the form of circles of red and white stripes to look like peppermint pattie hard candy.

Inside you could continue this theme by having bowls of peppermint for the youngsters when they have finished their meal. In fact, you might even call your restaurant "The Peppermint House." Now you have turned what originally seemed like a fault into a big advantage by changing the exterior building to match the image of the restaurant you wish to have.

In any new venture, the first thing you must do is decide what kind of restaurant you want to have and what kind of customers. Then, and only then, can you determine what type of building should house this restaurant. Remember, too, however, that sometimes all it takes is a little imagination to turn what may seem like an unsuitable building into just what you need and want.

Internal

The internal atmosphere of a foodservice is created in the area in which patrons dine or obtain their food. Because customers' eating pleasure is affected by their immediate surroundings, the operator who creates a pleasant, cheerful, and imaginative internal atmosphere will do much to satisfy customers.

The first step in creating an attractive internal atmosphere is to be sure that the customer is comfortable. The proper temperature should be maintained, with no cold drafts or hot air striking people. Sunlight should not create glare. Lighting should enable people to see well but should not be too bright. Contrasts of light in the area can give a pleasing effect. Restrooms should be readily available and immaculate.

The entire area should be clean, neat, and well-maintained. Furnishings should be uniform in style and should contribute to the overall décor. Tablecloths, if used, should hang neatly and evenly from the tables. If no tablecloths are used, place mats should be neatly set. Table settings should sparkle, and the entire place should convey a feeling of good organization and cleanliness.

A second step in achieving good internal atmosphere is to create a desirable mood for the operation. Some places want to appear busy and

yet efficient. Bright colors, a simple décor, and plenty of light can help do this. Cheery colors and lots of light should characterize operations geared toward families. Soft colors and dim lights help create a suitable mood for luxury operations. Low background music of good quality can be used to enhance a mood. Atmosphere can be further developed by the décor. Colors should follow through from walls to furnishings, draperies, and even tabletops.

Creating the right mood can do much to help win customer approval. Eating pleasure is greatly affected by how a customer feels. School lunchrooms, nursing homes, hospitals, and other institutions can raise the morale of patrons by providing a bright, cheery atmosphere. Other aspects—such as employee's uniforms, hair styles, and attitudes—contribute to an overall mood effect.

Developing Good Public Relations

Public relations is defined as the total effort of an operator to win and keep the goodwill of customers and the community. By maintaining goodwill, the operator encourages people to view the operation favorably. A community wants to feel that a foodservice is a part of it and is working toward its general welfare. By doing what it can to promote the good of the community, a foodservice can build tremendous goodwill and can take a position as an important member of the community family. Management should do what it can to promote community affairs and should join local groups such as the Kiwanis, Elks, or Rotary. Belonging to church groups and taking part in PTA and other activities also mark the operator as belonging. Supporting charitable drives by utilizing posters in the operation or even putting clip-ons on menus is good public relations. If the operator is in a tourist area, the business may distribute maps and other materials that are provided by the local chamber of commerce. Getting involved with the local welcome wagon agency, which offers free gifts from participating businesses to new community residents, is also a good idea. Foodservices from time to time have good-quality food that they cannot use. Giving this to charitable organizations builds goodwill.

Helping with food donations at Thanksgiving and Christmas also helps. Some operations sponsor little-league baseball teams or adult bowling teams.

Having good community relations is furthered by promotional news stories in the press and other media. If an operation can work up some good material of human and community interest, the media will use it. Matters of potential media interest include the following:

Opening a new restaurant

Complete remodeling or expansion

Announcing a new appointment at the executive level, the retirement of an old employee, or honors awarded to one

Inviting a celebrity to visit, with an acceptance received

Holding a special affair or meeting at the operation

Offering new services, such as catering or a take-out service

A news story should cover who, what, where, when, and why. The important facts should come first, followed by less important details. In this way, a story that is too long can be shortened without destroying the basic story. By keeping in touch with television stations, radio stations, and other communications media, the operation increases its chances of getting a news story about it aired.

Every guest who enters the operation provides it with an opportunity for promotion. One of the first aspects of promotion is to be sure that the guest enjoys the experience of eating there. Word-of-mouth advertising has been said to be the most effective form of promotion a foodservice can use. Suggestions can be solicited from guests on how better to serve them. Offering to help with social affairs—such as preparing special cakes, dishes, or other items they might need, or sending one's chef or head baker to give a demonstration at a woman's club meeting—also helps let guests know that their business is appreciated. Pleasant, efficient service and a cordial thank you and goodbye leave guests with a final impression that the operation appreciated their visit.

Using Promotional Materials

Publicity can play an important role in merchandising, and advertising can play a part in publicity. For some time McDonald's would not advertise, depending on word-of-mouth, and building customer volume by offering a good product at a reasonable price. With growing competition, however, McDonald's turned to advertising and found it an effective aid. Newspaper and magazine articles, direct mailings, and radio and television spots are effective with some markets. A recent study, however, showed that less than 1 percent of gross income is spent by the industry on advertising and that a substantial part of this did not achieve the results it should have because it was directed to the wrong market. Advertising must be carefully thought out and directed toward a specific market to achieve its objectives. Many things also can be done within an operation to advertise, such as posting information materials on backbars, in windows, or around the operation, using table tents and menu clip-ons, or even arranging for personnel whom customers see to wear badges.

Backbar, Window, and Other Signs

Informative materials on backbars, in windows, or around the operation can be quite effective in announcing things management wants customers to know. Coming promotional events such as special dinners on Mother's or Father's Day or a special bakery promotion can be broadcast by such signs. Showing a special dish of good gross profit in a colored photograph can improve sales for that item. In some operations, mobiles or small decorative signs hung by dark (almost invisible) thread can be used to advertise. Operators must be careful, however, not to clutter their dining area by using signs. A place's appearance is cheapened by having too many signs, too gaudy signs, or signs that are inappropriate to the décor or the operation.

Table Tents and Menu Clip

Table tents and menu clip-ons can be effective merchandisers, doing much what the signs previously discussed would do. Special luncheon or dinner features, the presence of a room kept open for late supper service, a catering service, or a cocktail lounge feature can be announced through table tents. A menu clip-on is a little printed or illustrated card that is affixed to the menu. It should not cover up other portions of the menu or clutter the menu's appearance.

Waiter and Waitress Badges

Waiter and waitress badges can be an effective means of attracting attention. They can carry the same types of messages as signs or clip-ons might. In one operation, a badge bearing the letters *AFFFT* was worn by waitresses. Whenever a curious customer asked what the letters meant, the answer was "Anyone for french fries today?" As with all promotional materials, management must be creative in devising badges and similar items.

Computers in Foodservice Merchandising

Today, many foodservices use in-house microcomputers that allow them to undertake many merchandising efforts that they formerly could not attempt. One example is that of the menu itself. Since the menu, if pleasantly created and designed, can act as a promotional tool for the foodservice, care should be taken in its design. Many foodservices have discovered that this can be accomplished by using a computer in the store. The commercial art packages available for computer-assisted design, for instance, can give the operator the ability to create menus immediately, according to need. These same programs can create table tents or other artwork for internal marketing.

Using various desk-top publishing software on microcomputers, operators can also generate an in-house newsletter or newspaper to promote special events or foods. This same software can also be used to promote a newsletter for the staff, and this is now being done in many larger foodservices to raise employee morale.

Computers can be used to merchandise a foodservice in many other ways as well. One such method might be the computerization of regular customers' preferences for table, food items, beverage, and

so on. By using a computer in this way, a foodservice could print out relevant information, based on daily reservations, for the servers to use. One operation that does this has found that it not only enables the operation to anticipate its needs better, but also gives the customer the feeling of receiving personalized attention.

In larger institutional foodservices, the computer has been employed as a merchandising tool to assist in the ordering process. By speeding up ordering in such foodservices as cafeterias and employee dining facilities, the computer ensures that the customer is accorded better service. This may involve either staff- or customer-activated computer ordering. Interactive video (the combination of computers with video disk players) has also recently been utilized to enhance customer satisfaction through merchandising. In such a case, a customer touches a screen to activate certain commands from the computer-controlled video disk. The screen might offer information on food products, local events around town, or other information that could serve to merchandise the operation.

SUMMARY

Both marketing and merchandising are forms of promotion for a foodservice. Marketing usually deals with external activities of the foodservice, while merchandising more often concentrates on internal promotion. Development of a marketing program is based on accurate descriptions of the market itself (which can be created from a market survey) and of customers' likes and dislikes. Once this information is compiled, a foodservice operator should plan the operation's position in the market so as to take advantage of the market's likes and dislikes in the best possible manner.

Merchandising should use as many factors as possible to entice people to purchase food. The following six activities are especially important in merchandising: training employees, planning special promotions, featuring special menu items, creating atmosphere, developing good public relations, and using promotional materials.

Personnel who come in contact with customers must be given special training if they are to merchandise well for the operation. Suggestive selling should occur to increase check averages. Customers are often far more pleased with their food and service if service personnel take the time to find out their needs and see that they are met.

Planning special promotions—such as giving special attention to guests' birthdays, anniversaries, family parties, and other special occasions, featuring special foods and meals for holidays, or building around athletic or other community events—can do much to merchandise.

Special menu items can be promoted by display, by promotional efforts of personnel, or by advertising. Three foods that lend themselves to such promotion are hors d'oeuvres, salads, and desserts, although other foods can also be used for this purpose. An operation can differentiate itself from others and can draw customers by having just a few special foods on the menu.

The proper atmosphere must be created by developing a good external appearance. Neatness, organization that facilitates entry, and special décor can be used to develop a good external atmosphere. Colors, signs, landscaping, good maintenance, and a host of other factors can also contribute to this. An attractive internal atmosphere is created by combining good décor, good colors, good lighting, neatness, and organization. Establishing a logo and following it through can help to set up an image that customers recognize and associate with the operation.

Good public relations can be developed by giving special attention to guests (such as through direct mailings), by helping guests in their special events, and by offering other personalized attentions. Community relations should also be developed to elicit the attention and goodwill of people in the community toward the operation.

Promotional materials inside an operation can take the form of signs, mobiles, clip-ons, table tents, waiter or waitress badges, and other items. They must be used with care and taste, however, to avoid giving the operation a cluttered or overly commercial appearance.

The use of computers in foodservices has greatly enhanced the ability of operations to cater to their customers' needs. This is done through creation of menus, table tents, and other merchandising displays, through newsletters, or through computer-assisted ordering systems.

CHAPTER REVIEW QUESTIONS

1. The Best Food in Town restaurant opened about six months ago. After an original flurry of activity, sales in the restaurant have consistently declined to a point where it is no longer feasible to operate. Because the owners are certain that their products are as good as or better than any others in town, they are confused as to how and why this happened.

   The restaurant is located in a converted service station at a busy intersection on the edge of town. The location seems good, especially because of the high level of visibility inherent in the location. The menu is primarily that of a steak house and closely resembles that of another restaurant in the area that has been in existence for sixteen years. In fact, Billy and Eric Idel, the two brothers who own "Best Food," both used to work at the other restaurant as cooks, so they are certain that their food is at least comparable. But while the other restaurant continues to flourish, Best Food is going downhill rapidly.

   In an effort to stem the downward slide, the brothers have increased the size of the steaks they offer by 1 to 2 oz each. While this was a risky proposition because of the damaging effect on food costs, the brothers thought it a wise move in order to attract more business. The increase has had little effect, however, as few customers even seem to know about it.

   In order to build their business, Billy and Eric must devise a way of distinguishing themselves from their competition and of promoting their restaurant as something different. They have asked you to devise a merchandising plan to promote their restaurant. In order to do so, you must first answer the following questions for the owners. What are the first steps to take toward the goal of creating a desirable image in the customers' minds? How should the brothers merchandise their products to emphasize the increased portions offered? Suggest specific promotional programs for the restaurant.

2. Discuss merchandising and the factors that can be used to promote business. Differentiate among the six factors discussed in this chapter.

3. How does an operation's atmosphere merchandise food? What is meant by external and internal factors in atmosphere? Find pictures of outside and inside areas of operations and indicate good and bad features as far as external and internal factors in atmosphere are concerned.

VOCABULARY

Marketing

Merchandising

Hors d'oeuvres

Table tents

Focused groups

Suggestive selling

Computer-assisted artwork

Menu clip-ons

Positioning

Market research

ANNOTATED REFERENCES

Brodner J.; Carlson, H. M.; and Maschal, H. T. 1962. *Profitable Food and Beverage Operation,* pp. 153-80, 228-44. Rochelle Park, N.J.: Ahrens Publishing. (Specifics of advertising and promotion, as well as service.)

Fisher, W. P. 1982. *Creative Marketing for the Foodservice Industry,* pp. 157-66. New York: John Wiley & Sons. (Merchandising through the menu.)

Hertzson, D. 1971. *Hotel-Motel Marketing,* pp. 131-61. New York: ITT Educational Services. (Developing food and beverage sales through merchandising.)

Laine, S., and Laine, I. 1972. *Promotion in Foodservice.* New York: McGraw-Hill. (Goal-oriented text stressing participation and premise promotion by the operator.)

Restaurant Business, Inc. 1971. *Menu Planning and Food Merchandising.* New York: ITT Educational Services. (Merchandising and its importance in a successful operation.)

Seaberg, A. G. 1983. *Menu Design— Merchandising and Marketing.* Boston: CBI Publishing. (Merchandising the menu through proper planning.)

Solomon, E. 1971. "Service Is an Honorable Profession." McGarvey's Boat Drive-in Restaurant. (Special emphasis on suggestive selling.)

Stenin, B. 1971. *Marketing in Action for Hotels, Motels, Restaurants.* pp. 1-16, 143-86. Rochelle Park, N.J.: Ahrens Publishing. (Marketing and merchandising for restaurants— past, present, and future.)

PART IV

Appendices

APPENDIX A

Menu Analysis

Some of the most commonly used methods of analyzing menus are discussed here. Evaluations of each of these methods follow. As aids to understanding how methods differ, data for seven dessert items are provided in tables A-1 and A-2.

SUBJECTIVE MENU EVALUATION

Menus are frequently evaluated on the basis of a cursory visual examination. This is a highly subjective method, and wide variation can be found in judgments. The comments of viewers of the winning menus in the annual National Restaurant Association's menu contest offer ample proof of this. The advantage of such a method is that it allows evaluation of a wider range of factors than other analytical methods assess. The method is also highly flexible. A scoring system can be used to identify factors and assign them numerical values. These numerical scores can then be used to compare menus. If this is done by a knowledgeable person, the method can be a good way of evaluating many aspects of menus.

MENU COUNTS (POPULARITY INDEXES)

Using a menu count or calculating a popularity index (the percentage of an item sold out of all items sold) is easy to do and gives highly informative data. Table A-1 shows a count and a popularity index. Volume is an important factor in successful operation; if other factors are favorable, large volume can indicate a high level of patronage satisfaction and a profitable operation. If records are maintained, managers can use them as a historical file of successful and unsuccessful menu items.

Unfortunately, it is often difficult to compare values obtained from different times when the underlying indexes are based on a different number of menu items studied. Thus, if five items are studied one time and eight are studied the next, the item with four "competitors" has a better chance of having a high index rating than the one with seven. Thus, if an item among eight has an index of 18 percent, it is likely to have a score of better than 1.0, while an item among five that has an index of 18 percent is likely to have a score of less than 1.0.

HURST'S MENU SCORING

Hurst's menu scoring is a good method for developing an overall numerical evaluation of how well a menu will do. It tests for the combined effect of items such as volume, selling price, food cost, and gross profit. Specifically, the method involves obtaining a score by multiplying the percentage of patrons who select a menu item belonging to an arbitrarily established group of items (such as the seven desserts identified in tables A-1 and A-2) by the items' average gross profit. Thus, if 143 out of

Table A-1. Menu Count and Associated Popularity Index for Seven Dessert Items

Menu Item	Menu Count	Popularity Index
Strawberry cake	~~LHT~~ ~~LHT~~ ~~LHT~~ /// **(18)**	13%
Lemon pie	~~LHT~~ ~~HHT~~ ~~LHT~~ ~~HHT~~ // **(22)**	15%
Fudge sundae	~~LHT~~ ~~HHT~~ // **(12)**	8%
Caramel custard	~~LHT~~ ~~LHT~~ ~~LHT~~ ~~LHT~~ ~~LHT~~ / **(26)**	18%
Cherry torte	~~LHT~~ ~~LHT~~ ~~LHT~~ ~~LHT~~ ~~LHT~~ /// **(28)**	20%
Key lime pie	~~LHT~~ ~~LHT~~ ~~LHT~~ ~~LHT~~ ~~LHT~~ //// **(29)**	20%
Brownie	~~HHT~~ /// **(8)**	6%
Total sold 143		100%

340 customers on a given day selected one of the seven desserts under study, the percentage would be equivalent to 143/340. If we also knew (as table A-2 indicates) that the average gross profit of the seven desserts was $1.07, we could then calculate the menu score for these seven items as 143/340 × 1.07 = 0.45.

Because it is highly flexible and sensitive even to slight changes in a single factor, menu scoring lends itself to simulation procedures that check ahead for possible beneficial or undesirable effects of changes in price, food cost, or other variable. Menu scoring is not difficult to do and relies on data that are readily available. The effects of changes on individual menu items cannot be evaluated by this method, but their effect on the whole menu can—an important consideration.

MENU FACTOR ANALYSIS

Kotschevar's menu factor analysis tests individual items, giving them numerical values that indicate how well each item measures up to management's expectations. It can test for variations in food cost, gross profit, dollar sales, volume, and other factors.

It is well-suited to simulations that involve trying out changes before running a menu item.

Understanding what the factors are is a prerequisite for drawing good information from them. The standard of 1.0 by which items are judged desirable or undesirable is like an average (mean) that marks the middle of the value range, with some items below it and others above it. If numerically significant changes are made in one item, some other item (or items) consequently will change with respect to the average (mean). For example, if one item increases in number sold but the total number sold does not change, its percentage sold of total sold increases and the percentages sold of other items decrease as illustrated in table A-3. In the first instance, item C has a factor of 1.08 (18/16.7), while in the second it has a factor of 0.96 (16/16.7); item A has gone from a factor of 0.65 (11/16.7) in the first instance to a factor of 1.08 (18/16.7) in the second. Even though it is below 1.0 in the second instance, item C may be a good item. It may just be that some items are better. Management must use menu factor values not as dictators of policy but as guides for decisions. Managers must look behind the index factor and weigh other variables before making a decision.

Table A-2. Sample Data for Menu Analysis of Seven Dessert Items

Menu Item	A (Count) No. Sold	B Selling Price	C Item Food Cost	D (A × C) Total Item Food Cost	E (A × B) Item Revenue	F (B − C) Gross Profit	G (A × F) Total Item Gross Profit	H (C/B) Item % Food Cost	I (A/K) Item % of Total Sold
Strawberry cake	18	$1.50	$0.28	$5.04	$27.00	$1.22	$21.96	19	13
Lemon pie	22	1.65	0.44	9.68	36.30	1.21	26.62	27	15
Fudge sundae	12	1.30	0.26	3.12	15.60	1.04	12.48	20	8
Caramel custard	26	1.00	0.22	5.72	26.00	0.78	20.28	22	18
Cherry torte	28	1.60	0.50	14.00	44.80	1.10	30.80	31	·20
Key lime pie	29	1.75	0.56	16.24	50.75	1.19	34.51	32	20
Brownie	8	1.00	0.20	1.60	8.00	0.80	6.40	20	6

Data derived from the above figures:

J = Number of items in the study = 7
K = Total sold in column A = 143
L = Total food cost (total of column D) = $55.40
M = Total revenues (total of column E) = $208.45
N = Total gross profit (total of column G) = $153.05

O = Average food cost percent (L/M) = 27%
P = Average gross profit (N/K) = $1.07
Q = Average number sold (K/J) = 20.43
R = Average selling price (M/K) = $1.46

Table A-3. Changes in Index Factor Caused by Changes in Number Sold

Item	Instance I			Instance II		
	No. Sold	Index (%)	Index Factor	No. Sold	Index (%)	Index Factor
A	15	11	0.66	25	18	1.08
B	20	14	0.84	18	13	0.78
C	25	18	1.08	22	16	0.96
D	18	13	0.78	18	13	0.78
E	22	16	0.96	17	12	0.72
F	40	29	1.74	40	29	1.74
Total	140	100		140	100	
Average (mean)	23.3	16.7%		23.3	16.7%	

MATRIX ANALYSIS

Matrix analysis can be used to test individual menu items for their suitability on a menu, but it is limited to testing the effect of two factors and not the effect of a number of factors. It allows for the testing of different factors such as volume, food cost, gross profit, and dollar sales, and factors can be weighted, as is done by Pavesic for gross profit and by Smith-Kasavana for volume. Because matrix analysis uses a mean or average as the standard for judging items, however, it has the same defect discussed previously relating to the standard of 1.0. The ideal, of course, would be to have all items exactly match the value of the average (mean). Any changes made in one item reposition the other items with respect to the mean. Matrix analysis lends itself to simulation study.

Matrix analysis has been treated by Miller, Smith-Kasavana, Pavesic, and Kotschevar. As figure A-1 indicates, Miller evaluates menu items on the basis of food cost and volume (Miller 1980). Smith and Kasavana use volume percentage and gross profit as their criteria; they call their method *Menu Engineering* (Kasavana and Smith 1982). Pavesic uses food cost and a weighted gross profit (Pavesic 1985). Kotschevar's method is modeled on Pavesic's, except that Kotschevar's weighted gross profit margin is calculated differently. His other standard is food cost. Table A-4 describes how each matrix method compares individual menu item values with an es-

tablished standard. In all four methods, the standard is subtracted from the item value to establish the item's matrix value. Thus, on the basis of data from tables A-2 and A-4, strawberry cake has the matrix values given in table A-5.

The matrices described in table A-5 each possess four possible combinations of values. These are given different names by the four developers, as indicated in figure A-2. Table A-6 gives the values for all four different matrices along with their calculations. Table A-7 summarizes these calculations, listing only the end values and their combination names.

GOAL ANALYSIS

The Hayes-Huffman goal analysis or numerical target method tests for the suitability of individual menu items and does not give an overall test for a menu. In this it resembles menu factor analysis and matrix analysis, but it considers more factors: gross profit (1 − food cost % = gross profit), selling price, volume, variable cost, and fixed cost (1 − [variable cost % + fixed cost %] = fixed cost). It is probably the best method yet developed for testing individual menu items. It is a very sensitive test and lends itself well to simulation. Because its standards are averages (means) and because some items are always going to be above and others below the standard, manipulation of items merely reorganizes the order.

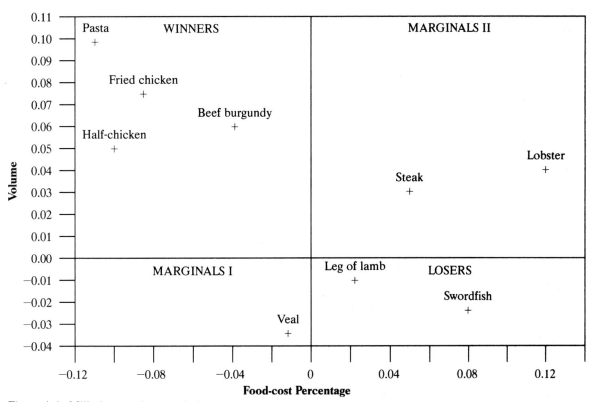

Figure A-1. Miller's menu-item analysis.

Table A-4. Methods of Calculating Matrix Values

Item Value	Standard Value	Item Value	Standard Value
Miller		**Pavesic**	
Food Cost: Item food cost	Average food cost	Food Cost: Item food cost	Average food cost
Volume: No. sold of an item	Average sold of all items	Weighted Gross Profit: Item gross profit	Total gross profit/no. items being studied
Smith-Kasavana		**Pavesic-Kotschevar**	
Gross Profit: Item's gross profit	Average gross profit	Food Cost: Item food cost	Average food cost
Volume: Percent sold of item	([1/no. of items studied] × 0.7 × 100)	Weighted Gross Profit: Item gross profit	Total gross profit/(no. of items sold/no. of items being studied)

Table A-5. Strawberry Cake Values

Miller

Food Cost: $(H - O)$
$\qquad$ $(19 - 27) = -8$

Volume: $(A - Q)$
$\qquad$ $(18 - 20.43) = -2.43$

Smith-Kasavana

Gross Profit: $(F - P)$
$\qquad$ $(1.22 - 1.07) = +0.15$

Volume: $(I - [1/J \times 0.7]) \times 100$
$\qquad$ $(13 - 10) = +3$

Pavesic

Food Cost: $(H - O)$
$\qquad$ $(19 - 27) = -8$

Weighted Gross Profit: $(G - [N/J])$
$\qquad$ $(21.96 - [153.05/7]) = +0.07$

Pavesic-Kotschevar

Food Cost: $(H - O)$
$\qquad$ $(19 - 27) = -8$

Weighted Gross Profit: $(G/[A/J])/(N/Q)$
$\qquad$ $(21.96/[18/7])/(153.05/20.43) = +1.05$

NOTE: The value of 10 is the Smith-Kasavana standard for volume obtained using the model $1/J \times 0.7 \times 100$, where J = number of items in the study group or 7. The calculation is then $1/7 \times 0.7 \times 100 = .10$. (The letters in parentheses refer to the values in table A-4).

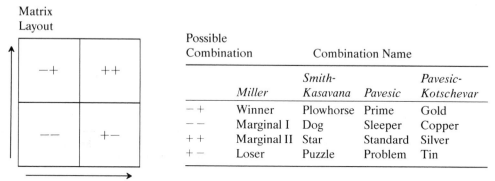

Possible Combination	Combination Name			
	Miller	Smith-Kasavana	Pavesic	Pavesic-Kotschevar
$- +$	Winner	Plowhorse	Prime	Gold
$- -$	Marginal I	Dog	Sleeper	Copper
$+ +$	Marginal II	Star	Standard	Silver
$+ -$	Loser	Puzzle	Problem	Tin

Figure A-2. Layout of matrix values, and names assigned each combination of values.

The Hayes-Huffman method of analysis has only one standard. The method involves developing a numerical target or goal for the standard and then calculating a similar value for each specific menu item to see how well it compares with the standard. The Hayes-Huffman method uses a mathematical formula $A \times B \times C \times D$ to derive the standard value and item values, where

$A =$ (1 − food cost %)
$B =$ number sold
$C =$ selling price
$D =$ (1 − [variable cost % + food cost %])

Using data in table A-2 and a variable cost of 32 percent, we may calculate the goal or numerical target as follows:

Table A-6. Four Matrix Calculations for Seven Menu Items

Menu Item	Miller		Smith-Kasavana	
	Food Cost	*Volume*	*Gross Profit*	*Volume*
Strawberry cake	$19 - 27 = -8$	$18 - 20.43 = -2.43$	$1.22 - 1.07 = +0.15$	$13 - 10 = +3$
Lemon pie	$27 - 27 = 0$	$22 - 20.43 = +1.57$	$1.21 - 1.07 = +0.14$	$15 - 10 = +5$
Fudge sundae	$20 - 27 = -7$	$12 - 20.43 = -8.43$	$1.04 - 1.07 = -0.03$	$8 - 10 = -2$
Caramel custard	$22 - 27 = -5$	$26 - 20.43 = +5.57$	$.78 - 1.07 = -0.29$	$18 - 10 = +8$
Cherry torte	$31 - 27 = +4$	$28 - 20.43 = +7.57$	$1.10 - 1.07 = +0.03$	$20 - 10 = +10$
Key lime pie	$32 - 27 = +5$	$29 - 20.43 = +8.57$	$1.19 - 1.07 = +0.12$	$20 - 10 = +10$
Brownie	$20 - 27 = -7$	$8 - 20.43 = -12.43$	$.80 - 1.07 = -0.27$	$6 - 10 = -4$

	Pavesic		Pavesic-Kotschevar	
	Food Cost	*Weighted Gross Profit*	*Food Cost*	*Weighted Gross Profit*
Strawberry cake	$19 - 27 = -8$	$21.96 - 21.89 = +0.07$	$19 - 27 = -8$	$21.96 - (18/7) - 7.49 = +1.05$
Lemon pie	$27 - 27 = 0$	$26.62 - 21.89 = +4.73$	$27 - 27 = 0$	$26.62 - (22/7) - 7.49 = +0.99$
Fudge sundae	$20 - 27 = -7$	$12.48 - 21.89 = -9.41$	$20 - 27 = -7$	$12.48 - (12/7) - 7.49 = -0.19$
Caramel custard	$22 - 27 = -5$	$20.48 - 21.89 = -1.61$	$22 - 27 = -5$	$20.28 - (26/7) - 7.49 = -2.02$
Cherry torte	$31 - 27 = +4$	$30.80 - 21.89 = +8.91$	$31 - 27 = +4$	$30.80 - (28/7) - 7.49 = +0.11$
Key lime pie	$31 - 27 = +5$	$34.51 - 21.89 = +12.62$	$32 - 27 = +5$	$34.51 - (32/7) - 7.49 = +0.85$
Brownie	$20 - 27 = -7$	$6.40 - 21.89 = -15.49$	$20 - 27 = -7$	$6.40 - (8/7) - 7.49 = -1.09$

$$\overset{(O)}{(1 - 0.27)} \times \overset{(Q)}{20.43} \times \overset{(R)}{1.46} \times \overset{(O)}{(1 - [0.32 + 0.27])} = 8.93$$

The calculation of the data shown for individual items in table A-8 according to the Hayes-Huffman model adopts the standard 8.93 as the means of determining whether individual items meet the goal or not. According to table A-8, only two desserts— fudge sundae (at -2.94) and brownie (at -5.86)—fail to meet the goal. Of those that meet the goal, custard (at $+0.40$) is least successful and key lime pie (at $+3.49$) is most successful.

BREAK-EVEN ANALYSIS

Break-even analysis is a good method to use to find out what must be achieved overall by a menu in dollar sales, volume, patron count, or some other category. It gives no information about how successful individual items will be or how they will react with others in the menu.

CORRELATION OF METHODS ANALYZING INDIVIDUAL ITEMS

Aside from the Pavesic-Kotschevar matrix method, we have discussed five methods that can be used to test the suitability of individual menu items: Kotschevar's menu factor analysis, Miller's matrix method, Smith-Kasavana's matrix method, Pavesic's matrix method, and the Hayes-Huffman goal method. How well do these six correlate on what is or is not a desirable menu item? Even a cursory visual examination of the data in table A-9 indicates that the methods varied considerably. Smith-Kasavana term one menu item a "plowhorse" that Miller calls a "winner." Smith-Kasavana call two other items "stars" that no one else gives a top rating. The others also had their disagreements.

Kendall's method for testing for coefficient of concordance was used to obtain a value to indicate whether or not any correlation existed between these five methods as a whole. Spearman's rank correlation and a test by Friedman were also run to

Table A-7. Results of Four Types of Matrix Analysis

Menu Item	Miller			Smith-Kasavana			Pavesic			Pavesic-Kotschevar		
	Food Cost	Vol-ume	Name	Gross Profit	Vol-ume	Name	Food Cost	Weighted Gross Profit	Name	Food Cost	Weighted Gross Profit	Name
Strawberry cake	−8	−2.43	Marg. I	+.15	+3	Star	−8	+.07	Prime	−8	+1.05	Gold
Lemon pie	±0	+1.57	Winner or Marg. II	+.14	+5	Star	±0	+4.73	Prime or Standard	±0	+.99	Gold or Silver
Fudge sundae	−7	−8.43	Marg. I	−.03	−2	Dog	−7	−9.41	Sleeper	−7	−.19	Copper
Caramel custard	−5	+5.57	Winner	−.29	+8	Plowhorse	−5	−1.61	Sleeper	−5	−2.02	Copper
Cherry torte	+4	+7.57	Marg. II	+.03	+10	Star	+4	+8.91	Standard	+4	+.11	Silver
Key lime pie	+5	+8.57	Marg. II	+.12	+10	Star	+5	+12.62	Standard	+5	+.85	Silver
Brownie	−7	−12.43	Marg. I	−.27	−4	Dog	−7	−15.49	Sleeper	−7	−1.09	Copper

Table A-8. Hayes-Huffman Goal Analysis of Seven Desserts

Item	(H)	(A)	(B)		(H)	Item Value $-$ Standard
Strawberry cake	$(1 - 0.19)$	$\times\ 18$	$\times\ 1.50$	$\times\ (1 - [0.32 + 0.19])$	$=\ 10.72$	$-\ 8.93 = +1.79$
Lemon pie	$(1 - 0.27)$	$\times\ 22$	$\times\ 1.65$	$\times\ (1 - [0.32 + 0.27])$	$=\ 10.86$	$-\ 8.93 = +1.93$
Fudge sundae	$(1 - 0.20)$	$\times\ 20$	$\times\ 1.30$	$\times\ (1 - [0.32 + 0.20])$	$=\ 5.99$	$-\ 8.93 = -2.94$
Caramel custard	$(1 - 0.22)$	$\times\ 26$	$\times\ 1.00$	$\times\ (1 - [0.32 + 0.22])$	$=\ 9.33$	$-\ 8.93 = +0.40$
Cherry torte	$(1 - 0.31)$	$\times\ 28$	$\times\ 1.60$	$\times\ (1 - [0.32 + 0.31])$	$=\ 11.44$	$-\ 8.93 = +2.51$
Key lime pie	$(1 - 0.32)$	$\times\ 29$	$\times\ 1.75$	$\times\ (1 - [0.32 + 0.32])$	$=\ 12.42$	$-\ 8.93 = +3.49$
Brownie	$(1 - 0.20)$	$\times\ 8$	$\times\ 1.00$	$\times\ (1 - [0.32 + 0.20])$	$=\ 3.07$	$-\ 8.93 = -5.86$

check against Kendall's. They both agreed with the Kendall finding, which indicated no significant correlation existed ($w = 0.04$).

Paired correlation tests were also run. The r's for these follow:

PAIR	r
Smith-Kasavana and Hayes-Huffman	0.90
Miller and Pavesic	0.75
Kotschevar and Hayes-Huffman	0.72
Kotschevar and Smith-Kasavana	0.53
Kotschevar and Pavesic	0.43
Miller and Smith-Kasavana	0.43
Miller and Hayes-Huffman	0.26
Pavesic and Hayes-Huffman	0.26
Smith-Kasavana and Pavesic	0.25
Kotschevar and Miller	0.15

Out of the twenty possible chances each author had for agreement with other authors, the following percentages of agreement occurred:

Hayes-Huffman	80%
Smith-Kasavana	75%
Pavesic	70%
Kotschevar	65%
Miller	40%

A check was also made to see how these five authors agreed on their evaluations of the various desserts. The greatest degree of agreement was found with respect to strawberry cake, lemon pie, and caramel custard.

RESULTS OF COMPARATIVE ANALYSIS

The most common analytical methods for analyzing menus can yield a wide variety of information; the kind depends on which method is used. There is probably no best method because each gives specific and different information from the others. The choice of which method to use should be made on the basis of the conditions and needs of the user.

Menu analysis is a way to focus management's attention on getting information about exactly what menus or menu items do or should do. At the very least, they are better than nothing, and too many operations do nothing—losing efficiency and profitability thereby. Methods of menu analysis force management to scrutinize, study, and evaluate menus or items. They develop a numerical value that facilitates objective comparison. They are helpful in pretesting or in simulations that do not require actually running the menu.

Probably the best way to perform menu analysis is to enlist a combination of methods. Certainly any menu greatly benefits from scrutiny by subjective methods because this enables management to consider factors that are not raised in any other way. Using a scoring method yields a numerical factor that can be used to compare other menus that are given subjective evaluation. This can be followed by a test of the menu, using Hurst's menu scoring method, to place a numerical value on the effects various factors have on menu acceptance

Table A-9. Hayes-Huffman Goal Analysis of Ten Entrées

(A) Menu Item Name	(B) Number Sold (MM)	(C) Menu Mix %	(D) Item Food Cost	(E) Item Selling Price	(F) Item CM (E − D)	(G) Menu Costs (D × B)	(H) Menu Revenues (E × B)	(L) Menu CM (F × B)	(P) FC% Category	(R) MM% Category	(S) Menu Item Classification
Half-chicken	24	12.0%	1.74	6.95	5.21	41.76	166.80	125.04	−0.10	0.05	WINNER
Steak	20	10.0%	4.78	11.95	7.17	95.60	239.00	143.40	0.05	0.03	MARGINAL II
Shrimp	16	8.0%	3.17	8.50	5.33	50.72	136.00	85.28	0.02	0.01	MARGINAL II
Veal	7	3.5%	3.01	8.95	5.94	21.07	62.65	41.58	−0.01	−0.03	MARGINAL III
Pasta	35	17.5%	1.28	5.50	4.22	44.80	192.50	147.70	−0.12	0.11	WINNER
Swordfish	9	4.5%	4.65	10.95	6.30	41.85	98.55	56.70	0.07	−0.02	LOSER
Lobster	22	11.0%	6.85	14.50	7.65	150.70	319.00	168.30	0.12	0.04	MARGINAL II
Beef burgundy	26	13.0%	2.17	6.95	4.78	56.42	180.70	124.28	−0.04	0.06	WINNER
Fried chicken	29	14.5%	1.78	6.75	4.97	51.62	195.75	144.13	−0.09	0.08	WINNER
Leg of lamb	12	6.0%	3.33	8.95	5.62	39.96	107.40	67.44	0.02	−0.01	LOSER

						(I) 594.50	(J) 1,698.35	(M) 1,103.85			
Total sold	(N) 200					$K = I/J$		$O = M/N$	$Q = (100\%/\text{items}) \times (70\%)$		
						35.0%		5.52	7.0%		
Number of items	10								$R = D/E - K$		

and profitability. Next, individual menu items should be tested for suitability. For this purpose, the Hayes-Huffman goal method may well be the best of those discussed for obtaining information on individual menu items. The last method used could be a check, using break-even analysis, to see how well the menu must perform overall in order to make a profit.

ANNOTATED REFERENCES

Hayes, D., and Huffman, L. 1985. "Menu Analysis: A Better Way." *Cornell Quarterly* (Feb. 1985) 25(4):64-70. (Gives a complete discussion of "goal analysis.")

Kasavana, M., and Smith, D. 1982. *Menu Engineering.* Okemos, Mich.: Hospitality Publishers. (Covers a wide range of computer applications in foodservices and gives a detailed discussion of menu engineering.)

Kotschevar, L. 1986. *Management by Menu.* New York: John Wiley & Sons. (A basic book on menu formulation, design, and application and how it affects management; has a detailed discussion of Hurst's menu scoring, subjective menu analysis, menu factor analysis, and goal analysis.)

Miller, J. 1980. *Menu Pricing and Strategy.* New York: Van Nostrand Reinhold. (Describes Miller's matrix method in menu analysis.)

Pavesic, D. 1985. "Cost-Margin Analysis." *Cornell Quarterly* (Nov. 1985) 25(3):70-77. (Offers a complete discussion of Pavesic's matrix method in menu analysis.)

APPENDIX B

Recommended Daily Dietary Allowances

Recommended Dietary Allowances For A Day For Selected Age Groups and Nutrients

| | | | | | | MINERALS | | VITAMINS | | | | |
| | | | | | | Calcium | Iron | A | C | Thia-mine | Ribo-flavin | Niacin |
Food energy in Calories	Protein Grams	Person	Age in years	Weight in pounds	Height in inches	Milligrams	Milligrams	International Units	Milligrams	Milligrams	Milligrams	Milligram equivalents
1,600	30	**Children**	4-6	42	43	800	10	2,500	40	0.8	0.9	11
2,000	35		6-8	51	48	900	10	3,500	40	1.0	1.1	13
2,200	40		8-10	62	52	1,000	10	3,500	40	1.1	1.2	15
2,500	45	**Males**	10-12	77	55	1,200	10	4,500	40	1.3	1.3	17
2,700	50		12-14	95	59	1,400	18	5,000	45	1.4	1.4	18
3,000	60		14-18	130	67	1,400	18	5,000	55	1.5	1.5	20
2,800	60		18-22	147	69	800	10	5,000	60	1.4	1.6	18
2,800	65		22-35	154	69	800	10	5,000	60	1.4	1.7	18
2,600	65		35-55	154	68	800	10	5,000	60	1.3	1.7	17
2,250	50	**Females**	10-12	77	56	1,200	18	4,500	40	1.1	1.3	15
2,300	50		12-14	97	61	1,300	18	5,000	45	1.2	1.4	15
2,400	55		14-16	114	62	1,300	18	5,000	50	1.2	1.4	16
2,300	55		16-18	119	63	1,300	18	5,000	50	1.2	1.5	15
2,000	55		18-22	128	64	800	18	5,000	55	1.0	1.5	13
2,000	55		22-35	128	64	800	18	5,000	55	1.0	1.5	13
1,850	55		35-55	128	63	800	18	5,000	55	1.0	1.5	13
+200	65	**Pregnancy**				+400	18	6,000	60	+0.1	1.8	15
+1000	75	**Lactation**				+500	18	8,000	60	+0.5	2.0	20

| CALORIE CARRIERS | | | | | | | MINERALS | | VITAMINS | | | |
| Fat | Carbo-hydrate | Protein | Food Energy in | | | Weight in | Calcium | Iron | A | C | Thia-mine | Ribo-flavin |
×9 Gm	×4 Gm	×4 Gm	Calories	Measure		Grams	Mg	Mg	I.U.	Mg	Mg	Mg
				Breakfast								
—	15	1	60	½ of 5″ melon	Melon	200	28	.8	6,800	66	.08	.06
2	17	4	98	⅔ cup	Rolled Oats, cooked	156	14	1.1	—	—	.15	.03
1	12	2	63	1 slice	Enriched Bread, toasted	20	20	.6	—	—	.06	.04
8	—	—	66	2 teaspoons	Margarine or Butter	9	2	—	308	—	—	—
9	12	9	159	1 cup	Milk	244	288	—	340	2	.07	.42
				Luncheon								
2	24	4	125	1 bun	Bun, enriched	46	42	1.2	—	—	.12	.09
10	—	23	185	3 oz. ground lean	Hamburger patty, broiled	85	10	3.0	20	—	.08	.20
9	—	7	107	1 oz. slice	Cheese (Processed) American	28	195	.3	340	—	—	.11
1	33	—	133	1 3″ diameter	Apple	220	16	.7	200	9	.07	.05
9	12	9	159	1 cup	Milk	244	288	—	340	2	.07	.42
				Dinner								
9	—	32	214	4 oz.	Halibut, broiled	125	20	1.0	850	—	.06	.09
11	—	—	100	1 tablespoon	Margarine or Butter	14	3	—	462	—	—	—
—	21	3	93	1 2½ inch	Baked potato	100	9	.7	—	20	.10	.04
—	9	4	53	½ cup cooked	Green Peas (fresh)	75	18	1.4	405	15	.21	.08
9	12	9	159	1 cup	Milk	244	288	—	340	2	.07	.42
80	**167**	**107**	**1,774**		**Total for Step I**	**1,810**	**1,241**	**10.8**	**10,405**	**116**	**1.14**	**2.05**
2	20	3	115	1 roll	Roll, enriched	38	28	.7	—	—	.11	.07
10	27	2	206	1 piece, 2″×2″×2″	Gingerbread	57	63	1.4	69	—	.07	.05
6	—	7	88	1 large	Egg	54	29	1.2	550	—	.06	.16
14	2	5	147	3 slices	Bacon, crisp	23	4	.6	—	—	.13	.07
—	1	—	4	1 large leaf	Lettuce	25	17	.3	500	4	.01	.02
—	5	1	22	1 small raw	Tomato	100	13	.5	900	23	.06	.04
2	22	5	110	2 slices	Whole-wheat Bread	46	46	1.0	—	—	.12	.10
34	**77**	**23**	**692**		**Total for Step II**	**343**	**200**	**5.7**	**2,019**	**27**	**.56**	**.51**
114	**244**	**130**	**2,466**		**Total for Steps I & II**	**2,153**	**1,441**	**16.5**	**12,424**	**143**	**1.7**	**2.56**

(STEP I) (STEP II)

Start with these minimum servings from four food groups:

Enriched and Whole Grain Bread-Cereal . . . *4 or more servings, daily (2 slices of bread equivalent to 1 serving of cereal)*

Lean Meat, Fish, Poultry, Eggs, Nuts, Peanut Butter, Dry Peas and Beans . . . *2 servings, daily (2 ounces, edible portion, to a serving)*

Fruit-Vegetable . . . *4 or more servings, daily*
Include potato or other vegetable or fruit
Include 1 rich in vitamin C
Include 1 dark green or yellow for vitamin A—at least every other day

Milk-Cheese . . . *daily, as such or in cooking (1 ounce of cheese equivalent to 1 cup of milk)*
Children 9-12 . . . . 3 or more cups
       under 9 . . . . 2 or more cups
Teenagers . . . . 4 or more cups
Adults . . . . 2 or more cups

Add more of these or other foods as you need them for growth, energy, ideal weight, or satisfying meals.

COMPARE these totals with NRC allowances for you.

ADD AND SUBTRACT foods as necessary.

FROM THE FOODWAY TO YOU

Did you add sugar? Did you add fat? Were some of the fats butter or margarine? Vegetable oil for salad dressing?

On the basis of recent nutrition research, many scientists are suggesting that adults limit calories from fat to 35 or 40 percent of total calories for the day. What does a 35 percent limit mean in terms of foods and the calories they carry?

An example: Ellen, a 21-year-old, needs 2000 calories a day. This means 700 calories (2000 × .35) may come from fat.

This is $\left(\dfrac{700 \text{ calories}}{9 \text{ calories/gram}} \right)$ 78 grams of fat.

In amounts of food this could be:

FOOD	MEASURE	GRAMS FAT
Milk	1 glass	10
Butter	2 tablespoons	22
Vegetable oil	1 tablespoon	14
Meat, lean	1 serving	12-25
Eggs	1	6

Note how quickly fat totals 64-78 grams, or 30-35 percent. A choicer cut of meat can easily shoot this percent to 40. Note that these figures do not include fat used in cooking, in cream, ice cream, candy, or other foods you are likely to add to complete the day's meals.

CALORIE CARRIERS	CALORIES
1 gram of fat	9
1 gram of protein	4
1 gram of carbohydrate	4

To hold a day's total calories from fat to 35 percent takes skill. It means that, as you grow older, you will have to know how to juggle . . . to balance a rich source of fat, if this is your food extravagance for the day, against a leaner source. You will have to learn how to balance all three—protein, fat, and carbohydrate. To do this:

▲ Meet your recommendations for protein. ▲ Carefully select your sources of fat and include vegetable oils. ▲ Turn to carbohydrates from selected sources to complete your nutrient and calorie quotas. As you turn to the tables of nutrients that follow, you will find selected sources are: enriched and whole-grain bread and cereal, skim milk, fruits and vegetables.

Through YOUR GUIDELINE TO NUTRIENTS, you can learn

★ that most foods carry many nutrients
★ which foods carry nutrients that are hard to get unless you plan for them
★ how to evaluate the food you eat for nutrients.

Continue to use your guideline to run a periodic double check on the way you manage the food in your life.

	CALORIE CARRIERS								MINERALS		VITAMINS			
Fatty Acids from fat		Fat	Carbo-hydrate	Protein	Food Energy in	Measure	**BREAD—CEREAL**	Weight in	Calcium	Iron	A	C	Thia-mine	Ribo-flavin
Linoleic Gm	Saturated Gm	×9 Gm	×4 Gm	×4 Gm	Calories			Grams	Mg	Mg	I.U.	Mg	Mg	Mg
Trace	1	6	16	3	129	1 biscuit, 2″ diam.	Biscuit, enriched	35	42	.6	—	—	.07	.07
—	—	1	23	3	101	¾ cup	Bran Flakes (40 percent bran) with thiamine added	28	16	1.3	—	—	.10	.05
							Bread							
—	—	1	20	2	93	1 slice, 3″×¾″	Boston brown bread	44	39	.8	—	—	.05	.03
—	—		12	2	60	1 slice	Cracked wheat bread, 20 slices per pound	23	20	.3	—	—	.03	.02
							French, Vienna, or Italian bread							
Trace	Trace	1	13	2	65	1 slice	Enriched, 20 slices per pound	23	10	.6	—	—	.06	.05
—	—	1	13	2	65	1 slice	Unenriched, 20 slices per pound	23	10	.2	—	—	.02	.02
—	—	1	12	2	60	1 slice	Raisin bread, 20 slices per pound	23	16	.3	—	—	.01	.02
—	—	—	12	2	55	1 slice	Rye bread, American, light, 20 slices per pound	23	17	.4	—	—	.04	.02
							White bread							
—	—	1	12	2	63	1 slice	Enriched, 20 slices per pound	23	20	.6	—	—	.06	.04
—	—	1	9	1	47	1 slice	Enriched, 26 slices per pound	17	16	.5	—	—	.04	.03
—	—	1	12	2	63	1 slice	Unenriched, 20 slices per pound	23	16	.2	—	—	.02	.02
—	—	1	9	1	47	1 slice	Unenriched, 26 slices per pound	17	16	.1	—	—	.01	.01
							Whole-wheat bread							
—	—	1	11	2	55	1 slice	20 slices per pound	23	23	.5	—	—	.06	.05
—	—	—	8	1	43	2 tablespoons	Bread crumbs, enriched, grated	11	13	.4	—	—	.03	.03
—	—	—	14	1	62	⅔ cup	Corn flakes, enriched, plain or pre-sweetened	16	3	.2	—	—	.07	.01
—	—	—	13	1	62	½ cup	Corn grits, enriched, cooked	121	1	.4	—	—	.05	.04
—	—	—	13	1	62	½ cup	Corn grits, unenriched, cooked	121	1	.1	—	—	.02	.01
—	—	—	26	2	119	1 cup	Cornmeal, enriched, cooked	238	2	1.0	142	—	.14	.10
—	—	—	26	2	119	1 cup	Cornmeal, unenriched, cooked	138	2	.5	142	—	.05	.02
Trace	2	5	23	3	151	1 muffin, 2¾″ diam.	Corn muffin, enriched	48	50	.8	144	—	.10	.11
—	—	1	10	1	60	2 medium	Crackers, graham	14	3	.3	—	—	.04	.02
—	—	1	6	1	35	2 crackers	Crackers, saltine	8	2	.1	—	—	—	—
—	—	—	20	4	98	¾ cup	Farina, enriched, instant cooking	179	138	11.5	—	—	.02	.02
—	—	—	32	5	155	1 cup	Macaroni, enriched, cooked (tender)	140	11	1.3	—	—	.20	.11
—	—	—	32	5	155	1 cup	Macaroni, unenriched, cooked (tender)	140	11	.6	—	—	.01	.01
1	14	25	44	18	475	1 cup	Macaroni (enriched) and cheese	220	394	2.0	970	—	.22	.46
Trace	1	4	17	3	118	1 muffin, 2¾″ diam.	Muffin, enriched	40	42	.6	40	—	.07	.09
Trace	1	1	19	4	100	½ cup	Noodles, enriched, cooked	80	8	.7	61	—	.12	.07
1	1	2	15	4	98	⅔ cup	Oatmeal or rolled oats, cooked	156	14	1.1	—	—	.15	.03
Trace	Trace	2	8	2	60	1 cake, 4″ diam.	Pancake, enriched	27	34	.3	30	—	.05	.06
Trace	3	6	23	8	180	1 piece, ⅛ of 14″ pie	Pizza pie, cheese	75	157	.7	570	8	.03	.09
—	—	1	11	2	55	1 cup	Popcorn, popped	14	2	.4	—	—	.05	.02
—	—	—	4	—	20	5 sticks	Pretzels, small stick	5	1	—	—	—	—	—
—	—	—	22	2	100	½ cup	Rice, white, cooked	84	7	.3	—	—	.01	.01
—	—	—	12	1	55	1 cup	Rice, puffed, enriched	14	2	.3	—	—	.06	.01
							Rolls							
Trace	1	2	20	3	115	1 roll	Plain, enriched	38	28	1.0	—	—	.11	.07
Trace	1	2	24	4	125	1 bun	Bun, enriched	46	42	1.2	—	—	.12	.09
Trace	1	2	31	5	162	1 roll	Hard, round, enriched	52	24	1.4	—	—	.14	.12
Trace	1	4	21	4	136	1 roll	Sweet, pan	43	37	.3	30	—	.03	.06
—	—	—	16	3	78	½ cup	Spaghetti, enriched, cooked (tender)	70	6	.7	—	—	.10	.06
Trace	5	18	33	11	339	1 cup	Spaghetti with meat sauce	250	23	1.8	771	20	.10	.10
Trace	2	7	37	9	261	1 cup	Spaghetti with tomato sauce, cheese	250	80	2.2	1,079	12	.27	.17
Trace	3	7.8	27	6.6	206	1 waffle, 5½″ diam.	Waffle, enriched	75	179	1.0	173	—	.11	.17
—	—	—	11	2	51	1 cup	Wheat, puffed, enriched	14	4	.6	—	—	.08	.03
—	—	—	17	2	74	¾ cup	Wheat flakes, enriched	21	9	.9	—	—	.13	.03
—	—	1	18	2	81	1 biscuit	Wheat, shredded	22	9	.7	—	—	.02	.03
—	—	—	11	2	51	2 tablespoons	Wheat flour, enriched, sifted	14	2	.3	—	—	.06	.04
—	—	—	11	2	51	2 tablespoons	Wheat flour, unenriched, sifted	14	2	.1	—	—	.01	.01

MEAT, POULTRY, FISH, ALTERNATES

	Fatty Acids from fat	Fat	Carbo-hydrate	Protein	Food Energy			Weight	Calcium	Iron	A	C	Thia-mine	Ribo-flavi
Linoleic Gm	Saturated Gm	×9 Gm	×4 Gm	×4 Gm	in Calories	Measure		in Grams	Mg	Mg	I.U.	Mg	Mg	Mg
							Meat							
							Beef, cooked							
Trace	5	10	15	15	209	1 cup	Beef and vegetable stew	235	28	2.8	2,303	16.5	.14	.16
Trace	2	4	—	19	114	4 thin slices, 4"×5"	Dried or chipped beef	56	12	2.8	—	—	.04	.18
Trace	5	10	—	23	185	3 ounces, lean	Hamburger, broiled	83	10	3.0	20	—	.08	.20
Trace	2	9	—	26	185	2 slices, 4"×1¼"×½"	Pot roast, rump, lean only	80	7	3.8	—	—	.08	.18
2	7	23	37	17	436	1 pie, 4¼" diam.	Potpie, baked	227	23	2.3	931	—	.07	.13
—	—	7	—	28	302	2 slices, 4"×2½"×½"	Rib roast, lean, some fat	106	8	3.5	—	—	.06	.22
Trace	2	2.6	—	11	70	2 slices, trimmed	Rib roast, lean only	41	4	1.4	—	—	.03	.09
Trace	7	13	—	25	222	1 slice, 4"×3"×⅜"	Round, broiled, lean and fat	85	10	2.6	—	—	.07	.19
Trace	1	4	—	22	134	2 pieces, 4"×1"×¼"	Round, broiled, lean only	71	9	2.6	—	—	.06	.17
1	13	27	—	20	329	3-ounce piece, 4"×2¼"×1"	Steak, sirloin, broiled, lean and fat	85	8	2.5	50	—	.05	.16
Trace	3	6	—	27	175	3-ounce piece, 4"×2¼"×1"	Steak, sirloin, broiled, lean only	85	11	3.3	15	—	.08	.21
							Cured Meat							
1	2	14	2	5	147	3 slices	Bacon, broiled or fried crisp	23	4	.6	—	—	.14	.07
1	7	16	1	7	173	2 slices, 4½"×⅛"	Bologna	57	4	1.0	—	—	.09	.12
1	13	26	—	20	316	3 slices, 3"×2¼"×¼"	Corned beef, medium fat	85	8	2.5	—	—	.02	.15
1	6	14	1	6	155	1 frankfurter	Frankfurter, cooked	51	3	.8	—	—	.08	.10
2	7	19	—	18	246	3 ounces	Ham, smoked, lean and fat	85	8	2.2	—	—	.40	.15
1	5	14	—	9	168	2 ounces	Luncheon meat, canned	57	5	1.3	—	—	.18	.12
							Lamb							
1	18	33	—	25	402	1 thick chop	Chop, broiled, lean and fat	112	10	3.1	—	—	.14	.25
Trace	3	6	—	21	139	1 thick chop	Chop, broiled, lean only	74	9	2.5	—	—	.11	.20
Trace	9	16	—	22	237	2 slices, 4"×3¼"×⅛"	Leg, roasted, lean and fat	85	9	2.8	—	—	.18	.23
1	13	23	—	18	287	2 slices, 4"×3½"×⅛"	Shoulder, roasted, lean and fat	85	8	2.4	—	—	.11	.20
Trace	3	6	—	17	131	2 slices, 3"×2¼"×⅛"	Shoulder, roasted, lean only	64	8	2.2	—	—	.10	.18
							Liver							
Trace	2	3	6	15	131	1 slice, 3"×2¼"×⅜"	Beef, fried	57	6	5.0	30,438	15	.14	2.38
							Pork							
3	12	27	—	26	359	1 thick chop	Chop, broiled, lean, low fat	100	12	3.5	—	—	1.00	.29
1	2	12	—	23	203	1 thick chop	Chop, broiled, lean only	75	10	2.9	—	—	.85	.25
1	4	11	—	20	173	2 slices, 3"×2½"×¼"	Roast, lean only	68	9	2.6	—	—	.83	.21
5	18	50	—	21	538	2 patties, 2¼" diam.	Sausage, bulk	113	8	2.7	—	—	.89	.21
Trace	4	9	—	23	183	3 ounces	Veal cutlet, broiled, lean only	85	9	2.7	—	—	.06	.31
Trace	7	14	—	23	229	2 slices, 3"×2"×⅛"	Veal roast, lean and fat	85	10	2.9	—	—	.11	.26
							Poultry							
2	3	3	—	20	116	¼ bird, boned	Chicken, broiled	85	8	1.4	68	—	.04	.16
2	3	8	—	25	185	½ breast, boned	Chicken, fried	79	9	1.2	103	—	.04	.21
2	4	12	—	27	234	Thigh and drumstick, boned	Chicken, fried	89	11	1.8	187	—	.06	.40
2	2	5	—	25	152	2 slices, 3½"×2⅝"×⅛"	Turkey, roasted	80	6	1.4	—	—	.04	.14
							Fish							
—	—	7	6	18	167	1 piece, 3"×3"×⅜"	Bass, average, oven-fried	85	71	.9	72	—	.05	.12
—	—	—	—	14	82	4 large or 9 small	Clams, raw meat only	100	—	3.4	—	—	—	—
—	—	5	—	24	145	3 ounces	Cod steak, broiled	85	26	.9	—	—	.04	.08
2	4	9	7	17	176	4-5 sticks	Fishsticks, breaded, cooked	100	11	.4	—	—	.04	.07
—	—	6	6	20	165	1 fillet, 3"×3"×½"	Haddock, fried	100	40	1.2	—	—	.04	.07
—	—	9	—	32	214	5 ounces	Halibut, broiled	125	20	1.0	850	—	.06	.06
—	—	3	1	20	108	1 small	Lobster, boiled	306	74	.7	—	—	.11	.06
—	—	2	3	8	66	5-8 medium	Oysters, raw	100	94	5.5	310	—	.14	.18
—	—	11	6	16	195	1 medium fillet	Perch, ocean, breaded, fried	85	14	1.3	50	—	.09	.10
—	—	7	—	27	182	1 small serving	Salmon, cooked, broiled or baked	100	—	1.2	160	—	.16	.04
Trace	3	8	—	17	145	3 ounces or ½ cup	Salmon, red, canned	85	220	1.1	200	—	.03	.14
4	2	9	1	22	180	6 sardines	Sardines, Atlantic, canned in oil	85	367	2.5	190	—	.02	.14
—	—	1	1	16	87	6-8 medium	Shrimp, raw	85	54	1.4	—	—	.02	.03
—	—	23	—	21	290	3 ounces	Trout, lake, broiled	88	27	1.1	460	—	.07	.20
4	2	7	—	25	170	½ cup	Tuna, canned	85	7	1.2	70	—	.04	.10

Linoleic Gm	Saturated Gm	Fat ×9 Gm	Carbohydrate ×4 Gm	Protein ×4 Gm	Food Energy in Calories	Measure	MEAT, POULTRY, FISH, ALTERNATES	Weight in Grams	Calcium Mg	Iron Mg	A I.U.	C Mg	Thiamine Mg	Riboflavin Mg
							Eggs							
1	2	6	—	7	88	1 egg, 24 oz./doz.	Egg, whole, large	54	26	1.2	550	—	.06	.16
—	—	—	—	4	17	1 white	Egg, white	33	3	—	—	—	—	.09
Trace	2	5	—	3	60	1 yolk	Egg, yolk	17	24	.9	550	—	.04	.07
							Nuts, peanuts, peanut butter							
4	2	19	7	7	215	¼ cup	Almonds, shelled	36	83	1.7	—	—	.09	.33
—	3	3	4	—	43	2 tablespoons	Coconut, shredded, sweetened	8	2	.2	—	—	.01	—
3	4	18	7	10	210	4 tablespoons	Peanuts, roasted, shelled	36	26	.8	—	—	.12	.05
2	2	8	3	4	93	1 tablespoon	Peanut butter	16	12	.4	—	—	.02	.02
6	Trace	10	2	2	104	8-12 halves	Walnuts	16	16	.4	—	—	.06	.02
							Dry beans and peas							
—	—	1	24	8	132	½ cup	Lima beans, cooked	96	28	2.8	—	—	.13	.06
—	—	—	21	8	115	½ cup	Red beans	128	37	2.3	—	—	.06	.06
—	—	1	26	10	148	½ cup	Split peas, cooked	125	14	2.1	60	—	.18	.11
—	—	1	60	16	308	1 cup	White beans, cooked without pork	261	183	5.2	140	5	.13	.10

FRUITS—VEGETABLES

Linoleic Gm	Saturated Gm	Fat ×9 Gm	Carbohydrate ×4 Gm	Protein ×4 Gm	Food Energy in Calories	Measure	**Fruits**	Weight in Grams	Calcium Mg	Iron Mg	A I.U.	C Mg	Thiamine Mg	Riboflavin Mg
—	—	1	33	—	133	1 apple, 3″ diam.	Apple, raw	220	16	.7	200	9	.07	.05
—	—	—	30	—	126	½ cup	Applesauce, sweetened	127	5	.6	51	1	.03	.02
—	—	—	27	1	105	4 halves, 2 tablespoons syrup	Apricots, syrup packed	122	13	.4	2,130	5	.02	.03
2	4	16	6	2	167	½ avocado, 3¼″×4″	Avocado, peeled	100	10	.6	290	14	.11	.20
—	—	—	22	1	85	1 banana, 6″	Banana, small	100	8	.7	190	10	.50	.60
—	—	1	15	2	64	¾ cup	Blackberries, raw	108	35	1.0	218	23	.04	.05
—	—	1	11	1	43	½ cup	Blueberries, raw	70	11	.7	70	10	.02	.04
—	—	—	14	1	60	½ melon, 5″ diam.	Cantaloupe	200	28	.8	6,800	66	.08	.06
—	—	—	11	1	40	½ cup or 9 large	Cherries, sweet, raw	57	13	.2	63	6	.03	.03
—	—	—	26	—	101	¼ cup	Cranberry sauce, sweetened	69	4	1.4	14	1	.01	.01
—	—	—	34	1	123	5-6 dates	Dates, pitted	45	26	1.4	25	—	.04	.04
—	—	1	25	1	98	½ cup	Fruit cocktail, syrup pack	128	12	.5	180	3	.02	.02
—	—	—	10	—	40	½ grapefruit, 4″ diam.	Grapefruit, medium	100	16	.4	440	36	.04	.02
—	—	1	20	1	75	1 cup	Grapefruit sections, raw	194	31	.8	20	72	.07	.03
—	—	—	23	1	95	1 cup	Grapefruit juice, fresh	246	22	.5	20	92	.09	.04
—	—	1	8	1	35	½ cup or 11-12 grapes	Grapes, raw, American type	77	7	.2	50	2	.03	.02
—	—	—	21	1	83	½ cup	Grape juice	127	14	.4	—	—	.05	.03
—	—	—	1	—	5	1 tablespoon	Lemon or lime juice	15	1	—	—	7	—	—
—	—	—	18	1	70	1 orange, 3″ diam.	Orange	150	63	.3	290	66	.12	.03
—	—	—	10	1	35	1 peach, 2″ diam.	Peach, raw	114	9	.5	1,320	7	.02	.05
—	—	—	17	—	66	¼ of 12-ounce carton	Peaches, sliced, frozen	85	5	.4	443	25	.01	.03
—	—	1	25	1	100	1 medium pear	Pear, raw	182	13	.5	30	7	.04	.07
—	—	—	23	—	90	2 halves, 2 tablespoons syrup	Pears, syrup pack	117	6	.2	—	2	.01	.02
—	—	—	10	—	40	2 halves, 2 tablespoons juice	Pears, water pack	122	6	.3	—	2	.01	.03
—	—	—	10	1	44	½ cup	Pineapple, raw, diced	84	13	.2	108	20	.07	.02
—	—	—	26	—	95	2 small slices, 2 tablespoons syrup	Pineapple, syrup pack	122	35	.7	100	11	.09	.02
—	—	—	15	1	55	2 small slices, 2 tablespoons juice	Pineapple, juice pack	100	29	.6	80	9	.07	.03
—	—	—	16	1	60	½ cup	Pineapple juice	125	19	.6	100	11	.07	.02
—	—	—	7	—	30	1 plum, 2″ diam.	Plums, raw	60	10	.3	200	3	.04	.02
—	—	—	19	1	70	4 prunes	Prunes, dried	32	14	1.0	430	1	.02	.05
—	—	—	31	1	115	4 tablespoons	Raisins, dried	40	25	1.4	8	1	.05	.03
—	—	1	13	1	53	¾ cup	Raspberries, red, raw	92	20	.8	120	23	.02	.07
—	—	—	18	1	70	¼ of 10-ounce carton	Raspberries, frozen	71	20	.4	55	11	.01	.03

		CALORIE CARRIERS							MINERALS		VITAMINS			
		Fat	Carbo-hydrate	Protein	Food Energy in Calories		FRUITS—VEGETABLES	Weight in Grams	Calcium	Iron	A	C	Thia-mine	Ribo-flavin
Fatty Acids from fat														
Linoleic Gm	Saturated Gm	×9 Gm	×4 Gm	×4 Gm	Calories	Measure			Mg	Mg	I.U.	Mg	Mg	Mg
—	—	—	49	1	193	½ cup	Rhubarb, cooked, sugar added	136	—	.6	35	9	.01	—
—	—	—	7	—	28	½ cup	Strawberries, raw, capped	75	15	.8	45	44	.02	.05
—	—	—	19	—	75	¼ of 10-ounce carton	Strawberries, frozen	71	16	.4	30	29	.01	.04
—	—	—	10	1	40	1 medium	Tangerine	114	34	.3	360	26	.05	.01
—	—	1	29	2	120	1 wedge, 4"×8"	Watermelon	925	30	.9	2,530	26	.20	.22
							Vegetables							
—	—	—	3	2	20	6 spears	Asparagus, cooked	96	18	1.8	770	17	.06	.08
—	—	—	3	1	13	½ cup	Beans, green, cooked in small amount water, short time	63	23	.5	415	9	.05	.06
—	—	1	15	4	75	½ cup	Beans, lima, immature, cooked	80	23	1.4	230	12	.11	.07
—	—	—	8	1	35	½ cup	Beets, cooked, diced	83	18	.6	15	6	.02	.04
—	—	—	5	3	26	1 large spear	Broccoli, cooked	100	88	.8	2,500	90	.09	.20
—	—	—	6	3	30	5-6 sprouts	Brussels sprouts, cooked	65	22	.9	260	31	.03	.08
—	—	—	3	1	13	½ cup	Cabbage, raw, finely shredded	50	23	.3	40	25	.03	.03
—	—	—	5	1	20	½ cup	Cabbage, cooked in small amount water, short time	85	39	.4	75	27	.04	.04
—	—	—	5	1	20	1 carrot, 5½"×1"	Carrot, raw	50	20	.4	6,000	3	.03	.03
—	—	1	5	1	23	½ cup	Carrots, cooked, diced	73	19	.5	9,065	3	.04	.04
—	—	—	5	2	23	¾ cup	Cauliflower, cooked	90	20	1.0	83	26	.05	.08
—	—	—	2	1	10	½ cup	Celery, raw, diced	50	25	.3	—	4	.03	.02
—	—	1	7	4	38	½ cup	Collards, cooked	95	237	1.5	7,250	42	.08	.23
—	—	1	16	2	65	From 1 ear, 5"×1¾"	Corn, sweet, yellow, cooked	85	4	.5	300	6	.09	.08
—	—	1	21	3	85	½ cup	Corn, canned, solids and liquid	128	5	.7	260	7	.04	.04
—	—	1	13	6	75	½ cup	Cowpeas, immature, cooked	80	30	2.0	310	16	.23	.07
—	—	—	1	—	5	6 slices	Cucumber, raw, pared	50	5	.2	—	4	.02	.02
—	—	1	8	3	40	½ cup	Dandelion greens, cooked	90	169	2.8	13,655	15	.12	.11
—	—	—	2	1	10	10 leaves	Endive, curly (including escarole)	57	45	1.0	1,700	6	.04	.07
—	—	1	8	4	45	1 cup	Kale, cooked	110	248	2.4	9,220	56	.08	.25
—	—	—	1	1	5	2 large or 4 small	Lettuce leaves	50	11	.2	270	4	.02	.04
—	—	—	5	2	15	½ cup	Mushrooms, canned	122	9	1.0	—	2	.02	.30
—	—	—	3	2	15	½ cup	Mustard greens, cooked	70	154	2.1	5,025	32	.04	.13
—	—	—	3	1	15	4 pods	Okra, cooked	43	35	.3	315	9	.03	.03
—	—	—	11	2	50	1 medium	Onion, raw	110	35	.6	60	10	.04	.04
—	—	—	5	—	25	6 small onions	Onions, young, green	50	68	.4	30	12	.02	.02
—	—	—	—	—	1	1 tablespoon	Parsley, raw, chopped	4	7	.2	290	7	—	.01
—	—	1	10	4	55	½ cup	Peas, green, cooked	80	18	1.5	575	12	.20	.11
—	—	—	3	1	15	1 pepper	Pepper, sweet, green	62	6	.4	260	79	.05	.05
—	—	1	9	2	50	1 tablespoon	Peppers, hot, red, dried; ground chili pepper	15	20	1.2	11,520	2	.03	.20
							Potatoes							
—	—	—	21	3	90	1 potato, 2½" diam.	Baked, peeled after baking	99	9	.7	—	20	.10	.04
—	—	—	23	3	105	1 potato, 2⅜" diam.	Boiled, peeled after boiling	136	10	.8	—	22	.13	.05
4	2	7	20	2	155	10 pieces	French-fried	57	9	.7	—	8	.06	.04
—	—	1	15	2	73	½ cup	Mashed, milk added	98	24	.5	25	9	.09	.06
4	2	7	10	1	110	10 chips	Chips	20	6	.4	—	2	.04	.02
—	—	—	2	—	10	4 radishes	Radishes, raw	40	15	.4	10	10	.01	.01
—	—	—	4	1	15	½ cup	Sauerkraut, canned, drained	75	27	.4	30	12	.03	.05
—	—	1	3	3	23	½ cup	Spinach, cooked	90	—	1.8	10,600	27	.07	.18
—	—	—	4	1	18	½ cup	Squash, summer, cooked	105	16	.4	275	12	.04	.08
—	—	1	12	2	48	½ cup	Squash, winter, baked	103	25	.8	6,345	7	.05	.16
—	—	1	36	2	155	1 medium	Sweet potato, baked	110	44	1.0	8,970	24	.10	.07
1	2	8	60	2	295	1 potato, 3½"×2¼"	Sweet potato, candied	175	65	1.6	11,030	17	.10	.08
—	—	—	6	2	30	1 medium	Tomato, raw	150	16	.9	1,640	35	.08	.06
—	—	—	5	1	23	½ cup	Tomatoes, canned	121	14	.8	1,270	20	.07	.04
—	—	—	5	1	25	½ cup	Tomato juice	121	9	.5	1,270	19	.06	.04
—	—	—	5	1	20	½ cup	Turnips, white, cooked	78	31	.4	—	14	.03	.05
—	—	—	6	1	26	½ cup	Turnips, yellow, cooked	80	44	.3	280	9	.04	.06
—	—	1	4	2	23	½ cup	Turnip greens, cooked	77	188	1.8	7,685	44	.05	.30

MILK—CHEESE

Linoleic Gm	Saturated Gm	Fat ×9 Gm	Carbo-hydrate ×4 Gm	Protein ×4 Gm	Food Energy in Calories	Measure		Weight in Grams	Calcium Mg	Iron Mg	A I.U.	C Mg	Thia-mine Mg	Ribo-flavin Mg
							Milk							
Trace	6	10	12	9	165	1 cup	Fluid, whole	244	285	.1	390	2	.08	.42
—	—	—	13	9	90	1 cup	Fluid, nonfat (skim)	246	298	.1	10	2	.10	.44
—	—	—	13	9	90	1 cup	Buttermilk	246	298	.1	10	2	.10	.44
Trace	1	2	7	4	60	½ cup	Yogurt	123	148	.05	85	1	.05	.22
—	—	—	11	7	73	4 tablespoons	Dry, nonfat	20	260	.1	5	2	.07	.36
1	11	20	24	18	345	1 cup	Evaporated, undiluted	252	635	.3	820	3	.10	.84
Trace	1	2	1	—	20	1 tablespoon	Half-and-half	15	16	—	70	—	—	.02
Trace	3	6	27	8	190	1 cup	Chocolate-flavored milk drink	250	270	.4	210	2	.09	.41
—	—	18	58	11	421	1 regular, 8 ounces milk	Chocolate milk shake	345	363	.9	687	4	.12	.55
Trace	6	11	26	9	235	1 cup	Cocoa	242	286	.9	390	2	.09	.45
							Cheese							
Trace	5	9	—	6	105	1 ounce	Blue mold (Roquefort-type)	28	122	.2	350	—	.01	.17
Trace	1	2	—	2	30	1 tablespoon	Cheddar, grated	7	55	.1	90	—	.02	.03
Trace	5	9	—	7	105	1 ounce or 1 slice	Cheddar, processed	28	214	.2	350	—	—	.12
Trace	1	1	1	4	30	2 tablespoons	Cottage cheese, creamed	28	25	.1	50	—	.01	.08
—	—	—	1	5	25	2 tablespoons	Cottage cheese, uncreamed	28	26	.1	—	—	.01	.08
Trace	3	6	—	1	55	1 tablespoon	Cream cheese	15	9	—	230	—	—	.04
Trace	4	8	1	7	105	1 ounce	Swiss	28	271	.3	320	—	.01	.06

FATS—OILS

Linoleic Gm	Saturated Gm	Fat ×9 Gm	Carbo-hydrate ×4 Gm	Protein ×4 Gm	Food Energy in Calories	Measure		Weight in Grams	Calcium Mg	Iron Mg	A I.U.	C Mg	Thia-mine Mg	Ribo-flavin Mg
Trace	2	3	1	—	35	1 tablespoon	Cream, light	15	15	—	130	—	—	.02
Trace	3	6	—	—	55	1 tablespoon before whipping	Cream, heavy, whipping	15	10	—	240	—	—	.02
							Fats—Cooking							
1	5	14	—	—	135	1 tablespoon	Lard	14	—	—	—	—	—	—
1	3	12	—	—	110	1 tablespoon	Vegetable fats, solid	13	—	—	—	—	—	—
							Oils, salad or cooking							
7	3	14	—	—	125	1 tablespoon	Corn, cottonseed, or soybean	14	—	—	—	—	—	—
1	2	14	—	—	125	1 tablespoon	Olive	14	—	—	—	—	—	—
							Salad Dressings							
5	2	10	1	1	90	1 tablespoon	Blue cheese	16	11	—	30	—	—	.02
3	1	6	2	—	60	1 tablespoon	Commercial, mayonnaise-type	15	2	—	30	—	—	—
3	1	6	2	—	60	1 tablespoon	French	15	3	.1	—	—	—	—
6	2	12	—	—	110	1 tablespoon	Mayonnaise	15	2	.1	40	—	—	—
4	1	8	1	—	75	1 tablespoon	Thousand Island	15	2	.1	60	2	—	—
							Spreads							
Trace	6	11	—	—	100	1 tablespoon	Butter	14	3	—	460	—	—	—
1	3	11	—	—	100	1 tablespoon	Margarine	14	3	—	460	—	—	—

SUGARS, SYRUPS, CANDIES

Linoleic Gm	Saturated Gm	Fat ×9 Gm	Carbo-hydrate ×4 Gm	Protein ×4 Gm	Food Energy in Calories	Measure		Weight in Grams	Calcium Mg	Iron Mg	A I.U.	C Mg	Thia-mine Mg	Ribo-flavin Mg
Trace	2	3	22	1	120	3 caramels	Caramels, plain	28	36	.7	50	—	.01	.04
Trace	5	9	16	2	145	1-ounce bar	Chocolate, sweetened, milk	28	61	.3	40	—	.03	.11
Trace	2	3	23	—	115	1¼" square	Fudge, plain	28	14	.1	60	—	—	.02
—	—	—	9	—	37	2 squares	Hard candy	10	—	—	—	—	—	—
—	—	—	23	1	90	1-ounce bar	Marshmallow	28	—	—	—	—	—	—
—	—	—	11	—	40	1 tablespoon	Chocolate syrup	20	3	.3	—	—	—	—
—	—	—	17	—	60	1 tablespoon	Honey	21	1	.2	—	1	—	.01
—	—	—	14	—	55	1 tablespoon	Jams, jellies, preserves	20	2	.1	—	1	—	—
—	—	—	6	—	23	1 marshmallow	Marshmallow, plain	7	—	—	—	—	—	—
—	—	—	13	—	50	1 tablespoon	Molasses	20	33	.9	—	—	.01	.01
—	—	—	15	—	55	1 tablespoon	Syrup, table blends	20	9	.8	—	—	—	—
—	—	—	4	—	17	1 teaspoon	Sugar, granulated, cane or beet	4	—	—	—	—	—	—
—	—	—	13	—	50	1 tablespoon	Sugar, brown, firmly packed	14	10	.4	—	—	—	—
—	—	—	8	—	30	1 tablespoon	Sugar, powdered	8	—	—	—	—	—	—

DESSERTS

MISCELLANEOUS

Linoleic Gm	Saturated Gm	Fat ×9 Gm	Carbo-hydrate ×4 Gm	Protein ×4 Gm	Food Energy in Calories	Measure		Weight in Grams	Calcium Mg	Iron Mg	A I.U.	C Mg	Thiamine Mg	Riboflavin Mg
						Cakes								
—	—	—	23	3	110	1/12 of 8" cake	Angel food cake	40	2	.1	—	—	—	.05
1	5	14	70	5	420	1/16 of 10" cake	Chocolate layer cake, fudge icing	120	118	.5	520	—	.03	.10
Trace	1	6	24	2	152	1 piece, 3"×3"×1/2"	Fruitcake, enriched, dark	40	29	1.0	48	—	.05	.06
Trace	2	10	27	2	206	1 piece, 2"×2"×2"	Gingerbread	57	63	1.4	69	—	.07	.05
Trace	1	5	31	4	180	1 piece, 3"×2"×1½"	Plain cake, no icing	55	85	.2	200	—	.02	.05
Trace	1	3	23	3	130	1 cupcake	Plain cupcake, no icing	40	62	.2	150	—	.01	.03
Trace	2	6	62	5	320	1/16 of 10" cake	Plain layer cake, with icing	100	117	.4	280	—	.02	.07
Trace	1	3	31	3	160	1 cupcake	Plain cupcake, with icing	50	58	.2	140	—	.01	.04
1	2	7	15	2	130	1 slice, 2¾"×3"×5/8"	Pound cake	30	16	.5	300	—	.04	.05
Trace	1	2	22	3	115	1/12 of 8" cake	Sponge cake	40	11	.6	210	—	.02	.06
						Cookies								
Trace	1	3	19	2	110	1 cookie, 3" diam.	Assorted	25	6	.2	—	—	.01	.01
—	—	6	15	1	116	1 cookie	Butterscotch, refrigerator	24	11	.5	22	—	.04	.03
—	—	4	3	—	17	1 small cookie	Chocolate or gingersnap	4	3	.1	3	—	.02	.02
—	—	1	12	1	55	1 small bar	Fig bar	16	11	.2	—	—	—	.01
—	—	2	10	9	63	1 cookie	Oatmeal with raisins	14	3	.4	7	—	.15	.11
—	—	2	8	—	17	1 small cookie	Vanilla wafer	4	4	—	14	—	.02	.08
Trace	3	5	24	4	152	½ cup	Cornstarch pudding, vanilla	125	144	.1	195	—	.04	.21
Trace	5	9	23	9	205	1 custard	Custard, baked (4 to 1 pt. milk)	157	163	1.1	607	—	.08	.32
Trace	1	6	16	2	125	1 average doughnut	Doughnut, cake-type	32	13	.4	26	—	.05	.05
						Ice cream and frozen custard								
Trace	5	8	15	3	137	1/8 quart or ½ cup	Regular, 10% fat	71	104	—	312	—	.03	.15
Trace	5	11	13	2	158	1/8 quart or ½ cup	Rich, 16% fat	71	55	—	469	—	.01	.08
Trace	3	5	21	5	143	1/8 quart or ½ cup	Ice milk	94	146	.1	195	1	.05	.21
						Pies								
1	4	15	51	3	346	1/7 of 9" pie	Apple	135	11	.4	40	1	.03	.03
1	4	15	52	4	352	1/7 of 9" pie	Cherry	135	19	.4	594	—	.03	.03
1	4	15	32	8	320	1/7 of 9" pie	Custard	135	130	.8	311	—	.07	.22
1	4	11	45	4	306	1/7 of 9" pie	Lemon Meringue	120	17	.6	204	4	.04	.10
1	2	16	56	3	366	1/7 of 9" pie	Mince	135	38	1.4	—	1	.09	.05
1	5	15	33	5	274	1/7 of 9" pie	Pumpkin	130	66	.7	3,211	—	.04	.14
—	—	1	30	1	140	½ cup	**Sherbet**	97	15	—	58	2	.01	.03
						Beverages, carbonated								
—	—	—	18	—	71	1 cup	Ginger ale	230	—	—	—	—	—	—
—	—	—	23	—	90	1 cup	Cola-type	230	—	—	—	—	—	—
—	—	—	—	—	5	1 cube	Bouillon cube	4	—	—	—	—	—	—
—	—	—	4	—	18	1 tablespoon	Chili sauce	17	3	.1	238	3	.02	.01
—	—	14	8	3	141	1 ounce square	Chocolate, unsweetened	28	22	1.9	17	—	.01	.07
—	—	—	—	9	34	1 tablespoon	Gelatin, dry, plain	10	—	—	—	—	—	—
							Gelatin dessert, ready-to-eat							
—	—	—	17	2	71	½ cup	Plain	120	—	—	—	—	—	—
—	—	—	20	2	80	½ cup	With fruit	120	—	—	4	—	—	—
Trace	Trace	2	—	—	35	4 extra large	Olives, green	22	14	.4	66	—	—	—
Trace	Trace	3	1	—	28	4 extra large	Olives, ripe	22	15	.3	13	—	—	—
—	—	—	3	1	15	1 pickle, 4"×1¾"	Pickle, dill	135	34	1.6	420	8	—	.09
—	—	—	7	—	29	1 pickle, 2¾"×¾"	Pickle, sweet	20	2	.2	18	1	—	—
							Soups, canned, ready-to-serve							
Trace	2	6	22	8	168	1 cup	Bean, with pork	250	63	2.3	650	3	.13	.08
Trace	1	1	5	2	38	¾ cup	Chicken, with rice	188	6	.2	113	—	—	.18
1	Trace	3	13	2	84	1 cup	Clam Chowder, Manhattan-type with water	255	36	1.0	918	—	.03	.03
4	4	11	13	5	168	¾ cup	Mushroom, Cream of, with milk	191	149	.4	191	—	.03	.27
1	Trace	3	21	9	148	1 cup	Pea, split	250	30	1.5	450	—	.25	.15
1	1	2	12	2	66	¾ cup	Tomato (water)	184	11	.6	754	9	.04	.04
Trace	1	2	10	5	80	1 cup	Vegetable, beef	250	13	.8	2,750	—	.05	.05
—	—	—	7	—	30	1 tablespoon	Starch, corn, arrowroot, etc.	8	—	—	—	—	—	—
1	5	8	6	3	107	¼ cup	White sauce, medium	66	74	.2	328	—	.02	.01

APPENDIX C

Ounce and Pound Amounts for Multiple Portions

Ounces: 25 to 1,000 Portions

25 PORTIONS	50	75	100	200	300	400	500	600	700	800	900	1000
—	—	1/8 oz	1/8 oz	1/4 oz	3/8 oz	1/2 oz	5/8 oz	3/4 oz	7/8 oz	1 oz	1 1/8 oz	1 1/4 oz
—	—	1/6 oz	1/6 oz	1/3 oz	1/2 oz	2/3 oz	5/6 oz	1 oz	1 1/6 oz	1 1/3 oz	1 1/2 oz	1 2/3 oz
—	—	1/5 oz	1/5 oz	2/5 oz	3/5 oz	4/5 oz	1 oz	1 1/5 oz	1 2/5 oz	1 3/5 oz	1 4/5 oz	2 oz
—	—	1/4 oz	1/4 oz	1/2 oz	3/4 oz	1 oz	1 1/4 oz	1 1/2 oz	1 3/4 oz	2 oz	2 1/4 oz	2 1/2 oz
—	—	1/3 oz	1/3 oz	2/3 oz	1 oz	1 1/3 oz	1 2/3 oz	2 oz	2 1/3 oz	2 2/3 oz	3 oz	3 1/3 oz
—	1/4 oz	3/8 oz	1/2 oz	1 oz	1 1/2 oz	2 oz	2 1/2 oz	3 oz	3 1/2 oz	4 oz	4 1/2 oz	5 oz
—	1/3 oz	1/2 oz	2/3 oz	1 1/3 oz	2 oz	2 2/3 oz	3 1/3 oz	4 oz	4 2/3 oz	5 1/3 oz	6 oz	6 2/3 oz
—	3/8 oz	5/8 oz	3/4 oz	1 1/2 oz	2 1/4 oz	3 oz	3 3/4 oz	4 1/2 oz	5 1/4 oz	6 oz	6 3/4 oz	7 1/2 oz
1/4 oz	1/2 oz	3/4 oz	1 oz	2 oz	3 oz	4 oz	5 oz	6 oz	7 oz	8 oz	9 oz	10 oz
1/2 oz	1 oz	1 1/2 oz	2 oz	4 oz	6 oz	8 oz	10 oz	12 oz	14 oz	1 lb	1 lb 2 oz	1 lb 4 oz
3/4 oz	1 1/2 oz	2 1/4 oz	3 oz	6 oz	9 oz	12 oz	15 oz	1 lb 2 oz	1 lb 5 oz	1 lb 8 oz	1 lb 11 oz	1 lb 14 oz
1 oz	2 oz	3 oz	4 oz	8 oz	12 oz	1 lb	1 lb 4 oz	1 lb 8 oz	1 lb 12 oz	2 lb	2 lb 4 oz	2 lb 8 oz
1 1/4 oz	2 1/2 oz	3 3/4 oz	5 oz	10 oz	15 oz	1 lb 4 oz	1 lb 9 oz	1 lb 14 oz	2 lb 3 oz	2 lb 8 oz	2 lb 13 oz	3 lb 2 oz
1 1/2 oz	3 oz	4 1/2 oz	6 oz	12 oz	1 lb 2 oz	1 lb 8 oz	1 lb 14 oz	2 lb 4 oz	2 lb 10 oz	3 lb	3 lb 6 oz	3 lb 12 oz
1 3/4 oz	3 1/2 oz	5 1/4 oz	7 oz	14 oz	1 lb 5 oz	1 lb 12 oz	2 lb 3 oz	2 lb 10 oz	3 lb 1 oz	3 lb 8 oz	3 lb 15 oz	4 lb 6 oz
2 oz	4 oz	6 oz	8 oz	1 lb	1 lb 8 oz	2 lb	2 lb 8 oz	3 lb	3 lb 8 oz	4 lb	4 lb 8 oz	5 lb
2 1/4 oz	4 1/2 oz	6 3/4 oz	9 oz	1 lb 2 oz	1 lb 11 oz	2 lb 4 oz	2 lb 13 oz	3 lb 6 oz	3 lb 15 oz	4 lb 8 oz	5 lb 1 oz	5 lb 10 oz
2 1/2 oz	5 oz	7 1/2 oz	10 oz	1 lb 4 oz	1 lb 14 oz	2 lb 8 oz	3 lb 2 oz	3 lb 12 oz	4 lb 6 oz	5 lb	5 lb 10 oz	6 lb 4 oz
2 3/4 oz	5 1/2 oz	8 1/4 oz	11 oz	1 lb 6 oz	2 lb 1 oz	2 lb 12 oz	3 lb 7 oz	4 lb 2 oz	4 lb 13 oz	5 lb 8 oz	6 lb 3 oz	6 lb 14 oz
3 oz	6 oz	9 oz	12 oz	1 lb 8 oz	2 lb 4 oz	3 lb	3 lb 12 oz	4 lb 8 oz	5 lb 4 oz	6 lb	6 lb 12 oz	7 lb 8 oz
3 1/4 oz	6 1/2 oz	9 3/4 oz	13 oz	1 lb 10 oz	2 lb 7 oz	3 lb 4 oz	4 lb 1 oz	4 lb 14 oz	5 lb 11 oz	6 lb 8 oz	7 lb 5 oz	8 lb 2 oz
3 1/2 oz	7 oz	10 1/2 oz	14 oz	1 lb 12 oz	2 lb 10 oz	3 lb 8 oz	4 lb 6 oz	5 lb 4 oz	6 lb 2 oz	7 lb	7 lb 14 oz	8 lb 12 oz
3 3/4 oz	7 1/2 oz	11 1/4 oz	15 oz	1 lb 14 oz	2 lb 13 oz	3 lb 12 oz	4 lb 11 oz	5 lb 10 oz	6 lb 9 oz	7 lb 8 oz	8 lb 7 oz	9 lb 6 oz

Pounds: 25 to 1,000 Portions

25 PORTIONS	50	75	100	200	300	400	500	600	700	800	900	1000
4 oz	8 oz	12 oz	1 lb	2 lb	3 lb	4 lb	5 lb	6 lb	7 lb	8 lb	9 lb	10 lb
5 oz	10 oz	15 oz	1 lb 4 oz	2 lb 8 oz	3 lb 12 oz	5 lb	6 lb 4 oz	7 lb 8 oz	8 lb 12 oz	10 lb	11 lb 4 oz	12 lb 8 oz
6 oz	12 oz	1 lb 2 oz	1 lb 8 oz	3 lb	4 lb 8 oz	6 lb	7 lb 8 oz	9 lb	10 lb 8 oz	12 lb	13 lb 8 oz	15 lb
7 oz	14 oz	1 lb 5 oz	1 lb 12 oz	3 lb 8 oz	5 lb 4 oz	7 lb	8 lb 12 oz	10 lb 8 oz	12 lb 4 oz	14 lb	15 lb 12 oz	17 lb 8 oz
8 oz	1 lb	1 lb 8 oz	2 lb	4 lb	6 lb	8 lb	10 lb	12 lb	14 lb	16 lb	18 lb	20 lb
9 oz	1 lb 2 oz	1 lb 11 oz	2 lb 4 oz	4 lb 8 oz	6 lb 12 oz	9 lb	11 lb 4 oz	13 lb 8 oz	15 lb 12 oz	18 lb	20 lb 4 oz	22 lb 8 oz
10 oz	1 lb 4 oz	1 lb 14 oz	2 lb 8 oz	5 lb	7 lb 8 oz	10 lb	12 lb 8 oz	15 lb	17 lb 8 oz	20 lb	22 lb 8 oz	25 lb
11 oz	1 lb 6 oz	2 lb 1 oz	2 lb 12 oz	5 lb 8 oz	8 lb 4 oz	11 lb	13 lb 12 oz	16 lb 8 oz	19 lb 4 oz	22 lb	24 lb 12 oz	27 lb 8 oz
12 oz	1 lb 8 oz	2 lb 4 oz	3 lb	6 lb	9 lb	12 lb	15 lb	18 lb	21 lb	24 lb	27 lb	30 lb
13 oz	1 lb 10 oz	2 lb 7 oz	3 lb 4 oz	6 lb 8 oz	9 lb 12 oz	13 lb	16 lb 4 oz	19 lb 8 oz	22 lb 12 oz	26 lb	29 lb 4 oz	32 lb 8 oz
14 oz	1 lb 12 oz	2 lb 10 oz	3 lb 8 oz	7 lb	10 lb 8 oz	14 lb	17 lb 8 oz	21 lb	24 lb 8 oz	28 lb	31 lb 8 oz	35 lb
15 oz	1 lb 14 oz	2 lb 13 oz	3 lb 12 oz	7 lb 8 oz	11 lb 4 oz	15 lb	18 lb 12 oz	22 lb 8 oz	26 lb 4 oz	30 lb	33 lb 12 oz	37 lb 8 oz
1 lb	2 lb	3 lb	4 lb	8 lb	12 lb	16 lb	20 lb	24 lb	28 lb	32 lb	36 lb	40 lb
1 lb 1 oz	2 lb 2 oz	3 lb 3 oz	4 lb 4 oz	8 lb 8 oz	12 lb 12 oz	17 lb	21 lb 4 oz	25 lb 8 oz	29 lb 12 oz	34 lb	38 lb 4 oz	42 lb 8 oz
1 lb 2 oz	2 lb 4 oz	3 lb 6 oz	4 lb 8 oz	9 lb	13 lb 8 oz	18 lb	22 lb 8 oz	27 lb	31 lb 8 oz	36 lb	40 lb 8 oz	45 lb
1 lb 3 oz	2 lb 6 oz	3 lb 9 oz	4 lb 12 oz	9 lb 8 oz	14 lb 4 oz	19 lb	23 lb 12 oz	28 lb 8 oz	33 lb 4 oz	38 lb	42 lb 12 oz	47 lb 8 oz
1 lb 4 oz	2 lb 8 oz	3 lb 12 oz	5 lb	10 lb	15 lb	20 lb	25 lb	30 lb	35 lb	40 lb	45 lb	50 lb
1 lb 5 oz	2 lb 10 oz	3 lb 15 oz	5 lb 4 oz	10 lb 8 oz	15 lb 12 oz	21 lb	26 lb 4 oz	31 lb 8 oz	36 lb 12 oz	42 lb	47 lb 4 oz	52 lb 8 oz
1 lb 6 oz	2 lb 12 oz	4 lb 2 oz	5 lb 8 oz	11 lb	16 lb 8 oz	22 lb	27 lb 8 oz	33 lb	38 lb 8 oz	44 lb	49 lb 8 oz	55 lb
1 lb 7 oz	2 lb 14 oz	4 lb 5 oz	5 lb 12 oz	11 lb 8 oz	17 lb 4 oz	23 lb	28 lb 12 oz	34 lb 8 oz	40 lb 4 oz	46 lb	51 lb 12 oz	57 lb 8 oz
1 lb 8 oz	3 lb	4 lb 8 oz	6 lb	12 lb	18 lb	24 lb	30 lb	36 lb	42 lb	48 lb	54 lb	60 lb
1 lb 12 oz	3 lb 8 oz	5 lb 4 oz	7 lb	14 lb	21 lb	28 lb	35 lb	42 lb	49 lb	56 lb	63 lb	70 lb
2 lb	4 lb	6 lb	8 lb	16 lb	24 lb	32 lb	40 lb	48 lb	56 lb	64 lb	72 lb	80 lb
2 lb 4 oz	4 lb 8 oz	6 lb 12 oz	9 lb	18 lb	27 lb	36 lb	45 lb	54 lb	63 lb	72 lb	81 lb	90 lb
2 lb 8 oz	5 lb	7 lb 8 oz	10 lb	20 lb	30 lb	40 lb	50 lb	60 lb	70 lb	80 lb	90 lb	100 lb
2 lb 12 oz	5 lb 8 oz	8 lb 4 oz	11 lb	22 lb	33 lb	44 lb	55 lb	66 lb	77 lb	88 lb	99 lb	110 lb
3 lb	6 lb	9 lb	12 lb	24 lb	36 lb	48 lb	60 lb	72 lb	84 lb	96 lb	108 lb	120 lb
3 lb 12 oz	7 lb 8 oz	11 lb 4 oz	15 lb	30 lb	45 lb	60 lb	75 lb	90 lb	105 lb	120 lb	135 lb	150 lb
4 lb 4 oz	8 lb 8 oz	12 lb 12 oz	17 lb	34 lb	51 lb	68 lb	85 lb	102 lb	119 lb	136 lb	153 lb	170 lb
4 lb 8 oz	9 lb	13 lb 8 oz	18 lb	36 lb	54 lb	72 lb	90 lb	108 lb	126 lb	144 lb	162 lb	180 lb
5 lb	10 lb	15 lb	20 lb	40 lb	60 lb	80 lb	100 lb	120 lb	140 lb	160 lb	180 lb	200 lb
5 lb 12 oz	11 lb 8 oz	17 lb 4 oz	23 lb	46 lb	69 lb	92 lb	115 lb	138 lb	161 lb	184 lb	207 lb	230 lb
6 lb 4 oz	12 lb 8 oz	18 lb 12 oz	25 lb	50 lb	75 lb	100 lb	125 lb	150 lb	175 lb	200 lb	225 lb	250 lb

APPENDIX D

Metric Conversion Tables

Metric Equivalents

1 centimeter = 0.3937 in.
1 decimeter = 3.937 in. = 0.328 feet
1 meter = 39.37 in. = 1.0936 yards
1 dekameter = 1.9884 rods
1 kilometer = 0.62137 mile

1 sq. centimeter = 0.1550 sq. in.
1 sq. decimeter = 0.1076 sq. ft.
1 sq. meter = 1.196 sq. yd.
1 are = 3.954 sq. rods
1 hectare = 2.47 acres
1 sq. kilometer = 0.386 sq. m.

1 cu. centimeter = 0.061 cu. in.
1 cu. decimeter = 0.353 cu. ft.
1 cu. meter = 1.308 cu. yd.
1 stere = 0.2759 cord
1 liter = 0.908 dry
1 liter = 1.0567 q. liq.
1 dekaliter = 2.6417 gal.
1 dekaliter = .135 peck
1 hectoliter = 2.8375 bu.

1 gram = .03547 ounce
1 kilogram = 2.2046 lbs.
1 metric ton = 1.1023 English ton

1 decimeter = 4 inches
1 meter = 1.1 yards
1 kilometer = ⅝ mile
1 hectare = 2½ acres
1 stere or cu. meter = ¼ of a cord

Linear Measure
1 in. = 254 centimeters
1 ft. = 3.048 decimeters
1 yard = 0.9144 meter
1 rod = 0.5029 dekameter
1 mile = 1.6093 kilometers

Square Measure
1 sq. inch = 6.452 sq. centimeters
1 sq. foot = 9.2903 sq. decimeters
1 sq. yd. = 0.8361 sq. meter
1 sq. rod = 0.2529 are
1 acre = 0.4047 hectare
1 sq. m. = 259 sq. kilometers

Measure of Volume
1 cu. in. = 16.39 cu. centimeters
1 cu. ft. = 28.317 cu. decimeters
1 cu. yd. = 0.7646 cu. meter
1 cord = 3.642 steres
1 qt. dry = 1.101 liters
1 qt. liquid = 0.9463 liter
1 gal. = 0.3785 dekaliter
1 peck = 0.881 dekaliter
1 bu. = 0.3524 hectoliter

Weights
1 ounce = 28.35 grams
1 lb. = 0.4536 kilogram
1 English ton = 0.9072 metric ton
1 kilogram = 1,000 grams

Approximate Metric Equivalents
1 metric ton = 2,200 lbs.
1 liter = 1.06 qt. liquid
1 liter = 0.9 qt. dry
1 hectoliter = 2⅝ bushel
1 kilogram = 2⅕ lbs.

Weights

The *Kilo,* or Kilogram (kg), has 1000 grams and is the standard metric weight unit. It is the *exact* equivalent of 2.205 American pounds. Conversions for recipes are:

GRAMS		OUNCES		OUNCES		GRAMS
1	=	0.035		1	=	28.35
2	=	0.07		2	=	56.70
3	=	0.11		3	=	85.05
4	=	0.14		4	=	113.40
5	=	0.18		5	=	141.75
6	=	0.21		6	=	170.10
7	=	0.25		7	=	198.45
8	=	0.28		8	=	226.80
9	=	0.32		9	=	255.15
10	=	0.35		10	=	283.50
20	=	0.70		11	=	311.85
30	=	1.05		12	=	340.20
40	=	1.40		13	=	368.55
50	=	1.75		14	=	396.90
				15	=	425.25
				16	=	453.59

Metrics is a system of weights and measures in which the gram is the basic unit of weight, the meter is the unit of length, and the liter is the measure of capacity or volume.

Metric measurements are made according to the decimal system, in units of 10. The meter, then, which is the approximate equivalent of one yard, contains 100 centimeters. One liter, which is approximately one quart liquid measure, contains 100 centiliters.

The basic vocabulary of the metric system is:

milli: 1/1000th of, as a millimeter equals 1/1000th of a meter.

centi: 1/100th of, as a centimeter equals 1/100th of a meter.

deci: 1/10th of, as a decimeter equals 1/10th of a meter.

kilo: 1,000 times, as a kilometer equals 1,000 meters.

Liquid Measure

The *Liter* (l) has 1000 milliliters (ml) and is the standard metric unit for liquid volume. The liter is commonly divided into tenths (deciliters or dl) and hundreths (centiliters or cl). One liter is the *exact* equivalent of 1.057 American quarts. Conversions for recipes are:

FLUID OUNCES		CENTILITERS		CENTILITERS		FLUID OUNCES
1	=	2.96		1	=	0.34
2	=	5.92		2	=	0.7
3	=	8.87		3	=	1.0
4	=	11.83		4	=	1.4
5	=	14.79		5	=	1.7
6	=	17.74		6	=	2.0
7	=	20.70		7	=	2.4
8	=	23.66		8	=	2.7
9	=	26.62		9	=	3.0
10	=	29.57		10	=	3.4
11	=	32.53		20	=	7.0
12	=	35.48		30	=	10.0
13	=	38.44		40	=	14.0
14	=	41.40		50	=	17.0
15	=	44.36		60	=	20.0
16	=	47.32		70	=	24.0
				80	=	27.0
				90	=	30.0
				100	=	34.0
				(liter)		

A major advantage of the metric system is that liquid volume and weights are related. One liter of water equals 1 kilo or 1000 grams.

APPENDIX E

Portion Measurement Data

Ounce and Cup Equivalents

FOOD ITEM	OUNCES PER CUP APPROXIMATE	CUPS PER POUND APPROXIMATE	FOOD ITEM	OUNCES PER CUP APPROXIMATE	CUPS PER POUND APPROXIMATE
Eggs, fresh or frozen, white	8⅔	2	Milk, nonfat, dry, crystal	2¾	5⅔
Eggs, fresh or frozen, yolks	8⅔	2	Mincemeat	8	2
Egg solids, whole, sifted	3	5	Molasses, cane	11½	1⅓
Egg solids, whole, packed	4	4	Noodles, 1″ piece, dry	2⅔	6
Egg solids, whites, spray dry, sifted	3	5	Nut meats, chopped	4	4
Egg solids, pan dried, powdered	4⅔	3½	Oats, rolled (quick)	3	5⅔
Egg solids, yolks, sifted	3	5⅔	Oils, all	8	2
Egg solids, yolks, packed	3½	4¾	Onions, dried	3½	4½
Egg, fresh, hard cooked, diced	6	2⅔	Peanuts	5	3¼
Figs, cut fine	6	2⅔	Peanut butter	8	2
Filberts, whole	4¾	3⅓	Peas, split	7	2¼
Flour, corn	4	4	Pecan halves	3¼	4¼
Flour, gluten	5	3¼	Pimiento	7	2¼
Flour, graham	5	3¼	Potato starch, sifted	5	3¼
Flour, rice	4½	3½	Prunes, pitted, dried, raw	7	2¼
Flour, rye	3	5⅔	Prunes, cooked, drained	8	2
Flour, soy, full fat	2	7½	Raisins, seeded, whole	5	3¼
Flour, soy, low fat	3	5½	Raisins, seeded, chopped	6½	2½
Flour, whole-wheat	7	2¼	Raisins, seedless, whole	5¾	2¾
Flour, white, all-purpose	4	4	Raisins, seedless, chopped	8	2
Flour, white, bread	4	4	Rice flour, sifted	4½	3½
Flour, white, cake	3⅓	4¾	Rice, white, long grain	6½	2½
Flour, white, pastry	3½	4½	Rice, white, medium grain	6¾	2⅓
Flour, white, self-rising	4	4	Rice, white, short grain	7	2¼
Gelatin, granulated	5⅓	3	Rice, wild	5½	3
Gelatin, flavored	7	2⅓	Rye flour	3	5⅔
Ginger, crystalized, diced	6	2⅔	Salt, free running	10¼	1½
Grapenuts	4	4	Salt, cooking	8	2
Hominy, grits	5½	3	Sorghum	11⅔	1⅓
Hominy, whole	6½	2½	Soybeans	7½	2¼
Honey	12	1⅓	Soy flour, full fat	2	7½
Hydrogenated fat	6⅔	2½	Soy flour, low fat	3	5½
Lard	8	2	Soy grits	5	3⅓
Lentils	7	2¼	Spaghetti, 2″ pieces	3⅓	4¾
Macaroni, 1″ piece, dry	4	4	Suet, chopped	4¼	3¾
Macaroni, shell, dry	4	4	Sugar, cane or beet		
Maple syrup	11	1½	confectioners	4½	3½
Margarine	8	2	granulated	7	2¼
Marshmallows	4	4	superfine	7	2¼
Milk, whole	8⅔	2	Tapioca, quick cooking	5½	3
Milk, buttermilk	8⅔	2	Tea	2½	6⅓
Milk, condensed	10¾	1½	Vermicelli, 2″ pieces	3	5⅔
Milk, evaporated	9	1¾	Walnuts, english, half	3½	4½
Milk, skimmed	8⅔	2	Wheat germ	2½	6⅔
Milk, whole, dry	3¾	4¼	Whole-wheat flour	7	2¼
Milk, nonfat, dry, powder	4	4	Yeast, dry	4¾	3⅓

COMMON CAN AND JAR SIZES

The labels of cans or jars of identical size may show a net weight for one product that differs slightly from the net weight on the label of another product, due to the density of the food. An example would be lima beans (1 lb), and blueberries (14 oz), in the same size can.

Can Size (Industry term)	Average Net Weight or Fluid Measure per Can (Check label)	Average Cups per Can	Cans per Case
No. 10	6 lb 8 oz (104 oz) to 7 lb 5 oz (117 oz)	12-13	6
No. 3 Cyl. or 46 fl. oz	3 lb 3 oz (51 oz) or 1 qt 14 fl. oz (46 fl. oz)	5¾	12
No. 2½	1 lb 13 oz (29 oz)	3½	24
No. 2	1 lb 4 oz (20 oz) or 1 pt 2 fl. oz (18 fl. oz)	2½	24
No. 303	16 to 17 oz	2	24
No. 300	14 to 16 oz	1¾	24
No. 1 Picnic	10½ to 12 oz	1¼	48
8 oz	8 oz	1	48 or 72

Meats, fish and seafoods are known and sold by weight of contents of can.

MEASURES FOR PORTION CONTROL

The most dependable method to use in measuring serving sizes or portions is to serve the food with dippers, scoops, ladles, or spoons of standard sizes.

Dippers or Scoops

The number of the scoop indicates the number of scoopfuls it takes to make 1 quart. The following table shows the level measures of each scoop in cups or tablespoons:

Dipper or scoop No.	Level measure
6	⅔ cup
8	½ cup
10	⅖ cup
12	⅓ cup
16	¼ cup
20	3⅕ tablespoons
24	2⅔ tablespoons
30	2⅕ tablespoons
40	1⅗ tablespoons

Scoops may be used for portioning such items as drop cookies, muffins, meat patties, and some vegetables and salads.

Ladles

Ladles may be used in serving soups, stews, creamed dishes, sauces, gravies, and other similar products.

¼ cup
½ cup
¾ cup
1 cup

COMMON FOOD MEASURES

3 teaspoons = 1 tablespoon
2 tablespoons = ⅛ cup or 1 fluid ounce
4 tablespoons = ¼ cup
8 tablespoons = ½ cup
12 tablespoons = ¾ cup
16 tablespoons = 1 cup
2 cups = 1 pint
2 pints = 1 quart
4 quarts = 1 gallon
8 quarts = 1 peck
4 pecks = 1 bushel

ABBREVIATIONS

AP	as purchased
EP	edible portion
Cyl	cylinder
tsp	teaspoon
T or tbsp	tablespoon
lb	pound
c	cup
pt	pint
qt	quart
gal	gallon
oz	ounce
fl. oz	fluid ounce
No.	number
wt	weight
incl	including
excl	excluding

Ounce equivalents in decimal parts of one pound

Number of ounces (1)	+0 ounces (2)	+¼ ounce (3)	+½ ounce (4)	¾ ounce (5)
	Pound	Pound	Pound	Pound
0	——	0.016	0.031	0.047
1	0.062	.078	.094	.109
2	.125	.141	.156	.172
3	.188	.203	.219	.234
4	.250	.266	.281	.297
5	.312	.328	.344	.359
6	.375	.391	.406	.422
7	.438	.453	.469	.484
8	.500	.516	.531	.547
9	.562	.578	.594	.609
10	.625	.641	.656	.672
11	.688	.703	.719	.734
12	.750	.766	.781	.797
13	.812	.828	.844	.859
14	.875	.891	.906	.922
15	.938	.953	.969	.984

To convert 10½ ounces to a decimal part of a pound, find 10 in column 1, then follow this line across to column 4, which shows that .656 pounds corresponds to 10½ ounces.

To convert a decimal part of a pound such as .531 to ounces, find .531 in the decimal pound readings—then refer to column 1 on the same line and find 8, the number of whole ounces. At the top of the column in which .531 is located, the +½ ounce should be added to the 8 ounces. Thus .531 pounds corresponds to 8½ ounces.

APPENDIX F

Food Equivalence Data

Table F-1. Approximate Equivalents in Quality Food Products

Ingredient	Substitute	Measure	Weight
Flour (2 c, 8 oz)	Cornstarch	1 c	
Cake flour (1 qt, 1 lb)	Hard or all-purpose flour	3¾ c and ¼ c cornstarch	13½ oz and 2½ oz cornstarch
Syrups, honey, etc. (1 pt, 1 lb 6 oz)	Sugar	2½ c sugar, ½ c water, ⅛ t cream of tartar	1¼ lb sugar, 4 oz water, ⅛ t cream of tartar
Chocolate, bitter (2 c, 1 lb)	Cocoa	3½ c, ¾ c shortening	12½ oz, 3½ oz shortening
Milk, whole (1 qt, 2 lb)	Dry milk, whole*	⅞ c, 3⅞ c water	3¾ oz, 1⅞ lb water
Milk, whole (1 qt, 2 lb)	Dry milk, nonfat*	¾ c, 3½ c water, 2 T shortening	3½ oz, 1¼ lb water, 1 oz shortening
Milk, nonfat (1 qt, 2 lb)	Dry milk, nonfat*	¾ c, 3⅞ c water	3½ oz, 1⅞ lb water
Milk, whole (1 qt, 2 lb)	Evaporated milk	No. 1 tall can plus water to equal qt	14½ oz plus water to equal 1 qt
Eggs, whole (1 pt, 1 lb)	Dried whole eggs	1¼ c, 1¾ c water	5 oz, 12½ oz water
Eggs, whites (1 pt, 1 lb)	Dried whites	1⅛ c, 1¾ c water	3 oz, 14 oz water
Eggs, yolks (1 pt, 1 lb)	Dried yolks	1⅛ c, 1¾ c water	6 oz, 11 oz water
Eggs, whole (1 pt, 1 lb)	Frozen whole	1 pt (10 eggs)	1 lb
Eggs, whites (1 pt, 1 lb)	Frozen whites	1 pt (18 whites)	1 lb
Eggs, yolks (1 pt, 1 lb)	Frozen yolks	1 pt (24 yolks)	1 lb
Butter (1 pt, 1 lb)	Margarine	1 pt	1 lb
Butter or margarine (1 pt, 1 lb)	Fat or oil	1⅞ c plus ½ t salt, 2 T water	14 oz, ½ t salt, 1 oz water
Cream, coffee, 18% (1 qt, 2 lb)	Milk, nonfat, and butter	3½ c milk, ¾ c butter	26 oz milk, 6 oz butter
Cream, whipping, 40% (1 qt, 2 lb)	Butter	Butter	40% of cream weight
	Milk, nonfat, and butter	3 c milk, 1⅓ c butter	20 oz milk, 12½ oz butter
Leavening agents			
Tartrate baking powder (¾ c, 4 oz)	SAS phosphate baking powder	⅜ c	2 oz
Tartrate baking powder (¾ c, 4 oz)	Soda and cream of tartar	3 t and ⅔ c	1 oz and 3 oz
SAS phosphate baking powder (⅝ c, 2 oz)	Phosphate baking powder	½ c plus 1 T	3 oz
SAS phosphate baking powder (⅝ c, 2 oz)	Soda plus liquid	3 T plus 1 c sour milk, or 1 c buttermilk, or 1 c milk, 1 T vinegar or lemon juice, or ½ to 1 c molasses	

* Measure equivalent is for regular dry milk; for instant use 1⅓ c for every ¾ of regular.

Table F-2. Food Equivalents, Weights and Measures

Food	Weight	Approximate Measure
Beverages		
Cocoa	1 lb	4½ c
Coffee, urn grind	1 lb	4½ c
Coffee, instant	1 oz	½ c
Tea	1 lb	1½ qt
Cereals and Cereal Products		
Barley, pearl	1 lb	2½ c
Bran, all-bran	1 lb	2 qt
Bran flakes	1 lb	3 qt
Bread, crumbs, dry	1 lb	1¼ qt
Bread, crumbs, fresh	1 lb	2½ qt
Bread, crumbs, dry sifted	1 lb	1 qt
Bread, soft, broken, ¾ in. cubes	1 lb	2¼ qt (packed 2 qt)
Bread, slices, ⅝ in.	1 lb	16 slices
Cake crumbs, soft	1 lb	1¼ qt
Crackers, crumbled	1 lb	2 to 2½ qt
Crackers, crumbs	1 lb	1¼ qt
Crackers, graham	1 lb	40 crackers
Crackers, small, square saltines	1 lb	108 crackers
Crackers, large, soda	1 lb	56 crackers
Cracked wheat	1 lb	3½ c (5 to 6 c cooked)
Cornflakes	1 lb	1¼ gal
Cornmeal	1 lb	3½ c (3 qt cooked)
Cornstarch, stirred	1 lb	3½ c (1 c = 4¾ oz, 1 oz 3½ T)
Farina	1 lb	2⅔ c
Flour, graham or whole-wheat	1 lb	3½ c
Flour, cake, unsifted	1 lb	3¾ c
Flour, cake, sifted	1 lb	1 qt
Flour, rye, straight grade, sifted	1 lb	1¼ qt
Flour, white, bread, sifted	1 lb	1 qt
Flour, white, bread, unsifted	1 lb	3¾ c
Farina	1 lb	2⅔ c
Hominy grits	1 lb	2½ to 3 c (6½ lb or 3¼ qt cooked)
Macaroni, 1 in. pieces.	1 lb.	3½ to 4 c (3¾ lb or 2½ qt cooked)
Noodles	1 lb	6 to 8½ c (3¾ lb or 2¼ qt cooked)
Oats, rolled	1 lb	4¾ c (2¼ qt cooked)
Rice	1 lb	2⅛ c (2½ lb or 2½ qt cooked)
Spaghetti, 2 in. pieces	1 lb	1¼ qt (4 lb or 2½ qt cooked)
Soya flour	1 lb	1¼ to 1½ qt
Tapioca, quick cooking	1 lb	2⅔ c (7½ c cooked)
Tapioca, pearl	1 lb	2¾ c (soaked and cooked 7½ c)
Wheat cereals	1 lb	2⅞ c (cooked 6 c)
Wheat, shredded	1 lb	20 small biscuits

Table F-2. *(cont.)*

Food	Weight	Approximate Measure
Dairy Products		
Butter or margarine (see also fats)	1 lb	2 c
Cheese, grated or ground	1 lb	2¼ c tight pack, 3¾ c loose pack
Cheese, cubed	1 lb 1 oz	1 qt
Cheese, cottage	1 lb	2¼ c
Cheese, Philadelphia cream	1 lb 9 oz	3 c
Cream, 18%	8¾ oz	1 c
Cream, 30 to 40%, whipping	1 lb	1 pt (doubles volume in whipping)
Milk, condensed, sweetened	11 oz	1 c
Milk, dry, instant	1 lb	5¾ c
Milk, dry, nonfat, regular	1 lb	1 qt
Milk, dry, whole, regular	1 lb	3¾ c
Milk, evaporated	1 lb	1⅞ c
Milk, fresh, liquid	8½ oz	1 c
*Eggs, large**		
Eggs in shell	1½ lb	1 doz
Eggs, whole	1 lb	1 pt (9 to 11)
Eggs, whites	1 lb	1 pt (17 to 20)
Eggs, yolks	1 lb	1 pt (19 to 23)
Eggs, hardcooked, chopped	1 lb	2½ c (1 doz = 3½ c)
Eggs, dry, whole, packed	1 oz	¼ c
Eggs, whole, dry	1 lb	1¼ qt (1½ c [6 oz] and 1⅞ c water = 1 doz eggs)
Eggs, whites, dry	1 lb	2 qt (¾ c [2 doz] and 1½ c water = 1 doz whites)
Eggs, yolks, dry	1 lb	4¼ c (1⅛ c [4 doz] and ⅝ c water = 1 doz yolks)
Meringue	6 oz	1 c
Fats and Oils		
Bacon fat	15 oz	1 lb (1 lb = 2⅛ c)
Butter or margarine	14 oz	1 pt
Creamed fat	1 lb	2½ c
Hydrogenated shortening	14½ oz	1 pt
Oil	1 lb	2¼ c
Suet, chopped	1 lb	3¾ c
Fruits		
Apples	1 lb	3 size 113 (3 c pared, diced, or sliced)
Apples, sliced	1 lb	4 to 4½ c
Apples, diced, half-inch	1 lb	1 qt
Applesauce	1 lb	1⅞ c
Apples, canned, solid pack	1 lb	1 pt
Apple nuggets	1 lb	6⅔ c
Apricots, dried	1 lb	3¼ c (1¾ lb or 5 c cooked)
Apricots, canned, heavy pack	1 lb	1 pt
Apricots, canned, halves, no juice	1 lb	1 pt (21 halves)
Apricots, fresh	1 lb	8 medium

*Eggs lose approximately 11 to 12% weight in shelling. Medium eggs are about 10% less in weight than large.

Table F-2. *(cont.)*

Food	Weight	Approximate Measure
Fruits (cont.)		
Avocados, Calavos, medium size	1 lb	2 to 3
Bananas, AP, medium size	1 lb	3 (peeled 10 oz)
Bananas, peeled	1 lb	2½ c diced, 1 medium banana = 30 ⅛ in. slices, or ¾ c, or ⅓ to ½ c mashed
Blackberries, fresh	1 lb	1 qt
Blackberries, water pack, drained	1 lb	3 c
Blueberries, fresh	1 lb	3 c
Cantaloupe	1 lb	1 melon 4 in. in diameter
Cherries, red, heavy pack, drained	1 lb	3 c
Cherries, Royal Anne, drained	1 lb	3 c
Cherries, candied	1 lb	3 c or 120 cherries
Cherries, Maraschino	1 qt	60 to 70 cherries
Citron, chopped	1 lb	2½ c
Cranberries, fresh	1 lb	1 qt (1 lb AP = 3¼ c sauce)
Cranberries, dehydrated	1 lb	8½ c
Cranberries, whole	2½ lb raw	1 qt cooked
Currants	1 lb	3½ c (1 c = 4½ oz)
Dates, pitted	1 lb	2¾ c (1 c = 6 oz, 1 c = 8¼ oz if packed)
Dates		
Dates, unpitted	1 lb	2½ c (1¾ c pitted)
Figs, dry	1 lb	3 c (1 c = 5 oz)
Grapefruit, 32s	1 lb	12 sections, 1¼ c juice
Grapes, whole, stemmed	1 lb	1 qt
Grapes, cut	1 lb	2⅔ c
Oranges, 88s, diced with juice	1 lb	2¼ c (1 orange = ½ c diced or ⅓ c juice)
Oranges, 88s, Florida	1 doz	1 qt juice
Oranges, rind, grated (also lemon)	1⅔ lb	¼ c (1 t = ⅛ oz)
Oranges, rind, grated (also lemon)	6½ oz	1 c
Peaches, canned, sliced with juice	1 lb	⅞ c
Peaches, fresh	1 lb	3 to 5 peaches
Peaches, dry, loose pack	1 lb	1 qt
Pears, canned, drained, diced	1 lb	2½ c
Pineapple, slices	1 lb	8 to 12 slices (2½ c)
Prunes, dried, size 30 to 40, uncooked	1 lb	3 c (2½ lb or 5 to 6 c cooked)
Prunes, cooked, pitted, with juice	1 lb	2¼ c
Pumpkin	1 lb	2½ c
Raspberries	1 lb	3½ c (2¼ c cooked)
Raisins	1 lb	3 c (1 c = 5¼ oz, 1 lb cooked = 1 lb 9½ oz or 1 qt)
Rhubarb, raw, 1 in. pieces	1 lb	1 qt (cooked 1⅜ lb or 2½ c)
Strawberries, fresh	1 lb	3¼ c
Meats		
Bacon, diced, packed	1 lb	2¼ c
Bacon, raw, sliced	1 lb	15 to 25 slices
Bacon, cooked	1 lb	85 to 95 slices

Table F-2. *(cont.)*

Food	Weight	Approximate Measure
Meats (cont.)		
Beef, dried, solid pack	1 lb	1 qt, scant
Beef, ground, raw	1 lb	1 pt
Beef, cooked, diced	1 lb	3 c
Chicken, ready-to-cook	5 lb	5 c cooked, diced meat (40% yield)
Chicken, cooked, cubed	1 lb	2½ c
Crabmeat, flaked	1 lb	3 c
Ham, cooked, diced	1 lb	3¼ c
Ham, cooked, ground, packed	1 lb	1 pt
Ham, raw, AP	1 lb	1 c fine diced cooked
Meats, chopped, cooked, moist, packed	1 lb	1 pt (loose pack = 1 qt)
Oysters, 1 qt, Eastern	2 lb	40 large, 60 small
Salmon, canned	1 lb	1 pt
Sardines, canned	1 lb	48, 3 in. long
Sausage, link	1 lb	16
Sausage meat	1 lb	1 pt
Shrimp, 2 lb AP	1 lb EP	3¼ c (5 lb in shell = gal)
Tuna fish	1 lb	1 pt
Turkey, ready-to-cook	30 lb	15 lb clear meat
Wieners	1 lb	10 (frankfurters 6 to 7)
Miscellaneous		
Chocolate, see spices		
Compressed yeast	½ oz	1 cake
Compressed yeast	8½ oz	1 c
Dry active yeast	1 lb	2½ lb compressed
Gelatin, granulated, unflavored	1 lb	3½ c (1 oz = 3½ T)
Gelatin, prepared, flavored	1 lb	2⅓ c (1 oz = ¼ c)
Marshmallows (1¼ in.)	1 lb	80
Nuts		
Almonds, shelled	1 lb	3½ c (¼ lb shelled)
Almonds, blanched	1 lb	3 c
Coconut, shredded	1 lb	4½ c to 7 c depending on type shred and tightness of pack
Coconut, ground or fine shred	2⅜ oz	1 c
Coconut, shredded, medium	1 oz	7 T
Filberts	1 lb	3⅓ c (½ lb shelled)
Peanut butter	1 lb	1⅞ c
Peanuts, chopped	1 lb	1 qt (⅔ lb shelled)
Pecans	1 lb	4¼ c (⅓ lb shelled)
Walnut meats	1 lb	4¾ c (½ lb shelled)
Walnut meats, chopped	1 lb	1 qt
Nut meats, ground	4¼ oz	1 c

Table F-2. *(cont.)*

Food	Weight	Approximate Measure
Salad Dressings and Condiments		
Catsup or chili sauce	9 oz	1 c
Cooked salad dressing	1 lb	1 pt
French dressing	1 lb	2⅛ c
Horseradish, ground	1 lb	2¼ c
Mayonnaise	1 lb	2⅛ c
Olives, small	1 lb	3½ c or 135 olives, 1 No. 10 = 4½ lb drained weight or 350 large olives
Pickles, chopped	1 lb	2½ c
Pickles, small	1 gal	80 (about 225 gherkins or 25 large per gal)
Spices, Seasonings, Leavenings		
Allspice, ground	1 lb	4½ c (1 oz=4½ T)
Baking powder	1 lb	2½ c (1 T = ⁷⁄₁₆ oz, 1 oz = 2½ T)
Celery seed	1 lb	1 qt (1 oz = ¼ c)
Chili or curry powder	1 oz	3 T
Chocolate, grated	1 lb	1 qt (1 lb = 16 squares)
Chocolate, grated	1 oz	5 T (1 c = 3¾ oz)
Chocolate, melted	1 lb	1⅞ c (1 oz = 2 T)
Cinnamon, ground	1 lb	1 qt (1 oz = ¼ c)
Cloves, ground	1 lb	3¾ c (1 oz = 3¾ T)
Cloves, whole	1 oz	5 T
Cream of tartar	1 lb	3 c (1 oz = 3 T)
Flavoring extracts	⅜ oz	1 T (⅛ oz = 1 t)
Ginger, ground	1 lb	4¾ c (1 oz = 4¾ T)
Mustard, ground	1 lb	5 c (1 oz = 5 T)
Nutmeg, ground	1 lb	3½ oz (1 oz = 3½T)
Paprika	3¼ oz	1 c (1 T = ⅜ doz)
Pepper	1 oz	¼ c
Sage, ground	1 oz	½ c
Salt	1 lb	1⅔ c (1 oz = 1 T, 2 t)
Soda	1 lb	2½ c (1 oz = 2 T, 6½ t = 1 oz)
Vinegar	1 lb	2 c (1 oz = 2 T)
Worcestershire sauce	9½ oz	1 c
Sugars and Syrups		
Corn syrup	11 oz	1 c
Honey	12 oz	1 c
Jam or jelly	1½ lb	1 pt
Sugar, cocktail cube	1 cubelet	½ t (small cube = 1 t, tablet = 1½ t, 96 cubes, medium, per lb)
Sugar, granulated	1 lb	2¼ c (superfine 2 c)
Sugar, confectioners, stirred	1 lb	3½ c
Sugar, confectioners, 4X, sifted	1 lb	4½ c (unsifted 2¾ c)
Sugar, brown	1 lb	3 c (packed 2¼ c)
Molasses	11 oz	1 c

Table F-2. *(cont.)*

Food	Weight	Approximate Measure
Vegetables		
Asparagus, fresh	1 lb	20 stalks
Asparagus, canned, tips, drained	1 lb	19 stalks
Asparagus, canned, cuts, drained	1 lb	2½ c
Beans, baked	1 lb	1⅞ c
Beans, dried, lima, small, AP	1 lb	2⅓ c (2½ lb or 1½ qt cooked)
Beans, lima, fresh, unshelled	1 lb	⅔ c shelled
Beans, lima, fresh, shelled	1 lb	2¼ c
Beans, lima, drained, cooked, fresh or canned	1 lb	2⅔ c (1½ lb = 1 qt)
Beans, kidney, dry, AP	1 lb	2⅓ c (2¼ lb or 1½ qt cooked)
Beans, string, cut, uncooked, EP	12 oz	1 qt
Beans, navy, dry, AP	1 lb	2⅓ c (2½ lb or 1¾ c cooked)
Bean sprouts	1 lb	1 qt
Beets, cooked, diced, drained	1 lb	2¼ c (3 to 4 medium whole)
Beets, cooked, sliced, drained	1½ lb	1 qt (1 lb = 2¾ c)
Brussels sprouts, AP	1 lb	1 qt
Cabbage, shredded, EP	12 oz	1 qt (1 lb = 5½ c or 1 lb = 7 c loose pack)
Cabbage, AP, shredded, cooked, drained	1 lb	3½ c
Carrots, half-inch cube, raw	1 lb	3¼ c
Carrots, diced, cooked, drained	1 lb	2½ to 3 c
Carrots, ground, raw, EP	1 lb	3¼ c
Carrots, AP	1 lb	4 medium, 6 small
Cauliflower, 1 crate	12½ lb, net, EP	10 qt
Cauliflower, head, medium	12 oz	4 to 5 portions
Celery, diced, EP	1¼ lb	1 qt (1 lb = 3¼ c)
Celery, dehydrated	1 lb	9½ c
Corn, cream style	1 lb	1⅞ c
Corn, whole kernel, drained	1 lb	2⅓ c
Cucumbers, diced	1 lb	2½ c
Eggplant, diced, half-inch cubes	1 lb	4½ c
Eggplant, sliced, 4 in. diameter, half-inch thick	1 lb	8 slices
Garlic, crushed	1 oz	6 to 9 cloves
Lettuce, average head	1 lb	10 to 12 leaf cups
Lettuce, shredded	1 lb	8 c (packed 5 c)
Lettuce, leaf	1 lb	30 salad garnishes
Onions, AP	1 lb	4 to 5 medium
Onions, chopped	1 lb	2½ to 3 c
Onions, grated or minced	5 oz	1 c
Onions, dehydrated	1 lb	9½ c
Mushrooms, fresh	1 lb AP	1⅓ c cooked
Parsley	1 lb	3 bunches (6 c chopped)
Parsnips, AP	1 lb	3 to 4 medium
Parsnips, diced, raw	1 lb	2½ to 3 c
Parsnips, diced, cooked	1 lb	2½ c

Table F-2. *(cont.)*

Food	Weight	Approximate Measure
Vegetables (cont.)		
Parsnips, mashed	1 lb	1 pt
Peas, fresh, 2½ lb AP	1 lb EP	1 pt scant, 5 portions
Peas, canned, dried	1 lb	2¼ c
Peas, dried, split	1 lb	2⅓ c (2½ lb or 5½ c cooked)
Peppers, green	1 lb	5 to 6 medium
Peppers, green, chopped	1 lb	3½ c
Pimientos, chopped	8 oz	1 c
Potatoes, white, medium, AP	1 lb	3 to 4 (¾ lb pared, 1 pt mashed)
Potatoes, dehydrated, cube	1 lb	4¾ c
Potatoes, dehydrated, flake	3½ oz	1 c
Potatoes, granule, dehydrated	7 oz	1 c
Potatoes, cooked, diced, half-inch cube	1 lb	3 c
Potatoes, sweet	1 lb	3 medium
Potato chips	1 lb	5 qt (20 1 c portions ¾ oz)
Pumpkin, cooked	1 lb	1 pt
Radishes, whole, topped and cleaned	1 lb	1 qt
Rutabagas, cubed, cooked	1 lb	3 c
Rutabagas, raw, cubed, EP	1 lb	3⅓ c
Sauerkraut, uncooked	1 lb	3 c
Spinach, raw	1 lb	5 qt, loose pack
Spinach, 1 lb raw, AP, cooked	13 oz EP	1½ c cooked, 3 portions
Spinach, canned, drained	1 lb	1 pt
Squash, summer, AP	1½ lb	1 3 in. diameter
Squash, Hubbard, cooked, mashed	1 lb	2⅛ c
Tomatoes, canned	1 lb	1 pt
Tomatoes, dried	1 lb	3½ c
Tomatoes, fresh	1 lb	3 to 4 medium
Tomatoes, fresh, diced	1 lb	2¼ to 2¾ c
Turnips, AP	1 lb	4 to 5 medium
Turnips, raw, diced	1 lb	3½ c
Watercress	1 lb	5 bunches

APPENDIX G

Troubleshooting Bread Failures

Table G-1. Troubleshooting Bread Failures

Fault	Possible Causes	Possible Remedies
Excessive volume.	Too much yeast.	Reduce yeast to 2 to 3%; check weighing procedures.
	Too little salt.	Maintain from 2 to 2½%; check weighing procedures.
	Excess dough.	Reduce scaling weights.
	Overproofed.	Reduce proofing time; keep between 70-30 or 80-20 fermentation time for sponges.
	Too cool oven.	Increase temperature.
Poor volume.	Weak flour.	Blend strong flour into flour or use a stronger flour; give less mixing, shorter fermentation, and less proofing time.
	Flour too old or too new.	Use aged flour; check age of flour.
	Water too soft or too alkaline.	Use a conditioner; additional salt improves too soft a water.
	Lack of leavening.	Use good yeast and handle it properly; have dough at proper temperature; reduce quantity of salt.
	Undermixing.	Increase mixing times until gluten in dough is properly developed; proper volume of dough to mixer is also a factor to check.
	Overfermented dough.	Reduce fermentation time.
	Overmixing.	Reduce mixing.
	Improper proofing.	Proof between 90° and 100° F and 80 to 85% relative humidity; watch proofing time and maintain proper ratio between fermentation and proofing procedures.
	Too much or too little steam in oven.	Open or close oven dampers; if steam is introduced into oven, establish better controls.
	Too hot oven.	Reduce temperature.
Too dark crust.	Excess sugar or milk.	Reduce; check diastatic action of flour; it may be breaking down too much starch into sugars.
	Overmixing.	Reduce mixing.
	Dough too young.	Increase fermentation and proof periods.
	Too hot oven.	Correct oven temperatures.
	Too long baking.	Reduce baking time.
	Too dry oven.	Close oven damper during part of baking, or use steam.
Too pale or dull color on crust.	Wrong proportion or lack of right ingredients.	Check ratios of sugar, salt, or milk, and diastatic action of flour; increase ingredients to proper ratios; add diastase syrup.
	Soft water.	Increase salt or add conditioner.
	Overfermentation.	Reduce temperature or time of fermentation.
	Excessive dusting flour.	Cover bench only with bare minimum.
	Too high proof temperature.	Reduce temperature.
	Cool oven.	Increase temperature.
	Improper use of steam.	Avoid excessive steam; open dampers to increase oven moisture.
Spotted crust.	Improper mixing.	Follow correct mixing procedures and sequence of adding ingredients.
	Excess dusting flour.	Reduce dusting flour.
	Excess humidity in proofing	Reduce relative humidity to between 80 and 85%.

Table G-1. *(cont.)*

Fault	Possible Causes	Possible Remedies
	Water in oven or excessive moisture in steam.	Check steam pipes and ovens; open dampers.
Hard crust or blisters.	Lack of sugar or diastatic action.	Increase sugars or check diastatic action of flour; check weighing of ingredients.
	Slack dough.	Reduce liquid; check mixing.
	Improper mixing.	Check mixing procedures and sequence of ingredient addition.
	Old or young dough.	Correct the fermentation time.
	Improper molding or make-up.	Correct procedures.
	Cool oven or too much top heat.	Check damper handling procedures and oven temperatures; check heating elements and heat source to see if functioning properly; check oven circulation.
	Cooling too rapidly.	Cool more slowly; keep out of drafts.
	Too much fat on product.	Reduce brushing of fat after make-up.
Poor shape.	Improper make-up or panning.	Correct procedures.
	Overproofing.	Reduce.
Flat top or sharp corner.	New flour.	Age flour six to eight months under proper conditions.
	Low salt.	Increase; check weighing procedures.
	Slack dough.	Reduce liquid; check mixing.
	Young dough.	Increase fermentation time.
	Excessive humidity in proofing.	Reduce humidity.
Excessive break on side.	Overmixing.	Reduce mixing.
	Improper molding.	Check molding, especially seam folds; place seam folds down on bottom of pan.
	Young dough.	Correct; check proofing time.
	Hot oven.	Reduce temperatures.
Thick crust.	Low shortening, sugar, or milk.	Increase; check scaling procedures.
	Low diastase.	Check diastatic action of flour; add malt syrup or diastase compound.
	Mixing improper.	Correct mixing procedures.
	Improper proofing.	Correct temperature, relative humidity, or time of proofing; check for wet crusts after proofing.
	Old dough.	Correct fermentation and/or proofing time.
	Improper baking.	Correct temperatures and times; reduce steam and check for excessive or insufficient moisture in ovens.
Tough crust.	Old or young dough.	Check fermentation times.
	Improper mixing.	Correct.
	Excess proof or wrong proof conditions.	Correct.
	Oven cold or excess steam.	Correct.
Lack of break or shred.	Excess diastase.	Decrease amount; use non-diastatic malt; check diastatic action of flour.
	Soft water.	Increase salt or use conditioner.
	Slack dough.	Reduce water substantially; check mixing.
	Improper fermentation or proof time.	Correct.

Table G-1. *(cont.)*

Fault	Possible Causes	Possible Remedies
	Too hot or too dry an oven.	Correct temperatures by damper control; introduce steam.
Ragged scaling or shelling on top.	Green or overly old flour.	Use flour properly aged.
	Old or young dough.	Check fermentation or proof times and conditions.
	Stiff dough.	Reduce flour or increase liquid.
	Crusting during proofing.	Increase relative humidity; brush lightly with shortening.
	Excess salt.	Reduce.
	Underproofing.	Increase proofing time.
	Excessive top heat in oven.	Check heat circulation and heat source in oven; check damper control.
	Cold dough.	Add warmer liquid; check mixing, fermentation, and proofing temperatures.
	Lack of salt or milk.	Check recipe and weighing procedures.
Too close grain.	Low yeast.	Increase; check weighing procedures.
	Underproofing.	Correct.
	Excess dough in pan.	Check scaling procedures.
Too coarse or open grain.	Hard or alkaline water.	Add vinegar or conditioner.
	Old dough.	Excess yeast; reduce fermentation time.
	Slack dough.	Reduce liquid; check mixing times.
	Improper molding.	Correct.
	Overproofing.	Reduce time or check temperatures.
	Improper pan size.	Check.
	Cold oven.	Increase oven temperature.
	Excessive greasing.	Check oiling or greasing of dough.
Gray crumb.	High diastatic action.	Reduce.
	High dough temperature or overfermentation.	Check mixing, fermentation, and proof temperatures and times.
	Cold oven.	Check temperatures and conditions of baking.
	Pans greasy.	Check greasing.
Streaked crumb.	Improper mixing.	Check ingredient sequence of adding in mixing.
	Too slack or stiff dough.	Check liquid or flour quantities; check to see if proper mixing times given.
	Excessive oil, grease, or dusting flour used.	Correct.
	High relative humidity.	Reduce relative humidity in fermentation or proofing.
	Crusting of dough in fermentation.	Increase relative humidity or brush with fat; cover to prevent moisture loss.
Poor texture.	Alkaline or very hard water.	Use conditioner or vinegar.
	Too slack or too stiff dough.	Reduce or increase ingredients to correct ratios; check mixing.
	High sugar or excess yeast.	Check ingredient ratios; check diastase, and decrease or increase as required.
	Lack of shortening.	Increase.
	High dough temperature.	Reduce liquid temperature or temperatures during fermentation or proofing.
	Overfermentation or proofing.	Reduce.

Herb, Spice, and Seasoning Data

	APPETIZERS	SOUPS	SALADS & DRESSINGS	VEGETABLES	EGGS AND CHEESE	MEATS AND SAUCES	POULTRY AND FISH	DESSERTS AND BAKED GOODS
ALLSPICE	Pickles, relishes, cocktail meatballs, pickled beets, fruit compote.	Green pea, vegetable, beef, minestrone, asparagus, tomato.	Cottage cheese, fruit salad, cheese dressing.	Eggplant, spinach, beets, squash, turnips, red cabbage, carrots.	Egg casserole, cream cheese.	Beef stew, meat loaf, hamburgers, baked ham, roast lamb, pot roast, cranberry sauce, meat gravies, tomato sauce.	Boiled fish, oyster stew.	Mincemeat, tapioca and chocolate puddings, spice cake, fruit cake, baked bananas, cookies, pie.
BAY LEAVES	Hot tomato juice, pickles, pickled beets.	Bouillon, bouillabaisse, fish chowders, lobster bisque, vegetable, minestrone, oxtail, potato, tomato, turtle.	Seafood salad, tomato aspic, chicken aspic, beet salad, French dressing.	Potatoes, artichokes, carrots, beets, eggplant, lentils, onions, rice, squash, zucchini.	Eggs Creole.	Beef stew, meat pie, corned beef, pot roast, roast beef, veal, meat sauces, lamb, spare ribs, gravies.	Capon, chicken boiled, à la king, fricassee, turkey (roast), boiled shrimp and lobster, fish stews, baked salmon.	
CARAWAY	Soft cheese spreads, pickles.	Cream soups, clam chowder, borsch, vegetable.	Potato salad, sour cream dressing, spiced vinegar, coleslaw.	Cabbage, cauliflower, potatoes, carrots, onions, turnips, broccoli, brussels sprouts, sauerkraut.	Cottage cheese, cream cheese.	Sauerbraten, roast pork, beef à la mode, liver, kidney stew.	Tunafish casserole, roast goose.	Rye bread, muffins, rolls, coffee cakes, cookies, loaf cake.
CAYENNE	Deviled eggs, seafood sauces, cottage and cream cheese dips and spreads, avocado dip.	Clam and oyster stews, fish chowder, cream soups, shrimp gumbo, vegetable.	Tuna, shrimp, chicken, macaroni, seafood, mayonnaise, thousand island dressing, sour cream.	Green beans, lima beans, cauliflower, cut corn, kale, broccoli.	Welsh rarebit, egg dishes, cheese soufflé, cottage and cream cheese.	Pork chops, veal stew, ham croquettes, barbecued beef, sandwich fillings, meat sauces.	Creamed chicken and croquettes, oysters, shrimp, poached salmon, tuna salad.	
CELERY SEED (salt, flakes, seeds)	Deviled eggs, ham spread, tomato juice, kraut juice, cream cheese spread, pickles.	Cream of celery or tomato, fish chowders and bisques, vegetable, bean, potato, bouillon.	Coleslaw, potato, egg, tuna, vegetable, kidney beans, salad dressings, sour cream dressing.	Cabbage, stewed tomatoes, potatoes, cauliflower, turnips, braised lettuce.	Welsh rarebit, boiled and fried eggs, cheese casserole, omelets, cheese sauce, deviled eggs.	Meat loaf, pot roast, meat stews, short ribs of beef, braised lamb.	Chicken croquettes, fish stews, chicken pie, oyster stew, stuffings.	Rolls, biscuits, salty breads.
CHILI POWDER	Avocado and cheese dips, seafood cocktail sauce.	Corn soup, pepperpot, fish and clam chowders, tomato, bean, shrimp gumbo, vegetable, chili soup.	French dressing, kidney bean salad, thousand island dressing, chili sauce.	Vegetable relishes, green peas, eggplant, rice, tomatoes, corn Mexicali, green beans, lima beans.	Omelets, soufflés, casseroles, boiled and scrambled eggs, cheese sauces, rarebits.	Chili con carne, arroz con pollo, tamales, meat loaf, hamburgers, stews, sauces.	Creamed seafood, shrimp, chicken and rice, chicken pie.	
CINNAMON (ground and stick)	Cinnamon toast, sweet gherkins, hot spiced beverages, pickled fruits.		Fruit salad dressings for fruit salads.	Sweet potatoes, squash, pumpkins, spinach, turnips, green beans, beets, parsnips.		Pork chops, ham, sauce for pork and lamb.	Boiled chicken (stick cinnamon), boiled fish, special chicken and fish recipes.	Chocolate and rice pudding, stewed fruits, apple desserts, buns, coffee cake, muffins, spice cake, molasses cookies.
CLOVES (whole and ground)	Sweet gherkins, pickled fruits, hot spiced wines, fruit punch.	Beef, bean, cream of tomato, cream of pea, mulligatawny.	Topping for fruit salad.	Beets, baked beans, candied sweet potatoes, squash.		(Whole) Ham and pork roast, stews, gravies, sausage, boiled tongue.	Baked fish, chicken à la king, roast or smothered chicken, chicken croquettes.	Preserved and stewed fruits, apple, mince, and pumpkin pies, chocolate, rice, and tapioca pudding, stewed pears.
CURRY POWDER	Tomato juice, sauce for dips, sweet pickles, deviled eggs, salted nuts.	Clam and fish chowders, tomato soup, cream of mushroom, oyster stew.	Fruit and meat salads, mayonnaise, French dressing.	Rice, creamed onions, creamed potatoes, scalloped potatoes, carrots, corn, celery, lima beans.	Sauce for eggs, deviled eggs, cottage cheese, cream cheese sauce.	Curried lamb, veal croquettes, stews.	Chicken croquettes, chicken hash, curried chicken and turkey, fish croquettes, shrimp.	
DILL	Cottage cheese, anchovy spread, cheddar cheese spread, pickles, sour cream dips, stuffed eggs.	Split pea soup, cream of tomato, navy bean, borsch, chicken, lobster bisque, turkey, fish chowder.	Coleslaw, cucumber, green bean, lettuce, mixed green, potato, seafood, mayonnaise, sour cream, French dressing.	Carrots, beets, cabbage, lima beans, green beans, turnips, eggplant, cauliflower, zucchini, squash.	Deviled eggs, omelets, scrambled eggs, cottage cheese, cream cheese, macaroni.	Beef: Pot roast, corned, stew, barbecued, hamburger; lamb chops or stew, roast pork.	Chicken pie creamed chicken, baked halibut, mackerel, salmon, creamed lobster, boiled and creamed shrimp.	

430

	APPETIZERS	SOUPS	SALADS & DRESSINGS	VEGETABLES	EGGS AND CHEESE	MEATS AND SAUCES	POULTRY AND FISH	DESSERTS AND BAKED GOODS
GINGER (ground)	Pickles, broiled grapefruit, chutney.	Bean soup, onion, potato.	Ginger pears, French dressing.	Beets, carrots, squash, baked beans.	Cheese dishes.	Broiled beef, lamb, veal, pot roast, stews, chopped beef.	Roast chicken, squab, cornish hen, sautéed chicken.	Gingerbread, cakes, cookies, pumpkin pie, custards, baked, stewed, preserved fruits, Indian pudding.
MARJORAM	Fruit punch, cream and cottage cheese dips, cheddar cheese spreads, pickles.	Onion soup, clam, oyster, Boston clam chowder, minestrone, oxtail, spinach.	Mixed green salad, asparagus, chicken, fruit, seafood.	Carrots, eggplant, peas, spinach, string beans, onions, summer squash, tomatoes, celery, broccoli, brussels sprouts.	Omelets, soufflés, creamed eggs, scrambled, cheese sauce, cheese soufflé, rarebits, cheese straws.	Roast beef, pork, veal, stews, meat pies, loaf, pot roast, short ribs, spare ribs.	Chicken croquettes, duck, goose, pheasant, guinea hen, codfish balls, halibut, salmon loaf, shad roe.	
MUSTARD (ground)	Pickles, pickled onions, ham spreads, Chinese hot sauce, hot English mustard, deviled eggs.	Lobster bisque, bean, onion.	Egg salad, shrimp, lobster, potato, fruit, salad dressings.	Asparagus, beets, broccoli, brussels sprouts, cabbage, onions, green beans, potatoes, baked beans.	Deviled eggs, casseroles, cheese sauces, cream cheese.	Baked ham, kidneys, pickled meat, sauces.	Shrimp, creamed and stewed oysters, boiled fish, fish sauces.	Molasses cookies, gingerbread.
OREGANO	Cheese spreads, pizza, vegetable juice, avocado dip, creamed and cottage cheese spreads.	Bean, beef, vegetable, tomato, lentil, minestrone, navy bean, onion, spinach.	Salad dressings, seafood, avocado, green bean, mixed green, potato, tomato, tomato aspic.	Peas, onions, potatoes, spinach, green beans, stewed tomatoes, mushrooms.	Creamed eggs, omelets, scrambled eggs, cheese sauce, soufflé, cottage cream, straws, rarebits.	Swiss steak, beef stew, broiled and roast lamb, meat loaf, sauces, gravies, spare ribs, veal scallopini.	Chicken cacciatore, sauté, roast, guinea hen, pheasant, stuffed fish, boiled shrimp, clams.	
PAPRIKA	Canapés, deviled eggs, cream cheese spreads, stuffed celery, creamed seafood, seafood cocktails.	Cream soups, chicken soup, chowders.	Coleslaw, potato salad, mayonnaise, French dressing.	Cauliflower, potatoes, celery, creamed vegetables.	Deviled eggs, scrambled eggs, Welsh rarebit, cottage cheese, cheese and egg dishes.	Hungarian goulash, ham, gravies.	Poultry and seafood dishes, shellfish, fried chicken.	
POPPY SEED	Cheese spreads, cottage cheese, cheese dips.	Onion soup.	Green salads, salad dressings.	Peas, potatoes, rutabaga, sweet potatoes, carrots, zucchini.	Fried and scrambled eggs, omelets, cottage cheese.	Noodle dishes.		Coffee cake, cookies, pie crusts, bread, rolls, pastries.
ROSEMARY	Deviled eggs, pickles, sour cream dips.	Mock turtle, chicken, lentil, minestrone, split pea, spinach, chowders.	Meat salad, fruit salad.	Peas, potatoes, mushrooms, onions, celery, lima beans, green beans, broccoli, cucumbers.	Deviled eggs, omelets, soufflés.	Roast and broiled lamb, beef, pork, veal, beef stew, pie, pot roast, swiss steak, spare ribs.	Capon, chicken fricassee, sauté, roast pheasant, partridge, quail, salmon, baked halibut, baked sole.	
SAFFRON		Chicken, bouillabaisse, lobster bisque, turkey.	Seafood salads.	Rice.	Scrambled eggs.	Gravy for roast chicken, roast turkey, roast veal, Spanish sauce, rabbit.	Arroz con pollo, bouillabaisse, chicken stew, chicken fricassee, creamed lobster, baked halibut, sole.	Rolls, breads, buns, cake, frostings and icings.
SAGE	Cheese spreads.	Consommé, fish and corn chowders, cream soups, asparagus, chicken, cream of tomato, minestrone, turkey.	Salad greens, salad dressings.	Brussels sprouts, onions, lima beans, peas, tomatoes, carrots, eggplant, winter squash, turnips.	Creamed eggs, soufflés, cheese sauce, rarebits, egg and cheese casseroles, cottage and cream cheese.	Beef, barbecue, stew, pie, roast, pot roast, barbecued lamb, roast lamb, pork, veal stew.	Capon, chicken stuffing, goose, duck.	
SESAME SEED	Soft cheeses.	Most soups.	Coleslaw, salad dressings.	Asparagus, green beans, tomatoes, spinach, noodle and vegetable casseroles, potatoes, rice.	Cream cheese.	Meat pies, Hawaiian ham steak.	Fried chicken, chicken casseroles, fish.	Top dressings on pies, cookies, coffee cake, rolls, breads, buns, crumpets.
TARRAGON	Vegetable juice cocktail, liver paté, herb butters, cheese spreads, seafood cocktails, stuffed eggs, pickles.	Bean, chicken, consommé, seafood chowders and bisques, mushroom, pea, tomato, turtle.	Asparagus, celery, chicken, coleslaw, cucumber, egg, green bean, kidney bean, mixed green, tomato.	Asparagus, beans, broccoli, cabbage, cauliflower, celery root, mushrooms, potatoes, spinach, tomatoes.	Deviled eggs, omelets, scrambled eggs, cottage cheese.	Meat marinades, broiled steak, pot roast, braised lamb, lamb stew, veal stew, bearnaise sauce, brown gravies.	Chicken, chicken sauté, broiled chicken, turkey, duck, broiled halibut, baked salmon, trout, tuna, broiled lobster.	

HERBS · PEPPERS · SPICES · SEEDS and SEASONING / Notes on How to Use Them

A

Allspice, ground—Flavor resembles combination of cinnamon, nutmeg and cloves. Delicious in cookies, cakes and relishes.

Allspice, whole—Use sparingly in soups, stews and sauces.

Anise Seed, ground—Originally from Southern Europe. These seeds lend a delightful flavor to salads, shrimp and crab dishes.

Anise Seed, whole—Delicious to sprinkle on cookies, sweet rolls and coffee cake before baking.

Apple Pie Seasoning—A delightful blend of seasonings to give apple pie the "spicy" touch.

Arrowroot—Used as a thickening agent in sauces such as vegetable and meat sauces. Neutral in flavor.

B

Barbecue Sauce Seasoning—A delicious blend of spices and herbs to use in making a barbecue sauce for meat, poultry and seafood.

Barbecue Seasoning—Skillfully blended all purpose barbecue seasoning. Can be used in dry form or as a base for barbecue or cocktail sauce.

Basil, leaf—Widely used in French and Italian dishes. Delicious flavoring in soups, stews and meat loaf.

Basil, powdered—Excellent in stuffings for fowl and sauces for spaghetti and other Italian dishes.

Bay Leaves—Lends a delicious flavor to fish, soups, tomato dishes and stuffings for fish and fowl.

Beef Soup Base—With a combination of the finest seasonings, to make beef soups and gravies.

Borie's Scotch Bonnet—A highly flavored sherry-and-pepper sauce for use in soups, dressings and stews.

Bouquet Garni—A blend of several fine herbs for use in making flavorful soups, stews and gravies.

C

Caraway Seed—Originally from Holland and North Africa, these seeds add greatly to the flavor of rye bread, sauerkraut, soup stock and stewed meats.

Cardamon Seed, whole and ground—Originally from India, cardamon lends a sweet flavor to breads, pastries and cookies.

Celery Seasoning Salt—Adds celery's delicate flavor to meats, stews, soups and salads.

Celery Seed, ground—From Southern France. Adds a delightful flavor to fish, salads, tomatoes, and salad dressing.

Celery Seed, whole—Adds delicious flavor to potato salad, soup and stews.

Charcoal Salt—A very special blended seasoning to use on steaks, chops and hamburgers for a delicious barbecue taste and appearance.

Chervil—Adds a moderately pungent flavor to salads, soups, fish sauces and egg dishes.

Chicken Soup Base—A delightful combination of herbs and spices for making chicken soup. Also use in casseroles and cream sauces.

Chili Powder—To use in adding that true Mexican flavor to chili con carne.

Cinnamon, ground—Indispensable seasoning for apple pie, apple sauce, sweet rolls, coffee cakes and sauces for game.

Cinnamon Stick—Used in sweet pickling, hot toddies, rum grogs and demitasse.

Cinnamon Sugar—Delicious on pancakes, toast, French toast, waffles, fruit sauces, cake and cookie batters.

Cloves, ground—The flower buds of an Indonesian tree, cloves, lend their delicious flavor to soups, stews and fruit desserts.

G

Ginger Garlic Seasoning Salt—A delicious blend of ginger and garlic to be used on lamb, in stews and roast meats. Use with cream cheese as a chip dip.

Ginger, whole and ground—The finest ginger comes from Jamaica and the British West Indies. Whole, it is used to give distinctive flavoring to chutney, pickles, conserves and applesauce. Ground, it is used widely for all types of spice cakes, cookies and sweet buns. Especially delicious in Oriental dishes.

Golden Rice Seasoning—A delicious blend of herbs and spices for flavoring rice dishes.

Good Taste—An all purpose seasoning salt prepared from the finest spices and herbs to add zest and savor to a wide variety of foods.

Gumbo Filé—To use in any gumbo soup.

H

Hamburger Seasoning—Excellent for indoor and outdoor cooking. Can be used on all ground meats before or after cooking.

Herb Blend for Eggs and Cheese—To make your egg and cheese dishes delightfully different and casually easier.

Herb Blend for Fish—A choice blend of fine herbs to add zest and savor to your fish dishes.

Herb Blend for Meat—The prize blend of a famous chef to add distinctive flavor to meats.

Herb Blend for Poultry and Game—Add small amount to dressing or sprinkle lightly on poultry or game before roasting.

Herb Blend for Salads—A blend of the finest obtainable herbs. Adds piquant distinction to dressings and salads.

Herb Blend for Soups—A correctly proportioned blend of herbs to make your cooking casually easy. Adds a delicious flavor to soups.

Herb Blend for Vegetables—A very special blend of seasonings to add a zestful touch to vegetables and spaghetti sauces.

Hickory Smoked Salt—A gourmet's seasoning to sprinkle on steaks, chops and hamburgers before cooking to impart a fine wood-smoke flavor.

Horseradish—A zesty horseradish powder to use in making prepared horseradish.

J

Juniper Berries—An aromatic berry in chopped form to use dry with poultry and meat.

L

Lemon Flavored Sugar—The ideal sweetening for tea—both hot and iced.

Lemon Peel—Use in sauces and marinade for poultry, lamb and veal. Add to cake batters, dessert sauces and toppings, meringues and custards.

M

Marjoram, leaf and powdered—The perennial herb of the mint family of France. Use in stuffings, chopped meats, stews, soups and salad dressings.

Meat Ball Seasoning—A famous chef's special seasoning for meat balls, spaghetti sauce, meat loaf, stuffed peppers and shrimp dishes.

Meat Tenderizer—Sprinkle on meat, fish or fowl before cooking.

Mint Leaves—Mint leaves impart an aromatic flavor popular for beverages, meats, confections and desserts.

Monosodium Glutamate—M.S.G. has no flavor of its own but increases the natural flavor of many dishes.

Mushroom Flakes—Cultivated in the heart of the mushroom country. Excellent added to sauces, gravies, meats and vegetables.

Mushroom Powder—A quick way of adding mushroom flavor to all foods.

P

Paprika—Widely used as a garnish and in goulash, meat stews, hashes, fish and game.

Parsley—Used as a colorful garnish. This herb is used in soups, sauces, baked fish, potatoes and salads.

Pea Soup Mix—A savory mixture for making a delicious pea soup.

Pepper, Cayenne—A very hot red pepper. Delicious to use with shrimp and crab dishes and chili sauce. Also add to hot Mexican and Spanish dishes.

Pepper, Creole—A Louisiana pepper similar to Cayenne. Very popular in Southern and Creole dishes.

Pepper, Lampong, black cracked—For those who prefer a more pungent pepper flavor. Especially good in soups and salads.

Pepper, Lampong, black ground fine—This rare extremely fine black pepper is a delight to all gourmets.

Pepper, Lampong, black ground—By far the most generally used of all spices. This pepper is ground immediately prior to packing to retain full flavor.

Pepper, Lampong, black medium—A pungent pepper particularly good in stews, soups and salads.

Pepper, Malabar, black ground—The finest of all black pepper. The most generally used of all spices at table and in cooking.

Pepper, White, ground—A mild variety of pepper. Ground white pepper is used chiefly in sauces where it is preferable not to have black pepper.

Peppers, Green Bell, diced—Dehydrated bell peppers. Use with spaghetti sauce, meat loaf and stews.

Peppers, Green Bell, ground—Dehydrated bell peppers to use in sauces for spaghetti, string beans, egg plant and liver.

Peppers, Red Bell, diced—Dehydrated bell peppers. Try in egg dishes, meat loaf and stews.

Peppers, Red, crushed—Use sparingly for a hot touch to Italian dishes, casseroles, stews, hamburgers and potted meats.

Peppercorns, Garlic—A delightful touch of garlic added to the finest available peppercorns.

Peppercorns, Lampong, black—Grown in the Netherlands East Indies. For use in peppermills to achieve pungent, freshly ground pepper.

Peppercorns, Malabar, black—These rare, extremely fine black peppercorns are used in soups, pickling and meat stews and whenever fine pepper is required. Used principally in peppermills.

Peppercorns, White—These are the finest of natural black peppercorns with the dark outer shell removed. Preferred by those who want a more delicate, less pungent flavor.

Pickling Spice, whole—A skillful blend of pungent spices and fine herbs to use in making a wide variety of pickles and relishes.

Pizza Seasoning—To use in making pizza sauce or to sprinkle over pizza at time of eating. Add to salads, veal cutlets and roast lamb.

Poivre Aromatique—Blended after the formula of an old French Huguenot family. Adds a delightful pungent taste to soups, stews, stuffings, meat loaf and tomato juice.

Poppy Seed—This Asian herb has a nut-like flavor and odor. Delicious for toppings on rolls, bread or cookies.

Pot Pie Seasoning—A famous old New England recipe to add that tangy flavor to your chicken or beef pot pies.

Poultry Seasoning—The ideal blend of herbs and spices to add to bread stuffing for fowl, fish and pork roasts.

Pumpkin Pie Spice—Developed by a famous pastry chef. Delicious in gingerbread, cookies, pies and buns.

C

Cookery Seasoning—Mixture of black pepper, salt, herbs and spices. Use in cooking or on the table. Adds zest to meats, soups, sauces, eggs and salad dressing.

Coriander, whole and ground—Native of the Mediterranean countries; for use in gingerbread, spice cookies, Danish pastries, roast pork, beef broth and meat sauces.

Cream of Tartar—Most frequently used in candy making and cake icings.

Corn-on-Cob Seasoning—Adds zest to meats, soups, sauces, salad dressings and corn on the cob.

Creole Seasoning—A blend of pungent spices indispensable in Creole recipes, thin soups, gumbos and ragouts.

Curry Powder—A subtle mixture of many Eastern herbs and spices imported from Madras, India. Used for lamb, rice, fish, soups, venison, kidney stews, sauces and mushrooms.

Cumin Seed—Native to the Mediterranean area, this spice gives a warm, aromatic taste to stews, roast meats and root vegetables.

D

Dill Seasoning Salt—An unusual, delightful seasoning. Use as you would salt to add flavor to eggs, cheese, meats, salads and potatoes.

Dill Seed—Famous for its use in pickling, meats, soups, salads, eggs and fried potatoes.

Dill Weed—This exceptional herb is delicious when used in creamed dishes, potatoes, salads.

F

Fennel Seed—A classic herb from the parsley family for use in Scandinavian hot breads, cakes and cookies. Delicious, too, in many Spanish and Italian dishes.

Fenugreek—A product of Morocco. Most frequently used in dishes of Greek origin. Also may be used as a substitute for curry.

Fried Chicken Seasoning—A delicious blend of spices and herbs to season chicken, roast turkey, Cornish hens, pheasant and egg plant.

G

Garlic Flakes—For every dish that requires garlic. These dehydrated flakes have eight times the strength of fresh garlic so should be used sparingly.

Garlic, Instant granulated—Delicious in sauces, all potato recipes, meats and stews. Can be used freely in any recipe which calls for garlic flavoring.

Garlic, minced—One of the oldest and widely used of spices. Delicious in stews, meat loaf, salad dressings, meat balls and potato salad.

Garlic Salt Chips—Sprinkle generously over roast beef and lamb before roasting. Use for that hidden garlic touch in soups, stews, gravies and sauces.

Garlic Seasoning Salt—Use to flavor meats, stews, fish and eggs.

Ginger Crystallized—Frequently used in Chinese and Japanese cookery. Also in making chutney and as a confection.

M

Mushroom Salt—Easy to use as a seasoning on roasts, sauces, gravies, eggs, barbecues and omelets.

Mustard Seed, ground and whole—A native to Europe and Southwest Asia this spice is widely used with meats, sauces, fish and mayonnaise.

N

Newburg Seasoning—Used by one of the leading chef's of Maryland's Eastern Shore to add a delicious flavor to lobster, shrimp or crabmeat.

Nutmeg, ground and whole—Originates in the East Indies. This spice gives an aromatic odor and slightly bitter taste to custards, puddings, pumpkin and fruit pies. Delicious sprinkled on egg-nog. Use a nutmeg grinder for the whole nutmeg.

O

Onion Chips—Small chips of onion to be used wherever onions are needed in soups, stews, roast meats and hamburger.

Onion Flakes, fried flavor—A delicious addition to any dish requiring an onion flavor.

Onion, Instant granulated—Use freely in any recipe which calls for onion flavoring. Delicious in sauces, potato recipes, meats and stews.

Onion, minced green—Colorful and delicious garnish for all salads, potato and tomato dishes, vichyssoise and tomato juice.

Onion, minced white—Adds delicate flavor to all dishes where onion is used—salad dressing, roast beef, steaks, chops, baked brown potatoes.

Onion Powder—For that "touch of onion" to be used in stews, roast meats, fish and fowl, potato salad and Italian sauces.

Onion Powder, roasted—Gives the delectable taste of roasted onions to meat gravies, sauces, fowl and hamburger.

Onion Seasoning Salt—Adds a delicious onion flavor to meats, stews, fish, salads and eggs.

Onion Soup, French—With a delightful combination of seasonings; for making onion soup and onion dips.

Orange Peel—Delicious in baked goods, duck and barbecue sauces. Add to butter, honey or syrup for toppings.

Oregano—This herb is widely used in the seasoning of Mexican and Italian dishes, pork and tomato sauces and bean dishes.

Oriental Mustard Seed—Used extensively in Oriental dishes. These seeds are very hot and should be used sparingly.

R

Red Bell Pepper and Onion Blend—A delicious combination to mix with cottage cheese.

Roast Meat Seasoning—For indoor and outdoor cookery. Excellent for stews, meat loaf, hash, croquettes, gravies, mock turtle soup, stewed rabbit and game.

Rosemary, leaf and powdered—Gives a pleasant delicate flavor to meats, soups, fish and salads.

S

Saffron—A native of Spain and the Mediterranean region. A true gourmet's flavoring for fish, soups, boiled rice, curry and fish sauces.

Sage Leaf—Grown in Dalmatia, this herb has a spicy aroma and should be used sparingly in soups, meats and all bread stuffings for fowl, fish and pork. Sage leaf powdered is delicious in vegetables, boiled fish and stews.

Salt Crystals—Salt in crystalline form. May be used as is in cooking or may be freshly ground in a salt mill for table use.

Savory, leaf and powdered—This fragrant Spanish herb lends a delightful flavor to soups, stuffings, cabbage, stewed meats and boiled mutton. In powdered form savory is delicious in egg dishes, cold sauces and salad dressings.

Seafood Seasoning—An expert blend of spices and herbs to sprinkle generously over fish or seafood.

Seasoning Salt—A mixture of peppers, salts, herbs and spices to be used in cooking or on the table.

Sesame Seed—A small seed from the Orient with a nut-like flavor to use on rolls, breads cookies and cakes.

Shrimp Seasoning—Add 1½ tsp. shrimp seasoning to 3½ cups water. Bring to boil. Add 1 lb. raw shrimp, boil 8 minutes. Remove from water.

Steak Seasoning, Garlic—For those who prefer a touch of garlic on their steak. Also excellent on lamb, pot roast, gravies, pork and rib roast.

T

Tarragon—Famous for flavoring turtle soup, eggs, meat sauces, salad greens and many vegetables, and a "must" for sauce Bearnaise.

Thyme—Delicious in bread stuffings, fish sauces, soups, gumbos, shellfish dishes, meats and vegetables.

Tomato Puree Flakes—Dehydrated tomatoes to use in tomato sauces and purees.

Turmeric—Used in soups, pickles and other dishes where a rich yellow color is desired. Use to color rice where saffron is not used.

V

Vanilla Bean—A dried, cured fruit of the orchid family. The vanilla bean is used for baking, desserts, candy and syrups.

Vanilla Flavored Sugar—A combination of vanilla beans and sugars to use in baking and desserts.

Vegetable and Salad Blend—An ideal mixture of dried vegetables to use in soups, cottage cheese salads and cheese dips.

John Wagner & Sons Inc.

Iryland, Pa.

Purveyors to Epicures

Since 1847

Copyright 1961 by John Wagner & Sons, Inc.

Standard Portions

Table I-1. Standard Portions

Food	Portion and Serving Method
Meats	
American chop suey	4 oz ladle, rounded
with corn soya	2 T, No. 32 scoop
with rice	No. 16 scoop
Baked hash, beef or corned beef	No. 10 scoop or heaped serving spoon, 5 to 6 oz
Beef or other meat and noodles	No. 8 scoop rounded or 6 oz ladle rounded, about 7 oz (¾ c)
Beef patty	No. 8 scoop before cooking, use tongs
Beef or other meat stew	6 oz (¾ c), ladle
Chili con carne	6 oz ladle rounded to give 8 oz
Corned beef and cabbage	3 or 4 oz sliced beef, tongs; 3 to 4 oz cabbage, spoon
Cold cuts	3 oz, tongs or spatula
Cabbage rolls	2 rolls, 3 oz each (use 2 oz meat filling), use spoon
Creamed meats	½ c, 4 oz ladle; use 8 to 10 lb cooked meat per 100; serve over toast, biscuits or No. 16 scoop rice
Croquettes	No. 10 or 12 scoop for 1; No. 20 scoop for 2; 1½ oz sauce
Frankfurters, 6 to 7 lb	2, tongs
with sauerkraut	1 rounded serving spoon, 3 oz
Fritters	2, tongs; portion with No. 20 scoop; 2 strips bacon
Ham à la king	4 oz ladle rounded
Ham, baked, boned	5 to 6 oz before cooking, tongs
Ham, baked, slices	3 to 4 oz after cooking, tongs
Ham, fried	6 oz before cooking, tongs
Hamburgers	2, portion with No. 20 dipper, tongs
Liver, braised	3 to 4 oz before cooking, 2 strips bacon, tongs
Meatballs and spaghetti	No. 20 scoop, 2 balls, 2 serving spoons spaghetti and sauce
Meat sandwich, hot	2 oz meat, 1 or 2 slices bread, tongs; 2 oz ladle gravy
Meatloaf	4 to 5 oz cooked, slice and use spatula or tongs
Meat pie	2 serving spoons, rounded 8 oz
with pie crust	Cut 17 × 25 baking pans 5 by 9, 45 portions
with biscuit	2½ in diameter, serve 1 with 6 oz stew
Meat turnover	2 oz meat, No. 16 scoop; serve with 2 oz gravy, ladle
Mock drum sticks	5 oz before cooking, serve 1
New England boiled dinner	6 oz before cooking, 3 to 4 oz after, tongs, 5 oz vegetables and 5 oz potatoes
Pork chop	3 to lb before cooking, serve 1; 6 to lb serve 2
with dressing	2 to 3 oz; use serving spoon or No. 16 scoop
Pork chop with pocket	3 to lb, 1½ oz stuffing; tongs
Roasts, meat or poultry	3 oz cooked, tongs
with dressing	2 to 3 oz meat cooked; 4 oz (½ c), No. 10 scoop rounded of dressing
Sausage, bulk	3 oz before cooking, tongs
Sausages, link, 14 to 16 per lb.	2, tongs
Spareribs	8 to 12 oz before cooking, tongs
Steak, braised, swiss, etc.	6 to 7 raw, 4 to 5 oz cooked, spoon
Steak, dinner, dry-heat type	8 oz AP, no bone, tongs; size may vary with institution
Steak, ground	3 to pound, No. 8 scoop rounded; 4 oz cooked, tongs
Steak, stuffed	5 to 6 oz before cooking; 1½ oz dressing, tongs
Stew	No. 8 scoop rounded or 6 oz ladle rounded (¾ c)

Table I-1. *(cont.)*

Food	Portion and Serving Method
Meats (cont.)	
Veal birds	5 oz before cooking; 1½ oz dressing; spoon
Veal cutlet	4 oz before breading; 5 oz breaded
Veal chop	5 oz
Wieners, 10 to lb	2, tongs
Fish	
Fillet, baked or fried	3 to pound before cooking; 4 oz if breaded
Steak	3 to pound unless wasteful in eating, then 6 oz
Creamed fish dishes	4 oz ladle rounded; 1 slice toast, 1 biscuit, or No. 16 scoop of rice
Shrimp wiggle	4 oz ladle rounded; slice of toast or biscuit or No. 16 scoop of rice
Shrimp, deep-fried, fantail	4 to 5, tongs
Strips, breaded and deep-fried	1 oz each, serve 3, tongs; about 35% breading
Croquettes	No. 10 scoop for 1; No. 20 scoop for 2; 1½ oz sauce
Loaf	4 oz slice; in 17 × 25 pan, cut 5 by 9, in 12 × 20 pan, cut 4 by 6: bake in these 1 in. deep
Scalloped salmon, tuna, etc.	1 4 oz ladle rounded, 5 to 6 oz; if thick, rounded serving spoon
Fish and noodles	Serving spoon rounded, 5 to 6 oz
Tunafish, potato chip dish	Serving spoon rounded, 5 to 6 oz
Soufflé	Cut 17 × 25 pan, 5 × 9, 12 × 20 pan 4 by 6
Poultry	
Chicken fricassée, unboned	12 oz raw meat, spoon
Chicken, creamed	6 oz (¾ c); about 2 oz cooked chicken meat per portion
Chicken, fried	2 pieces or half (12 oz before cooking)
Chicken or turkey, roast	2 to 3 oz with dressing, 4 oz without, 2 oz gravy
Duck or geese	12 oz to 1 lb before cooking
*Luncheon Entrées**	
American noodles	5 oz, serving spoon well-rounded
Baked beans	6 oz ladle or two serving spoons or one heaped
Baked lima beans	6 oz, serving spoon heaped
Baked eggs, Creole	4 oz ladle, rounded
Beef biscuit roll	1, 4 in. diameter, 2 oz ladle gravy
Buttered apples with sausage	3 apple halves, 2 sausages
Cheeseburgers	1 No. 16 scoop, 2 each, slice cheese ¾ to 1 oz each
Cheese fondue	4 oz, 1 oz sauce; cut 12 × 20 pan 4 by 6, spoon and ladle
Rice and cheese baked	5 oz (⅔ c), well-rounded serving spoon
Creole spaghetti	1 serving spoon well-rounded (6 oz)
Eggs à la king or creamed eggs	2 halves egg on half slice of toast; 2 oz sauce
Omelet	4 oz, spoon; if cut, use spatula
Goulash	6 oz ladle
Italian delight	4 oz ladle
Italian spaghetti	1 heaped serving spoon spaghetti, 4 oz ladle sauce
Macaroni and cheese	1 heaped serving spoon, 5 to 6 oz
Macaroni hoe	1 heaped serving spoon, 5 to 6 oz
Meat soufflé	1 heaped serving spoon, 1½ oz sauce
Pizza pie	Cut 18 × 20 in baking sheet 4 by 5, use spatula

*A 12 × 20 in. baking pan 4 in. deep with food (16 to 18 lb of food) may be cut 5 by 8 to give 40 6 to 7 oz portions. (Use 6 in. deep pan.)

Table I-1. *(cont.)*

Food	Portion and Serving Method
Luncheon Entrées (cont.)	
Scalloped ham and potatoes	1 heaped serving spoon, 5 to 6 oz
Scalloped meat dishes	1 heaped serving spoon, 5 to 6 oz
Scrapple	4 oz, 2 slices
Spanish rice	1 well-rounded serving spoon, 5 oz
Stuffed cabbage	1 or 2
Swedish meatballs	2 2 oz each after cooking; portion with rounded No. 20 scoop
Tamale pie	1 heaped serving spoon, 5 to 6 oz
Welsh rarebit	½ c, 4 oz ladle, on toast, biscuit, or No. 16 scoop rice
Vegetables	
Most canned vegetables	3 oz (½ c), 1 rounded serving spoon
Apples, buttered	½ c, 3 to 4 pieces, serving spoon
Asparagus tips	3 to 5 canned, 4 to 6 fresh
Beans, navy, lima, or other	4 to 5 oz, serving spoon
Beets, Harvard	½ c, serving spoon rounded
Beet greens, other greens	3 oz (½ c), tongs or serving spoon
Broccoli, buttered	2 to 3 pieces, 3 to 4 oz, tongs
Cabbage, steamed, fried, etc.	3 oz (½ c), serving spoon
Onions, creamed	2 to 3 small onions, serving spoon
Potato puff	5 oz, ⅔ c, spoon
Potato, browned, steamed, etc.	5 oz, serving spoon
Potato, au gratin, creamed, etc.	4 to 5 oz, serving spoon
Potato, baked	5 to 6 oz, tongs
Potato, hash brown, etc.	4 to 5 oz, serving spoon
Potato, mashed	1 No. 10 scoop or serving spoon, 4 oz
Potato, french-fried	4 oz, 8 to 10 pieces, tongs or spoon
Potato cakes	4 oz, serving spoon
Rice, steamed	No. 10 scoop rounded (⅔ c)
Squash, acorn, baked or steamed	⅓ or ½ squash
Squash, hubbard	6 to 7 oz piece before baking
Squash, mashed	4 oz, rounded serving spoon
Sweet potatoes, baked	5 to 6 oz, tongs
Sweet potatoes, candied or glazed	2 slices, 4 oz
Scalloped sweet potatoes and apples	4 oz, serving spoon
Tomatoes, escalloped or stewed	4 oz ladle
Vegetable pie	5 oz, well-rounded serving spoon
Vegetables, creamed	3 to 4 oz
Salads	
Coleslaw	3 oz, serving spoon
Cottage cheese	No. 20 scoop
Deviled egg	2 halves
Gelatin	12 × 20 pan, 1 in. deep, cut 5 by 10, 50 portions
Mixed fruit	1 rounded serving spoon, No. 2 scoop
Mixed vegetable	1 rounded serving spoon
Sliced tomato	2 large or 3 medium slices

Table I-1. *(cont.)*

Food	Portion and Serving Method
Salads (cont.)	
Head lettuce, 1 lb average	⅛ head, 2 oz serving
Potato, cold or hot	1 No. 10 or No. 12 scoop (4 to 5 oz)
Waldorf	1 rounded serving spoon, 3 oz
Fish or meat salad, entrée-type	5 to 6 oz, 1 c
Brown bean	4 to 5 oz
Dressings and Sauces	
Mayonnaise, boiled, etc.	1 to 2 T; portion depends upon salad size
French or other liquid	1 to 2 T; portion depends upon salad size
Cranberry sauce, applesauce, etc.	2 to 2½ oz, scant serving spoon or No. 16 scoop
Soup	
Cup	6 oz, ¾ c
Bowl	8 oz, 1 c
Tureen	10 to 12 oz, 1¼ to 1½ c
Breads	
Biscuits	2 to 3 1 oz each**
Bran rolls	2 1 oz each
Cinnamon rolls	2 1½ oz each
Cornbread, coffee cake, etc.	1 piece 2 oz, cut 18 × 26 in. baking sheet 6 by 8
Muffins	2 2½ oz each
Griddle cakes	3 3 to 4 oz each
Potato doughnuts	2 2 oz each
Hot rolls	2 1 oz each
Sweet dough items, breakfast	1 3 oz each
White or other bread, sliced	1 to 2 slices, 1 oz each

Desserts	Pan Size	Portion
Cakes, butter		
Sheet, 1 layer	18 × 26 in.	Cut 6 by 8, 48 portions
	13½ × 22⅞ in.	Cut 5 by 9 or 6 by 8, 45 or 48 portions
	12¾ × 23 in.	Cut 5 by 9 or 6 by 8, 45 or 48 portions
Sheet, 2 layer	18 × 26 in.	Cut 12 by 5, 60 portions
	13½ × 22⅞ in.	Cut 3 by 20, 60 portions
	12¾ × 23 in.	Cut 3 by 20, 60 portions
Square, 1 layer	9½ × 9½ in.	Cut 3 by 4, 12 portions
Square, 2 layer	9½ × 9½ in.	Cut 3 by 7, 21 portions
Round, 2 layer	8 in. diameter	Cut 12

Eight 8 in. round layer cakes will serve 96
Six 9 × 13 in. sheets will serve 96
One 9 × 13 in. sheet, two layer, will serve 30
Four 12 in. round layer cakes will serve 120   (See also portioning information in
Three 14 in. round layer cakes will serve 120   chapter on cakes and cookies)

Angel food	16 oz	Cut 16
Chocolate roll, jelly, etc.	18 × 26 in. rolled	34 to 36 portions

**Weight is calculated from raw weight before baking.

Table I-1 *(cont.)*

Desserts	Pan Size	Portion
Cakes, butter (cont.)		
Cup cakes	1 No. 16 scoop	1 each
Doughnuts, cake	1 oz.	2
Cookies		
Brownies, date bars, etc.	18 × 26 in.	Cut 54, serve one
	13½ × 22⅞ in.	Cut 5 by 9, 45 portions
Pies		
One or two crust	10 in.	Cut 8
(use marker)	9 in.	Cut 7
	8 in.	Cut 6
Crust, double	9 in.	12 oz
Crust, single	9 in.	6½ oz
Filling, cream	9 in.	1½ to 2 pt (1½ to 2 lb)
Filling, custard-type	9 in.	1½ pt (1½ lb)
Filling, fruit	9 in.	1½ pt (1½ lb)
Puddings		
Apple crisp, brown betty, etc		4 oz
Apricot whip		¾ c
Bread pudding	13½ × 22⅞ in.	½ c, cut 5 by 9
Cobblers, etc.	13½ × 22⅞ in.	½ c, cut 5 by 9
	12 × 20 in.	½ c, cut 6 by 8
Cream, rice, tapioca, etc.		½ c, No. 10 scoop
Cream puff or éclair batter		1 oz (small), 2 oz (large)
Cream puff or éclair filling		1½ oz, No. 20 scoop
Icebox cake	12¾ × 23 in.	Cut 5 by 10
Icebox pudding		No. 20 scoop
Jello	12¾ × 23 in.	Cut 5 by 9
	12 × 20 in.	Cut 6 by 8
Whipped cream topping		2 T; 2 qt whipped topping per 100 portions
Ice Cream, etc.		
Brick	quart	Cut 8
Bulk		No. 12 scoop
Sundae		No. 16, 2 oz sauce
(See also portioning information in frozen desserts)		
Miscellaneous		
Graham cracker roll, etc.	Loaf 9⅝ × 5½ × 3¼ in.	Cut 16
Pineapple delicious		½ c, No. 10 scoop rounded
Shortcake		2½ in. diameter biscuit, ⅓ c fruit, 2 T whipped cream
Steamed pudding	1 qt mold	Cut into 12 (3½ oz); 2 oz sauce
	12 × 20 in.	Cut 6 by 10
Meringues		⅓ c, 2 oz ladle syrup or sauce, 2 T whipped cream
Sauces for topping		3 T, vary with richness

Index

POINT LOMA NAZARENE COLLEGE RYAN LIBRARY

Conversion Scales

Weights and Liquid Measures

Weights

½ oz	=	14 grams		9	oz	=	254 grams
¾ oz	=	21 g		10	oz	=	283 g
1 oz	=	28 g		11	oz	=	311 g
1½ oz	=	43 g		12	oz	=	340 g
1¾ oz	=	50 g		13	oz	=	368 g
2 oz	=	57 g		14	oz	=	396 g
2½ oz	=	71 g		15	oz	=	425 g
2¾ oz	=	78 g					
3 oz	=	85 g		1	lb	=	453 g
3½ oz	=	99 g		1¼	lb	=	566 g
4 oz	=	114 g		1½	lb	=	679 g
5 oz	=	142 g		1¾	lb	=	792 g
6 oz	=	170 g		2	lb	=	905 g
7 oz	=	199 g		2¼	lb	=	1018 g
8 oz	=	226 g					

Liquid Measures

1 teaspoon	=	0.005 liters		1½ cups	=	0.36 liters
1 tablespoon	=	0.015 l		1¾ cups	=	0.42 l
2 tablespoons	=	0.03 l				
				1 US pint	=	0.47 l
¼ cup	=	0.06 l		1¼ US pt	=	0.60 l
½ cup	=	0.12 l		1½ US pt	=	0.72 l
¾ cup	=	0.18 l		1¾ US pt	=	0.83 l
1 cup	=	0.24 l		1 US quart	=	0.94 l
1¼ cups	=	0.30 l				

Note: Throughout this volume, quantities quoted in pints and quarts refer to the US measures.